UNDERSTANDING
PASTORAL COUNSELING

Elizabeth A. Maynard, PhD, is associate professor and chair of Clinical Mental Health Counseling programs at the University of St. Thomas in Houston, Texas. She is trained and licensed as a clinical psychologist and has focused her work on adult clients. Her emphasis in research, training, and clinical work is on the intersection of sexuality and religion/spirituality. Dr. Maynard has a further interest in the intersection of religion and coping, particularly the use of faith in coping with prejudice. She received her PhD in clinical psychology from the School of Psychology at Fuller Theological Seminary in Pasadena, California. Her research has been published in peer-reviewed journals such as *Mental Health, Religion & Culture, American Journal of Pastoral Counseling,* and *Journal for the Scientific Study of Religion.* She recently edited *Self-Renewal Themes in Psychotherapy: A Guide for Clinicians* (2014) and a special edition of the journal *Research in the Social Scientific Study of Religion* on religion, spirituality, and sexuality.

Jill L. Snodgrass, MDiv, PhD, is assistant professor of pastoral counseling at Loyola University Maryland. She is a certified pastoral counselor, a Fellow in the American Association of Pastoral Counselors, and an ordained minister in the United Church of Christ. Her research interests include spiritual care and counseling with traditionally marginalized populations, with specific emphasis on individuals and families experiencing homelessness and women transitioning from incarceration. From 2008 to 2011, Dr. Snodgrass was the associate director of the Clinebell Institute for Pastoral Counseling and Psychotherapy in Claremont, California. She is president of the Mid-Atlantic Region of the American Academy of Religion, vice chair of the Atlantic Region in the American Association of Pastoral Counselors, and a member of the Society for Pastoral Theology. In addition to her work as a researcher and minister, Dr. Snodgrass has served as a pastoral counselor in churches, shelters, transitional housing facilities, and community centers. She has published articles in such peer-reviewed publications as *Journal of Pastoral Care & Counseling, Pastoral Psychology,* and *Journal of Pastoral Theology.*

UNDERSTANDING PASTORAL COUNSELING

Elizabeth A. Maynard, PhD
Jill L. Snodgrass, MDiv, PhD

Editors

SPRINGER PUBLISHING COMPANY
NEW YORK

Springer Publishing Company, LLC
11 West 42nd Street
New York, NY 10036
www.springerpub.com

Acquisitions Editor: Nancy S. Hale
Composition: Westchester Publishing Services

ISBN: 978-0-8261-3005-1
e-book ISBN: 978-0-8261-3006-8
Instructor's Manual ISBN: 978-0-8261-7175-7
Student Resources ISBN: 978-0-8261-3009-9

Instructor's Materials: Qualified instructors may request supplements by e-mailing textbook@springerpub.com

Student Resources are available from *www.springerpub.com/maynard-snodgrass*

15 16 17 18 19 / 5 4 3 2 1

The author and the publisher of this Work have made every effort to use sources believed to be reliable to provide information that is accurate and compatible with the standards generally accepted at the time of publication. The author and publisher shall not be liable for any special, consequential, or exemplary damages resulting, in whole or in part, from the readers' use of, or reliance on, the information contained in this book. The publisher has no responsibility for the persistence or accuracy of URLs for external or third-party Internet websites referred to in this publication and does not guarantee that any content on such websites is, or will remain, accurate or appropriate.

Library of Congress Cataloging-in-Publication Data

Understanding pastoral counseling / Elizabeth A. Maynard and Jill L. Snodgrass, Editors.
    pages cm
   ISBN 978-0-8261-3005-1 (hard copy : alk. paper) — ISBN 978-0-8261-3006-8 (ebook) 1. Pastoral counseling.
   I. Maynard, Elizabeth A., editor. II. Snodgrass, Jill Lynnae, editor.
   BV4012.2.U53 2015
   253.5—dc23

                                                                                2015004652

Printed in the United States of America by McNaughton & Gunn.

CONTENTS

CONTRIBUTORS

Iain Tucker Brown, PhD, Licensed Mental Health Counselor and Nationally Certified Counselor, Clinical Counselor, Eastern Oregon University, La Grande, Oregon

Stephen Clarke, MS, Licensed Clinical Professional Counselor, Therapist in Private Practice and PhD Candidate, Loyola University Maryland, Shastri in the Shambhala Buddhist Tradition, Baltimore, Maryland

Jim Coffield, PhD, Licensed Psychologist, Professor of Counseling, Reformed Theological Seminary, Orlando, Florida

Russ Curtis, PhD, Licensed Professional Counselor, Associate Professor of Counseling, Western Carolina University, Cullowhee, North Carolina

Christina Jones Davis, MDiv, ThD, Licensed Marriage and Family Therapist, Clinic Director of the Counseling Center and Assistant Professor of Pastoral Care and Counseling, Christian Theological Seminary, Indianapolis, Indiana

Paul J. Deal, PhD, Nationally Certified Counselor, Assistant Professor of Clinical Mental Health Counseling, SUNY Plattsburgh, Plattsburgh, New York

Carrie Doehring, MDiv, PhD, Professor of Pastoral Care, Iliff School of Theology, Denver, Colorado

F. Morgan Enright, PhD, Licensed Marriage and Family Therapist and Supervisor, Licensed Professional Counselor and Supervisor, Private Practitioner and Adjunct Professor, Gordon Conwell Theological Seminary and Pfeiffer University, South Hamilton, Massachusetts

L. Mickey Fenzel, PhD, Licensed Psychologist, Chair and Professor of Pastoral Counseling, Loyola University Maryland, Columbia, Maryland

Serena A. Flores, PhD, Licensed Professional Counselor, Certified School Counselor, Assistant Professor and Chair of School Counselor Program, The University of St. Thomas, Houston, Texas

Jesse Fox, PhD, Nationally Certified Counselor, Assistant Professor of Pastoral Counseling, Loyola University Maryland, Columbia, Maryland

Michael T. Garrett, PhD, Eastern Band of the Cherokee Nation, Licensed/Certified School Counselor, Broward County Public Schools, Fort Lauderdale, Florida

Kathleen J. Greider, MDiv, PhD, Edna and Lowell Craig Professor of Practical Theology, Spiritual Care, and Counseling, Claremont School of Theology, Claremont, California, Fellow, American Association of Pastoral Counselors, ordained Christian minister

Daniel Gutierrez, PhD, Licensed Mental Health Counselor, Nationally Certified Counselor, Assistant Professor of Counseling, University of North Carolina at Charlotte, Charlotte, North Carolina

Timothy S. Hanna, MTS, MS, Nationally Certified Counselor, PhD Candidate, Loyola University Maryland, Columbia, Maryland

Jason Hays, PhD, Pastoral Counselor in Private Practice, Associate Minister for Pastoral Care and Congregational Life, First Congregational United Church of Christ, Boulder, Colorado

Danielle LaSure-Bryant, EdD, Licensed Clinical Professional Counselor and Approved Clinical Supervisor, Nationally Certified Counselor, Director of Clinical Education and Division Director for Pastoral Counseling at the Loyola Clinical Centers, Loyola University Maryland, Columbia, Maryland

Lawrence M. LeNoir, PhD, Licensed Clinical Professional Counselor, Director of the Master's of Science in Pastoral Counseling, Loyola University Maryland, Columbia, Maryland

Michael Lockman, MS, Licensed Graduate Professional Counselor, Hope Health Systems, Inc., Baltimore, Maryland

Gina Magyar-Russell, PhD, Licensed Clinical Psychologist, Associate Professor of Pastoral Counseling, Loyola University Maryland, Columbia, Maryland

Joretta L. Marshall, MDiv, PhD, Diplomate in the American Association of Pastoral Counselors, Professor of Pastoral Theology, Care, and Counseling and Executive Vice President and Dean, Brite Divinity School, Fort Worth, Texas

Elizabeth A. Maynard, PhD, Licensed Clinical Psychologist, Associate Professor and Chair of Clinical Mental Health Counseling Programs, The University of St. Thomas, Houston, Texas

Joanne L. Miller, PhD, Certified Pastoral Counselor, Consultant, Germantown, Maryland

Bonnie J. Miller-McLemore, PhD, E. Rhodes and Leona B. Carpenter Professor of Religion, Psychology, and Culture, Divinity School and Graduate Department of Religion at Vanderbilt University, Nashville, Tennessee

Bill Moulder, PhD, Professor of Biblical Studies, Trinity International University, Deerfield, Illinois

Konrad Noronha, SJ, PhD, Licensed Clinical Professional Counselor and Nationally Certified Counselor, Coordinator and Lecturer, Pastoral Management Program, Lecturer, Theology Department, Jnana Deepa Vidyapaeeth, Pune, India, Spiritual Director, De Nobili College, Pune, India

Kari A. O'Grady, PhD, Assistant Professor of Pastoral Counseling, Loyola University Maryland, Columbia, Maryland

Rodney Parker, ThM, MS, Licensed Graduate Professional Counselor and Nationally Certified Counselor, Director of ALANA Services and PhD Candidate, Loyola University Maryland, Baltimore and Columbia, Maryland

Mark Parrish, PhD, Licensed Professional Counselor, Chair and Associate Professor of Counselor Education and College Student Affairs, University of West Georgia, Carrolton, Georgia

Tarrell Awe Agahe Portman, PhD, White River Cherokee Nation, Licensed Mental Health Counselor and Nationally Certified Counselor, Professor and Dean of the College of Education, Winona State University, Winona, Minnesota

James W. Pruett, DMin, PhD, Licensed Professional Counselor, Licensed Marriage and Family Therapist, and Diplomate in the American Association of Pastoral Counselors and College of Pastoral Supervision and Psychotherapy; Clinical Fellow in the American Association for Marriage and Family Therapy; Founding Director of the Integrative Psychotherapy Training Program, Carolinas HealthCare System, Charlotte, North Carolina

Thomas E. Rodgerson, BD, PhD, Diplomate in the American Association of Pastoral Counselors and Licensed Clinical Professional Counselor, Director of the Master of Arts in Spiritual and Pastoral Care, Loyola University Maryland, Columbia, Maryland

Shahnaz Savani, MSW, MA, Licensed Social Worker, Adjunct Professor, University of Houston–Downtown, Houston, Texas

Heidi Schreiber-Pan, PhD, Licensed Clinical Professional Counselor, Private Practitioner, Towson, Maryland

Jill L. Snodgrass, MDiv, PhD, Fellow, American Association of Pastoral Counselors, Assistant Professor of Pastoral Counseling, Loyola University Maryland, Columbia, Maryland

Joseph A. Stewart-Sicking, MTS, EdD, Ordained Episcopal Priest, Associate Professor and Director of the PhD in Pastoral Counseling, Loyola University Maryland, Columbia, Maryland

Elizabeth Denham Thompson, MDiv, Licensed Marriage and Family Therapist, Ordained in Cooperative Baptist Fellowship, Fellow, American Association of Pastoral Counselors, Clergy and Congregational Consultant, Owner, Eremos Consulting Group, Denver, Colorado

Loren Townsend, MS, MDiv, PhD, Diplomate in the American Association of Pastoral Counselors, Approved Supervisor by the American Association for Marriage and Family Therapy, and Licensed Marriage and Family Therapist, Henry Morris Edmonds Professor of Pastoral Ministry, Professor of Pastoral Care and Counseling, and Director of the Marriage and Family Therapy Program, Louisville Theological Seminary, Louisville, Kentucky

Sharanya Udipi, PhD, Licensed Counseling Psychologist, Private Practitioner and Staff Psychologist, Texas Woman's University, Houston, Texas

Kenneth White, MA, MDiv, PhD Candidate, Loyola University Maryland, Columbia, Maryland

Cyrus Williams, PhD, Licensed Mental Health Counselor and Nationally Certified Counselor, Assistant Professor of Psychology and Counseling, Regent University, Virginia Beach, Virginia

PROLOGUE

During the first half of the 20th century, psychology infused American culture: Returning veterans, manual laborers, housewives, businessmen, and Americans in a plethora of cultural contexts read popular psychology, sought counseling, and embarked on the journey toward self-realization. Ministers studied Freud. Seminarians embarked on clinical education in hospital contexts. Divinity schools and seminaries began offering courses in psychodynamic theory. In response to these and other cultural shifts, "pastoral counseling," an approach to mental health care grounded in the ancient art of Judeo–Christian soul care, quickly developed into a formalized profession. Ministers established pastoral counseling practices both within and outside congregational contexts. The American Association of Pastoral Counselors was formed and offered standards detailing who pastoral counselors were and what they did. Pastoral counselors positioned themselves alongside an increasingly diverse group of mental health professionals. Clinebell (1966) published the first edition of *Basic Types of Pastoral Care & Counseling: Resources for the Ministry of Healing and Growth,* perhaps the most widely read book on the subject. Pastoral counseling emerged as an approach to mental health treatment and a specialized ministry predominantly offered by clergy in Judeo–Christian traditions.

The clarity and popularity of the discipline, however, did not endure. By the time I (Snodgrass) began my own pastoral counseling training in 2005, who pastoral counselors were and what they did were markedly different than during the discipline's nascent days. "What makes pastoral counseling *pastoral*?" This query was posed so frequently during my (Snodgrass) doctoral studies in spiritual care and counseling that it quickly became rhetorical. The question was not intended to elicit a definitive, static answer, for a universal definition of pastoral counseling was elusive. Moreover, a postmodern outlook and propensity to deconstruct cautioned us against explanations that claimed to be true for *all* peoples in *all* places.

During graduate school, I (Snodgrass) enjoyed reflecting on the *pastoral* nature of pastoral counseling with colleagues and mentors. The discussion was generative, and the explanations offered resulted in as many questions as answers. I embraced the ambiguity of the discipline.

Then in 2011, we (Snodgrass and Maynard) both joined the faculty of Loyola University Maryland, and I (Snodgrass) was tasked with teaching "Introduction to Pastoral Counseling" in a CACREP (Council for Accreditation of Counseling and Related Educational Programs)-accredited program that prepares students to become licensed clinical professional counselors. The shift in position, from student to professor, from pastoral counselor-in-training to fellow of the American Association of Pastoral Counselors, compelled me to cultivate a different view on and experience of the discipline's ambiguity. Although studying the discipline's history and debating its future remained an engaging pastime, we (Snodgrass and Maynard) realized that if pastoral counselors-in-training could not succinctly define what made their counseling practice *pastoral*, they simply abandoned the adjective. They graduated from the program, became licensed and employed, and left pastoral counseling to the generations before who fit the mold that, long ago broken, has yet to find new form.

We needed help. We wanted to educate students not only about the practice of pastoral counseling 50 years ago but about what it is today. Myriad excellent articles were available to aid in this effort, but large holes still remained. There did not seem to be a text that offered a comprehensive overview of the diversity of who pastoral counselors are, our psychospiritual frameworks of understanding, and our ways of intervening (Cheston, 2000). Although now in its third edition, *Basic Types of Pastoral Care & Counseling* (Clinebell & McKeever, 2011) is not the definitive text that it once was because it no longer reflects the diversity of pastoral counseling practices and practitioners. We began voicing our concerns with colleagues teaching, supervising, and practicing pastoral counseling and quickly realized that our longing for a comprehensive text portraying the landscape of pastoral counseling today was felt by many.

This volume originated from a shared desire to articulate what makes pastoral counseling *pastoral* in an age of increasing religious diversity, rapid changes in managed health care, and technological capabilities that unite peoples across cultural and geographic divides. This text does not posit a static, universal understanding of pastoral counseling. Rather, it illuminates the diversity within the discipline that is already occurring and offers suggestions regarding how pastoral counselors can navigate the changing landscape of mental health care in our current context to maintain unity amid our diversity.

The authors are long-term clinicians and educators as well as doctoral-level pastoral counselors-in-training; professionals trained in psychology, marriage and family therapy, social work, and counseling; and religiously endorsed and lay adherents of a variety of religious traditions. This multiplicity of voices and perspectives reflects what pastoral counseling is today as well as where the discipline is headed.

Pastoral counseling continues to evolve from its origins as a specialized ministry to an approach to mental health care offered in a wide array of contexts, including both religious and secular settings. Pastoral counselors, while sharing a common identity, are also bicultural as the result of our training and spiritual and religious commitments. This is a pivotal time in the field as practitioners and academics assess both the history and future directions of the discipline, consider the place of pastoral counseling alongside allied professions, and even explore new language to describe the work of pastoral counseling. This introductory text, aimed at an audience of pastoral counseling professionals, students, and allied professionals in ministry and mental health settings (clergy, psychologists, social workers, and professional counselors), provides an overview of key issues in the history, current practice, and future of pastoral counseling.

The text is organized into seven sections. In addition, for faculty and other professionals choosing to adopt the book as a course text, an electronic Instructor's Manual is available featuring sample syllabi, assignments, class activities, and tools to evaluate student understanding of the material. **Requests for the Instructor's Manual can be made by e-mailing textbook@springerpub.com. The appendices mentioned in Chapter 27 are available for download from Springer Publishing Company's website: www.springerpub.com/maynard-snodgrass.** The text itself begins with Chapters 1 and 2, which offer an introduction to the discipline of pastoral counseling by outlining a brief history of pastoral counseling as well as an understanding of how the discipline maintains unity amid the vast diversity of practices and practitioners.

The next three sections are modeled after Cheston's (2000) "ways paradigm" and detail pastoral counseling theory and practice according to three precepts: a way of being, a way of understanding, and a way of intervening. The first of these three sections explores pastoral counselors' ways of being. Chapter 3 addresses the common roles and functions of pastoral counselors as mental health professionals whose identities and/or practices are grounded in both religious and lay contexts.

The second of these three sections describes pastoral counselors' ways of understanding. Chapters 4 and 5, respectively, describe understandings of the human condition and suffering that are often shared among pastoral counselors. In Chapter 6, the uniqueness of pastoral counselors as bilingual mental health professionals, professionals who, based on their training, speak the languages of both psychology and religion, is explored, and a description of how the integration of languages occurs is given. Chapter 7 elucidates how pastoral counselors understand the art of diagnosis in relation to more dominant models of conceptualizing psychopathology and disease. Because spiritual assessment is a key element of effective pastoral counseling practice, Chapter 8 presents methods and tools pastoral counselors can employ to aid in such assessments. Chapter 9 describes the common spiritual and theological content, both explicit and implicit, that arises in pastoral counseling and guides the reader in attending to these themes. Finally, because pastoral counselors are themselves multicultural and exist in increasingly multicultural contexts, Chapter 10 explains how pastoral counselors can navigate the liminal space that arises within cross-cultural encounters.

The fourth section presents the ways of intervening common to pastoral counseling. Chapter 11 offers the reader a sense of the interventions employed by both pastoral counselors and allied mental health professionals, whereas Chapter 12 depicts the distinctiveness of interventions unique to the discipline. Chapter 13 then differentiates pastoral counseling from spiritual direction, a related but discrete discipline that is also grounded in the ancient practice of soul care.

The book's fifth section reflects the religious diversity present among pastoral counselors and those they serve. Based on the assertion that every individual occupies a unique religious location, both within and outside religious traditions, Chapter 14 explores how pastoral counselors can compassionately and ethically counsel in the midst of religious difference. Building on this recognition that all counselors and clients possess different religious locations, the next six chapters present understandings of pastoral counseling from the perspective of distinctive religious and/or cultural traditions. Chapter 15 focuses on a Torah-based approach to counseling within the Jewish faith. Chapter 16 explores pastoral counseling within an Islamic tradition. Chapter 17 offers a Buddhist approach to pastoral counseling grounded in an understanding of the counselor as *kalamitra* or spiritual friend. Chapters 18 and 19, respectively, depict conceptions of pastoral counseling in relation to Hinduism and Native American spirituality. Finally, Chapter 20 focuses on pastoral counseling with queer-identified persons, individuals whose sexual and/or gender identities are fluid or do not conform to traditional binary understandings of gender and sexuality.

The sixth section of the text illustrates special issues in pastoral counseling. These special issues further exemplify the distinctiveness of pastoral counseling as evidenced by the functions of referral, consultation, and collaboration (Chapter 21); the education and supervision of pastoral counselors (Chapter 22); and the use of both qualitative and quantitative research methods (Chapter 23). In recognition of our increased technological abilities, as well as the dearth of mental health resources available in some geographic regions, Chapter 24 guides the reader in understanding distance counseling and how to engage in an ethical distance counseling practice. Finally, because the traditional focus of pastoral counseling has been on the counsel of adults, Chapter 25 presents literature in the area of childhood studies and offers implications for the theory and practice of pastoral counseling.

The seventh and concluding section of the text builds on the theory and practice of pastoral counseling as presented in the first sections by offering a prophetic call for the future of the discipline. In Chapter 26, the reader is invited to consider how the core values of the pastoral counseling tradition might be abandoned, amended, or retained in an effort to move the discipline into the future. Chapter 27 illustrates one model for incorporating pastoral counseling within an integrative, medical context of care. New practices such as these may continue to increase as a result of the changing landscape of managed care and the implementation of the Affordable Care Act. Finally, Chapter 28 offers a reflection on pastoral counseling from beyond the discipline from the perspective of the psychology of religion and spirituality. Understanding how relationships can be formed among and between allied professionals will be an important component of moving the field of pastoral counseling into the future.

At the conclusion of each chapter, the reader is presented with a series of questions for critical reflection. We hope that these questions will help to generate discussion about the theory and practice of pastoral counseling as well as where the discipline is headed. We are grateful to the many authors who helped to nurture this book to fruition and the clients, counselors, and communities who will carry the discipline forward into the future.

Elizabeth A. Maynard and Jill L. Snodgrass

REFERENCES

Cheston, S. E. (2000). A new paradigm for teaching counseling theory and practice. *Counselor Education and Supervision, 39*, 254–269. doi:10.1002/j.1556-6978.2000.tb01236.x

Clinebell, H. C. (1966). *Basic types of pastoral care & counseling: Resources for the ministry of healing and growth*. Nashville, TN: Abingdon Press.

Clinebell, H. C., & McKeever, B. C. (2011). *Basic types of pastoral care & counseling: Resources for the ministry of healing and growth* (3rd ed.). Nashville, TN: Abingdon Press.

Jill L. Snodgrass

1

PASTORAL COUNSELING: A DISCIPLINE OF UNITY AMID DIVERSITY

When I was 6 years old, my maternal great-grandmother died. She lived 400 miles away, and I don't recall seeing her much or being particularly affected by her death. My middle sister, however, at age 11, was quite struck by this loss. It was not that she grieved, per se; rather, she developed existential anxiety and became aware, as Tillich (1952/2000) would maintain, of her own finitude, thus struggling to muster the courage to be. I, of course, did not understand this event in those terms at the time; however, I knew something was "wrong with her" as she begged me, night after night, to share her twin-sized bed.

My parents, concerned for their middle daughter's well-being, decided to make an appointment for her to meet with our congregation's pastoral counselor. Rev. Arnold Schaper, PhD, an ordained United Church of Christ minister, operated a pastoral counseling practice from the congregation's ancillary building. At 6 years old, I didn't understand how, exactly, "Arn" could help my sister. I knew he was a representative of the church, a person of faith. I knew he had a kind and caring disposition. I knew my family respected him. And I knew he was tall. Surely these were the characteristics of someone who could help. I was hopeful that he could lessen my sister's anxiety and free me from the nightly captivity of her twin bed. Eventually, it worked.

In many ways, Arn represented the archetypal pastoral counselor of the early 1980s: male, European American, Protestant, and ordained. After pursuing theological education and earning an MDiv, he served in a church for many years before earning a doctorate in humanistic psychology. He provided pastoral counseling services to the community with the fiscal and material support of a congregation. He personified what J. Claude Evans (1983) described as the norm of the American Association of Pastoral Counselors (AAPC): "that its membership is mostly white, male, Anglo-Saxon, Western and middle-class" (p. 587).

Pastoral counselors with a long tenure in the discipline may recognize Arn as a representative of what Townsend (2009b) refers to as the metanarrative or "grand narrative": a time in the discipline when there was a clear definition of what pastoral counseling was and who pastoral counselors were (p. 10). Townsend claims, "If you had asked me in 1979 what pastoral counseling was, I would have had a swift and certain answer" (p. 1). For those with decades of clinical practice behind them, as well as pastoral counseling educators, it is easy to romanticize the past and long for a clear metanarrative about the discipline and practice of pastoral counseling.

In the past, greater clarity may have existed about the discipline and practice of pastoral counseling. However, this understanding was created, perpetuated, and represented by those at the center, and not the margins, of practice. As Townsend (2009a) asserted, this clear definition of pastoral counseling obscured the plurality of the practice and rendered "non-European-American contributions invisible" (p. 39).

Panikkar's (1979) exegesis on the Tower of Babel can serve as a helpful metaphor for understanding the blessings that may result from the end of pastoral counseling's metanarrative. As recounted in Genesis 11, following the flood, everyone on Earth spoke one language. The people settled in Shinar and attempted to build a tower of brick, a tower reaching to the heavens that would declare their unity and prevent the spread of the people. But God confused their speech, and the sole language gave way to the "babel" of languages. God diversified the languages in an act of privileging plurality. Pastoral counselors at the center of practice in the 1950s to 1970s may have claimed to speak in a singular tongue and envisioned a monolithic tower representing the theory and practice of the discipline. But just like those who settled in Shinar, pastoral counselors at the center "thought themselves to be alone bearers of a flag with absolute standards" (Panikkar, 1979, p. 199) rather than recognizing that "there is no territory belonging exclusively to the pastoral counselor" (Patton, 1981, p. 230). The people who settled in Shinar were made to abandon "the dream of a unitarian," monolithic language and to accept plural tongues and diverse languages (Panikkar, 1979, p. 199). Similarly, pastoral counsels have been challenged to move beyond a grand narrative toward recognizing the plurality present within the discipline and fostering communication and communion among those allied in the goal of nurturing greater psychospiritual well-being within and among today's societies.

Rather than offer yet another grand narrative of what pastoral counseling is and who pastoral counselors are, the goal of this chapter is to describe the plurality present within the discipline, summarize the discipline's use of the adjective *pastoral*, and offer a broad, fluid understanding of pastoral counseling. The chapter then explores the diversity of professionals engaged in pastoral counseling, the characteristics of those professionals within the ever-expanding landscape of mental health care, and the settings in which pastoral counseling most often occurs. It then elucidates the commonly held spiritual assumptions influencing pastoral counseling practice as well as their impact on practice. Finally, the chapter concludes by outlining a clarion call for pastoral counselors to embrace the discipline's unity amid its diversity by "building roads of communication . . . [and] communion" among partners allied toward common goals (Panikkar, 1979, p. 199).

WHAT MAKES PASTORAL COUNSELING "PASTORAL"?

In teaching graduate courses in an introduction to pastoral counseling, I often joke with students about the common misunderstandings we hear when sharing with others that we are aspiring or practicing pastoral counselors: "I'm so glad! A lot of pastors are really messed up. It's so good that you can help them." "Does that mean you work in pastures?" "Are you a minister?" "Is that like counseling sheep or farm animals or something? Are you like the horse whisperer?" Although the adjective *pastoral* may be multivalent or even ambiguous to many in today's culture, the shepherding metaphor on which it is based is grounded in early religious traditions. The adjective *pastoral* refers to the metaphor of the shepherd present in Jewish and Christian scriptures; shepherds are key figures throughout these sacred texts. Moses spent time as a shepherd. David, a young shepherd, was chosen by God to become king. God was depicted as a shepherd in Psalm 23, highlighting God's caring and protective natures. Jesus, "The Good Shepherd," guided, protected, and gave his life for his "sheep." And Abel, Abraham, and Rachel spent time in the pastures caring for and guiding their flocks. The adjective *pastoral* not only refers to this rich religious heritage but also indicates how, through "careful listening, through sensitive responses, and with compassionate understanding, the pastoral counselor shepherds persons into a new grazing land, leads people to cooler waters" (Blanchette, 1991, p. 31).

Townsend, in Chapter 2 of this volume, chronicles the Judeo–Christian history of the discipline of pastoral counseling and demonstrates why the adjective *pastoral* was relevant to the profession given both its historical roots and the religious identities of many pastoral counselors in the 1940s to 1950s. However, as noted earlier, the definition of "pastoral counseling" operant in those early days reflected the practice and its practitioners at the center and not those at the margins; early definitions of pastoral counseling failed to recognize the plurality of practices that were already occurring, and pastoral counselors, much like those who settled in Shinar, only opened their ears to hear the voices of those who spoke the same language and sounded just like them.

As the discipline burgeoned and grew in the mid-20th century, multiple understandings of pastoral counseling were already emerging. For example, in the 1966 edition of *Basic Types of Pastoral Care & Counseling*, one of the most widely read books on the subject, Howard Clinebell differentiated pastoral *counseling* from pastoral *psychotherapy*. He understood pastoral counseling to be more short term and needed throughout the life span and pastoral psychotherapy as a long-term enterprise employing "reconstructive therapeutic methods" to address the growth debilitation that occurs from early life deficits (Clinebell, 1984, p. 26). In 1980, Carroll A. Wise, a pioneer in the modern pastoral counseling movement, contended that use of the term *pastoral counseling* was an effort to put up a fence that said more about who was out rather than who was in. Pastoral counselors who constructed these fences worked to prevent clergy from offering spiritual care to the mentally ill and psychiatrists from attending to matters of religious belief. According to Wise,

> Pastoral "counseling" has been defined by several methods. One is by building professional fences. In this method, one group says, "This is my province. You stay out." Such fences may be supported by certain cultural sanctions or practices. The point is that such a method aims at exclusion. (p. 5)

Not only does building this fence promote the belief that religious leaders should not care for the psyche, but it also furthers the fallacy that mental health professionals should not attend to a client's spiritual or religious beliefs.

Wise and Clinebell were both European American men, both Methodist pastors, and both faculty who taught pastoral care and counseling at Methodist seminaries. In many ways, they were at the center of pastoral counseling and represented the meta-narrative or "grand narrative" of who pastoral counselors were (Townsend, 2009b). Yet their understandings of the theory and practice of pastoral counseling were distinct in numerous ways.

As previously stated, privileging a monolithic understanding of pastoral counseling, both *who* does it and *what* it is, was an attempt, much like the Tower of Babel, for pastoral counselors to make a name for themselves. One way in which many in the discipline have attempted to respect difference and honor diversity, while not discarding the core theories and practice of pastoral counseling, is by renouncing the term *pastoral* altogether due to its Judeo–Christian heritage. The adjective *pastoral* is considered by many to be limiting and narrow. As Doehring (2006) contends, if *pastoral* is understood to refer to the care provider, then it "cannot be used to describe the [counsel] offered by Buddhist, Muslim, or Hindu caregivers" (p. 6). In contexts with rich religious diversity, many hospitals and other organizations have opted to replace the adjective *pastoral* with the seemingly more inclusive term *spiritual* (Doehring, 2006). Hospitals have changed the names of their pastoral care services departments to spiritual care services, for example. Pastoral counseling centers, including many affiliated with the Samaritan Institute, have dropped the adjective *pastoral*, replaced it with *spiritual*, or abandoned it all together.

In addition, many individuals who were trained in pastoral counseling now prefer monikers with less religious heritage and, in some cases, more. They identify as spiritually integrated counselors, spiritually integrated psychotherapists, or spiritual counselors, or they opt for titles such as pastoral psychotherapist, Christian counselor, or Bible counselor. Others have chosen to adopt the titles granted through their licensure, such as marriage and family therapist, social worker, or professional counselor, although their academic training and degrees were in pastoral counseling.

Therefore, for many individuals and institutions with ties to pastoral counseling, the shift from "pastoral" to "spiritual" was considered an attempt to recognize the plurality of practice and practitioners and to value diversity and inclusion. Bruce Rogers-Vaughn (2013), however, posited a compelling argument indicating that neoliberalism is driving the shift in discourse from "pastoral" to "spiritual." Neoliberalism is a capitalist approach to economics that promotes privatization, reduction in social services, free trade, and a trickle-down approach to the distribution of wealth. Neoliberalism favors the privatization of health care rather than universal or comprehensive approaches. Therefore, Rogers-Vaughn argued that the verbiage of pastoral counseling has changed from "theology, pastoral, and soul" to "spiritually-integrated and best practices" because the core tenets of the discipline have been replaced with "neoliberal-friendly terms" that reflect the only grand narrative that remains—that of the "free market" (p. 6). Pastoral counseling, according to Rogers-Vaughn, has abandoned theological reflection and the practice of soul care and is focused instead on best practices, which are largely determined by efficiency and render the counselor a tool of production more than a spiritual companion. Whether one agrees with this assessment or not, semantics and neoliberal economic pressures are among many factors that have contributed to the fragmentation of pastoral counseling.

The Fragmenting of Pastoral Counseling[1]

The tower, the monolithic understanding and approach to the discipline, that many pastoral counselors worked to build was destroyed long before its completion, causing pastoral counselors to scatter and settle in different environs. In addition to the destruction that resulted from semantic changes and the shifting landscape of health care, other dynamics have contributed to the fracturing of a monolithic understanding and practice of pastoral counseling over the past 30 years. First, ordination and religious endorsement have served to fragment the discipline. The AAPC emerged in the early 1960s from a desire to formalize pastoral counseling as a distinctive practice and to "set and maintain standards for individual pastoral counselors and pastoral counseling centers" (Van Wagner, 1992, p. v). This included the creation of membership standards or qualifications to establish structures of accountability and constrain the laxity of practice that was growing within the discipline. As membership standards were discussed and later concretized in 1963, it was simply assumed that "pastoral counselors were by definition ordained ministers" (Townsend, 2009a, p. 28). According to Evans (1983), "The emphasis on ordination during the AAPC's early years came from the supremacy of psychoanalytic theory, with its origin in 19th century patriarchal culture and from the patriarchy of the priesthood still dominant in the majority of churches today" (pp. 587–588). Therefore, early membership standards requiring ordination or religious endorsement resulted in the marginalization of many women, and some men, whose traditions denied them such status on the basis of gender, race/ethnicity, and/or sexual orientation.

The discipline was further fragmented due to a schism that developed regarding how pastoral counseling relates to the life of the local congregation. As most pastoral counselors practicing in the 1950s to 1980s were ordained and serving in what was considered a specialized ministry, questions about the appropriate contexts of pastoral counseling emerged. According to Townsend (2009a), in the mid-1950s, "pastoral counseling claimed a model of ministry that was increasingly segregated from general parish ministry. . . . Many believed the most appropriate place for counseling was a clinic or center separated from broader congregational life" (p. 23). The distance between the church and the pastoral counseling office grew, both literally and metaphorically. For a compelling overview on the divide regarding "private practice," the reader is referred to Van Wagner's (1992) brief book *AAPC in Historical Perspective 1963–1991*.

The schism relating to congregational affiliation emerged, in part, from questions about accountability. Who was the pastoral counselor, functioning in a private practice, accountable to, if not the congregation or denomination? This question was considered in the late 1980s to early 2000s with changes in both licensing and managed care. Whereas pastoral counselors-in-training with seminary education were previously eligible to sit for mental health licensing examinations in most states, this privilege was rescinded in many states (Greider, Clements, & Lee, 2006). In addition, without licensure, many pastoral counselors were no longer eligible for reimbursement through managed care (Townsend, 2009b). As Marshall writes in Chapter 26 of this volume, "Maintaining clinical work as a pastoral counselor who does not carry any other professional license made the work increasingly difficult" (p. 436). For this and other reasons, most modern pastoral counselors-in-training attend training programs that prepare them to become licensed mental health professionals in a variety of allied professions, thus contributing to the pastoral counselor's bicultural identity.

Each of these issues presents challenges to the discipline. As a result of these and other concerns, pastoral counseling has not been able to achieve "unity without uniformity and diversity without fragmentation" (Lalonde, 1994, para. 1). Without a tower, without universal understandings of pastoral counseling theory, practice, and training, the discipline has failed to "[build] roads of communication . . . [and] communion" (Panikkar, 1979, p. 199). According to Townsend (2009a), "To avoid fragmentation of the field, pastoral counselors must develop theories and theologies of difference that allow mutual respect and room for multiversal practices" (p. 63). Toward this goal of fostering unity amid diversity and combatting fragmentation, a fluid definition of pastoral counseling is in order.

Creating Unity Amid Diversity: Definition(s) of Pastoral Counseling

Pastoral counseling is an approach to mental health care that draws on the wisdom of psychology and the behavioral sciences alongside spirituality/religion/theology.[2] Pastoral counseling focuses on the promotion of well-being, symptom alleviation, increased coping, positive behavioral changes, and improved relationships with self and others, and it "regards changes in one's spiritual life, one's values, meanings, and ultimate commitments" (Clinebell, 1984, p. 373) as central.

Pastoral counselors are *bilingual* because they are trained in the languages of both spirituality/religion/theology and psychology. Pastoral counselors integrate the languages of spirituality/religion/theology and psychology by using a diversity of methods (see Chapter 6 in this text by Doehring for further explanation of the various ways pastoral counselors integrate these languages in assessment and intervention). In addition, for reasons of spiritual or religious belief and/or in response to client concern and context, pastoral counselors may place primacy on one language over and above another (van Deusen Hunsinger, 1995).

Pastoral counselors are *bicultural* because they have graduate training in both religious/spiritual/theological education and a mental health discipline. These disciplines have distinct but related cultures, with the former housed more in the humanities and the latter in the social sciences. Pastoral counselors' religious/spiritual/theological education and competence are perhaps the discipline's foremost distinction. According to Doehring (2009),

> What makes us unique in the field of mental health is that we draw upon our theological education to understand our own spirituality, and the spirituality of those we counsel. . . . Our theological education, including its ongoing process of spiritual formation, makes our counseling different from other mental health professionals. (p. 7)

Because the term *theological* refers only to the study of God and therefore excludes the study of many religious and spiritual traditions, I find the term to be too narrow. Yet if this adjective is broadened to include religious and spiritual education as well, then I concur with Doehring (2009) that the primary uniqueness of pastoral counselors is our formal, most often, graduate education in spirituality/religion/theology.

In addition, pastoral counselors are often drawn to spiritual/religious/theological education and the discipline of pastoral counseling in response to "a call" in their lives, whether or not that call is understood to be from God or a transcendent source. This means that pastoral counselors' own faith and spiritual/religious commitments often guide them toward pastoral counseling as well as or rather than other allied mental health disciplines. Nevertheless, pastoral counselors are spiritually, religiously, and theologically flexible and curious. According to Wise (1980), maintaining this flexibility can at times be challenging as it is not simply the regurgitation of "intellectual learning of ideas and systems as presented in the classroom or in a book" (p. 62). Rather, "it requires the growth of the [counselor] in his emotional and spiritual life, the accumulation of insight and understanding into processes and relationships, and the formulation of these insights in theological [spiritual/religious] concepts" (pp. 62–63). The task of pastoral counseling is not to apply static doctrine or sacred texts to clients' presenting concerns. Rather, pastoral counseling entails a more nuanced art of integrating spiritual/religious/theological and psychological wisdom in response to the uniqueness of each client's beliefs and situation.

In addition, pastoral counselors' bicultural identities are often formed by their own religious cultures alongside the cultures espoused by their clinical training programs, which may be in one of many allied mental health disciplines such as social work, marriage and family therapy, professional counseling, or psychology. For example, where I teach at Loyola University Maryland, the pastoral counseling program is accredited by both the Council for Accreditation of Counseling and Related Educational Programs (CACREP) and the AAPC. Therefore, students are formed with bicultural identities as clinical mental health and pastoral counselors with psychological and spiritual/religious/theological education.

Many believe that the distinction of pastoral counseling is about the identity and formation of the pastoral counselor rather than about the practice itself. For example, on the basis of his study of 85 pastoral counselors "selected for maximum variation of religious affiliation, race, gender, ethnicity, geographic location, sexual orientation, social class, training history, and location of current practice" (p. xi), Townsend (2009a) reported that the majority of participants indicated that "pastoral is who I *am* [emphasis added], not what I *do* [emphasis added]" (p. 60). However, in exploring the participants' pastoral identities, many of the identity markers were practices shared by most allied mental health professionals: "bringing my spiritual self into the room," "asking the big questions about meaning in therapy," or "being in relationship" (p. 61). The idea that pastoral counseling is about "who I am" worked better in the early days of the profession when all pastoral counselors were ordained religious leaders, formed in similar theological and psychological ways. Today, in seeking to recognize the unity amid the diversity of the discipline, pastoral counseling cannot be defined solely by the identities of its practitioners. In an attempt to recognize the unique practices and contributions of pastoral counseling within the vast landscape of mental health care, it is important to articulate pastoral counselors' way(s) of being with clients in counseling, way(s) of understanding clients and common clinical concerns, and way(s) of intervening in therapy (Cheston, 2000). This, indeed, is the overarching goal of this text.

PASTORAL COUNSELORS AND OTHER ALLIED MENTAL HEALTH PROFESSIONALS

The bulk of this text focuses on what pastoral counselors *do*, and less attention is spent addressing who pastoral counselors *are*. Therefore, we now turn to explore the diversity of professionals engaged in the field and who pastoral counselors are in relation to other allied mental health professionals. As previously stated, when the AAPC created membership standards in the early 1960s, it was assumed that all pastoral counselors were ordained or "religiously endorsed" (C. Doehring, personal communication, June 11, 2014). Today, the number of religiously endorsed pastoral counselors entering the profession is markedly decreased; unfortunately, the AAPC does not maintain statistics indicating the percentage of religiously endorsed members (B. Nyman, personal communication, July 28, 2014). In Chapter 3 of this volume, Maynard and Parker articulate the common roles and functions of pastoral counselors whose identities are grounded in secular rather than religious contexts. Therefore, it is important now to note briefly the uniqueness of religiously endorsed pastoral counselors.

Religiously endorsed pastoral counselors are, like all pastoral counselors, bilingual and bicultural. They speak the languages of spirituality/religion/theology and psychology, and they are formed in two related but distinctive cultures. Religiously endorsed pastoral counselors are, however, ordained, licensed, or commissioned by their religious traditions or communities. Therefore, they are accountable to the religious organization and, at times, to an ordaining community to which they are called. They may be *acharyas* (Buddhist teachers), *rinpoches* (Tibetan Buddhist teachers), rabbis, imams, deacons, ministers, pastors, priests, or a plethora of other religious leaders. According to Doehring, "What distinguishes religiously endorsed counselors is that their endorsement makes them accountable for how they use their [spiritual, religious, and] theological education and formation in *publicly* representing their religious tradition" (C. Doehring, personal communication, June 11, 2014). In most cases, pastoral counselors are accountable to both their religious organizations and mental health organizations and to licensing boards.

Although licensure laws vary by state, pastoral counselors, like most allied mental health professionals, are also accountable to state licensing boards and cannot practice based solely on their religious standing or accountability to religious orders or organizations. In states where licensure may not be required, it is often very difficult for pastoral counselors (and other mental health counselors) to join insurance panels, which is required in order to see clients wishing to use insurance. Therefore, many aspiring pastoral counselors, both those with and without religious endorsement, opt to attend accredited programs that prepare them to meet state licensing requirements. As previously noted, this contributes to pastoral counselors' bicultural identities as they hold degrees such as MFT, MSW, MS, MA, PhD, and PsyD.

Often as a result of their academic training and the degrees earned, pastoral counselors are active in a variety of professional organizations. Although attention has been paid in this chapter to the AAPC and its historical role in the concretization of the discipline, pastoral counselors are also active in Division 36: the Society for the Psychology of Religion and Spirituality of the American Psychological Association (APA); the Association for Spiritual, Ethical, and Religious Values in Counseling (ASERVIC) that is affiliated with the American Counseling Association (ACA); the Society for Spirituality and Social Work; the Christian Association for Psychological Studies (CAPS); and other professional organizations and associations. Membership and activity in these organizations reflect pastoral counselors' bicultural identities and, according to Townsend (2009a), "Thinking about multiple pastoral identities holds more promise for the field's future, especially as it continues to diversify and migrate away from institutional identity lodged only in AAPC membership" (p. 63).

Formation, both within and beyond academic training and participation in professional organizations, is an important part of ongoing development for all mental health professionals. Formation is the "set of experiences that act to structure knowledge by shaping a perceptual field and cognitive–emotional interpretive framework[s]" (Townsend, 2006, p. 31). Formation results from external and internal, conscious and subconscious, dialogue between theory (or structured knowledge) and practice (or experiences). The formational processes of religiously endorsed pastoral counselors are unique and differ from the formation typical among pastoral counselors whose identities are grounded in secular rather than religious contexts. This is because for many, but not all, pastoral counselors, their formation as religious leaders precedes their formation as mental health professionals. Religiously endorsed pastoral counselors have most often spent years dedicated to a religious or spiritual formation process. This commonly entails religious/spiritual education and study, spiritual direction as it is understood within the tradition, supervision of ministerial practice, and reflection on integrating one's spiritual, emotional, relational, financial, and physical health toward greater well-being. Although formation differs markedly among religiously endorsed pastoral counselors from diverse spiritual and religious traditions, the continuing formational journey of becoming a pastoral counselor is often built on a solid foundation of mutual accountability between the individual and her or his religious organization. Bidwell and Marshall's (2006) book *The Formation of Pastoral Counselors:*

Challenges and Opportunities is a helpful resource for educating the reader on how the formation of pastoral counselors has changed as fewer pastoral counselors undergo the formational processes related to religious endorsement.

THE SETTING AND CONTEXT OF PASTORAL COUNSELING

Given the multiplicity of professionals engaged in pastoral counseling, it is no surprise that pastoral counselors operate in a diversity of settings and contexts. For millennia, spiritual and religious leaders offered care and counsel to and on behalf of their spiritual/religious communities. It was not until the 1950s, however, that pastoral counseling became a specialized form of ministry. As explained by Townsend in Chapter 2 of this text, pastoral counseling in the 1950s was predominantly conducted by religiously endorsed professionals, mostly Protestant clergy, and often occurred in church settings. The advent of pastoral counseling as a specialized ministry was accompanied by an increasing sense of professionalism that often entailed adopting a secular, medical model of care and moving one's practice beyond the walls of the church. Therefore, according to McClure (2010), "Over time, pastoral counselors' identity and work was less aligned with religious communities and more with the secular medical and psychological body" (p. 85). This shift away from the congregational or parish context influenced both the theory and practice of pastoral counseling. On the basis of his analysis of the pastoral counseling literature published between 1949 and 1999, Stone (2001) concluded that:

> most of the pastoral counseling theorists studied either fail to demonstrate a good grasp of the kind of counseling that occurs in parish ministry, or they show little interest in it. Many seem more in tune with classical theology, psychotherapy, or specialized pastoral counseling than with the counseling that happens in local congregations. (p. 187)

Although counsel outside the congregational setting often entailed charging fees for services and was thus a theologically contentious issue, it was also believed that "clients were more likely to be honest outside the walls of the church, client confidentiality was easier to protect, and counseling could be unconstrained by theological, ideological, or practical boundaries usually associated with the church and its clergy" (Townsend, 2009b, p. 2).

In the past 30 to 40 years, however, many pastoral counselors have sought to reclaim the contextual influence of the church. As previously mentioned, many criticisms were leveraged against the discipline of pastoral counseling for distancing itself from parish and congregational contexts. However, there has been a growing recognition in the discipline that communal and systemic factors exert tremendous influence on an individual's mental and spiritual well-being. Therefore, numerous community pastoral counseling centers have reclaimed the congregational context and are now housed in religious buildings, most often churches, in exchange for the provision of free or reduced-fee counseling services to congregants. Religious communities offer hospitality to pastoral counselors and counseling centers and then depend on them as a referral resource. According to Kelcourse (2002), "In response to congregational needs, church based and Samaritan counseling centers have arisen around the country" (p. 144). Such relationships between congregations and pastoral counselors are often experienced as mutually beneficial and considered a mission or outreach to the community by some congregations. Recounting the experience of Dan Moseley, senior pastor at Vine Street Christian Church in Nashville, Tennessee, Kelcourse wrote,

> While those who came to his church for counseling generally did not join the congregation, the church based counseling center was recognized as a significant service to the community. Members of other churches, grateful for an effective referral, felt even greater loyalty to their own minister and congregation than before. (p. 145)

Nevertheless, with changes in managed health care, "pastoral counselors increasingly find their vocational home in public agencies rather than churches or church-related centers" (Townsend, 2009b, p. 9). As licensed mental health counselors, pastoral counselors often work alongside a diversity of allied mental health professionals in academic counseling centers, nonprofit counseling agencies, hospice and bereavement organizations, youth services bureaus, Veterans Affairs medical centers, government-supported agencies, correctional institutions, retirement communities, hospitals, shelter contexts, and more. Given that many of these settings are public or "secular" in nature and, as such, do not often overtly support the integration of spiritual/religious/theological wisdom within mental health care, pastoral counselors are at times challenged to retain the uniqueness of their bilingual and bicultural approach to mental health care. However, an increasing number of mental health professionals now recognize that clients' spiritual/religious beliefs affect their mental well-being. Moreover, culturally competent practice requires the acknowledgment and incorporation of clients' various cultures (i.e., ethnic/racial, educational, sexual, religious) within the counseling process. Therefore, it is hoped that the push toward greater cultural competence, in addition to the growing religious diversity in most U.S. regions, will, in time, contribute to the wider acceptance of incorporating spiritual/religious/theological wisdom within mental health care in public and private agencies alike.

THE DISCIPLINE'S SPIRITUAL ASSUMPTIONS

After describing the discipline of pastoral counseling in all its diversity and outlining pastoral counselors' bilingual and bicultural identities, it may seem hypocritical to posit any assumptions or beliefs shared among pastoral counselors. However, the following three assumptions about human nature seem to fit with most pastoral counselors, even though they are conceptualized uniquely within each counselor's spiritual or religious tradition and lived experience. They are the belief that humans are inherently relational, humans are co-created, and humans are both blessed and depraved.

Humans Are Inherently Relational

Every religious and spiritual tradition possesses its own creation story. Whether one believes that the world was formed when a cosmic egg was split it two, when a rival god emerged from the primeval ocean, when a singular deity spent a week forming life *ex nihilo* (out of nothing), or a plethora of other beliefs, most pastoral counselors concur that creation is interconnected. For pastoral counselors, whose work with humans reveals the positive and negative impacts we have on one another, this recognition of the interconnectedness of creation is witnessed in the intrinsic relationality of all humans (Cooper-White, 2007). Human beings are born from relationship, in relationship, and spend a significant amount of life's energy navigating relationships with self, other, and, for those in theistic traditions, God. According to Cooper-White (2007), "Human beings are thus connected with all creation and with one another, knit into the entire fabric of creation, and interwoven in an unfathomably deep and wide 'living human web'" (p. 39). Pastoral counselors' recognition that humans are inherently relational influences how individual, couple, family, and community problems are assessed and the interventions employed.

Humans Are Co-Created

In the 1940s and 1950s, pastoral counseling drew heavily on psychoanalytic and psychodynamic theories (Clinebell, 1984). In the early days of pastoral counseling, the counselor was often viewed as the "expert" who possessed the ability to uncover aspects of the client's psyche that were considered previously inaccessible to the client and to direct the client toward health and wholeness. The modern pastoral counseling movement was also highly influenced by client-centered therapy and the educative approach to counseling advocated by Carl Rogers and Seward Hiltner. This approach drew "more and more of the solutions to the situation out of the creative potentialities of the person needing help" (Holifield, 1983, p. 304). The client was considered to possess innately the aptitude to move from self-realization to self-actualization.

Grounding these theories, as well as most approaches to pastoral counseling, is the belief that humans are co-created. We do not become who we are in isolation. As inherently relational beings, we are continuously created in and through relationship. Moreover, although pastoral counselors are grounded in a variety of spiritual and religious frameworks, most do not believe that life is fully scripted or predetermined. Humans possess agency that allows us to create our own stories and, with varying degrees of control, to influence our life courses. Writing from a Christian perspective, Wise (1980) contended that "man [sic] as a creature has the power to take a hand in the creation of himself by utilizing and fulfilling the potentials which God has placed in him" (pp. 34–35). As relational beings, at times we benefit from cooperating toward this end with a counselor whose unique expertise also aids in cocreating our journeys. "The pastor[al counselor] has no blueprint of what another person should be" (Wise, 1980, p. 35) but works alongside clients, from his or her own expertise, to help clients to move toward their desired goals and outcomes.

Humans Are Both Blessed and Depraved

Pastoral counselors regularly encounter clients attempting to cope with the pain, suffering, and heartache of the human condition. Spiritual and religious traditions most assuredly differ in their understandings of why humans suffer. Yet whether suffering is perceived as the result of original sin or attachment, divine wrath or fate, most pastoral counselors concur that, at least in some ways, humanity is depraved. Humans will suffer and commit sinful and evil acts, some more egregious than others. Nevertheless, pastoral counselors are also witness to the myriad blessings in clients' lives. Again, whether this is understood as God's favor, coincidence, or the direct result of hard work and perseverance, most pastoral counselors concur that "good" and "evil," however broadly understood, exist simultaneously in individuals, communities, and all creation. As Fox, Gutierrez, Coffield, and Moulder note in Chapter 4 of this text, this is the paradox of human existence. Therefore, recognition of humanity's goodness and depravity requires humility on the part of the pastoral counselor. Wise (1980) wrote that the pastoral counselor is "called upon to accept his [*sic*] basic humanity and to experience within himself the truth that ultimately he stands in the same need as others, and that he has the same potential for sin and illness [and I would add blessing] as do all others" (p. 32). Pastoral counselors are more apt to recognize in others the creative potential toward both creation and destruction, good and evil, if they first identify it in themselves.

BUILDING ROADS OF COMMUNICATION AND COMMUNION

The metanarrative or "grand narrative" (Townsend, 2009b, p. 10) of what pastoral counseling is and who pastoral counselors are no longer holds true (if, indeed, it ever did). Therefore, given the diversity of spiritual/religious/theological backgrounds and training experiences among pastoral counselors, the religious diversity of clients, and the religious heritage of the term *pastoral*, why retain the name *pastoral counseling?* Is use of the name today, as Wise (1980) contended 35 years ago, simply an attempt to build a fence and keep people out? It seems that fences and towers have never truly served the discipline. Therefore, as we strive toward unity among the diversity of practices and practitioners of pastoral counseling, the adjective *pastoral* must be changed or redefined.

Yet fostering connection and unity amid such diversity will not be accomplished by something as simple as a name change. Because there is currently no clear consensus regarding a new moniker for pastoral counseling, perhaps an attempt at redefinition is in order. Pastoral counseling is "pastoral" on the basis of the training, formation, and spiritual/religious/theological orientations of pastoral counselors—that is, "who we are" and "what we do," as well as the uniqueness of our assessments and interventions. Pastoral counselors recognize that "whether or not we are religious, all persons inhabit a particular location relative to religion" (Greider, Chapter 14, p. 235). This means that all counselors and clients possess distinct religious locations, and thus all clinical encounters, even those between two Methodists, two Orthodox Jews, or two Muslims from the Shia Ismaili tradition, are interreligious. Pastoral counselors employ distinct methods of integrating psychology and spirituality/religion/theology (see Chapter 6 by Doehring, this volume). Pastoral counselors have unique ways of listening for and responding to implicit and explicit spiritual and theological themes in counseling (see Chapter 9 by Snodgrass and Noronha, this volume). Finally, although pastoral counselors draw from the same schools of psychotherapy and utilize therapeutic modalities identical to those used by most mental health professionals (see Chapter 11 by Hanna, this volume), there are also distinct interventions employed in pastoral counseling (see Chapter 12 by Jones Davis, this volume).

In order for the discipline of pastoral counseling to move forward with unity amid diversity, pastoral counselors of various faith traditions, working in various contexts, and trained in various cultures, need to engage in greater communication and communion with one another. I urge you to read and reflect on Chapter 26 of this volume, written by Joretta Marshall, which outlines in a prophetic manner the values of pastoral counseling that can help to move the discipline into the future. In addition, the reader is encouraged to:

- Seek out religiously diverse dialogue partners. Form a case consultation group or cultivate a supervisory relationship with someone doing the work of pastoral counseling (as defined previously) who may or may not identify as a pastoral counselor—for example, a Christian counselor, a spiritually integrated psychotherapist, a social worker serving in a Jewish community center, a Torah-based therapist, a biblical counselor, or a Buddhist psychotherapist. In addition, remember that diversity within religious traditions can be as great as that found among them.
- Commit to ongoing spiritual/religious/theological education. Pastoral counselors do not impose their own spiritual/religious/theological views or assessments on clients. Rather, such wisdom is created collaboratively through critical reflection with clients and communities. Although counselors are committed to continuing clinical education, most do not put forth the same effort to continuing spiritual/religious/theological growth. At least not formally.
- Attend the annual meeting of an allied professional organization such as APA's Society for the Psychology of Religion and Spirituality (Division 36), ASERVIC, the AAPC, the Society for Spirituality and Social Work, and others. Most pastoral counselors are bi- or multicultural as a result of their training and professional memberships. Pastoral counselors, with their training in spiritual/religious/theological reflection, have much to offer to colleagues in other organizations but also much to learn from them.
- Consider your title. If you were trained as a pastoral counselor and have dropped the *pastoral* adjective, consider reclaiming it. You no doubt had a compelling reason for doing so; however, the future of the discipline is dependent on many voices and perspectives coming together to influence both the practice and the public's perception. Your uniqueness is an essential part of the whole. Or, if the description of pastoral counseling presented earlier mirrors your own practice and you do not identify as a pastoral counselor, reflect critically on why this is. Perhaps this is a culture in which you are already acculturated and may benefit from greater engagement with. As Patton (1981) asserted,

> The goal of pastoral counseling is never simply unimpaired function, but function *for* something, for one's commitments and meanings. The pastoral counselor is not the only health practitioner who has this understanding of healing. He or she is, however, the only one whose role and identity, as well as function, *represent* [emphasis added] this understanding. (p. 230)

- Advocate on behalf of the discipline. Doing this requires knowing enough about the unity and diversity of pastoral counseling and counselors that one can confidently share with others "who we are" and "what we do" (Townsend, 2009a). Speaking out on behalf of the discipline entails more than serving clients and connecting with other professionals. It includes affecting our communities by responding to current events from a psychospiritual perspective, facilitating workshops and serving on panels within secular and religious communities, contributing to the local chapters of organizations such as the National Alliance on Mental Illness or Active Minds, and volunteering to participate in events such as the National Depression, Alcohol, and Eating Disorder Screening Days. Advocating on behalf of the profession entails influencing federal policies that affect both mental health providers and consumers; forming partnerships that enable pastoral counselors to provide services to underserved and marginalized populations; correcting misconceptions, which may result from religious discrimination, about the practice of pastoral counseling among individuals, allied mental health professionals, and wider communities; and helping emerging professionals to navigate the landscape of managed care by getting credentialed for insurance panels.

Pastoral counselors, like the people who settled in Shinar, have been forced to abandon "the dream of a unitarian," monolithic discipline in favor of recognizing plurality and fostering communication and communion among those allied in the goal of nurturing greater psychospiritual well-being within and among today's societies (Panikkar, 1979, p. 199). Therefore, pastoral counselors are called to the work of continuously defining and redefining who we are and what we do, communicating with allied mental health professionals and consumers about who we are and what we do, and challenging the construction of fences and towers that may result in greater exclusion than inclusion.

REFLECTION QUESTIONS

1. Do you feel the profession should retain the use of the term *pastoral* or replace it with something more inclusive, such as *spiritual?* Why or why not?
2. What are uniquely pastoral ways that a counselor can "be" with, understand, and therapeutically intervene in clients' lives?
3. According to Snodgrass, pastoral counselors share core spiritual beliefs that humans are inherently relational, humans are co-created, and humans are both blessed and depraved. How do these assumptions relate to your own religious/spiritual tradition and lived experience? What implications do these assumptions have for you as a pastoral counselor?
4. Do you currently (or will you in the future) identify yourself distinctly as a *pastoral* counselor? Explain your reason(s) for this decision.

NOTES

1. I am indebted to Loren Townsend for his use of the verb *fragmenting* to describe the discipline of pastoral counseling in his Opening Convocation at Louisville Seminary on February 5, 2009.
2. It is inaccurate to say that pastoral counselors draw on the wisdom of theology, because not all pastoral counselors or clients identify with theistic traditions. In the same way, it is inaccurate to say that pastoral counselors draw on the wisdom of religion, as, for example, some contend that Buddhism is a "philosophy" and not a "religion." For this reason, spirituality/religion/theology are each essential to pastoral counseling practice in various contexts.

REFERENCES

Bidwell, D. R., & Marshall, J. L. (2006). *The formation of pastoral counselors: Challenges and opportunities.* Binghamton, NY: Haworth Pastoral Press.

Blanchette, M. C. (1991). Theological foundations of pastoral counseling. In B. K. Estadt, M. C. Blanchette, & J. R. Compton (Eds.), *Pastoral counseling* (2nd ed., pp. 18–35). Englewood Cliffs, NJ: Prentice Hall.

Cheston, S. E. (2000). A new paradigm for teaching counseling theory and practice. *Counselor Education and Supervision, 39,* 254–269. doi:10.1002/j.1556-6978.2000.tb01236.x

Clinebell, H. C. (1966). *Basic types of pastoral care & counseling: Resources for the ministry of healing and growth.* Nashville, TN: Abingdon Press.

Clinebell, H. C. (1984). *Basic types of pastoral care & counseling: Resources for the ministry of healing and growth* (Rev. ed.). Nashville, TN: Abingdon Press.

Cooper-White, P. (2007). *Many voices: Pastoral psychotherapy in relational and theological perspective.* Minneapolis, MN: Fortress Press.

Doehring, C. (2006). *The practice of pastoral care: A postmodern approach.* Louisville, KY: Westminster John Knox Press.

Doehring, C. (2009). Theological accountability: The hallmark of pastoral counseling. *Sacred Spaces: The e-Journal of the American Association of Pastoral Counselors, 1,* 4–34. Retrieved from http://www.aapc.org/media/75733/theologicalaccountability3.pdf

Evans, J. C. (1983). Pastoral counseling comes of age. *Christian Century, 100,* 586–588.

Greider, K. J., Clements, W. M., & Lee, K. (2006). Formation of care of souls: The Claremont way. *American Journal of Pastoral Counseling, 8,* 177–195. doi:10.1300/J062v08n03&#x0331l13

Holifield, E. B. (1983). *A history of pastoral care in America.* Nashville, TN: Abingdon Press.

Kelcourse, F. (2002). Pastoral counseling in the life of the church. *Encounter, 63,* 137–146.

Lalonde, R. (1994). *Unity in diversity: Acceptance and integration in an era of intolerance and fragmentation.* Retrieved from http://bahai-library.com/lalonde_unity_diversity

McClure, B. J. (2010). *Moving beyond individualism in pastoral care and counseling: Reflections on theory, theology, and practice.* Eugene, OR: Cascade Books.

Panikkar, R. (1979). The myth of pluralism: The Tower of Babel—A meditation on non-violence. *Cross Currents, 29,* 197–230.

Patton, J. (1981). Pastoral counseling comes of age. *Christian Century, 98,* 229–231.

Rogers-Vaughn, B. (2013). Pastoral counseling in the neoliberal age: Hello best practices, goodbye theology. *Sacred Spaces: The e-Journal of the American Association of Pastoral Counselors, 5,* 5–45. Retrieved from http://www.aapc.org/media/127298/2_rogers_vaughn.pdf

Stone, H. W. (2001). The congregational setting of pastoral counseling: A study of pastoral counseling theorists from 1949–1999. *Journal of Pastoral Care, 55,* 181–196.

Tillich, P. (2000). *The courage to be* (2nd ed.). New Haven, CT: Yale University Press. (Original work published 1952)

Townsend, L. L. (2006). Theological reflection and the formation of pastoral counselors. *American Journal of Pastoral Counseling, 8,* 29–46. doi:10.1300/J062v08n03_03

Townsend, L. L. (2009a). *Introduction to pastoral counseling.* Nashville, TN: Abingdon Press.

Townsend, L. L. (2009b). *What's pastoral about pastoral counseling?* Retrieved from http://caldwell chapel.blogspot.com/2009/02/whats-pastoral-about-pastoral.html

van Deusen Hunsinger, D. (1995). *Theology & pastoral counseling: A new interdisciplinary approach.* Grand Rapids, MI: William B. Eerdmans.

Van Wagner, C. A. (1992). *AAPC in historical perspective 1963–1991.* Fairfax, VA: American Association of Pastoral Counselors.

Wise, C. A. (1980). *Pastoral psychotherapy: Theory and practice.* New York, NY: Jason Aronson.

Loren Townsend

2

PASTORAL COUNSELING'S HISTORY[1]

The *Dictionary of Pastoral Care and Counseling* (Clinebell, 1990) identifies pastoral counseling as a 20th-century phenomenon. It emerged among North American Protestant pastors who incorporated new psychological information into their ministries and, by midcentury, was a ministry specialty requiring distinctive training (Clinebell, 1990). However, pastoral counselors also claim a genealogy anchored in ancient Hebrew and Christian understandings of care, expanded through the history of the Western Christian church and the Protestant Reformation, and later focused in the confluence of modern theology and behavioral sciences in late 19th-century Europe and North America. This genealogy highlights contemporary pastoral counseling's Euro-American characteristics and the dominant Protestant, clerical interpretive tradition that anchors its identity. Equally important, historical review helps us appreciate what practices, traditions, and people are marginalized or excluded by the particularity of this genealogy.

CONTEXT: JUDEO–CHRISTIAN CARE OF THE SOUL

In his *Introduction to Pastoral Care*, Charles Gerkin (1997) noted that structured care and counseling has existed "back as far as the collective memories of the Christian community can be extended" (p. 23). He observed that the oldest Judeo–Christian model of care rests on a threefold tradition. Prophets assured continuity of tradition, priests organized worship, and wise men and women provided practical guidance in daily life. Noting the constancy of these three elements through history, Gerkin concluded that care of God's people always rests in a "trialogical interactive tension" among these three central elements (p. 26). This tension was consolidated in Jesus, "the good shepherd." Central to the Gospel of John, this metaphor depicts Jesus' ministry as the unified expression of wisdom (parables), prophetic action (cleansing of the temple), and priestly leadership (relationship with his followers). It was a metaphor so compelling that "shepherd of the flock" became the prototypical image of a pastor in the early church.

   Details of Jesus' ministry in the Synoptic Gospels anticipate pastoral counseling practices. In *A History of the Cure of Souls*, John McNeill (1977) observed that these writers emphasize Jesus' difference from other scribes, rabbis, teachers, and masters of wisdom. Although he was sometimes called Rabbi, Jesus appears most often as a healer of souls who conversationally engaged male and female disciples, public leaders, and moral outcasts. Unlike other religious leaders, his ministry was marked by a clear focus on human need and God's care for those who suffer. Instead of gathering large crowds intentionally, Jesus seemed to prefer transformational conversations with individuals or small groups. These were often structured to encourage lively dialogue that led others to discover important truths or to offer spiritual renewal and rest. McNeill pointed to gospel stories such as the rich ruler (Mark 10:17–22), Zacchaeus (Luke 19:1–10), and his encounter with the Samaritan woman (John 4:7–14) as characteristic of Jesus' personal, conversational approach.

Jesus' example was carried into the early church by pastors who responded personally to human need. Their interventions nurtured and protected Christian faith and offered guidance for living. The Apostle Paul expressed this through his "anxiety for all the churches" (2 Cor. 11:28 American Standard Version), which motivated him frequently to provide practical—and sometimes very personal—guidance to congregations and individual church leaders. His letters are rich with examples of pastoral responses to specific problems. These included, for example, questions of sexual ethics (1 Cor. 7:1–9), decision making in situations of personal difference (Rom. 14:2–12), personal failure and depression (2 Cor. 1:8, 11), marital problems (Eph. 4–5), divorce (1 Cor. 7:10–16), self-destructive lifestyles (1 Cor. 5:4–6; 2 Cor. 2:5–11; Gal. 6:1), and mutual support within the community of believers (Rom. 14:7, 15, 19; 1 Thess. 5:11). Paul's interventions often addressed specific personalities and interpreted the local context of problems.

In their analysis of pastoral care, Clebsch and Jaekle (1967) note that through most of Christian history, *pastoral* has described a specific constellation "of helping acts, done by *representative Christian persons*, directed toward the *healing, sustaining, guiding,* and *reconciling* of *troubled persons* whose troubles arise *in the context of ultimate meanings and concerns*" (p. 4). Care begins when an individual[2] experiencing an insoluble problem turns to a person who represents the resources, wisdom, and authority of religion. This person need not be clergy or an official representative of a faith tradition. However, *pastoral* does specifically require one who offers care to be grounded in the resources of a specific faith tradition, to have access to the wisdom generated by the heritage of Christians' experience, and to be able to claim the authority of a "company of believers." This foundation allows a carer to engage troubled persons at the point of deep religious meaning and ultimate concerns, which are often hidden or unconscious.

Clebsch and Jaekle (1967) identify four basic functions of pastoral care that emerged in the early church (healing, sustaining, guiding, and reconciling) and trace how these are variously emphasized through eight "epochs" of Western church history. For example, all four functions can be found in records of care from the period of church persecution, but pastors were more concerned with reconciliation rather than healing, guiding, or sustaining. On the other hand, guiding took a focal role in the period of church consolidation after Constantine and during the Dark Ages. The medieval church codified care in a sacramental system to emphasize illness and healing. During The Enlightenment, care was organized around sustaining souls in a treacherous world, and care in post-Christendom (late 18th and 19th centuries) emphasized pluralism, voluntarism, and guidance toward personal value systems and norms. Gerkin (1997) uses these epochal stories of Western Christianity to develop his thesis that pastoral care is always formed in a specific sociocultural location that must balance four tensions. Care must attend (a) to the foundational tradition that grounds faith and practice within the Christian community, (b) to the life of the community of faith itself, (c) to the needs and problems of individuals and families, and (d) to the "issues and concerns of the contemporary cultural context" (p. 36). American history provided a unique context for these tensions that helped shape pastoral counseling into a 20th-century specialized ministry and professional practice.

CONTEXT: CARE AND COUNSELING IN AMERICAN RELIGIOUS LIFE

In *A History of Pastoral Care in America*, E. Brooks Holifield (1983) charted how elements of pastoral counseling emerged more than 300 years ago as part of a larger sociopolitical story. It is important to note that Holifield's history—which is the most comprehensive history of pastoral care to date and the basis for most other writers' discussion of that history—excludes accounts of slave and Black churches, which had little of their history documented. The Euro-American church's story is tied to a narrative of change in American culture and economy, changes in how the church and ministers functioned in society, profound advances in medicine and psychology, and theologians' efforts to interpret these shifts and integrate them into a vision for American religious life. American pastors:

> brought to their tasks conflicting traditions, clashing temperaments, disparate methods of "pastoral conversation," and differing views of theology. Indeed, to trace the changing styles of "pastoral care" in America is to tell a story of transformations in theology, psychology, and society. . . . If one listens throughout a period of three centuries, one can trace a massive shift in clerical consciousness—a transition from salvation to self-fulfillment—which reveals some of the forces that helped to ensure "the triumph of the therapeutic" in American culture. (p. 16)

In practice, this meant that the central focus of care in the church shifted from concern with salvation and church membership to personal counseling. Rapid evolution of psychological and clinical sciences was a driving force for this changing vision of humans' primary needs. Although theology and ministry had always interacted with the psychologies of their day, Holifield saw America as a special case. American religious thought coalesced around introspective piety that required pastors to know something of parishioners' inner world. This influence was powerful enough for him to claim that "America became a nation of psychologists in part because it had once been a land of Pietists" (Holifield, 1983, p. 65). This basic relationship between religion and psychology, nurtured by the trajectory of American social and political life over three centuries, created a context from which pastoral counseling emerged as a Protestant ministry specialty.

CARE IN EARLY AMERICAN HISTORY

Holifield (1983) highlighted how early American pastoral care reflected social and theological issues of the time. Although approaches to care were embedded in four separate Christian traditions—Catholic, Lutheran, Anglican, and Reformed—all were anchored one way or another in helping parishioners manage sin in their internal lives. The purpose of care was to foster spiritual growth. Pastors were expected to be expert on inner experience, equipped to help people become sensitive to sin, and able to map personal progress toward religious growth. How pastors understood this was firmly grounded in the American intellectual context. Seventeenth-century pastoral manuals showed a dynamic interplay between pastoral activity, changing social conditions, and innovations in American theology, philosophy, psychology, and ethics. The result was not so much a systematic theology of care as it was a "complex of inherited ideas and images subject to continued modification in changing social and intellectual settings" (Holifield, 1983, p. 30). Care during this period reflected the hierarchies of a colonial social order, most clearly seen in a theological dichotomy between body and soul. People experienced problems in living because they defied established order, especially supernatural authority. This was an internal problem because defiance expressed failure of "higher" mental and spiritual functions to control "lower" dimensions of physicality. Pastoral care most often was wise counsel to support an inner life of obedience. One grew spiritually by learning to subject bodily life to the rule of the spirit and by obeying God, the highest of all authorities.

The Great Awakening of the mid-1700s added complexity to this hierarchical notion. In the light of revivalism, "Old Light" and "New Light" religious leaders debated how emotion and rationality should be balanced in spiritual growth. New Light revivalists called for primacy of emotional experience, whereas Old Light pastors challenged emotion unbridled from reason. This struggle pressed disagreeing pastoral theologians such as Charles Chauncy, Jonathan Edwards, and Gilbert Tennent to examine philosophical, psychological, and theological interpretations of human affect and rationality in religious experience. Holifield (1983) identified Jonathan Edwards as a master of integration who turned to John Locke's psychology to help answer theological questions raised by revivalism and to revise Puritan understanding of internal religious life. The result was a forceful, theologically and psychologically balanced position on human volition, emotion, and behavior that helped stabilize care in a revivalist context. Edwards also provided a practical model for care. He frequently invited troubled persons into his study for conversation and encouraged pastors to attend diligently to the needs of parishioners beset by life's problems (Edwards, 1743).

The Great Awakening raised significant questions in American religious life. How should rationality and sentiment be managed in the internal life of the soul? How did right behavior and belief relate to feelings and convictions? These questions "popularized a psychological vocabulary and hence a way of thinking about society, politics, and piety. It was that vocabulary and that way of thinking that would shape the cure of souls in America for half a century" (Holifield, 1983, p. 106). This focus inspired pastoral theologians to observe the struggles of spiritual growth, consider classification systems of spiritual maturity, and develop guides for pastoral listening. Counseling consisted of firm advice giving (most often related to effective moral living), finding the religious source of true happiness, and preventing parishioners from pursuing wrong ways of living.

Nineteenth-century life in America shifted away from agrarian roots and toward urbanization, privatization, industrialization, and social segmentation. By midcentury, economic life began to organize loosely around hierarchies of owner and laborer. Factory and merchant trade replaced the home as the center of economic production. Work and family—now separate spheres—were structured around more sharply defined gender roles. Men worked away from home in private industry, whereas women guarded the private domestic retreat insulated from the concerns of economic production (Hereven, 1984). Religious life paralleled social developments as evangelical Protestantism became a majority in cities and towns and normalized religious life as private and voluntary.

By the mid-1800s, the church's role in American life had changed. Churches, particularly in towns and cities, were no longer primary representatives of a community's identity or arbiters of social values. Instead, they became private communities consisting of volunteers. Pastoral emphasis turned from defining right values, beliefs, and behaviors toward fostering voluntary personal conversion and nurturing individual spiritual life. Clergy became shepherds of a private congregation that could, like a private business, grow and prosper or fail and die. On one hand, this change signaled a significant loss of ministers' central role in a community. On the other hand, ministry gained status as a career endowed with advancement possibilities similar to vocations in private industry. Turmoil over the abolition of slavery also "prompted many Protestant congregations to define themselves as 'sanctuaries,' centers of devotion secure from the outside world" (Holifield, 1983, p. 125). Church became a private sphere with congregational life focused on devotionalism and personal experience. As social and religious life segregated, pastors turned their attention almost exclusively toward parishioners' inner lives. *Pastoral* now stood in contrast to *public*. This new religious "culture of the self" sparked intense pastoral interest in emerging psychologies and innovative care.

Holifield (1983) offers Ichabod Spencer as a prototypical pastoral innovator. Conscious of his diminished pastoral authority, Spencer (1850/2001) modeled a new form of pastoral intervention in *A Pastor's Sketches*. Here he constructed a broad vision of the inner world of the human mind influenced by 19th-century psychologists and mental philosophers (Francis Bacon, John Locke, David Hume, Thomas Upham, and Dugald Stewart). By understanding internal states, emotions, and motivation, a pastor could help parishioners make the sentimental conscious and reach deeper levels of self-understanding. Spencer's case studies showed how pastoral conversation could enhance self-understanding and help "anxious enquirers" make decisions while also sustaining their connection to a worshipping community. Although controversial, his method was influential.

As the culture of self gained strength in the late 19th century, congregations expected their pastors to provide individual counseling about moral matters and to lead church-based small groups focused on expression of feeling and honest conversation about difficult matters. Pastors needed to be students of human nature and psychology who could classify persons and their problems and guide the individual toward a healthy, balanced sense of self and salvation. Pastoral counseling in this period helped church members develop conscience, form character, balance emotion and rationality, experience religious conviction, exhibit good moral behavior, and find ways to move beyond despair. A few pastoral leaders advocated for a new discipline of clinical theology based in the case methods of law and medicine (Holifield, 1978).

Gerkin (1997) notes that by the end of the 19th century, two changes had transformed pastoral care and counseling. First, churches that formerly were centers of worship and evangelism became the center of social life for a voluntary, private community. Congregations were expected to meet social needs, including counseling, to enhance emotional and psychological life. Second, the style of pastoral presence in counseling had shifted from direct moral instruction to quiet conversations with parishioners. This "natural" style reflected psychologists' discovery of the unconscious mind and liberal theologians' focus on God's immanent presence in nature. These two shifts supported a culture of self-mastery and prepared the way for what Gerkin calls "the full-blown appropriation of the rapidly developing psychological sciences" (p. 49).

TWENTIETH-CENTURY CONTEXT

By the early 20th century, most mainstream American pastors were less concerned about helping parishioners balance emotion and rationality and more concerned about subconscious dynamics influencing men's and women's feelings and behavior. This was coupled with a liberal Protestant doctrine of divine immanence that supported fundamental trust in the creative action of nature. It was important, therefore, to understand human psychology, especially as it applied to helping parishioners organize their internal lives and daily behavior. This matched a dramatic expansion in academic and therapeutic psychology between 1880 and 1910. These disciplines were asking many of the same questions posed by ministers and pastoral theologians: What is the relationship between human feeling, thought, volition, and action? Is conscious activity more important than unconscious activity? How do these factors influence mental and behavioral healing? How can human religious life be understood psychologically? Several significant developments helped form pastoral counseling as a mid-20th-century specialty.

Psychology and Psychotherapy

Prior to the 20th century, most academic psychologists were busy conducting studies to describe states of consciousness, levels of attention, or perception. Few were concerned about therapeutic application. However, in the late 1890s, William James at Harvard University pressed for more clinical attention. Psychology, he believed, offered little if it could not contribute to real human life. James proposed a functionalist[3] psychology to bridge scientific study of the brain and clinical need. He believed it was useless to study mental structures in isolation. Sensation and mental experience must be understood in the context in which they occurred. Mind and body were a psychophysical unity. Psychology must attend to how the mind adapts to changing physical circumstances as well as to states of mind. This shift provided psychology a way to relate directly to the concerns of everyday human life and problems.

James's approach had much to offer. Functional psychology made room for the idea that human perception and thought could be organized by will. Furthermore, his vision of an integrated mind and body resolved much of the split between rationality and sentimentality that had dominated nearly a century of pastoral theology. Linking mental activity and behavior provided a pathway for self-fulfillment—an idea that quickly appealed to clergy counselors. For example, James (1892) defined *habit* as a reciprocal exchange between neurological activity and behavior. That is, the mind stimulated a tendency toward action, but action also influenced the activities of the mind. Habits could be developed systematically or controlled because individuals could decide where to direct their attention. In these decisions, individuals partially create their environments and their destinies. James's concept of the "willing self" supported counseling that encouraged character development through self-mastery and self-control. These themes made sense in the masculine ethos of early pastoral counselors.

In his later work, James set the stage for more passive approaches to counseling by emphasizing a "subliminal self" that was not accessible to active, conscious awareness. James (1902) refined these ideas in *The Varieties of Religious Experience*, in which he proposed saving transformation was grounded in subconscious processes that were beyond the control of conscious action and effort. Religious behavior could be "healthy-minded" or "sick-minded" depending on the underlying internal processes from which it emerged. "Sick souls" would find relief from their internal struggle not through effort but through surrender to internal life.

The new psychology of religion developed by James, Edwin Starbuck, and James Leuba suggested that religious transformation was not so much an effect received from a transcendent God but a function of human psychology. This position fit well with liberal Protestant thought and 19th-century Transcendentalism (Holifield, 1983;

Schmidt, 2012), both of which emphasized the authority of personal experience and God's immanent presence in human life. Salvation was a human process. Problems of the soul were about inner, emotional experience, not about right belief or doctrine. Pastoral counseling in liberal congregations began to shift away from cognitive, intellectual answers and toward helping parishioners surrender to a "wider self" that would lead to transformation.

James's (1890/1983) idea of balance between action and receptivity, the influence of 19th-century New Thought,[4] and an emerging psychology of religion expanded Protestant preference for a "natural" approach to counseling. At the same time (c. 1910), Freud was emphasizing unconscious mental processes that drove behavior and was pressing neurology toward a "natural" cure for sick souls through psychoanalysis. For pastoral counselors and theologians, psychoanalysis raised awareness that human emotional, spiritual, and volitional life was more complex and mysterious than supposed by earlier theological anthropologies. This implied that effective clergy counseling would require specialized training in the methods of psychotherapy.

The Emmanuel Movement

Advances in psychotherapy quickly attracted the attention of counseling clergy. As early as 1905, parish clergy incorporated psychotherapy as a central part of pastoral care. Emmanuel Church (Episcopal) in Boston was an important model. Believing that all pastors were psychotherapists whether they meant to be or not, Rector Elwood Worcester pressed for parish care to be guided by science rather than tradition. He led the church to sponsor lectures about therapy and psychological disorders, collaborate with physicians to conduct diagnostic sessions at the church, and form treatment teams to cure "nervous diseases resulting from defects of character" (Holifield, 1983, p. 206). Physicians would make diagnoses and refer appropriate cases to church-centered therapists. This new approach quickly spread to well-to-do Protestant congregations in the United States, Europe, Asia, and Africa. The Emmanuel model included features of James's attention to relaxation and receptivity, Freud's concept of the unconscious, and an expectation that psychotherapy would produce stronger character and moral control.

By the early 1920s, conflict between physicians and clergy began to erode the movement. Physicians initially welcomed clergy as partners in treatment, expecting them to work under the direction of physicians and limit their work to moral education or suggestive therapy. However, clergy partners wanted to build a pastoral psychotherapy that included work with the unconscious to help build character. Physician critics responded that pastoral counselors were confusing theology with therapy and making a substandard attempt to become psychotherapists without medical training. Although short-lived (1905–1929), this movement was the first effort by Protestant clergy to claim treatment authority over psychological problems, address the scientific materialism of early 20th-century medicine, and offer a model of care that integrated a nonreductionistic vision of body, mind, and spirit (McCarthy, 1984).

The Social Gospel and Christian Education

The decade following World War I was what Holifield (1983) called a "psychological revival" that left no American institution untouched. This revival was influenced by American soldiers who had received psychological services in the military, a shift toward the Social Gospel in Protestant thought, and popular fascination with Freud. Psychology promised success through self-realization to a culture that was quickly becoming urban, white collar, and middle class. Popular psychology shifted its focus from character building to developing personalities able to adapt to industry and work well with others. Ministers were expected to offer care informed by these psychological trends. In a 1934 study of ministry education, Mark May (May, Brown, Shuttleworth, Jacobs, & Feeney, 1934) found that nearly 80% of Protestant clergy had regular private consultations with congregants about personal problems. These ministers felt unprepared by seminaries to manage these consultations. May concluded that individual counseling was likely to become a permanent and critically important dimension of ministry in the future. Harry Emerson Fosdick, pastor of Riverside Church in New York (1926–1946), argued that the success of the Social Gospel[5] required better adjusted individuals. He claimed pastoral counseling as the center of his ministry and insisted that the best preaching was personal counseling at a group level. Fosdick's outspoken advocacy for counseling was a model for pastors "who were eager to learn from Freud but disinclined to pronounce him savior" (Holifield, 1983, p. 221).

Pastoral counseling entered seminaries through religious education departments in the 1920s and 1930s. Religious educators were attracted to John Dewey's claim that education was a form of personal growth in which experience was reorganized to inform future action. Influenced by Dewey, George Albert Coe at Union Theological Seminary taught that religious education should promote individual self-realization and insisted that care of souls should be organized by the psychological method. Consequently, early pastoral counselors studied psychology of religion, developmental psychology, and the increasingly popular theories of Sigmund Freud, Alfred Adler, and Carl Jung. Seminary-trained pastoral counselors found homes in congregations where they became resident psychologists carrying on some of the tradition of the failed Emmanuel movement. Carl Rogers, a leading 20th-century humanist psychologist who had a profound later influence on pastoral counseling, credits his education at Union Theological Seminary as central to his focus on the value of helping relationships.

Clinical Pastoral Education

Gerkin (1997) described the 1920s as a profoundly transitional time for pastoral care. The Emmanuel and Social Gospel movements were waning. The brutality of wars and oppression in the early 20th century led neo-orthodox theologians—particularly Karl Barth—to challenge liberalism's optimism and focus on human sinfulness and the need for salvation.[6] During this time, a small group of ministers organized to offer clinical training in hospitals and social agencies. The group was led by congregational pastor Anton Boisen. His personal struggle with psychosis prompted him to explore links between theology, mental suffering, and effective ministry. In 1925, clinical pastoral education (CPE) was born as Boisen and Boston neurologist Richard Cabot began training a small group of theological students using medical case study methods. Their agenda was to transform the Protestant ministry by engaging ministers in concrete episodes of human conflict and pain. This clinical pastoral training model shaped how pastoral counselors would later appropriate psychotherapeutic theory. New pastoral counseling centers at Wellesley Hills Congregational Church and Old South Church in Boston in the early 1930s gave concrete expression to these innovations. In 1937, the American Foundation of Religion and Psychiatry (AFRP) was established by psychoanalytic psychiatrist Smiley Blanton and author Norman Vincent Peale at the Marble Collegiate Church in New York City. The AFRP's success in training counselors and providing psychotherapy in a religious context anchored later efforts to form a professional guild and an institutional identity for pastoral counselors.

In the mid-1930s, Cabot and Boisen disagreed about the nature of mental illness and parted ways. Cabot maintained a strict physical, organic view of mental illness, whereas Boisen focused on psychological factors. Two traditions of clinical training emerged. The Boston group, led by Cabot and Russell Dicks, was grounded in an organic metaphor focused on physical illness, growth, and stability. Their model of counseling (Cabot & Dicks, 1936) assumed that the healing power of God was present in each person's life. The counselor's task was to listen and help individuals find the "growing edge" of their lives presented by their current problem. As counselees discovered God's immanent presence, counselors could help troubled people face and assimilate God's plan for their lives. Competent clergy counselors, they believed, were formed through persistence, effort, and personal discipline.

Boisen's (1936) focus on psychiatry defined the New York tradition of clinical training. He believed that the "living human documents" of psychiatric patients' internal lives showed a theological picture of the human self defined by turmoil, struggle, and irrational chaos rather than the positive, divine immanence images of growth proposed by Cabot and Dicks. Boisen's turbulent picture of human personality drew clinical supervisors toward psychoanalysis and a treatment ethic that valued liberation from internal chaos through insight. Rather than focus on discipline and competence, clinical training in this tradition introduced pastoral counselors to deeper motivations of the self experienced in disorder, conflict, and guilt. Insight into one's own pathological motivation through psychoanalysis became the focus of both clinical training and counseling practice. Rollo May's (1939/1967) book, *The Art of Counseling*, provided a firm platform for this position. May, a minister trained at Alfred Adler's Vienna clinic, promoted counseling as a means to insight through psychological interpretation and theological clarification. Good counseling was based in the person of the counselor, not in learned technique. Citing Adler and Freud, May (1939/1967) asserted that personal analysis was necessary to be an effective therapist. Alongside these clinical developments, Paul Tillich and H. Richard and Reinhold Niebuhr developed theologies in dialogue with psychoanalysis. These reinforced the value of insight over adjustment in pastoral counseling.

In the 1940s and 1950s, clinical pastoral training spread quickly through seminaries, hospitals, and prisons in the United States. In 1967, the Boston and New York groups reunited and were joined by Southern Baptist[7] and Lutheran supervisors to form the Association for Clinical Pastoral Education. The association standardized clinical pastoral education (CPE) as a professional education program for ministry with a focus on pastoral identity, interpersonal competence, and chaplaincy skills. By the 1950s, pastoral theologians and clinicians were drawing clear distinctions between *pastoral care* and *pastoral counseling*. Pastoral care, in its broadest sense, was an attitude engendered in faith communities to nurture individuals, families, and the community in times of need or distress. Specialized pastoral care, often expressed by chaplains, required specific training to help individuals and families find emotional support, manage life tasks, and provide religious guidance in times of need. Pastoral counseling was targeted to individual problems (and later family problems) through psychotherapy.

PASTORAL COUNSELING: A CLINICAL MINISTRY SPECIALTY

The clinical pastoral training movement set the stage for pastoral counseling to develop as a ministry specialty in at least five ways. First, it solidified a frame of reference for ministry specialists to focus on mental health needs. Second, it provided clinically trained leaders to stimulate pastoral counseling specialization. Third, it consolidated an interdisciplinary medical, psychological, and theological context for ministers to borrow psychotherapeutic theories and implement them as integrated forms of ministry. Boisen's legacy located this integration not in technique but in personal transformation of the counselor through insight into her or his own disorders, chaos, and motivations. As a result, psychoanalysis and depth psychologies became privileged models of therapy. Research 80 years later (Townsend, 2006) showed that most contemporary pastoral counselors continue to see skill development as secondary to personal formation through insight.

Fourth, clinical education defined ministry to troubled souls in a way that bridged congregational life and other contexts of health care. This made room for counseling as a ministry unconstrained by congregational boundaries or traditional tasks of parish ministers.

Fifth, the CPE movement advocated for basic CPE as part of Protestant seminary education. Ministers exposed to this training were more likely than their predecessors to interpret parishioners' problems as mental health issues rather than sin or disobedience. Clinically trained pastors understood that intervention in complex religious–mental health problems required substantial skill beyond the training of most congregational pastors. This understanding motivated many to seek psychotherapeutic training or to refer individuals to clergy counselors with psychotherapy training. Both responses encouraged pastoral counseling as a specialty.

Rich interactions between clinical ministry, psychiatry, and psychology in the late 1930s and 1940s sparked an explosion of pastoral counseling centers, training programs, and literature interpreting the relationship between psychotherapy, theology, and ministry. This was part of a multilayered post–World War II environment that included "a theological revolt against legalism, the recovery of older Protestant doctrines [through neo-orthodoxy's critique of liberalism], a white-collar economy, a burgeoning cultural preoccupation with psychology, postwar affluence, . . . a critique of mass culture, and an ethic of self realization" (Holifield, 1983, p. 260). Sociologist Philip Rieff (1966/1987) noted that by mid-20th century, "I believe" had been replaced by "I feel," which anticipated psychotherapy as the secular spiritual guide of the future. This "culture of the therapeutic" idealized individualized happiness and an ethical responsibility to "find one's self" (Bellah, Madsen, Sullivan, Swidler, & Tipton, 1985). In growing numbers, postwar Americans turned to counseling to manage life and achieve success. Popular psychology literature had religious overtones and often appeared a more accessible faith than Christianity. Norman Vincent Peale (1952), for instance, believed that his self-mastery techniques were a form of applied Christianity that would ensure health and success.

With therapeutic thought so close to the heart of American culture, it is no surprise that ministers were drawn increasingly to pastoral counseling. Postwar America was prosperous enough to pay them. It is also no surprise that pastoral theologians criticized the culture of the therapeutic. Several called for a more critical and thoughtful integration of psychotherapy into religious life. Seward Hiltner (1951, 1959) observed that popular psychological techniques alone might offer some temporary problem relief but could impede spiritual growth without careful theological consideration. Wayne Oates (1954) criticized popular psychology as a cult of reassurance that failed to address internal human contradictions and relegated religion to a personal resource for selfish benefits. Pastoral counselor training responded to popular interest in psychotherapy but also promised theological depth that transcended temporary relief or a cult of reassurance.

Pastoral counseling specialization gained credibility partly through academic interest in seminaries and graduate schools. Prior to 1940, few seminaries offered counseling courses. By the 1950s, pastoral counseling was a separate area of seminary training with a unique curriculum. Several universities, including the University of Chicago and Boston University, developed advanced degree programs in personality and theology, pastoral psychology, pastoral theology, and pastoral counseling.

Holifield (1983) points to four seminal pastoral theologians who helped define this emerging specialty. Seward Hiltner, a Presbyterian minister and student of Anton Boisen, was professor of pastoral theology at the University of Chicago and Princeton Theological Seminary. His *Pastoral Counseling* (1949) was a primary text for pastoral counselors through the 1950s. It provided a theoretical foundation for pastoral practice grounded in psychodynamic theory and the emerging work of Carl Rogers. Hiltner's *Preface to Pastoral Theology* (1958) was the first comprehensive method through which reflection on pastoral counseling could inform theology. Carroll Wise, also a student of Boisen, was professor of pastoral psychology and counseling at Garrett Biblical Institute. Wise (1951, 1966, 1980), influenced by personalist theology,[8] taught that the accepting, caring therapeutic relationship communicated the gospel at the point of counselees' human need. His writing illustrated a thorough commitment to Freudian analytic psychology, Rogerian methods of counseling, and psychotherapy as pastoral intervention. Paul Johnson, professor of psychology and pastoral counseling at Boston University, integrated the work of neo-Freudian Harry Stack Sullivan with personalist theology. Like Hiltner and Wise, Johnson relied heavily on Rogers. Wayne Oates (1962), professor of pastoral care and psychology at Southern Baptist Theological Seminary, provided a conservative, evangelical vision of pastoral counseling that was less reliant on psychoanalysis and Rogers. Instead, he saw the pastoral counselor as the representative of Christ's care for persons in need of God's saving grace. By defining pastoral counseling in theological terms—as action that affirmed the lordship of Christ, personal dialogue between Creator and creature, the priesthood of all believers, and the power of the Spirit—he was able to integrate behavioral sciences into more conservative patterns of clergy counseling.

Holifield (1983) and other historians of pastoral care overlooked Thomas Pugh's contribution to this era of pastoral counseling. Pugh, an African American pioneer in pastoral theology and pastoral counseling, completed his PhD at Boston University and was deeply influenced by personalist theology and dynamic personalism. He developed relationships with Sullivan, Johnson, Oates, Wise, Hiltner, Beck, and family therapy pioneer Emily Mudd through his study in Boston and postgraduate work at the University of Chicago, the Menninger Clinic, and the University of Pennsylvania. As a professor at the Interdenominational Theological Seminary (1959–1994), he integrated pastoral counseling into the seminary curriculum, defined an enduring paradigm for African American pastoral counseling, and worked to provide clinical training for African American students in segregated Atlanta. Like his contemporaries, his model of practice was influenced by Rogers and psychoanalysis. However, as a deeply practical and culturally observant innovator, he was one of the first pastoral counselors to integrate family systems and communal models into pastoral counseling theory and practice.

The 1950s and early 1960s produced rich interaction between theology, psychology, and pastoral practice. Theologian David Roberts (1950) suggested that theology and psychotherapy were correlative. Psychotherapy could not do its job without a Christian view, and insights from psychotherapy could deepen theology. Tillich (1952), who maintained close personal relationships with psychoanalysts, defined a way to balance theology and psychology by making a distinction between pathological anxiety grounded in unresolved human conflicts and existential anxiety related to human finitude. Psychotherapy could help resolve pathological anxiety, but relief from existential anxiety was found only in acceptance "by that which infinitely transcends one's individual self" (p. 165). Howard Stone (2001b) noted that Tillich was referenced by pastoral counseling literature nearly twice as often as any other 20th-century theologian.

By the mid-1950s, pastoral counseling was defined by two characteristics that dominated its practice and theory. First, pastoral counseling claimed a model of ministry increasingly segregated from general parish ministry. Early pastoral counselors had been trained as psychotherapists in medical and social service contexts. Many believed the most appropriate place for counseling was a clinic separated from congregational life. More than 85 Protestant counseling centers were established between 1950 and 1960. Second, pastoral counselors relied heavily on psychodynamic personality theories and long-term models of therapy that were inaccessible to most parish pastors. According to Stone (2001a), this influence defined pastoral counseling for the next half-century.

Psychodynamic theories developed by Harry Stack Sullivan, Karen Horney, and Erich Fromm emphasized an ethic of therapeutic self-realization that broke free of social convention, moralism, and authoritarian control. One could not love others, claimed Fromm (1956), without loving one's self. Psychotherapy aimed to uncover and release "who we really are." These ideas found consonance with contemporary theology. Bultmann (Bartsch & Bultmann, 1953) claimed that only by being free to be one's self could one be open to an unknown future in God. Bonhoeffer (1959) resisted legalism and moralism. Barth (2009) pronounced the death of legalism in favor of human freedom to respond to God's grace. Tillich (1952) claimed that to become a free and integrated human person was a moral imperative. Self-realization was required to obey the command of love. Pastoral theologians saw long-term psychotherapy as a way to plumb the depths of the unconscious and free individuals for new life. Hiltner (1945) believed that psychotherapy, like forgiveness, helped sinful clients confront, objectify, and transcend their internal law-conscience. This made room to manage more rational and important ethical concerns. For Wise (1951, 1980) and Johnson (1967), the purpose of psychotherapy was not to change behavior or values but to form a relationship that valued the person and expressed acceptance and understanding. Holifield (1983) notes that this theological and psychotherapeutic distrust of moralism, rejection of authoritarian institutions, and focus on individual growth prepared the way for Carl Rogers's profound influence on pastoral counseling.

In his review of 50 years of pastoral literature, Stone (2001a) observed that "pastoral counseling clearly owes a debt to Freud . . . but the influence of Carl Rogers is greater than that of Freud or any other psychotherapeutic theorist or theologian. . . . The heavy reliance of an entire field on the thinking of one person—Carl Rogers—is astonishing" (p. 185). Rogers studied with religious educators at Union Theological Seminary and completed his doctorate in educational psychology at Columbia University. He was deeply influenced by liberal Protestant ideas that the authority for individual action and belief was internal. The human person, according to Rogers (1951), was inherently driven toward health and self-actualization. Therapeutic insight could uncover and overcome "subception" of self created by authoritarian parents and damaging institutions. Unconditional positive regard expressed through nondirective, empathic therapy helped clients know themselves and accept their own perceptions, values, and goals. Good therapists must also know and accept themselves. This allowed them to be "genuine" by maintaining "congruence" with their own internal lives as they empathically connected with their clients (Rogers, 1942, 1951).

A number of pastoral theologians and counselors were skeptical of Rogers's absolute focus on inherent human goodness (particularly those influenced by Boisen or neo-orthodox and evangelical theologies) and remained tied to conflict-oriented psychoanalytic personality theories.[9] However, by the mid-1950s, nondirective Rogerian counseling methods (if not his theory of personality) served as the foundation of most pastoral counseling training and practice. Pastoral theologian Don Browning (1966) drew parallels between Rogerian therapy and God's action in atonement, whereas popular pastoral writers saw Rogers's nondirective style as an embodiment of what good priests and ministers had always done. Counseling communicated the gospel at the point of human need not through words but through a relationship in which deep feelings found expression and acceptance.

Rogers's nondirective approach fit well with the commitments and theological anthropologies of a quickly growing discipline. Furthermore, Rogers's nondirective methods could be taught in a short period of time, were relatively safe for pastors with little counseling training, and provided a foundation on which pastoral counseling specialists could build. It is no surprise that Rogers was one of the first recipients of the American Association of Pastoral Counselor's (AAPC's) Distinguished Contribution Award or that many pastoral counselors today prefer reflective, nondirective models of intervention combined with psychodynamic personality theory.[10]

DEVELOPMENT OF A PROFESSION

By 1960, psychotherapy was rapidly expanding beyond Freudian psychoanalysis and Rogers's client-centered therapy. Pastoral counselors found options in gestalt therapy, Viktor Frankl's logotherapy, a variety of humanistic and existential approaches, and object relations theory. Many trained alongside other mental health professionals in new schools of psychotherapy and began to identify themselves as psychotherapists informed by ministerial training rather than clergy counselors. By the early 1960s, voices within the pastoral counseling movement were calling for a professional guild to affirm this emerging specialty, to support pastoral counseling in nonparish contexts, and to set professional standards for the field.

In 1963, leaders of the AFRP in New York, the largest multidisciplinary church counseling center in the country, initiated a conference of 100 pastoral counselors. The meeting was led by Frederick Kuether, AFRP training director, financed by a New York insurance magnate, and restricted to pastoral counselors "who were actually doing pastoral counseling in a self-aware and publicly announced center" (Van Wagner, 1991, p. 4). Professors from theological schools were not invited. Denominational representatives and colleagues from allied psychotherapeutic professions were invited as observers only. This meeting highlighted pastoral counseling's rapid growth. There were then 149 pastoral counseling centers in 29 states, most founded after 1960. Conference speakers called for a new guild, the AAPC, to set standards and regulate pastoral counseling as a clergy specialty. Kuether (1963) argued for a clear distinction between pastoral care and pastoral counseling. The former sought to bring people closer to the church and to sustain an institution. The latter engaged the inner lives of individuals. Pastoral counseling was religious only to the extent that it helped people manage religious aspects of personal problems. Kuether believed that to limit pastoral counseling to the institutional church was to deny its deepest meaning. Clinebell, the first president of the AAPC,[11] extended this argument. A counselor was not pastoral because of institutional connections. Instead, his or her theological training, clergy standing, use of religious symbols in therapy, and therapeutic attention to spiritual growth defined *pastoral* (Clinebell, 1964).

The new AAPC defined pastoral counseling as a clinical specialty centered on and regulated outside of parish life. Pastoral counselors were located mostly in counseling clinics and private practice. Their primary responsibility was to the psychological needs of individuals and only secondarily to the broader mission of the institutional church. Standards of practice and training were removed from denominations and seminary curricula and placed in a regulating agency (AAPC). This stand met with sharp criticism from Seward Hiltner and Wayne Oates, both excluded from the New York meeting because they were seminary professors. Hiltner rejected Clinebell's location of "pastoral" in the person of the therapist and vigorously resisted segregating pastoral counseling from the institutional church. By definition, *pastoral* presupposed the symbols of the church and firm connections with parish life. Furthermore, the new guild encouraged ministers to become psychologists disguised by the mantle of ordination. It also encouraged private practice. Private *pastoral* practice, asserted Hiltner (1964), was a contradiction in terms. Oates (1962) contended that private practice of pastoral counseling was "a violation of the basic character of the ministry and very likely unethical" (p. 31). Neither Hiltner nor Oates joined the new organization, and both continued to focus on parish pastoral counseling.[12] Hiltner eventually separated himself from the pastoral counseling movement. Oates joined the AAPC in 1969.

Despite these conflicts, the fledgling AAPC grew and gained national attention. *The New York Times* highlighted the founding meeting. A *Newsweek* story (May 6, 1963), titled "Minister as Therapist," quoted the president of the National Psychological Association for Psychoanalysis as saying the need for psychotherapists was so great that he welcomed "anyone with training."

In 1963 and 1964, Howard Clinebell led the process to give the AAPC structural shape. Tension about membership standards arose immediately. Standards defined identity. Who would be in? Who would be out? Where do pastoral counselors work? What do they do? What is their relationship to the church? These questions were centered in conflict about how clinical or pastoral members should be. The first set of proposed standards required pastoral counselors to hold doctoral degrees with training similar to psychoanalysts and few pastoral concerns. Clinebell and others resisted an elite membership. Instead, they called for broader standards that guaranteed basic clinical competence and a church relationship but avoided a "mental health clinical" model. After much debate and a series of position papers, charter members of AAPC defined pastoral counselors as "clergymen who do counseling as part of their parish ministry and . . . those clergymen who have acquired specialized training and experience and have become identified as specialists" (AAPC, 1964). The membership also approved standards that emphasized clinical competence, pastoral identity, and denominational connections. Van Wagner (1991) speculated that this compromise reflected the fact that most charter members could not meet the highly restrictive standards originally proposed. Tension between pastoral and clinical also appeared in governance. The Parish Division set standards for parish counselors, whereas the Clinical Division set standards for nonparish counselors. This distinction was eliminated in 1969 in favor of hierarchical membership—pastoral counselor in training, member, fellow, and diplomate. Congregational ministers without extensive clinical training were set apart as nonvoting pastoral affiliates. Although AAPC members were firmly committed to institutionalizing pastoral counseling as a clinical specialty, church relationships were retained through the association's legal incorporation as a religious, not-for-profit entity, and ordination was required for membership. AAPC and denominational leaders established religious endorsement processes that held pastoral counselors accountable to ecclesial authority while also affirming separate clinical identities.

The tension between clinical and pastoral continued to be a central dialogue from 1965 through 1985. Could pastoral counselors be in private practice like other mental health professionals? How should pastoral counselors relate to other professionals? What contexts were appropriate for pastoral counseling services? One set of voices, led by Oates (1964), opposed fee-for-service, private pastoral counseling. The practice would erode pastoral identity and make it indistinguishable from other kinds of counseling. The AAPC moderated this dispute by allowing private practice so long as pastoral counselors maintained a clear pastoral identity and some ecclesial accountability. Remarkably absent from these early formative debates was any substantial question about what models of psychotherapy were appropriate for pastoral counseling. Psychodynamic and Rogerian approaches were the default position of the guild, which probably reflected training programs' strong commitment to these theories. Alternative models were largely ignored by pastoral counselors. Theological questions apart from pastoral identity were equally absent. Van Wagner (1991) suggests early leaders agreed to "let theological issues lie" in favor of establishing an organization (p. 82).

In the 1970s, legislative pressure was building in the United States to regulate all mental health practice, which intensified clinical–pastoral tension. Should pastoral counselors seek licenses as clinical mental health professionals or claim a ministerial exemption? This question was answered by a 1974 AAPC resolution that pastoral counselors, as clergy and religious leaders, were exempt from licensing laws and would "neither seek nor accept certification or licensure by the state" (American Association of Pastoral Counselors, 1974). This same issue would arise again in the 1990s.

Pastoral counselors' clinical preoccupation was not universally appreciated. Cultural observers were concerned that pastoral counselors were no longer willing to challenge individuals' value systems. Ministers as pastoral counselors "have come to look and act more and more like psychotherapists, just as psychotherapists have come to look and act more and more like priests" (Sprecht & Courtney, 1994, p. 13). Social analyst Barbara Dafoe Whitehead (1996) concluded that pastoral counselors' commitment to psychotherapy undercut their ability to confront clients' value systems theologically. Fear that theological challenge would undercut individual self-realization, or be interpreted as moralistic, led pastoral counselors to cede moral decision making to the authority of psychotherapy. This profoundly influenced pastoral approaches to marriage and marital counseling. Pastoral counselors had traded the wisdom of religious teachings for a psychological "canon" that had very little evidence of success in marital counseling. Whitehead contends that this shift escalated divorce in the 1960s and 1970s and shifted marital counseling from the domain of the church to civil society. This perception likely reflects pastoral counselors' early reliance on individual psychotherapy. Although some early innovators were trained as family therapists, systemic models of therapy were not widely accepted or central to pastoral counselor training until the mid-1990s (Townsend, 2013). Edwin Friedman's (1985) bestselling book *Generation to Generation: Family Process in Church and Synagogue* applied Bowenian family therapy to parish life and stimulated pastoral interest in family therapy.

Between 1970 and 1990, pastoral counseling grew and consolidated as a ministry specialty. Pastoral theologian Larry Graham (1988) observed that pastoral counseling began as a loosely organized movement led by charismatic leaders but by the end of the 1980s was "on the verge of becoming institutionally autonomous" (p. 7) with its own executive leadership, financial bases, standards of practice, socially accepted service and training centers, and ideological orthodoxies. Pastoral counseling had shifted away from ecclesial connections and toward autonomous existence. This gave pastoral counselors more authority for their own ministry and allowed them to rethink their work in relationship to church and society.

By 1988, there were nearly 3,000 AAPC members who provided an estimated 1.5 million hours of counseling per year and produced approximately $51 million in fees. There were more than 100 pastoral counseling centers in the United States and Canada. Pastoral counselor training was also well integrated into seminary and graduate school curricula. Most Protestant seminaries had professors of pastoral counseling. Several offered doctorate degrees. Institutional autonomy was clearly evident as new corporate business models (like the Samaritan Institute[13]) gained priority over parish-based models of practice. James Ewing (1988), former executive director of the AAPC, saw these developments as formation of "a new religious institution" (pp. 28–29).

One effect of institutionalization was that pastoral counseling was no longer countercultural. It had become integrated into what Bellah et al. (1985) called the "culture of the therapeutic." Graham (1988) suggested that this integration required careful theological reflection to assess how changed practices "fracture the communal web of life" (p. 12). His hope was that autonomous pastoral counseling would continue to help shape the theology of the church—the historic task of pastoral theology—but also bring new life to the church and other communities.

TWENTY-FIRST CENTURY

In the mid- and late 1990s, cultural and religious shifts abruptly slowed the institutional growth of pastoral counseling. First, Mainline Protestant denominations were compromised by conflict and declining membership. This reduced pastoral counselors' access to congregational and denominational support. Second, increasing cultural diversity (racial, ethnic, class, sexual, and international) raised serious questions about pastoral counseling defined by Euro-American, primarily male, Protestant clergy who advocated privatized, individualistic practices. In the mid-1980s, the AAPC's ordination requirement for certification was challenged by women and gay and lesbian counselors who could not be ordained. The AAPC responded by providing ordination equivalencies for those barred from ordination. Three decades of conflict and compromise ended with a bylaws revision in 2011 that removed ordination requirements.

In the late 1990s, groups of culturally diverse counselors increased resistance to embedded Euro-centric values, theologies, and models of counseling expressed by the AAPC's standards and operating procedures. These were often inhospitable to other-than-Christian and cultural minorities. Edward Wimberley noted that these dynamics often made pastoral counseling feel like "the last bastion of racism in mainline Protestantism" (as cited in Townsend, 2009, p. 47). This was highlighted by the fact that accepted histories of pastoral care and counseling (Gerkin, 1997; Holifield, 1983; Patton, 1990; Van Wagner, 1991) made no reference to non–Euro-American contributions. These lacunae reflect historical methods that disregard unpublished narrative, the fact that minorities had little access to centers of power that widely promoted and published accomplishments, and the perception that minority contributions were not generally relevant to the entire field of pastoral counseling. By 2005, the AAPC identified 199 non–Euro-American members who represented 8% of the association's total membership. This stood in sharp contrast to increasing numbers of trained non–Euro-American pastoral counselors who rejected AAPC certification. These facts motivated the AAPC in 2007 to launch the Multicultural Competencies—Racial Justice Project to end systemic and individual racism in the AAPC. The project's final report (AAPC, 2010) recommended substantial changes in governance, procedures, and standards and became a central guiding document for the AAPC's future.

Although racial and multicultural tensions contributed to slow growth in the United States, pastoral counseling gained strength in Asia and Africa. Lartey (2004) noted that international growth was stimulated by innovative leaders who integrated pastoral counseling into indigenous cultural patterns. This often meant a shift away from North American individualistic assumptions and practices in which these leaders had been trained. Pastoral counseling in Singapore, for example, is focused on the whole community's resilience. In Africa, it must be integrated into a cultural milieu that is fundamentally spiritual, holistic, and synthetic. Young Gweon You (2011) showed how indigenous cultural and religious forces transformed American translations of pastoral counseling (1950s–1990s) into a vibrant, rapidly growing, and specifically Korean/Korean American movement with its own institutional identities, methods, associations, training, and standards. In the second decade of the 21st century, Korean and Korean American scholars are deconstructing American hegemony of pastoral counseling and constructing new models informed by Korean and Korean American experience (Lee, 2011; Moon, 2011; Park, 2011).

A third factor affecting pastoral counseling's growth in the United States was a shift in how mental health services were delivered. By the late 1980s, most pastoral counselors relied on fee-for-service and health insurance reimbursement. By the mid-1990s, payments were controlled by managed care companies that reimbursed only state-licensed therapists. In response, some pastoral counselors returned to parish ministry and provided psychotherapy as an extension of a congregation's religious care. Others lobbied state legislators to define pastoral counseling as a licensable mental health discipline equal to marriage and family therapists, professional counselors, and social workers. This produced theological and First Amendment concerns: Authority and responsibility for ministry would shift from ecclesial bodies to state regulatory bodies. Pastoral counselors argued that citizens have a right to state-regulated faith-based services. Legislation was successful in six states (New Hampshire, North Carolina, Maine, Kentucky, Tennessee, and Arkansas). A third, and largest, group of pastoral counselors opted to do what was necessary to qualify for licenses as professional counselors, marriage and family therapists, social workers, or psychologists. As mental health professionals, they could claim a pastoral identity expressed through theological education, expertise in managing the connection between spirituality and therapy, or expertise in faith-based services. Functionally, "pastoral" became a bridge linking religious and spiritual concerns and behavioral sciences. This metaphor releases the notion that pastoral counseling is a distinct model of psychotherapy.

Today, pastoral counseling is not a unified discipline or a counseling guild shaped primarily by the AAPC. Instead, it is emerging in the 21st century as an interpretive location where psychotherapists, in all their diversity, engage in multicultural, multi-religious reflective practice as a way to provide high-quality spiritually integrative or faith-based care.

REFLECTION QUESTIONS

1. Holifield (1983) described a transition from "salvation to self-fulfillment." How might this shift in consciousness and the growth of a uniquely American "culture of the self" have helped pave the way for the development of pastoral counseling in early American history?

2. Contrast the Boston and New York traditions of clinical training that emerged in the mid-1930s. If you had been an ordained clergy member and a pastoral counselor during that time, which tradition would you have been more attracted to and why?

3. Who had more influence on pastoral counseling, Sigmund Freud or Carl Rogers? Explain your answer.

4. Philip Rieff (1966/1987) observed that by mid-20th century, "I believe" was replaced by "I feel." How might this shift reflect parallel changes in the modern use of the term *pastoral*? How would you define the term *pastoral* in relation to counseling today?

NOTES

1. This chapter is a revision of "Pastoral Counseling: A Genealogy," in Townsend (2009).

2. Clebsch and Jaekle saw care primarily as an individual, intrapsychic enterprise. This reflects the fact that their interpretive tradition was guided by a modern, Cartesian vision of the human person not yet informed by general systems theory, feminist critique of individualism, postmodern critique of the Cartesian self, or contemporary theological anthropology's attention to social location as central to the human self. Their insistence that pastoral care ends when it departs from the interest of one individual fails to account for fundamental social networks in which people live, are formed, and are sustained. It also fails to appreciate the mutual and recursive social nature of problems in living.

3. James's functional approach departed from the predominant structuralist approach of the day. Structuralists, such as Edward Tichener, focused on the *content* of the mind and asserted that all mental experience could be understood by examining combinations of simple elements or events within the mind. Functionalists, such as William James, John Dewey, and G. Stanley Hall, rejected this simple view in favor of understanding the mind in its functional context—what it does and how it acts in particular contexts.

4. New Thought was a controversial movement in the late 19th century usually credited to Phineas Parkhurst Quimby. Success and health were gained by learning techniques of self-abandonment through mental discipline. Based on Christian teachings and 19th-century metaphysical traditions, it emphasized spirituality, mystical experience, and the power of mind over the body. In addition to influencing many Protestant clergy, the movement is credited with inspiring Emanuel Swedenborg, Mary Baker Eddy, Ralph Waldo Emerson, and Franz Mesmer. See Braden (1963).

5. The Social Gospel was a late 19th- and early 20th-century liberal movement in American churches that emphasized application of Christian principles to the problems of urbanization and industrialization. Leading figures, such as Washington Gladden and Walter Rauschenbusch, defocused personal, individual sin and emphasized the social nature of sin. Social Gospel leaders believed that society could progress and realize at least some of the kingdom of God. The movement was idealistic and optimistic about humanity's future, which was expressed in pragmatic social action. Charles Sheldon's 1897 book, *In His Steps*, highlighted one Social Gospel position—American society would be transformed if people's public and private actions were guided by the question, "What Would Jesus Do?"

6. Sigmund Freud's thought was also deeply affected by these same issues. Freud observed that his primary concept, the pleasure principle, could not explain the brutality of war or cultural oppression. He subsequently revised his theory to include new structures of the mind and a *thanatos* drive.

7. See Russell Moore's (2005) essay, *Counseling and the Authority of Christ: A New Vision for Biblical Counseling at Southern Baptist Theological Seminary*. Moore, dean of Southern Baptist Theological Seminary, cites Wayne Oates's introduction of clinical training and pastoral counseling into seminary curricula and Southern Baptist congregational life as a primary contribution to the seminary and denomination's drift into liberalism. This drift was corrected between 1996 and 2006 by reversing Southern Baptists' participation in clinical training, rejecting any form of ministry influenced by behavioral or psychotherapeutic sciences, and asserting that the Bible alone is sufficient for instruction in all matters of human life and problems in living.

8. Personalism is a philosophical stand (related to idealism) that highlights the person as ontologically ultimate. This position asserts the priority of mind and spirit; that is, it rejects the idea that the human person is subordinate to any universal mind or spirit and any form of psychology that confuses the "true person" with "personality" that is "learned or socially motivated." This philosophical stand is central to humanistic theorists such as Rogers, Allport, Maslow, and Perls. Pastoral counseling was especially influenced by personalist theology developed at Boston University, which emphasized the personal nature of God and the unity of all in a Cosmic Person.

9. Russell Dicks in *Pastoral Work and Pastoral Counseling* (1944) opposed Rogers by asserting that nondirective counseling did not exist. All counseling was directive. This criticism resurfaced in family therapy, feminist critique of pastoral counseling, and postmodern expressions of pastoral therapy.

10. Howard Stone's (2001a) literature review shows this pattern clearly. Townsend (2011) showed that almost all certified pastoral counselors sampled relied on psychodynamic theory to understand human personality and client-centered (Rogerian) methods for counseling practice. Those claiming other positions felt marginal to the main body of pastoral counselors.

11. At the time of the meeting, Howard Clinebell was director of the Pasadena area Pastoral Counseling Center and associate professor at the Southern California School of Theology at Claremont. Van Wagner (1991) suggests Clinebell was selected for president because of his relationship with Methodist pastoral counselors at Marble Collegiate Church in New York, his lack of connection with the CPE movement, and his association with Frederick Kuether.

12. Van Wagner (1991) suggests that personal conflicts between Oates and Hiltner and the leaders of the Council for Clinical Training who helped shape the AAPC may have been as important as ideological differences in their resistance to the new guild.

13. The Samaritan Institute (organized in 1972) developed a model of management that assisted local religious leaders to build financially successful counseling centers. In 2015, the Samaritan Center reported 60 Samaritan Centers in the United States and Japan (http://www.samaritaninstitute.org).

REFERENCES

American Association of Pastoral Counselors. (1964). *Constitution of the American Association of Pastoral Counselors*. Fairfax, VA: Author.

American Association of Pastoral Counselors. (1974). *Council Minutes, April 1974*. Fairfax, VA: Author.

American Association of Pastoral Counselors. (2010). *Multi-cultural competencies—Racial justice task force: Final report: American Association of Pastoral Counselors*. Fairfax, VA: Author.

Barth, K. (2009). *Church dogmatics*. New York, NY: T & T Clark.

Bartsch, H. W., & Bultmann, R. (1953). *Kerybma and muth: A theological debate*. London, UK: S.P.C.K. Publishing.

Bellah, R. N., Madsen, R., Sullivan, W. M., Swidler, A., & Tipton, S. M. (1985). *Habits of the heart: Individualism and commitment in american life*. Berkeley, CA: University of California Press.

Boisen, A. T. (1936). *The exploration of the inner world: A study of mental disorder and religious experience*. Chicago, IL: Willett, Clark & Company.

Bonhoeffer, D. (1959). *The cost of discipleship*. New York, NY: Macmillan.

Braden, C. S. (1963). *Spirits in rebellion: The rises and development of new thought*. Dallas, TX: Southern Methodist University.

Browning, D. S. (1966). *Atonement and psychotherapy*. Philadelphia, PA: Westminster.

Cabot, R., & Dicks, R. (1936). *The art of ministering to the sick*. New York, NY: Macmillan.

Clebsch, W. A., & Jaekle, C. R. (1967). *Pastoral care in historical perspective*. New York, NY: Harper & Row.

Clinebell, H. J. (1964). The challenge of the specialty of pastoral counseling. *Pastoral Psychology, 15*, 17–28. doi:10.1007/BF01762003

Clinebell, H. (1990). Pastoral counseling movement. In R. Hunter (Ed.), *Dictionary of pastoral care and counseling* (p. 177). Nashville, TN: Abingdon.

Dicks, R. (1944). *Pastoral work and personal counseling*. New York, NY: Macmillan.

Edwards, J. (1743). *The great concern of a watchman for souls*. Boston, MA: Green, Bushnell & Allen.

Ewing, J. W. (1988). Theological implications of the institutionalization of pastoral counseling. *Journal of Pastoral Psychotherapy, 1*(3/4), 23–31.

Friedman, E. (1985). *Generation to generation: Family process in church and synagogue*. New York, NY: Guilford.

Fromm, E. (1956). *The art of loving*. New York, NY: Harper & Row.

Gerkin, C. V. (1997). *An introduction to pastoral care*. Nashville, TN: Abingdon.

Graham, L. (1988). The institutionalization of pastoral counseling. *Journal of Pastoral Psychotherapy, 1*(3/4), 7–22.

Hereven, T. K. (1984). Themes in the historical development of the family. In R. D. Parks (Ed.), *Review of child development research: The family* (Vol. 7, pp. 137–138). Chicago, IL: University of Chicago Press.

Hiltner, S. (1945). Toward an ethical conscience. *Journal of Religion, 25*, 1–9. Retrieved from http://www.jstor.org/discover/10.2307/1197680?uid=308711881&uid=3739680&uid=2129&uid=2&uid=70&uid=3&uid=16751760&uid=67&uid=62&uid=3739256&sid=21105956454231

Hiltner, S. (1949). *Pastoral counseling*. Nashville, TN: Abingdon.

Hiltner, S. (1951). *Self understanding*. New York, NY: Scribner's.

Hiltner, S. (1958). *Preface to pastoral theology*. Nashville, TN: Abingdon.

Hiltner, S. (1959). *Pastoral counseling*. Nashville, TN: Abingdon.

Hiltner, S. (1964). The American Association of Pastoral Counselors: A critique (pp. 8–16). *Pastoral Psychology, 15.*

Holifield, E. B. (1978). *The gentlemen theologians: American theology in southern culture, 1795–1860*. Durham, NC: Duke University Press.

Holifield, E. B. (1983). *A history of pastoral care in America: From salvation to self-realization*. Nashville, TN: Abingdon.

James, W. (1892). *Psychology, briefer course*. New York, NY: Henry Holt.

James, W. (1902). *The varieties of religious experience*. New York, NY: Longman.

James, W. (1983). *The principles of psychology*. Cambridge, MA: Harvard University Press. (Original work published 1890)

Johnson, P. E. (1967). *Person and counselor*. Nashville, TN: Abingdon Press.

Kuether, F. (1963). Pastoral counseling: Community or chaos. *The Pastoral Counselor, 1*, 3–10.

Lartey, E. (2004). Globalization, internationalization, and indigenization of pastoral care and counseling. In N. Ramsay (Ed.), *Pastoral care and counseling: Redefining the paradigms* (pp. 87–108). Nashville, TN: Abingdon.

Lee, I. (2011). Korean American women's relationality. *Sacred Spaces: The e-Journal of the American Association of Pastoral Counselors, 3*, 44–61. Retrieved from http://www.aapc.org/news-events/sacred-spaces/volume-3-2011/

May, M. A., Brown, W. A., Shuttleworth, F. K., Jacobs, J. A., & Feeney, C. V. (1934). *The education of American ministers* (Vol. 1). New York, NY: Institute of Social and Religious Research.

May, R. (1967). *The art of counseling*. Nashville, TN: Abingdon. (Original work published 1939)

McCarthy, K. (1984). Psychotherapy and religion: The Emmanuel movement. *Journal of Religion and Health, 23*(2), 92–105. Retrieved from jstor.org/stable/27505768

McNeill, J. T. (1977). *A history of the cure of souls*. New York, NY: Harper & Row.

Moon, H. (2011). The "living web" revisited. *Sacred Spaces: The e-Journal of the American Association of Pastoral Counselors, 3*, 14–39. Retrieved from http://www.aapc.org/media/76013/hmoon_pastoral_care.pdf

Moore, R. (2005). *Counseling and the authority of Christ: A new vision for biblical counseling at Southern Baptist Theological Seminary*. Louisville, KY: Southern Baptist Theological Seminary.

Oates, W. E. (1954). The cult of reassurance. *Religion and Life, 24*, 72–82. doi:10.1177/003463735405100306

Oates, W. E. (1962). *Protestant pastoral counseling*. Philadelphia, PA: Westminster.

Oates, W. E. (1964). Association of pastoral counselors: Its values and its dangers. *Pastoral Psychology, 15*(3), 5–7.

Park, S. (2011). Come and eat. *Sacred Spaces: The e-Journal of the American Association of Pastoral Counselors, 3*, 62–87.

Patton, J. (1990). Pastoral counseling. In R. Hunter (Ed.), *Dictionary of pastoral care and counseling*. Nashville, TN: Abingdon.

Peale, N. V. (1952). *The power of positive thinking*. New York, NY: Prentice-Hall.

Rieff, P. (1987). *The triumph of the therapeutic: Uses of faith after Freud*. Chicago, IL: University of Chicago Press. (Original work published 1966)

Roberts, D. E. (1950). *Psychotherapy and a Christian view of man*. New York, NY: Scribner's.

Rogers, C. (1942). *Counseling and psychotherapy*. Boston, MA: Houghton Mifflin.

Rogers, C. (1951). *Client-centered therapy*. Boston, MA: Houghton Mifflin.

Schmidt, L. E. (2012). *Restless souls: The making of American spirituality* (2nd ed.). Berkeley, CA: University of California Press.

Sheldon, C. M. (1985). *In his steps*. Grand Rapids, MI: Zondervan.

Spencer, I (2001). *A pastor's sketches: Conversations with anxious souls concening the way of salvation*. Vestavia Hills, AL: Solid Ground Christian Books. (Original work published 1850)

Sprecht, H., & Courtney, M. (1994). *Unfaithful angels: How social work has abandoned its mission*. New York, NY: Free Press.

Stone, H. W. (2001a). The congregational setting of pastoral counseling: A study of pastoral counseling theorists from 1949–1999. *Journal of Pastoral Care, 55*(2), 181–196. Retrieved from jpcp.org/samples/stone_55_2

Stone, H. W. (2001b). *Strategies for brief pastoral counseling*. Minneapolis, MN: Fortress.

Tillich, P. (1952). *The courage to be*. New Haven, CT: Yale University Press.

Townsend, L. L. (2006). Theological reflection and the formation of pastoral counselors. In D. Bidwell & J. Marshall (Eds.), *The formation of pastoral counselors: Challenges and opportunities* (pp. 29–46). Binghamton, NY: Haworth Pastoral Press.

Townsend, L. L. (2009). *Introduction to pastoral counseling*. Nashville, TN: Abingdon.

Townsend, L. L. (2011). Pastoral counseling: A grounded theory description. *Journal of Pastoral Care and Counseling, 65*(3), 1–16.

Townsend, L. L. (2013). Pastoral counseling and family therapy. In D. A. Leeming (Ed.), *Encyclopedia of psychology and religion* (2nd ed.) New York, NY: SpringerReference.

Van Wagner, C. A. (1991). *AAPC in historical perspective, 1963–1991*. Fairfax, VA: American Association of Pastoral Counselors.

Whitehead, B. D. (1996). *The divorce culture: Rethinking our commitments to marriage and family*. New York, NY: Vintage.

Wise, C. (1951). *Pastoral counseling: Theory and practice*. New York, NY: Harper & Brothers.

Wise, C. (1966). *The meaning of pastoral care*. New York, NY: Harper & Row.

Wise, C. (1980). *Pastoral psychotherapy: Theory and practice*. New York, NY: Jason Aronson.

You, Y. G. (2011). History and future of Korean pastoral counseling. *Sacred Spaces: The e-Journal of the American Association of Pastoral Counselors, 3*, 120–137. Retrieved from http://www.aapc.org/media/76028/youyounggweonfinal.pdf

Elizabeth A. Maynard and Rodney Parker

3

PASTORAL COUNSELORS: MENTAL HEALTH PROFESSIONALS

Among the most significant transformations in the field of pastoral counseling over the past half-century have been the entrance of laypersons into the profession and the increasing numbers of pastoral counselors who identify as both religious leaders and licensed mental health professionals. The face of pastoral counseling has indeed changed from its early days of predominantly White, Protestant, ordained clergymen to a group that is more diverse than ever before in terms of ethnicity, gender, sexual orientation, religious/spiritual tradition, and professional identity.

This chapter explores who pastoral counselors are as mental health professionals, in terms of their professional identities, training, and licenses. We consider the settings in which pastoral counselors offer care, including both explicitly religious/spiritual and nonreligious contexts. We also consider what pastoral counselors as licensed mental health professionals do in their everyday work and the functions they serve in their practices and communities.

PROFESSIONALS AT THE CROSSROADS

Pastorally inclined professionals are found in multiple professions and care settings. Today, professionals who identify as pastoral counselors include ordained and religiously endorsed leaders, religiously or spiritually committed laypersons, spiritually sensitive or curious laypersons not affiliated with specific spiritual or religious traditions or communities, and a small group of practitioners who do not themselves identify as religious or spiritual but pursue training in pastoral counseling because they understand the important role that spirituality plays in the lives of clients.

As state laws and licensing requirements have changed over the past half-century, an increasing number of pastoral counselors maintain multiple identities both as religiously endorsed or ordained religious leaders and as licensed mental health professionals. At the same time, some of the largest growth in the profession has occurred among laypersons seeking training in pastoral counseling and licensure as mental health professionals. Many religiously endorsed pastoral counselors begin their careers with theological training and later pursue pastoral counseling as an outgrowth and specialization of their ministries. Other pastoral counselors begin their training as mental health professionals and later pursue training in pastoral counseling. Today, a growing number of individuals seek training as pastoral counselors without the intent to pursue or participate in traditional clergy roles. For many of these professionals, religious endorsement is either unavailable or undesirable. This is particularly true in traditions in which the individual may not be accepted into ordained leadership roles due to gender, sexual orientation, marital status, or other personal characteristics. Still others are drawn to the distinctive roles and functions of pastoral counseling and may not be interested in performing the other traditional functions of clergy such as teaching/preaching, pastoral care, staff supervision, or the administration of religious organizations.

Clergypersons as Pastoral Counselors

Pastoral counselors who are both religiously endorsed and licensed mental health providers are often challenged to discern the boundaries and intersections between these roles. In particular, these pastoral counselors must work to create clear distinctions between the pastoral care work related to their clergy roles and the more distinctive work of pastoral counseling. They often need to identify the limitations of their clergy roles and the benefits accrued when they decide not to try to be all things to all people. These pastoral counselors often make distinctions among times when they are serving as religious leaders, pastoral counselors, or both. For example, to make clear distinctions between their work with their religious communities and their pastoral counseling practices, many pastoral counselors refrain from offering pastoral counseling to members of their own organizations or traditions. These professionals may choose to refer members of their own religious communities to other pastoral counselors for ongoing care. Others choose to offer pastoral counseling to members of their religious communities, while clarifying the times, places, and functions of pastoral counseling that are distinct from their other roles and responsibilities.

Laypersons as Pastoral Counselors

Laypeople have come to see the value of pastoral counseling, both alongside and distinct from other forms of pastoral ministry, and have sought opportunities to care for others in this way. Many laypersons now seek training to become pastoral counselors and to pursue mental health licensure or certification in their jurisdictions. As more laypeople are trained as pastoral counselors, several important issues arise. The lay pastoral counselor must discern what types of formal and informal relationships to maintain with religious leaders and established communities, how to work in collaboration with clergy and other religious leaders for the well-being of their clients, how to offer distinctive contributions to the spiritual and mental well-being of clients without duplicating or supplanting the role or authority of the client's religious leaders, and how to challenge the roles and authority of the client's religious leaders when it may be necessary for client well-being or growth. It is also important that lay practitioners understand that the integration of spirituality alone into a helping relationship does not make one a pastoral counselor, nor does one's own commitment as a spiritual or religious person make one automatically qualified to offer counsel of this type.

Distinct and Intersecting Identities

Although religious and spiritual traditions often differ markedly in their use of ordained or endorsed religious leaders and the roles that those individuals are asked to play, religious leaders often have responsibilities for teaching/instruction in both the formal teachings and practices of the tradition, exhortation of participants to moral or desirable behavior, participation with adherents of the tradition in the rites and rituals of the tradition, consultation with adherents during significant life transitions or challenging periods such as illness and grief, facilitation of growth opportunities such as retreats, administration of the religious organization, supervision of volunteers and lay leaders, and training and supervision of other staff and leaders in training. In the Christian tradition, the pastoral metaphor evokes the image of shepherds leading and tending to the needs of their flocks (as in Psalm 23). The religious leader most often understands herself or himself as one who tends particularly to the spiritual growth and well-being of parishioners, while she or he may also attend to some of the more practical daily material, psychological, and social needs of parishioners through referral and coordination of social services.

Although pastoral counselors as mental health professionals are often engaged in this type of case management with their clients, understanding the biological, psychological, social, and spiritual needs of those in their care, the primary focus of the mental health professional is on the client's psychological or emotional and social well-being. Psychoeducation may be an important part of the counseling or psychotherapy offered to the client but is most often focused on specific skills that the client may learn to change her affective state or improve her interpersonal functioning rather than instruction in religious/spiritual principles. Mental health practitioners often discuss moral conflicts with clients, without the expectation (at least on the practitioner's part) that he is expected to uphold the moral standard of a particular tradition. In fact, mental health professionals often avoid the endorsement of moral teachings from particular traditions, exploring instead with the client what she or he finds meaningful. Religiously endorsed pastoral counselors must often carefully navigate these situations, reflecting on both their roles as moral leaders and their reflective counseling roles. On occasion, both religiously endorsed and lay pastoral counselors may explore moral instruction or guidance with clients, always attentive to issues of both authority and the means of intervening with clients that are most appropriate for their level of development and current concerns.

Mental health professionals may also share other similarities and differences with religious leaders. For example, mental health professionals often have the benefit of exploring the client's psychological needs in more depth and over a longer period of time than many religious leaders are able to do, whereas religious leaders are often able to observe clients in their broader social systems and relationships. Like their clergy counterparts, many mental health professionals also maintain responsibility for administration of their agencies, as well as training and supervision of other professionals.

Pastoral Paradigms

Pastoral counselors are committed to the development and safeguarding of the spiritual wholeness of their clients. As noted by other authors in this volume (see Snodgrass, Chapter 1, this volume), pastoral counseling work is bicultural, multicultural, and intercultural by its nature. For many practitioners, it is *bicultural* in the sense that professionals bridge the worlds of spirituality/religion/theology and professional mental health disciplines such as psychology, professional counseling, marriage and family therapy, social work, or drug and alcohol counseling. For other practitioners, it is *multicultural*, as the individual or organization bridges the worlds of spirituality/religion/theology, professional mental health disciplines, and other disciplines such as medicine (see work by Pruett and Enright, Chapter 27, this volume, for discussion of these tricultural intersections). Pastoral counseling work is also often multicultural work in the sense that the application of spirituality/religion/theology and mental health disciplines varies widely in response to dimensions of human diversity. The work of dialogue and integration among these domains often looks quite different based on the ethnicity, culture, gender, sexual orientation, economic status, language, and specific faith traditions of the counselor and her clients. Ultimately, pastoral counseling may be understood as an *intercultural* or *transcultural* enterprise, as practitioners not only draw on and move between the perspectives and paradigms of religion/ spirituality/theology and mental health disciplines but also forge paradigms and ways of working with clients that are distinct from the other perspectives.

As the pastoral counselor engages in this multidimensional work, it is important that he consider the often differing assumptions of the mental health and religious/ spiritual worldviews. First, understandings of well-being and pathology often differ between religious traditions and mental health models. For example, many Abrahamic (Jewish, Christian, Muslim) models of well-being assume that a right relationship with God is necessary for human flourishing, but this assumption is not part of the dominant secular mental health models. Models of pathology, suffering, and disease are also quite different between religious and secular models (please see the chapters by Fox et al. [Chapter 4], LeNoir [Chapter 5], and Rodgerson [Chapter 7] in this volume for a fuller exploration of these themes).

Ultimately, the practitioner must consider his ultimate referents. For many clergypersons, including those who are psychologically savvy, theological or spiritual truths trump psychological principles as ultimate referents. For many in mental health roles, psychological principles usually trump theological or spiritual principles. For pastoral counselors, the prioritizing of theological, spiritual, and psychological principles varies by role, context, client, and the work to be done in counseling.

PASTORAL COUNSELORS AS MENTAL HEALTH PROFESSIONALS

The preparation of pastoral counselors as mental health professionals is distinct from that of religious leaders. This process differs particularly in terms of the nature and models of training, licensure, and certification to meet state or provincial practice requirements. Mental health professionals also differ from religious leaders in the ways in which they approach assessment/diagnosis, present their services to the public, endorse particular ethical standards, and employ unique interventions.

Professional Training

The curricula of mental health training programs are most often designed to meet national standards outlined by professional organizations and state/provincial licensing board requirements. The most widely adopted professional standards for graduate-level training are those of the American Psychological Association (2013), Commission on Accreditation for Marriage and Family Therapy Education (2005), Council on Social Work Education (2008), and Council for Accreditation of Counseling and Related Educational Programs (2009). These professions and state/provincial licensing boards outline specific content that should be covered in training programs (e.g., human growth and development across the life span, atypical/pathological symptoms in individuals and families, group processes, assessment or appraisal of client concerns). The emphasis in mental health training programs is on the mastery of a body of professional knowledge and the development of foundational assessment and helping skills such as empathic listening, assessment, treatment interventions, and crisis management. Some programs go further to encourage personal reflection on the part of the trainee and the development of the trainee's identity as a helping professional. Few mental health training programs emphasize the spiritual growth and formation of the practitioner. In contrast, many clergy training programs place an emphasis on the spiritual formation and growth of the trainee as an essential element of effective ministry/practice.

Although an increasing number of mental health training programs briefly address spirituality as a human diversity issue, few graduate programs systematically address issues of religion and spirituality in client care. Students in graduate training programs may receive explicit training in spiritually integrated psychotherapy or similar practices when an individual faculty member offers courses or maintains a research agenda in these areas. The notable exceptions to this are integrative training programs in psychology and marriage and family therapy such as those at Fuller Theological Seminary, Rosemead School of Psychology at Biola University, Wheaton College, Azusa Pacific University, and George Fox College. However, most licensed mental health professionals receive training in nonintegrative training programs, both religious and secular. That is, even though an institution may be religiously affiliated, the mental health graduate programs within that institution may not explicitly address issues of religion and spirituality. Pastoral counseling training programs designed to prepare trainees to meet professional standards and licensing requirements (an exemplar of which is the Pastoral Counseling Department at Loyola University Maryland) are thus important in their work of cultivating the pastoral sensitivities and practices of trainees.

What should pastoral counseling mental health training programs emphasize that distinguishes them from other mental health training programs? Effective training in pastoral counseling requires exploration of the trainee's ways of being with clients and colleagues, ways of understanding and assessing client concerns, and ways of intervening with clients (Cheston, 2000). This involves the cultivation of pastoral sensitivity and sensibility and may significantly inform the counselor's choice of therapeutic orientation(s). This often involves the skillful interweaving of the counselor's openness, skill, and pastoral nature.

First, students should be challenged and supported in the development of a pastoral *identity*. Over time, the trainee is able to articulate what is *pastoral* about pastoral counseling, as well as what is distinctively pastoral in her own counseling work. These definitions and identities vary significantly, including both traditional understandings of pastoral identities and roles (Clinebell & McKeever, 2011; Nouwen, 1972) and emerging views and models of pastoral counseling identity (Graham, 1995; Ramsay, 2004). As the profession shifts and changes, elements of these definitions and identities may also change.

Second, students should be encouraged to cultivate a pastoral *presence* with clients and colleagues. This presence may be connected to the student's emerging theoretical orientation (e.g., a nondirective Rogerian approach) as well as distinct from it. This presence may involve elements of spiritual companionship, seeking, guiding, and colaboring. This pastoral presence may also be a *prophetic* presence as students learn to both listen and speak into the lives of others with courage and care. Although many practitioners understand a pastoral presence as a gentle presence, a pastoral presence is also often a bold presence, as when clients and counselor are inspired to speak truth to power.

Third, the student is encouraged to learn both the prevailing religious/spiritual/theological models of understanding the human condition and those that are dominant among mental health professionals. This includes exploration of spiritual models of human development and thriving (e.g., Fowler, 1981), secular meaning-making models (e.g., Frankl, 1959/1984), and spiritual and secular models of assessment and diagnosis (see Chapter 7 by Rodgerson in this volume; Maynard, 2013).

Fourth, the student is encouraged to develop her skill in pastoral counseling interventions. These may include both distinctively pastoral interventions (such as those described in this volume by Jones Davis [Chapter 12] and Stewart-Sicking [Chapter 13]), as well as those shared with other mental health professions (see chapters in this volume by Deal and Magyar-Russell [Chapter 8], Snodgrass and Noronha [Chapter 9], and Hanna [Chapter 11]). The student is also encouraged to explore the commonalities and differences between pastoral counseling methods and those of other spiritually integrative approaches (Aten, O'Grady, & Worthington, 2012; Cashwell & Young, 2011; G. Miller, 2003; W. R. Miller, 1999; Pargament, 2007; Sperry & Shafranske, 2005). The student is trained in both implicit and explicit methods of integration and intervention, understanding that the inclusion of or openness to religious and spiritual themes in mental health work is not the same thing as intentional psychospiritual integration (Tan, 1996). She is also tuned to the client's interest in and openness to integration, the client's experiences of spiritual development, the expectations of the setting in which she works, and the client's distinctive culture and the roles that religion and spirituality play in it.

Fifth, the student is encouraged to engage in ongoing and intentional spiritual and professional *formation* that extends beyond the mastery of *knowledge* and development of *skills*. That is, emphasis is placed not only on what she *knows* and what she *does* but also *who she is* (and for some, *whose* she is) and how she is present with others. Thus, the student's personal spiritual growth is an essential element of a pastoral counseling education. This growth may be facilitated through readings, course assignments, dialogue with peers and faculty, and spiritual practices beyond the training program.

Sixth, pastoral counseling programs encourage the student's openness to spiritual traditions beyond her own. This includes openness to learning more from clients and colleagues about their meaning-making systems, as well as openness to questioning the assumptions and values of one's own tradition and practice. The pastoral counseling student is encouraged to refrain from religious instruction or proselytizing, electing instead open reflection and exploration of the client's paradigms and her own. The student is not asked to abandon her own values and tradition so much as to open herself to truths from both within and beyond her tradition. The student is encouraged to cultivate an *interreligious, interspiritual,* and *intercultural* perspective that not only tolerates but also embraces the wisdom of many traditions and values the dialogue among perspectives. This perspective involves the enrichment and transformation of both the counselor and the client. Although this enrichment and transformation may sometimes be the fruit of serendipity, the pastoral counseling student is encouraged to intentionally engage in these transformative dialogues.

Although these emphases in training and formation may be most fully realized in pastoral counseling mental health training programs, professionals trained in other types of mental health programs may pursue these types of developmental experiences through continuing-education activities, supervision, and consultation with pastoral counselors.

Mental Health Licensure

The practices of psychology, professional counseling, marriage and family therapy, and social work are regulated by state/provincial laws and licensing boards. In most jurisdictions, it is illegal to offer mental health services unless one is licensed as a mental health professional, completing requirements for licensure under supervision, or a student enrolled in a graduate training program in a mental health discipline. Pastoral counselors must ensure that they are practicing counseling in accordance with the laws in their areas.

Most licensing boards do not recognize graduate degrees in religion or theology as satisfying the educational requirements for mental health licensure. For example, the Texas State Board of Examiners of Licensed Professional Counselors (TSBELPC) accepts graduate degrees in counseling, psychology, and related fields to meet the educational requirements for licensure as a licensed professional counselor but specifically does not accept graduate degrees in theology to meet licensure requirements. Thus, an individual in Texas and states with similar licensing requirements who holds a Master of Divinity (MDiv) degree from an accredited educational institution must either practice pastoral care and counseling within the scope of his clergy role and responsibilities or seek an additional mental health graduate degree and professional licensure if he would like to practice as a clinical pastoral counselor.

Mental Health Practice Settings

Today, pastoral counselors trained as mental health professionals offer care in a variety of settings. These include explicitly religious settings such as churches, synagogues, temples, and mosques and the counseling centers affiliated with them; hospital chaplaincies; integrative health care settings; independent pastoral and secular counseling centers; public agencies; detention facilities; shelters; and private practices. The roles, titles, and professional identities that pastoral counselors take on in these settings vary considerably. Professionals may offer their services in these settings with or without identifying their pastoral or mental health identities. In some settings, particularly those that are religiously affiliated, the "pastoral" identity and title may be particularly prized by clients seeking care. In other settings, the pastoral counselor may be "closeted" in her pastoral identity, using her professional degrees and licenses as her primary identity marker.

Pastoral counselors serving as mental health professionals in secular settings often experience distinctive challenges. Some may be required to conceal their pastoral identities while serving clients, whereas others may be identified as "the religious counselor" on staff and receive client referrals because of this identification by others, whether or not these are appropriate referrals. They are engaged in recurring cycles of dilution or intensification of identity based on their settings, clients, supervisors, and professional affiliations. Clergy and vowed religious persons who serve as pastoral counselors in secular settings may also experience additional challenges such as dress codes that prohibit the expression of their pastoral identities. For example, the first author has trained pastoral counselors serving in mental health settings who were either encouraged or required to remove their clerical collars or religious habits to be accepted as trainees at secular sites. Although there are certainly issues of projection and transference to be addressed with clients and colleagues when a pastoral counselor is clearly identifiable as a religious professional, the religious identity of the counselor should ideally be a topic for discussion rather than exclusion.

Marketing and Public Identity

These training, licensure, and setting issues also affect the ways in which pastoral counselors present themselves and their credentials to the public. Depending on her practice setting and responsibilities, the pastoral counselor may describe herself in marketing materials as a pastoral counselor, a licensed mental health professional, or both. If potential clients and referral sources are knowledgeable about pastoral counseling, she may need to do little to explain the nature and scope of her work. However, if she primarily serves clients unfamiliar with pastoral counseling, she may need to offer education to potential clients and referral sources about who pastoral counselors are, what they do, and how they are both similar to and different from other religious, spiritual, and mental health professionals. The pastoral counselor must also consider if she will describe herself specifically as a pastoral counselor or according to her spiritual tradition (e.g., "Christian counselor"), although the meanings of these religious titles vary considerably by practitioner, consumer, and jurisdiction.

Mental Health Paradigms

In addition to training models and licensure requirements, pastoral counselors who work as mental health professionals are also exposed to and often endorse the prevailing paradigms, ethical codes, and standard practices of their mental health disciplines. Most practicing mental health professionals endorse one or more of the commonly accepted theoretical orientations to clinical work (e.g., psychodynamic, cognitive/behavioral, humanistic/existential, systems, postmodern). Most of these approaches to clinical work, although not explicitly hostile to the pastoral perspective, pose challenges for the religious practitioner (Jones & Butman, 1991; Vitz, 1977). That is, many of the models of personality, views of disorder and distress, and approaches may be mismatches for specific religious traditions. Pastoral counselors often resolve these mismatches by adopting aspects of the models without accepting all dimensions of a model. Here, the pastoral counselor may distinguish among the ways of *being* with the client outlined by each model, the ways of *understanding* the client's experience proposed by the model, and the means of *intervening* proposed by the model (see Cheston, 2000, for a fuller explanation of this paradigm). That is, the counselor may find that the ways of being with the client are congruent with his tradition, but he may not endorse the models for understanding or intervening with the client when those are in conflict with his beliefs and values. Please see Chapter 11 by Hanna in this volume for further exploration of this issue.

Assessment and Diagnosis

Most mental health professionals in North America and many other parts of the world are trained in and expected to use the prevailing models for assessment and diagnosis found in the fifth edition of the *Diagnostic and Statistical Manual of Mental Disorders* (*DSM-5*; American Psychiatric Association, 2013) or *International Statistical Classification of Diseases and Related Health Problems,* 10th Revision (*ICD-10;* World Health Organization, 2010) to comply with the best practices of their organizations or professions. Although useful in many ways, these diagnostic systems are not inherently pastoral, and pastoral counselors have noted a number of challenges in the use of these diagnostic systems with clients (Maynard, 2013). The most commonly expressed concerns with these diagnostic systems are their tendencies toward reductionism (seeing the client as an amalgam of symptoms rather than in her or his wholeness) and the tendency to either overlook or pathologize religious or spiritual concerns.

Professional Ethical Standards

Pastoral counselors trained as mental health professionals are obliged to adhere to the ethical standards of their professions and may also endorse the ethical standards of the American Association of Pastoral Counselors (2012). Fortunately, most professional ethical standards are aligned with the values and priorities of most spiritual/religious traditions, particularly in their emphasis on the value and dignity of the human person. However, conflicts may occasionally arise between professional ethical requirements and practices in some faith communities. For example, the expectations for client confidentiality may be experienced as overly restrictive in many faith settings, and pastoral counselors may be challenged to maintain both the legal and ethical standards of confidentiality while navigating the particular culture of their religious communities.

Pastoral counselors trained as mental health professionals may also experience challenges when commonly accepted interventions supported by research in their fields appear to be in conflict with the values or teachings of their clients or faith communities. For example, solo or mutual masturbation is a treatment technique often endorsed in sexuality research. However, some religious clients may balk at the use of this method because it is at odds with the teachings of their tradition. The first author once served a client referred by her physician due to an inability to reach orgasm. The client reported that she was unable to reach orgasm with two previous spouses but was motivated to reach orgasm in the future with a spouse. She was unmarried at the time of treatment and unwilling to engage in masturbation for religious reasons. Without an acceptable partner with whom to engage in sexual behaviors (herself or another), the counseling stalled. To respect the client's religious beliefs, the focus of counseling then turned to ways in which the client might cultivate her sensuality, self-care, and self-appreciation so that she might be prepared for a future sexual relationship.

Compensation

Pastoral counselors must also address the means by which they are compensated for their services. The work of some pastoral counselors is compensated for by their faith communities or donors who either entirely or partially subsidize the costs of care. Others practice in fee-for-service settings, with clients or their family members paying directly for care. Pastoral counselors who are licensed as mental health professionals may also be eligible for third-party reimbursement (insurance), through either public (Medicare, Medicaid, and state programs) or private insurance entities. The policies for third-party payments vary by state, profession, and licensure status.

INTEGRATED PROFESSIONALS

Pastoral counselors trained and licensed as a mental health professional bring much to the profession. Although the occasional traditionalist from the religious or psychological realm may view these pastoral counselors as traitors or outsiders, they are uniquely poised to serve as bridge builders and integrators between the historical practices of pastoral counseling and the increasingly professionalized and guild-based world of mental health.

REFLECTION QUESTIONS

1. Do you think ordained and/or religiously endorsed leaders are better equipped to serve as pastoral counselors? Why or why not?
2. In your role as a pastoral counselor, have you experienced conflicts between your theological/spiritual and psychological principles? How can such conflicts be managed?
3. The authors advocate engaging in "transformative dialogues" to develop awareness of others' spiritual traditions. What are some specific ways you might actively seek out and engage in transformative dialogues?
4. Pastoral counselors are employed in a diversity of settings. What are the benefits and limitations of this for the profession? For your practice?

REFERENCES

American Association of Pastoral Counselors. (2012). *Code of ethics*. Retrieved from http://www .aapc.org/about-us/code-of-ethics/

American Psychological Association, Office of Program Consultation and Accreditation. (2013). *Guidelines and principles for accreditation of programs in professional psychology*. Retrieved from http://www.apa.org

American Psychiatric Association. (2013). *Diagnostic and statistical manual of mental disorders* (5th ed.). Arlington, VA: American Psychiatric Press.

Aten, J. D., O'Grady, K. A., & Worthington, E. L. (Eds.). (2012). *The psychology of religion and spirituality for clinicians*. New York, NY: Routledge.

Cashwell, C. S., & Young, J. S. (Eds.). (2011). *Integrating spirituality and religion into counseling: A guide to competent practice* (2nd ed.). Alexandria, VA: American Counseling Association.

Cheston, S. E. (2000). A new paradigm for teaching counseling theory and practice. *Counselor Education and Supervision, 39*, 228–269. doi:http://dx.doi.org/10.1002/j.1556-6978.2000 .tb01236.x

Clinebell, H., & McKeever, B. C. (2011). *Basic types of pastoral care and counseling: Resources for the ministry of healing and growth* (3rd ed.). Nashville, TN: Abingdon.

Commission on Accreditation for Marriage and Family Therapy Education. (2005). *Accreditation standards: Graduate and post-graduate marriage and family therapy training programs* (Version 11.0). Retrieved from http://www.aamft.org

Council for Accreditation of Counseling and Related Educational Programs. (2009). *2009 CACREP accreditation manual*. Retrieved from http://www.cacrep.org

Council on Social Work Education. (2008). *Educational policy and accreditation standards*. Retrieved from http://www.cswe.org

Fowler, J. W. (1981). *Stages of faith: The psychology of human development and the quest for meaning*. New York, NY: HarperCollins.

Frankl, V. E. (1984). *Man's search for meaning*. New York, NY: Pocket Books/Simon & Schuster. (Original work published 1959)

Graham, L. (1995). From relational humanness to relational justice: Reconceiving pastoral care and counseling. In P. Couture & R. Hunter (Eds.), *Pastoral care and social conflict* (pp. 220–234). Nashville, TN: Abingdon.

Jones, S. L., & Butman, R. E. (1991). *Modern psychotherapies: A comprehensive Christian appraisal.* Downers Grove, IL: IVP Academic.

Maynard, E. A. (2013). The diagnostic and statistical manual: Sacred text for a secular community? *Mental Health, Religion & Culture, 17*(2), 136–142. doi:10.1080/13674676.2012.762574

Miller, G. (2003). *Incorporating spirituality in counseling and psychotherapy: Theory and technique.* Hoboken, NJ: John Wiley.

Miller, W. R. (Ed.). (1999). *Integrating spirituality into treatment: Resources for practitioners.* Washington, DC: American Psychological Association.

Nouwen, H. J. M. (1972). *The wounded healer: Ministry in contemporary society.* New York, NY: Random House.

Pargament, K. I. (2007). *Spiritually integrated psychotherapy: Understanding and addressing the sacred.* New York, NY: Guilford.

Ramsay, N. (2004). Contemporary pastoral theology: A wider vision for the practice of love. In N. Ramsay (Ed.), *Pastoral care and counseling: Redefining the paradigms* (pp. 155–176). Nashville, TN: Abingdon.

Sperry, L., & Shafranske, E. P. (Eds.). (2005). *Spiritually oriented psychotherapy.* Washington, DC: American Psychological Association.

Tan, S. Y. (1996). Religion in clinical practice: Implicit and explicit integration. In E. P. Shafranske (Ed.), *Religion and the clinical practice of psychology* (pp. 265–387). Washington, DC: American Psychological Association.

Vitz, P. C. (1977). *Psychology as religion: The cult of self-worship* (2nd ed.). Grand Rapids, MI: William B. Eerdmans.

World Health Organization. (2010). *International statistical classification of diseases and related health problems* (10th rev.). Geneva, Switzerland: Author. Retrieved from http://www.who.org

Jesse Fox, Daniel Gutierrez, Jim Coffield, and Bill Moulder 4

THE HUMAN CONDITION: PASTORAL PERSPECTIVES

The *human condition* is a complex theological, philosophical, and psychological term that refers to the nature of our human experience. Typically, discussions of the human condition from a pastoral perspective are framed within the terminology of existential theory, exploring themes relating to life and death, meaning and despair, freedom and limitation, being and becoming, and so forth (see Guthrie, 1990)—what Yalom (1980) calls the "givens" of human existence (p. 8). Significant pastoral concerns arise directly from the givens of human existence, as well as the contexts in which those experiences occur. However, we see no need to repeat what has already been written and therefore explore the topic from a slightly different angle. We assume that readers will have some understanding of existential approaches to counseling and refer readers who may be unfamiliar with existential theory to Cooper's (2003) comprehensive, yet relatively accessible, review of the existential therapies.

Instead, the organization and method of our discourse cover six key contexts for understanding the human condition: (a) human dignity and depravity, (b) story, (c) relational style, (d) family, (e) gender, and (f) view of God. These six key contexts not only offer philosophical value in organizing a perspective of human nature but also possess salient power for understanding the human condition within the context of therapeutic relationships and the unique vocation of pastoral counseling. It is our hope, then, that readers will find our explanation of these key terms to be both intellectually stimulating and of great practical value when addressing difficult questions about the human condition with clients who sometimes seek help in understanding them.

It is not our intention, nor is it possible in a chapter of this scope, to survey every perspective that has developed in history to answer those fascinating and sometimes daunting questions about our common ancestry and human predicament. Thus, transparency about our authorial assumptions is in order. As authors, we share a common Christian worldview, and readers familiar with the Christian tradition will likely see various points of contact between our responses and those already in circulation. At the same time, we are passionate learners of the world's great wisdom traditions, and we do not expect readers to be able to use our discussion without qualification in their unique contexts, knowing that some would disagree even within our own tradition about our approach to the human condition. That being the case, and when it is possible, we have chosen to build on the foundation of the Judeo–Christian perspective and draw points of connection to philosophy, psychology, and Eastern thought, referring to Hinduism and Buddhism as these traditions are often called on as exemplars of the Eastern worldview.

HUMAN DIGNITY AND DEPRAVITY

At their very foundation, human beings are a paradox. During his internment in the Nazi concentration camps, Viktor Frankl (1992) captured the seemingly contradictory nature of his fellow inmates in the following description of his experiences:

> In this living laboratory [the Nazi concentration camps], we watched and witnessed some of our comrades behave like swine while others behaved like saints. Man has both potentialities within himself: which one is actualized depends on decisions but not on conditions. (p. 135)

Likewise, St. Ignatius of Loyola (1991) in his guide to spiritual formation, the *Spiritual Exercises*, noticed the same potential within human nature and developed a method for discerning the movement of the spirit toward either desolation or consolation as a way of spiritual transformation. Respect for purity, and identifying when that purity is defiled, is a hallmark of all religious belief and praxis (Paden, 1988). In line with those writers, as well as the world's wisdom traditions in general, we suggest that the lens through which to understand the human condition is equal part light and dark, glorious and shameful, remarkable and disappointing. As with any paradox, addressing only one end of the continuum will inevitably result in quick counterclaims to the contrary. So you say human beings are wondrous creatures, what of all the genocides in human history that came at the hands of so-called divine image bearers, not to mention the daily acts of violence inflicted on the innocent and vulnerable in countless numbers? If people possess inherent dignity, why are they so capable of inflicting such suffering onto their fellow human beings? Or the opposite: So you say humanity is wretched, what about the great beauty humans are capable of creating, the relief work for the suffering, sacrificial love, or the museums filled with the powers of human creativity? So without providing some explanation of human dignity *and* depravity, our capacity for glory *and* shame, an understanding of the human condition lacks explanatory power; too much data are lost if one side is ignored. Therefore, as we begin this chapter, we first address the importance of understanding the dignity of human nature and from there grasp at the opposite pole.

Human Dignity

In his treatise on the human condition, St. Basil the Great (2005) instructed his readers to begin their understanding of humanity, and thereby the human condition, through its unique distinction and heritage by quoting the first book of the Pentateuch, Genesis 1:26. St. Basil built his theory of the human condition by comparing and contrasting the narrative flow of Genesis 1, pointing out a key feature of the narrative as the biblical writer described the created order, from light, to plants, to animals, and finally to the human race. It is the human race alone, said St. Basil, that is given the distinction of sharing or reflecting the divine essence. Although St. Basil was undoubtedly speaking from his Christian worldview, it is not difficult to surmise that most if not all spiritual and religious traditions can be united in the central belief that human beings possess inherent dignity. And so we begin there: glory, mystery, and dignity.

In the Judeo–Christian tradition, what is meant by "human dignity" is that God endowed human beings with a unique identity as *image bearers* (Genesis 1:26–28). Several scholars have posited theories of what this might mean; some options include the uniqueness of the human soul being inextricably linked to the human body, the rational faculties of the human mind, the freedom of the human will, the responsibilities of abiding by a moral conscience, a designated vocation to rule over the created order, or some combination of all these (see Erickson, 1998; Harrison, 2005; Hoekema, 1986; Steckel, 1987). We need not side with one theory over another at this point. Instead, what each writer has suggested, and what concerns us most here, is that human beings have inherent worth *because of their likeness to the creator God*, whatever that likeness may be. Human beings are sacred or holy because of how God made them. It is here that the Hebrew language can provide some assistance. The word *image* is a translation of the Hebrew words *tselem* and *demuth*, with the underlying thought being *likeness*; human beings were made to be like God much like a mirror or a representative of the divine essence (Hoekema, 1986). Human beings are holy because God is holy and are to remain as such (Leviticus 19:2).

It is this basic premise, that human beings reflect God's character, that provides the foundation for human dignity. Moreover, the Genesis myth seems to suggest that it is the divine will that human beings be intimate with God, with one another, and the "garden" in which they were to cultivate (this likely means that human beings were created to serve as stewards over all created order), with the phrase ultimately amplifying this wish being, "Adam and his wife were both naked, and they felt no shame" (Genesis 2:25 New International Version). Cistercian monk and a founding figure of the Centering Prayer movement, Thomas Keating (2002), has written extensively on the human condition and updated the language of the Genesis myth in terms accessible to modern psychology. Keating suggests that human beings possess three innate dispositions that, in and of themselves, are both good and wholesome. The three desires are for (a) survival/security, (b) affection/esteem, and (c) power/control and are our companions from birth, finding their perfect rest and fulfillment in God (as the Genesis story seems to imply). St. John of the Cross (1962), in his manifesto on the heights of spiritual experience called the *Living Flame of Love*, summed up the human desire for God in these words:

Oh Living Flame of Love . . .
How gently and how lovingly
Thou wakest in my bosom,
Where thou dwellest secretly and alone!
And in thy sweet breathing,
Full of blessing and glory,
How delicately thou inspirest my love. (p. 30)

In the Judeo–Christian Tradition, Jesus as Messiah exemplified the infinite God (to borrow Lewis's [1991] phrase) *operating under human conditions*. It therefore should come as no surprise that St. John the Evangelist depicted the high priestly prayer of the 17th chapter of his Gospel with language of "oneness," where Jesus as the Messiah draws all God's people to himself and into the intimacy he has with the Father (see John 17:11, 21–23 for telling examples). Equally unsurprising, some theologians like Karl Barth, based on key passages such as those we have already reviewed, concluded that to be fully human is to live in relationship (see Erickson, 1998; Price, 2002), and without relationship, we cease to fulfill the divine design for our human condition.

It is important to remember that respect for human dignity appears to be ubiquitous, to varying degrees, within most religions. For instance, the three great Abrahamic traditions, at the beginning of their sacred texts, all concur that human beings demand respect due to their divine origin (Smith & Smith, 1991). Likewise, by studying the sacred texts of several religious traditions, Sant Kirpal Singh (2007) concluded that all agree on the following premise about human beings: " 'Know ye not that ye are the temple of God and God verily resides therein?' " (p. 81).

Although we suggested that a review of world religions is beyond the scope of this chapter, we believe it is worthwhile to draw connection here to some Eastern traditions to provide context. Specifically, with Hinduism, respect for the human person stems from the central dogma that within all living things resides the divine *Brahman*. And so, it is common for Hindu priests to begin temple ceremonies with the following prayer:

O Lord, forgive three sins that are due to my human limitations:
Thou art everywhere, but I worship you here;
Thou art without form, but I worship you in these forms;
Thou needest no praise, yet I offer you these prayers and salutations.
Lord, forgive three sins that are due to my human limitations. (Smith & Smith, 1991, p. 34)

In looking over the crowd of devotees, the priest sees the spark of the divine in the faithful. Followers of Hinduism, if so moved, can take upon themselves the path of love exemplified in *Bhakti Yoga*, which emphasizes acts of compassion for others (one of four paths to God in Hinduism, the other three being knowledge [*Jnana Yoga*], work [*Karma Yoga*], and psychophysical exercise [*Raja Yoga*]). Therefore, similar to Judaism and Christianity, the Hindu belief in the dignity of all living things (and as a result, worthiness of love and devotion) is an outgrowth of the belief in the *Atman–Brahman* unity (Smart, 2000). Like Hinduism, the Buddha taught the importance of recognizing the essential unity that lies behind reality, albeit positing a different sort of unity—the void or nothingness. Although Buddhism rejected the notion of an all-powerful, creator God, the emphasis on compassion for others is obviously at the forefront of the Buddha's teaching and likely stems doubly from the centrality of *nirvana* (nothingness) and the belief in the reincarnation of all living things (Paden, 1988). First, nirvana is the central goal of all spiritual progress that comprises the essence of reality, and ethical misconduct toward others invariably defies the purity of consciousness required for enlightenment. And second, because all living things are connected through the cycle of rebirth, there is no living thing that is unworthy of compassion.

Human Depravity

As we have already said, a discussion of the human condition is incomplete without an honest look at the human capacity to commit serious grievances against self, others, and the cosmos in general. We need not provide a litany of the atrocities rendered by human means throughout history; to deny these would simply be naïve. We would argue that pastoral counseling is a profession in part because the human condition is already in a state of fragmentation. But where did this human potential for destruction come from in the first place? Although the origin of evil has consumed pages of philosophical and theological inquiry, the exact origin of evil is a mystery to the laymen and the learned alike (Wright, 2006). For instance, the Genesis myth never really explains how evil came to exist in the first place. Did evil exist before the serpent or was the serpent its creator? Who is the serpent anyway? What is the significance of the fruit, and why were the first parents not allowed to consume it? Were human beings the inventors of evil, or did it come about by collaboration with supernatural sources?

Such questions may never be put fully to rest. However, suffice it to say that the Genesis story clearly does provide some direction in the manner in which the human condition is *affected* by evil. Or as Rabbi Cassuto (1989) taught,

> The central theme of our section [Gen. 3] does not aim to give a philosophical explanation of the origin of evil in the world, but has the practical purpose of providing moral instruction and of assuaging the feeling of perplexity in the heart of man, who finds a contradiction between the creator's paternal love and the multitudinous troubles that throng his world. (p. 139)

As we noted earlier, human beings find solace in their intimacy with God, which simultaneously provides the context for their dignity. However, the intimacy that human beings were intended to enjoy is now deeply distorted. For instance, the freedom of *being naked without shame* is now universally experienced as the *fear of exposure*: "But the Lord God called to the man, 'Where are you?' He answered, 'I heard you in the garden, and I was afraid because I was naked; so I hid'" (Genesis 3:9–10 New International Version). The reverberation of the Fall can be felt within the human psyche, as John Powell (1969) so wryly put it in his book *Why Am I Afraid to Tell You Who I Am?* The answer: Because if I tell you who I am, you might reject me. Or as Irvin Yalom, the renowned existential and group therapy theorist, said, every client he has ever seen has feared being exposed for secrets that relate to a sense of personal inadequacy, alienation from other people, or sex (Yalom & Leszcz, 2005).

Keating (1999, 2002) suggests that the human condition was affected by the Fall in at least four significant ways that concern us here: (a) separation from God, (b) separation from each other, (c) separation from ourselves, and (d) separation from the cosmos in general. Our ontological and existential fragmentation therefore affected our three innate needs for survival/security, affection/esteem, and power/control. Instead of those needs finding their rest and fulfillment in the infinite resources of God's love, they instead become "sources of human misery that will never work" (Keating, 1999, p. 18). In an attempt to respond to a broken world, the three desires become compulsive and unconscious, what Keating (1999, 2002) calls the *false-self*. The false-self system is a way of describing the three innate needs (survival/security, affection/ esteem, and power/control) after becoming self-centered and therefore create a persona based on the image of oneself as opposed to the image of God (Keating, 1994). Despite their inability to be fully satisfied in the human psyche, they remain humanity's programs for happiness and are the source of our afflicted emotional states and our inability to love each other. At least within the three most influential monotheistic traditions (Judaism, Christianity, and Islam), human beings consistently fail to fulfill the divine moral law and have done so since recorded history.

The Judeo–Christian myth is not the only tradition that has had to grapple with the reality of the human sickness; as Keating (2002) has said,

> The doctrine of the Fall was an effort on the part of theologians to explain how the pervasive disease of human nature came about. Taoism, Hinduism, Buddhism, and other religions also bear witness to the experience of a universal illness that has afflicted the human family from the beginning. (p. 152)

It is striking to note that most if not all religions have developed codes of moral conduct, the core of which are often remarkably similar and testify to the human potential for error in an equally uniform fashion (Singh, 2007; Smart, 2000). In the East, the law of justice is called *karma* (the term refers to "work" in the practical sense, or the law of cause–effect, but refers to justice when applied to moral contexts) and is the reason for the cycle of reincarnation that all living beings must come to terms with (Smith & Smith, 1991). The justice for past misdeeds is carried out through one's particular time and place and within the social order, which would also include the misdeeds of past lives (i.e., the transmigration of souls). Specifically within Hinduism, all of reality can be understood from a succession of three tiers of experience: the material world, the soul of God, and the unity of all living things; beginning at the bottom (the material), each successive tier elucidates the lower levels of consciousness (Smart, 2000). Material reality (including the human body) is therefore a manifestation of God or the oversoul that provides life to the whole cosmos. The same is true of the various manifestations of God or gods cross-culturally. In the theological sect of Hinduism called the Advaita Vedanta (the term refers to the "nondualistic" meaning of the Vedas), union is the highest reality, not God. Therefore, the experiences of the body and the physical world are illusory or a mirage, the Indian term being *maya*, which must be transcended to end the otherwise endless cycle of rebirth (i.e., reincarnation). The path of transcendence in both Hindu and Buddhist thought (although Siddhartha Gautama himself was a devout critic of traditional Hindu doctrine, especially the concept of an untouchable caste; see Smith & Smith, 1991; Zacharias, 2000) is generally achieved through a strict practice of meditation and ethical behavior that eventually purifies the practitioner's consciousness until all forms of duality are extinguished. Pure consciousness is liberation, called *moksha*. In Hinduism, the soul is released from its bodily prison, and the cycle of karma is brought to an end in divine union with the human spirit (at least until the next cycle of cosmic reincarnation commences). However, in Buddhism, the path to enlightenment does not involve the absorption of the spirit into an oversoul; what lies on the other side of enlightenment is emptiness because what underlies everything, according to the Buddha, is a constant and dynamic transience (Smart, 2000).

The traditional Hindu and Buddhist perspectives about enlightenment and liberation demonstrate how, alongside a problem or disease of the human spirit that all people experience in their specific time and place in the cosmos, there exists also a solution to that problem in all religions. In the Christian schema, the solution is found in the faithfulness of Jesus as the vindicated Messiah (Wright, 1996), who, by his death and resurrection, liberated humanity from the tension of their existential predicament of life and death, meaning and meaninglessness, being and nothingness, and so on (Guthrie, 1990); the term exemplifying this all-encompassing victory is *resurrection* (Wright, 2003). Although interpretations of the resurrection of Jesus differ dramatically, varying from a transformed human physicality to an abiding spiritual presence (see Borg & Wright, 2007), the need to fashion one's life after the resurrected Jesus is a perennial teaching within Christianity. The well-known "now, but not yet" tension in Christian theology refers to the sufficiency of Jesus' life, death, and resurrection that took place in first-century Palestine to right the wrongs of the world past, present, and future, while still awaiting the day in which the entire cosmos will be put to right and the restoration of the entire created order will be fully consummated (see Cole, 2009; Erickson, 1998). Likewise, liberation from the human tendency for error in the present tension between past and future is found in the grace of God through the free gift of faith; as St. Paul said, "For it is by grace you have been saved, through faith— and this is not from yourselves, it is the gift of God" (Ephesians 2:8 New International Version).

STORY

The precarious dance of humanity between dignity and depravity is described, understood, and expounded on routinely in the stories we tell one another. From the most ancient expressions of humanity in cave drawings to the most recent Hollywood movie, it is clear that humanity expresses, defines, explains, understands, and heals itself narratively. "God made man because He loves stories" has now become a Yiddish proverb attributed to Holocaust survivor and winner of the Nobel Peace Prize, Elie Wiesel (1966, p. 10). Our belief systems and our values are often more "caught" than "taught." The very first Christian spiritual directors (the so-called Desert Fathers) were acutely aware of the implicit storylines we pick up in our lived experience and tailored their methods of offering pastoral and spiritual care accordingly (Ward, 1975). Culture after culture, as well as diverse faith communities, capture the hearts and minds of their constituents through story. Sometimes these stories take center stage in a particular religion. For instance, New Testament scholar N. T. Wright's (1992, 1996, 2003, 2013) magnum opus detailing the development of the Christian faith has dramatically and comprehensively demonstrated that at its very foundation, the Bible is first and foremost a story. Although some religious sects may reject the need for a sacred text or may even view a text that espouses to be sacred as inherently suspect, many religions still refer to a particular text or a group of texts they see as either revelatory or at least insightful teachings about God or ultimate reality (whether it be the Quran, the Torah, the Bible, or the Gita; see Smith & Smith, 1991). Although not every sacred text espouses to depict historical referents in its storytelling, most do in some sense place the story of their faith in some parabolic form (such as the Zen teachings). Moreover, story is not only the way that humans understand deity or the nature of ultimate reality; it is also how they try to connect and understand one another and self. Each person's life is her own, individual story that is a segment of a larger story that inevitably creates and sustains her belief system.

Every story possesses a complex network of themes and subplots, and the same is true of the human condition. It is therefore important to understand how a person portrays the thematic material of his story. Is the theme a tragedy, a comedy, the tale of an epic hero, or merely a documentary? Just as literature has genre and novels have plots, human lives have themes and tendencies that seem to repeat themselves or look for a common denouement. It is best to understand more than only the themes of the narrative but also the setting, much like the hermeneutical discipline of a sacred text. When theologians study the sacred text to attempt full understanding, they look for genre, context, meaning, and application (see Klein, Bloomberg, & Hubbard, 1993). The sacred text of humanity is read in a similar way.

Just as the setting is central in a story, the setting is important in the human narrative. In analyzing a novel, one must consider the minor and major characters and how they influence development and movement of the story. To understand the human condition, the relational interplay between the people who shape the story and the setting must be understood. Developmental psychology is dependent on the art of watching character development, which includes physical, moral, cognitive, emotional, social, and spiritual development. How the character interacts with the environment and his or her innate abilities determines the outcome of the individual belief system.

As pastoral counselors develop, they inevitably grapple with the diverse theoretical orientations available to provide them a foundation for practice. I (Jim Coffield) am often asked by students what characteristics are imperative to become a good counselor. Is it some sort of cognitive spelunking, looking for deep insights in the mind?

Or what about an archeological dig of the client's soul? Or is effective counseling simply good listening and feedback techniques? Because human beings are stories that need to be read, my most common answer is that counselors need to be humble and curious. But most important, they need to love stories.

RELATIONAL STYLE

Any discussion of the human condition would be incomplete without some mention of the human capacity for deep connection to other people. We are relational beings. From the moment we are born (and even before then), we are completely dependent on another person. Throughout all of childhood, we look to another for guidance, safety, and to help us meet our needs. As we get older, our desire for relationship and our ability to relate may change, but it seldom goes away. From the Judeo–Christian perspective, our innermost being longs for a satisfying, close, and personal relationship with God (as already discussed previously). The image of God in Christianity is that of a mysterious trinity, where God exists within a perfect network of relationship (Coppedge, 2007). Likewise, human beings are designed to be in perfect unity with God. When we fail at achieving intimacy with God, we attempt to meet these needs with objects of attachment. Gerald May (1988) describes it this way:

> God wants to be our perfect lover, but instead we seek perfection in human relationships and are disappointed when our lovers cannot love us perfectly. God wants to provide our ultimate security, but we seek our safety in power and possessions and then find we must continually worry about them. We seek satisfaction of our spiritual longing in a host of ways that may have little to do with God. (p. 93)

Or as the 17th-century philosopher Blaise Pascal (1995) said in his well-known work, *Pensees*,

> What is it then, that this desire and this inability proclaim to us, but that there was once in a man a true happiness of which there now remain to him only the mark and empty trace which he in vain tries to fill from all his surroundings, seeking from things absent the help he does not obtain in things present? But these are all inadequate, because the infinite abyss can only be filled by an infinite and immutable object, that is to say, only God himself. (p. 52)

According to May (1988), each of us searches for the *easiest* way to fill the God-shaped hole within us, and this compulsion to fill our longing for God is most apparent in the human propensity for addiction. The Christian scriptures are replete with stories of God seeking to connect with people in relationship and humanity seeking to satisfy their spiritual hunger with the created instead of the creator. From the Christian perspective, only God can satisfy our true need for relationship. Thus, Christians seek to establish redemptive relationships both with God and with each other (i.e., the body of Christ).

May (1988) said, "Relationships are the vehicle through which we most directly love and are loved" (p. 33). Without relationships, it is impossible to meet our basic needs (see Glasser, 2010) and defend against feelings of existential anxiety and isolation (see Yalom, 1980). In essence, we need to have contact with fellow travelers and companions who can help us walk through our struggles (Allender, 1999).

Relationships that exhibit acceptance, unconditional positive regard, and warmth create an atmosphere conducive to personal growth and healing (see Rogers, 1957). When researchers examine the most effective components of counseling, the relationship between the counselor and the client is the strongest predictor of counseling success (Norcross, 2009). Yalom (1989) stated that his professional rosary was "it's the relationship that heals, the relationship that heals, the relationship that heals" (p. 91). Thus, as tempting as it is to credit clients' successes to our knowledge of technique or flawless performance in session, the relationship is what does the most good in counseling, across the board.

In addition to seeing the healing benefits of relationship, theorists such as Kohut (1971), Wolf (2002), and Cashdan (1988) believed that our ability to relate to others is at the core of our sense of self. As we saw in our discussion of human dignity, some theologians believe that our ability to relate is an aspect of the divine. For example, if the only way we know to relate to others and satisfy our needs is through demonstrating dependency, power, sexuality, or ingratiation, then we begin to mar our view of ourselves and no longer feel prized, valued, or worthy outside of relationships (Cahsdan, 1988; Wolf, 2002). We begin to treat everyone in the relational style that we believe brings us the most attention and affection, regardless of how far this image is from our authentic selves. If we believe that no one will love us unless we are in need, then we always present ourselves as being a victim and eschew any responsibility for change. In other words, we can behave in ways that manipulate others for the sake of filling ourselves with a sense of belonging, acceptance, and love (May, 1988). Conversely, when someone accepts us into relationship without "falling for" our manipulating techniques (e.g., acting helpless), we are set free to be genuine, to be authentic, and to grow. One could argue that part of the healing power of the therapeutic relationship occurs because a counselor allows the client to have an authentic encounter with his or her own self.

FAMILY

To be human is in some way to be indebted to a family. We did not choose our families, yet they are ours nonetheless. The expression of relational style, colored as we saw by our confluence of inner drives for wholeness, intimacy, and fulfillment, is perhaps no more apparent than within the context of family. Equally likely, our family members are also the ones who are most likely to be familiar with our capacities for glory and brokenness. In a thought-provoking chapter on family dynamics in the context of human development (particularly those dynamics within conservative, Protestant churches), Kimball (2001) lamented that two often-repeated, yet subliminal messages about family are held as an almost absolute in American church culture:

> Every therapist and pastor we went to communicated either explicitly or implicitly that we were the sources of our son's acting out. . . . We thought we'd done our best. . . . If we had just done things right, he would have turned out happy. He would be working hard and loving God. (p. 346)

This view of family places the onus of responsibility for the health and development of the family unit entirely on the shoulders of the parent(s) or caregiver(s). The second message is similarly extreme, with a slightly different thrust:

> Our daughter is willful and rebellious. She has turned from God and disobeys us. We need help getting her under control. We need a therapist or pastor who will support our authority (as the Bible asserts it) and show her the error and potential destruction of her ways. (p. 346)

This message holds that it is within the power of the pastoral counselor to somehow "control" family members' behavior by means of reinforcing parental authority. Unfortunately, both messages are inadequate to address the complexity of the human condition as it manifests within family contexts.

Instead of the narratives just described, Kimball (2001) offered an alternative perspective using an integration of Jesus' teachings on family with Bowlby's (1982) attachment theory and Vygotsky's (1962) cognitive development theory. In short, our relational style is significantly influenced by our attachment to primary caregivers early on in our development (Bowlby, 1982); when caregivers are available, responsive, and helpful, we tend to internalize models of self that are loveable and valuable that extend outward toward other figures in our relational world. Conversely, if our parent(s) (or surrogate parent[s]) do not provide us with an available and safe presence, we tend to relate defensively with others, assuming an inherent danger in the risk of interpersonal relationship. Most important, our attachment style from earlier stages of our development filters into our parenting style; if those styles of relating are not dealt with, they run the risk of passing onto future generations dysfunctional relational strategies. Moreover, families, as well as children within families for that matter, do not develop within a vacuum and are inevitably influenced by a myriad of contextual or environmental factors (Vygotsky, 1962). Therefore, families function through the transformation of their psychological (and for us spiritual) raw material (i.e., memory, perception, language) by sociocultural influences that either help or hinder our development. Vygotsky used the term *proximal development* to refer to figures in our lives who teach us to grow (stretch us so to speak) to higher levels of our development as human beings. The important message for us here is that human relationships are powerful for our growth, *even if those relationships exist outside the blood relative bond*. It is here that Kimball (2001) refers to the teachings of Jesus on familial relationships. One day while teaching the crowds, his relatives sent a messenger to bring Jesus to them. His response was unexpected:

> He replied to him, "Who is my mother, and who are my brothers?" Pointing to his disciplines, he said, "Here are my mother and my brothers. For whoever does the will of my Father in heaven is my brother and sister and mother." (Matthew 12:48–50 New International Version)

Keating (2002) has pointed out that for Jesus to say this within the cultural climate of his day would have been shocking to those who heard him because familial, blood relationship was a cultural boundary marker. Instead of identifying his blood relatives as his family, Jesus redefined family to be those who sincerely seek the will of God, or as St. Paul later said, "There is neither Jew nor Gentile, neither slave nor free, nor is there male and female, for you are all one in Christ Jesus" (Galatians 3:28 New International Version). Jesus is speaking to what Wilber's (1981) theory of transpersonal evolution called *mythic membership consciousness*, where Jesus is calling on his contemporaries to evolve beyond their tribal tendencies and welcome all of humanity into the fold (what Keating [2002] called the *contemplative dimension of the gospel*).

The essential unity of the human family with God, as we already saw, is part of the dignity inherent to the human condition (and for some religious traditions, this would include the animal order) and is often described by the mystics. John Donne, the 17th-century English poet, in a work that would later inspire the titles of both Hemingway's (1940) novel *For Whom the Bell Tolls* and Merton's (1955) spiritual *No Man Is an Island*, put it this way:

> No man is an island, entire of itself; every man is a piece of the continent, a part of the main. If a clod be washed away by the sea, Europe is the less, as well as if a promontory were, as well as if a manor of thy friend's or of thine own were: any man's death diminishes me, because I am involved in mankind, and therefore never send to know for whom the bells tolls; it tolls for thee. (Donne, 1624/1999, p. 103)

The simple, but profound, message: We are one family. Or as St. Paul wrote, "You are all one in Christ Jesus" (Galations 3:28 New International Version).

GENDER

A diversity of views on gender, as well as its relation to biological sex, is evident today and grounded within one's epistemological assumptions. In other words, describing one's views of gender is a way of determining the epistemology lens (positivist, constructivist, critical realist, etc.) that one brings to the discussion. It is little wonder that people who are drawn to postmodern, relativistic paradigms tend to also see gender as a fluid, socially constructed concept that shifts depending on a myriad of cultural conditions (i.e., gender is a cultural construction). It is equally unsurprising that those who tend to favor modernist or positivist epistemologies tend to see gender as a discrete entity that can be categorized (i.e., gender is determined by whatever kind of genitals the person possesses). As authors, we tend to adhere to more of a middle-ground approach between the two. In other words, we agree with the postmodern critique that people bring to every discussion their biases, which are undoubtedly affected by time and place. At the same time, we hold that there is a reality outside the mind of the knower that can be interacted with, tested, and understood. Walking the path to knowledge, then, is done in constant dialogue with reality, where initial hypotheses are tested and confirmed or revised through a critical examination of the evidence while simultaneously acknowledging the need to reexamine cultural presuppositions that may help or hinder the investigation (see Wright, 1992, for a more thorough discussion of this approach).

Returning to an awareness of the philosophical presuppositions that undoubtedly play a role in how individuals understand issues of gender is, perhaps, a much-needed starting place for wider discourse. In Christian theological circles, discussions of gender invariably circle back to St. Paul's statements about Christian households in Ephesians 5:21–33 (see Piper & Grudem, 1991) and have centered on the following question: Do men and women assume basic roles in their families, and therefore their communities and society at large, on the basis of their gender? At the risk of oversimplifying an enormously complex scholarly issue, the arguments from competing camps (e.g., egalitarian vs. complementarian) have not spent enough time focusing on St. Paul's summation of the entire issue, "This is a profound mystery" (Ephesians 5:32 New International

Version). In context, and similar to the dignity inherent in the human condition we have already covered, the starting place for understanding the genders is awe-inspiring mystery. This is perhaps the reason why reductionist views of gender (whether they hold that gender is nothing more than culture or nothing more than hormonal compounds) tend to fall flat; mystery can be puzzled at, admired, but never fully explained until new revelation comes to light. If it can be accepted that gender is in fact part of the "divine revelation," then how an individual chooses to understand and live out gender matters, and this is part of the way the human condition is understood and interpreted.

To understand the human condition and not be curious about how a culture, group, faith, and individual perceives and lives out gender would be naïve. How people define and express masculinity and femininity determines much about how they interact and engage their world. It becomes a part of how they express themselves sexually, socially, and even parentally. For example, is femininity seen as dangerous or delightful? Is physical beauty to be hidden or displayed? Are emotions to be expressed or hidden? Is it courageous to sacrifice or to fight? Although it is oversimplified to say that these questions are just about gender, clearly the lens through which one understands the role of gender influences the life one lives.

There are several great theological debates about the nature of God. One of them is the question of choice—did God choose us or did we choose God? Within the Christian tradition, the debate has raged. Yet, the mystery may be reflected in the very image of the divine found in gender. The question could be rephrased by asking whether God pursues us or whether we invite or choose God. The traditional view of masculinity might suggest a God who pursues, whereas the same view of femininity might point to the mystery of a God who is creative, nurturing, and inviting. Of course, men can be nurturing and women can pursue and be aggressive. Again, reductionist approaches rarely have explanatory power within the mystery of gender. However, if one assumes that God's nature is revealed through creation, then gender says something unique and important about God. Conversely, the way we understand ourselves as gendered will reveal something about how we see ourselves and relate to the world.

Most religious systems recognize some difference between masculinity and femininity and recognize that there is dignity in both maleness and femaleness. Likewise, most religious systems attach meaning to sexuality, and some even consider sexual expression sacred. For instance, in the Hindu tradition, sexual expression corresponds to the second of the seven major chakras. The word *kama*, or pleasure, is often misunderstood by Westerners as vain, sexual self-indulgence but is actually believed to be part of the spirit's ascent to divine union (Goleman, 1996). During intercourse, the devout Hindu will repeat specific passages of the Sutra to both honor the uniqueness of gender expression in sex as well as move forward in his or her spiritual development to aligning the final five chakras.

One of the truly unique aspects of the human condition is our ability and our propensity to put meaning to events and actions. At the most basic level, gender and one's sexuality can be understood either as the meaningless expressions of a high-functioning animal or as part of meaningful expressions of a creature who is sacred—a lower form of the divine. To state this simply, you are either a high form of animal or low form of angel. In his novel *The World, The Flesh and Father Smith*, Bruce Marshall's (1945) character Father Smith says during a debate about sexuality and religion that " 'the young man who rings the bell at the brothel is unconsciously looking for God' " (p. 108). He was speaking of the core desire in the human condition to connect with the divine, and it may be helpful to note that it is often through and with our understanding of gender and sexuality that we live out that desire for significant and divine connection.

VIEW OF GOD

What does one's view of God have to do with the human condition and pastoral counseling? First, it is important to note that one's view of God often influences how one interprets distress and injustice, as well as makes meaning of one's suffering (Park, 2013). For example, someone experiencing a stressful event may interpret it as part of the plan of a benevolent and loving God and thus more effectively cope with the negative circumstances (see Mickley, Pargament, Brant, & Hipp, 1998; Park, 2013). In addition, some would argue that how you view God relates to how you view yourself. For example, if you view God as a parent, do you see yourself as a child of God? If God is your judge, do you feel like you are on the side of the prosecution or the defense? Is your life marked by the struggle with guilt that typically accompanies someone on trial? Existential psychotherapist Frankl (1978) noted that religion and spirituality are a central component to how one discovers one's "ultimate" meaning in life and that finding meaning is the primary motivation of the human condition. Likewise, we suggest that how one views God, or the nature of the ultimate, influences how one copes with life circumstances and how one makes meaning in life. Therefore, one's view of God has direct implications on one's understanding of the human condition and thus one's counseling practice.

Given the crucial role that belief plays in our lives, it is not surprising that our view of God also has a significant influence on our way of living. Matters of faith are issues of ultimate concern (Tillich, 1951, 2005); therefore, they are, in essence, strong beliefs that have strong implications. C. S. Lewis (2014) once said, "I believe in Christianity as I believe that the Sun has risen, not only because I see it, but because by it I see everything else" (p. 15). Accordingly, our view of God has the ability to alter our human experience. For instance, someone who envisions a God who is caring and merciful may experience less guilt after wrongdoing than someone whose only conception of God is of an unforgiving, moral lawgiver. Conversely, one who sees God as having no use for laws may feel overwhelmed by the injustice of the world. Therefore, one cannot truly understand the human condition without first examining how humanity views the divine.

In the 1950s, Milton Rokeach carried out an unorthodox (and unethical) psychological study to examine the influence of confrontation on schizophrenic patients. He arranged a meeting between three psychiatric patients who all believed they were Jesus Christ. *The Three Christs of Ypsilanti* (Rokeach, 1984) describes the quarrel between these three individuals, as each tried to prove that he was a holier, more authentic, Jesus than the others. Regardless of how much they confronted each other and how often the research team intervened, nothing served to weaken their delusional belief systems. In fact, each found methods of rationalizing the existence of the other two (e.g., believing the others were operated by machines or mental patients) and further ingrain themselves in their beliefs that they were the one true Christ.

Whereas the *Three Christs of Ypsilanti* failed to prove that outward confrontation had any effect on delusional belief systems, it did provide a treatise on how core beliefs are inextricably tied to our sense of identity, how we see others, and how we make sense of our worlds. No matter how rational or philosophically sound they are, human beliefs shape our perceptions and ultimately influence the way we live. For example, to my (Daniel) 5-year-old daughter, the world is a magical and safe place. She has never seen a ball not worth chasing after, a costume too expensive to buy, or known a legitimate reason why we could not just drop everything and go to Walt Disney World that very moment. Her world is boundless and limitless, full of kind, compassionate people, who always manage to triumph over evil. Consequently, she lives a carefree life. In contrast, for most adults, our childlike beliefs of limitless opportunities and endless good have been forced to adapt to a world in which *not* every good deed gets rewarded and "good" and "underserving" people die in sometimes horrific and dishonorable ways. Thus, we live with more caution, a stronger sense of responsibility, and a tendency to see the world around us with a more critical eye. In either case, how we see the world makes a considerable difference.

As noted in the introduction to this chapter, our goal is not to provide a comprehensive survey of comparative religion. Every religion and denomination has its own unique understanding of what is sacred or divine, and within a faith practice, views of God often overlap and are integrated. For example, in Christianity, there are elements of God as a father, a law-giving judge, and an oversoul. Therefore, any attempt to review comprehensively each of these faith practices in this short chapter would be ineffective at best. Instead, we provide five major conceptions of God that readers will likely encounter in clients they may help and we briefly describe how these views may influence human behavior. The views we briefly examine here are (a) God as judge, (b) God as love, (c) God as parent, (d) God as benevolent (but senile) grandfather, and (e) God as oversoul.

God as Judge

The image of God as judge might be the most commonly found in popular culture. In movies, stories, and even cartoons, God is often conceptualized as the great and powerful overlord who sits on a throne in the heavens, keeps records of rights and wrongs, and is looking to dispense judgment. Whereas this image is often perverted in the popular culture, there is some grounding for this image in many faith traditions, and it makes logical sense that the creator of the universe would have both the power and authority to judge humanity. For some, this belief might induce feelings of fear, guilt, and an overall impression that God is callous and lacks empathy. In addition, some form of compensatory behavior is also almost always a response (e.g., offering sacrifice, prayer, confession, etc.) to avoid punishment. However, this might be a welcomed image for others, who are overwhelmed with the depravity and injustice of the world and are comforted by the idea of a just ruler who can make all things right.

God as Love

Another way of viewing God is to place an emphasis on God's love, or rather that God somehow embodies love. This image is available in much of the faith literature. The santguru Kirpal Singh (1988) stated, "God is love, our soul is love and the way back to God is also through love" (p. 50). Or as St. John put it, "Whoever does not love does not know God, because God is love" (1 John 4:8 New International Version). Those who see God as love often recognize God as being full of grace, mercy, and compassion. A God of love would encourage believers to be compassionate and kind. This image of God may seem more welcoming and inviting to those who eschew the idea of God as judge. However, this belief may not sit well with individuals who feel it provides a license for unethical living or who find it difficult to accept a God who loves those who commit acts of violence in the world.

God as Parent

Among other views, Christianity adopts the view of God as a parent (father and mother). This approach understands God as balancing both the roles of authority figure (i.e., judge) and nurturer (i.e., love), as well as disciplinarian (i.e., justice) and comforter (i.e., mercy). In short, viewing God as father involves recognizing God as being an authority that is personally concerned with one's well-being. This can likewise be balanced by viewing God as a mother, who provides new life and nurturance for the world. The image of God as a parent is an inviting image for many. However, it is important to recognize that many may have had negative and even traumatizing relationships with their earthly parents and may abhor the image of God as some replicated version of their primary familial bonds.

God as Benevolent (but Senile) Grandfather

Using his typical penetrating insight and penchant for a turn of phrase, C. S. Lewis (1962) once wrote that human beings possess a propensity to desire

> not so much a Father in Heaven as a grandfather in heaven—a senile benevolence who, as they say, "liked to see young people enjoying themselves," and whose plan for the universe was simply that it might be truly said at the end of each day, "a good time was had by all." (p. 40)

The benevolent, but senile, grandfather God stands juxtaposed to the view of God as parent described earlier. Instead of being a balance of discipline and comfort, this view resembles the deistic God who is distant and remote and only "shows up" to make sure that people get what they wanted during holiday visits. That being the case, people who drift toward this perspective would likely respond negatively to circumstances that do not offer immediate gratification and would likely reject concepts such as divine obedience or submission.

God as Oversoul

It is also important to recognize that God is not always seen as a single being. Some religions (especially in the Eastern practices) identify God as being a supreme soul and each human being as a separate piece of that cosmic consciousness. To use a typical analogy from this perspective, God is the ocean and each human being is a drop. Through this lens, one would recognize all living beings as God. Thus, if God is in everyone, then to honor or care for another is to honor or care for God. Some traditions expand their understanding of the indwelling of God to all living things so that animals are not just lower order species but are also our mother, our father, our brother, our sister, and so on. Consequently, this view of God lends itself to caring for others, showing hospitality, and introspection.

CONCLUSIONS

Our study of the human condition has taken us through a systematic use of six categories to conceptualize the human condition. In human dignity and depravity, we saw that at their very foundation, human beings possess a potentiality for light and dark, glory and shame, comedy as well as tragedy. We also suggested that the human condition is best understood within the context of story—that the lives of individuals, and indeed their very understanding of the sacred, are ordered within narrative frameworks that sometimes include complicated subplots and important settings. Within the story of human life, we also interact with other characters who expose our relational style as we play out our dignity and depravity within the context of our relational inclinations. Our relational style is, perhaps, best understood in light of the family or families we come from. We suggested that gender is a mystery to be puzzled about, and attempts to reduce it to an atomistic system have not done justice to its profundity. Last but not least, our concept of who God or the ultimate is might be one of the most important cognitive frameworks we possess. How we think about the nature of ultimate reality likely influences the way we behave toward God and, consequently, toward other people.

Of course, this will not be the last chapter ever written on the human condition, and there are many good chapters that already exist. At the very least, a chapter like this reminds us just how complex the human condition is and how difficult it can be to encapsulate in any one system of thought. This should be even more evident in the lives of people who seek the help of pastoral counselors, who bring with them stories of hardship and heartbreak, shame about secret misdeeds, as well as the glory of the human soul when it shines with God's light. There will likely always be something about human beings to be wondered at, even confused about. This is the joy of the mystery of the human condition.

REFLECTION QUESTIONS

1. According to the authors, "at their very foundation, human beings are a paradox." What does this statement mean to you?
2. Think about an important time or incident in your life. Who were the main characters involved in this chapter of your personal story? Would you consider the overarching storyline a comedy, a tragedy, or perhaps a heroic tale? How has this story contributed to your belief system, or what values did you "catch" by living it?
3. Consider a particular relationship with someone with whom you feel accepted, a sense of unconditional love or positive regard, and as having space to grow and sometimes heal. How might being in this relationship help you to be a more effective pastoral counselor?
4. What ramifications does the concept of the *human family* as described in this chapter have for you as an individual? As a part of a community? As a pastoral counselor?

REFERENCES

Allender, D. B. (1999). *The healing path: How the hurt in your past can lead you to a more abundant life.* Colorado Springs, CO: Waterbrook.

Basil the Great. (2005). *On the human condition.* Crestwood, NY: St. Vladimir's Seminary Press.

Borg, M. J., & Wright, N. T. (2007). *The meaning of Jesus: Two visions*. New York: Harper One.

Bowlby, J. (1982). Attachment and loss: Retrospect and prospect. *American Journal of Orthopsy-chiatry, 52*(4), 664–678. doi:10.1111/j.1939-0025.1982.tb01456.x

Cashdan, S. (1988). *Object relations therapy: Using the relationship*. New York, NY: W. W. Norton.

Cassuto, U. (1989). *A commentary on the Book of Genesis: Part I From Adam to Noah Genesis I–VI 8*. (I. Abrahams, Trans.). Jerusalem, Israel: Magnes Press, The Hebrew University.

Cole, G. A. (2009). *God the peacemaker: How atonement brings shalom*. Nottingham, UK: Apollos.

Cooper, M. (2003). *Existential therapies*. London, UK: Sage.

Coppedge, A. (2007). *The God who is triune: Revisioning the Christian doctrine of God*. Downers Grove, IL: IVP Academic.

Donne, J. (1999). *Devotions upon emergent occasions and death's deue*. New York, NY: Vintage.

Erickson, M. J. (1998). *Christian theology* (2nd ed.). Grand Rapids, MI: Baker. (Original work published 1624)

Frankl, V. E. (1978). *The unheard cry for meaning: Psychotherapy and humanism*. New York, NY: Washington Square Press.

Frankl, V. E. (1992). *Man's search for meaning: An introduction to logotherapy* (4th ed.). Boston, MA: Beacon.

Glasser, W. (2010). *Choice theory: A new psychology of personal freedom*. New York, NY: Harper-Collins.

Goleman, D. (1996). *The meditative mind: The varieties of meditative experience*. London, UK: Thorsons.

Guthrie, S. C. (1990). Human condition/predicament. In R. J. Hunter, H. N. Malony, L. O. Mills, & J. Patton (Eds.), *Dictionary of pastoral counseling* (pp. 541–543). Nashville, TN: Abingdon.

Harrison, V. F. (2005). *On the human condition*. Crestwood, NY: St. Vladimir's Seminary Press.

Hemingway, E. (1940). *For whom the bell tolls*. New York, NY: Scribner's.

Hoekema, A. A. (1986). *Created in God's image*. Grand Rapids, MI: W. B. Erdmans.

Ignatius of Loyola. (1991). *Spiritual exercises and selected works* (G. E. Ganss, P. R. Parmananda, E. J. Malatesta, & M. E. Palmer, Trans.). New York, NY: Paulist Press.

John of the Cross. (1962). *The living flame of love* (E. A. Peers, Trans.). Garden City, NY: Image Books.

Keating, T. (1994). *Intimacy with God*. New York: The Cross Road.

Keating, T. (1999). *The human condition: Contemplation and transformation*. New York, NY: Paulist Press.

Keating, T. (2002). *Foundations for centering prayer and the Christian contemplative tradition*. New York, NY: Continuum.

Kimball, C. N. (2001). Family brokenness: A developmental approach. In M. R. McMinn & T. R. Phillips (Eds.), *Care for the soul* (pp. 346–362). Downers Grove, IL: InterVarsity Press.

Klein, W. W., Bloomberg, C. L., & Hubbard, R. L. (1993). *Introduction to biblical interpretation*. Dallas, TX: Word Publishing.

Kohut, H. (1971). *The analysis of the self*. New York, NY: International Universities Press.

Lewis, C. S. (1962). *The problem of pain*. New York, NY: Macmillan.

Lewis, C. S. (1991). *The four loves*. New York, NY: Harcourt Brace Jovanovich.

Lewis, C. S. (2014). *Is theology poetry?* Samizdat University Press.

Marshall, B. (1945). *The world the flesh and Father Smith*. Cambridge, MA: Riverside Press.

May, G. (1988). *Addiction and grace*. San Francisco, CA: HarperCollins.

Merton, T. (1955). *No man is an island*. New York, NY: Harcourt, Brace.

Mickley, J. R., Pargament, K. I., Brant, C. R., & Hipp, K. M. (1998). God and the search for meaning among hospice caregivers. *Hospice Journal, 13*, 1–8.

Norcross, J. C. (2009). *Psychotherapy relationships that work: Therapist contribution and responsiveness to patents*. New York, NY: Oxford University Press.

Paden, W. E. (1988). *Religious worlds: The comparative study of religion*. Boston, MA: Beacon.

Park, C. L. (2013). Religion and meaning. In R. F. Paloutzian & C. L. Park (Eds.), *Handbook of the psychology of religion and spirituality* (pp. 357–379). New York, NY: Guilford Press.

Pascal, B. (1995). *Pensees and other writings* (H. Levi, Trans.). Oxford, UK: Oxford University Press.

Piper, J., & Grudem, W. A. (1991). *Recovering biblical manhood and womanhood: A response to evangelical feminism*. Wheaton, IL: Crossway.

Powell, J. (1969). *Why am I afraid to tell you who I am?* Allen, TX: Argus Communications.

Price, D. J. (2002). *Karl Barth's anthropology in the light of modern thought.* Grand Rapids, MI: W. B. Erdmans.

Rogers, C. (1957). The necessary and sufficient conditions of psychotherapeutic personality change. *Journal of Counseling Psychology, 21*(2), 95–103. doi:10.1037/0033-3204.44.3.240

Rokeach, M. (1984). *The three christs of Ypsilanti.* New York, NY: New York Review of Books.

Singh, K. (1988). *Morning talks* (5th ed.). Anaheim, CA: Ruhani Satsang, Divine Science of the Soul.

Singh, K. (2007). *The wheel of life.* Blaine, WA: Ruhani Satsang.

Smart, N. (2000). *Worldviews: Crosscultural explorations of human beliefs.* Upper Saddle River, NJ: Prentice Hall.

Smith, H., & Smith, H. (1991). *The world's religions.* New York, NY: HarperSanFrancisco.

Steckel, C. J. (1987). The emergence of morality and faith in stages: A theological critique of developmental theories. In P. W. Pruyser (Ed.), *Changing views of the human condition* (pp. 159–177). Macon, GA: Mercer University Press.

Tillich, P. (1951). *Systematic theology* (Vol. 1). Chicago, IL: University of Chicago Press.

Tillich, P. (2005). *The new being.* Lincoln, NE: Bison.

Vygotsky, L. S. (1962). *Thought and language* (E. Haunfmann & G. Vakar, Trans.). Cambridge, MA: MIT Press.

Ward, B. (1975). *The sayings of the desert fathers.* Kalamazoo, MI: Cistercian.

Wiesel, E. (1966). *The gates of the forest* (F. Frenaye, Trans.). New York, NY: Holt, Rinehart and Winston.

Wilber, K. (1981). *Up from Eden.* Garden City, NY: Anchor Press/Doubleday.

Wolf, E. S. (2002). *Treating the self.* New York, NY: Guilford.

Wright, N. T. (1992). *The New Testament and the people of God.* Minneapolis, MN: Fortress.

Wright, N. T. (1996). *Jesus and the victory of God.* Minneapolis, MN: Fortress.

Wright, N. T. (2003). *The resurrection of the Son of God.* Minneapolis, MN: Fortress.

Wright, N. T. (2006). *Evil and the justice of God.* Downers Grove, IL: InterVarsity Press Books.

Wright, N. T. (2013). *Paul and the faithfulness of God.* Minneapolis, MN: Fortress.

Yalom, I. D. (1980). *Existential psychotherapy.* New York, NY: Basic Books.

Yalom, I. D. (1989). *Love's executioner.* New York, NY: Basic Books.

Yalom, I. D., & Leszcz, M. (2005). *Theory and practice of group psychotherapy* (5th ed.). New York, NY: Basic Books.

Zacharias, R. (2000). *Jesus among other gods.* Nashville, TN: Word Publishing.

THE NATURE AND FUNCTION OF SUFFERING

Viktor Frankl, a 20th-century psychiatrist, neurologist, and survivor of Auschwitz, created a form of psychotherapy called logotherapy, which provides individuals with pathways to attain meaning. In his internationally acclaimed book, *Man's Search for Meaning*, Frankl (1959/1984) states, "If there is a meaning in life at all, then there must be a meaning in suffering. Suffering is an ineradicable part of life, even as fate and death. Without suffering and death human life cannot be complete" (p. 76). More generally, the *Merriam-Webster Online Dictionary* (2014) states that suffering is "pain that is caused by injury, illness, loss, etc. : physical, mental, or emotional pain" (Definition section). Thus, suffering, in its basic form, always involves some type of pain. Yet, is it fair to say that all subjective experiences of pain automatically suggest that the person is suffering? For the purposes of this chapter, suffering is understood as a highly subjective, complex, universal phenomenon and, thus, an ordinary dynamic of the human condition. It is integrally associated with physical pain and/or emotional distress, mitigated, at times, by the individual's intrapersonal and interpersonal processes related to resilience or hardiness. Although the extent and degree to which individuals suffer varies significantly, suffering can be the source of tremendous spiritual and psychological growth or a profoundly overwhelming and impairing experience no matter the resilience or hardiness the person possesses.

If the opinion of Frankl (1959/1984) is adopted, the omission of suffering from human existence would render human life incomplete. He further explores how individuals can be "worthy" of their suffering and how suffering provides human beings opportunities to access deeper meaning and attain moral values. Frankl does believe, however, that "only a few people are capable of reaching such high moral standards" (p. 76). Suffering that possesses hidden opportunities for deeper meaning and moral development emerges from the effective employment of various aspects and/or dynamics of the human condition. Some of these dynamics involve the person's constitution and the effects of suffering on the body; intrapersonal processes such as cognitive appraisals and emotional management; interpersonal processes, including various types of human support; and the interaction between intrapersonal and interpersonal processes (Cassell, 2004). Yet, the subjective experience of suffering attests to the fact that no one can have full and complete understanding or knowledge of what another's suffering must feel like (Cassell, 1991).

Individuals who have lived through the most brutal of humanity's treatment of humanity, as Frankl certainly did, know that suffering can strip human dignity like piranhas after their prey. Suffering, at its worst, is the behemoth that reconstitutes ordinary mental processes such as managing one's anxiety, engulfing an individual's existence in blocks of rigid or chaotic patterns of perception and behavior as if danger lurked at every turn. In these situations, the individual's meaning-making mental processes have become overtaxed, and surviving, not thriving, is the only way to proceed. The person is left with overwhelming mental images of vulnerability, disturbing emotions, unsettling dreams, the loss of meaning, attitudes of hostility or rejection, and dispositions that reinforce avoidant behaviors that may, in effect, perpetuate suffering. Pain is experienced and internalized in repeated and familiar ways, exacerbating an individual's suffering, and can solidify the person's self-identity with feelings of inadequacy and vulnerability, leaving the individual with disturbing assumptions about the nature of the world that inadvertently produce more isolation.

Suffering, as it emerges, functions as a signal that alerts the self that human coping has momentarily reached its limits. These intrapersonal dynamics involve many complex processes such as appraisal (the individual's evaluation of what is happening and its impact on the self), attention (the individual's focus that works in tandem with the person's appraisal capacities), emotion regulation (the individual's capacity to manage distress, anxiety, and pain), and the affective (emotional) quality of the individual's personal narrative (the story the person tells the self that assists in helping the person make sense out of the event[s]). The interpersonal dynamics associated with defusing or exacerbating suffering that include seeking support from others, learning how to talk about one's pain, and recognizing one's needs during and in the aftermath of experiencing pain are oftentimes rooted in the caregiver–child relationship, most especially the ability and quality of the caregiver's attunement with the child: the caregiver's ability to know what the child must be feeling, needing, and wanting coupled with an effective response to the child's feeling, needing, and wanting. The more consistently attuned the caregiver is with the child, the more resilient the child may become, thus establishing a more effective foundation from which the child may learn to manage pain. The less attuned the caregiver is with the child, the more difficult it will be for the child to trust others, trust himself or herself, and develop adequate coping strategies to manage pain and suffering. The effects from the reciprocal relationship between intrapersonal and interpersonal processes are difficult to separate at times. However, to appreciate the nature of suffering, it is important to analyze how the intrapersonal and interpersonal processes defuse or exacerbate an individual's experience of suffering.

THE ORIGINS OF INTRAPERSONAL PROCESSES AND SUFFERING

How can two individuals experience roughly the same event and one suffers terribly, whereas the other does not? Are there universal assumptions about suffering that no matter the person's constitution (genetic predispositions, temperament), anyone experiencing certain events will suffer? Observing how individuals, societies, and "mother earth" treat human beings, one recognizes that oppression, coercion, brutality, racism, tsunamis, earthquakes, or tornados cause individuals to feel pain; however, all of us know someone who has experienced such events and "moved on" or developed more resilience or hardiness with apparently no ill effects from the trauma. When suffering is present, some type of pain will always be present. When pain is present, suffering does not necessarily follow. How is that so?

Consider this scenario: One child falls off a bike, lands hard on the pavement, cries, and refuses to get back on the bike; another child falls off a bike, lands hard on the pavement, and cries, yet jumps back on the bike and rides off. The pain that both children experienced after hitting the pavement was processed differently by each child, leading one to attend to the pain through tears and avoidance, whereas the other tended to his pain without avoidance. Imagine later that day the first child saying, "Mommy, I'm never going to ride a bike. I hate it," whereas the second child says, "Can I ride my bike over to Jenny's?" Is it possible to say which of these two children has suffered or which one has suffered more?

The pain experienced by both children produced motivational schemas, that is, patterns of thinking that led to behavior regarding the use of bikes in the aftermath of falling off the bike. The first child developed a schema that left the child fearful and wanting to avoid the bike. The second child developed a schema that appears to accept falling off the bike within a framework in which fear is absent or regulated. Much more must be known about each of these children before suggesting that one is more resilient than the other. However, most would probably agree that the first child has suffered more in the wake of falling off the bike than the second child.

The scenario just described addresses one component of the nature–nurture interaction that all human beings experience throughout their lives. This interaction is a way of discussing how the environment influences a person's physiology, including the social brain, and the manner in which the person's physiology influences the environment. Nature and nurture operate to affect physiological structures within the brain that organize a coordinated framework by which the individual thinks, feels, and behaves (Fraley, Roisman, Booth-LaForce, Owen, & Holland, 2013; Siegel, 2012). The events leading to the fear and avoidance responses for the first child may be associated with specific natural or biological processes within that child. In other words, the first child's constitution may leave the child vulnerable to suffering from such events as falling off a bike. The capacity of humans to recognize or register fear (the first child's perception about riding a bike) and respond to that fear or threat (the first child's desire to avoid the bike) is embedded deeply within the social brain and reflects inborn capacities that are enhanced or diminished through experience.

Pillay (2010) describes evolutionary forces that influenced the "hardwiring" of the fear circuits in an individual's social brain. The experience of fear for most individuals operates like an emotional bully, butting to the head of the line for attention. Once fear is sensed, the brain implements primitive processes to assess the degree of danger or threat. Such primitive processes are greatly influenced by experience and add to the "hardwiring" of the fear circuits. In this manner, the less capable the person is in defusing the fear circuits, the more vigilant the person becomes within his or her environment, and the more the person avoids situations that can cause the fear.

When an individual experiences pain, be that emotional or physical, evolutionary processes within the brain are immediately triggered, creating a cascade of electrochemical reactions, demanding that the person produce some type of response to the unwanted stimulus (Ochsner & Gross, 2004). Furthermore, these natural processes within the social brain are so sensitive to danger and threat that the fear circuits can be triggered before conscious awareness emerges and thus leave the person less apt to determine what is causing the fear (Pillay, 2010). In fact, fear circuits can register fear in one twelfth of a second (Cozolino, 2010), putting the body on alert, generating subjective expectations about the presenting danger that may leave the individual running from feared phenomena, literally or figuratively. Yet, it is critically important for humans to have this innate capacity to recognize danger and threat—sometimes avoidance is the most prudent thing to do. Hence, this innate, natural capacity to register fear needs a second, slower circuit that allows humans time to process the initial fears, dangers, or threats in order not to be subjected to them (Cozolino, 2010).

The second fear circuit operates to recruit other physiological structures of the brain in the service of appraisal (Cozolino, 2010). Appraisal, as noted previously, describes an individual's ability to evaluate the forces seeking one's attention; in this case, it is the stimulus causing the danger or fear. The appraisal processes take longer and are secondary to the work of the initial fear circuits for significant reasons. When an individual is frightened, the circuits that put the body on alert do so for immediate action when the stimulus is clearly something from which one ought to escape. When the danger, threat, or frightening stimulus is not so clear, the second, slower circuit can be activated, providing the individual an assessment of the nature of the feared stimulus (Cozolino, 2010). When a course of action fails to remove the fear, the individual remains alert to his or her surroundings, and the cycle of appraisal repeats (fear that is not removed or defused has a deleterious effect on the physiological structures of the social brain). Eventually, these processes form a mind-set within the person, placing the individual on one of two trajectories: resilience and hardiness or various degrees of personal vulnerability. So, what does all of this have to do with suffering?

The social brain is hardwired to sense fear, danger, threat, or distress. Any pain, therefore, is automatically filtered through the fear circuits and processed as a stimulus to be avoided or approached. Avoidance may serve the individual in the short run; however, when an avoidance mind-set endures, the individual suffers from an ever-growing store of perceived threats, generating more vigilance in his or her environment and sowing the seeds of personal vulnerability. Ironically, that which encourages vigilance and avoidance increases the likelihood of more suffering and pain, narrowing one's capacity for personal agency and resilience. As individuals rely on avoidance to manage their pain and suffering, personal growth is blocked.

The individual who does not address the origins of his or her suffering activates fear-maintaining cognitive schemas (predictable ways of thinking and behaving) that enhance self-doubt and feelings of inadequacy, prompting the development of defensive coping strategies for emotional protection that impede emotional growth. Such defensive coping strategies are intended to defuse anxiety, tension, and distress, yet often operate at the expense of adaptation, personal growth, and resilience. This is not to suggest, however, that an individual's resilience can always protect him or her from suffering. Suffering is an ordinary dynamic of the human condition. All humans suffer, yet the more resilience an individual possesses, the greater capacity the individual has to defuse suffering. However, each person has a breaking point at which the individual's resilience can no longer serve to defuse pain and suffering.

The Social Brain and the Experience of Suffering

The concept of a social brain has been around since the 1970s (Cozolino, 2006). Research tools such as positron emission tomography scans, single-photon emission computed tomography scans, magnetic resonance imaging, and functional magnetic resonance imaging have revolutionized the neuroscience field, leading to a plethora of information on the inner workings and complexities of the brain. To understand the place of pain and suffering within the context of one's social brain, one must first appreciate the biology of survival and the pivotal role that pain plays in that process.

The capacity to recognize or feel pain represents an evolutionary asset essential to survival (Cassell, 1992). The experience of pain aids the individual in determining what behaviors or events cause harm, and thus it requires strategies to deal with the painful behaviors or events. Pain is a marker or motivating force for survival; it serves an individual's quality of life. Without the capacity to experience pain, an individual's life would be cut short due to a failure to measure personal harm (Cassell, 1992). Thus, ignoring physical and emotional pain often reinforces avoidance schemas and can ultimately become lethal.

It is beyond the scope of this chapter to provide an extensive review of the neuroscience research in the area of the social brain. However, when an individual registers fear, danger, or threat, the individual's rational, logical, problem-solving capacities (representing the operations of the executive functioning regions of the prefrontal cortex—that part of the brain behind the forehead and above the eyes) are impeded, triggering the fight, flight, or freeze responses (Panksepp & Biven, 2012). These are natural processes for humans. Without these processes, an individual can overlook a dangerous situation, making a very bad choice that leads to painful consequences. However, the more that these primitive responses are triggered, the more the person is conditioned to expect them to occur, and the more deeply the experiences are embedded in the individual's memory. Memory will then serve to protect the individual from such triggering events (Siegel, 2012). In this regard, these intrapersonal dynamics will promote escapist, avoidant, and reactive responses to perceptions of danger and threat. Hence, pain and suffering are compounded as the person's memory prepares the person to anticipate pain and suffering, whereas others encountering similar experiences may only anticipate a benign encounter or event (Siegel, 2012). Imagine someone who expects to be hurt or mistreated by others due to the individual's experiences. In this case, the perception of anticipated pain generates the cycle of suffering for the individual; and unfortunately, it is not uncommon for this dynamic to operate at an unconscious level.

When these natural processes of self-protection are triggered within an environment of care, nurturance, warmth, love, and appropriate levels of challenge and accountability through the ministrations of the primary caregivers (evidence of an elaborative, enriched environment), the individual internalizes this environment and develops resilience and a secure attachment (Bowlby, 1988). Furthermore, through the elaborative, enriched environment, the experiences of threat and/or harm are mitigated with each new experience of threat or harm managed, thus amending the soil of resilience, personal agency, and a secure attachment (Siegel, 2009). When such enriched environments are absent, the fear circuits are strengthened, leaving individuals with an ever-increasing sense of personal vulnerability and anxiety.

The fear circuits, as mentioned earlier, are extensive and process stimuli very quickly, compromising the person's capacity to appraise the event accurately and generating the fight, flight, or freeze responses (Panksepp & Biven, 2012). Individuals who are constitutionally vulnerable to anxiety, distress, and tension will register danger and threat more quickly, resulting in patterned or predictable behaviors (e.g., being and acting overly cautious, unwilling to take risks, hypervigilant with an increased sensitivity to emotional dysregulation; Hannan & Orcutt, 2013). If the first child in the preceding illustration possessed an inborn vulnerability to anxiety or distress, the child would likely be tentative about getting on the bike and would avoid the bicycle after falling off. The child's internal processing would make associations between bikes and danger. These associations would be reinforced each time the child sees and then avoids a bike. In this situation, the response to pain and suffering (falling off the bike and wanting to avoid bikes) would be embedded through conditioned thoughts, emotions, and behaviors (seeing or perceiving and avoiding bikes) that exacerbate rather than alleviate the child's distress.

The original experience of riding and falling off the bike, as well as the resulting internalization of the pain and fear, leads to avoidance and shapes the child's behavior toward bikes. When one's intrapersonal processing has been affected by more profound experiences of emotional or physical pain (e.g., daily interactions with an alcoholic parent, being bullied in school, having an emotionally abusive teacher or coach, or personal violations such as robbery, rape, or other forms of harm and oppression), the fear circuits are strengthened. When this occurs, the individual expects more pain and distress. In this regard, individuals can generate pain and suffering from past experiences that leave them anxious and depressed while believing that danger and threat are pervasive in the present (Cozolino, 2010).

The individual who leaves childhood without having dealt with his or her experiences of pain will develop rigid or chaotic (or a combination of both) behavioral tendencies, thoughts, choices, and perspectives, thus laying the foundation for more pain and suffering. In such cases, pain often overwhelms the individual's capacity to make sense of the pain, leaving the individual with few resources to engage in meaning-making processes. Individuals either become too frightened to reflect on the pain experienced or develop impenetrable defensive coping strategies that disrupt healthy self-awareness. These tendencies result in impeded resilience and hardiness.

Thoughts on Memory, the Mind, and the Counselor
Neuroscientists today have many theories about how the mind emerges amid the chemical and electrical processes occurring in the brain (Cozolino, 2010; Edelman, 2006; Panskepp & Biven, 2012; Siegel, 2012). Yet, it is still not completely clear how the physiological workings of the brain create a *mind*. What is clear from the research on the developing mind, however, is that a person's temperament and genetic disposition, and how those intersect with one's environment—the nature–nurture interaction—including the type of care and nurturing the individual experiences, create a mind-set that impedes or facilitates one's ability to engage the world with resilience, hardiness, and personal agency (Berlin, Cassidy, & Appleyard, 2008; Mikulincer & Shaver, 2007; Vaughn, Bost, & van Ijzendoorn, 2008). Through the elaborative, enriched environment discussed earlier, individuals experience sustained support that can turn pain and suffering into personal growth and avenues for meaning making that enrich life. The counselor–client alliance provides for such an environment.

Working with individuals who are constitutionally vulnerable to fear, distress, danger, or threat requires that the counselor possess accurate empathy and the ability to assess the client's emotional reactions on a moment-to-moment basis throughout the session. The "dance" of psychotherapy with clients involves knowing how to be fully present to the client in a nonanxious, nondefensive, nonpejorative, and nonthreatening manner while gently nudging the client toward increasing levels of personal agency. This "dance" is not exclusive to pastoral counselors but is expected of all counselors. Pastoral counselors, however, are in a position to recognize the salience, and thus the power, of the client's spirituality for the purposes of not only increasing personal agency but also expanding the client's healthy spirituality.

INTERPERSONAL PROCESSES AND SUFFERING

Consider the scenario between the two children previously described and imagine a parent of the first child witnessing the child fall off the bike and hitting the pavement, racing to the child, picking up the child, and brushing off the child. Imagine the child reaching for the bike with the intention of wanting to get back on it when the parent says, "Are you sure you should do that? I'm just so nervous about you hurting yourself. Are you sure you're not hurt? That was a terrible fall. Look, you're rubbing your elbow. Oh my, it's all scraped up! I can't believe your uncle bought you that stupid thing! I told him you wouldn't be able to ride it. C'mon, let's go home. I have to make sure you're okay." Or imagine this scenario: The parent witnesses the child fall, the child sees the parent witnessing his fall, and the parent does nothing. Or the parent sees the child fall off the bike and the tears streaming down the child's face, and says, "Get back on that bike. There's nothing wrong with you." Each of these interactions leaves the child with an impression about what he or she just experienced with a concomitant and potentially deleterious effect on the child's resilience and capacity to tolerate pain and suffering. The interactions individuals have on a daily basis from the time of their birth until their launching from the home influence their mind-set regarding the boundaries of personal agency, degree of perceived personal vulnerability, and their pain or frustration tolerance.

According to Siegel (2012), an individual's mind-set is an elusive and complex phenomenon that is highly influenced by and susceptible to the energy and information flow from others in his or her environment. In this way, "The human brain is a 'social organ of adaptation' stimulated to grow through positive and negative interactions with others" (Cozolino, 2010, p. 12). A newborn's behavior can be said to activate the caregiving system of primary caregivers, ensuring caregiver proximity and response to the infant's needs, depending on the caregiver's appraisal of those needs (Solomon & George, 2008). Two dynamics emerge from these experiences. The first dynamic involves the newborn's experience of pain and distress when his or her needs are not met. The second dynamic involves the newborn's reactions when the caregiver fails to adequately address the newborn's distress.

Think for a moment about the person whose core identity (i.e., the deeply "felt" belief that the person has regarding himself or herself) is founded on a consistent experience of care and nurturance with appropriate levels of challenge and accountability in an elaborative enriched environment. Being raised in an enriched environment of care, warmth, support, engagement, and accurate caregiver–child attunement results in the person possessing an ability to maintain a positive and robust core sense of self despite conflicts or crises (Siegel, 2012). The person possesses the capacity to accurately judge his or her needs and the clarity to choose strategies that will thwart the threat or harm perceived. Clearly, even the healthiest environments will not protect the individual from every threat or harm. Yet, the daily interactions between primary caregivers and the developing child establish patterned reactions to distress that have implications for the remainder of that individual's life, establishing intrapersonal and interpersonal skills used to defuse threats and manage pain across the life span (Fraley et al., 2013).

Attachment and Interpersonal Suffering

Bowlby (1988) developed the concept of attachment from observing children interacting with their parents. Bowlby's work on attachment theory, as well as the work of those who have followed, explains the "hardwiring" processes of interpersonal relationships. Attachment theory speaks to a fundamental aspect of the nature of pain and suffering and the development of resilience—namely, that suffering is not always associated with a recent experience and may have its origin in early caregiver–child interactions.

The human person is hardwired for relationships, including proximity-seeking behavior, and the needs for a secure base and safe haven (Bowlby, 1988). Proximity-seeking behaviors are necessary to attract others, such as primary caregivers, so that they turn their attention toward the child to respond to the child's needs. A secure base emerges when the caregiver's attention provides the infant with an experience of consistent welcome, warmth, acceptance, and need fulfillment. Such experiences promote a sentiment best described as a "safe haven" for the child where protection from or response to the child's distress is optimized. However, distress is a universal experience, and no parent or primary caregiver is capable of attuning perfectly to the child's needs and rhythms. In this regard, the key to a secure attachment is the caregiver's capacity to not only be attuned to the child but to effectively repair the relationship when the caregiver has failed.

Bowlby (1988) developed the concept of "internal working models" to describe an internalized set of rules that govern emotions, impulses, thoughts, and behavior that arise from the manner in which the child was treated. These internal working models develop during a time when the child's capacity for conscious awareness is primitive at best. Thus, as the child internalizes the treatment that he or she experiences at the hands of his or her caregivers, a dual process involving how the child "should" treat others and how the child "should" treat himself or herself will be played out in the child's behavior, most especially when it comes to managing personal pain and distress. The "internal working models" of how the child feels and relates to the self and the other ultimately suggest the type of attachment the child develops: secure or insecure. Attachment in this regard bespeaks a person's capacity to trust himself or herself and another, bond with others, and use effective coping measures when in pain, as well as the freedom and curiosity to explore the world.

No matter what happens between the primary caregivers and the infant, the infant will form an attachment. Whether the attachment is secure or insecure depends on the child's environment and experiences with the primary caregivers. The child's experience of distress is mitigated by the consistent ministrations of the caregiver in the caregiver–child interactions. When the infant is hungry or needs changing, affection, play, sleep, or comfort, the parent who is capable of recognizing the infant's needs responds appropriately and sows the seeds of effective self-regulatory intrapersonal behaviors and a secure attachment (Weinfield, Sroufe, Egeland, & Carlson, 2008). When the parent fails to recognize the child's needs or fails to attune to the child's distress on a consistent basis, the seeds of self-doubt, poor self-image, and poor emotion regulation are sown, resulting in an insecure attachment. This legacy of early childhood relationships has a direct effect on how well an individual may attenuate pain and suffering throughout his or her life.

Furthermore, the experience of pain that an infant ultimately learns to tolerate and manage is directly related to the manner in which the infant was treated at those times. The infant will internalize the treatment that he or she experiences and develop conclusions that have lasting implications about the self as a result of that treatment (Zimmermann & Becker-Stoll, 2002). The conclusions become answers to questions such as "Do I matter?" or "Do I have worth?" or "How dangerous are people?" Keep in mind that this is not a reflective process; the child does not possess the maturity to engage in reflective processing; therefore, these conclusions are felt. Such conclusions reflect aspects of the internal working models, and when those conclusions are negative, individuals will avoid or develop poor defensive coping strategies from feeling the effects of those internalized responses.

Those children with a secure attachment possess internal working models that allow them to manage and alleviate the distress (Bowlby, 1988). Secure attachment lends itself to other important intrapersonal–interpersonal systems such as the exploration of the environment. When a child feels safe and secure and recognizes that he or she has access to a secure base, the child will become curious about his or her environment and begin to explore. The promotion of exploratory behaviors via secure attachment enhances a child's ego resilience, emotional regulation, and personal agency (Grossmann, Grossmann, Kindler, & Zimmermann, 2008). Children with an insecure attachment possess internal working models that impede their capacity to manage distress effectively. Thus, when a child's ability to manage distress is impeded because of caregiver misattunement, a child does not experience the alleviation of stress without an intrapersonal and interpersonal toll. The toll, represented by insecure attachment, is the generation of self-preservation or self-survival strategies that leave the child with deficits in his or her ability to trust that his or her emotional needs will be met, a propensity to employ defensive strategies to ward off distress that increase self-doubt or isolation, and an impeded sense of imagination and exploration (Fraley et al., 2013; Grossmann et al., 2008).

Insecure Attachment and the Experience of Pain and Suffering

The brain is wonderfully plastic (Cozolino, 2010); physiological structures of the brain can change due to interactions with a person's environment. Despite childhood experiences that result in an insecure attachment, research suggests that an individual can develop an "earned" secure attachment through a process of "facing and dealing" (Fonagy, 2010) with past experiences. Insecure attachment is marked by vigilance about one's environment that reinforces the insecure attachment. In this regard, distress is experienced or perceived more quickly, and impedes the individual's ability to engage the social brain's executive functioning, reasoning, and logic capabilities. Thus, the individual with an insecure attachment will tend to be compromised in his or her ability to manage distress in a satisfactory manner (Ginot, 2012).

The rules that govern distress management for the individual with an insecure attachment are employed without conscious awareness. This dynamic is akin to a battleship shooting down a flock of birds before determining the type or level of threat. If the defensive measures of those who are insecurely attached are ready for deployment at the first indication of threat or harm, the experience of emotional pain can be misapplied or misattributed. These reactions reinforce the need for defensive measures, and the cycle of vigilance and/or unsatisfying interactions continues (Lipton & Fosha, 2011).

Imagine an individual raised in an environment in which the norm was drama, crisis, violence, and neglect. The constitutionally hardier members within that family will be less affected; however, no one within that environment will emerge unscathed. Each individual emerging from that environment, based on the family member's constitution and the treatment each received at the hands of caregivers, will have a capacity to tolerate distress. When attachment is insecure, the person's capacity to manage impulses and other emotional triggers will be compromised. The person's reactions will reinforce the insecure attachment and leave the person struggling to manage pain and distress.

Brain Plasticity and Suffering

The effects of the historical experiences of emotional pain lurk in the shadows of an insecurely attached individual's memory. The insecurely attached individual's memory organizes interactions with others "into an unshakable storyline that becomes an inseparable part of a dysregulated self-state" (Ginot, 2012, p. 60). In other words, the person with an insecure attachment suffers from an inability to regulate his or her emotions. Emotional pain that is not addressed or poorly regulated generates memories that act like walls of an individual's emotional fort. The emotional fort serves to protect the person from feeling or experiencing certain emotions. When a person perceives danger, the immediate reaction is self-protection, a retreat into one's emotional fort. Individuals self-protect in various ways (e.g., avoidance, passive resistance, withdrawal and isolation, overt hostility, creating drama), and self-protection can play a role in perpetuating suffering.

Remember the individual raised in an environment with a bounty of drama, crisis, violence, and neglect? Imagine that she was raised in a family in which both parents were alcoholics. She developed a way of thinking and managing her emotions that keeps her vigilant (her social brain perceiving fear, danger, and threat) when she smells alcohol. Many individuals smell alcohol and do not find themselves feeling anxious, alert for danger, or expecting a crisis to drop like a bomb, yet she does. Her internal working model for managing distress, connecting with others, and feeling safe and secure have been forged in the fires of a chaotic alcoholic family. Her default mode for pain tolerance is activated by the smell of liquor. The message emerging from her vigilance, in the wake of smelling alcohol, is something like this: "I am terribly vulnerable right now and in danger of harm." This message zips from her olfactory senses to those regions of the social brain that she cannot defuse fast enough (the fast fear circuit); the onslaught or power of those impulses, thoughts, or emotions leaves her feeling like a child trapped in an adult's body.

She is engaged in a repeated and familiar intrapersonal battle among other competing forces, thoughts, emotions, and impulses that leave her with a compromised ability to manage distress. She knows that this is "crazy." She cannot figure out why she is so uptight. She has been this way ever since she was a child. She cannot stand the man to whom she was attracted just seconds ago who holds a beer in his hand just like her father did. However, she cannot stop herself from being attracted to him. He has something that she has always found attractive in men, and this frightens her even more. She feels as if she is on the verge of a panic attack, just like the one she had at the office party a couple of months ago. She wants to disappear. She knows how to disappear, become a nonperson, and blend in with the patterns on the wall; she is well practiced in using those defensive behaviors. She can do this and make her way to the exit. If someone catches her before she leaves, she has the ready excuse, "I'm not feeling well," or "I have another commitment." When she finally makes it to her car, she flops down on the front seat and sobs. She asks herself, "What is wrong with me?" When she arrives back at her house, she reaches for the pitcher of gin and tonic that she made earlier for these occasions. The pain of her childhood is avoided while she employs negative defensive coping strategies that perpetuate her pain and suffering.

The individual described here has experienced terrible trauma. The lasting impact of that trauma leaves her compromised when dealing with distress. Her vigilance keeps her body alert for danger while emotional and psychological healing is impeded. All who suffer with an insecure attachment are compromised, to some extent, in managing their affect and emotions. Despite all of this, our brains possess the capacity to repair. Anyone who has lived through difficult and trying circumstances, compromised in his or her capacity to manage distress, can change these old patterns of thinking, feeling, and behaving and develop more flexible and adaptive ways of thinking, feeling, and behaving.

THE FAMILY AND SUFFERING

In various Western societies, the family is the primary educational environment. Parents establish a particular type of emotional sentiment (climate) within the home that enhances or detracts from the child's quality of life. As discussed previously, the type of environment that leads to secure attachment involves patterns of caring behaviors consistently demonstrated, most especially during times when the child experiences distress. When those behaviors are inconsistently demonstrated or absent, the tendency is for children to develop an insecure attachment.

In their research on the dynamics that lead to stability and satisfaction in marriages, Gottman and Silver (1999) found evidence for the importance and influence of sentiment created by a couple. This emotional climate is highly influenced by culture, socioeconomic status, local demographics, and other types of affiliations. When the sentiment is positive, it is likely that certain ways of communicating are operative during times of conflict, whereas other types of communication are operative when conflict is at a minimum (Fainsilber-Katz & Gottman, 1993). These communication dynamics have a direct effect on the manner in which the rules and regulations for "right" behavior are communicated to children.

Each family determines the behaviors to which all members must adhere. When the rules and regulations of a family are established, a pattern of interaction becomes predictable or expected. The rules and regulations established within a family indicate the type of boundaries the family will employ during periods of calm or conflict. The boundaries can be rigid or chaotic, enmeshed or disengaged (Olson, 1999). Boundaries tend to be permeable and change when roles within the family are altered. For example, a father who develops a debilitating illness and cannot work or perform his duties/responsibilities around the house may cause other members of the family to alter their roles in an effort to stabilize the family operations (Olson, 1999).

The rules and regulations that are established within a family produce a degree of stability (homeostasis) that is not easily changed once those rules are in place (Olson, 1999). The rules and regulations govern things such as emotional expression, recognition of pain or distress, and routines and activities. In this regard, each family determines the extent to which emotions are expressed and suppressed, the range of acceptable behaviors, and what to do with members who attempt to push the boundaries. Therefore, the family system that emerges, influenced by external and internal forces, operates to encourage conformity to the prevailing authority, however that authority is defined.

Families must establish norms, rules, and regulations to survive or thrive. The more rigid or chaotic the boundaries within the family, the less tolerance the family has for conflict (Olson, 1999). Families that are less adaptive or flexible tend to lean toward rigidity or chaos (or a combination of both). The messages that each family member internalizes about the world, connecting with others, managing emotions, risk taking, and exploration plant the seeds of future success, intimacy, resilience, and the management of pain or suffering. The family that encourages the expression of emotions, tolerates mistakes, employs forgiveness, encourages development, and honors the uniqueness of each member operates out of the elaborative enriched environment (Grossmann et al., 2008).

When an individual is launched from the family of origin, that person is equipped with a unique mind-set that can adapt, adjust, and expand or crumble, isolate, or cling as life unfolds. When pain is managed well, suffering is minimized, and opportunities for personal growth and agency are possible. When pain is not managed well, suffering will be exacerbated. Unfortunately, some rules and regulations within the family inadvertently predispose members to additional pain and suffering. For example, the family member raised to believe that emotions such as anger or sadness are not acceptable to feel or express will struggle when interacting with those who do not share such beliefs or when these feelings are triggered within him or her.

Yet, such dilemmas and conflicts produce a type of pain and suffering that has the potential to enhance well-being, build personal agency, and expand an individual's horizons. When such encounters result in defensiveness, a clinging to the past, protectionism, or a failure to reconsider the skewed, biased, or prejudicial value system of the family of origin, threat and danger will be experienced and cause the individual to use familiar mechanisms to hinder change. Changing an attitude or value is often considered a threat to the "harmony" of the family system and will lead the family members to cling to the familiar, even if "harmony" is defined by values that cause depression, anxiety, isolation, or hostility. When these family members engage those outside the family, they will seek out others who can serve to protect and maintain their entrenched values and beliefs. Resilience, hardiness, maturation, and personal growth are clipped at the plinth of tradition—a subtle and effective mask for exclusionary strategies. The enriched environment is not only meant for human development at its earliest stages but also intended to be the environment in which individuals prosper throughout the life span. This cannot happen when clinging to traditions or "old familiar ways" that impede the thinking and behaving that promote flexibility and adaptability.

When a family crisis emerges, the more rigid or chaotic the family system, the less capable that family system will be in coping effectively with the crisis, thus increasing the likelihood of compounding the family's pain. In these families, the more severe the crisis, the more debilitated the family's ability to assist its members in coping effectively. Yet, even the most resilient, robust family can be overwhelmed, traumatized, and dismantled by certain events, creating a lasting impact for generations that follow.

CULTURE'S INFLUENCE ON PAIN AND SUFFERING

Culture is a powerful force influencing behavior and mind-sets, dictating how a society ought to raise its children, what behaviors or emotions are acceptable within that culture, who is the authority, and what are considered painful, threatening, or distressing experiences. Culture answers questions such as the following: What is appropriate discipline for children? What are good personal dreams for members from that culture to have? Who may participate in attaining those dreams? How important is empathy in the culture, and for whom is empathy deserved? How ought one respond to being wronged? What determines national interest, and what ought nations do when those interests are being threatened? Answers to such questions have direct implications for what is understood as pain and suffering ("There's nothing wrong with you, get back up on that bike") and the appropriate interpersonal and intrapersonal behaviors used to alleviate such pain and suffering in a particular culture.

History has shown in cruel ways how human beings can adopt attitudes and value systems that devalue differences and establish industries marked by prejudice, racism, judgment, and bias that contribute to an individual's pain and suffering. Such cultural survival initiatives reflect evolutionary dynamics generating the "us versus them" mentality in which the prevailing or dominant culture enhances its position and defends against alternative values by punishing those who seek to change the prevailing culture. As mentioned previously, human beings are hardwired for relationships, and belonging to a group is an evolutionary survival need; conformity not only ensures the survival of the group but also promotes stereotypic ways of perceiving the outside world. Culture, as with families, influences the generation of rules and regulations, and once those are set, they are very difficult to change (Doidge, 2007).

Imagine a culture in which respect and dignity were automatically extended to all, regardless of race, ethnicity, sexual orientation, gender, socioeconomic status, place of birth, or area of the world in which one currently resides. Imagine, too, every human possessing the desire to protect others from distress due to prejudicial or oppressive behaviors or beliefs. Imagine a cultural norm in which the transgressor humbly sought the harmed individual's forgiveness while working to repair the relationship no matter the clan, tribe, ethnicity, or race.

Suffering, distress, and pain are ordinary, and yet, some of these experiences happen as a result of the culture's synthetic pressure and influence. In this context, "synthetic" represents the pressures that cultures adopt to behave in predetermined ways simply because those in authority say so. The culture's value system emerges to maintain conformity to survive. Survival represents a primitive evolutionary force, and in order for the culture to survive, individuals must adhere to cultural norms, or the culture will die. Leaders within the culture have responsibilities to establish the elaborative enriched environment for all to thrive. When the culture's value system operates out of an "us versus them" mentality, pain and suffering will be forever built into the system and paradoxically cause the very thing the culture operates to protect against: its own death. Pastoral counselors are in the unique position to contribute to the global effort for social justice and peace, in which all individuals are given opportunities to thrive and grow personally, one client or one group at a time.

PAIN AND SUFFERING BEYOND ATTACHMENT, FAMILY, AND CULTURE

The stories of counselors serving the unsung heroes who face chronic or terminal illnesses, cruel forms of violence, and similar hardships are rich with powerful signs of both human resilience and fortitude, as well as heartbreaking misery. Such stories point to the capricious nature, and yet ordinariness, of pain and suffering. All suffer; yet, all do not suffer equally. Isolation and helplessness generate an emotional cocktail of rage, fear, fatigue, and profound sadness when individuals are placed in categories that leave them feeling profoundly different from others. Individuals who suffer from genetic maladies, oppressive societal forces, and accidents that produce disfigurement can experience their suffering compounded when meaning-making mechanisms feel absent or elusive.

Suffering represents a human system that is out of balance. Failure to readjust the system can eventually lead to apathy, including apathy toward one's or another's death and decay (Richard, 1992). Suffering wears on the individual or collective psyche like a woolen coat covered in molasses. As suffering increases its hold on the person and society, the body, mind, and spirit wear down, leaving the person and society helpless, engaged in personal survival, inured to others' suffering. In the face of suffering, all individuals sometimes face the great task of making sense out of the senseless (Wilkison, 2013).

"Who could possibly appreciate, understand, or patiently listen to what I have lived through? Who could possibly help me touch such despair and make sense out of the darkness, this black hole of my psyche, and not evaporate within it?" These and other questions are often raised by those who have lived through unimaginable pain and suffering. Think of the mother unable to give the hoped-for response to her son who is in the final stages of a terminal illness when he says, "I don't think I'll be here for Christmas"; the community shattered by a deranged gunman on a killing spree; the neglected and physically or sexually abused man who drank away his pain until he committed vehicular homicide; the soldier who has lost limbs protecting his country, unable to get treatment because someone wanted a bonus; or the person afflicted with a genetic disorder living day in and day out with physical pains while knowing how he or she is different from everyone else. The list of unimaginable suffering as a result of uncontrollable events or careless behavior is too long to name. The nature of suffering, as an important and ordinary phenomenon, reflects the proverbial double-edged sword: Individuals will suffer, yet how individuals respond intrapersonally and interpersonally to that suffering determines whether suffering is an opportunity to create meaning and wisdom or an affliction. In this regard, the counselor, invited on her client's journey of healing and personal growth, understands what is beyond the client's current suffering and what is immediate, what is present that is tethered to the past, and what is possible as the past is used to transform the present.

THE PASTORAL COUNSELOR'S RESPONSE TO THOSE WHO SUFFER

The counselor must turn anxiety and avoidance into triggers for curiosity and exploration (Cozolino, 2010). Curiosity is an important tool for counselors and clients to cultivate, as it affords a measure of distance from the toxic effects of emotional dysregulation (Waehler, 2013). Curiosity emerges from the executive functioning regions of the prefrontal cortex and serves as a mechanism of exploration, learning, and development (Barkley, 2004; Panksepp & Biven, 2012). The client who experiences accurate empathy from a finely attuned counselor receives assurances that abandonment, isolation, and loneliness will be mitigated (DeGeorge & Constantino, 2012). On the other hand, for those clients whose pain and suffering have left them with little or no desire for closeness, especially closeness with a counselor, a different skill set is required. In these cases, the counselor–client working alliance operates without subtle inferences to promote closer bonds of attachment (Byrd, Patterson, & Turchik, 2010) and emphasizes the nonjudgmental attitude and unconditional positive regard necessary for healing to occur (Rogers, 1960/1995). In either situation, the client's capacity to manage pain and suffering is enhanced as the counselor provides a corrective experience from that which originally caused the client's disturbance.

These counseling skills are taught across counseling programs and do not distinguish pastoral counselors from other types of counselors. Today, most counselors recognize that the requisite conditions for change include counselor warmth, flexibility, unconditional positive regard, accurate empathy, and counselor-to-client attunement. The theory of counseling adopted by the counselor serves as a guide for assessment and treatment, and it provides the counselor with a structure for understanding human development and psychopathology. In addition, the place of spirituality in the therapeutic context has been well researched and documented (Crook-Lyon et al., 2012; Worthington & Sandage, 2001), with emphasis on training future counselors to engage the aspects of a client's spirituality that are salient for coping (Pargament, 2007). Yet, what are the specific and distinguishing counseling methods and counselor traits that pastoral counselors are challenged to possess when working with suffering clients, and how does the pastoral counselor develop such skills?

Turning again to Frankl (1959/1984) and his discussion of suffering, one recognizes that suffering can turn bodies into wisps of bone and flesh, yet suffering's most heinous impact is often on the mind. A loss of dignity can eventually give way to rumination on the past in a manner that stifles the individual's capacity to recognize meaning and purpose in the current situation (Frankl, 1959/1984). Processes that clip this spiral toward meaninglessness replace these tendencies with self-curiosity, self-compassion, and a spirit animated by love that enlivens the intrapersonal culture for the pastoral counselor. Ultimately, what the pastoral counselor has done for herself through her transpersonal practices, she wishes to model and animate within the client. The distinguishing dynamics associated with pastoral counseling and the pastoral counselor are eventually found in the pastoral counselor's way of being that works in tandem with the training the pastoral counselor receives to comfortably and accurately address religion and spirituality in its diverse forms.

A Note on Counselor Pitfalls

In the presence of another's suffering, most new counselors have the knee-jerk reaction to identify and fix a problem. The helpless feelings associated with a client's suffering are perceived as a burden that must be eradicated. If suffering continues, the new counselor internalizes the client's helplessness, doubt, confusion, and shame. The temptation to resort to tricks of the trade grows as the counselor imagines using techniques from a class in cognitive behavioral therapy (CBT) or Adlerian therapy. The new counselor finds herself overwhelmed by the client's distress, which is often exacerbated by a plethora of counselor "shoulds" (e.g., I should be able to help, I should be better at this, I should solve this problem, I should fix this person). This perspective continues until the counselor is able to self-soothe, tune into the client's pain and suffering more accurately, and demonstrate the warmth and acceptance that comes with unconditional positive regard. The recognition that counselor–client attunement is a better index for client improvement than theory and technique (Goldman, Hilsenroth, Owen, & Gold, 2013) represents a movement toward maturation for lay and pastoral counselors alike. The paradox inherent in the counselor's work is that by letting go of fantasies of counselor omnipotence and becoming skilled in the practice of unconditional positive regard, counselor–client attunement, and establishing an emotional safe haven and secure base for the client, the client's suffering is attenuated.

SUMMARY AND CONCLUSIONS

Suffering is a complex, universal, highly subjective phenomenon caused by enduring physical or emotional pain that can be broadly understood through intrapersonal and interpersonal processes and their interaction with constitutional factors. The individual's inherited genetic makeup, the quality of caregiver–child attunement that produces either secure or insecure attachment, and the interpersonal processes associated with the family, culture, and the larger society are implicated in the individual's tolerance for and generation of pain and suffering. Hardiness and resilience are highly influenced by the nature–nurture matrix. The elaborative enriched environment is the optimum environment within which to be raised. Yet, even the most robust among us, those with secure attachment, may experience trauma that can rip apart emotional adaptability and flexibility, leaving the person in a state of helplessness, isolation, and terror. All environments, however, will plant the seeds for resilience and hardiness or a self-perpetuating cycle of defensive coping strategies that impede personal growth. The power of brain plasticity should be a comfort to all who were raised in a less-than-ideal environment and/or who have experienced traumatic events that have left them with overwhelming feelings of vulnerability and hypervigilance. Patterned reactions and thoughts deeply embedded in the social brain can change if the person is willing to address his or her pain and suffering.

Counselor effectiveness in responding to a client's suffering emerges through a maturation process involving much more than a counselor's theoretical orientation. The skills associated with counselor–client attunement, establishing warmth and compassion through unconditional positive regard, and providing a safe haven and secure base support client improvement and afford a corrective experience for client transformation. The pastoral counselor is tasked with assessing and recognizing the salience of religious and spiritual processes and determining how best to use them. However, just as Frankl (1959/1984) observed that not every problem or conflict represents a neurotic process, not every issue presented before the pastoral counselor represents a spiritual or religious matter. The effective work of the pastoral counselor results in the client possessing an enhanced sense of self that is firmly rooted in this world and a recognition that he or she is a critical player in the world's transformation through an increased capacity to love both self and other.

REFLECTION QUESTIONS

1. According to the author, "When suffering is present, some type of pain will always be present. When pain is present, suffering does not always follow." How would you describe the difference between pain and suffering? Give examples from your own life experience.
2. Reflect on your experiences and environment growing up. How might your past affect your ability to manage pain and suffering in the present?
3. Is there someone in your life whose response to uncontrollable events or afflictions exemplifies suffering as an opportunity for meaning and wisdom? Briefly summarize his or her story as it relates to the chapter.
4. Do you find yourself naturally and consistently turning to someone specific when you experience pain and suffering? Why do you think you turn to that person? Compare your answer to the skills the author describes as essential for pastoral counselors when dealing with clients going through pain and suffering.

REFERENCES

Barkley, R. A. (2004). Attention-deficit/hyperactivity disorder and self-regulation: Taking an evolutionary perspective on executive functioning. In R. F. Baumeister & K. D. Vohs (Eds.), *Handbook of self-regulation: Research, theory, and applications* (pp. 301–323). New York, NY: Guilford.

Berlin, L. J., Cassidy, J., & Appleyard, K. (2008). The influence of early attachments on other relationships. In J. Cassidy & P. R. Shaver (Eds.), *Handbook of attachment: Theory, research, and clinical applications* (2nd ed., pp. 333–347). New York, NY: Guilford.

Bowlby, J. (1988). *A secure base: Parent–child attachment and healthy human development*. New York, NY: Basic Books.

Byrd, K. R., Patterson, C. L., & Turchik, J. A. (2010). Working alliance as a mediator of client attachment dimensions and psychotherapy outcome. *Psychotherapy Theory, Research, Practice and Training, 47*(4), 631–636. doi:10.1037/a0022080

Cassell, E. (1991). Recognizing suffering. *The Hastings Center Report, 21*(3), 24–31. doi: 10.2307/3563319

Cassell, E. (1992, March). The nature of suffering: Physical, psychological, social, and spiritual aspects. *NLN Publications*, pp. 1–10. doi:10.1093/acprof:oso/9780195156164.003.0003

Cassell, E. J. (2004). *The nature of suffering and the goals of medicine* (2nd ed., Kindle ed.). London, UK: Oxford University Press.

Cozolino, L. (2006). *The neuroscience of human relationships: Attachment and the developing social brain*. New York, NY: W. W. Norton.

Cozolino, L. (2010). *The neuroscience of psychotherapy: Healing the social brain*. New York, NY: W. W. Norton.

Crook-Lyon, R. E., O'Grady, K. A., Smith, T. B., Jensen, D. R., Golightly, T., & Potkar, K. A. (2012). Addressing religious and spiritual diversity in graduate training and multicultural education for professional psychologists. *Psychology of Religion and Spirituality, 4*(3), 169–181. doi: 10.1037/a0026403

DeGeorge, J., & Constantino, M. J. (2012). Perceptions of analogue therapist empathy as a function of salient experience similarity. *Journal of Psychotherapy Integration, 22*(1), 52–59. doi:10.1037/a0027365

Doidge, N. (2007). *The brain that changes itself: Stories of personal triumph from the frontiers of brain science*. New York, NY: Penguin.

Edelman, G. M. (2006). *Second nature: Brain science and human knowledge*. New Haven, CT: Yale University Press.

Fainsilber-Katz, L., & Gottman, J. M. (1993). Patterns of marital conflict predict children's internalizing and externalizing behavior. *Developmental Psychology, 29*(6), 940–950. doi: 10.1037/0012-1649.29.6.940

Fonagy, P. (2010). Psychotherapy research: Do we know what works for whom? *British Journal of Psychiatry, 197*(2), 83–85. doi:10.1192/bjp.bp.110.079657

Fraley, R. C., Roisman, G. I., Booth-LaForce, C., Owen, M. T., & Holland, A. S. (2013). Interpersonal and genetic origins of adult attachment styles: A longitudinal study from infancy to early adulthood. *Journal of Personality and Social Psychology, 104*(5), 817–838. doi:10.1037/a0031435

Frankl, V. E. (1984). *Man's search for meaning: An introduction to logotherapy* (3rd ed.). New York, NY: Touchstone. (Original work published 1959)

Ginot, E. (2012). Self-narratives and dysregulated affective states: The neuropsychological links between self-narratives, attachment, affect, and cognition. *Psychoanalytic Psychology, 29*(1), 59–80. doi:10.1037/a0023154

Goldman, R. E., Hilsenroth, M. J., Owen, J. J., & Gold, J. R. (2013). Psychotherapy integration and alliance: Use of cognitive-behavioral techniques within a short-term psychodynamic treatment model. *Journal of Psychotherapy Integration, 23*(4), 373–385. doi:10.1037/a0034363

Gottman, J., & Silver, N. (1999). *The seven principles that make marriage work*. New York, NY: Three Rivers Press.

Grossmann, K., Grossmann, K. E., Kindler, H., & Zimmermann, P. (2008). A wider view of attachment and exploration: The influence of mothers and fathers on the development of psychological security from infancy to young adulthood. In J. Cassidy & P. R. Shaver (Eds.), *Handbook of attachment: Theory, research, and clinical applications* (2nd ed., pp. 383–416). New York, NY: Guilford.

Hannan, S. M., & Orcutt, H. K. (2013). Emotion dysregulation as a partial mediator between reinforcement sensitivity and posttraumatic stress symptoms. *Personality and Individual Differences, 55*, 574–578. doi:10.1016/j.paid.2013.04.028

Lipton, B., & Fosha, D. (2011). Attachment as a transformative process in AEDP: Operationalizing the intersection of attachment theory and affective neuroscience. *Journal of Psychotherapy Integration, 21*(3), 253–279. doi:10.1037/a0025421

Merriam-Webster Online Dictionary. (2014). Retrieved from http://www.merriam-webster.com/dictionary/suffering

Mikulincer, M., & Shaver, P. R. (2007). *Attachment in adulthood: Structure, dynamics and change*. New York, NY: Guilford.

Ochsner, K. N., & Gross, J. J. (2004). Thinking makes it so: A social cognitive neuroscience approach to emotion regulation. In R. F. Baumeister & K. D. Vohs (Eds.), *Handbook of self-regulation: Research, theory, and applications* (pp. 229–255). New York, NY: Guilford.

Olson, D. H. (1999). Circumplex model of marital & family systems. *Journal of Family Therapy*. Retrieved from http://eruralfamilies.uwagec.org/ERFLibrary/Readings/Circumplex ModelOfMaritalAndFamilySystems.pdf

Panksepp, J., & Biven, L. (2012). *The archeology of mind: Neuroevolutionary origins of human emotions.* New York, NY: W. W. Norton.

Pargament, K. I. (2007). *Spiritually integrated psychotherapy: Understanding and addressing the sacred.* New York, NY: Guilford.

Pillay, S. S. (2010). *Life unlocked: 7 revolutionary lessons to overcome fear* (Kindle ed.). New York, NY: Rodale.

Richard, L. (1992). *What are they are saying about the theology of suffering?* Mahwah, NJ: Paulist Press.

Rogers, C. (1995). *On becoming a person: A therapist's view of psychotherapy.* New York, NY: Houghton Mifflin. (Original work published 1960)

Siegel, D. J. (2009). Mindful awareness, mindsight, and neural integration. *The Humanistic Psychologist, 37,* 137–158. doi:10.1080/08873260902892220

Siegel, D. J. (2012). *The developing mind: How relationships and the brain interact to shape who we are.* New York, NY: Guilford.

Solomon, J., & George, C. (2008). The measurement of attachment security and related constructs in infancy and early childhood. In J. Cassidy & P. R. Shaver (Eds.), *Handbook of attachment: Theory, research, and clinical applications* (2nd ed., pp. 383–416). New York, NY: Guilford.

Vaughn, B. E., Bost, K. K., & van Ijzendoorn, M. H. (2008). Attachment and temperament: Additive and interactive influences on behavior, affect, and cognition during infancy and childhood. In J. Cassidy & P. R. Shaver (Eds.), *Handbook of attachment: Theory, research, and clinical applications* (2nd ed., pp. 192–216). New York, NY: Guilford.

Waehler, C. A. (2013). Curiosity and biculturalism as key therapeutic change activities. *Psychotherapy, 50*(3), 351–355. doi:10.1037/a0033029

Weinfield, N. S., Sroufe, L., Egeland, B., & Carlson, E. (2008). Individual differences in infant–caregiver attachment: Conceptual and empirical aspects of security. In J. Cassidy & P. R. Shaver (Eds.), *Handbook of attachment: Theory, research, and clinical applications* (2nd ed., pp. 78–101). New York, NY: Guilford.

Wilkison, I. (2013). The problem of suffering as a driving force of rationalization and social change. *British Journal of Sociology, 64*(1), 123–141. doi:10.1111/1468-4446.12009

Worthington, E. L., & Sandage, S. J. (2001). Religion and spirituality. *Psychotherapy, 38*(4), 473–478. doi:10.1037//0033-3204.38.4.473

Zimmermann, P., & Becker-Stoll, F. (2002). Stability of attachment representations during adolescence: The influence of ego-identity status. *Journal of Adolescence, 25,* 107–124. doi: 10.1006/jado.2001.0452

Carrie Doehring 6

THE CHALLENGES OF BEING BILINGUAL: METHODS OF INTEGRATING PSYCHOLOGICAL AND RELIGIOUS STUDIES

The purpose of this chapter is to describe how pastoral counselors draw on religious and theological studies along with psychological studies. How do counselors bring these distinct disciplines to bear on their counseling practice? This is a question about interdisciplinary methods, which are shaped by implicit or explicit religious orientations. Pastoral counselors can be described as bilingual and bicultural. Their graduate education teaches them the languages of both psychological and religious studies. They learn methods for bridging these disciplines more often by example than explicit discussions about methodology. As this chapter illustrates, the near history of American pastoral counseling in the 20th century generated several distinct ways of relating psychological studies with religious and theological studies. I trace this history and outline two dominant methods and one emergent method of relating psychological and religious studies to the practice of counseling.

Is there something unique about the kind of help that people get from pastoral counselors who bridge psychological studies and religious and theological studies? How is such counseling shaped by the private faith commitments of lay pastoral counselors and the public vocations of religiously endorsed counselors? This chapter explores these questions by looking at the ways that pastoral counselors draw on both psychological and religious/theological knowledge in the counseling they do. A brief look at history highlights why questions about interdisciplinary method became important in the second half of the 20th century.

HISTORICAL BACKGROUND

Pastoral counseling by religious leaders has been going on for centuries. Historically, such counseling relied on religious sources of authority, such as the Hebrew Bible and the New Testament; commentaries on these sacred texts, such as the Midrash; and authoritative religious texts, such as the spiritual writings of the Desert Fathers, and rabbinical, ecclesial, monastic, or denominational writings that ordered communal and spiritual life. Generally speaking, the goal of pastoral care and counseling was to guide and save the souls of those seeking care.

In the late 19th century, the landscape of counseling started to change with the rise of psychology as a science. Counseling developed within a variety of contexts and professional arenas throughout the 20th century, including psychotherapy, social work, psychiatric care, community mental health counseling, and marriage/family counseling. In the 1950s, mainline Protestant and Roman Catholic seminaries began to offer academic and training programs incorporating psychological studies and psychotherapeutic training into theological education. Psychologically informed pastoral counseling and chaplaincy became specialized vocations as religious leaders pursued education and training in psychological counseling. Some seminaries developed doctoral programs in pastoral psychology that combined psychodynamic models of personality, existential theologies such as Paul Tillich's (1953) theology of ultimate concerns, and client-focused counseling such as Carl Rogers's (1961) approach of unconditional acceptance. Clinical pastoral education (CPE) within psychiatric hospitals was recognized as a form of clinically based theological education and was required by some seminaries and denominations as preparation for ministry. Pastoral counseling centers opened across the country, and the American Association of Pastoral Counselors was established as an organization that certified pastoral counselors and accredited pastoral counseling centers.

A new orientation to pastoral care and counseling came into being. This clinical paradigm of pastoral care and counseling used psychological research and therapeutic strategies to heal care seekers, unlike the classical paradigm of pastoral care, which had historically relied primarily on religious sources of authority to provide spiritual guidance to save the *souls* of care seekers (Patton, 1993). There was widespread enthusiasm among mainline Protestant and Catholic clergy for the healing potential of psychotherapy in the 1950s without much awareness of how this emerging clinical paradigm of pastoral care and counseling was different from historical classical paradigms of pastoral care and counseling.

Pastoral counselors became enamored with using psychological perspectives and psychotherapeutic practices because they resonated with many post–World War II middle-class Euro-American values—such as individualism, growth, and progress—that could, it was thought, promote healing and self-actualization in pastoral care and counseling (Holifield, 1983; McClure, 2010; Myers-Shirk, 2009). This enthusiasm for all things psychological and psychotherapeutic in the 1950s and 1960s made pastoral counselors want to leave behind traditional theological ways of understanding human nature as sinful. Many pastoral counseling enthusiasts rebelled against the moral exhortation of pastoral guidance in the classical paradigm of pastoral counseling (Snodgrass, 2007). These counselors embraced the nonjudgmental and compassionate language of psychotherapists such as Carl Rogers (1961).

As psychological ways of understanding life experience became popular throughout the 20th century, people began to speak about psychological experiences using everyday language—"I feel depressed/anxious" or "I'm addicted to. . . ." Psychological terms such as *anxiety, addiction,* and *depression* were used as first-order language for talking about psychological struggles in everyday ways. First-order language is the common parlance of how people talk about experience—in this case, psychological or religious experiences (Jennings, 1990). Theoretical perspectives, such as using psychological or theological studies, can be thought of as second-order ways of talking about experiences using formal or informal education to understand and think about psychological and religious experiences (Jennings, 1990). Third-order language involves the interdisciplinary methods one uses to bring psychological and theological perspectives together in thinking about clinical experiences (Jennings, 1990). Many pastoral counselors of the 1950s, 1960s, and 1970s preferred first-order psychological rather than religious language when it came to talking about human struggles and suffering because it seemed less moralistic, and this made them less fluent in using second-order perspectives from theological studies in thinking about their clinical practice. Instead, they became fluent in using second-order psychological perspectives. Psychology rather than theology became the second-order language they shared when conferring and writing about counseling. For pastoral counselors, the dominance of psychological second-order languages made them less adept at using the theological second-order languages they learned through theological education. In addition, increasing awareness of the need to respect religious differences made them hesitant to use any tradition-specific theological perspectives, for fear of imposing their theology on others (Doehring, 2009).

At the risk of simplifying the complex history of pastoral counseling in the second half of 20th century, I describe three interdisciplinary methods that emerged over this time. In different ways, these methods address the methodological challenges of being bilingual in both psychological and religious/theological studies. All of these methods are integrative but in different ways. To highlight their differences, I have labeled these integrative methods as foundational, dialogical, and liberative/postmodern. The first two methods date back to the 1980s and 1990s, whereas the third method is emerging across psychological and theological studies that use postmodern approaches to knowledge and explicitly explore social oppression.

THE INTERDISCIPLINARY METHODS OF PASTORAL COUNSELORS

Foundational Method

The first method, which I will call a *foundational* method, emerged from within explicitly Christian PhD programs accredited by the American Psychological Association (APA).[1] It uses a common foundational religious worldview, which is described as evangelical Christian or more broadly theistic. Counselors become theologically fluent in describing this common religious worldview, which helps them be accountable for tracking how this worldview:

- influences their clinical practice (Richards & Bergin, 2000, 2005a),
- is shared by those in theistic religious traditions (Richards, 2005; Richards & Bergin, 1997), and
- supports or calls into question the often assumed naturalistic worldview of psychology (Slife, Reber, & Lefevor, 2012).

A foundational approach to integrating psychological and theological/religious studies is most relevant for those who share a common religious worldview. This foundational method fosters fluency in theological and religious studies based on evangelical Christianity as well as an inclusive comparative approach to the study of religion that looks for a common core to theistic traditions. It is less compatible with a comparative approach to religion that focuses on differences across religious and spiritual orientations (Moyaert, 2012; Prothero, 2010). A foundational approach makes it harder for pastoral counselors to use theological and religious studies that are not oriented to evangelical Christianity (Helminiak, 2010; Hoffman, 2012).

Dialogical Method

The second method of integration is more *dialogical*, bringing into conversation questions and answers arising from within relevant disciplines, such as psychological and religious/theological studies, without searching for a common religious or theological worldview. This approach is represented by practical theologians (Browning, 1991; Browning & Cooper, 2004; E. Graham, Walton, & Ward, 2005a; Wolfteich, 2014) who exemplify the use of what is called a correlational method for interfacing social sciences and theological studies, as well as by psychologists of religion such as Pargament (1997, 2007; Pargament, Mahoney, Shafranske, Exline, & Jones, 2013), Shafranske (2009, 2014), and Mahoney (Mahoney, LeRoy, Kusner, Padgett, & Grimes, 2013). They combine research and clinical approaches in the psychology of religion using a comparative approach to religious studies that acknowledges irreducible differences between traditions. The recently published two-volume *APA Handbook of Psychology, Religion and Spirituality* (Pargament, Mahoney, & Shafranske, 2013) represents this dialogical approach. Although most of the chapters in the *Handbook* do not employ explicit theological language, they provide room for a full range of theological and religious perspectives. This dialogical approach is also represented in a helpful standard of care used when engaging in spiritually oriented counseling (Vieten et al., 2013); the approach enumerates 16 competencies in attitudes, knowledge, and skills that respect the diversity and distinctiveness of spiritual and religious experiences, practices, and beliefs, which develop and change over time and may be resources or liabilities in psychological and spiritual crises and coping.

Postmodern/Liberative Method

A third emergent method uses a more explicitly *postmodern* approach to *liberative* spiritual integration that builds on the dialogical method described earlier in several ways. First, it draws on postmodern and social constructive approaches to knowledge in both psychological studies (Gergen, 2001, 2002, 2006; Stolorow, Atwood, & Orange, 2002) and religious and theological studies in practical and pastoral theology (Beaudoin, 2014; Doehring, 2015; E. Graham, 1996; E. Graham, Walton, & Ward, 2005b; L. K. Graham, 1992, 2013). This liberative method looks at individual, family, and social change within a broad goal of social justice. For example, it uses theories and practices of intersectionality that highlight the ways in which various kinds of social systems of oppression, such as fundamentalist religious systems, sexism, racism, classism, and heterosexism, intersect from one moment to the next, sometimes affording and sometimes denying privilege (Doehring, 2014, 2015; Ramsay, 2013; Weber, 2010). The need to take into account social systems of privilege has become even more important within a postcolonialist global horizon where varieties of counseling, with their indigenous practices and contextual theologies, have often been suppressed and devalued by Western models of care (Lartey, 2004). This liberative postmodern method of integration is compatible with both the dialogical method as well as clinical approaches oriented toward social justice—particularly those using theories of intersectionality (Conwill, 2010; Kamya, 2007; Liasidou, 2013; McDowell & Hernandez, 2010).

Readers are invited to consider which of these three approaches helps them become more fluent in using both psychological and religious/theological studies in their clinical practice. I use a fictional case study to describe how I put into practice first a dialogical method and then a postmodern liberative method. I then draw on chapters written by theistic psychologists to imagine how to use a foundational method and what is distinctive about this method.

AN ILLUSTRATION

Anita is an African American middle-aged woman living in an urban setting in the northeastern United States. She sought counseling after discovering her brother's body after he committed suicide in the midst of lifelong struggles with substance use and depression. She had helped him relocate to her city a few years before when, yet again, his substance use caused him to lose his job, his home, and his driver's license. Having him close at hand made their relationship more complex and conflictual. She witnessed his suicidal tendencies when he emerged from binges to face the wreckage of his life—another lost job, his trashed apartment, and his hung-over body, along with the hate-filled e-mails he sometimes sent her during alcohol-fueled rages. She had tried to help him by encouraging him to find routines that sustained him—exercise, healthy eating, going to Alcoholic Anonymous, and doing well at manual labor jobs. The last binge was too much for him. He couldn't face starting over again, and he ended his life. Anita went to check up on him after she had not heard from him for a couple of weeks and has had flashbacks of the experience of discovering his body. Her grief, anger, and guilt over his suicide have threatened to unravel her tightly woven and demanding responsibilities toward family, work, and church.

She sought pastoral counseling because her Baptist religion and community of faith, usually a lifeline for her in times of stress, seem to be exacerbating her traumatic grief. She dropped out of singing in the church choir. Being in worship brings her face-to-face with trauma-related feelings she can usually avoid by focusing on work and family commitments. Her minister met with her, heard about these spiritual struggles, and recommended pastoral counseling. How will counseling combine psychological and theological ways of responding to her suffering? We use this case study to explore how pastoral counseling helps people like Anita to change.

A Dialogical Method of Integration

Similar to their counterparts in other methods of integration, those using a dialogical method understand the therapeutic relationship itself as a means of change. Psychological research identifies the most significant factor in therapeutic change as the therapeutic alliance—the quality of the collaborative work between client and counselor and how well the counselor's ways of helping interface with the client's goals and expectations (Barber, Khalsa, & Sharpless, 2010; Hatcher, 2010)—especially her expectations of a counselor who is able to use both theological and psychological perspectives to understand her grief. A dialogical method explicitly responds to Anita's goals and expectations for spiritually integrative trauma care (Kusner & Pargament, 2012; Murray-Swank & Murray-Swank, 2013; Pargament & Cummings, 2010).

Pastoral counselors bring into dialogue an array of theological perspectives that help Anita discern whether particular beliefs, values, and spiritual practices alleviate or exacerbate posttraumatic stress. Using research on religious coping and spiritual struggles, counselors will not assume that religious and spiritual practices always help Anita feel safe when she reexperiences trauma. Indeed, psychological research on religious coping has found that religion and spirituality are multidimensional and, hence, related to acute stress and trauma in a variety of life-enhancing, life-limiting, and destructive ways. "The critical question isn't *whether* religion and spirituality are good or bad, but *when, how,* and *why* they take constructive or destructive forms [in the aftermath of trauma]" (Pargament, Mahoney, Exline, Jones, & Shafranske, 2013, p. 7). Psychological studies on religious coping and trauma have demonstrated that Anita will likely experience transitory religious and spiritual struggles that often involve questioning and searching for spiritual and religious practices and meanings. Anita seems unable to conserve practices and beliefs that have helped her in the past; she needs to discover new beliefs and practices that become integrated into her life. Anita is more likely to experience psychospiritual growth if she can find and use positive religious coping strategies that include believing in and experiencing God as benevolent, collaborating with God in problem solving rather than deferring to God or being self-directing, and seeking spiritual support in her community of faith. If she becomes stuck in chronic religious struggles and uses negative religious coping, she may believe in and experience God as punitive and abandoning, questioning God's love, and she may become discontented with her religious community (Pargament, Murray-Swank, Magyar, Murray, & Ano, 2005). Ongoing struggles and negative coping are associated with increased psychological and spiritual distress. Anita may well experience a transitory or chronic sense of spiritual violation and desecration of that which is sacred (e.g., her caregiving role with her brother), which threatens her spiritual well-being (Murray-Swank & Pargament, 2005; Pargament, 2007; Pargament, Magyar, Benore, & Mahoney, 2005). Her traumatic experience may well include many "sticking points"— conflicts between pretrauma beliefs/values and trauma-related doubts and questions, such as, "How could a loving God allow this to happen to me?" (Murray-Swank & Waelde, 2013). Pastoral counselors can help Anita elaborate these conflicts and help her think about them theologically, using whatever theological perspectives are most relevant and meaningful for Anita.

A Postmodern Liberative Method of Integration

Pastoral counselors using a liberative postmodern method will listen for distinctive features of Anita's spiritual orienting system, made up of formative values, ultimate beliefs, and practices that connect her with God and help her to cope with stress. How do Anita's trauma-related feelings, such as fear, shame, and guilt, pull together values, beliefs, and coping practices that may be shaped by family and social systems? How has her internalization of these social systems shaped the ways she responds spiritually to the trauma of her brother's death? On one hand, her religious community helps her draw on centuries of African American spirituality. On the other hand, she can easily feel inadequate in traditional roles of African American women that make them the emotional centers of family systems. Spiritual practices that foster self-compassion can uncover and alleviate the shame that often is part of privatized religious meaning making (Doehring, 2015; Herman, 2011) and the devaluation incurred by interacting social systems of racism and sexism. Spiritual practices authentic to Anita's religious tradition will help her compassionately counteract hyperarousal, intrusive memories, and avoidant coping.

Emerging research on trauma and moral distress suggests that, in addition to issues of fear, shame and guilt may also feature in Anita's posttraumatic stress (Herman, 2011). Pastoral counselors are uniquely equipped to help morally distressed trauma survivors such as Anita find spiritual practices that help her experience a sense of self-compassion and/or a transcendent experience of the compassion of God

(Bingaman, 2014; Doehring, 2015; Kinghorn, 2012). When shame is compassionately addressed at the outset of counseling, morally distressed trauma survivors such as Anita can use spiritual practices that increase self-compassion and decrease the sense of responsibility for suffering that leads to moral distress.

Once Anita has found and begun to use spiritual practices that help her experience safety, she will be invited to become theologically reflexive about this "lived theology": the grief- and trauma-related values, beliefs, and coping practices she is implicitly using to make sense of and live with the trauma of her brother's death. Counselors' religious and theological education gives them a historical and comparative understanding of various religious and theological ways that people have tried to make sense of and live with suffering. There are, of course, innumerable philosophical and theological treatises on evil and the problem of suffering. Theologian Nelson (2003) provides a helpful introductory typology of five ways of understanding suffering within Christian traditions. In reviewing various ways that religious traditions have struggled to make sense of suffering, pastoral counselors can consider how such understandings may be life giving or life limiting for Anita in the process of coping with trauma-related symptoms and also in the long-range meaning-making process.

Theological reflexivity involves understanding how beliefs and values are shaped not only by Anita's family system and religious community but also by social systems of advantage and privilege internalized throughout her life and enacted now as she struggles with grief. Anita might consider what values and beliefs were important to her in how she cared for her brother. Anita describes her role as the eldest sibling who became the emotional ballast for the family after her parents died. She felt very responsible for her brother and wanted him to have a sense of belonging to the family when she relocated him to her city. She believed that if she worked alongside God in caring for him, he would finally be able to overcome his substance use disorder and return home like the prodigal son. Verbalizing this belief energizes her anger toward God for not doing more to return this "lost sheep" to the fold. Now she understands why she feels irritated at church, especially when images of an all-powerful God are used. Anita could be invited to say more about this anger, as she begins to question where God was and what God wants of her. Anita may decide to seek out a conversation with her pastor about these questions and about her guilt about not praying or singing in the choir—two practices that were the mainstay of her religious coping in the past. She used to be able to offer up her worries in prayer at the end of the day and felt that God lifted these burdens from her each night before she fell asleep. Now when she tries to fall asleep, images of her brother's dead body haunt her.

In conversations with her counselor, Anita can now see how much of her guilt is connected with feeling responsible for protecting her brother, who seemed much more disadvantaged by racism throughout his life than she was. She realizes that she has discounted the ways that racism, classism, and sexism intersected in her life, generating a fear-based spiritual orientation to the world. It was up to her to hold onto a job, fulfill religious duties, and protect her brother—especially by trying to keep him out of jail. She realizes that her physical exhaustion, along with her aches and pains, are symbolic of this heavy burden of responsibility and guilt she has carried. She begins to create space in her day to put her feet up and listen to music that releases sadness as she feels held within God's compassion and the compassion of those who care for her, especially in her religious community. Her pastor, who has been meeting with her every month or so, realizes how much her story resonates with other women in the congregation, and he begins a sermon series on the burdens of guilt that African American women can so easily carry. He offers an evening service of remembrance so that family members who carry burdens of guilt can be invited to lay these at the communion table. Anita participates and describes to her counselor the outpouring of grief that so many experienced. Anita's relationship with God and her community of faith have changed. These relationships are energized now by sadness and compassion and not by guilt. Her values and beliefs are changed, with more emphasis now on interconnected responsibility and belonging, as well as beliefs that God suffers with her. Her pastor and community have changed as well, with more awareness of each other's burden and with more communal ways of caring.

This integrative liberative method first allows lived theologies—enacted beliefs, values, and habitual ways of coping and connecting spiritually—to emerge and be compassionately understood and then brings these theologies into conversation with various public and comparative theologies that have stood the test of time and are relevant and meaningful for someone like Anita. In the process of exploring the benefits and liabilities of Anita's lived theology, she and her counselor will co-construct life-giving theologies of suffering that are deeply anchored in Anita's values and beliefs. Life-giving beliefs and values can be used to counter automatic trauma-related thoughts based on life-limiting embedded theologies and to build an intentional theology about the trauma of her brother's death and her role in his life. Posttraumatic growth will increase as Anita develops a well-integrated spirituality that is "broad and deep, responsive to life's situations, nurtured by the larger social context, capable of flexibility and continuity [and] large enough to encompass the full range of human potential and luminous enough to provide the individual with a powerful guiding vision" (Pargament, 2007, p. 136).

A Foundational Method of Integration

What distinguishes a foundational method from the dialogical and postmodern/liberative methods I have described? While being respectful of Anita's unique religious values and beliefs (Richards & Bergin, 2000, 2005a), pastoral counselors using a foundational method will explore the ways that Anita is experiencing her traumatic loss through a Baptist and biblical worldview. They will listen for how God features in Anita's spiritual struggles and hopes, and they will draw on their own theistic worldview, which includes God as an active agent of change. Perhaps the most distinctive feature of the foundational worldview of theistic counseling is supernaturalism, a key feature in describing the purpose and goals of therapy:

> The most distinctive feature about our orientation that differentiates it from the major secular therapeutic systems is the idea that God can intervene in the lives of human beings to help them cope, heal, and change. (Richards & Bergin, 2005b, p. 154)[2]

Anita's counselor will look for empirically based approaches to trauma that can help to identify Anita's theistic beliefs, which might be intensifying her religious struggles (like beliefs in a punitive God). Psychospiritual education about trauma and journaling that tracks various aspects of trauma-related symptoms are strategies used in cognitive behavioral therapy (CBT), one of the best evidence-based treatments that can be aligned with the foundational method, especially when drawing on biblical texts to examine and counteract Anita's beliefs in a punitive God (Tan, 2001, 2007). Assuming that Anita shares values and beliefs in the authority of the Bible, a pastoral counselor using a biblical, Christian approach to CBT would be justified in using "only those techniques that are *consistent with biblical truth* [emphasis added] . . . reaffirm[ing] scriptural perspectives on suffering . . . and overcoming mental anguish due to unbiblical erroneous beliefs (i.e., misbeliefs)" (Tan, 2007, p. 102).

Following CBT strategies, Anita will keep a daily record of when she experiences trauma-related symptoms, how disruptive they are (on a 10-point scale), what seems to have triggered symptoms, and how she coped, particularly by drawing on biblical texts in her spiritual practices. These journal entries help Anita and her counselor to track type, frequency, and severity of trauma-related symptoms and the ways she copes. As pastoral counseling moves from the assessment and psychoeducational phase into a psychospiritual focus on coping, a biblical, Christian approach to CBT will "use *biblical truth* (John 8:32), not *relativistic values* [emphasis added], to conduct cognitive restructuring and behavioral change interventions" (Tan, 2007, p. 102).

Her counselor will engage Anita's belief system in searching for and helping her use biblical beliefs about God's grace and forgiveness. The benefit of a foundational approach is that it might well fit the evangelical and/or theistic worldview that Anita uses in making sense of her trauma and trying to connect with God and her community of faith. The liability is that it may fail to take into account the ways Anita's worldview is not traditionally Baptist. On one hand, sociological surveys demonstrate that nearly one third of Americans continue to believe that the Bible "is the actual word of God and is to be taken literally, word for word" (Blow, 2014). Nearly half believe that it is "the inspired word of God but not everything in it should be taken literally" (Blow, 2014). These survey data could explain why foundational methods of interfacing theistic worldviews and psychotherapy may be particularly meaningful in the United States but less so in other countries.

A liability of using a foundational method in counseling Anita is that she may be one of those Christians whose religious identity is less conformist and more plural and particular, as sociological research by the Pew Foundation has demonstrated (Lugo, Green, & Smith, 2008). For example, the religious identity of a person who was raised and is still within a Christian tradition may be based on Christian beliefs and practices, with additions from other religious traditions, such as beliefs in reincarnation. That person's religious identity might well look like postmodern architecture that includes contrasting architectural styles within one edifice. Pastoral counselors using a theistic worldview will likely retain a more conformist religious identity, especially religiously endorsed pastoral counselors who feel responsible for explicitly representing the cornerstone beliefs of their religious tradition. They may unwittingly exacerbate Anita's spiritual struggles if she is worried about being shunned by her religious community for her nonconformist beliefs. In addition, the full range of second-order theological studies of suffering that span both modern and postmodern approaches to religious and theological knowledge may not be as readily available to those working within foundational approaches, who typically use theological studies congruent with an evangelical Christian belief system. In other words, the theological fluency of those using a foundational approach may be limited to theological studies within their own tradition. For example, a theistic counselor may not access theological perspectives, such as womanist liberation theologies, that might be especially meaningful for Anita.

CONCLUSIONS

I have identified and illustrated three interdisciplinary methods of bringing both psychological and religious/theological studies and professional allegiance to bear on clinical practice. Readers will want to consider carefully which methods best fit their education, training, professional/religious affiliations, and credentials, along with their clinical contexts. As my use of recent publications indicates, this is an exciting time to be engaged in pastoral counseling. The territory of this kind of clinical care is expanding, and the map I have provided in demarcating three methods is a provisional, bird's-eye view from someone much more familiar with dialogical and postmodern/liberative methods than foundational methods. I invite readers to engage in their own third-order reflections on the methods they use to become bilingual and bicultural in these exciting and challenging times and to stay abreast of research and clinical publications on theistic counseling and spiritually integrated counseling that draws on dialogical and postmodern/liberative methods.

REFLECTION QUESTIONS

1. The author describes pastoral counselors as *bilingual* and *bicultural*. Explain what this means to you. What other "languages" do you speak?
2. Which of the three methods of integration (foundational, dialogical, and postmodern/liberative) is most attractive to you and why?
3. The author illustrates how each of the three methods of integration can be applied in the fictional case study of Anita. Based on this illustration, which of these methods best fits your own education, training, professional/religious affiliations, and credentials? Why?

NOTES

1. In the 1950s, the Christian Association for Psychological Studies (CAPS) was organized by "practicing psychologists mostly from a Reformed theological persuasion" (Johnson & Jones, 2000, p. 35). Their interest in providing clinical psychology programs accredited by the American Psychological Association (APA) for Christians led to the establishment of PhD programs in clinical psychology at Fuller Theological Seminary in 1964 and Rosemead School of Psychology at Biola University in 1970. Since then, other explicitly Christian APA-accredited programs have come into being at Baylor University (Baptist) and Brigham Young University (Church of Jesus Christ of Latter-day Saints).
2. These four beliefs are necessary to qualify as a theistic counselor: (a) God exists, (b) humans are created by God, (c) humans are in immediate communication with God, and (d) God regularly and miraculously intervenes in worldly affairs, especially when prevailed upon by believers (Richards & Bergin, 2005b).

REFERENCES

Barber, J. P., Khalsa, S., & Sharpless, B. A. (2010). The validity of the alliance as a predictor of psychotherapy outcome. In J. C. Muran & J. P. Barber (Eds.), *The therapeutic alliance: An evidence-based guide to practice* (pp. 29–43). New York, NY: Guilford.

Beaudoin, T. (2014). Postmodern practical theology. In K. A. Cahalan & G. S. Mikoski (Eds.), *Opening the field of practical theology: An introduction* (pp. 187–202). New York, NY: Rowman & Littlefield.

Bingaman, K. A. (2014). *The power of neuroplasticity for pastoral and spiritual care.* Lanham, MD: Lexington Books.

Blow, C. M. (2014, June 8). Religious constriction. *The New York Times*, p. A19.

Browning, D. S. (1991). *A fundamental practical theology: Descriptive and strategic proposals.* Minneapolis, MN: Augsburg Fortress Press.

Browning, D. S., & Cooper, T. D. (2004). *Religious thought and modern psychologies* (2nd ed.). Minneapolis, MN: Fortress.

Conwill, W. L. (2010). Domestic violence among the Black poor: Intersectionality and social justice. *International Journal for the Advancement of Counselling, 32*(1), 31–45. doi:10.1007/s10447-009-9087-z

Doehring, C. (2009). Theological accountability: The hallmark of pastoral counseling. *Sacred Spaces, 1*(1), 4–34.

Doehring, C. (2014). Emotions and change in intercultural spiritual care. *Pastoral Psychology, 63*(5), 583–596. doi:10.1007/s11089-014-0607-3

Doehring, C. (2015). *The practice of pastoral care: A postmodern approach* (Rev. and expanded ed.). Louisville, KY: Westminster John Knox.

Gergen, K. J. (2001). Psychological science in a postmodern context. *American Psychologist, 56*(10), 803–813. doi:10.1037/0003-066x.56.10.803

Gergen, K. J. (2002). *Relational being: Beyond self and community.* New York, NY: Oxford University Press.

Gergen, K. J. (2006). *Therapeutic realities: Collaboration, oppression and relational flow.* Chagin Falls, OH: Taos Institute.

Graham, E. (1996). *Transforming practice: Pastoral theology in an age of uncertainty.* New York, NY: Mowbray.

Graham, E., Walton, H., & Ward, F. (2005a). "Speaking of God in public": Correlation. In E. Graham, H. Walton, & F. Ward (Eds.), *Theological reflection: Methods* (pp. 138–169). London, UK: SCM Press.

Graham, E., Walton, H., & Ward, F. (2005b). "Theology-in-action": Praxis. In E. Graham, H. Walton, & F. Ward (Eds.), *Theological reflection: Methods* (pp. 170–199). London, UK: SCM Press.

Graham, L. K. (1992). *Care of persons, care of worlds: A psychosystems approach to pastoral care and counseling.* Nashville, TN: Abingdon.

Graham, L. K. (2013). Political dimensions of pastoral care in community disaster responses. *Pastoral Psychology, 63*(4), 471–488. doi:10.1007/s11089-013-0571-3

Hatcher, R. L. (2010). Alliance theory and measurement. In J. C. Muran & J. P. Barber (Eds.), *The therapeutic alliance: An evidence-based guide to practice* (pp. 7–28). New York, NY: Guilford.

Helminiak, D. A. (2010). "Theistic psychology and psychotherapy": A theological and scientific critique. *Zygon, 45*(1), 47–74.

Herman, J. (2011). Posttraumatic stress disorder as a shame disorder. In R. L. Dearing & J. P. Tangney (Eds.), *Shame in the therapy hour* (pp. 261–275). Washington, DC: American Psychological Association.

Hoffman, L. (2012). Religious experience in a cross-cultural and interfaith context: Limitations and possibilities. *Pastoral Psychology, 61*(5/6), 809–822. doi:10.1007/s11089-011-0394-z

Holifield, E. B. (1983). *A history of pastoral care in America: From salvation to self-realization.* Nashville, TN: Abingdon.

Jennings, T. W. (1990). Pastoral theological methodology. In R. J. Hunter (Ed.), *Dictionary of pastoral care and counseling* (pp. 862–864). Nashville, TN: Abingdon.

Johnson, E. L., & Jones, S. L. (2000). A history of Christians in psychology. In E. L. Johnson & S. L. Jones (Eds.), *Psychology and Christianity: Four views* (pp. 11–53). Downers Grove, IL: InterVarsity Press.

Kamya, H. (2007). Narrative practice and culture. In E. Aldarondo (Ed.), *Advancing social justice through clinical practice.* (pp. 207–220). Mahwah, NJ: Lawrence Erlbaum.

Kinghorn, W. (2012). Combat trauma and moral fragmentation: A theological account of moral injury. *Journal of the Society of Christian Ethics, 32*(2), 57–74.

Kusner, K., & Pargament, K. (2012). Shaken to the core: Understanding and addressing the spiritual dimension of trauma. In R. A. McMackin, E. Newman, J. M. Fogler, & T. M. Keane (Eds.), *Trauma therapy in context: The science and craft of evidence-based practice* (pp. 211–230). Washington, DC: American Psychological Association.

Lartey, E. Y. (2004). Globalization, internationalization, and indigenization of pastoral care and counseling. In N. J. Ramsay (Ed.), *Pastoral care and counseling: Redefining the paradigms* (pp. 87–108). Nashville, TN: Abingdon.

Liasidou, A. (2013). Intersectional understandings of disability and implications for a social justice reform agenda in education policy and practice. *Disability & Society, 28*(3), 299–312. doi:10.1080/09687599.2012.710012

Lugo, L., Green, J., & Smith, G. (2008). *Transcript: U.S. Religious Landscape Survey Report II.* Pew Forum on Religion & Public Life. Retrieved from http://www.pewforum.org/2008/06/01/u-s-religious-landscape-survey-religious-beliefs-and-practices/

Mahoney, A., LeRoy, M., Kusner, K., Padgett, E., & Grimes, L. (2013). Addressing parental spirituality as part of the problem and solution in family psychotherapy. In D. F. Walker & W. L. Hathaway (Eds.), *Spiritual interventions in child and adolescent psychotherapy* (pp. 65–88). Washington, DC: American Psychological Association.

McClure, B. (2010). *Moving beyond individualism in pastoral care and counseling: Reflections on theory, theology, and practice.* Eugene, OR: Cascade Books.

McDowell, T., & Hernandez, P. (2010). Decolonizing academia: Intersectionality, participation, and accountability in family therapy and counseling. *Journal of Feminist Family Therapy, 22*(2), 93–111. doi:10.1080/08952831003787834

Moyaert, M. (2012). Recent developments in the theology of interreligious dialogue: From soteriological openness to hermeneutical openness. *Modern Theology, 28*(1), 25–52. doi:10.1111/j.1468-0025.2011.01724.x

Murray-Swank, A., & Murray-Swank, N. A. (2013). Spiritual and religious problems: Integrating theory and clinical practice. In K. Pargament, A. Mahoney, & E. P. Shafranske (Eds.), *APA handbook of psychology, religion, and spirituality: An applied psychology of religion and spirituality* (Vol. 2, pp. 421–437). Washington, DC: American Psychological Association.

Murray-Swank, N. A., & Pargament, K. (2005). God, where are you? Evaluating a spiritually-integrated intervention for sexual abuse. *Mental Health, Religion & Culture, 8*(3), 191–203. doi:10.1080/13694670500138866

Murray-Swank, N. A., & Waelde, L. C. (2013). Spirituality, religion, and sexual trauma: Integrating research, theory, and clinical practice. In K. Pargament, A. Mahoney, & E. P. Shafranske (Eds.), *APA handbook of psychology, religion, and spirituality: An applied psychology of religion and spirituality* (Vol. 2, pp. 335–354). Washington, DC: American Psychological Association.

Myers-Shirk, S. (2009). *Helping the good shepherd: Pastoral counselors in a psychotherapeutic culture 1925–1975.* Baltimore, MD: The Johns Hopkins University Press.

Nelson, S. L. (2003). Facing evil: Evil's many faces: Five paradigms for understanding evil. *Interpretation, 57*(4), 399–413. doi:10.1177/002096430005700405

Pargament, K. (1997). *The psychology of religion and coping: Theory, research, practice.* New York, NY: Guilford.

Pargament, K. (2007). *Spiritually integrated psychotherapy: Understanding and addressing the sacred.* New York, NY: Guilford.

Pargament, K., & Cummings, J. (2010). Anchored by faith: Religion as a resilience factor. In J. W. Reich, A. J. Zautra, & J. S. Hall (Eds.), *Handbook of adult resilience* (pp. 193–210). New York, NY: Guilford.

Pargament, K., Magyar, G. M., Benore, E., & Mahoney, A. (2005). Sacrilege: A study of sacred loss and desecration and their implications for health and well-being in a community sample. *Journal for the Scientific Study of Religion, 44*(1), 59–78. doi:10.1111/j.1468-5906.2005.00265.x

Pargament, K., Mahoney, A., Exline, J., Jones, J., Jr., & Shafranske, E. (2013). Envisioning an integrative paradigm for the psychology of religion and spirituality: An introduction to the APA handbook of psychology, religion and spirituality In K. Pargament, A. Mahoney, & E. Shafranske (Eds.), *APA handbook of psychology, religion and spirituality* (Vol. 1, pp. 3–19). Washington, DC: American Psychological Association.

Pargament, K., Mahoney, A., & Shafranske, E. P. (Eds.). (2013). *APA handbook of psychology, religion, and spirituality* (2 vols.). Washington, DC: American Psychological Association.

Pargament, K., Mahoney, A., Shafranske, E. P., Exline, J. J., & Jones, J. W. (2013). From research to practice: Toward an applied psychology of religion and spirituality. In K. Pargament, A. Mahoney, & E. P. Shafranske (Eds.), *APA handbook of psychology, religion, and spirituality: An applied psychology of religion and spirituality* (Vol. 2, pp. 3–22). Washington, DC: American Psychological Association.

Pargament, K., Murray-Swank, N., Magyar, G., Murray, N., & Ano, G. (2005). Spiritual struggle: A phenomenon of interest to psychology and religion. In W. R. Miller & H. Delaney (Eds.), *Judeo-Christian perspectives in psychology: Human nature, motivation, and change* (pp. 245–268). Washington, DC: American Psychological Association.

Patton, J. (1993). *Pastoral care in context: An introduction to pastoral care.* Louisville, KY: Westminster John Knox Press.

Prothero, S. (2010). *God is not one: The eight rival religions that run the world and why their differences matter.* New York, NY: HarperOne.

Ramsay, N. J. (2013). Intersectionality: A model for addressing the complexity of oppression and privilege. *Pastoral Psychology.* *63*(4), 453–469. doi:10.1007/s11089-013-0570-4

Richards, P. S. (2005). Theistic integrative psychotherapy. In L. Sperry & E. P. Shafranske (Eds.), *Spiritually oriented psychotherapy* (pp. 259–285). Washington, DC: American Psychological Association.

Richards, P. S., & Bergin, A. E. (1997). A theistic, spiritual view of psychotherapy. In P. S. Richards & A. E. Bergin (Eds.), *A spiritual strategy for counseling and psychotherapy* (pp. 115–142). Washington, DC: American Psychological Association.

Richards, P. S., & Bergin, A. E. (2000). Religious diversity and psychotherapy: Conclusions, recommendations, and future directions. In P. S. Richards & A. E. Bergin (Eds.), *Handbook of psychotherapy and religious diversity* (pp. 469–489). Washington, DC: American Psychological Association.

Richards, P. S., & Bergin, A. E. (2005a). Ethical and process issues and guidelines. In P. S. Richards & A. E. Bergin (Eds.), *A spiritual strategy for counseling and psychotherapy* (2nd ed., pp. 183–217). Washington, DC: American Psychological Association.

Richards, P. S., & Bergin, A. E. (Eds.). (2005b). *A spiritual strategy for counseling and psychotherapy* (2nd ed.). Washington, DC: American Psychological Association.

Rogers, C. R. (1961). *On becoming a person: A therapist's view of psychotherapy.* Boston, MA: Houghton Mifflin.

Shafranske, E. P. (2009). Spiritually oriented psychodynamic psychotherapy. *Journal of Clinical Psychology, 65*(2), 147–157. doi:10.1002/jclp.20565

Shafranske, E. P. (2014). Psychotherapy with Roman Catholics. In P. S. Richards & A. E. Bergin (Eds.), *Handbook of psychotherapy and religious diversity* (2nd ed., pp. 53–76). Washington, DC: American Psychological Association.

Slife, B. D., Reber, J. S., & Lefevor, G. T. (2012). When God truly matters: A theistic approach to psychology. *Research in the Social Scientific Study of Religion, 23,* 213–237.

Snodgrass, J. (2007). From Rogers to Clinebell: Exploring the history of pastoral psychology. *Pastoral Psychology, 55*(4), 513–525. doi:10.1007/s11089-007-0066-1

Stolorow, R. D., Atwood, G. E., & Orange, D. M. (2002). *Worlds of experience: Interweaving philosophical and clinical dimensions in psychoanalysis.* New York, NY: Basic Books.

Tan, S.-Y. (2001). Emprically supported treatments. *Journal of Psychology and Christianity, 20*(3), 282–286.

Tan, S.-Y. (2007). Use of prayer and scripture in cognitive-behavioral therapy. *Journal of Psychology and Christianity, 26*(2), 101–111.

Tillich, P. (1953). *The courage to be.* New Haven, CT: Yale University Press.

Vieten, C., Scammell, S., Pilato, R., Ammondson, I., Pargament, K., & Lukoff, D. (2013). Spiritual and religious competencies for psychologists. *Psychology of Religion and Spirituality, 5*(3), 129–144. doi:10.1037/a0032699.supp

Weber, L. (2010). *Understanding race, class, gender, and sexuality: A conceptual framework* (2nd ed.). New York, NY: Oxford University Press.

Wolfteich, C. E. (2014). Hermeneutics in Roman Catholic practical theology. In K. A. Cahalan & G. S. Mikoski (Eds.), *Opening the field of practical theology: An introduction.* New York, NY: Rowman & Littlefield.

Thomas E. Rodgerson

7

TO DIAGNOSE OR NOT TO DIAGNOSE: PASTORAL COUNSELING DISTINCTIVES IN CONCEPTUALIZING AND ENGAGING HUMAN DISTRESS

Consciousness of the fragility of life in an unpredictable world has led to a multitude of interpretive systems aimed at helping human beings navigate life's choices and make sense of life events in order to endure, thrive, or minimize the effects of human suffering. For thousands of years, these interpretive systems have been embodied in the narratives, doctrines, ethical codes, rituals, and social constructs (Smart, 2000) of religious traditions, or what some have called religious "communities of meaning" (Rogers-Vaughn, 2013, p. 29). From creation stories about light and darkness, to narratives about paradise lost, to enlightenment about Four Noble Truths, to yogic paths leading to bliss, to understanding the nature of submission to Allah, human beings have received and created ways of understanding the human condition often motivated by the desire to enhance human flourishing and minimize human distress.

Although not completely absent on the stage of world thought prior to the 17th century, The Enlightenment brought ideas of a scientific method as a way of understanding the order and disorder of the world, the functioning of the human body and mind, and the conceptualization of human suffering. Medical and social scientific advances in the 20th century offered alternative, if not competing, interpretive systems to the centuries-old wisdom of religious thought. Rational and scientific approaches to human dysphoria were often seen as moving the understanding of physical dysphoria from attributions of sin to scientific diagnosis of disease, moving the understanding of social dysphoria from religious constructs of covenant or community to economic theory, and moving the understanding of mental dysphoria from penance and exorcism to medication and talk therapy. In that movement, social science, attempting to avoid the label of being a "soft" science, increasingly emphasized the medical model of diagnosis for mental disorders based on an empirically derived biopsychosocial understanding of mental dysphoria with recommended evidenced-based treatments.

In the 20th century, pastoral counseling emerged as a discipline that attempted to bring the wisdom of religious interpretive systems into dialogue with the scientific (and especially social scientific) interpretive systems, aimed at helping human beings navigate life's choices and make sense of life events in order to endure, thrive, or minimize the effects of human suffering. This process of dialogue has often been defined by ambiguity and ambivalence, nowhere seen more clearly than in the idea of *pastoral diagnosis* as a unique way of conceptualizing human distress. After stepping back to look at the history and meaning of *pastoral diagnosis*, this chapter proposes a way of understanding pastoral diagnosis as a process of discernment that seeks to bring into dialogue alternative ways of knowing, while at the same time being grounded in a larger interplay between knowing and unknowing, which brings a unique experience to the engagement with human distress.

THE MODERN EMERGENCE OF AND AMBIVALENCE ABOUT PASTORAL DIAGNOSIS

Historical Roots of Pastoral Diagnosis

It can be argued that any interpretive system that attempts to make sense of human suffering will devise some form of diagnosis aimed at understanding the meaning of the suffering and usually leading to some form of intervention. In religious systems, usually priests, pastors, teachers, prophets, gurus, rabbis, imams, or the like are looked to as authorities for diagnosing the meaning of suffering and recommending responses to alleviate suffering. The idea of pastoral diagnosis that developed in the 20th century had its roots in the worldwide pattern of religious interpretive systems in general and more particularly in the centuries-old practice of pastoral care from the Judeo–Christian (mostly Christian) tradition (see Townsend, Chapter 2 in this volume, for a wider history of pastoral counseling).

Hiltner (1976) suggested that if diagnosis were defined in terms of appraisal, examination, or evaluation, then the first appearance of diagnosis in Christian history had to do with the evaluation for membership in the church. This was not only in terms of evaluating readiness for membership, but in times of persecution when persons recanted their faith, it was also for diagnosing their ability to be readmitted to the church. Once Christianity became the official religion of the Roman Empire, there emerged books of penitentials with guidelines for "diagnosing" the nature of an offense against the community or God and the penance to be done for restoration. The penitentials were followed by pastoral theology and moral theology in Roman Catholicism. "Moral theology became the codification of moral principles based on religious premises and pastoral theology codified the individual situations" (Hiltner, 1976, p. 575). Although Protestants refused to have case books, they, too, made evaluations of sin and determinations about the genuineness of repentance in their form of pastoral diagnosis as part of a larger religious interpretive system that aimed at helping human beings navigate life's choices and make sense of life events in order to endure, thrive, or minimize the effects of human suffering.

Holifield (1983) notes that, whether Protestant or Roman Catholic, clerical counselors in the 16th and 17th centuries focused on diagnoses that allowed for the remedy of sin for the cure of souls. Following the directives of the Fourth Lateran Council, which required every adult to confess at least once a year to the local priest seeking absolution, "the Catholic moral theologians of the sixteenth century completed the process by elaborating a complex body of casuistry—the application of general principles to particular cases—which promised to solve every spiritual dilemma that anyone could imagine" (Holifield, 1983, p. 17). Protestants, on the other hand, sought ways of detecting sin as faithlessness, spiritual deadness, idolatry, or disorder with innovative methods for diagnosing the emotional components of repentance, the nature of a rebellious will, spiritual pride, or temptation, with a later turn to the intricacies of inward piety and the assurance of salvation. The diagnostic tone of these initiatives might be seen in the title of a book authored by Greenham (1599), *Godly Instructions for the Due Examinations and Direction of All Men* (as cited in Holifield, 1983). By 1656, when Baxter wrote *The Reformed Pastor*, urging clergy to spend more time in personal conversations with parishioners, "he could assume the existence of a comprehensive literature teaching the pastor how to converse with individuals about spiritual matters" (Holifield, 1983, p. 24). Accompanying this focus on remedies for sin variously defined, by the 17th century, Protestants followed the Catholic initiative, seen often in spiritual direction, of envisioning the cure of souls as a process marked by development through identifiable stages or levels. "If sin were one side of the pastoral equation, salvation was the other, and salvation was obtained through a process of development" (Holifield, 1983, p. 25).

The Modern Ambivalence About Pastoral Diagnosis

As the subtitle of Holifield's (1983) book suggests, the nature of pastoral care and pastoral diagnosis moved from themes of salvation to themes of self-realization in the 19th and 20th centuries. As theological winds shifted, as the progression of human knowledge emerged, and as social and political climates changed, pastoral diagnosis altered its language and approach. However, the process of evaluating the nature of a problem for the purpose of helping human beings navigate life's choices and make sense of life events in order to endure, thrive, or minimize the effects of human suffering remained constant.

Pastoral diagnosis in the 20th century was affected by two very different trends. On one hand, pastoral diagnosis, which had become focused on sin and salvation, gravitated toward moralistic and behavioral advice giving. This led Hiltner (1976) to remark,

> I draw the general conclusion that pastors and churches, far from having had no experience with diagnosis, have had so many bad experiences with it that, when they move out of a legalistic framework and genuinely want to help people, the last resource they are likely to look for is diagnosis. . . . We cannot, therefore resurrect pastoral diagnosis without reconstructing it. (p. 578)

On the other hand, diagnosis in the 20th century became the prerogative of the medical profession, and pastoral care became enamored with psychological ways of understanding and categorizing the human condition. Holman (1932) suggested a program of religious diagnosis that was informed by the scientific method and would guide all religious work. Draper (1965) coined the term *pastoral diagnosis*, advocating for pastors, like physicians, to offer their treatment only after correct diagnosis, yet staying away from a system of classification. Lake (1965) argued for ministers to be trained mostly in psychiatric diagnosis while adding theological analysis in what he called a "clinical theology" (Townsend, 2013). Stein (1980), commenting on the possibility that pastoral caregivers had lost their identity, said,

> One reason Freud and Jung "rescued" theology for the modern age . . . is that they gave us tools to deal with man's true iconic depths, depths that pious and banal moralisms and preaching often missed by a thinly disguised legalism and/ or grace so generally applied that it resembled a doctor lining up his pneumonic patients and spraying penicillin at them instead of injecting it in their veins. One

can scarcely fault the enthusiasms that carried pastoral psychology along when pastors began to discover the "injection methods" depth psychology and pagan doctors introduced to us. (p. 22)

But the excitement around new "injection methods" of care was tempered by a concern that the "pastoral" was being left out of pastoral diagnosis and that "diagnosis" had become overly focused on pathology as in the medical model. This led Hiltner (1976) to remark that:

a valid new pastoral diagnosis must, in addition to exploring what is uniquely pastoral, rethink the basic meaning of any diagnosis, and not permit medicine or psychiatry to dictate the definition of what is to be included in and excluded from the meaning of diagnosis. (p. 581)

This ambivalence around pastoral diagnosis was picked up by Pruyser (1976) in his classic work, *The Minister as Diagnostician*. He suggested that the hesitation to diagnose came from a history of pastoral diagnosis that tended toward advice, judgment, direction, control, and being limited to the "examination of conscience." As well, there was the antidiagnostic bias of the then popular client-centered ways of listening and the modern tendency to relinquish "diagnosis" to the medical profession. Advocating for a form of evaluation that was both pastoral and diagnostic while being sensitive to advances in modern medicine, Pruyser (1976) suggested six diagnostic variables for use in pastoral assessment: (a) the person's *awareness of the Holy* (Is anything sacred to the person or held in reverence? What is regarded as untouchable or inscrutable?); (b) the person's understanding of *Providence* (What is the "Divine Purpose" in its intention toward myself? Why am I so besieged? Why me?); (c) the person's living out of *Faith* not as a set of beliefs but in terms of engagement with life and the "courage to be"; (d) the person's understanding of *Grace or Gratefulness* (Is there an attitude of gratitude toward life? Can one accept and offer forgiveness?); (e) the person's understanding of *Repentance* (Does the person accept responsibility for their situation, neither too little or too much?); and (f) the person's understanding of *Communion* (Is the person fundamentally embedded or estranged, open to the world or encapsulated, in touch or isolated, united or separated?).

It could be argued that in his attempt to resolve the modern ambivalence around pastoral diagnosis, Pruyser (1976) followed one of the threads woven into the pre-20th-century history of pastoral diagnosis by developing diagnostic categories, just as earlier theologians had developed diagnostic categories for sin and moral behavior. Fowler (1981, 1987), on the other hand, picked up on the other thread in pre–20th-century pastoral diagnosis, seen often in spiritual direction, in which the cure of souls was marked by identifiable stages. Attempting to integrate spirituality (from any faith tradition) with modern psychological (structural–developmental) theories of human development, Fowler (1987) suggested seven stages of faith: *Primal Faith* (infancy, the incorporative self), *Intuitive–Projective Faith* (early childhood, the impulsive self), *Mythic–Literal Faith* (childhood and beyond, the imperial self), *Synthetic-Conventional Faith* (adolescence and beyond, the interpersonal self), *Individuative–Reflective Faith* (young adulthood and beyond, the institutional self), *Conjunctive Faith* (early midlife and beyond, the interindividual self), and *Universalizing Faith* (midlife and beyond, the God-grounded self). Reflecting on Fowler's work, Schneider (1986) saw it as a major advance over alternative attempts to develop a pastoral diagnostic framework because it was organized around faith itself and did not reduce faith to some other category, had a developmental approach, was multidimensional and interdisciplinary, was structural rather than thematic and universally applicable, and organized a variety of aspects of human existence into a coherent framework.

Since the classic works of Pruyser and Fowler, there have been further developments of Pruyser's work by Maloney (1988) and Brun (2005) and a lone call by Denton (2008) for research toward an Axis VI for spiritual issues, building on the multiaxial diagnostic approach of the fourth edition of the *Diagnostic and Statistical Manual of Mental Disorders* (American Psychiatric Association, 1994). Townsend (2013) further illustrates the ambivalence about pastoral diagnosis as he identifies two broad diagnostic attitudes in the pastoral counseling literature of the 1980s and 1990s: one that emphasized theological reflection to examine a client's behavior, thought, and emotion and one that emphasized more formal diagnostic practices while juxtaposing religious and psychotherapeutic language.

Overall, there remains an ambivalence about pastoral diagnosis, which raises the question of whether to diagnose or not to diagnose as pastoral counselors and caregivers. Is *pastoral diagnosis* the best way to conceptualize human distress from a pastoral counseling perspective? Townsend (2013) even suggests "that the time has come to retire the notion of a specialized 'pastoral diagnosis' in favor of 'pastoral engagement with interdisciplinary diagnostic practices'" (p. 94). Interestingly, this is happening at the same time as the means of spiritual assessment proliferate in the wider social scientific literature, emerging from research in the psychology of religion that now distinguishes spirituality from religion and embraces spirituality as an important multicultural variable (see Deal & Magyar-Russell, Chapter 8 in this volume). For someone like Rogers-Vaughn (2013), that very proliferation of spiritual assessment is indicative of a loss of a distinctive pastoral and theological approach to human distress and is, in his opinion, a capitulation to neoliberal capitalism and its focus on what can be controlled and sold in the marketplace.

PASTORAL DIAGNOSIS AS A DIAGNOSIS OF *GNOSIS*

Rather than retiring the term *pastoral diagnosis* because of the aforementioned ambivalence, perhaps it is possible to *live into* the ambivalence by retaining and further refining the possible pastoral counseling distinctives for conceptualizing and engaging human suffering suggested by the term. For instance, implicit in this ambivalence is the call in *pastoral* diagnosis to evaluate the meaning of *diagnosis* itself from a pastoral perspective and even to diagnose the meaning of *gnosis* (Greek for "knowledge"), or the ways of knowing, that are brought to the interpretive process of conceptualizing and engaging human suffering. In this case, the evaluative process would start with an evaluation of the assumptive world of the pastoral caregiver or counselor.

The Importance of Assumptions in Pastoral Diagnosis

Ramsey (1998) says, "Diagnosis is an evaluative process of discerning the nature of another's difficulty in order to provide an appropriate and restorative response. *Diagnosis is never neutral. It always reiterates the anthropological and philosophical assumptions of the practitioner* [emphasis added]. It is an inherently hermeneutical process" (p. 1). Without suggesting any pastoral diagnostic categories, Ramsey says, "Pastoral diagnosis differs from diagnosis defined by various therapeutic paradigms because of the explicit theological contexts in which the anthropological and philosophical assumptions of practitioners are rooted" (p. 1). The key to pastoral diagnosis, she says, is the formation of pastoral identity, the intentional process of developing and articulating a theological self-consciousness on the part of the practitioner and, with this pastoral identity, *attending to* the religious significance of experience.

Essential to the formation of pastoral practitioners is the very process not only of what they *attend to* but also what they *attend from*. The "wisdom" that underlies the caregiver's choice of questions for spiritual assessment, evaluation, or diagnosis; the ways of thinking about the answers to those questions; and the suggestions for intervention based on those questions are the result of the caregiver's own history, training, and assumptive world *from which he or she attends*. Those engaged in *pastoral* diagnosis, as suggested by this author, bring a distinctive assumptive world to the interpretive process of conceptualizing and engaging human distress that would allow for an understanding of *diagnosis* as "wise discernment" and would include in that discernment ways of knowing that go beyond a social scientific assumptive world.

From a Kataphatic to an Apophatic Understanding of *Gnosis*

Living in the ambivalence of *pastoral* diagnosis would mean that the pastoral counselor or caregiver brings an assumptive world to the interpretive process that allows for subject material and experience that is at its core essentially unspeakable. It is unspeakable in the same way that the Jewish tradition refrains from speaking God's sacred name. It is unspeakable in the same way that the apophatic (*via negativa*) tradition of prayer acknowledges that one can know only by entering a cloud of unknowing, resting in God beyond concepts and particular acts in an exercise of pure faith (Keating, 1994). In this case, the pastoral counselor or caregiver has an assumptive world that allows for the *diagnosis* of *gnosis*, or ways of knowing, that would also include "unknowing."

The apophatic approach (*via negativa*) to prayer differs from the kataphatic (*via positiva*) approach to prayer. The apophatic approach to prayer strips away all of the attitudes, mental images, and ideas that are considered to stand in the way of a relationship with God because God transcends all human language. It is the "unsaying" (*apophasis*) of language for God, and it leads eventually from the negation of knowing to the "negation of negation," in which the mind shifts beyond unknowing to an inexpressible, hidden union with God (Howells, 2005). Conversely, the kataphatic approach to prayer emphasizes God's immanence. *Kataphatic* means "with images," and kataphatic praying focuses on things such as the beauty of nature, the gospels, the symbols of faith in the creed, an affective relationship with Christ, and participation in the liturgical life of a faith community. A kataphatic process such as the Spiritual Exercises of Saint Ignatius leads to a progressive simplification and eventual transparency of the Christian mysteries (Ruffing, 2005). Many would argue that the fullness of prayer includes a dialectical dynamic between affirmation and negation, *via positiva* and *via negativa*.

It can be enlightening to apply this distinctive language of prayer as different approaches to *pastoral* diagnosis are considered. Just as a kataphatic (*via positiva*) approach to prayer would exercise the rational faculties enlightened by faith, a kataphatic approach to pastoral diagnosis might look to research and finding theological categories that could be a "knowing apart or through" (Greek: *dia* + *gnosis*), seeking clarity, distinction, and transparency. An apophatic approach to *pastoral* diagnosis regards diagnosis more as a wise discernment that specifically looks to the unknown and unknowable for the possibility of revelation that is beyond words (Greek: *apophasis* coming from the verb *apophemi* and meaning "saying no" or "saying negatively" or *apophasis* coming from the verb *apopaino* with overtones of "revelation"; Coakley & Stang, 2009).

Pastoral conversations incorporate a respectful attitude of "not knowing" that attempts to set aside the preconceived ideas and prejudgments of any person, problem, or worldview so that the caregiver might truly be present and listen, not unlike Nicholas of Cusa's "learned ignorance" before God (Casarella, 2009). Pastoral conversations seek to enter the unspeakable, incomprehensible darkness in a person's life that may be connected with trauma, unconscious patterns, doubts about God, or emerging thoughts still beyond words, not unlike Gregory of Nyssa's discovery that darkness could be an appropriate way to find God as he reflected on Exodus 20:21: "And the people stood afar off while Moses drew near to the thick darkness where God was" (Meredith, 1999). Pastoral conversations wait for, are not afraid of, and enter into moments of deep silence, not unlike Dionysius' plea to the Trinity to:

Guide us to that topmost height of mystic lore which exceedeth light and more thanexceedeth knowledge, where the simple, absolute, and unchangeable mysteries of heavenly Truth lie hidden in the dazzling obscurity of the secret Silence, outshining all brilliance with the intensity of their darkness. (Rolt, 1920, p. 191)

Pastoral conversations invite those who receive care into a true forgetting, forgetting their intellectual constructions of self and life, forgetting the negative self-talk, guilt, and pain, not unlike the anonymous author of *The Cloud of Unknowing* who advises those on the apophatic path to "try to destroy all understanding and awareness of anything under God and tread everything down deep under the cloud of forgetting . . . a sort of cloud of unknowing" (Walsh, 1981, pp. 82, 120). Pastoral conversations invite the ones receiving care into unspeakable moments when only love can make a connection, as the author of *The Cloud of Unknowing* says, "When we try to draw close to God, only love can take the final step, drawing us into the dark yet dazzling mystery of God" (Walsh, 1981, p. xiv), and as Teresa of Avila conveys in her reflection on Song of Songs 2:3, "It seems that while the soul is in this delight that was mentioned it feels itself totally engulfed and protected in this shadow and kind of cloud of Divinity" (Giron-Negron, 2009, p. 169).

In an apophatic approach, an essential element of *pastoral* diagnosis would include attention to whether and how the counselor *attends to* these unspeakable experiences. Do such experiences occur in the pastoral conversation? Are they noticed? Do they occur in the life of the one receiving care? Can the caregiver invite clients to *attend to* these unspeakable moments in the pastoral conversations, or in the whole of their lives, and to notice the "shifts" in their lives that result or the "revelation" that occurs out of the silence?

The most important diagnostic element then becomes the pastoral counselor's own experience and the commensurate personal *attention to* the unspeakable in his or her own life. Does the counselor have a spiritual practice that allows for the "revelation" that comes out of silence? Schlauch (1993) suggests that this attention would constitute the primary "root metaphor" informing the "clinical attitude" of the counselor. In suggesting a revisioning of *pastoral* diagnosis, he contends that "in this re-visioning pastoral diagnosis is an ongoing activity within a clinical perspective that is the expression of root-metaphors, which are enacted in a clinical attitude and made operational in the diagnostic variables" (Schlauch, 1993, p. 54). Building on the work of Shapiro (1989), Kohut (1971), and Schafer (1983), Schlauch reminds counselors that everything done in a pastoral conversation is guided by the *counselor's* attitude. The one receiving care is influenced by this attitude, and the attitude itself is learned from the counselor: "As a tacit map it guides every feature of the clinician's activities. As a map that the client may (will) internalize, at least in part, it will come to influence many features of the client's activities" (Schlauch, 1993, p. 59).

Polanyi (1974, 1983) refers to this feature as the "tacit dimension" in which knowledge is transmitted tacitly from one generation to another. What is passed on tacitly is that which has come to "indwell," or has been "interiorized," in the life of the teacher or, in this case, the pastoral counselor. The teacher *attends from* this "indwelling" in any focused *attention to* the process. From an apophatic vantage, it is this internalized experience of the unknowable and unspeakable that the caregiver *attends from*, which allows the caregiver to *attend to* these unspeakable experiences in the lives of the ones receiving care. A nontheistic tradition might characterize this concept similarly:

> From the standpoint of Zen, the experience is the essential content of Buddhism, and the verbal doctrine is quite secondary to the wordless transmission of the experience itself from generation to generation. . . . Yet the actual content of the experience was never and could never be put into words. For words are the flames of *maya*, the meshes of its net, and the experience is of the water which slips through. (Watts, 1957, pp. 54–55)

A Kataphatic and Apophatic Interplay

A kataphatic and apophatic interplay is similar to the process that emerges from considerations of power and privilege. Bidwell (2004) invites spiritual directors into a self-emptying, not-knowing approach that requires a turn to God in humility with a contemplative attitude and a replacing of linear, logical thinking with "heart" knowledge. Such an attitude enables spiritual directors to risk suspending what they think they know in order to understand fully the experience of the directee. "Then, listening to God through the heart, the practitioner of brief spiritual direction turns to *appropriate knowing* to evaluate what the directee has said about God against what is known about God through Scripture, tradition, experience, and reason" (p. 24). The "heart" approach, grounded in unknowing and what is known through scripture, tradition, experience, and reason, replicates this interplay. Similarly, Townsend (2009) encourages a "not knowing" form of empathy that becomes a "qualified 'not knowing' that rejects the privileged position of the therapeutic 'expert' but takes seriously mutual exploration of larger formative cultural, racial ethnic, gender, and class concerns" (p. 112).

At some level, this call to "interplay" catches what Hunter (2006) identified as "the deepest theological issue confronting liberal pastoral theology today . . . to bring these two complementary understandings of God, and all that is related to them in terms of ministry theory and practice, back into a proper unity" (p. 7). Here, Hunter was referring to the thinking that emphasizes the immanence of God in the world and the thinking that emphasizes the transcendence of God separate from the world and humans. By extraction, Hunter's point suggests an interplay between the kataphatic and the apophatic.

Applying these examples specifically to the issue of *pastoral* diagnosis suggests the importance for counselors in following a kataphatic approach to know and understand the categories associated with the levels of faith development, the identification of ways of being religious, ways of praying, or categories of virtues and vices emerging out of scripture and tradition. In a kataphatic approach, the pastoral counselor would also want to know categories and distinctions emerging from the social scientific research on spiritual assessment mentioned earlier in this chapter (see also Deal & Magyar-Russell, Chapter 8 in this volume) and the diagnostic categories of mental health disorders such as those found in the fifth edition of the *Diagnostic and Statistical Manual of Mental Disorders* (*DSM-5*; American Psychiatric Association, 2013). This way of knowing that is a "knowing apart" with distinctions and clarifications based on evidence-based research is an important part of the pastoral counselor's repertoire of understanding and is a part of what Townsend (2013) means by "pastoral engagement with interdisciplinary diagnostic practices" (p. 94).

However, *pastoral* diagnosis would also allow for other ways of knowing and even ways of not knowing. Therefore, simultaneous with any kataphatic understanding, pastoral counselors following an apophatic approach could recognize and experience the suspension of all knowledge and would be willing to enter the "negation of negation." And then, *attending from* the wordless, unknowable, unspeakable experience that is internalized through an ongoing contemplative practice in his or her life, the counselor can be present in any context of pastoral conversation and can use any form of spiritual assessment discerned with wisdom to *attend to* the "revelation" that will come out of silence. This interplay between the kataphatic and the apophatic ways of pastoral diagnosis will maintain a certain ambivalent quality of pastoral diagnosis, being beyond words and essential to the process. It will function similarly to the necessary interplay of kataphatic and apophatic practices in contemplative prayer (Keating, 1994).

In its call to evaluate the assumptive world of the clinician and in its ability to call on ways of knowing and unknowing in the evaluative process of human distress, *pastoral* diagnosis has the ability to evaluate *gnosis* (any particular way of knowing) itself and avoids the limitation of forcing all *diagnosis* onto the Procrustean bed of empiricism and social science. In so doing, those practicing *pastoral* diagnosis avoid the danger of becoming mental and spiritual technicians who have been born on that Procrustean bed. Rather, they are formed as wise and discerning guides with a wider understanding of how to help human beings navigate life's choices and make sense of life events in order to endure, thrive, or minimize the effects of human suffering.

MOVING BEYOND CONCEPTUALIZATION TO ENGAGING EXPERIENCE

Implicit in *pastoral* diagnosis is not only a way of conceptualizing human distress but also a way of engaging human distress with a particular focus on experience. This is inclusive of oft-repeated findings beginning with Frank (1961) that it is the nature of the relationship more than any particular theoretical approach that contributes to improvement in counseling (Sparks, Duncan, Cohen, & Antonuccio, 2010). The very word *pastoral* is indicative of a relational experience in counseling that is nurturing (from *pascere*, "to feed, to shepherd") with spiritual overtones of being a shepherd of souls.

Among other things, the implication here is that this is more than a cognitive experience. As Panksepp and Biven (2012) point out, much of psychotherapy research and practice deals with secondary and tertiary processes of the brain that are largely cognitive, whereas the primary, affective consciousness of the brain affected by experience is less researched and less targeted in counseling. They conclude that affects, not cognitions, are the very base of the psychological being. They say, "We make the case for the conclusion that raw affective feelings lie at the primordial foundation of the mental apparatus—that they are the primal biological substrates of a core-SELF—perhaps the neural foundation of the concept of the 'soul'" (Panksepp & Biven, 2012, p. 46).

Only certain types of communal, social, and relational experiences can effect change at this primordial foundation of the mental apparatus. "When affects maintain the upper hand, the talking cure is apt to fail because the interpretive method, the cardinal psychotherapeutic tool, can frequently be ineffective in the face of our primal passions" (Panksepp & Biven, 2012, p. xviii). The *pastoral* experience implied in the process of *pastoral* diagnosis with its inclusion of various ways of knowing engages these primary, raw, affective aspects of "core-consciousness" (Panksepp & Bivens, 2012, p. 389) that often underlie human distress.

This *pastoral* experience with its evaluation of ways of knowing is also similar to non-Western approaches to psychology that are concerned less with the content of consciousness and more with "consciousness itself" (Childs, 2011, p. 290) and the "stance" or "presence" in which consciousness itself is experienced. Childs (2011) says,

> Mindfulness can first offer awareness of lifeworld and then, by a further refinement, a more radical stance in which consciousness and world are not divided. The establishment of mindfulness in the first sense can be seen as the therapeutic agent while cultivation of presence goes further to offer the foundation of the lifeworld to psychological investigation. (p. 292)

Childs (2011) further states that clinicians are called in clinical practice to the "experience of presence" and to "maintain attention, to bear affect, to trust intuitions of the client's mind and 'not to know'" (p. 294) with an extension of psychology into the "informal" where it is "open to the less rational aspects of experience, to unjustified and intuitive knowledge" (p. 296). This is another way from a non-Western perspective to describe the *pastoral* experience of presence, which comes from the indwelling of knowing and unknowing in the clinician and is tacitly present and communicated to the other in a counseling or caregiving situation.

Similarly, the *pastoral* experience included in *pastoral* diagnosis is inclusive of a relational engagement described by Miller (2011) in her suggestions for spiritual awareness in psychotherapy:

> *Spiritual Awareness* is attunement with a loving and guiding universe around us, in us, and through us. Spiritual awareness in psychotherapy focuses on our human dialogue with the universe in daily living. Developing our dialogue with the universe is a form of healing and growth understood within a postmaterialist view of psychology, namely, that consciousness exists in states other than matter and that there exists a teleological process that is guided by the source. . . . Our daily-lived dialogue with the universe evolves through direct experience such that psychotherapists must engage their own spiritual path if they are to accompany clients through a process of spiritual awareness. (p. 325)

The *pastoral* experience implicit in the process of *pastoral* diagnosis is certainly inclusive of this "postmaterialistic" view where the lived spiritual experience of the unspeakable and unknowable through the spiritual practice of the clinician or caregiver becomes available tacitly and directly in the *pastoral* engagement that waits for "revelation" to come out of silence. In this process, a new "lived experience" is created for both the client and the counselor.

Perhaps unique to the *pastoral* experience of engagement called for in the process of *pastoral* diagnosis is the necessity for the inclusion of social justice in which there is as much a diagnosis of the culture and the context as there is of the presenting problems of the individual. On one hand, as suggested by Townsend (2013), this includes an awareness of power and privilege embedded in any attempt at diagnosing an individual in which the very categories of diagnosis have been culturally constructed by those in power (whether religious or secular). This is another way in which *pastoral* diagnosis is called to give a diagnosis of the ways of *gnosis*/knowing embedded in the culture and to do so from the perspective of justice.

On the other hand, as suggested by Rogers-Vaughn (2013) and others, the justice component of the *pastoral* experience involves the raising of a prophetic critique in society. In the *pastoral* experience implicit in *pastoral* diagnosis, not only is there a "presence" that comes from the spiritual practice of the counselor who has learned to dwell in unspeakable silence, but also there is a "presence" from the lived experience of the counselor who has named and given voice to the unspeakable injustice embedded in society. Not only must there be a practice of stillness in the life of the pastoral counselor or caregiver, but there must also be the practice of advocacy on behalf of the poor whose condition of poverty contributes to their suffering and to mental dysphoria that is then given a diagnosis by those in power. Such advocacy would also include giving voice to unspeakable injustice on behalf of those who are excluded from or mistreated in a broken and unjust health care system. This advocacy work outside of the counseling room becomes a part of the *pastoral* presence inside the counseling room, as does the nature of fee setting and choice of clients who are seen, which are embedded in the institutional structures of the pastoral counseling practice itself. The inclusion of justice in the process of *pastoral* diagnosis allows for a *pastoral* experience in which the ancient prophetic announcements of hearing the cry of the enslaved, of bringing comfort to the marginalized, of bringing light into darkness, of bringing love to the unlovable still reverberate at many levels and, when truly *experienced*, provide a distinctive antidote to human suffering.

REFLECTION QUESTIONS

1. What is the chapter's position regarding pastoral diagnosis? How does this relate to the way diagnosis was taught in your own counselor education and training?
2. Describe in your own words the difference(s) between the kataphatic and apophatic approaches to diagnosis. Are these approaches in conflict with one another? How might they be used together?
3. Do any of your spiritual practices or disciplines reflect the apophatic tradition? How does this inform your practice as a pastoral counselor at present or in the future?
4. What part does the chapter suggest that social justice plays within the context of pastoral diagnosis? What are your reactions to this aspect of the pastoral counseling role?

REFERENCES

American Psychiatric Association. (1994). *Diagnostic and statistical manual of mental disorders* (4th ed.). Washington, DC: American Psychiatric Press.

American Psychiatric Association. (2013). *Diagnostic and statistical manual of mental disorders* (5th ed.). Arlington, VA: American Psychiatric Press.

Bidwell, D. R. (2004). *Short term spiritual guidance.* Minneapolis, MN: Fortress.

Brun, W. (2005). A proposed diagnostic schema for religious/spiritual concerns. *Journal of Pastoral Care and Counseling, 59*(5), 425–440. Retrieved from www.jpcp.org/jpcc.htm

Casarella, P. (2009). Cusanus on Dionysius: The turn to speculative theology. In S. Coakley & C. M. Stang (Eds.), *Rethinking Dionysius the Areopagite* (pp. 137–148). Chichester, UK: Wiley-Blackwell.

Childs, D. (2011). Mindfulness and clinical psychology. *Psychology and Psychotherapy: Theory, Research and Practice, 84,* 288–298. doi:10.1348/147608310X530048

Coakley, S., & Stang, C. M. (Eds.). (2009). *Rethinking Dionysius the Areopagite.* Chichester, UK: Wiley-Blackwell.

Denton, D. (2008). *Naming the pain and guiding the care: The central tasks of diagnosis.* Lanham, MD: University Press of America.

Draper, E. (1965). *Psychiatry and pastoral care.* Englewood Cliffs, NJ: Prentice Hall.

Fowler, J. (1981). *Stages of faith: The psychology of human development and the quest for meaning.* San Francisco, CA: Harper & Row.

Fowler, J. (1987). *Faith development and pastoral care.* Philadelphia, PA: Fortress.

Frank, J. D. (1961). *Persuasion and healing.* Baltimore, MD: The Johns Hopkins University Press.

Giron-Negron, L. M. (2009). Dionysian thought in sixteenth-century Spanish mystical theology. In S. Coakley & C. M. Stang (Eds.), *Rethinking Dionysius the Areopagite* (pp. 163–176). Chichester, UK: Wiley-Blackwell.

Hiltner, S. (1976). Toward autonomous pastoral diagnosis. *Bulletin of the Menninger Clinic, 40*(5), 573–592. Retrieved from menningerclinic.com/research/bulletin

Holifield, B. (1983). *A history of pastoral care in America: From salvation to self-realization.* Nashville, TN: Abingdon.

Holman, C. T. (1932). *The cure of souls.* Chicago, IL: University of Chicago Press.

Howells, E. (2005). Apophatic spirituality. In P. Sheldrake (Ed.), *The new Westminster dictionary of Christian spirituality* (pp. 117–119). Louisville, KY: Westminster John Knox Press.

Hunter, R. (2006). Pastoral theology: Historical perspectives and future agendas. *Journal of Pastoral Theology, 16*(1), 7–30. Retrieved from spt-jpt.org/index.php/jpth/index

Keating, T. (1994). *Intimacy with God.* New York, NY: Crossroad.

Kohut, H. (1971). *The analysis of the self.* Madison, CT: International Universities Press.

Lake, F. (1965). *Clinical theology: A theological and psychiatric basis to clinical pastoral care.* London, UK: Darton, Longman, & Todd.

Maloney, N. (1988). The clinical assessment of optimal religious functioning. *Review of Religious Research, 30*(1), 3–19. doi:10.2307/3511836

Meredith, A. (1999). *Gregory of Nyssa.* New York, NY: Routledge.

Miller, L. (2011). An experiential approach for exploring spirituality. In J. D. Aten, M. R. McMinn, & E. L. Worthington (Eds.), *Spiritually oriented interventions for counseling and psychotherapy* (pp. 325–343). Washington, DC: American Psychological Association.

Panksepp, J., & Biven, L. (2012). *The archaeology of mind.* New York, NY: W. W. Norton.

Polanyi, M. (1974). *Personal knowledge.* Chicago, IL: University of Chicago Press.

Polanyi, M. (1983). *The tacit dimension.* Gloucester, MA: Peter Smith.

Pruyser, P. (1976). *The minister as diagnostician.* Philadelphia, PA: Westminster.

Ramsey, N. (1998). *Pastoral diagnosis: A resource for ministries of care and counseling.* Minneapolis, MN: Fortress.

Rogers-Vaughn, B. (2013). Pastoral counseling in the neoliberal age: Hello best practices, goodbye theology. *Sacred Spaces: The e-Journal of the American Association of Pastoral Counselors, 5,* 5–45. Retrieved from http://www.aapc.org/media/127298/2_rogers_vaughn

Rolt, C. E. (Ed.). (1920). *Dionysius the Areopagite: On the divine names and the mystical theology.* Whitefish, MT: Kessinger.

Ruffing, J. (2005). Kataphatic spirituality. In P. Sheldrake (Ed.), *The new Westminster dictionary of Christian spirituality* (pp. 393–394). Louisville, KY: Westminster John Knox Press.

Schafer, R. (1983). *The analytic attitude.* New York, NY: Basic Books.

Schlauch, C. (1993). Re-visioning pastoral diagnosis. In R. Wicks & R. Parsons (Eds.), *Clinical handbook of pastoral counseling* (Vol. 2, pp. 51–101). Mahwah, NJ: Paulist Press.

Schneider, C. (1986). Faith development and pastoral diagnosis. In C. Dykstra & S. Parks (Eds.), *Faith development and Fowler* (pp. 221–250). Birmingham, AL: Religious Education Press.

Shapiro, D. (1989). *Psychotherapy of neurotic character.* New York, NY: Basic Books.

Smart, N. (2000). *Worldviews: Crosscultural explorations of human beliefs* (3rd ed.). Englewood Cliffs, NJ: Prentice Hall.

Sparks, J. A., Duncan, E. A., Cohen, D., & Antonuccio, D. O. (2010). *The heart and soul of change* (2nd ed.). Washington, DC: American Psychological Association.

Stein, E. (1980). Reactions to Dr. Oden's "Recovering lost identity." *Journal of Pastoral Care, 34*(1), 20–23. Retrieved from www.jpcp.org/jpcc.htm

Townsend, L. (2009). *Introduction to pastoral counseling.* Nashville, TN: Abingdon.

Townsend, L. (2013). Best practices: Re-thinking pastoral diagnosis. *Sacred Spaces: The e- Journal of the American Association of Pastoral Counselors, 5,* 66–101. Retrieved from http://www.aapc .org/media/127304/4_townsendpastc

Walsh, J. (Ed.). (1981). *The cloud of unknowing.* Mahwah, NJ: Paulist Press.

Watts, A. (1957). *The way of Zen.* New York, NY: Mentor Books.

RELIGIOUS AND SPIRITUAL ASSESSMENT IN PASTORAL COUNSELING

With so many related and overlapping approaches to assessing contemporary religious and spiritual lives—psychology of religion and spirituality, spiritual direction, spiritually oriented psychotherapy, spiritually integrated psychotherapy, pastoral psychology, pastoral care, Jungian psychotherapy—what is unique to pastoral counseling, and how might it collaborate with other spiritually minded disciplines? Religious and spiritual assessment within pastoral counseling is an interdisciplinary practice insofar as it understands the human being from both theological and psychological traditions (Doehring, 2009; Dueck & Reimer, 2009; Ramsay, 1998; Townsend, 2006; van Deusen Hunsinger, 1995). Practices of assessment are always linked to methods of integration. In short, how and which disciplines we integrate drive how we assess. This chapter explores pastoral counseling assessment through an integrated interdisciplinary framework.

AN INTEGRATED INTERDISCIPLINARY FRAMEWORK

The Dimensions of Assessment

Although this chapter is located in a pastoral counseling text, the hope is that its use will extend across professionals from the American Association of Pastoral Counselors (AAPC) to the American Psychological Association (APA). Allied mental health disciplines assess religiousness and spirituality in similar and unique ways, each with its own strengths. One way to draw on the strengths of the respective guilds is through a comprehensive framework of tacit, implicit, and explicit dimensions of assessment. Each dimension approaches religiousness and spirituality in unique ways, and differential allied disciplines are inclined to assess using particular dimensions. For example, the primary aim of the tacit dimension of assessment is to identify the theological and philosophical lenses through which pastoral counselors understand the sacred narrative of their clients (Doehring, 2009; Townsend, 2006). As such, pastoral theology plays a central role in tacit assessment. The primary aim of the implicit dimension is to understand the psychospiritual themes operating in the client's everyday lived experience (Pargament, 2007). Religious and theological studies feature prominently in the implicit assessment process. Last, the explicit dimension of assessment focuses on how religiousness and spirituality contribute to the overall psychological health and unhealth of the client (Pargament, 2007). Here, the psychology of religion and spirituality is the vital contributing discipline. In sum, the dimensions of assessment are similar insofar as they share a common interest in religiousness and spirituality and are different in terms of the extent to which they draw on theological and psychological understandings.

The benefits of applying this three-dimensional, interdisciplinary, and integrated framework are that it encourages dialogue and collaboration among allied mental health disciplines; brings a trifocal lens of theological, phenomenological, and psychological understanding to the assessment of religiousness and spirituality; and prepares pastoral counselors to skillfully and sensitively assess a plurality of religious and spiritual forms populating the diverse American landscape. Each dimension brings a distinct interpretive framework to the assessment process. Subsequently, each dimension approaches the client's religious and/or spiritual life with a different question. For example, the tacit dimension asks, "How does my own unspoken theological formation inform the assumptions through which I define what it means to be religiously and spiritually whole?" The implicit dimension asks, "In what way(s) does the client experience psychospiritual themes associated with the sacred or sacredness in his or her everyday life?" Last, the explicit dimension asks, "In what ways do religiousness and spirituality, as psychological constructs alongside other biopsychosocial–cultural domains, contribute to the health and unhealth of the human person?" Although the importance of each dimension may vary by client, taking a comprehensive approach, attuned to the complex layers of the religious and spiritual life, helps ensure ethical and competent assessment. Please see Table 8.1 for an overview of criteria discussed in this framework.

Statement of Positionality

One way of respecting diversity is by acknowledging one's positionality. Coming from the qualitative traditions, positionality refers to the worldview, judgments, biases, and cultural backgrounds of the researchers (Guba & Lincoln, 2005). Positionality

TABLE 8.1 Summary of the Major Criteria for the Three Dimensions of Religious and Spiritual Assessment

DIMENSION	TACIT	IMPLICIT	EXPLICIT
Primary aim	Developing a pastoral identity; encounter mystery of the other	Understanding psychospiritual themes in lived experience	Assessment of religious and spiritual constructs
Primary focus of assessment	Self and client	Client	Client
Primary interpretive discipline	Pastoral theology	Religious and theological studies	Psychology of religion and spirituality
Primary hermeneutic	Theological formation	Phenomenological	Psychological universals
Method of integration	Bilingual formation of theology and psychology: allows for critical correlation	Correlates religious studies and psychology on the psychospiritual themes	Correlates religious and spiritual constructs with psychological theory of health and unhealth

comprises the contingent qualities of our being through which we apprehend and give value to our world.

The positionality through which I, Paul Deal, come to this chapter is as a White, middle-class man. I was raised in New England in a Reformed Presbyterian Christian tradition. Because my undergraduate degree was at a Christian liberal arts institution, my BA in psychology was integrated with theological and philosophical studies. During my undergraduate education, I also studied in two other educational settings whose diversity and plurality gave me the opportunity to grapple with the implicit values of my assumptive world. I have an MS/PhD from an ecumenical pastoral counseling program located in a Jesuit university, where I was formed by professors from various educational backgrounds, ranging from pastoral counseling and social work to clinical, personality, and educational psychology. Several of my professors also had advanced degrees in theology or were ordained. My worldview might be categorized as a form of postmodern critical realism influenced by phenomenological hermeneutics.

The positionality through which I, Gina Magyar-Russell, come to this chapter is as a White, middle-class woman. I was raised in the Midwestern United States in the Roman Catholic tradition. My undergraduate degree in psychology and history was from a large, state university noted for its liberal philosophical and political leanings. My master's and doctoral degrees in clinical psychology were also earned from a state university in the Midwest. My training was in an APA–approved clinical psychology program, and my mentor was a renowned psychologist of religion and spirituality. None of my professors had advanced degrees in theology, nor were they ordained clergy. My worldview might be categorized as a form of postmodern critical realism in which the intersection among religion, spirituality, and the health sciences holds promise for revealing human truths.

The Tacit Dimension

The parallel to owning one's positionality in the context of pastoral assessment brings us to the first major dimension of assessing the religious and spiritual lives of our clients—the tacit dimension. There are two critical aspects of tacit assessment. The first is that tacit assessment is preconscious and always occurring, which suggests that practicing ethically means first recognizing and becoming critically conscious of our own theological assumptions. The second key component is that the tacit assessment process is part of pastoral identity formation, which is aided by recognizing how we are socioculturally located (Townsend, 2011) and moving from theological naïveté to theological sophistication (Doehring, 2009). Ultimately, this critical focus on the self is about learning how to be present and encounter the mystery of the other, without projecting and inflicting our own unresolved faith difficulties on those seeking care. Of the three dimensions of assessment, the tacit most clearly affirms the value of understanding and reflecting on religious and spiritual lives through a theological perspective (American Association of Pastoral Counselors, 1986, p. I-1). The theologically reflective counselor is sensitive to the ways sacred narratives enact powerful sources of meaning and identity for the client.

Although best practices frequently refer to what we actively do to assess religiousness and spirituality while in session, the tacit dimension hones in on the assumptions we bring *into* session. In other words, tacit assessment concentrates on uncovering what *we do through*. Competent assessment begins with comprehensive self-assessment of our ways of being religious and spiritual. In sum, the important point is that the tacit dwells at the level of *being*:

> In the end, men [*sic*] choose between ultimate values; they choose as they do, because their life and thought are determined by fundamental moral categories and concepts that are, at any rate over large stretches of time and space, a part of their being and thought and sense of their own identity. (Berlin, 1969, pp. 171–172)

This speaks to the stuff of the tacit dimension. It is the way our being is formed and how we encounter the world. It is the way the spirit inhabits us as people and how it shapes, transforms, and sanctifies what we do—including spiritual assessment. The tacit highlights that "much of what we accept as normative is deeply anchored in our past and identity" (Taylor, 2007, p. 582).

The tacit dimension of assessment requires one to make a hermeneutic turn toward unearthing what is difficult to speak because it dwells within the preconscious assumptions embedded within our own worldview. In this sense, the tacit is both partially revealed and concealed in the words and practices used for assessment. For example, a counselor's preferred use of a God-image inventory (Christian, theistic, religious, individual/personal relationship, transcendent, belief oriented) as opposed to the Daily Spiritual Experience Scale (spiritual, theistic and nontheistic, immanent, experience oriented; Underwood & Teresi, 2001) may reveal the values or assumptions of the counselor's tacitly held theological and philosophical worldview, while inadvertently obscuring other representations of the sacred. Identifying these tacit assumptions is a prerequisite for offering a space of genuine curiosity and being able to encounter the mystery of the client's world.

Borrowing from Polanyi (2009), Rodgerson (2012) refers to the tacit dimension as the ways of knowing, *through* which and *from* which the pastoral caregiver attends to and assesses the spiritual and religious themes of the client's narrative. In other words, the ways through which knowing occurs—prejudgments and presuppositions, tradition knowledge, inherited practices—coalesce into a particular way of being present with the client. Some questions raised by the tacit dimension of assessment are, "To what extent can we codify the traditioned knowledge and inherited practices we bring into session?" and "How do we discern between what is yet to be made explicit and the unknowing that is truly beyond words?" There are no easy answers to these questions. Learning to attend to the tacit is an evolving process and practice that is both at the heart of the formation of pastoral identities and connected to the overall comprehensive quality of our conceptualization, assessment, and diagnosis of religion and spirituality in psychotherapy. Attention to the following two topics is a step toward making the tacit more explicit.

Problem of Context-Independent Pastoral Identities

Context-independent pastoral identities tend to assume that one particular way of being spiritual and religious is sufficient for all people, in all times, and in all places. They tend to assume that there is one way of being pastoral. The problem of context-independent pastoral identities is that they tend to overlook the question of "assessment by whom and from where?" Without attention to the tacit dimension, a specific type of pastoral identity risks masquerading as a view free from all instantiating contexts and values. The problem of assuming a context-independent pastoral identity manifests when a particular approach is assumed to be universally applicable (Lee,

2010). When treated as such, the tacit assumptions of the assessing counselor remain behind a veil of ignorance, above reproach, and beyond contestability. Context independence promotes blindness to religious and spiritual diversity.

Overcoming context independence means recognizing that the choice of where and with whom to train is to commit to a "particular philosophy of formation guided by specific models of therapy and theological reflection" (Townsend, 2011, p. 7). Consequently, all formational processes enact a system of socially located and culturally constructed meanings. Embedded in every formational program is a tradition of implied values and prejudgments about human wholeness and what makes for a good life. In selecting a program for study, knowingly or not, the pastoral counselor is demonstrating a "willingness to apprentice oneself to a craft and submit oneself to the wisdom and authority of a master teacher who embodies the tradition" (Dueck & Reimer, 2009, p. 153). The tacit dimension of assessment protects against the dogma and ignorance of context-independent pastoral identities by encouraging reflexivity and dialogue in master and apprentice alike. Bypassing this crucial step increases the chance of theological projection and countertransference seeping into the assessment process, thereby contaminating the potential for authentically encountering the client's world.

From Context Independent to Socioculturally Located

Each pastoral identity is formed within a particular sociocultural context. Having a well-informed identity means cultivating awareness of the specific tradition and assumptions of the context through which one was formed. It means striving to balance the guiding insights that traditions provide about human suffering and flourishing with the humility to extend a space wherein the uniquely traditioned resources of the client's worldview may emerge. These are formidable challenges for the pastoral counselor.

Pastoral counseling is characterized by the formational experience of developing an identity capable of practicing spiritually sensitive and theologically integrated assessment. However much identity may be central to formation, its meanings are as subjective and multiple as the contexts in which these identities are formed. Therefore, Townsend (2011) recommends that pastoral counselors engage the interdisciplinary discourse as a way to socially and culturally locate pastoral identities in "local contexts, solidify what 'pastoral' means in that location, and clarify how 'identity' is expressed through specific practices" (p. 12). If we aspire to move from context-independent to socioculturally located pastoral identities, then familiarity with historical, sociological, and religious studies can help trace and reveal the ways our unique identities are "like all others, like some others, and like no others" (Cooper-White, 2011, p. 96). In this sense, the formation of a pastoral identity is also a pathway to appreciate new theological vistas, including those perceived as misguided or previously stigmatized.

From Theological Naïveté to Sophistication

According to Doehring (2009), theological education and the ongoing process of spiritual formation help the pastoral counselor develop beyond theological naïveté toward theological sophistication. Part of this process involves being held accountable to the spiritual, religious, and theological assumptions that are implicit in all training programs. Like a code of ethics, theological traditions prescribe standards of excellence against which we can weigh, critically argue, and consciously engage issues ranging from theological anthropology to ethics to teleology.

According to Cooper-White (2011), pastoral assessment is "grounded in theological training of its practitioners," which introduces the unique element of theological reflection to pastoral assessment (p. 98). Theologically reflective pastoral counselors discern and use first-order (premodern), second-order (modern), and third-order (postmodern) religious and theological languages as part of assessment (Doehring, 2009). First-order languages address the theologies in which we are embedded and therefore are disposed to speak spontaneously and in largely precritical ways. For instance, instinctively, we draw on first-order languages to make sense of crisis. Second-order languages make our embedded theologies explicit and develop them through formal and informal theological education. Frequently, the use of second-order languages is precipitated by challenges posed by theodicy, postmodernism, science, and religious pluralism. In a self-authoring culture, the spiritual seeking that accompanies second-order reflection is encouraged, if not expected. Failing to engage in second-order reflection diminishes the ability to adequately assess and support the spiritual struggles that may arise with individuation. Third-order reflection focuses on the methods pastoral counselors are trained to use to integrate psychology and theology in spiritual assessment.

As a last step, Doehring (2009) also raises the important issue of competently assessing the religious and spiritual worlds of those from other traditions, where we may be prone to religious collusion, collision, or collaboration (Jordan, 1986). Here again, overcoming naïveté means critically and consciously owning our paradigms for theological comparison (theological, universal, phenomenological), discerning the context in which each comparison approach is appropriate, and understanding the associated risks and benefits of each—for example, minimizing religious difference versus finding common ground versus encountering the nuances of the client's religious world. In sum, the deconstructive and contextualizing processes of the tacit dimension—reflection, formation, location, sophistication — are a means to consciously recognize and critically evaluate the theological and philosophical inheritance of one's assumptive world. If the adage that clinicians are their own best tool is true, then the task for every pastoral counselor is to craft a heuristic for comprehensive assessment not only of the client but also for oneself.

Pastoral Assessment: Understanding Religiousness and Spirituality as Sacred Narratives

As noted earlier, theologically informed pastoral assessment involves the contextualizing process of critically and consciously owning one's theological tradition. Going through this individuation process and forming a pastoral identity—via the owning of social location (Townsend, 2006) and becoming theologically sophisticated (Doehring, 2009)—permits a more reflexive relationship to theological assumptions, therefore increasing the ability to recognize the essential differences between our own and our clients' theological worlds. The other unique quality of pastoral assessment to be taken up here involves understanding religiousness and spirituality as sacred narratives.

From the perspective of sacred narratives, religiousness and spirituality are not something one has or is but ways of being through which the world is apprehended and encountered. The truth value of sacred narratives is not restricted to the values of modernism, such as objective facts and quantifiable knowledge. On the contrary, the narrative perspective understands them as a coherent body of integrated meanings able to illuminate proverbial existential and cosmological questions, such as "Who are we?" "Why are we here?" "From where do we come?" and "How should we live?"

Because every story carries an ethos, sacred narratives bring immense resources to nurture and sustain meaning through the practices, experiences, relationships, coping methods, knowledge, and strivings they prescribe.

Understanding religiousness and spirituality as a sacred narrative is a unique quality of pastoral assessment and enormously advantageous for understanding the religious and spiritual worlds in which clients dwell. Pastoral assessment is unique not only because of formational theological training but because many pastoral counselors have themselves dwelt or dwell in deeply religious worlds—granting the distinct advantage of empathic attunement (*verstehen*) to the particular nuances of sacred narratives. For example, the struggles of reconciling what it means for a client to "be in the world, but not of the world" or follow Christ's example so that they might "have life, and have it abundantly" (John 10:10 New Revised Standard Version) or "know that all things work together for good for those who love God" (Romans 8:28 New Revised Standard Version) manifest in distinct forms from within a given context. An intimate familiarity with the logic and values informing sacred narratives provides a window of understanding into the benefits and detriments that accompany living a sacred narrative in the modern world.

From the perspective of a sacred narrative, the cravings and destructive impulses that drive so many problem behaviors, from personal battles with alcohol or food to cultural patterns of consumerism, are recast as holy desire. This need not negate the science of neurochemistry. Rather, pastoral assessment takes a form of suffering commonly called addiction and imbues it with additional meanings—spiritual restlessness (Augustine, 1998), the disordering of desires (Ignatius, 1548/1964), being ensnared by hungry ghosts (Buddhism), spiritual thirst for wholeness (Jung, 1961)—capable of casting this diagnosis in a fresh light with new possibilities for healing and wholeness. Being equipped with two lenses allows the pastoral counselor not only to move back and forth between the psychological and theological dimensions of the client's world but to bring them to bear on one another.

The pastoral application of theological reflection situates human desire within a narrative of self-transcendence able to enact a telos suggesting that the fulfillment of human desire depends on the reshaping (Dueck & Reimer, 2009) and healing (Farley, 2005) of desire. The assumption here is that normative constructions of health and flourishing in psychological discourses need theological narratives to actualize fully the moral and ethical dimensions of psychotherapy (Murphy, 2005). Interpreting the human experience through sacred narratives does not give license to impose our sacred narratives or even to suppose we possess wisdom enough to deem the best course of action for our clients. What the pastoral assessment of sacred narratives does, however, is provide a lens able to access respectfully some of the client's most prescriptive and life-sustaining sources of meaning.

Sacred narratives open the assessment process to questions of who and what kind of creature the human being is in light of being created in the image of a transcendent, yet immanent, sacred in whom we live and move and have our being. In addition, they expand a teleology of health and well-being to include wholeness, relational hope, sacrifice, forgiveness, transformation, and a mature capacity for love—all of which provide meaning to integrate and transcend suffering. Symptoms of psychological pathology are weighed against the possibility of a spiritual suffering or holy disease indicating the growing pains of maturing one's worldview with fear and trembling. Through this lens, the language of diagnostic categories reified in the psychopathology bible of the *Diagnostic and Statistical Manual of Mental Disorders* (DSM-5; American Psychiatric Association, 2013) takes on the complexity of a multilayered understanding of the human being.

Reenvisioning Sociocultural Norms

Within the context of the religious and spiritual assessment process, sacred narratives also provide a way to evaluate and reenvision the normative values of American culture used to define psychological health. For example, sacred narratives provide a lens to recognize and critique the ways the subjective turn and expressive individualism in modern culture have also, at least in part, imbued our ways of being spiritual and religious. Increasingly, these phenomena require shopping the spiritual marketplace, whether for individual practices or a spiritual community, for a fit that is comfortable and costs little in terms of accommodating one's personal values. This means that the self is a primary source of authority and, as such, is responsible to seek out and construct a uniquely self-styled narrative of meaning. This stands in stark contrast to the religious imperative to structure our lives in obedience to a self-transcending narrative and order. Nonetheless, finding and expressing a unique self increasingly equates with authenticity in American culture (Taylor, 2007). The task of understanding the growing population of varied religious and spiritual manifestations leads to the dimension of implicit assessment.

Implicit Assessment: Understanding Psychospiritual Themes in Lived Experience

In addition to the tacit dimension of spiritual and religious assessment, best practices also include attention to the implicit dimension. Implicit approaches to spiritual assessment "refer to a more covert approach that does not initiate the discussion of religious or spiritual issues and does not openly, directly, or systematically use spiritual resources" (Tan, 1996, p. 368). The advantage of the implicit approach is its strength in assessing those less versed or less comfortable with explicitly religious or spiritual language. If Pargament (2007) is correct in observing that "many people find it increasingly difficult to locate the sacred in their lives" (p. 245), pastoral counselors will find implicit assessment essential. For many clients, the search for meaning and significance may not yet, or ever, be consciously recognized as religious or spiritual. Moreover, strivings and ultimate concerns are often hidden and embedded in forms that fall beyond the purview of religion traditionally defined. In light of this, Townsend (2009) implores pastoral counselors to develop "skills that respond to ultimate concerns that are expressed implicitly through problems in living" (p. 5).

Compared to the hermeneutic turn of the tacit dimension, the implicit dimension of spiritual and religious assessment makes a decidedly phenomenological turn toward lived experience. In the framework previously outlined, the implicit dimension was epitomized in the question, "How do pastoral counselors attend to the way(s) in which the client experiences psychospiritual themes associated with the sacred or sacredness in their everyday life?" The answer to this question, to be explored in this section, is to begin by understanding religiousness and spirituality in terms of the psychospiritual themes grounded in everyday lived experience.

Basic Assumptions

The import of implicit spiritual assessment is grounded in several assumptions. The first is that spirituality—the search for ultimate concerns of significance—is an essential quality of the overall human experience, regardless of spiritual or religious background and whether it is practiced in secular or sacred contexts (Pargament, 2007). The second assumption is that the spiritual and psychological dimensions of the human experience are related (Sperry & Mansager, 2007), and as such, exploring the client's psychological experiences of ultimate significance is a way of understanding the lived experience of religiousness and spirituality. According to Fuller (2001), psychotherapy is so imbued with religious consciousness as to merit a kind of "psychological religiousness," which he understands as "the expression of a post-theological spirituality" (p. 6). The third reason for including an implicit dimension within religious and spiritual assessment is that Americans' spiritual and religious lives exist within a diverse and pluralistic sociocultural context. Moreover, pluralism dwells within as well as between. Different contexts may elicit different forms of religious and spiritual discourse—even within the same person—ranging from premodern to modern and postmodern (Bender, 2007). The aspiration to recognize and understand the breadth and complexity of religious worlds precipitates the growing willingness within pastoral counseling and related disciplines to emphasize and embrace a multi-level interdisciplinary paradigm (Emmons & Paloutzian, 2003)—multiple levels of analysis (quantitative and qualitative) and interdisciplinary collaboration (psychology of religion, theology, religious studies).

Interdisciplinary Approach

Taking an interdisciplinary approach helps illuminate trends within the sociocultural context in which pastoral counselors are actively practicing assessment. Attention to context is useful not only to identify the horizons of the pastoral counselor's formation but also to expand their horizons of understanding with regard to evolving constructions of spirituality and religiousness in the contemporary American landscape. Scholarship from sociological and religious studies research illuminates important trends—pluralism, globalism, secularism, postmodernism—that are shifting the terrain of American religious life (Bender, 2010; Taylor, 2007). For example, consider the growing identification with categories of "spiritual not religious" and "nones" among the millennial generation (Pew Poll, 2012). Butler-Bass (2012) describes this shift as a turn from the *what* of religion to the *how*, from what one believes to how one lives. Scholars have dubbed this trending phenomenon as the emergence of a middle ground (Heelas & Houtman, 2009; Taylor, 2007), which is an expanding space between traditional poles of theism and atheism. Implicit assessment gives the pastoral counselor full access to middle-range experiences engaged with the realities of everyday life.

To date, the bulk of research and practice in pastoral counseling has focused on traditional theists and religious dwellers to the neglect of seeking and practice-oriented spiritualities (Wuthnow, 1998). Much may be learned about the middle-ground varieties by looking outside the pastoral literature (see Heelas, 2011). The emergence of middle-range spiritualities raises the import of widening spiritual and religious assessment to include a broader range of syncretistic and nontraditional beliefs, practices, and experiences. On this note, the relationship between the tacit and implicit dimensions becomes clear. If tacit formation shapes the varieties of religiousness and spirituality pastoral counselors are willing to recognize, implicit methods of spiritual assessment will depend on a well-developed tacit dimension. If tacit formation is lacking and one is more theologically naïve than sophisticated, the range of religiousness and spirituality will likely remain restricted to one's own experience. Still, many sophisticated assessors may find themselves stretched between the familiar territory of their own tradition's view about religious and spiritual flourishing and encountering the mystery of the other and their unique religious and spiritual worldview.

Assessing Traditional Religious and Spiritual Lives

Implicit assessment is pivotal for traditional as well as nontraditional middle-range spiritualities. Even if the client is affiliated and active in a religious tradition, it remains important to proceed with a comprehensive implicit assessment. Years of immersion in religious worldviews, for example, can produce layered accretions of *religionese*—a kind of private denominational language—(e.g., "laying down my life for Christ," "rooting myself in the vine," "taking up the cross") encrusted over the basic elements of a living faith. Implicit assessment returns to the concrete elements by taking detailed accounts of what these expressions mean, look, and feel like in practice.

Implicit assessment disaggregates the categories of religion and spirituality from the elementary behaviors, beliefs, attitudes, and actions that comprise and are constructed as religiousness by focusing on lived experiences of "specialness" (Taves, 2010, p. 175). Asking about special things includes sacred matters and formal religiousness, but as a subset of the more encompassing term, *special*. Attention to the building blocks of what counts as special provides the benefit of temporarily bypassing the explicit system of religion and its presumed meanings in order to explore the particular aspects of experiences that are consciously or unconsciously set apart as special (Taves, 2010). In sum, implicit assessment can help reveal the level of continuity between ultimate concerns and the actual behaviors through which they are sustained. For example, one might profess the God of religion as his or her ultimate concern, while worshipping the local sports teams in terms of actual everyday behaviors.

Overall, psychologists of religion such as Pargament (2007) view implicit assessment primarily as a stepping stone: "Important as they are, however, they cannot yield rich, detailed, information about spirituality and the degree to which it is well integrated or poorly integrated in the client's life. For that, a more explicit and extensive spiritual assessment is required" (p. 220). For traditional forms of religious and spiritual life, this is likely true. Herein, the language of struggles, pathways, destinations, and transformations provides a clear praxis for situating the client's relationship with a sacred consciously recognized as such and identified with God, Yahweh, Allah, Jesus, Mohammed, or Buddha. However, the overtly religious language of explicit assessment will likely be out of sync with understanding middle-ground spiritual and religious lives, especially if they are not consciously recognized as such. Given that the literature on explicit assessment (Pargament, 2007) focuses predominantly on traditional religiousness, the dimension of implicit assessment is best situated to understand the nontraditional middle range.

Assessing Nontraditional Middle-Ground Religiousness and Spirituality

Assessing spirituality and religion in the contemporary landscape of American culture is remarkably complex not only because of the multiplicity of self-authored forms but also because clients may be unsure of how to characterize their unique collection of practices, ideas, and experiences (Murray & Nielsen, 2006). Depending on their religious upbringing, particularly if it was damaging, they may also be reluctant or opposed to associating their current stance with the language of religion and spirituality. Here, the task of implicit assessment is to attend to the language of the client as signals of significance. Learning their language will validate the importance of their unique posture and engage them in a process of clarifying resources as well as latent spiritual needs. For example, perhaps a client recalls a moment of losing herself in the elemental force of the current while kayaking, the gift of sharing a space with a deer on a morning walk, or the meditative stillness she experiences while hanging laundry. Perhaps she is seeking a regular practice to deepen these experiences or a community of belonging with whom she might share them. Pastoral counselors, as attendants to the spiritual and religious lives of our clients, should strive to familiarize ourselves with nontraditional avenues within the middle ground. Otherwise, we may inadvertently overlook the exploration of strivings and ultimate concerns.

A General Approach

Given the ambiguity and plurality surrounding middle-ground spiritualities, implicit assessment should clarify several questions: How did the clients arrive at, and how do the clients experience, this middle space? Is it syntonic or dystonic? In what ways are they finding vitality and liberation in this middle space as opposed to feeling lost and overwhelmed? To what extent are the clients experiencing this space as affirming of spiritual meaning versus a space of retreat and refuge from religious trauma? Leaving religion because one was wounded is different from finding it irrelevant and boring. Conversely, other clients may simply lack a palate for religion or spirituality, having never been engaged along these lines of thinking and experiencing. Still others may be experiencing religion relocated in extra-ecclesial contexts (Gould, 2005), wherein their sacred destinations and pathways have been reconstructed in a new context of living one's ultimate concerns (e.g., from church to social justice movement). For those in the midst of spiritual struggles, the middle ground can afford some additional breathing room while working out challenges posed by postmodernism, plurality, or theodicy. Discerning these questions will help clarify the language congruent with clients' worldviews. Caution must be taken not to impose a spiritual or religious worldview, even implicitly and tacitly conceived, on clients for whom it lacks resonance.

One way to translate the search for significance for clients without an explicit sense of connection or spiritual/religious identity is to conceptualize the risk of attending counseling as a search for more: more sleep in a busy schedule, more self-control over cravings, more freedom from anxious thoughts, more connection with friends, more happiness in work and career. Nested within these searches for more are the raw materials for bridges yet to be built: to deeper meaning, significance, and the possibility of sacred discovery. For example, consider the desire for more sleep in a client working 60 hours per week. Assuming that basic financial needs are met, we might explore the tacit spiritual strivings found in taking on more work to achieve the goal of promotion and increased salary. Perhaps the client tells herself a story about how status and recognition will make her happier or more desirable, making lost sleep a worthwhile sacrifice. Having identified these latent strivings, we can explore and possibly even expand the meaning of these destinations and the pathways traveled in their pursuit. What begins as a desire for more sleep becomes an opportunity to reevaluate deeper longings for significance.

A Specific Approach: Exploring the Psychospiritual Themes

Implicit spiritual and religious assessment involves the exploration of psychospiritual themes. This section addresses how psychospiritual themes may be used to assess and cultivate psychospiritual health and flourishing through two primary questions. First, how are psychospiritual themes applied in assessing lived forms of religiousness and spirituality? Second, how are psychospiritual themes identified? In other words, which themes provide useful markers for assessing the client's psychospiritual flourishing?

Applying Psychospiritual Themes

Psychospiritual themes are applied through structuring our ways of listening and questioning during the assessment process. With regard to listening, the themes provide an interpretive framework through which potential strivings in the client's story may be recognized and organized. For example, if a client makes a passing remark about the best part of his day being a 20-minute walk through the woods with his dog, the counselor can flag that as a possible life-giving experience worth exploring in greater detail. In this sense, the themes also structure the questioning process by actively guiding the counselor in discerning which parts of the client's story to follow up on and explore in greater detail.

What differentiates implicit assessment questions from those of explicit assessment is that they are functionally oriented rather than substantive. For example, rather than asking about the client's spiritual practices, functional questions refer to the functions of spiritual practice, such as, "What nurtures a sense of vitality in your life?" or "In what ways do you experience rest?" Functional questions are a respectful and inclusive way to get acquainted with the latent psychospiritual themes of the client's narrative. By probing the client's worldview for resources of meaning, equanimity, and vitality, any number of singular experiences (holding a baby, tending the garden, civic participation) might be connected within an orienting system that enacts the function of a spiritual or religious practice, yet they will be understood through the language of the client.

Another way to conceptualize the functional approach used in implicit assessment is to consider St. Augustine's (1998) revelatory question, "What then do I love when I love my God?" (p. 185). Across numerous theistic stances (theist, pantheist, animist, atheist, agnostic), this question invites reflection on the "gods," or things set apart as most special and ultimate, we love in our everyday lived experience. The "gods" or ultimate concerns around which a life is ordered enact the functional role of the sacred—the provision of passion, meaning, purpose, coherence, identity, vitality, resilience, and transformation. Understanding sacredness functionally is a widely applicable method of assessment because it expands beyond traditionally religious content to explore the psychospiritual meanings derived through participating in one's ultimate concerns.

Identifying Psychospiritual Themes

As the tacit dimension of assessment asserts, the themes we gravitate toward are inevitably informed by our own formation, and there is no single definitive list. However much the implicit dimension departs from religiously explicit language and instead relies on the language of psychospiritual themes, it still depends on being clear about the criteria used to define and recognize lived experiences of religiousness and spirituality. In keeping with the interdisciplinary character of pastoral counseling, phenomenological studies of religion and theology provide a rich body of literature well versed in the various themes punctuating human experiences of sacredness. As such, they offer a variety of psychospiritual themes to loosely structure the implicit assessment of religiousness and spirituality.

The broadest, most inclusive category from which to begin delineating any number of themes associated with the spiritual, religious, mystical, or sacred is specialness (Taves, 2010; e.g., what is special or significant in your life?). Given the diversity of theistic stances in the middle ground and the aversion some clients may have toward the term *sacred*, specialness offers a spectrum on which to order all things clients set apart, from the more ordinary (a valued piece of art) to extraordinarily sacred (a transformational experience of oneness-with-everything). By narrowing in on more specific themes, other inquiries may be formed, such as, "What has been the most 'life-giving' (Ignatius, 1548/1964) moment of your week?" or "Describe a time when you felt fully alive" (Irenaeus of Lyons). Other important themes include the client's history of "peak" (Maslow, 1964), "mystical" (James, 1929), and "mysterium tremendem et fascinans" or numinous (Otto, 2012) experiences. Assessing such experiences functionally may be done through exploring spiritual emotions—gratitude, wonder, awe, reverence, dependency—via questions, such as, "When and/or for what have you felt gratefulness or gratitude?" (Stendl-Rast, 1984), "In what ways have you experienced a sense of wonder or awe?" (Heschel, 1983), and "How do you imagine and respond to the sources upon which your life depends?" (Dewey's [1934] natural piety or Schleiermacher's [1799] reverent feelings of absolute dependence).

Another dimension of the sacred from which psychospiritual themes may be gleaned is transcendence/immanence. In other words, pastoral counselors can listen for and explore the ways in which the immanent world of the here and now arouses the client's imagination for what is self-transcending or beyond. Moreover, what contexts and experiences awaken primordial intuitions for hierophany (the eruption of what feels sacred in the immanent world; of the invisible in the visible) wherein the client may experience the world, or part of the world, as an "epiphany of God" (Schmemann, 1973) or revealing of the "wholly other" (Eliade, 1987)? Relatedly, in what ways do clients feel a part of something greater and larger than the self? Examples may range from political movements and grassroots organizing (social justice, environmentalism, civil rights) to aesthetics and the arts (dance, drama, theatre, poetry, symphony, literature, architectural design) to nature and ecology (food systems, biodiversity, natural beauty) to science and physics (evolution, astronomy, quantum entanglement) to human and animal relationships (riding a horse, playing a team sport, nursing a child, caring for an ailing parent).

As social and relational beings, other psychospiritual themes to listen for and explore include the ways clients experience a sense of belonging and home, connectedness and compassion, inspiration and elevation. Because humans are relational, questions exploring the nature and content of their connections, such as, "For what are you willing to spend your time and energy?" and "For what are you willing to suffer?" may excavate hidden resources. Last, given that relationship includes vulnerability and pain, where do the clients draw the "courage to be" (Tillich, 2000) and affirm life in the face of uncertainty? How do they practice the art of letting go, surrender, and serenity? In what ways do they engage the mindful practice of being awake and aware of the present moment (Hahn, 1992)?

By applying the psychospiritual themes, polarized dichotomies between sacred/ secular, religious/spiritual, and theist/nontheist may be circumvented to assess clients' experience of what is most special and significant in their lives. Across worldviews, we can learn about the ways clients experience a sense of enchantment, exercise a poetic or imaginative sensibility, connect to a self-transcending story or purpose, and respond

TABLE 8.2 Example Questions for Implicit and Explicit Religious and Spiritual Assessment

IMPLICIT	EXPLICIT
What do you do when you feel really stressed out (angry/hurt/sad/mad/tired)?	To what organizations do you belong, including any that are religious or spiritual? How regularly do you attend?
How do you comfort yourself or help yourself feel better?	What religious/spiritual practice(s) do you participate in (prayer, saying grace, meditation, singing, going to church/temple/synagogue/mosque)? How often for each?
What gives your life purpose? (Or, what purpose would you like to serve? What leads you to be happy? What gives you joy?)	How do you define/describe and express your spirituality? (Try to resist the temptation to define the term for your client. You want to hear what the client thinks.)
For what are you grateful?	When do you feel most religious or spiritual?
How easy is it to forgive yourself/others?	How has your religion/spirituality helped and/or hurt you?

Note: Example religious and spiritual assessment questions used by Loyola University Maryland pastoral counseling graduate students at the Loyola Clinical Centers (Columbia, MD); adapted from various sources (D. Lasure-Bryant, personal communication, May 22, 2014).

to the sources on which they feel their existence depends. Although technical, these terms provide phenomenological categories to assess lived experiences. Additional examples of implicit assessment questions are described in Table 8.2.

The Explicit Dimension of Religious and Spiritual Assessment

Given their unique position to interact with clients on sacred matters and the need to be conversant with other mental health professionals, pastoral counselors should engage in explicit, formal assessment of religiousness and spirituality when clinically indicated. From the psychological perspective, Hodge (2013) defines religious and spiritual assessment as "the process of gathering, analyzing, and synthesizing information about these two interrelated constructs into a framework that provides the basis for practice decisions" (p. 93). Thus, from this framework, assessment of religiousness and spirituality has a purpose: to inform clinical decision making. In addition, explicit religious and spiritual assessment can provide the clinician with a better understanding of the client's worldview and improve the ability to work with the client effectively and sensitively. Although explicit assessment may be appropriate for clients from a variety of religious and spiritual worldviews, it is specifically oriented and perhaps most beneficial for working with clients from traditional religious and spiritual backgrounds.

Other important functions of explicit religious and spiritual assessment are to explore whether the client's religious or spiritual orientation is healthy or unhealthy (Zinnbauer, 2013), to determine whether the client's religiousness or spirituality affects the presenting problem, to discover whether the client's religious and spiritual practices and community can be used as a resource, and to determine whether religious or spiritual interventions might be used in counseling (Hodge, 2013; Pargament, 2007). All of these reasons for conducting explicit religious and spiritual assessment point to the importance of more precisely tapping into a unique source for change within the pastoral counseling relationship. As previously mentioned, this source moves beyond the biopsychosociocultural model of assessment and intervention. This powerful dimension is the sacred (Pargament, Magyar-Russell, & Murray-Swank, 2005). When sacred matters are overtly explored with the client, they in turn hold considerable repercussions for motivations, beliefs, and behaviors, all essential elements for therapeutic change and growth in the pastoral counseling relationship.

Preliminary Religious and Spiritual Assessment

Hodge (2013) provides a helpful overview and practical outline of the purpose and function of an explicit preliminary religious and spiritual assessment from the psychological perspective. He raises the important point that time is limited in the counseling intake process and that the religious and spiritual realms are but two of many domains that should be considered during the initial assessment. Thus, preliminary questions that help determine (a) the *significance* of religiousness or spirituality to the client, (b) whether the client has a specific religious or spiritual *affiliation* and/or community to which he or she belongs, (c) whether the client views his or her religiousness or spirituality as a *resource* for daily living to cope with problems, (d) and whether religiousness or spirituality may be *related to the presenting problem* represent important starting points in the pastoral counselor's initial explicit assessment of religiousness and spirituality.

Shafranske (2005) suggests the use of tentative language for framing initial religious and spiritual questions to create a neutral environment that will allow the client the freedom to respond in a genuine manner. For example, to inquire about religious or spiritual affiliation, the question to the client could be phrased, "Do you happen to belong to a religious or spiritual community?" (adapted from Hodge, 2013). Moreover, responses to initial inquiries should help frame subsequent questions. For instance, if one question reveals that the client identifies with a certain faith tradition (e.g., Judaism), subsequent questions should incorporate the appropriate terminology (e.g., synagogue) when possible. The aim of a preliminary explicit assessment is to determine whether a more comprehensive religious and spiritual assessment is indicated. Because contemporary pastoral counselors practice in a variety of secular settings, it is essential to note that the preliminary assessment may suggest that religion and spirituality do not appear to be relevant to the presenting problem, at least at the present time. If this is the case, religious and spiritual assessment might be considered a dynamic, ongoing process that might be encountered later, perhaps implicitly, as the counseling relationship develops over time. Additional examples of explicit assessment questions are provided in Table 8.2.

Moving to a Comprehensive Assessment

The goals of an explicit, comprehensive religious and spiritual assessment are to obtain a more thorough understanding of the client's beliefs, experiences, and practices and how these factors affect the presenting problem(s) and possible resolution(s) (Hodge, 2013; Pargament, 2007; Pargament & Krumrei, 2009). Moving into a more in-depth religious and spiritual assessment process with clients requires several essential areas for contemplation. Paramount is professional ethical considerations. For instance, many pastoral counselors are also licensed clinical professional counselors (LCPCs) falling under the professional authority of the American Counseling Association (ACA). According to the 2014 ACA Code of Ethics, "Counselors respect the diversity of clients and seek training in areas in which they are at risk of imposing their values onto clients, especially when the counselor's values are inconsistent with the client's goals or are discriminatory in nature" (ACA, 2014, p. 6, Standard A.11.b). Thus, pastoral counselors must ensure they have adequate training, engage in authentic self-reflection, and/or seek professional case consultation when working with clients from diverse religious and spiritual backgrounds.

Another critical consideration prior to engaging in a comprehensive religious and spiritual assessment is determining the client's degree of openness to the process and confirming ongoing informed consent to delve deeper into the client's religious and spiritual life. Although many clients desire to discuss their religious and spiritual lives in counseling, some clients may believe discussing religion and spirituality in a professional counseling relationship is inappropriate or uncomfortable, or clients may simply not want to share personal or painful religious and spiritual information until rapport is established (Richards & Bergin, 2000; Rose, Westefeld, & Ansley, 2008).

Consistent with the spirit of following professional ethical codes for mental health counselors, the practitioner's level of cultural competence with the client's specific religious or spiritual culture and its related value system is another necessary factor to evaluate before proceeding. Given the many differences in cultural norms and religious and spiritual worldviews, the counselor must be aware of types of questions and interactions that may be incongruent with the clients' value system as they might adversely affect the client and/or the therapeutic relationship. For instance, Dein (2013) described the use of magic, traditional healers, and *jinn* ("beings created with free will, living on earth in a world parallel to mankind [who] can possess a human body thus inflicting physical or mental harm to the possessed person" [p. 199]) by Bangladeshi Muslims in the United Kingdom to understand and cope with physical and mental health problems. If the pastoral counselor is not aware of these aspects of "folk Islam," they might dismiss or attempt to change these beliefs and practices, which could be destructive to the client's well-being and the counselor–client relationship.

The salience attributed to religiousness and spirituality as an organizing principle in the client's life is also a significant factor to consider before embarking on an extensive religious and spiritual assessment process. In other words, the degree to which religiousness and/or spirituality are integrated into the client's daily life and worldview, as well as the relevance of religiousness and spirituality to the presenting issue(s), are important factors to consider. If, for instance, the client describes himself or herself as "believing in God, not belonging to a faith community, and typically not giving God much thought," a comprehensive religious and spiritual assessment may not be warranted at that point in the counseling relationship. Traditional religiousness and spirituality do not appear to be central forces regarding how the client functions in the world. Finally, the extent to which the client's religious and spiritual values allow for pastoral counseling and mental health service provision is another important consideration (Hodge, 2013). For instance, in the qualitative study of Bangladeshi Muslims using folk Islam practices in the United Kingdom referenced earlier, Dein (2013) reported that:

> individuals generally did not discuss religious and cultural issues with their doctors maintaining that health professionals would not accept their beliefs, and in many instances, felt that these professionals lacked cultural sensitivity. Only rarely would they admit to consulting traditional healers to their health professionals. (p. 210)

In such instances, comprehensive, explicit assessment may not be advisable at all times (or at any time) in the counseling relationship. Once all of these factors are carefully considered, and the decision is made to proceed, a number of useful religious and spiritual assessment techniques have been developed.

Of Tools and Traditions

The clinician should select assessment modalities that best meet the needs of the client, the setting, the clinician's knowledge and abilities, and the clinical situation. Although not an exhaustive list, options for explicit religious and spiritual assessment include (a) the use of open-ended questions to elicit the client's religious and spiritual history, current story, future ambitions, beliefs and attitudes, and experiences and practices; (b) quantitative instruments designed for assessing religion and spirituality in psychotherapy; and (c) diagrammatic tools that aid both the clinician and the client and capture a great deal of information in a creative and relatively succinct manner (Hodge, 2013).

The use of open-ended questions is often helpful for gaining detailed information and building a therapeutic alliance with the client. When asked with careful consideration, open-ended questions demonstrate the pastoral counselor's interest and sensitivity to the religious and spiritual lives of their clients, while simultaneously allowing clients to share to the extent of their comfort level. For instance, some clients may choose to tell their religious and spiritual histories and experiences in great detail, whereas others might pick and choose aspects of their religious and spiritual stories they feel comfortable and safe sharing early in the counseling relationship. Examples of open-ended questions or statements about past religious and spiritual experiences are, "What religious or spiritual experiences stood out for you as you were growing up?" and "Tell me about the religious or spiritual tradition you grew up in" (adapted from Pargament, 2007). Questions that tap into the client's current conceptualizations, expressions, and experiences of religiousness and spirituality are, "What do you hold sacred in your life?" "How would you describe your current religious or spiritual orientation?" "What has damaged or hindered your spirituality?" and "Who supports you spiritually, and how do they offer this support?" (adapted from Hodge, 2013; Pargament, 2007). Example questions that inquire about future spirituality are, "How do you see yourself changing spiritually in the future?" and "How does your religiousness or spirituality relate to your goals in life?" (adapted from Hodge, 2013; Pargament, 2007). Additional examples of explicit, open-ended questions are displayed in Table 8.2.

Quantitative instruments designed for assessing religion and spirituality in psychotherapy can be an effective means of screening for problematic religious and spiritual issues, for efficiently identifying areas in need of clinical attention, and for identifying religious and spiritual resources and strengths. Here again, the counselor must consider the information gathered from the preliminary religious and spiritual assessment and determine whether assessment instruments in general, or specific self-report questionnaires, are appropriate for a given client. Specifically, "counselors recognize the effects of . . . religion [and] spirituality . . . on test administration and interpretation, and they place test results in proper perspective with other relevant factors" (ACA, 2014, p. 12, Standard E.8). Thus, when selecting and using quantitative measures to aid in assessment of religiousness and spirituality, pastoral counselors should use multiple means of assessment to gain a comprehensive picture of the role religiousness and spirituality play in the lives of their clients (Hodge, 2013). Dozens of instruments have been developed to measure different dimensions of religiousness and spirituality. Table 8.3 provides examples of useful measures for assessing various dimensions of religiousness and spirituality within the context of the counseling relationship.

Finally, diagrammatic tools such as genograms, eco-maps, and life maps can be used to gather a great deal of client information in a nonverbal (or less verbal) and concise manner. Detailed instruction on how to construct genograms, eco-maps, and

TABLE 8.3 Example Instruments Used for Assessing Different Dimensions of Religiousness and Spirituality

SCALE NAME	AUTHORS	MEASURES/SUBSCALES
Quest Scale	Batson and Schoenrade (1991)	The degree to which an individual's religiousness or spirituality involves an open dialogue with existential questions
Spiritual Transformation Scale (STS)	Cole, Hopkins, Tisak, Steel, and Carr (2008)	Spiritual growth and decline/worldview, goals and priorities, sense of self, relationships
The Religious and Spiritual Struggle Scale	Exline, Pargament, Grubbs, and Yali (2014)	Six domains of religious and spiritual struggle/divine, demonic, interpersonal, moral, doubt, and ultimate meaning
Brief RCOPE	Pargament, Smith, Koenig, and Perez (1998)	Positive religious coping methods and negative religious coping methods
Spiritual Assessment Inventory (SAI)	Hall and Edwards (1996)	Two dimensions of spiritual experience: awareness of God and quality of relationship with God
Religious Commitment Inventory–10 (RCI-10)	Worthington et al. (2003)	How much an individual is involved in his or her religion/intrapersonal and interpersonal commitment
FACIT-Spiritual Well-Being Scale	Peterman, Fitchett, Brady, Hernandez, and Cella (2002)	The religious and spiritual components of quality of life following illness/meaning, peace, faith
Sacred Loss and Desecration	Pargament, Magyar, Benore, and Mahoney (2005)	Appraisals of negative life events as sacred losses and/or desecrations
The Daily Spiritual Experience Scale	Underwood and Teresi (2001)	Perception of the transcendent in daily life; the involvement of the transcendent in one's life

Note: See also Pargament (2007) and Pargament et al. (1998) for a more extensive list of assessment measures. Brief RCOPE, Brief Measure of Religious Coping; FACIT, Functional Assessment of Chronic Illness Therapy.

life maps is beyond the scope of this chapter; however, Hodge (2013) describes general strategies and techniques for using these tools with clients, along with their relative strengths and limitations, and a decision tree used for aiding in selection of comprehensive assessment modalities. Although each diagrammatic technique has unique features depending on the need for assessment in different domains, such as the importance of generational factors (genogram) or depicting connections between relational and environmental factors (eco-map), these visual approaches may cultivate new insights, honor nonverbal styles of communication and creative expression, and foster client–counselor rapport in the religious and spiritual assessment process (Hodge, 2013).

Limitations and Challenges due to Clinical Setting
Ideally, clinicians might combine open-ended/qualitative and more structured quantitative approaches to integrate the client's religious and spiritual information into an effective assessment that leads to accurate, effective, and sensitive diagnosis; treatment planning; and intervention (see Chapters 7 and 11 in this volume). However, such a thorough approach and process represents the ideal. Many settings in which pastoral

counselors work, such as prisons, residential treatment facilities, and hospitals, do not allow for private or lengthy assessments. For instance, in medical settings, assessment of religiousness and spirituality is often limited to general markers of religiousness, such as religious affiliation and frequency of religious service attendance. These indices, however, have not been shown to identify adequately the salience of religion and spirituality in clients' lives, nor do they identify individuals at risk for religious and spiritual struggles and their associated psychological distress (Magyar-Russell, Pargament, Trevino, & Sherman, 2013).

To address the need for brief assessment, specifically for religious and spiritual struggle in the hospital setting, Fitchett and Risk (2009) developed the Rush Protocol (RP). The RP is a three-item screening protocol (six items total; a decision tree is followed for each patient with a maximum of three questions possible per patient) that can be administered by any health professional with brief training to identify potential cases of religious and spiritual strain that require more in-depth assessment by a pastoral counselor or chaplain. Following Fitchett and Risk's (2009) protocol, the first question asked of all patients is, "Is religion or spirituality important to you as you cope with your illness?" If the patient answers "yes," the second question is, "How much strength/comfort do you get from your religion/spirituality right now?" However, if the patient answers "no" to the initial question, the follow-up question is, "Has there ever been a time when religion/spirituality was important to you?" (p. 3). Based on patient responses to each of the second questions, referral for a comprehensive religious and spiritual assessment is immediately made, or patients are asked whether they would like a visit from a hospital chaplain or pastoral counselor. The intent of the instrument is to assist the clinician administering the protocol to take one of three actions: (a) referral for comprehensive religious and spiritual assessment because screening indicated possible spiritual struggle; (b) referral for routine spiritual care (which may uncover religious/spiritual struggle) because a chaplain/pastoral counselor visit was requested by the patient, even though no indication of spiritual struggle was present; or (c) no referral or further action because no chaplain/pastoral counselor visit was requested and there was no indication of religious or spiritual struggle.

Of import, among 200 newly admitted medical and surgical patients, those who were in high need of spiritual intervention and had few spiritual resources were less likely to request spiritual assistance in comparison to those with less need and greater spiritual resources (Fitchett, 1999), underscoring the importance of clinician-based religious and spiritual assessment. Moreover, hospital staff members often refer patients who identify themselves as having strong religious and spiritual beliefs and who typically have moderate or high levels of spiritual resources (Fitchett, 1999). Thus, in the hospital setting, those in greatest need are most likely to be overlooked by pastoral counselors and chaplains. The RP represents the type of brief and explicit religious and spiritual assessment tools that pastoral counselors should be using, and developing, for use in challenging and time-limited clinical situations. Such brief assessment protocols could increase the efficiency and productivity of pastoral counselors by focusing their therapeutic efforts on individuals in greatest need of religious and spiritual intervention.

CONCLUSIONS

Assessment is always provisional and subject to revision, making it more like a working hypothesis than a definitive conclusion. When a religious and spiritual assessment is useful, it lends pragmatic value to clients' ability to recognize the self-transcending and transformative aspects of their lives. The three-dimensional interdisciplinary and integrative framework presented in this chapter offers a comprehensive and nuanced approach to assessing religiousness and spirituality. The tacit dimension helps with differentiating between various pastoral identities and being present without inflicting one's own biases and struggles onto the client. The pastoral counselor must develop a sophisticated pastoral identity to offer a sacred space able to encounter the mystery of the client's world. The phenomenological focus of implicit assessment on lived psychospiritual themes makes it applicable to multiple language worlds, particularly those ambivalent, middle-ground, nontheistic (Pargament, 2007), extratheistic (Ammerman, 2013), and hybrid (Bender, 2007) forms. What's more, modes of implicit assessment unearth resources and build bridges for cultivating and integrating the tacitly spiritual into everyday life.

Although implicit methods of assessment apply sensitizing themes and questions to draw out the unspoken strivings and concerns linked to what the client holds most special and sacred, explicit methods are most adept in assessing traditional forms of religiousness and spirituality. Explicit assessment affords a clear and detailed picture of the relationships among clients' psychological distress, well-being, and their religiousness and/or spirituality. As the pastoral counselor moves from the tacit to implicit to explicit forms of assessment, the issue at stake is not merely the adoption of religious, spiritual, or sacred terms but evaluating the client's ability to consciously access the practices, experiences, beliefs, relationships, and actions that enact sacredness in life. Regardless of the particular names assigned to ultimate concerns, consciousness raising opens the way to new possibilities for religious and spiritual integration and resources.

REFLECTION QUESTIONS

1. Craft your own "statement of positionality" similar to those offered by the authors at the beginning of the chapter. Based on your own cultural background and experience, what context-independent assumptions might you bring into a session based on your own pastoral identity? What impact do those assumptions have on your understanding of or approach to diagnosis?

2. In what ways might the apophatic approach to diagnosis discussed in Chapter 7 be related to or inform the tacit dimension of assessment?

3. Consider your own spiritual or religious tradition: What is one example of how the sacred manifests to you through the tacit dimension, the implicit dimension, and the explicit dimension?

REFERENCES

American Association of Pastoral Counselors. (1986). *The constitution of the American Association of Pastoral Counselors*. Fairfax: VA: Author.

American Counseling Association. (2014). *ACA 2014 code of ethics as approved by the ACA governing council*. Alexandria, VA: Author.

American Psychiatric Association. (2013). *Diagnostic and statistical manual of mental disorders* (5th ed.). Arlington, VA: American Psychiatric Press.

Ammerman, N. (2013). Spiritual but not religious? Beyond binary choices in the study of religion. *Journal for the Scientific Study of Religion, 52,* 258–278. doi:10.1111/jssr.12024

Augustine. (1998). *Confessions*. New York, NY: Oxford University Press.

Batson, C. D., & Schoenrade, P. (1991). Measuring religion as quest: II. Reliability concerns. *Journal for the Scientific Study of Religion, 30*, 430–447. Retrieved from http://www.jstor.org.ezp .lndlibrary.org/stable/1387278

Bender, C. (2007). Religion and spirituality: History, discourse, measurement. In *Essay forum on the religious engagements of American undergraduates*. Retrieved from http://religion.ssrc.org/ reforum/Bender.pdf

Bender, C. (2010). *The new metaphysicals: Spirituality and the American religious imagination*. Chicago, IL: University of Chicago Press.

Berlin, I. (1969). *Four essays on liberty*. London, UK: Oxford University Press.

Butler-Bass, D. (2012). *Christianity after religion: The end of church and the birth of a new spiritual awakening*. New York, NY: HarperCollins.

Cole, B. S., Hopkins, C. M., Tisak, J., Steel, J. L., & Carr, B. I. (2008). Assessing spiritual growth and spiritual decline following a diagnosis of cancer: Reliability and validity of the spiritual transformation scale. *Psycho-Oncology, 17*, 112–121. doi:10.1002/pon.1207

Cooper-White, P. (2011). *Many voices: Pastoral psychotherapy in relational and theological perspective*. Minneapolis, MN: Fortress.

Dein, S. (2013). Magic and jinn among Bangladeshis in the United Kingdom suffering from physical and mental health problems: Controlling the uncontrollable. *Research in the Social Scientific Study of Religion, 24*, 193–219. doi:10.1163/9789004252073_009

Dewey, J. (1934). *A common faith*. New Haven, CT: Yale University Press.

Doehring, C. (2009). Theological accountability: The hallmark of pastoral counseling. *Sacred Spaces: The e-Journal of the American Association of Pastoral Counselors, 1*, 4–34. Retrieved from http://www.aapc.org/media/75733/theologicalaccountability3.pdf

Dueck, A., & Reimer, R. (2009). *A peaceable psychology: Christian therapy in a world of many cultures*. Grand Rapids, MI: Brazos.

Eliade, M. (1987). *The sacred and the profane: The nature of religion*. Orlando, FL: Harcourt.

Emmons, R. A., & Paloutzian, R. F. (2003). The psychology of religion. *Annual Review of Psychology, 54*(1), 377–402. doi:10.1146/annurev.psych.54.101601.145024

Exline, J. J., Pargament, K. I., Grubbs, J. B., & Yali, A. M. (2014). The Religious and Spiritual Struggles Scale: Development and initial validation. *Psychology of Religion and Spirituality*. Retrieved from http://dx.doi.org/10.1037/a0036465

Farley, W. (2005). *The wounding and healing of desire: Weaving heaven and earth*. Louisville, KY: Westminster John Knox Press.

Fitchett, G. (1999). Screening for spiritual risk. *Chaplaincy Today, 15*(1), 2–12. Retrieved from http://journals.sfu.ca/jpcp/index.php/jpcp/index

Fitchett, G., & Risk, J. L. (2009). Screening for spiritual struggle. *Journal of Pastoral Care & Counseling, 63*, 1–12. Retrieved from http://journals.sfu.ca/jpcp/index.php/jpcp/index

Fuller, R. C. (2001). *Spiritual, but not religious: Understanding unchurched America*. Oxford, UK: Oxford University Press.

Gould, R. K. (2005). *At home in nature: Modern homesteading and spiritual practice in America*. Berkeley, CA: University of California Press.

Guba, E. G., & Lincoln, Y. S. (2005). Paradigmatic controversies, contradictions, and emerging confluences. In N. K. Denzin & Y. S. Lincoln (Eds.), *The Sage handbook of qualitative research* (3rd ed., pp. 191–215). Thousand Oaks, CA: Sage.

Hahn, T. N. (1992). *Peace is every step*. New York, NY: Bantam.

Hall, T. W., & Edwards, K. J. (1996). The initial development and factor analysis of the spiritual assessment inventory. *Journal of Psychology and Theology, 24*, 233–246. doi:10.1111/1468-5906 .00121

Heelas, P. (Ed.). (2011). *Spirituality in the modern world: Within religious tradition and beyond (critical concepts in religious studies)*. New York, NY: Routledge.

Heelas, P., & Houtman, D. (2009). Research note: RAMP findings and making sense of the 'god within each person, rather than out there.' *Journal of Contemporary Religion, 24*, 83–98. doi: 10.1080/13537900802630521

Heschel, A. (1983). *I asked for wonder: A spiritual anthology*. New York, NY: Crossroad.

Hodge, D. R. (2013). Assessing spiritualty and religion in the context of counseling and psychotherapy. In K. I. Pargament, A. Mahoney, & E. P. Shafranske (Eds.), *APA handbook of psychology, religion, and spirituality* (Vol. 2, pp. 93–123). Washington, DC: American Psychological Association.

Ignatius. (1964). *The spiritual exercises of Saint Ignatius: Saint Ignatius profound precepts of mystical theology* (A. Mattola, Trans.). New York, NY: Doubleday. (Original work published 1548)

James, W. (1929). *The varieties of religious experience*. New York, NY: Modern Library.

Jordan, M. R. (1986). *Taking on the gods: The task of the pastoral counselor*. Nashville, TN: Abingdon.

Jung, C. (1961). *Letter to Bill Wilson*. Retrieved from http://www.barefootsworld.net/jungletter

Lee, S. K. (2010). Much depends on the kitchen: Pastoral practice in multicultural society. In K. Grieder, D. van Duesen Hunsinger, & F. B. Kelcourse (Eds.), *Healing wisdom: Depth psychology and the pastoral ministry* (pp. 34–56). Grand Rapids, MI: Eerdmans.

Magyar-Russell, G., Pargament, K. I., Trevino, K., & Sherman, J. E. (2013). Religious and spiritual appraisals and coping strategies among patients in medical rehabilitation. *Research in the Social Scientific Study of Religion, 24*, 93–135. doi:10.1163/9789004252073_006

Maslow, A. (1964). *Religions, values, and peak-experiences*. New York, NY: Penguin.

Murphy, N. (2005). Constructing a radical-reformation research program in psychology. In A. Dueck & C. Lee (Eds.), *Why psychology needs theology: A radical-reformation perspective* (pp. 53–78). Grand Rapids, MI: Eerdmans.

Murray, R., & Nielsen, M. E. (2006). The spiritualistic tradition. In E. T. Dowd & S. T. Nielsen (Eds.), *The psychologies in religion: Working with the religious client* (pp. 255–269). New York, NY: Springer Publishing Company.

Otto, R. (2012). *The idea of the holy: An inquiry into the non-rational factor in the idea of the divine and its relation to the rational*. Cambridge, UK: Oxford University Press.

Pargament, K. I. (2007). *Spiritually integrated psychotherapy: Understanding and addressing the sacred*. New York, NY: Guilford.

Pargament, K. I., & Krumrei, E. J. (2009). Clinical assessment of clients' spirituality. In J. D. Aten & M. M. Leach (Eds.), *Spirituality and the therapeutic process: A comprehensive resource from intake to termination* (pp. 93–120). Washington, DC: American Psychological Association.

Pargament, K. I., Magyar, G. M., Benore, E., & Mahoney, A. (2005). Sacrilege: A study of sacred loss and desecration and their implications for health and well-being in a community sample. *Journal for the Scientific Study of Religion, 44*(1), 59–78. doi:10.1111/j.1468-5906.2005.00265.x

Pargament, K. I., Magyar-Russell, G., & Murray-Swank, N. A. (2005). The sacred and the search for significance: Religion as a unique process. *Journal of Social Issues, 61*(4), 665–687. doi: 10.1111/j.1540-4560.2005.00426.x

Pargament, K. I., Smith, B. W., Koenig, H. G., & Perez, L. (1998). Patterns of positive and negative religious coping with major life stressors. *Journal for the Scientific Study of Religion, 37*(4), 710–724. doi:10.2307/1388152

Peterman, A. H., Fitchett, G., Brady, M. J., Hernandez, L., & Cella, D. (2002). Measuring spiritual well-being in people with cancer: The Functional Assessment of Chronic Illness Therapy Spiritual Well-Being Scale (FACIT-Sp). *Annals of Behavioral Medicine, 24*, 49–58. doi:10.1207/S15324796ABM2401_06

Pew Poll. (2012). "Nones" on the rise: One in five adults have no religious affiliation. *The Pew Forum on Religion and Public Life*. Retrieved from http://www.pewforum.org/2012/10/09/nones-on-the-rise/

Polanyi, M. (2009). *The tacit dimension*. Chicago, IL: University of Chicago Press.

Ramsay, N. J. (1998). *Pastoral diagnosis: A resource for ministries of care and counseling*. Minneapolis, MN: Fortress.

Richards, P. S., & Bergin, A. E. (Eds.). (2000). *Handbook of psychotherapy and religious diversity*. Washington, DC: American Psychological Association.

Rodgerson, T. E. (2012). Apophatic attending: An essential for pastoral diagnosis. *Journal of Pastoral Care & Counseling, 66*(1), 1–8.

Rose, E. M., Westefeld, J. S., & Ansley, T. N. (2008). Spiritual issues in counseling: Clients' beliefs and preferences. *Psychology of Religion and Spirituality, S*(1), 18–33. doi:10.1037/1941-1022.S.1.18

Schleiermacher, F. (1799). *On religion: Speeches to its cultured despisers.* London, UK: Kegan Paul, Trench, Tribner.

Schmemann, A. (1973). *For the life of the world.* Crestwood, NY: St. Vladimir's Seminary Press.

Shafranske E, P. (2005). The psychology of religion in clinical and counseling psychology. In R. F. Paloutzian & C. L. Park (Eds.), *Handbook of the psychology of religion and spirituality* (pp. 496–514). New York, NY: Guilford.

Sperry, L., & Mansager, E. (2007). The relationship between psychology and spirituality: An initial taxonomy for spiritually oriented counseling and psychotherapy. *Journal of Individual Psychology, 63*(4), 359–370. Retrieved from http://utpress.utexas.edu/index.php/journals/journal-of-individual-psychology

Stendl-Rast, D. (1984). *Gratefulness, the heart of prayer: An approach to life in fullness.* Ramsey, NJ: Paulist Press.

Tan, S. Y. (1996). Religion in clinical practice: Implicit and explicit integration. In E. P. Shafranske (Ed.), *Religion and the clinical practice of psychology* (pp. 365–387). Washington, DC: American Psychological Association. doi:10.1037/10199-013

Taves, A. (2010). No field is an island: Fostering collaboration between the academic study of religion and the sciences. *Method & Theory in the Study of Religion, 22*(2–3), 170–188. doi: 10.1163/157006810X512356

Taylor, C. (2007). *The secular age.* Cambridge, MA: Belknap Press of Harvard University Press.

Tillich, P. (2000). *The courage to be.* New Haven, CT: Yale University Press.

Townsend, L. (2006). Theological reflection and the formation of pastoral counselors. *American Journal of Pastoral Counseling, 8*(3–4), 29–46. doi:10.1300/J062v08n03_03

Townsend, L. (2009). *Introduction to pastoral counseling.* Nashville, TN: Abingdon Press.

Townsend, L. (2011). A grounded theory description of pastoral counseling. *Journal of Pastoral Care & Counseling, 65*(3), 1–16. Retrieved from http://journals.sfu.ca/jpcp/index.php/jpcp/article/viewArticle/263

Underwood, L. G., & Teresi, J. A. (2001). The Daily Spiritual Experience Scale: Development, theoretical description, reliability, exploratory factor analysis, and preliminary construct validity using health-related data. *Annals of Behavioral Medicine, 24*(1), 22–33. doi:10.1207/S15324796ABM2401_04

van Deusen Hunsinger, D. (1995). *Theology and pastoral counseling: A new interdisciplinary approach.* Grand Rapids, MI: Eerdmans.

Worthington, E. L., Jr., Wade, N. G., Hight, T. L., Ripley, J. S., McCullough, M. E., Berry, J. W., ... O'Conner, L. (2003). The Religious Commitment Inventory-10: Development, refinement, and validation of a brief scale for research and counseling. *Journal of Counseling Psychology, 50*, 84–96. doi:10.1037/0022-0167.50.1.84

Wuthnow, R. (1998). *After Heaven: Spirituality in America since the 1950's.* Berkeley, CA: University of California Press.

Zinnbauer, B. J. (2013). Models of healthy and unhealthy religion and spirituality. In K. I. Pargament, A. Mahoney, & E. P. Shafranske (Eds.), *APA handbook of psychology, religion, and spirituality* (Vol. 2, pp. 71–89). Washington, DC: American Psychological Association.

Jill L. Snodgrass and Konrad Noronha

9

RESPONDING TO EXPLICIT AND IMPLICIT SPIRITUAL CONTENT IN PASTORAL COUNSELING

Pastoral counseling, an extension of the Judeo–Christian practice of soul care, privileges the integration of clients' spiritual beliefs within mental health care. Pastoral counselors are trained to listen for spiritual content in clients' presentations and to respond and intervene in ways that facilitate both spiritual and mental well-being. This chapter focuses on the common themes of meaning and the sacred that emerge in pastoral counseling practice. It elucidates explicit (unambiguous and overt) and implicit (embedded or covert) spiritual content that is commonly presented by clients. Because our social locations inform the way we understand the discipline and practice of pastoral counseling, the chapter's first section outlines the authors' backgrounds and the assumptions grounding the chapter's approach and content. The chapter continues by exploring the explicit spiritual content commonly raised by clients within the Abrahamic traditions (Judaism, Christianity, Islam), and implications for pastoral counseling are then outlined. The final section explores implicit spiritual content, which is seemingly inherent to the human condition and often occupies the subtext of a client's presentation. Implications for pastoral counseling are offered for each of these themes as well.

THE AUTHORS' CONTEXTS AND ASSUMPTIONS

In our postmodern milieu, it is essential to contextualize this chapter by clarifying the authors' social locations and the overarching assumptions that guide our assertions regarding the practice of pastoral counseling. First, the authors approach this subject from the positions of their own social locations. Jill Snodgrass is a married, heterosexual, European American woman, raised and ordained in the United Church of Christ, a liberal Protestant denomination. She received a PhD in practical theology and teaches spiritual care and pastoral counseling in the Mid-Atlantic region of the United States at a Jesuit university. Konrad Noronha is a Roman Catholic priest, belonging to the Society of Jesus (Jesuits), who received a PhD in pastoral counseling. He lives in India, where he teaches at an institute of pastoral management that is part of a seminary wherein laity, clergy, and vowed religious are trained. Both authors are grounded in the Christian tradition and yet recognize that all encounters between counselor and client are truly interreligious (see Chapter 14 in this volume). Therefore, the explicit spiritual content noted in this chapter reflects the historical Judeo–Christian bias of the discipline of pastoral counseling as well as the authors' training and religious locations. However, attempts are made to broaden theistic conceptions to incorporate the Abrahamic faiths and to employ a specific, inclusive understanding of spirituality and religion.

Defining Spirituality and Religion

In contrast to popular narratives in the West and a significant portion of research in the psychology of religion, the authors disagree with Ellingson (2001) and other social scientists regarding a "growing division between organized religion and spirituality" in the United States (p. 257). Rather, in accordance with Ammerman (2013), the authors claim that the perceived binary between religion and spirituality promotes a false "either/or discourse" (p. 260). For example, in a study sampling both religious and nonreligious individuals in Boston and Atlanta, "for a large majority, spirituality is defined by and interchangeable with the experiences their religious communities have offered them and taught them how to interpret" (Ammerman, 2013, p. 273). This "either/or discourse" (p. 260) ignores the fact that most spiritual beliefs and practices derive their meaning from religious traditions. For example, an individual may contend that her desire to live in accordance with the Golden Rule, an ethic of reciprocity, is a foundation of her spiritual beliefs and practices. However, derivations of the Golden Rule are present in dozens of religious traditions, and most likely the individual's understanding of this ethic is conceptualized within a religious framework. This does not mean that the individual practices that religious tradition. Rather, it means her understanding of the Golden Rule is colored by the religious cultures to which she has previously participated (if any), been exposed to, or which are dominant in her culture. Thus, the authors contend that spiritual beliefs and practices are often derived from or refer to religious beliefs and practices, and the growing division between spirituality and religion is most likely more theoretical than practical.

As such, the authors adopt Lartey's (2003) definition of spirituality, which recognizes the place of the transcendent, which for many refers to God or the meaning contexts of institutionalized religion, in its structural framework. According to Lartey, spirituality:

> refers to the human capacity for relationship with self, others, world, God and that which transcends sensory experience, which is often expressed in the particularities of given historical, spatial and social contexts, and which often leads to specific forms of action in the world. (pp. 140–141)

Therefore, when using the terms *spiritual* and *spirituality*, the authors understand this to include religious beliefs and practices. When using the term *theological*, the authors understand this to refer only to the beliefs and doctrines of theistic religious traditions, which in this chapter is almost always used in reference to the Abrahamic traditions.

Spiritual Growth as the Goal of Counseling

From the authors' perspectives, spiritual growth, broadly conceived, is the goal of all pastoral counseling. This goal is in addition to those at the foundation of most mental health practices (i.e., the promotion of mental health, symptom alleviation, and increased coping) and is considered equally important. Clinebell (1984) posits nine basic spiritual needs that serve as goals for the pastoral counseling process, five of which the authors deem relevant in today's spiritual landscape: the need to "maintain hope in the midst of losses and tragedies"; "[discover] ways to move from the alienation of guilt to the reconciliation of forgiveness"; "undergird self-esteem and reduce alienating narcissism (pride)"; engage in and facilitate "moments of transcendence, mystical 'peak experiences'"; and belong to a "caring community . . . that nurtures and sustains" (p. 110). It is imperative on the part of the counselor to help the client discover a salient, salugenic (i.e., health- and life-producing) spirituality; to discover God, the Ultimate, a higher power, or his or her understanding of the transcendent; and to bring that into the therapeutic process. This aids the counselor and the client in collaboratively working toward client wholeness, which is the aim of counseling. Although this will not be accomplished in all counseling relationships, whether due to duration, the client's presenting concerns, or client resistance, the authors believe spiritual growth to be primary among the *teloi* or aims of pastoral counseling practice.

Pastoral Counseling and a Willingness to Unlearn and Relearn Theology

Grounding our exploration of explicit and implicit spiritual content in pastoral counseling is the belief that competent practice requires counselors to be spiritually and theologically flexible. Few individuals are raised or educated in contexts that engender doctrinal malleability. More often than not, people are "taught theology as an objective mode of thought" (Wise, 1980, p. 62) and engage in types of catechesis or religious education that offer answers, often in the form of centuries-old doctrines, to the questions that arise within the vicissitudes of life. In contrast, the pastoral counselor's practice is grounded in pastoral theology—an understanding of God and God's creation that derives as much from revelation and lived experience of God as from systematic theology or ethics. Therefore, as Wise (1980) contends, the pastoral counselor "faces the experience of learning, unlearning, and relearning theology" (p. 62). Pastoral counselors are charged with exploring the client's understanding of spirituality and "living religious language" rather than making assumptions about or attempting to control another's beliefs (p. 63). Although pastoral counselors are often drawn or called to the profession because of their personal faith commitments, the pastoral counselor occupies a perilous position when approaching others with a spiritual foundation grounded in anything other than curiosity and questions. Therefore, according to Shafranske (2005),

> The incorporation of religious or spiritual interventions or resources should not be determined by the psychotherapist's personal faith orientation; rather, it should correspond to the salience and function of religion in the client's life, with informed consent, and within the scope of the clinician's competence, established through appropriate training and supervision. (p. 502)

All Modalities

As evidenced throughout this volume, pastoral counselors employ a diversity of treatment modalities and are not limited to one model or school of psychotherapy. Therefore, listening for and responding to explicit and implicit spiritual content is possible within all theoretical approaches (i.e., client centered, cognitive behavioral, relational cultural, family systems, psychodynamic) and regardless of the client's presenting concerns. The following sections consider explicit and implicit spiritual content common to clinical pastoral counseling practice and offer appropriate responses to each.

EXPLICIT SPIRITUAL CONTENT IN PASTORAL COUNSELING

Pastoral counselors offer counsel and guidance to a diversity of clients with a variety of presenting concerns. Some clients seek pastoral counselors with the specific desire to incorporate their spiritual beliefs into mental health treatment, some seek pastoral counselors out of an assumed trust based on shared tradition or spiritual understanding, and some do not seek pastoral counselors but find themselves in such relationships based on problems accessing treatment, the pastoral counselor's use of a sliding scale, or poor research as a mental health consumer. Pastoral counseling with this variety of clients necessitates a preparedness to engage explicit spiritual content. However, this content may at times be peripheral rather than central to the process of counseling. According to Clinebell (1984),

> Obvious and explicit theological issues—e.g., problems of belief, doubt, doctrine, the nature and methods of prayer—are the presenting problem in only a small minority of those seeking pastoral help. One study found that only 10 percent of pastoral counseling clients were perceived as having problems primarily in the religious area. (p. 103)

Nevertheless, competence in recognizing and engaging explicit spiritual content is one of the hallmarks of pastoral counseling and requires significant exploration. The following section examines three explicit types of spiritual content common to the practice of pastoral counseling: God images, scripture or sacred texts, and prayer.

God Images

The God of the Abrahamic traditions is described in scriptures in myriad ways, including as king, ruler, master, servant, father or Abba, spirit, warrior, destroyer, breath, fire, and eternal power. Jewish, Christian, and Islamic writers of sacred texts used anthropomorphisms to describe God, attributing human characteristics, emotions, and behaviors to God in an attempt to understand and cultivate intimacy with God. Islam posits 99 names of Allah (God), such as the creator, the provider, and the truth, many of which are present in Judaism and Christianity as well. Classical Christian theologies describe God as all-good, all-knowing, omnipresent, eternal, and unchanging (Burke, 1977). God is often depicted in Western Christian cultures as an older, White, powerful male, which has been contested by contemporary theologies describing God as young or Black or female, or all three in combination (Popovici, 2011).

Grounded in, or at times in opposition to, such scriptural and cultural conceptions of God, individuals frequently possess, consciously or not, God images. God images are material or abstract representations of a deity or a figure of worship that have emotional and relational components (Moriarty & Hoffman, 2007). Both theological reflection and one's psychological history contribute to God image formation. Yet God images are conceptually distinct in theology and psychology (Sorajjakool, 1999).

God Images in Theology

As noted earlier, Abrahamic theologies and sacred texts afford many God images, yet according to Christian scripture, "No man has ever seen God" (1 John 4:12 New International Version). Thomas Aquinas (2006) said that God always exceeds every kind of human knowledge (Summa Theologiae 1.12.1.ad 1, 3; 1.12.7.ad 2) and that "man is best united to God by realizing that in knowing God he knows nothing about him" (q. 7.a.5 arg. 14). Therefore, when considered theologically, God images are thought to be revealed through the world of nature, the events of history, the life of the community, and individual personal experience (Wright, 1987).

From a theological perspective, speech about God and God images influence both our corporate and individual relationships with God. According to Johnson (1992), "The way in which a faith community shapes language about God implicitly represents what it takes to be the highest good, the profoundest truth, the most appealing beauty" (p. 4). Communities that speak of God's vengeful power will understand and relate to God in a manner markedly nuanced from those communities that speak of God's beneficence and forgiveness. As a result, understandings of and relationships with God are always mediated by historical contexts and milieus.

> Neither abstract in content nor neutral in its effect, speaking about God sums up, unifies, and expresses a faith community's sense of ultimate mystery, the world view and expectation of order devolving from this, and the concomitant orientation of human life and devotion. (Johnson, 1992, p. 4)

Because worldview and historical contexts guide theological understandings of God, God has been known through many analogies and by many names since the beginning of the Abrahamic traditions. Therefore, insight from Thomas Aquinas, a medieval theologian and philosopher, offers age-old wisdom about how we speak of God.

Aquinas offered three rules governing how language can be used to describe God:

> The first rule is that "God is incomprehensible, meaning that the infinitely creating, redeeming and life-giving mystery is so beyond us, and so within us, that the human mind can never fully grasp the divine essence." The second rule says that "no expression for God can be taken literally," and the third says "there must be many names and images for God since no one alone is adequate or absolute." (as cited in Popovici, 2011, p. 11)

God Images in Psychology

Unlike theological conceptions of God, most psychological theories relate God images to actions of the psyche, the mind, and early childhood influences. According to psychological literature, God image refers to the way an individual relationally or emotionally experiences God. It is a person's heart knowledge of God (O'Grady & Richards, 2007) and is complex, subjective, and emotional (Moriarty & Hoffman, 2007). God images are not exactly the same as ideas or feelings but dynamically relate to the affective and cognitive aspects of the person (Jonker, Eurelings-Bontekoe, Zock, & Jonker, 2007). Research indicates that God images are internally and phenomenologically constructed and experienced and are independent of any ontological questions about the external reality of God (Kunkel, Cook, Meshel, Daughtry, & Hauenstein, 1999; O'Grady & Bartz, 2012).

People form God images in various ways. According to Freud, a God image originates from law and guilt and has strong paternalistic overtones (Rizzuto, 1979). Other theorists posit that people's God images resemble their maternal relationships, that children's God images model whoever is more salient in their lives, and that the God images of young adults are determined by their self-concepts and self-esteem. Many approaches tie God image development to the development of the changing self—as the self changes, the God image changes (Moriarty, Thomas, & Allmond, 2007). Factors influencing an individual's experience and thereby God image include:

> (1) caregiver relationships, (2) other significant relationships, (3) church experience, (4) world experiences (e.g., general experience of the world as a safe or unsafe place), (5) gender, (6) sexual orientation, (7) cultural experience, (8) God concept/beliefs, (9) wish fulfillment/compensation, (10) personality factors, (11) psychological health, (12) ability/disability, (13) self-image/self-esteem, and (14) developmental factors (including religious/spiritual/faith development and psychological development). Additional factors which may need further consideration include biological factors and direct relational factors with God. (Hoffman, Knight, Boscoe-Huffman, & Stewart, 2007, p. 260)

The Pastoral Counselor Responds to God Images

Before investigating how pastoral counselors can effectively explore and draw on a client's God image, it is important to note the dangers one faces in misinterpreting another's God image. Wyatt (2004) offered a poignant illustration when recounting how, despite a client's depiction of her God as "an observer" who is "powerless to act in the world," Wyatt projected and falsely assumed the client's God to be "fierce" and condemning as that mirrored her paternal relationship (p. 30). Pastoral counselors are forewarned to avoid assuming that a client's God image is either in relation or opposition to a primary or parental relationship, adheres to the client's religious doctrine or scripture, or is wholly healthy or unhealthy.

According to O'Grady and Richards (2007), spiritually mature individuals are able to move beyond narrow theological and psychological manifestations of God image to form a God image inclusive of their personal experiences in relationship with the divine. In contrast, "spiritually immature individuals tend to have God concepts that are based primarily on other's accounts of God, projections carried over from their childhoods, or projections of their personality disorders or other pathologies" (p. 192). Helping clients to explore their God images and how such images relate to the client's presenting problem and/or primary relationships can, for some, be an important pathway to healing. Outlined in the text that follows are three assessment and intervention techniques related to God images.

Spiritual life map.   One way to assess clients' God images throughout the life span is by asking clients to draw a spiritual life map. Although creative liberties are encouraged, the simplest approach entails drawing a line depicting birth to the present with markers identifying key spiritual experiences or turning points throughout one's chronological journey (Hodge, 2005). The counselor then asks the client to share his spiritual journey highlighting what he recalls about his God image and relationship with God at each significant experience. As Hodge reminds us, the counselor "should attempt to place their own beliefs on the shelf and seek to understand [clients'] phenomenological spiritual reality" (p. 80). Based on this narrative and the content of the client's God images, counselors can help the client to consider how his God image has changed in response to life experiences; how those God images relate to the client's own religious education, understanding, and key relationships; and what resources the client may have at his disposal that were previously forgotten or ignored.

Critical reflection on God images.   Pastoral counselors can help clients by facilitating critical and reflective conversation about God images by recounting personal experiences with God and how God was known to and experienced by the client in the past and in the present. Counselors may help clients to identify the attributes of their God image(s) and consider how those attributes are similar to or distinct from those of their primary caregivers, parents, and other key relational figures (O'Grady & Richards, 2007, p. 194). The client and counselor may collaboratively decide that aspects of the client's God image are more pathogenic (i.e., toward the client's disease) than salugenic (i.e., toward the client's health and well-being). In such cases, O'Grady and Richards (2007) recommend employing the following approaches to augment or revise one's God images:

> Specific goals that therapists may wish to consider for God image change might include: (a) helping clients examine what impact their God image and relationship with God may be having on their presenting concerns, (b) helping clients look at ways their experiences with others may be contributing to their conceptions of God, (c) encouraging clients to use their religious teachings to help them learn more about God's true character. (p. 197)

Using measures.   Another means of fostering conversation and reflection about clients' God images is through the use of inventories and scales. Over the past 40 years, psychologists of religion have endeavored to measure various aspects of individuals' God images through the creation and validation of inventories and scales. Counselors can employ these measures to initiate critical discussion about clients' beliefs in God, particulars about their God images, and how such concepts relate to clients' experiences with their families of origin. Inventories and scales can facilitate exploration of the adjectives clients use to describe God, invite clients to identify certain statements about God as either true or false, determine how God is similar to and distinct from primary caregiving figures, and more. For examples of particular scales and inventories, Hill and Hood's (1999) edited volume offers a chapter overviewing seven God concept scales, noting for each the variables, considerations of use, and reliability and validity.

Scripture and Sacred Texts

Scriptures and sacred texts are an important component of most religious traditions as they outline the tradition's beliefs and serve as the foundation for religious doctrines. "Adherents of that system use these writings as a guideline to define, develop, and clarify their belief systems" (Cook, Dixon, & Fukuyama, 2011, p. 279). The Tanakh, Talmud, and Midrash in the Jewish tradition; the Old and New Testaments in Christianity; and the Quran in Islam all offer adherents insights into understanding God, the faith, and their own lives. In each of these Abrahamic traditions, adherents believe that God reveals Godself within the sacred writings. Sacred texts in the Abrahamic traditions offer both life wisdom and a greater intimacy and understanding of God. Sacred writings from other traditions (e.g., Hinduism and Buddhism) are not viewed as divine revelation but do serve as sources for spiritual and moral wisdom. Nevertheless, adherents within each religious tradition approach sacred writings in unique ways. Some believe scriptures to be infallible and quite literally the direct revelation of God. Others consider scriptures to be important sources of wisdom that are translated or authored by humans and thus fallible and subject to error. Pastoral counselors need to understand not only how clients view the sacred texts of their traditions but also how they read or engage these texts in living out their faith.

Although definitions and practices of Christian counseling and pastoral counseling are equally numerous and diverse, when addressing the use of sacred texts in counseling, it is imperative to differentiate the two allied but distinctive practices. Christian counseling is most simply defined as "counseling conducted by a Christian who is Christ-centered, biblically based, and Spirit filled" (Tan, 2011, p. 363). Christian counselors employ the Bible in myriad ways, but all counseling approaches and interventions are understood to be biblically based and Christ centered. In contrast, pastoral counselors, when relevant, employ the sacred writings and scriptures of the client's religious tradition irrespective of the counselor's own faith and tradition. Pastoral counselors draw on sacred texts and writings in a manner that invites "wisdom to inform the process, spirit, and goals of caring/counseling relationships" (Clinebell, 1984, p. 124); "to comfort and strengthen people in crisis" (p. 124); and "to help heal spiritual pathology and change pathogenic beliefs" (p. 125).

The Pastoral Counselor Incorporates Scripture and Sacred Texts

Scripture and sacred texts can be used effectively in counseling for myriad purposes. According to Richards and Bergin (2005), sacred writings are used to help clients:

> (a) challenge and modify their dysfunctional beliefs; (b) reframe and understand their problems and lives from an eternal, spiritual perspective; (c) clarify and enrich their understanding of the doctrines of their religious tradition; (d) strengthen their sense of spiritual identity and life purpose; and (e) seek God's enlightenment, comfort, and guidance. (p. 261)

Depending on the knowledge, expertise, and comfort level of the pastoral counselor, scriptures and sacred texts can be both implicitly and explicitly integrated in counseling (Tan, 1996). Implicit integration of sacred texts is less directive, waiting for the client to initiate discussion of a text if desired, and less critical, accepting the client's perspectives and interpretations rather than employing critical, contextual examination of the text. Pastoral counselors may find that when forming therapeutic rapport and gaining an understanding of the client and his or her presenting concerns, implicit integration of sacred texts and scriptures is more appropriate than explicit integration. Before explicitly integrating sacred texts into counseling, pastoral counselors need to explore and acknowledge their own feelings and beliefs about sacred writings lest incorporation of such writings becomes fertile ground for unhealthy countertransference. Pastoral counselors need to adopt an attitude of curiosity and a willingness to explore clients' beliefs about sacred texts rather than rigidly limiting discussions to "right" and "wrong" interpretations or beliefs. Finally, pastoral counselors should be clear about the purpose and goal for incorporating sacred texts at any given time within the counseling process. Drawing on the work of Monroe (2007), Tan (2007) suggests asking oneself,

Why do I want to have the client read this [sacred] text? What do I hope to accomplish through it (e.g., to be provoked, taught, comforted, connected to something greater than self, to change one's focal point)? What barriers might hinder this goal? How might the client misinterpret my intervention? (p. 108)

After exploring the responses to the preceding questions, the pastoral counselor may then consider explicitly integrating scripture and sacred text in the following ways.

Interpreting and discussing scripture and sacred text. Once the pastoral counselor understands her own and the client's views about the role and function of sacred texts, she may wish to identify particular scripture verses or excerpts from sacred texts within the client's tradition that offer a helpful hermeneutic or lens for reflecting on the client's presenting problems. The pastoral counselor's job is not to teach a "correct" understanding of the text. As noted previously, pastoral counselors must be spiritually and theologically flexible. However, by discussing and reflecting on the client's understanding of the text, the counselor may facilitate within the client a sense of intimacy and connection to God, the transcendent, or an eternal spiritual truth. As Clinebell (1984) observed, "Having a sense of the sustaining presence of God, as communicated for example in the familiar words of the twenty-third or the ninetieth Psalm can be a source of great strength for some people in handling shattering losses" (p. 124). Interpreting and discussing scripture can also help clients to explore more critically their unexamined or preconscious spiritual and theological beliefs. For example, Mary, a 43-year-old single mother of two, shares with her counselor the following: "I was always taught, as it says in Proverbs 3:5, to trust in the Lord with all my heart and not to lean on my own understanding. But what does that really mean? I've been unemployed for almost 2 years, and I don't understand why God would wait like this to give me a job." The counselor's job is to help the client to give voice to her own understanding of this scripture and what it means to her at this moment in her spiritual journey. The counselor needs to explore why the client selected this particular passage, what it means to her at this particular point in time, and how her previous understanding may or may not resonate with her current lived experience.

Drawing on sacred stories or parables recounted in spiritual writings. Sacred stories or parables have a powerful way of helping clients to reflect on their experiences and to reauthor their own narratives toward greater empowerment and resilience. According to Harney (2000), parables and stories "allow the client to go out of his or her currently stuck mind-set and observe a similar situation being resolved. Ideally, the knowledge gained by following the analogy will transfer back into the client's issue" (p. 222). Clients may benefit from selecting a biblical or scriptural figure (e.g., Job or Ruth) whose story, experience, or personality mirrors the client's own. The stories and metaphors of these characters' lives can enable the client to connect both affectively and spiritually (Richards & Bergin, 2005). The client and counselor can then explore the similarities and differences between the client's problems and those of the scriptural figure and reflect on how that material can guide the client in future thoughts and behaviors.

Clinebell (1984) suggests asking clients to share their most and least favorite scriptural stories. He recounts a client who, after years of feeling trapped, recounted the Exodus story as her favorite due to the assurance of the Promised Land (p. 125). Discussing with clients their most and least favorite scriptural stories can uncover the metaphors and plotlines operant in their own lived experiences.

Working from a feminist, narrative perspective, Neuger (2001) advocates employing parables to illustrate how "God's spirit and wisdom are present in what might otherwise seem like a routine moment" in a manner that transforms the characters in the parable (p. 135). Parables can help clients to reflect on God's work in all aspects of their lives, even the mundane, and the counselor can then help clients to reframe their own situation toward "more life-giving directions" (p. 137).

Using scriptures to explore client's dysfunctional or irrational beliefs.   The role of pastoral counselors is not to teach correct belief, doctrine, or scriptural understandings. With few notable exceptions, the pastoral counselor should not present herself as a religious, moral, or scriptural authority. However, it is not uncommon for pastoral counselors to pause when clients' exegesis or interpretation of sacred texts seem to be dysfunctional or not supportive of their greater health. In such situations, it is helpful to discuss such interpretations in depth and to explore how the belief is consonant with the client's tradition. The pastoral counselor is encouraged to practice caring, empathic confrontation rather than aggressively challenging the client. One way this can be done is by providing the client with additional readings that may help the client to reflect on his or her previous understanding and consider other possible interpretations. Such exploration can help the client and counselor to work collaboratively toward reframing dysfunctional beliefs into beliefs that are both traditionally grounded and life giving to facilitate greater psychological and spiritual well-being.

Bibliotherapy.   Bibliotherapy does not entail referring clients to read and pray for the cessation of all problems. However, effective psychological counseling and intervention can be strengthened through the reading of scriptures and both canonical and noncanonical sacred texts. Although the Bible, Book of Mormon, Talmud, Torah, Quran, Tao Te Ching, and Bhagavad Gita are commonly accepted sacred texts, counselors should also recognize that clients may apply sacred meaning to texts that are not acknowledged or accepted by any of the major religious traditions (Cook et al., 2011). Nevertheless, "Bible studies, sacred scripture commentaries, and biographies of great religious leaders, saints, prophets, and others all help interested readers to grow and deepen their faith and understanding of their religious-spiritual traditions" (Plante, 2009, p. 36). Counselors may refer clients to read aspects of particular sacred texts or counselors may ask clients to share with them the texts that have been meaningful to the clients' spiritual and psychological journeys.

Prayer

According to Clinebell (1984), prayer and meditation occupy three roles in the pastoral counseling relationship:

> They are important resources for the [counselor's] own spiritual preparation for facilitating spiritual growth in counseling; they can be used by the counselor on behalf of the counselee; they are skills that the counselee can be taught for use in self-healing. (p. 128)

Yet pastoral counselors frequently overlook the power of prayer with clients (O'Connor & Meakes, 2008). This is especially striking because more than 90% of Americans state that they regularly engage in prayer (Gallup & Jones, 2000). According to Cheston and Miller (2011), counselors avoid prayer for myriad reasons:

For some counselors, there is an element of fear ("I don't want to offend or impose my beliefs"), an element of safety in the clinical distance ("I'm a counselor, not a pastor or priest"), or an element of relief ("I don't have to address this uncomfortable area"). (p. 243)

Pastoral counselors need to acknowledge these or other feelings regarding prayer to become comfortable discussing prayer with clients, praying for and with clients, and, when relevant, guiding clients in their prayer lives.

Before turning to examine the role of prayer in pastoral counseling today, a definition of prayer is essential. Theological understandings and practices of prayer differ among the world's spiritual traditions. However, generally prayer is understood as "a dynamic form of communion of the religious person with the deity or transcendent Other" (LeFevre, 1995, p. 937). Prayer is considered by many to be "primary speech" and "primordial human language" (LeFevre, 1995; Ulanov & Ulanov, 1982). It is universal and not dictated by the confines of one's language or cultural construction. Through prayer, we communicate with the interior of our being as well as with God or the transcendent other. Yet prayer can be both individual and corporate. It is manifest both within and beyond numerous set forms, and prayer may be an attempt to petition God to intercede, to confess our wrongdoings, to dialogue in intimacy with God, and more. Across individuals and traditions, prayer may be verbal or silent, individual or communal, with our lips or our feet (thus passive or active), expressive or meditative, and yet always with the goal of deeper relationship with self, other, and God. It is the authors' belief, a position shared by Ulanov and Ulanov (1982), that "everybody prays. People pray whether or not they call it prayer. We pray every time we ask for help, understanding, or strength, in or out of religion" (p. 1).

A significant number of studies aim to explore the effectiveness of prayer in addressing various conditions and ills. However, according to a review and meta-analysis conducted by Masters and Spielmans (2007), most research on prayer entails methodological limitations such as an overdependence on observational studies, poorly formulated operationally defined constructs with operational definitions that were poorly formulated and thus difficult to measure, and a lack of longitudinal studies. Although numerous studies demonstrate the efficacy of prayer in "induc[ing] favourable psychological and possibly physiological effects" (Bernardi et al., 2001, p. 1446), the meta-analysis conducted by Masters and Spielmans (2007) evidences "no discernable effects" of intercessory and other forms of prayer (p. 329). According to Gubi (2008), the pastoral counselor is encouraged to consider prayer as a resource rather than a remedy as "in most spiritualities prayer exists for the purpose of developing and deepening a personal relationship with God (Richards, 1991) rather than as a psychological intervention" (p. 35).

The Pastoral Counselor Incorporates Prayer

This section examines three prayer practices relevant to pastoral counseling: prayer on behalf of clients, prayer between client and counselor, and guiding clients in prayer. Yet given that all pastoral counseling relationships are interreligious, how can pastoral counselors ethically incorporate prayer within clinical practice? Foremost, the use of prayer in pastoral counseling practice is unethical when (a) it is not part of the client's agenda and/or the client has not provided informed consent, (b) it does not match the client's religious tradition or beliefs, (c) it imposes the counselor's own faith perspective and/or agenda, and (d) the counselor uses prayer as a defense or to avoid or to influence the power dynamic between client and counselor (Gubi, 2009). Therefore, ethical prayer entails consistency with the client's faith and use of language relevant to the client, and ethical prayer is engaged in with the aim of facilitating the client's spiritual growth. For additional guidance on helpful versus unhelpful prayer with clients, please refer to Cheston and Miller (2011), Gubi (2004, 2008), and Richards and Bergin (2005).

Prayer on behalf of clients.   Pastoral counselors may find praying for clients to be a meaningful ritual before, following, or in between sessions. Gubi (2004) refers to this as covert prayer in that the client is not directly engaged. Pastoral counselors may petition God or the transcendent for assistance in helping clients, may entrust clients to God when their concerns are overwhelming, and may come to find that praying for a client effects change in both client and counselor. According to Cheston and Miller (2011), pastoral counselors might even consider using times of silence during the session as opportunities to engage in covert prayer on the client's behalf.

Prayers between client and counselor.   Many pastoral counselors and those in allied mental health professions recognize that prayer, when used ethically, can facilitate transformation within the client and the clinical process. According to Gubi (2008), prayer and counseling share numerous similarities: "Both prayer and counselling develop the capacity for mature dependence; they create a transitional space in which persons can discover their uniqueness; they encourage symbolizing the true self to an 'other'" (p. 32). Some pastoral counselors consider counseling itself to be a prayer that emerges from the three-way encounter among the counselor, the client, and the transcendent.

Explicit or overt forms of prayer (Gubi, 2008) can enable both counselor and client to give voice to thoughts, feelings, concerns, or desires that may otherwise be difficult to communicate. Overt prayers between client and counselor can serve as a helpful opening or closing to the session and function as a meaningful ritual within the relationship. The counselor may choose to offer prayers that aim to empower and uplift the client, that invite the client into a new way of relating to the transcendent, and that give voice to lament but simultaneously engender hope during times of despair. According to Clinebell (1984), "Inviting people during caring and counseling relationships to pray (if that is meaningful to them) may be helpful in a different way than for the counselor to pray" (p. 123). Doing so not only empowers the client in his or her relationship with the transcendent but also invites the client to disclose profound matters of the heart in a trusting and sacred moment.

Guiding clients in prayer.   Beginning in the early 1980s, mindfulness practices have gained increasing popularity within most mental health disciplines due in part to the empirically supported benefits of the practice (Davis & Hayes, 2011). Numerous books and workbooks guide clinicians on incorporating and teaching mindfulness practices within counseling and psychotherapy (Dunkley & Stanton, 2014; McCown, Reibel, & Micozzi, 2010). For this reason, teaching clients methods and practices of prayer and meditation in counseling may be more culturally acceptable now than at any point in the past 60 years.

Nevertheless, there is debate among counselors and therapists regarding whether one needs to maintain his or her own practice of the prayer or spiritual discipline before offering guidance to a client. The maintenance of one's own practice can be especially problematic for pastoral counselors as, given the diversity of clients' traditions, one is likely to be unfamiliar with the prayers and spiritual practices of all clients' traditions. Therefore, when guiding clients in prayer, it is advised that the counselor be familiar with the prayer or spiritual practice so that the guidance is grounded in at least a minimal level of personal experience. For example, a Buddhist pastoral counselor should not be guiding a Catholic client to pray the rosary unless the counselor is familiar with this prayer and understands its significance within the Catholic tradition, and the client is connected to additional resources within his religious community to help facilitate his prayer practice. Likewise, a Christian pastoral counselor should not be guiding a Jewish client to pray a nighttime prayer sung in Hebrew without an understanding of its use and significance within the Jewish tradition and without connecting the client to her rabbi or another authority to help in cultivating the practice. Pastoral counselors are advised to only teach prayer practices that resonate with the client's spiritual and theological beliefs and to follow the client's lead, in addition to consulting relevant and reputable resources, when the client shares a practice with which the counselor was previously unfamiliar.

For a helpful overview of prayer practices and techniques that transcend spiritual traditions and can be readily incorporated within the counseling session, we refer the reader to Cheston and Miller's (2011) summary of using the Gestalt empty-chair technique in prayer and the use of "off-road prayer" that is extemporaneous, unscripted, and responsive to what is raised in silence. Finally, it is important to heed Clinebell's (1984) caution that one should "never feel that one has to use religious words or resources. God is continually active in all relationships, whether or not formal religious words or practices are used" (p. 123).

IMPLICIT SPIRITUAL CONTENT IN PASTORAL COUNSELING

All mental health professionals are trained to listen to both what is said and what is unsaid. We apply various hermeneutics in listening to the content of client concerns: the interpretive lens produced by our own experiences (countertransference), the modality or therapeutic approach employed, and the guidance and biases offered to us by supervisors, past or present. Therefore, according to Clinebell (1984),

> It is easy to miss the hidden spiritual dimensions of the problems a [pastoral counselor] encounters in counseling. If, for whatever reasons, counselors are tuned mainly to the wavelength of psycho-social aspects of human problems, they tend not to hear the profound spiritual longings often present. Such deafness is a serious handicap. (p. 105)

Implicit spiritual content needs to be drawn out and counselors need to help clients to articulate and uncover the deeper meaning within clients' spiritual belief systems. Therefore, the following section attempts to attune pastoral counselors' ears to the implicit spiritual content most often encountered in clinical practice. Absent from this exploration are numerous additional implicit themes such as suffering, shame, guilt, and forgiveness. Although these are profoundly spiritual issues, an extensive body of literature is available to guide the pastoral counselor toward effective practice with these issues, including Chapter 5 in this volume, which features pastoral responses to suffering. Therefore, the three themes of implicit spiritual content examined in this chapter include existential anxiety, hope and despair, and loneliness and isolation.

Existential Anxiety

Existential anxiety entails trepidation related to the meaning of life and death and is a part of the human condition. It derives, according to Tillich (1952), from our awareness that "being has nonbeing 'within' itself" (p. 34), our awareness that life inherently entails death. Existential anxiety is nonpathological. Unlike fear, it has no object, nothing concrete toward which it is directed. Rather, "its object is the negation of every object" (p. 36). Our being is threatened by our finitude and, according to Tillich, thus manifests in the anxiety of death and the anxiety of meaninglessness (p. 41).

First, the anxiety of death and fear of death are not synonymous. Fear, unlike anxiety, has an object. Clients may present with a fear of death when wellness is threatened and illness or disease evident. In contrast, the anxiety of death is an awareness of our contingent nature. We exist only in this one time and place, and our existence is contingent on the outcome of each causal factor and moment. We have no "ultimate necessity," the world will keep turning without us, and our finitude and death is assured (Tillich, 1952, p. 44). As a result of this knowledge, many experience an anxiety of meaninglessness and question the meaning of existence. According to Tillich (1952), in grappling with an anxiety of meaninglessness, "One is [often] driven from devotion to one object to devotion to another and again on to another, because the meaning of each of them vanishes and the creative eros is transformed into indifference" (p. 47). The anxiety of meaninglessness causes us to find meaning in various practices or devotions (i.e., devotion to a television show), or objects or outlets (i.e., material possessions or consumption), and therefore we grapple to cope with the "being" of existence.

The Pastoral Counselor Responds to Existential Anxiety

According to Wise (1980), pastoral counselors are frequently called to care for and respond to the anxieties of existence. "Human beings are caught between creative and destructive forces throughout their existence, between conflicting aspirations, or between aspirations and a sense of inadequacy" (Wise, 1980, p. 290). Such experiences of anxiety, of tension between creative and destructive forces, place us at what Clements (2001) describes as the "edge of experience" (p. 405). The edge of experience is a place of both threat and growth and therefore invites us to respond with either creativity or rejection.

Our task as pastoral counselors is to help clients respond with courage and creativity. According to Clinebell (1984), "Whatever one uses to cope with existential anxiety is, psychologically speaking, one's religion" (p. 108). Pastoral counselors risk supporting idolatry or the deification of meaningless objects or concerns if clients' existential anxiety is not properly recognized and addressed. Therefore, the first step in doing so is to discern whether the presenting anxiety is a fear of death in the bodily form, in the form of self or spirit, or is more accurately a fear of living (Wise, 1980). Fear of bodily death in the face of an objective threat to existence, in the face of illness or disease, necessitates working with a client's spiritual or ultimate beliefs. Anxiety regarding the death of self or spirit requires helping clients to draw on the resources of their spiritual tradition or to make meaning of life through work, love, or courage (Frankl, 2006). At times, this may require a restructuring of the self and "may mean moving into another developmental stage, rearranging one's value system, or exercising one's freedom to more fully be one's self" (Ashby, 1990, p. 48). In addition, it requires a willingness to engage life "intensely and fully" (Clinebell, 1979, p. 113). Belief in a viable philosophy of life and creative values, whether grounded in a theistic or other cultural worldview, helps to imbue one with the trust required to cope with life's vicissitudes in a meaning-centered and growth-producing manner.

Hope and Despair

Many clients seek pastoral counseling in response to feelings of profound hopelessness and, at times, despair. Contemporary psychology, most notably the work of Snyder (2000), offers considerable insight into hope as a psychological construct. Understanding, listening for, and leveraging hope are fundamental responsibilities in pastoral counseling. But psychological and spiritual constructs of hope are distinct. Pastoral counselors conceptualize hope not only within a psychological framework but within clients' meaning-contexts and spiritual belief systems. As Kinghorn (2013) suggests, limiting ourselves to psychological models of hope traps us in hope's immanence and negates the profound transcendent qualities of hope. Psychological constructs of hope are grounded in what is and can be achieved on earth and in the here and now. Spiritual constructs of hope acknowledge the existence of a divine or other transcendent force and thus recognize that hope can be placed in something or someone chronologically and spatially beyond the here and now.

Hope as a Psychological Construct
Nevertheless, understanding hope as a psychological construct and cognitive process is an important first step before turning our attention to the transcendent significance of hope. Snyder (2002) began researching hope in the mid-1980s as a cognitive rather than emotional process. According to Snyder, hope relates to learned optimism, self-efficacy, and self-esteem. It is a way of thinking directed toward an objective or goal that may be short or long term, insignificant or substantial. Simply stated, hope as a psychological construct is the cognitive process of formulating pathways toward the accomplishment of a goal and enacting agency toward the achievement of that goal. A hopeful person demonstrates what Snyder (2002) calls "pathways thinking," which "entails the production of one plausible route, with a concomitant sense of confidence in this route," toward the completion of a goal (p. 251). "Hope can exist as a relatively stable personality disposition (i.e., a trait) or as a more temporary frame of mind (i.e., a state)" (Lopez et al., 2004, p. 388). Hopeful individuals think through the possible pathways that would enable the accomplishment of a goal. In addition, hope requires a sense of agency and the motivation to enact one's pathways thinking. The cognitive process associated with pursuing a goal produces positive emotions, and when stressors and barriers impede the pursuit of a goal, individuals with high levels of hope are able to perceive the intrusion as a challenge rather than a threat (Snyder, 2002). Simply stated, hope as a psychological construct is grounded in goal-oriented cognition.

Hope as a Spiritual Construct
This psychological understanding of hope delimits hope to a cognitive process with a focus on immanent goals and fails to recognize the transcendent qualities of hope that are often grounded in clients' meaning-contexts or spiritual frameworks. As Kinghorn (2013) argues, "If therapists and clients really want to engage the richly subtle contours of hope, it would be wise to look beyond the language of modern psychology to the languages of cultural and religious traditions that have been shaping the context of hope for thousands of years" (p. 377). Hope serves as a spiritual anchor in many religious traditions. The hope evidenced by Noah, Moses, Isaiah, and Jeremiah

is a prominent theme in Judaism and the Hebrew scriptures. The hope engendered by Christ's resurrection and the coming of the Kingdom of God constitute a foundational doctrine in the Christian tradition. And in Islam, the absence of hope, despair, is in itself considered sinful. How a client understands hope within the framework of his or her meaning-context is essential knowledge for the pastoral counselor to explore. Yet clients of all or no spiritual traditions will benefit from exploring hope not only as goal-oriented cognitions, as advocated by Snyder (2000), but as transcendent-oriented cognitions as well.

To understand what is meant by transcendent-oriented cognition, it is first necessary to define our use of *transcendent*. Transcendence in this sense is not limited to the supernatural or the other-worldly, the "vertical" aspects of our spiritual ways of relating. Rather, transcendence entails both the vertical aspects of our spiritual lives as well as the immanent, the "horizontal" aspects of our being (Hood, 2005, p. 350). Therefore, whereas goal-oriented cognition entails thinking and acting toward goals, transcendent-oriented cognition focuses on our temporal existence, how we understand the human condition within and beyond the bounds of time, and the dialectic nature of human existence as we continuously participate in beginnings and endings, creation and destruction.

First, transcendent-oriented cognition engenders hope by embracing the paradox of humans' temporal existence. We exist in the space of "no longer" and "not yet" (Moltmann, 1977, p. 193). We are grounded in our personal and collective histories, what is no longer, the past, and yet we are endowed with the creative potential to contribute to the not yet. Our temporal state, our existence in the present moment, results from a dialect interchange between the past and the future. Individuals engaged in transcendent-oriented cognition do not see the past and future as binaries with only the future offering the promise of goal attainment. The temporality of existence is understood on a much grander scale that includes but is not limited to our individual, finite experience. Therefore, goals often transcend our existence and include reappraisals of the past as well as future occurrences well beyond our tenure on earth.

In addition, transcendent-oriented cognition recognizes generativity in birth and death, accomplishment and setback, as such seeming binaries are all part of the ebb and flow of creation. Transcendent-oriented cognition facilitates a "patient and confident surrender to uncontrollable" forces or events with a nonattached attitude toward the goals themselves (Pruyser, 1990, p. 532). It is not simply a cognitive reframing of the pathways to one's goal. Rather, it is a more much generalizable hope that features "waitpower even if change is not happening" (Worthington, 2005, p. 31). Transcendent-oriented cognition is more akin to faith, although it may or may not have a divine referent. Kwan (2010) summarized such a hope well when he wrote,

> Having specific goals means closing off the possibility of novelty and taking present knowledge to be final. To the contrary, the hoping person "is open to gaining new knowledge, for he [*sic*] sees the universe itself as an open-ended process, far from being finished." (p. 63)

Hopeful persons are grounded in the histories from which they emerged but also endowed with the creative potential to contribute to the generative endeavors of the future. Through transcendent-oriented cognition, our hope is not grounded simply in the goals we are (or are not) capable of accomplishing within our own finitude; rather, hope is grounded in the knowledge of a transcendent element, that which surpasses human knowledge and cognition, as well as creates in ways not limited by finitude. Therefore, according to Pruyser (1990),

In all paradigms [of hope] there is a belief (despite insufficient objective demonstration of its tenability) that the world, the cosmos, is a process and thus has a forward edge moving into the unknown, the not-yet-revealed, the creative—in a word, into the transcendent that can throw new light on or even alter present conditions. (p. 534)

The Pastoral Counselor Responds to Hope and Despair

Our task then as pastoral counselors is to be holders of hope for our clients. This entails understanding hope within the client's worldview, listening for pathways thinking and evidence of agency/motivation, and leveraging the client's hope, however minimal it may be, toward its development. Pastoral counselors may find the following approaches helpful toward this end.

First, pastoral counselors work to enhance hope by facilitating goal-oriented cognitions in clients. According to Lopez et al. (2004),

Hope-enhancing strategies typically involve enlisting clients in tasks that are designed to
- Conceptualize reasonable goals more clearly
- Produce numerous pathways to attainment
- Summon the energy to maintain pursuit
- Reframe insurmountable obstacles as challenges to be overcome (p. 390)

Lopez et al. (2004, p. 398) suggest using scales or measures to assess hope; offering clients psychoeducation about hope theory; creating lists of the important components in clients' lives; outlining creative, attainable, and specific goals related to these components; visualizing and verbalizing the effective pathways to these goals; and continuing to evaluate clients' progress toward the desired goals.

Enhancing clients' hope is best accomplished not only through goal-oriented cognitions but through transcendent-oriented cognition as well. Pastoral counselors aid clients by (a) helping clients to identify generalizable hope within their own and others' lives that may not be directed toward particular goals, (b) empowering clients to recognize the transcendent power of their creative abilities as beyond the finitude of their individual existence, (c) reminding them to remain open to knowledge not yet revealed, and (d) helping clients to recognize that creation is never static but dynamic and ever changing, which at time requires "waitpower" or faith.

Finally, pastoral counselors can serve as holders of hope for clients by exploring with them a healthy view of suffering consonant with the clients' traditions. By understanding suffering within one's spiritual framework, clients are better equipped to use goal-oriented and transcendent-oriented cognitions toward a healthy and hopeful appraisal of their current circumstances.

Loneliness and Isolation

Pastoral counseling is built on the Judeo–Christian spiritual assertion that humans are made in connection and relationship. However, loneliness and isolation are common experiences in our Western, individualistic context. Pastoral counselors are equipped to recognize the profound spiritual and existential concerns at the root of such experiences and to help clients to cope and grow toward profound connection. Loneliness and isolation are not synonymous, but they are more often than not comorbid if experienced for a significant duration. Loneliness is:

an enduring condition of emotional distress that arises when a person feels estranged from, misunderstood, or rejected by others and/or lacks appropriate social partners for desired activities, particularly activities that provide a sense of social integration and opportunities for emotional intimacy. (Rook, 1984, p. 1391)

In contrast, "*Isolation* is the condition of being separated from all important persons, things, or relationships" (Grant, 1990, p. 663). Situational loneliness and/or isolation are more common than loneliness and isolation resulting from characterological issues. "Situational isolation and transitory loneliness" (Grant, 1990, p. 663) may be the result of grief, loss, or crisis. The precipitating event may be experienced as negative (e.g., the sudden death of a spouse or partner) or positive (e.g., a promotion at work that causes one to relocate, leaving relationships and familiarity behind).

The Pastoral Counselor Responds to Situational Loneliness and Isolation
In responding to situational loneliness and isolation, a helpful first step is to explore the client's theological or philosophical anthropology. This means discussing and critically reflecting on the client's understanding of the human condition. Are humans made in and for community? Are humans inherently relational? What implications do the client's beliefs have on his experience of loneliness and isolation? For adherents of the Abrahamic traditions, this means exploring what it means to say that humans are made in the image of God. Exploring these and other questions can help counselors to identify clients' core beliefs and their spiritual import.

Building on this exploration, Grant (1990) posits a two-step response to experiences of situational and transitory loneliness and isolation. First, the pastoral counselor needs "to assess the nature of the loneliness and its readiness for resolution" (p. 663). Regardless of the cause, pastoral counselors need not move clients too quickly through processes of grief or adjustment. In addition, pastoral counselors should avoid allowing the establishment of a therapeutic rapport and the counselor–client bond to be substituted for true remediative or rehabilitative change. Therefore, "the second step is an environmental manipulation, putting the isolated person in contact with others who are resources for relationship and/or may be similarly afflicted" (p. 663). The second step requires behavioral changes intended to manipulate the client's behaviors and environment in a manner congruent with the client's theological and philosophical anthropology.

The Pastoral Counselor Responds to Characterological Loneliness and Isolation
In contrast to situational or transitory experiences of loneliness and isolation, some clients may present with similar concerns that are truly more characterological in nature. Loneliness rooted in the client's personality structure is often "the result of the person's anger, suspicion, and anxiety. Such persons, due to their painful experiences in formative relationships, experience others primarily as targets for their anger or as potential sources of danger" (Grant, 1990, p. 663). Therefore, shifts in the client's environment will do little to ameliorate loneliness or isolation until other therapeutic issues are addressed. Pastoral counselors are aided, foremost, by not allowing the client's presentation or behaviors to be off-putting. Such clients are seeking isolation and engaging the therapist in the dance. The pastoral counselor's therapeutic orientation will influence how she responds in situations of characterological loneliness and isolation; however, it can still be helpful to explore, as noted earlier, the client's philosophical and theological anthropology. Identification of these core beliefs can help counselors to confront clients regarding dissonance and consonance between their beliefs and behaviors. Pastoral counselors can then help clients by identifying the

behaviors that result in isolation and exploring with clients the motivations and assumptions driving them. According to Grant (1990), "Identification of new choice points about those assumptions and about continuing to use those behaviors" enables the pastoral counselor and client to explore collaboratively new ways of proceeding (p. 664).

CONCLUSIONS

Responding to explicit and implicit spiritual content within mental health practice is a hallmark of pastoral counseling. This chapter offered an initial overview of explicit spiritual content commonly encountered in pastoral counseling—God images, scripture and sacred text, and prayer—as well as the implicit spiritual content presented by clients from a diversity of spiritual traditions—existential anxiety, hope and despair, and loneliness and isolation. Readers are encouraged to employ the chapter's reference list as a recommended reading list for further information on these themes and additional guidance on how they can be addressed within clinical practice. Whether spiritual content is explicit or implicit, one primary goal of pastoral counseling is to facilitate spiritual growth. Therefore, listening for and learning to respond to these spiritual concerns, however subtle they may be, is essential in helping clients to "maintain hope in the midst of losses and tragedies"; "[discover] ways to move from the alienation of guilt to the reconciliation of forgiveness"; "undergird self-esteem and reduce alienating narcissism (pride)"; engage in and facilitate "moments of transcendence, mystical 'peak experiences'"; and belong to a "caring community ... that nurtures and sustains" (Clinebell, 1984, p. 110).

REFLECTION QUESTIONS

1. According to the authors, "The pastoral counselor occupies a perilous position when approaching others with a spiritual foundation grounded in anything other than curiosity and questions." What meaning(s) does this statement have for you?
2. How comfortable or familiar are you with the sacred texts of your own faith tradition? How might you approach incorporating the sacred texts of a client who has a different tradition from your own? What concerns do you have regarding ethical use of sacred texts you are not familiar with?
3. If requested to do so, would you feel at ease praying with a client during a session? Why or why not? Would you feel comfortable praying with a client from another faith tradition? How does the client's religious tradition influence your response?
4. Briefly write down what "hope" means to you. Has there been a time in your life when you felt like you had lost hope? Describe that experience and what/who was instrumental in your regaining your sense of hope.

REFERENCES

Ammerman, N. T. (2013). Spiritual but not religious? Beyond binary choices in the study of religion. *Journal for the Scientific Study of Religion, 52*(2), 258–278. doi:10.1111/jssr.12024

Ashby, H. U., Jr. (1990). Anxiety. In R. J. Hunter (Ed.) *Dictionary of pastoral care and counseling* (pp. 47–48). Nashville, TN: Abingdon.

Bernardi, L., Sleight, P., Bandinelli, G., Cencetti, S., Fattorini, L., Wdowczyc-Szulc, J., & Lagi, A. (2001). Effect of rosary prayer and yoga mantras on autonomic cardiovascular rhythms: Comparative study. *British Medical Journal, 323*, 1446–1449. doi:10.2307/25468612

Burke, R. (1977). Rahner and Dunne: A new vision of God. *Iliff Review, 34*(3), 37–49.

Cheston, S. E., & Miller, J. L. (2011). The use of prayer in counseling. In C. S. Cashwell & J. S. Young (Eds.), *Integrating spirituality and religion into counseling* (pp. 243–260). Alexandria, VA: American Counseling Association.

Clements, W. M. (2001). Issues in pastoral care and counseling for the fourth quarter of life. *Pastoral Psychology, 49*(6), 403–411. doi:10.1023/A:1010397417014

Clinebell, H. J. (1979). *Growth counseling: Hope-centered methods of actualizing human wholeness.* Nashville, TN: Abingdon.

Clinebell, H. J. (1984). *Basic types of pastoral care and counseling: Resources for the ministry of healing and growth* (Rev. ed.). Nashville, TN: Abingdon.

Cook, S. W., Dixon, L. S., & Fukuyama, M. A. (2011). Integrating sacred writings in therapy. In J. D. Aten, M. R. McMinn, & E. L. Worthington Jr. (Eds.), *Spiritually oriented interventions for counseling and psychotherapy* (pp. 227–301). Washington, DC: American Psychological Association. doi:10.1037/12313-011

Davis, D. M., & Hayes, J. A. (2011). What are the benefits of mindfulness? A practice review of psychotherapy-related research. *Psychotherapy, 48*(2), 198–208. doi:10.1037/a0022062

Dunkley, C., & Stanton, M. (2014). *Teaching clients to use mindfulness skills: A practical guide.* New York, NY: Routledge.

Ellingson, S. (2001). The new spirituality from a social science perspective. *Dialog, 40*(4), 257–263. Retrieved from http://onlinelibrary.wiley.com/doi/10.1111/dial.2001.40.issue-4/issuetoc

Frankl, V. E. (2006). *Man's search for meaning.* Boston, MA: Beacon.

Gallup, G., Jr., & Jones, T. (2000). *The next American spirituality: Finding God in the twenty-first century.* Colorado Springs, CO: Cook Communications.

Grant, B. W. (1990). Loneliness and isolation. In R. J. Hunter (Ed.), *Dictionary of pastoral care and counseling* (pp. 663–664). Nashville, TN: Abingdon.

Gubi, P. M. (2004). Surveying the extent of, and attitudes toward, the use of prayer as a spiritual intervention among British mainstream counsellors. *British Journal of Guidance and Counseling, 32,* 461–476. doi:10.1080/03069880412331303277

Gubi, P. M. (2008). *Prayer in counselling and psychotherapy: Exploring a hidden meaningful dimension.* London, UK: Jessica Kingsley.

Gubi, P. M. (2009). A qualitative exploration into how the use of prayer in counselling and psychotherapy might be ethically problematic. *Counselling & Psychotherapy Research, 9*(2), 115–121. doi:10.1080/14733140802685312

Harney, K. F. (2000). Visualizing psychological concepts in stories, parables, and riddles. *Counseling and Values, 44*(3), 222–227. doi:10.1002/j.2161-007X.2000.tb00174.x

Hill, P. C., & Hood, R. W., Jr. (Eds.). (1999). *Measures of religiosity.* Birmingham, AL: Religious Education Press.

Hodge, D. R. (2005). Spiritual lifemaps: A client-centered pictorial instrument for spiritual assessment, planning, and intervention. *Social Work, 50*(1), 77–87. doi:10.1093/sw/50.1.77

Hoffman, L., Knight, S., Boscoe-Huffman, S., & Stewart, S. (2007). Diversity issues and the God image. *Journal of Spirituality in Mental Health, 9*(3/4), 257–279. doi:10.1300/J1515v09n03-13

Hood, R. W., Jr. (2005). Mystical, spiritual, and religious experiences. In R. F. Paloutzian & C. L. Park (Eds.), *Handbook of the psychology of religion and spirituality* (pp. 348–364). New York, NY: Guilford.

Johnson, E. A. (1992). *She who is: The mystery of God in feminist theological discourse.* New York, NY: Crossroad.

Jonker, H., Eurelings-Bontekoe, E. M., Zock, H., & Jonker, E. (2007). The personal and normative image of God: The role of religious culture and mental health. *Archiv Für Religionspsychologie, 29,* 305–318. doi:10.1163/008467207X188883

Kinghorn, W. (2013). "Hope that is seen is no hope at all": Theological constructions of hope in psychotherapy. *Bulletin of the Menninger Clinic, 77*(4), 369–394. doi:10.1521/bumc.2013.77.4.369

Kunkel, M. A., Cook, S., Meshel, D. S., Daughtry, D., & Hauenstein, A. (1999). God images: A concept map. *Journal for the Scientific Study of Religion, 38*(2), 193. doi:10.2307/1387789

Kwan, S. M. (2010). Interrogating "hope": Pastoral theology of hope and positive psychology. *International Journal of Practical Theology, 14*(1), 47–67. doi:10.1515/IJPT.2010.5

Lartey, E. Y. (2003). *In living color: An intercultural approach to pastoral care and counseling* (2nd ed.). London, UK: Jessica Kingsley.

LeFevre, P. (1995). *Modern theologies of prayer*. Chicago, IL: Exploration Press.

Lopez, S. J., Snyder, C. R., Magyar-Moe, J. L., Edwards, L. M., Pedrotti, J. T., Janowski, K., . . . Pressgrove, C. (2004). Strategies for accentuating hope. In P. A. Linley & S. Joseph (Eds.), *Positive psychology in practice* (pp. 388–404). Hoboken, NJ: John Wiley.

Masters, K., & Spielmans, G. (2007). Prayer and health: Review, meta-analysis, and research agenda. *Journal of Behavioral Medicine, 30*(4), 329–338. doi:10.1007/s10865-007-9106-7

McCown, D., Reibel, D., & Micozzi, M. S. (2010). *Teaching mindfulness: A practical guide for clinicians and educators*. New York, NY: Springer.

Moltmann, J. (1977). *The church in the power of the spirit*. New York, NY: Harper & Row.

Monroe, P. G. (2007). *Guidelines for the effective use of the Bible in counseling*. Unpublished manuscript.

Moriarty, G. L., & Hoffman, L. (Eds.). (2007). *God image handbook for spiritual counseling and psychotherapy*. New York, NY: Routledge.

Moriarty, G. L., Thomas, M., & Allmond, J. (2007). God image psychotherapy: Comparing approaches. *Journal of Spirituality in Mental Health, 9*(3/4), 247–255. doi:10.1300/J515v 09n03-12

Neuger, C. C. (2001). *Counseling women: A narrative, pastoral approach*. Minneapolis, MN: Augsburg Fortress.

O'Connor, T. S., & Meakes, E. (2008). Connection to early church theologians: Canadian ethnographic study on the similarities and differences between prayer and theological reflection in pastoral care and counseling. *Pastoral Psychology, 56*(5), 497–506. doi:10.1007/s11089-008-0128-z

O'Grady, K. A., & Bartz, J. D. (2012). Addressing spiritually transcendent experiences in psychotherapy. In J. D. Aten, K. A. O'Grady, & E. L. Worthington (Eds.), *The psychology of religion and spirituality for clinicians: Using research in your practice* (pp. 161–188). New York, NY: Routledge/Taylor & Francis.

O'Grady, K. A., & Richards, P. S. (2007). Theistic psychotherapy and the God image. *Journal of Spirituality in Mental Health, 9*(3/4), 183–209. doi:10.1300/J515v09n03-09

Plante, T. G. (2009). *Spiritual practices in psychotherapy: Thirteen tools for enhancing psychological health*. Washington, DC: American Psychological Association.

Popovici, A. (2011). Speakers discuss images of God. *National Catholic Reporter, 47*(15), 11. Retrieved from http://ncronline.org/

Pruyser, P. W. (1990). Hope and despair. In R. J. Hunter (Ed.), *Dictionary of pastoral care and counseling* (pp. 532–534). Nashville, TN: Abingdon.

Richards, D. G. (1991). The phenomenology and psychological correlates of verbal prayer. *Journal of Psychology and Theology, 19*(4), 354–363. Retrieved from http://journals.biola.edu/jpt/volumes/19/issues/4

Richards, P., & Bergin, A. E. (2005). Religious and spiritual practices as therapeutic interventions. In P. Richards & A. E. Bergin (Eds.), *A spiritual strategy for counseling and psychotherapy* (2nd ed., pp. 251–279). Washington, DC: American Psychological Association. doi:10.1037/11214-009

Rizzuto, A. (1979). *The birth of the living god: A psychoanalytic study*. Chicago, IL: University of Chicago Press.

Rook, K. S. (1984). Promoting social bonding: Strategies for helping the lonely and socially isolated. *American Psychologist, 39*(12), 1389–1407. doi:10.1037/0003-066X.39.12.1389

Shafranske, E. P. (2005). The psychology of religion in clinical and counseling psychology. In R. F. Paloutzian & C. L. Park (Eds.), *Handbook of the psychology of religion and spirituality* (pp. 496–514). New York, NY: Guilford.

Snyder, C. R. (Ed.). (2000). *Handbook of hope: Theory, measures, and applications*. San Diego, CA: Academic Press.

Snyder, C. R. (2002). Hope theory: Rainbows in the mind. *Psychological Inquiry, 13*(4), 249–275. Retrieved from http://www.jstor.org/stable/1448867

Sorajjakool, S. (1999). Theories of personality: Interpretations of reality and the formation of personality. *Pastoral Psychology, 48*(2), 143–158. doi:10.1023/A:1022046811192

Tan, S. Y. (1996). Religion in clinical practice: Implicit and explicit integration. In E. P. Shafranske (Ed.), *Religion and the clinical practice of psychology* (pp. 365–387). Washington, DC: American Psychological Association. doi:10.1037/10199-013

Tan, S. Y. (2007). Use of prayer and scripture in cognitive-behavioral therapy. *Journal of Psychology & Christianity, 26*(2), 101–111. Retrieved from http://www.questia.com/library/journal/1P3-1492333351/use-of-prayer-and-scripture-in-cognitive-behavioral

Tan, S. Y. (2011). *Counseling and psychotherapy: A Christian perspective.* Grand Rapids, MI: Zondervan.

Thomas Aquinas. (2006). *Summa theologiae: Latin text and English translation, introductions, notes, appendices and glossaries* (T. Gilby, Trans.). New York, NY: Cambridge University Press.

Tillich, P. (1952). *The courage to be* (2nd ed.). New Haven, CT: Yale University Press.

Ulanov, A., & Ulanov, B. (1982). *Primary speech: A psychology of prayer.* Atlanta, GA: John Knox Press.

Wise, C. A. (1980). *Pastoral psychotherapy: Theory and practice.* New York, NY: Jason Aronson.

Worthington, E. L. (2005). *Hope-focused marriage counseling: A guide to brief therapy* (2nd ed.). Downers Grove, IL: InterVarsity Press.

Wright, J. H. (1987). God. In J. A. Komonchak, M. Collins, & D. A. Lane (Eds.), *A new dictionary of theology* (pp. 423–436). Collegeville, MN: The Liturgical Press.

Wyatt, J. (2004). Counselling and religious faith. *Psychodynamic Practice, 10*(1), 27–43. doi:10.1080/14753630310001655992

Kari A. O'Grady, Kenneth White, and Heidi Schreiber-Pan

10

CROSS-CULTURAL COUNSELING: THE IMPORTANCE OF ENCOUNTERING THE LIMINAL SPACE

After spending several years in a seminary run by White men, Malidoma Patrice Some (1994) returned to his African tribe with a conflicted soul. His tribal elders proposed that he undergo a tribal initiation that would require him to step into a liminal space with the certainty of either significant transformation or death. Malidoma Patrice's father explained that the Whites are animated by a powerfully restless spirit that imposes a "new order—the order of unrest" (p. 177). He stated that the apparent strength of the White man is an illusion masking terror: The intrinsic tension and conflict within the White man's soul is the articulation of his battle with an overwhelming fear of himself. His wrestle with himself unsettles the world and all those who inhabit it with him. His father instructed further that the only way to settle the White man within Malidome Patrice was to immerse him in a tribal rite of passage that had both the potential to heal his soul and to kill it. His father was clear about the risks of both undergoing the ritual and avoiding it. He warned Malidome Patrice that his previous training among the Whites would be a barrier to his transformation and survival, "like a wall in front of you that will want to keep you from digging into yourself the way the people are expected to during this kind of experience" (p. 178).

We, as pastoral counselors, cannot be afraid of fear and enter into that kind of transformation. A great deal of courage is required to engage ourselves fully with the experience of the *other*. This kind of transformation requires us to move beyond intellectual multicultural engagement toward a willingness to live in a more authentic, vulnerable way. Marshall (2010) states,

> Pastoral care and counseling is not simply about caring for those who come to us; it is also about moving beyond our counseling offices and our communities of faith in order to have an impact on the world in which we live. There are risks, of course, in this kind of pastoral work. To engage ourselves in the critical issues of the day puts our beliefs out front for people to see, and for them to challenge. (p. 431)

Marshall seems to be suggesting that the call to be a pastoral counselor is the beckoning to expose ourselves in meaningful and vulnerable ways on the behalf of the *other*, especially the *marginalized* other. Perhaps being "pastoral" necessarily means letting go of control and accepting fear as a requisite of courage and change. Are we brave enough to disrobe ourselves of the privileges that bring us comfort and opportunity? What would compel us to engage in this sort of exposure to the elements of injustice, and what would we become if we did? What would pastoral counseling look like if transformation of society and of the pastoral counselor was an essential criterion of effective care for the client? Perhaps the first step would be the step into the space of the other.

When we are initially challenged in this way, we cannot see what we will later become and how dramatically our lives might change, but we sense that change must come, and this sensation can be breathtaking. We must rally enough courage to step into the liminal space (Franks & Meteyard, 2007). The liminal space is a dangerous space, but change cannot come without it, and pastoral counselors are called to be change agents.

In this chapter, we present a type of culturally open pastoral counseling that requires a transformation of self and society beyond an educated mind and a politically sensitive vocabulary. This kind of transformation is patterned after the transformation that can be found in the initiation rites inherent in many religions and cultures. We assume that this movement will be a difficult, but necessary, one toward deep and meaningful cross-cultural engagement with clients and grassroots societal transformation. In the remainder of this chapter, we discuss the current state of multicultural competence and social justice discourses and challenge the reader to move beyond the current approaches to these topics. We then present a case that illustrates transformation that can occur when we step into the liminal space with another. The case presentation is followed by a commentary of the case through the perspective of Turner's (1969) discussion of liminal space. This discussion will include Turner's three phases of personal and societal transformation: separation, margin, and aggregation. We then offer a few guiding principles that are intended to foster a more open approach to cross-cultural training for pastoral counselors.

MULTICULTURAL COMPETENCE AND SOCIAL JUSTICE IN PASTORAL COUNSELING

Traditionally, training in issues of diversity in pastoral counseling has consisted of two components: training in cultural competence and attention to social justice. Although we are proposing that the field move beyond these traditional approaches to training, we believe that counselors should be familiar with them. We begin by exploring multicultural competence.

Multicultural Competence

Cultural competence can be defined as the "extent to which an individual has embodied the skills and knowledge necessary to live, survive, and thrive in a particular culture" (Chao, Okazaki, & Hong, 2011, p. 264). Training in this area in pastoral counseling and related fields focuses on meeting the ethical guidelines established by professional organizations. The American Psychological Association (APA), the American Counseling Association (ACA), the National Association of School Psychologists (NASP), and the American Association of Pastoral Counselors (AAPC) have established guidelines that accredited programs are required to maintain to produce competent practitioners. For instance, the AAPC created a task force to draft a set of principles that illustrate the profession's commitment to training and supporting antiracist multiculturally competent pastoral counselors (see Table 10.1). The guidelines serve as a mandate to the profession to be mindful of the dynamics that create and perpetuate individual and institutional racism. Ethical standards such as these, in conjunction with well-written textbooks, offer structure, an occasion to explore issues of diversity in a "safe" and intellectually rigorous environment, and an opportunity to notice diversity of that which constitutes the self (see Jones, Sander, & Booker, 2013, for a list of textbooks).

TABLE 10.1 American Association of Pastoral Counselors (AAPC) Statements on Antiracist
              Multicultural Competencies

To be antiracist multiculturally competent, AAPC must commit itself for deep care for the governance, policy, and clinical training and practice that is intentionally inclusive and through which members are willing to hear the pains of those who have been historically, intentionally, and systemically excluded and disadvantaged.

The process of becoming antiracist multiculturally competent includes AAPC members' commitment to (a) examine racial and cultural identity formation of pastoral counselors and its implications in personal life and clinical practice; (b) analyze critically how AAPC's training, certification, and accreditation standards may reflect racism and monoculturalism; (c) engage in contextual and multicultural analysis of all governance, policy, and practices; and (d) explicitly express concern for managing differences and justice.

Furthermore, members of AAPC commit themselves to become antiracist multiculturally competent pastoral counselors by embodying the following values:

Antiracist multiculturally competent pastoral counselors are committed to pursuing social justice and democratic ideals in which all persons are regarded as having equal worth regardless of identity markers, including but not limited to race, gender, age, sexual orientation, difference in ability, religion, language, and cultural or national origins.

Antiracist multiculturally competent pastoral counselors appreciate human diversity as *a gift*, not a barrier, and engage in training and the practice of pastoral counseling in order to serve peoples from diverse backgrounds by acquiring the attitudes, knowledge, and skills needed for competent clinical practice.

Antiracist multiculturally competent pastoral counselors acknowledge that the pastoral counseling movement in the United States has been significantly formed by White Anglo-Saxon Protestants and that AAPC's organizational structure, culture, governance, and public programs and documents have contributed to systemic exclusion of racial and cultural minorities.

Antiracist multiculturally competent pastoral counselors are committed to bringing about individual, organizational, and societal changes to undo the devastating effects of ever-evolving forms of racism and prejudice and are always alert for and responsive to persons and groups experiencing new or newly recognized forms of exclusion.

Antiracist multiculturally competent pastoral counselors engage in critical self-reflection about ourselves as well as the communities and societies to which we belong. Especially when we belong to dominant groups, multiculturally competent pastoral counselors acknowledge the privileges accorded to us by virtue of our identity and seek to distribute power equitably among all communities.

Antiracist multiculturally competent pastoral counselors are committed to creating a safe space where all persons can work through the painful realities and conflicts that arise out of the history of domination and subjugation and out of the differences we bring from our traditions.

Antiracist multiculturally competent pastoral counselors are committed to seeking justice "now" because they see the urgency of the individual, organizational, and societal changes that must take place, and thus ask, "If not now, when?"

Source: American Association of Pastoral Counselors (2014).

Hansen (2010) suggested that a "missing component of this laudable emphasis on diversity . . . is *intraindividual diversity* (i.e., diverse components of being that exist within individuals)" (p. 16). This diversity within the self may play a significant role in introducing an underappreciated, yet ever-present, aspect of the conversation about and training of culturally competent pastoral counselors. What doors of understanding are opened when one is able to both see and appreciate what makes one not like the others?

The Multicultural Counseling Inventory (MCI; Sodowsky, 1996) was designed to "operationalize the commonly accepted constructs of multicultural counseling competence . . . and to uncover other potential dimensions of MCC [multicultural cultural counseling]" (p. 44). MCC represents the counselor's multicultural knowledge, beliefs, and attitudes (or self-awareness) and skills. In his study of counseling students, Ivers (2012) found that there was significant difference in scoring between Latino and European Americans on the MCI, with Latino counseling students scoring higher overall than their European counterparts. There was also a significant difference found between minority groups on the MCI scale overall and on the Skills, Awareness, and Relationship subscales, with Latino counseling students scoring higher than other peers (Ivers, 2012). Despite a number of limitations in this study, Ivers concluded that the reason for these differences is self-perception within the cultural context. Latinos may see themselves as outside of the cultural norm and, therefore, hold to those distinct aspects of Latino culture that differentiate them from the larger White culture. This may be largely due to their proximity to their nations of origin and a constant flow of new immigrants that keep the culture of origin fresh within the context of the host culture. He also suggested that it is possible that this form of differentiation may reflect aspects of self-determination. The results from the Ivers study provide a degree of support for the idea that a person's ability to both notice and appreciate what makes him or her different from others contributes to the development of multicultural competence. It is also possible that when we explore the diversity within the self and between self and the other, people become too dimensional to be placed in conceptual boxes. Perhaps the complexity of identity compels complex conceptualizations that consider aspects of self that both overlap with and provide contrast to the shared and unique aspects of the other.

Social Justice

Social justice can be defined as:

> the commitment to ensuring change locally, nationally, and internationally based on the valuing of fairness and equity in resources, rights, and treatment for marginalized individuals and groups of people who do not share equal power in society because of their immigration, racial, ethnic, age, socioeconomic, religious heritage, physical ability, or sexual orientation status groups. (Constantine, Hage, Kindaichi, & Bryant, 2007, p. 24)

Training and discussions of social justice in pastoral counseling and related fields are aimed at drawing attention to the injustices inflicted on marginalized populations and motivating privileged populations to address and eradicate the resulting disparities. Historically, such focus on social justice has brought about critically important societal change in the United States. The women's suffrage movement led to the Nineteenth Amendment to the U.S. Constitution, guaranteeing women the right to vote. The American civil rights movement led to the 1964 Civil Rights Act, which prohibited discrimination based on race, color, religion, sex, or national origin. Moreover, the long and less publicized actions of disabled Americans and their advocates resulted in the Americans With Disabilities Act of 1990. Professional counselors, including pastoral counselors, have also contributed to advancements in issues of diversity. Hanna and Cardona (2013) noted that "for well over 30 years, the counseling field has been increasingly focused on the importance of developing the therapeutic relationship between counselors and members of oppressed groups and diverse cultures" (p. 349).

Most would agree that attention to issues of justice has indeed increased over the past few decades in the United States. However, immigration reform, the rights of the mentally ill, and the rights for those who are of the same sex to be married are matters yet to be sufficiently addressed. Furthermore, despite the advances that have been made in civil rights, most would argue that socioeconomic disparity is increasing (particularly in the United States) and that, despite our best intentions, we have a long way to go before we can declare ourselves a just society in all aspects of diversity.

For example, the January–February 2014 issue of the *Harvard Magazine* featured a cover story entitled "Disrupted Lives: Sociologist Matthew Desmond Studies Eviction and the Lives of America's Poor." The magazine cover displayed a photo of two African American males standing in the middle of household furniture, one with boxes in hand, the other with hands on hips. The article itself was illustrated with a picture over a two-page spread of one African American adult female, two African American female youths, and one young African American male looking out of a window. The subsequent pages also featured images of African Americans, along with the European American sociologist Desmond, until finally on the sixth page of the article, a White female was presented. The caption stated, "She was evicted from her apartment after missing a court date while she was in the hospital recovering from a stroke" (Gudrais, 2014, p. 43). The 10 individuals pictured, nine African American and one European American, all reside in Milwaukee, Wisconsin, a city that, according to the 2010 census, is 44.78% White (http://censusviewer.com/city/WI/Milwaukee). Although this article was intended to draw attention to socioeconomic disparity, it inadvertently endorsed an oppressive system. The captions and pictures could have just as easily read, "Evicted: poor, black, uneducated, oppressed and unable to help themselves; Evicted: white woman with extenuating circumstances."

Wilson (2003) cautions against focusing on society's structural and institutional "attitudes, values and actions" (p. 22) from the perspective that individuals' experiences are the result of oppression and powerlessness. She warned about the *seduction of dependency* and suggested that advocates of the social justice model often overlook the secondary gains of the client. Although her work specifically focuses on disabled clients, her assertion can be generalized. She defined the seduction of dependency as "the tendency of some disabled people to develop a high degree of dependency and accept diminished autonomy" (p. 22). She further asserted that as long as the focus is on society's attitudes, values, and actions, the focus is not on the needs of the client and, therefore, weakens the resilience of the client. She suggested that a focus on client needs may be resisted because a strong client functioning autonomously does not contribute to the needs of "the cause" (p. 22). This corroborated the positions of Gushue and Constantine (2007) and Helms (1995), who argued that the desire to rescue those one considers disadvantaged may nurture a perspective of implied racial superiority and inadvertently and subconsciously justify White social justice advocates maintaining an identity of superiority.

We propose that the seduction of dependency points in both directions. The effects of structures and institutions on those classified as *special groups* or *minority groups* are obvious. For those who lack exposure to, or awareness of, these effects, there is a plethora of information and training available. However, what about those who are viewed as the mythologized institutionally and structurally privileged (e.g., White, male, heterosexual, high socioeconomic status, Christian)? Is there a seduction to remain dependent on the structures and institutions that maintain their privilege? Have we structured multiculturalism (e.g., ecological model within community counseling) such that once the privileged populations have acquired the skills and knowledge necessary to score in the acceptable range on an MCC or MCI, they can use their privilege to assist those who are oppressed in a way that emphasizes superiority of the privileged population over those whom they are assisting? Does cultural competence training, with its underlying focus on social justice, maintain the status quo of the different *others* (Chao et al., 2011) and circumvent the possibility of a transformative experience for those who are called to address issues of diversity in pastoral counseling? Have we romanticized the ideal of the benevolent and privileged helper who has "empathy" for those disadvantaged people who so desperately need "our" help? Could this focus be simply a more nuanced and sophisticated way of "White" or "male" or "able-bodied" maintaining privilege? In other words, we are asserting that, despite our best intentions, our current approach to multiculturalism may inadvertently reinforce the systems and structures we are seeking to overcome.

THE ENCOUNTER: A CASE STUDY

I (Kari) serve as the multicultural and diversity affairs committee chair for the pastoral counseling department in which I work. We recently hired a new chair for our department. The new chair called me into his office a few weeks prior to the beginning of the fall semester and issued an assignment. He wanted me to meet with Dr. Skipp Sanders, director of the Reginald F. Lewis Black History Museum of African American History and Culture in Baltimore, Maryland, to see if we might set up an event for our students at the museum. I was eager to please my new chair but also mindful of the growing mound of tasks in my "inbox." Nevertheless, I made a call to Dr. Sanders's assistant and made arrangements for me, a European American woman and member of The Church of Jesus Christ of Latter-day Saints (LDS), and the student representative, fellow author, Ken, an African American Southern Baptist man, to meet with Dr. Sanders, so that I could check this item off my ever-growing "to-do list."

We were greeted warmly by Dr. Sanders, who welcomed us to his "home" and invited us to join him on a tour of the museum. Our tour began with a sneak preview of a renowned African American art collection that was being assembled in a private room in the back of the museum. He spoke with pride and excitement about each of the precious artifacts that had been placed in the museum's care for the duration of the exhibit. Next, we moved into the heart of the museum. The displays were arranged with a tasteful mixture of past and present, highlighting both the ordinary and the extraordinary experiences of African Americans in Maryland.

Ken and Dr. Sanders engaged with the displays nostalgically as they reminisced about their shared African American heritage. I was learning both from the displays and from the interaction of the two men, hoping to bring back with me something of use for the students I teach in our diversity course. At this point in my observation, Ken enthusiastically asked me whether I was able to relate to the experiences of oppression in the display due to the history of oppression of my faith tradition. His question caught me by surprise. I admitted, "I was observing as a teacher, not a student, so I had not considered that level of empathy."

Ken's question challenged me to a deeper level of authentic engagement with the tour. Was I willing to relate with the narratives within the displays? As the tour continued, Ken and Dr. Sanders grew more and more energized. At one point in the tour, they directed my attention to a life-sized portrait of an immaculately dressed gentleman. They explained the need for African American men to dress with dignity to preserve the respectability of the whole community. As we moved through the remaining exhibits, I continued to learn from the displays as well as the dialogue, but I grew increasingly aware of an internal discomfort. Near the end of the tour, I approached Ken and Dr. Sanders and said, "It appears that the two of you are feeling inspired, enlightened, and energized by the stories captured in the displays. You seem very joyful. I am having a different emotional experience than the two of you. I feel a great deal of pain. I am feeling the suffering of the experiences and the weight of the expectations placed upon the people highlighted in these exhibits."

Dr. Sanders responded by touching my arm and looking me warmly in the eyes. He said, "Dr. O'Grady, this is not the history of African Americans in Maryland alone; this is your history. This is the history of all Americans. It is the story of all people. We can all relate to stories of struggle and triumph and everyday experiences." At the end of the elevator ride down to the main level, Dr. Sanders touched my arm again and said, "You are welcome here anytime. Consider this your home."

His words of wisdom not only informed my understanding but also transformed me. I realized that until that moment, I (and most likely countless others in the United States) had bifurcated history into history and other people's history. What would it mean for me to see African American history as my history—not the history of the wrongs I (and people like me) had committed and continue to perpetuate but rather just my history? What if I attached to their story the way I connected to the displays in the Smithsonian National Museum of American History? What would I have to relinquish to embrace the narratives in this museum as my narrative? I knew then at an epistemological level, deeper than ordinary ways of knowing, that I would have to soften the edges of my being that separate me from the edges of the other. I would have to allow my frame to blur into the shape of the other. I would be changed.

The Case Continues: Another Voice

As a 47-year-old African American man, I (Ken) find myself thinking very differently about diversity these days. I am from rural west Texas, certainly from the wrong side of the tracks, and yet I found my way to Harvard Divinity School, where I completed a Master of Divinity degree. While there, I completed 2 years of seminarian-in-residence training at an Episcopal church in Concord, Massachusetts. At present, I serve as an ordained associate pastor at a culturally conservative, biblically fundamentalist, all-White evangelical church in southern Maryland. Recently, after I preached at the morning service, the senior pastor stood at the podium and said, "Pastor Ken is a true man of God. He has broken down some of the cultural barriers that I have."

The senior pastor still has not taken down the Confederate flag from the wall in his office. I do not need him to. I was not there to gain power, to assert power, or to use power to convince him to take down a flag. I did not join that church to fight a culture war. Nor did I join it to make this congregation of people of faith feel guilt for remaining an all-White congregation for 50 years in a community that has changed into a majority minority neighborhood. I did not join it to show the senior pastor that he is blind to ways in which he has siloed himself and his church while preaching Sunday after Sunday that "we have to leave these walls and reach this community." I went there to engage in the hard work of cross-cultural understanding and authentic engagement of *other* through openness, through vulnerability, and through patience. I cannot say that it has not been painful and that there have not been moments when I have been frustrated, disconcerted, and at times incensed. But this is the work of inclusion. I was there to be transformed, to allow them to bear witness to that transformation, and, therefore, to be impinged upon by the power of the transformation and see themselves as being transformed alike. I did so not knowing exactly what the result would be, how long it would take, or the challenges that lay ahead; I only knew that I am willing to pay the price of admittance and commit to the process. I share this to communicate that the transformative process of cross-cultural learning takes vulnerability, it takes not knowing, it takes intentionality. Diversity is not what we do; diversity is who we are, each one of us. I do need them and they need me. We need one another to be the lens through which we interpret what it means to "be."

In April 2013, I (Ken) gave a presentation entitled "Identity as a Dynamic Component of Pastoral Counseling" at Loyola University Maryland as one in a series of presentations given on diversity. Its assertion was that diversity is a construction and that individuals are made of many parts: "Identity is not stagnant but constantly under construction" (K. White, 2013). At the end of my presentation, a short, blonde-haired professor approached me. Immediately, two things struck me: her calm demeanor and a knowing glint in her eye. She asked whether I would be willing to join the diversity taskforce at Loyola. The reply came from my lips so quickly it was as though I saw the words after they left my mouth, and it was too late to reach out and grab them back. "Yes ma'am, thank you." I wondered, "What have I gotten myself into this time?"

Subsequently, Kari asked whether I would accompany her to the Reginald F. Lewis Black History Museum of African American History and Culture in Baltimore, Maryland. It was a brisk day, and the drive from southern Maryland took over an hour, giving me plenty of time to think of the several possible experiences that might happen. At the time, I was also a student in her diversity issues in counseling class, and we had previously engaged in intense, enlightening conversations about the complexities of diversity, culture, engagement, and the value of processing encounters of *other* in meaningful and transformative ways.

When I arrived, Kari was there waiting. She met me with a smile. Shortly thereafter, Dr. Skipp Sanders stepped through the door. When Dr. Sanders approached us, we were standing side by side. He reached out his hand and introduced himself. I replied, "Ken White, and this is Dr. Kari O'Grady, professor of pastoral counseling at Loyola University Maryland." My reply was intentional and important for the process. Both Dr. Sanders and I are male and African American. It was important for me in this space to invite Kari in with all of the value she would bring. My introduction illustrated that I viewed myself as accompanying her rather than indicated that I was devaluing myself. I wanted each component of the experience to stand on its own.

As we toured, I immediately noticed two things: the physical space and the narrative articulated by the artifacts and pictures. First, the physical layout of the museum was fascinating. The combinations of bright and dim light surrounding the items displayed were themselves impactful, highlighting one display while drawing attention to another. Life-sized pictures were prominently displayed along with other artifacts that had been strategically placed to draw attention, for each had a story to tell. Near the end of the tour, Dr. Sanders explained that the museum represented the history of African Americans in Maryland. As we spoke and fleshed out the museum's deeper implications, we noted that what was being spoken as a subtext was that African American history in Maryland, and in the United States as a whole, is not a separate and distinct history but America's history. We spoke about the important contributions of the populations who are allowed an identity within the constructs that presently guide conversations about diversity (i.e., racial minorities, women, the poor). We also discussed the value of empowering those who appear to be without power based on multifaceted analysis of institutions and structures. However, the conversation took a turn.

As we toured the museum, Kari spoke about the pictures of struggle and the obvious desire to rise above the complicated circumstances of African Americans' past experiences of injustice in the United States. I responded by asking her about the shared experience of "her people" in America. Kari is a member of the Church of Jesus Christ of Latter-day Saints, a group with its own history of struggle and experiences with the vicissitudes of minority group status, a group with its own *identity*. Change the color of the faces and the narrative of struggle, progress, identity pride, and the articulation of a rich and meaningful history, and the stories were hers as well. The women in dresses, the children working and playing, the men standing with their families, and the many "firsts" could be said as easily about the LDS community. Yes, African American history is American history, and LDS history is American history.

At that moment, one of Dr. Sanders's assistants walked in, and they began a conversation. This gave Kari and me an opportunity to talk privately. The commonality and shared experience of people in America struck her. We spoke about the value of understanding the common experience and the value of understanding oneself and cultural history as a part of a larger narrative. My question was, "But what's the price of admittance to this narrative?" Her eyes glistened. The price of admittance is declaration of or sacrifice of identity, the price of one's individual group identity to be a part of the whole so that its history can really be seen and known as American history. The price required is not the sacrifice of identity as defined as component parts with equivalent value but rather the letting go of the conception of identity as rigid and even forced, "identification with groups of people who have been socialized as belonging to a group" (Helms, 1993, p. 241). The price requires the relinquishing of siloed identities to see the varied identities that construct the self. The price of admittance is authentic engagement of *other* with openness to the possible opportunity for transformation endemic in the process.

Case Commentary Through the Lens of Turner

What follows is an assessment of this encounter interpreted through the work of the anthropologist Victor Turner (1969) as presented in his analysis of specific ritual processes in *The Ritual Process: Structure and Anti-Structure*. The work of Turner, based on Arnold van Gennep's (1960) cultural interpretation of rites of passage, is seminal in its presentation of grassroots change and transformation. Although this short presentation is not meant to be exhaustive, it is intended to be an introduction to a methodological approach to in-depth work in the area of diversity and, more specifically, to the potentially transformative experiences to be had in the education of clinical pastoral counselors. We consider the transformation of individual and group identification into the holy/wholly *one* to be a sacred ritual that can be viewed within the framework of initiates who are entering a rite of passage that transforms them and allows them to enter into *communitas*.

Space and narrative can serve as ground for transformation. Turner (1969) noted that the processes of transition, here termed *transformation*, "are marked by three phases: separation, margin, and aggregation" (p. 94). Often these phases co-occur rather than occur linearly; however, for purposes of cross-cultural training, it can be helpful to describe them in a linear fashion.

Separation

During the first phase, *separation*, the individual or group exhibits behavior that represents the willingness to detach from the structures that represent, set, and secure positions and locations within the present social and cultural construct. When approached by Dr. Sanders, it was important to meet the societal tendency to preference commonalities in gender and race with a deferential introduction of Kari by Ken. Dr. Sanders approached Ken first as a fellow African American male, at which point Ken intentionally pivoted attention to Kari. He introduced her without reference to gender and with body language that articulated comfort with her in this space, which represented African American culture and power. Much of what one communicates is paralinguistic. Ken was intentional with his body position, hand gestures, and tone of voice to communicate, "Doc, she should be here." It would have been easy to make the common ethnic and gender connection, to maintain the traditional ways we have been socialized to connect. In other words, men are socially trained to connect to men in ways that often marginalize women, and races are trained to band together against other races. However, moving from the structured into the second phase consists of an intentional stripping of norms and a willingness to assume ambiguous and indeterminate attributes.

Margin

The space in the margins is amorphous, and one must be aware of the power that can be gained upon entry into this space. There is a cost of entry: humility. Turner (1969) noted that there is a humbling that is requisite in the second phase, also known as the liminal phase or period. In this phase, individuals are undifferentiated and equal. Individuals are stripped of those things with which they identify and that which would identify them and their status within the existing social construct. With the handshake, Ken acknowledged the social norms of gender and race. He then sought to move beyond his Blackness and *maleness* through his introduction of Kari. When presented with an opportunity to restructure the experience, Kari did not identify Ken as a student or assistant but engaged with him as a colleague, a fellow initiate. Persons in a liminal state may be disguised, scantily clothed, or naked. Liminality, or the liminal state, is likened to death. Not only must those entering into this liminal space leave identifying markers at the point of entry, but liminal persons must be willing to allow those markers of identity to die. This was illustrated when Ken moved beyond race and gender and Kari superseded the traditional hierarchy of teacher and student so that they could enter into the liminal space as fellow initiates. At some point during the journey into the liminal space, the initiate becomes keenly aware that he or she is entering into a dangerous state and that a death of sorts is likely to occur.

The museum space offered itself as that liminal space. The liminal space is mystical, unfamiliar, other, and the lines of space and time are blurred. Furthermore, it is *sacred*. In the biblical sense, it is *holy ground*. The physical space and the story or stories narrated within signify detachment "from an earlier fixed point in the social structure, from set cultural conditions (a state)," or from "a set of cultural conditions" (Turner, 1969, p. 94). Not only did Kari and Ken become ambiguous to one another, but the space presented them with a narrative unfamiliar enough, morphed enough, disconcerting enough to unlearn, to become new in the experience. They journeyed into the museum as new and ready to be written upon by the wisdom of the museum as they listened to and followed the instruction of their *shaman*, Dr. Sanders. They presented themselves to a process of *unknowing to not knowing*, so that they might emerge "endowed with additional powers to enable" (Turner, 1969, p. 95) for the work they felt lay ahead of them and that they were called to engage (p. 95). Stepping into the liminal space during a rite of passage into a new station or status, although not a new path, is a seminal step into the process of meaningfully following a path.

Reaggregation
Individuals or groups that have experienced the first two stages of the process are to emerge into the third state or phase, reaggregation or reincorporation. They are brought once again back into a stable and structured state within the existing cultural structure. However, the newly reintegrated person(s) have newly bestowed rights, responsibilities, and powers that are incumbent by virtue of the privilege of having this experience. They are obligated to use these powers for the good of all. They are bound by a new set of ethical standards conferred by the community. As Turner (1969) wrote,

> It is as though there are two major "models" for human interrelatedness, juxtaposed and alternating. The first is of society as a structured, differentiated, and often hierarchical system of politico-legal-economic positions with many types of evaluation, separating men [*sic*] in terms of "more" or "less." The second, which emerges recognizably in the liminal period, is of society as an unstructured or rudimentarily structured and relatively undifferentiated *communitas*, community, or even communion of equal individuals who submit together to the general authority of the ritual elders. (p. 96)

This reaggregation into the existing structure is essential for transformation. The infusing of all aspects of the individual's past, released and reinterpreted in and by the liminal experience, allows the individual to emerge into the culture empowered to, and with the responsibility of, fulfilling the mandate placed on him, her, or them in the liminal state. The mandate is bound by the ethical standards that are incumbent in the standards. One emerges from this sacred process with the pride and responsibilities "of a higher position or office" (Turner, 1969, p. 97). We, like Turner, prefer the term *communitas*, "to distinguish the modality of social relationship from an 'area of common living'" (p. 96). This is a reordering of the structure of community functionally through the change of one's understanding of place and purpose within the larger cultural structure. *Communitas* is representative of people experiencing liminality together.

The museum was just an ordinary space that became liminal because Kari and Ken encountered it in a new and open way. Kari did not continue to engage as a White woman viewing a Black person's experience but rather as someone sharing in and deeply relating to that experience. This was possible because Dr. Sanders was courageous enough to offer Kari his history as hers, even though people much like her had abused and rejected his space in the past. He was generous enough to open the doors of his history, his identity, not only to allow her to look at it but to invite her to adopt it as her own. She might have rejected it, but the *shaman* knew that he had to face that death of sorts or all would die. Because of Dr. Sanders's openness, Kari's and Ken's experience with the liminal space of the museum created a reinterpretation of peoples and cultures that moved them from a traditional view of multiculturalism into the new space of *communitas*. With this transformation comes a mandate.

A CULTURALLY OPEN APPROACH TO TRAINING
IN PASTORAL COUNSELING

As an immigrant to the United States, I (Heidi) was able to take a step back and view the multicultural nature of this country from an outsider's viewpoint. In my naïveté, I came to this country without a comprehensive understanding of the history of race relations and the depth of conflict among people of various racial backgrounds. It was troubling to accept that my new home was flawed with overt discrimination and systematized racism.

Kari noted earlier that African American history is American history and contains within it the history of all suffering. As a native-born German, it is part of my heritage to acknowledge the extensive suffering of the Jewish people as a result of my ancestors' actions. I have had powerful interactions with Jewish community members that can be described as mutually healing. This healing was the result of thoughtful reflection and ownership of one's individual cultural story. The act of embracing the United States as my new home, comprehending the complexity of its multicultural nature, and acknowledging the roots of my heritage prepared me to enter the sacred ground of liminality. I had a significant awakening experience during a diversity class where I gained profound insight into the deeply hidden biases and unconscious projections that affect oppressed minorities on a daily basis. Consequently, these experiences launched my passion for cross-cultural work and prepared me to engage in a number of ways and settings as a fellow sojourner among people from all walks of life. This walk included participating in a teaching assistantship with Kari in the diversity issues in counseling course, a university-sponsored fieldwork trip that Kari and I took to Haiti, and the implementation of special forums on racism, heterosexism, and prejudice for pastoral counseling students aimed at enhancing cross-cultural awareness. This work forced me to explore the liminal space I inhabit. Even today, feelings of unease continue as I settle into my liminal space. Nevertheless, the appreciation of my unique cultural formation story, in addition to an attitude of humility and openness, provides safety and a sense of deep groundedness. This groundedness or anchoring provides fuel for the unending work of transformation—transformation of an egalitarian and pluralistic nature. Engaging in the type of transformation described by Turner is an ongoing process that cannot be easily addressed in training through a simple, step-by-step plan. However, in this portion of the chapter, I add to my colleagues' case study and analysis by distilling experiences from both my personal history and my professional work into some clinically relevant guidelines. We wish to offer a few guiding principles intended to foster a more culturally open approach to cross-cultural training for pastoral counselors and other helping professionals. These principles are the result of multiple conversations with pastoral counseling students and faculty, presentations, and research. They are a unique compilation of innovative ideas and expert recommendations targeted toward creating crossculturally competent counselors. Furthermore, these principles suggest foundational standards that introduce counselors to the essential skills of working with a diverse clientele. The following principles and their accompanying exercises can be viewed as part of the ritual of preparing a pastoral counselor for engagement in the liminal space in such a way that he or she can step into *communitas*.

Principle 1: Know Thine Own Story and Tell It

Narrative therapy (M. White, 2007) is a compelling approach to counseling that places an individual in the expert role of his or her own life. This approach emphasizes the broader context of an individual's life, paying special attention to a variety of dimensions such as race, gender, class, sexual orientation, ethnic heritage, age, and mental and physical abilities and characteristics (M. White & Epston, 1990). This framework provides a valuable context for counselors to examine their own *cultural* story, including assumptions, values, and biases. A meaningful and therapeutically useful exercise is to write one's cultural formation story. A cultural formation story is similar to writing a life story but focuses on the cultural underpinnings of one's personal history. This exercise may provide new meaning for one's past experiences and generate fresh insights. The following prompts are beneficial when writing one's cultural formation story:

- What were the most important values in my family of origin, and do they still hold true for me today?
- How has my understanding of my cultural heritage evolved over time?
- How did my family of origin address issues of diversity; how did they interact with people of different racial, sexual, or socioeconomic backgrounds?
- Were there differences in opinion among family members regarding issues of diversity?
- What are some key (multicultural) experiences I had as a child/adolescent, and how have those experiences formed me?
- Did my family of origin show any bias toward a particular group of people (e.g., poor, African American, Asian, LGBTQI [lesbian, gay, bisexual, transgender, queer, and intersex], mentally ill, overweight, women)?
- Were there stereotypical remarks made regarding a specific race (e.g., "Blacks are lazy," "Mexicans aren't clean," "Asians are smarter than other races")?
- How was my family of origin affected by issues of discrimination, oppression, racism, and stereotyping?
- What was my experience with direct or indirect benefits of individual, institutional, or cultural racism?
- How have my experiences with people of diverse backgrounds formed me?
- How have experiences of discrimination, oppression, racism, and stereotyping benefited or harmed me?

Culturally skilled counselors should strive for a thorough understanding of how their upbringing has influenced their views of others. It is essential to reflect on one's own cultural background and experiences, attitudes, values, and biases to ensure a continual experience of self-awareness. Furthermore, to become a culturally skilled counselor, one must develop knowledge about his or her multifaceted aspects of self, particularly how this self forms one's attitudes and biases and shapes one's counseling approach (Sue, Arredondo, & McDavis, 1992). An attitude of self-awareness often leads to insight on issues of countertransference, fostering a more effective therapeutic relationship. A central element of successful cross-cultural counseling is the counselor's awareness of his or her position in the social hierarchy. This includes an honest evaluation of one's place of privilege, which requires a systematic assessment of societal benefits due to one's race, gender, physical attributes, sexual orientation, or socioeconomic background.

Principle 2: Become Aware of Cognitive Dissonance

Cognitive dissonance "describes the state of psychological disequilibrium experienced when we are facing, but have not yet resolved, information that contradicts our worldview" (Newton, 2010, p. 144). In other words, cognitive dissonance leads to feelings of discomfort that result from holding two conflicting beliefs or a conflict between a belief and a behavior. A common experience of cognitive dissonance occurs for counselors in training who reflect on issues of diversity. Most students want to hold the belief that they do not discriminate or engage in racism (Sue, 2001). When a lecture exposes them to the reality of systematized racism or White privilege, it often conflicts with their previously held belief about their ability to refrain from discrimination. The following excerpt, from a pastoral counseling student, describes this sentiment:

> In discussing some of the more emotional subjects—heterosexism, racism, and classism—in this class, I realized how much these social constructs have shaped my identity, relationships, behaviors, and beliefs. Consequently, I often felt moments of discomfort. The conflict between my belief and experience created cognitive dissonance. For example, I always thought that I was a pretty independent, progressive thinker who had overcome racism (belief), but discussing White privilege evoked many visceral reactions (emotions). As such, I realized that I still have a long way to go. I also learnt that there are aspects of internalized racism, heterosexism, and classism that I still need to address. (Male student, personal communication, May 2013)

Unfortunately, some students who experience cognitive dissonance during their cross-cultural training tend to meet issues of diversity with resistance to preserve their prior beliefs and to avoid the inherent risks of true transformation. Diversity training highlights issues that are often experienced in direct opposition to one's worldview. Consequently, students fear disconnection from their communities. The education field has, in recent years, drawn attention to the ways that students encounter dissonance and has developed potential resistance reduction strategies. For example, McFalls and Cobb-Roberts (2001) proposed that creating awareness of cognitive dissonance (i.e., metadissonance) prior to the student experiencing dissonance can help reduce resistance. One hundred twenty-four undergraduate education students were divided into two groups; students in both groups were instructed to read "White Privilege: Unpacking the Invisible Knapsack" by Peggy McIntosh (1989). This article highlights many hidden White privileges and is capable of eliciting cognitive dissonance in the reader. Both groups were directed to engage in a reflective written response to the article, but the second group received a lecture on cognitive dissonance theory prior to writing the response. As a result of becoming aware of possible mental discomfort due to dissonance, members of the second group showed less resistance to discrepant information than their peers who did not receive the lecture. In other words, when students received information on cognitive dissonance theory and the role of metadissonance prior to reflecting on diversity issues, fewer responses revealed themes of denial, anger, and rejection in response to the article. Therefore, bringing attention to the notion of metadissonance promises to be a beneficial way of reducing resistance and opening oneself to the phases of transformation that are necessary for effective counseling (McFalls & Cobb-Roberts, 2001).

Principle 3: Broaden Your Cultural Horizon

> To become neighbors is to bridge the gap between people. As long as there is distance between us and we cannot look into one another's eyes, all sorts of false ideas and images arise. (Nouwen, 2013)

Nouwen's words highlight the need to encounter people whose lives differ from one's own. By directly experiencing the *other*, the potential to gain new meaning and broaden one's cultural horizon grows substantially. With an increasingly diverse population in the United States, an ever more integrated society as interfaith and interracial marriages peak, and unprecedented access to people from various cultural backgrounds, it is more important than ever that pastoral counseling students are able to seek out and leverage cross-cultural experiences for the benefit of personal development and professional effectiveness. Yalom (2002) asserted that the best counseling is the counseling that transforms both the counselor and the client. By stepping into the space of the *other*, we are able to create a new space with our clients that allows for authentic discourse in which both the client and the counselor emerge from the experience as something new. Pastoral counselors prepare themselves for transformative experiences with all clients by exposing themselves to diverse populations and experiences. The counselor must soften his or her edges so he or she does not merely observe the experience but rather truly engages in the experiences of the *other*.

Efforts to broaden one's cultural horizon should not only involve the professional domain but also include settings of a personal and social nature. For example, joining a community meeting with a racially diverse population helps the counselor gain another perspective aside from the experience she or he encounters at her or his academic or clinical institutions (Sue et al., 1992). The following list provides suggestions for ways to broaden one's cultural horizon:

- Attend a worship service at a religious community that differs from your own.
- Attend a Buddhist meditation group.
- Attend an Alcoholics Anonymous (AA) or other support group meeting.
- Seek out people of different racial or socioeconomic backgrounds at work, school, or church and initiate a conversation.
- Serve at a soup kitchen or homeless shelter.
- Visit a LGBTQI community center.
- View and discuss the educational documentary film *Color of Fear* (Lee, Hunter, Goss, & Bock, 1997).
- Volunteer at an immigrant or refugee community organization.
- Participate in a mission trip or study abroad.

Exposure and engagement are essential for counselors' professional and personal self-development as they provide experiential, hands-on encounters. Such encounters have the potential to facilitate understanding and familiarity with people and situations that previously have been thought of as foreign, perplexing, or even inferior. An authentic cross-cultural experience is a fundamental ingredient of professional competency.

Principle 4: Practice Cultural Humility

As pastoral counselors and pastoral counselors-in-training, it may be helpful to reinforce that the strength of cross-cultural competency is defined by the openness one has toward the *other* (Fowers & Davidov, 2006). Moreover, openness integrates the interpersonal dimension of humility, a trait that is a characteristic of respect for others and a lack of self-focus. Therefore, a cultural humility approach advocates for self-evaluation and awareness that one's own culture is not superior to other cultures. Educating counselors-in-training to become culturally humble requires critical thinking skills in addition to continuous reflections on cross-cultural experiences (Schuessler, Wilder, & Byrd, 2012). Cultural humility challenges an individual's sense of superiority that often arises when one is confronted with cultural differences. Therefore, an attitude of cultural humility is a way of being that is *other* oriented. The preceding guiding principles in this section describe elements of cross-cultural competence; however, cultural humility proposes that such feelings of competence can lead to overconfidence and failure to notice the complexity and uniqueness of the clients' culture and experience (Hook, Davis, Owen, Worthington, & Utsey, 2013). Therefore, it is vital that counselors maintain an attitude of cultural humility and commit to its lifelong development. The following list of objectives may be helpful for counselors to reflect on when considering a viewpoint of cultural humility:

- Promote an interpersonal stance of openness rather than superiority.
- Reflect on cross-cultural experiences through dialogue or journaling.
- Trust in the value of self-reflection and self-critique.
- Become aware of one's own cultural lens through which one perceives the client.
- Take an open stance toward others, recognizing one's ability to learn from all clients.
- Become less authoritative and more collaborative, less of an expert and more of a learner.
- Understand one's own prejudices and biases.
- Readily enter into the client's world.
- Acknowledge one's limited knowledge and understanding of the client's cultural background and experiences.

The primary focus of cross-cultural training for pastoral counselors is awareness, knowledge, and self-reflection. Developing cultural competence requires knowing oneself and actively processing consequential insights. Furthermore, it requires heightened awareness of personal cognitive dissonance when confronted with conflicting beliefs. Experiential encounters with cultures different from one's own are essential when gaining multicultural counseling skills. Finally, it is indispensable that counselors cultivate an attitude of cultural humility; culturally humble counselors approach their clinical work through a lens of persistent openness, self-critique, and lifelong learning.

CONCLUSIONS: THE MANDATE

The call to be a pastoral counselor beckons us to expose ourselves in meaningful and vulnerable ways on the behalf of the other and the all. To engage in this work means that we may have to not only acknowledge and abandon privileges but also relinquish our previously held perspectives and allow our sense of identity or identities to be altered. We must be willing to learn anew without the constraints of well-rehearsed cognitive structures. We must be willing to reconsider that which we thought we understood, even that which we hold sacred. We must be willing to be fellow initiates who are opening ourselves to the liminal spaces before us by engaging in rituals that soften the edges that separate us from the edges of the *other*, thus allowing us to create *communitas*.

Traditionally, training in issues of diversity within clinical pastoral counseling has focused on cultural sensitivity training by making one aware of dos and don'ts and discussing social injustices. This traditional approach tends to target those in power whether by identifying cultural blind spots and White privilege or by including more people from *special groups* as participants, authors, students, and counselors to provide an outlet for the guilt and power that is endemic to White privilege.

Our approach, however, is distinct. We are not proposing the Herculean task of reordering structures and institutions that maintain the status for White power. Rather, we propose intentionally stripping oneself of prior knowledge of self (cultural identity) and revisiting oneself on the sacred ground created in the liminal space regardless of one's power status or religious position. As noted in the preceding case study, both Kari and Ken abandoned self to enter a liminal space together. To help achieve this objective, we shared Turner's three phases of transformation, suggesting that these phases represent the process of transformation required for pastoral counselors who wish to open themselves to the liminal space so that they may be effective counselors and engage in authentic societal change. This chapter presented practices that can help prepare pastoral counselors for the kind of transformation that moves beyond tolerance or even acceptance to *communitas*. These processes were illustrated through the authors' experiences and struggles with psychological, spiritual, and societal transformation.

When we encourage people to change at the grassroots level, the institutions and structures that feed and are fed by these unjust systems will change. We acknowledge that this type of transformation requires much from people and from the field of pastoral counseling. We recognize that this type of change is risky and that it is certainly not for everyone. For some, cultural sensitivity training and the social justice mandate to use their position of privilege to help "those" people is enough. However, for others, there is a desire to go further, to be transformed. Sojourners who strip themselves of cultural identity, embrace equity, and recognize their pluralistic composition can emerge truly transformed.

Who are we as pastoral counselors after each encounter with the liminal space? With what additional *knowing* and power do we emerge after experiencing the liminal space, whether it is a visit to a museum, a session with a client, or reading a chapter in a book? Such encounters become transformative when we routinely prepare to enter into ritual processes, courageously step into liminal spaces, and thoughtfully emerge with a new state, mandate, and responsibility. When such encounters are experienced together as fellow thinkers, scholars, educators, and human beings, the transformation is *communitas*. We encourage pastoral counselors across the globe to courageously step into the liminal space.

> I was not afraid of dying. Wasn't I already dead in some sense, trapped between worlds as I was? If [stepping into the liminal space] was a way out of this trap, could I really say no? (Some, 1994, p. 177)

REFLECTION QUESTIONS

1. What fears do you currently hold onto that keep you from being fully present with your clients?
2. What is needed for you to relinquish or attend to those fears appropriately so that you can have an empathic compassion for your clients who are from different cultural backgrounds than your own?
3. What activities listed in this chapter would be most likely to broaden your horizons of cultural awareness?
4. Have you had an experience of stepping into the liminal space? If so, what helped you step into that space? If not, what practices, beliefs, and perspectives would you need to adjust in your life to prepare to step into the liminal space?
5. Have you ever experienced a sense of communitas? If so, how did you experience it? If not, what holds you back from experiencing communitas?

REFERENCES

American Association of Pastoral Counselors. (2014). *Anti racist multicultural competencies*. Retrieved from http://www.aapc.org/about-us/anti-racist-multicultural-competences/

Chao, M., Okazaki, S., & Hong, Y. (2011). The quest for multicultural competence: Challenges and lessons learned from clinical and organizational research. *Social & Personality Psychology Compass*, 5(5), 263–274. doi:10.1111/j.1751-9004.2011.00350.x

Constantine, M. G., Hage, S. M., Kindaichi, M. M., & Bryant, R. M. (2007). Social justice and multicultural issues: Implications for the practice and training of counselors and counseling psychologists. *Journal of Counseling and Development*, 85, 24–29. doi:10.1037/0735-7028.38 .3.321

Fowers, B. J., & Davidov, B. J. (2006). The virtue of multiculturalism: Personal transformation, character, and openness to the other. *American Psychologist*, 61, 581–594. doi:10.1037/0003-066X.61.6.581

Franks, A., & Meteyard, J. (2007). Liminality: The transforming grace of in-between places. *Journal of Pastoral Care & Counseling*, 61(3), 215–222.

Gudrais, E. (2014). Disrupted lives: Sociologist Matthew Desmond studies eviction and the lives of America's poor. *Harvard Magazine*, 116(3), 38–43. Retrieved from http://harvardmag .com/pdf/2014/01-pdfs/0114-38.pdf

Gushue, G. V., & Constantine, M. G. (2007). Color-blind racial attitudes and White racial identity attitudes in psychology trainees. *Professional Psychology: Research and Practice*, 38(3), 321–328. doi:10.1037/0735-7028.38.3.321

Hanna, F. J., & Cardona, B. (2013). Multicultural counseling beyond the relationship: Expanding the repertoire with techniques. *Journal of Counseling & Development*, 91(3), 349–357. doi: 10.1002/j.1556-6676.2013.00104.x

Hansen, J. T. (2010). Counseling and psychoanalysis: Advancing the value of diversity. *Journal of Multicultural Counseling and Development*, 38(1), 16–26. doi:10.1002/j.2161-1912.2010 .tb00110.X

Helms, J. E. (1993). I also said White racial identity influences White researchers. *The Counseling Psychologist*, 21, 240–243. Retrieved from dx.doi.org.ezp.lndlibrary.org/10.1177/00110000 93212007

Helms, J. E. (1995). An update of Helms' White and people of color racial identity models. In J. G. Ponterotto, J. M. Casas, L. A. Suzuki, & C. M. Alexander (Eds.), *Handbook of multicultural counseling* (pp. 181–198). Thousand Oaks, CA: Sage.

Hook, J. N., Davis, D. E., Owen, J., Worthington, E. L., & Utsey, S. O. (2013). Cultural humility: Measuring openness to culturally diverse clients. *Journal of Counseling Psychology*, 60, 353–366. doi:10.1037/10032595

Ivers, N. N. (2012). The effect of ethnicity on multicultural competence. *Journal of Professional Counseling: Practice, Theory & Research, 39*(2), 40–52. Retrieved from http://www.highbeam.com/doc/1P3-2725908391.html

Jones, J. M., Sander, J. B., & Booker, K. W. (2013). Multicultural competency building: Practical solutions for training and evaluating student progress. *Training and Education in Professional Psychology, 7*(1), 12–22. doi:10.1037/a0030880

Lee, M. W., Hunter, M., Goss, R., Jr., & Bock, R. (Producers). (1997). *The color of fear* [Motion picture]. Oakland, CA: Stir-Fry Seminars and Consulting.

Marshall, J. (2010). Pro-active intercultural pastoral care and counseling with lesbian women and gay men. *Pastoral Psychology, 59*(4), 423–432. doi:10.1007/s11089-009-0203-0

McFalls, E. L., & Cobb-Roberts, D. (2001). Reducing resistance to diversity through cognitive dissonance instruction: Implications for teacher education. *Journal of Teacher Education, 52*, 164–172. doi:117/0022487101052002007

McIntosh, P. (1989, July–August). White privilege: Unpacking the invisible knapsack. *Peace and Freedom Magazine*, pp. 10–12.

Newton, P. E. (2010). Thinking about linking. *Measurement: Interdisciplinary Research and Perspectives, 8*(1), 38–56. doi:10.1080/15366361003749068

Nouwen, H. (2013, July 22). *Bridging the gap between people* [Online forum]. Retrieved from http://myemail.constantcontact.com/Daily-Meditation--Bridging-the-Gap-Between-People.html?soid=1011221485028&aid=aYkWnblK7g8

Schuessler, J. B., Wilder, B., & Byrd, L. W. (2012). Reflective journaling and development of cultural humility in students. *Nursing Education Perspectives, 33*(2), 96–99. doi:10.5480/1536-5026-33.2.96

Sodowsky, G. R. (1996). The Multicultural Counseling Inventory: Validity and applications in multicultural training. *Multicultural Assessment in Counseling and Clinical Psychology*. Paper 13. Retrieved from http://digitalcommons.unl.edu/burosbookmulticultural/13

Some, M. P. (1994). *Of water and the spirit: Ritual, magic, and initiation in the life of an African Shaman*. New York, NY: Penguin.

Sue, D. W. (2001). Multidimensional facets of cultural competence. *The Counseling Psychologist, 29*(6), 790–821. doi:10.1177/0011000001296002

Sue, D. W., Arredondo, P., & McDavis, R. J. (1992). Multicultural counseling competencies and standards: A call to the profession. *Journal of Counseling and Development, 70*, 477–486. doi:10.1002/j.1556-6676.1992.tb01642.X

Turner, V. (1969). *The ritual process: Structure and anti-structure*. New York, NY: Aldine Transaction.

van Gennep, A. (1960). *The rites of passage*. Chicago, IL: University of Chicago Press.

White, K. (2013, April). *Identity as a dynamic component of pastoral counseling*. Paper presented at the Everyone is Diverse to Someone seminar. Baltimore, MD: Loyola University Maryland.

White, M. (2007). *Maps of narrative practice*. New York, NY: W. W. Norton.

White, M., & Epston, D. (1990). *Narrative means to therapeutic ends*. New York, NY: W. W. Norton.

Wilson, S. (2003). *Disability, counseling and psychotherapy: Challenges and opportunities*. New York, NY: Palgrave Macmillan.

Yalom, I. D. (2002). *The gift of therapy: An open letter to a new generation of therapists and their patients*. New York, NY: HarperCollins.

Timothy S. Hanna

11

COMMON GROUND: PASTORAL COUNSELING AND ALLIED PROFESSIONAL INTERVENTIONS

The first step to take is to become aware that love is an art.
—Erich Fromm (1956)

The prior chapters have explored who pastoral counselors are and how they think. What remains is to delineate what pastoral counselors *do*. This question is often asked by laypeople and professionals alike and may even beleaguer a discerning student of pastoral counseling. Much as Erich Fromm (1956) averred that love is an art, pastoral counseling too can be conceived of as *an art*. To be sure, however, in this modern age of mental health care, pastoral counseling should also be considered *a science*. As an art, pastoral counseling requires a personal formation rooted in ways of being and understanding and forged through careful practice, training, and supervision. This foundation also reflects the discipline's scientific bases, which are further evidenced by the pursuit and inclusion of research-driven and empirically based practices.

This text has made efforts thus far to outline the theory and practice of pastoral counseling through an examination of the particular ways of being and understanding that demarcate this unique discipline. Inasmuch as all mental health care practices stem from a common psychological foundation, pastoral counseling shares many similarities with other allied mental health professions. This chapter explores the interventions employed within pastoral counseling that resonate with those used in other mental health professions, whereas Chapter 12 presents interventions unique to the practice of pastoral counseling.

TOWARD A COMMON GROUND OF INTERVENTION

Mental health professionals define themselves in unique ways reflective of their experiences and orientations. At the same time, overarching commonalities exist across those definitions, providing an element of relation and cohesion within the field. The actual interventions employed by different allied health professions similarly share a common ground, and the pages that follow present examples of such communal practices and demonstrate the parallels they reflect across disciplines and theoretical orientations.

Intervention

What is an intervention? Although the term *intervention* is defined differently by different mental health disciplines, an intervention is nonetheless widely understood among therapists as some skill, method, or practice used to facilitate change in one or more individuals (Ballou, 1995). Interventions may target the thoughts, feelings, or behaviors of the clients and in some cases may directly affect their experiences or larger world perspectives. Interventions stem from and correspond to the treatment plan developed in response to the client's presenting concerns. Cheston (2000) explains,

> Once the goals are formulated, the counselor draws from knowledge of and relationship with the client to challenge, interpret, reflect, and support the client toward the therapeutic goals. The job is to assist the client by structuring the change process and using counseling knowledge to implement steps toward the goal. (p. 257)

Put simply, interventions may be thought of as the "work" of therapy.

Cheston (2000) adds that "a way of intervening refers to the means by which a counselor interrupts the client's cycle of dysfunction and allows for the processing of healthier alternatives of thinking, feeling, and behaving" (p. 257). One might imagine that there are numerous ways of achieving such a goal, and surely there are more possible interventions than can be counted here. Interventions are implemented by the practitioner with a timing and intention that can vary according to that professional's personal and theoretical orientations. What unites the multitude of interventions, however, is the common goal or intention of promoting a particular change at a particular time for a particular individual.

Most of the interventions used by pastoral counselors stem from a psychotherapeutic perspective informed by psychological theories and the historical, collective experience of the mental health disciplines (see Chapter 2, this volume). As Cheston (2000) states, "Theories not only help to explain how change occurs but what technique will enhance a client's movement toward the goal of increased mental health" (p. 257). Although this formation heavily informs mental health practitioners' interventions, common ground persists across the allied professions due in large part to the overlap of those collective academic and practical traditions. In addition, the health professions at large have long participated in a collaborative effort to respond to the particular needs of an individual. Gladding and Newsome (2010) note,

> Although it is important to establish a specialized identity within the broad arena of therapeutic professions, it is equally important to recognize the ways in which professions interrelate . . . to collaborate and complement each other's work so that clients' needs are served effectively. (p. 27)

Indeed, such an "alliance" allows for a holistic inclusion of multiple facets of health care—medical, social, community, and religious/spiritual.

Allied Health Professions

The term *allied health professions* as I employ it refers to the array of professions committed to aiding individuals in their pursuit of a healthier life. In this chapter, the term refers specifically to those professions with a shared psychotherapeutic component to their craft. A brief list may include psychiatrists, psychologists, mental health counselors, social workers, school counselors, marriage and family therapists (MFTs), and alcohol and drug counselors. A more extensive list would reveal the true breadth and level of specialization with which, at least, "Western" societies respond to mental health concerns today—other cultures and societies may vary in their levels of specialization with regard to health care. For instance, the website "www.FindCounseling.com" lists more than 50 different "types of mental health professionals" (Table 11.1). In addition, according to the American Association of Pastoral Counselors (AAPC), there are at least 12 certifications or licensures that pastoral counselors may hold, revealing a variety of training paradigms (Table 11.2).

TABLE 11.1 Sample of Different Types of Mental Health Professionals

- Alcohol and drug counselor (LADC)
- Art therapist (CAT, LPAT)
- Educational psychologist
- Hypnotherapist
- Learning specialist
- Licensed certified social worker–clinical (LCSW-C)
- Licensed clinical pastoral therapist (LCPT)
- Licensed clinical professional counselor (LCPC)
- Licensed clinical psychologist (PsyD, LCP)
- Licensed marriage and family therapist (LMFT)
- Licensed mental health counselor (LMHC)
- Licensed professional counselor (LPC)
- Licensed psychologist (PsyD, PhD, LP)
- Master's degree-trained social worker (MSW)
- Pastoral counselor (see Table 11.2)
- Psychiatric nurse
- Psychiatric social worker (PSW)
- Psychiatrist (MD)
- Psychoanalyst
- Psychologist
- Psychotherapist
- School psychologist
- Substance abuse counselor (SAC)

Adapted from FindCounseling.com (2014).

TABLE 11.2 Sample Certifications/Licensures That a Pastoral Counselor Might Hold

- CCPT—Certified clinical pastoral therapist
- CpastC—Certified pastoral counselor
- LPC—Licensed professional counselor
- LPP—Licensed pastoral psychotherapist
- LCPC—Licensed clinical professional counselor
- LCPT—Licensed clinical pastoral therapist
- LMHC—Licensed mental health counselor
- LMFT—Licensed marriage and family therapist
- CPC—Certified professional counselor
- LMFC—Licensed marriage and family counselor
- LPCMH—Licensed professional counselor of mental health
- LCMHC—Licensed clinical mental health counselor

Adapted with permission from the American Association of Pastoral Counselors (2014).

The different professions included under this category are unified by a common attention and response to behaviors, thoughts, and feelings that may arise in service of another's mental well-being. Different "allies" will serve in different roles and different (although sometimes similar or the same) settings, united toward the common end of the individual's wholeness and mental well-being. Imagine the physician serving in a hospital, responding with a comprehensive medical understanding of the individual's physiological system; a social worker in a consulting room, locating resources to connect the individual better with her or his community or gain stability in employment or housing; a psychologist in an agency setting, offering an assessment of the individual's ability to respond effectively to social demands; a pastoral counselor in a private office working with the individual to facilitate a fuller life by breaking through specific personal barriers impeding well-being; and the counselor educator offering a local workshop to offer information that can inform a community on how to prevent or respond to certain psychological difficulties. These allies respond collectively to meet the individual on various levels and in an overarching, holistic manner that augments the successfulness of their response. And they do so united on common ground—employing insights and techniques drawn from psychological disciplines with the aim of helping and healing individuals in specific contexts and settings.

COMMON-GROUND INTERVENTIONS

Although interventions differ by definition and discipline, this chapter intends to elucidate the common ground shared across professions that serve to promote mental well-being. The language and references that link these approaches reflect the depths and breadth of professional academic endeavors that have contributed to a collective understanding of psychological well-being—an area of health that includes physical, emotional, behavioral, cognitive, and spiritual dimensions but whose common tongue is currently rooted in psychological discourse. Pastoral counselors and other allied professionals are equally likely to draw from this shared pool of therapeutic interventions.

Most mental health interventions are grounded in four major theoretical orientations: psychodynamic, cognitive behavioral, humanistic/existential, and family systems. Although some argue that the pastoral orientation is a unique theoretical orientation altogether (Clinebell & McKeever, 2011; Estadt, Blanchette, & Compton, 1991; Ramsay, 2004; Wicks, Parsons, & Capps, 1993), I contend that the uniqueness of pastoral counseling stems largely from the pastoral counselor's way of being and understanding. Pastoral counselors employ distinctive interventions to be sure (see Chapter 12, this volume), but many of the interventions employed align with the four major theoretical approaches noted earlier. In the pages that follow, each of these four orientations, along with other additional perspectives meriting consideration, is explored in terms of their particular interventions and the way in which pastoral approaches align. Within this common ground, the pastoral aspect of those interventions reveals itself in the content of those practices, as well as the timing, motivation, and intention that direct them.

Psychodynamic Approaches

> Psychoanalysis is not . . . only a therapeutic modality but an art, a way of thinking and of looking at the world. It is an aesthetic as much as a hermeneutic, and certainly more than a science. It is a commitment to the belief that

things—including people, faces, words, behaviors—are never only as they seem, and that everything potentially has multiple layers of meaning. (Cooper-White, 2007, p. 4)

An exploration of traditional psychotherapeutic strategies often begins with one of the original schools of thought—psychodynamic (within which psychoanalysis exists as a particular approach). Developed in the early 20th century by Sigmund Freud (1940/1964), Carl Jung (1954), Alfred Adler (1964b), and others, the psychodynamic model persists today in both mainstream culture and professional practice. Each of these theorists was trained in medicine, and modern psychiatry and other mental health professions historically linked to medicine continue to reveal the influences of psychodynamic theory. In addition, as noted earlier, according to Cooper-White (2007) the particulars of this theory allow for considerations of a perhaps less "medical" or "scientific" nature (or perhaps these extra components serve to further inform what "medical" and "scientific" approaches truly entail). Either way, an array of helping professions uses traditionally psychodynamic strategies in their practices—from psychiatrists and nurse practitioners, to psychologists and social workers, to counselors, chaplains, and pastoral counselors alike.

Modalities and Interventions

The psychodynamic orientation consists of a number of different modalities, including Freudian psychoanalysis (Freud, 1940/1964), Jungian analysis (Jung, 1954), Adlerian psychology (Adler, 1964b), and object-relations theory (Winnicott, 1965). What characterizes the psychodynamic school of thought at large is the recognition of and attention to unconscious meanings and motivations and a view of the human psyche as a complex, dynamic, and powerful entity. Accordingly, interventions that stem from the psychodynamic orientation focus primarily on raising individuals' awareness of the unconscious dimensions of their psyche. Psychodynamic strategies exist along a "supportive–interpretive continuum" (Leichsenring & Leibing, 2007, p. 218). Along this continuum, the practitioner intervenes to develop new abilities and raise awareness in the client by directly *interpreting* and challenging client patterns and providing *support* through the therapeutic relationship itself.

Interpretation.   Several interventions emerge from this focus on the unconscious realm of an individual's psyche. Along with other allied professionals, pastoral counselors may use these practices to approach that "hidden" content and offer the client varying degrees of "expert" interpretation. Several strategies can be employed to gain access to the unconscious. One of the more traditional methods engages the unconscious via *stream of consciousness* or *free association*, in which the client says whatever comes to mind, "flow[ing] with any feelings or thoughts . . . without censorship" (Corey, 2009, p. 75). Some professionals, regardless of pastoral identity, may even employ a form of hypnosis to invite the client into greater contact with unconscious content. The therapist can subsequently offer interpretations of what these thoughts and feelings suggest in terms of the client's overall presenting problem.

Clients may eventually become more careful with what they say in session, and this can be subsequently understood by psychodynamic practitioners as *resistance* and further explored and interpreted in terms of the individual's avoidance of progress or issues with trust or vulnerability (Wolitzky, 2003). The focus on resistance is a classic psychodynamic tool that has been widely adopted not merely across professions but across theories as well. The concept of resistance resonates with another psychodynamic concept, *defense mechanisms*, which provide another rich ground for therapeutic intervention. According to classic psychoanalytic theory, the human psyche develops various defenses to protect itself against otherwise unbearable or unacceptable feelings, thoughts, and expressions. By pointing these out to the client, psychodynamic professionals can help shine a light on these unconscious phenomena, thereby raising awareness in the client and facilitating change.

Common ground also exists for helping professionals who may employ some form of *dream analysis*, another classic psychodynamic intervention. The approach to understanding and interpreting dreams varies across the different subsets of psychodynamic theory (Curtis & Hirsch, 2003), but what remains uniform is the belief that the unconscious can express itself more freely in dreams. Psychodynamic pastoral counselors and other professionals will thus interpret the manifest content of the client's dream to identify and raise to the client's awareness the latent content that the unconscious is expressing and explore its significance.

The therapeutic relationship.   Psychodynamic practitioners focus on the therapeutic relationship as a key component in promoting client change. Indeed, research indicates the therapeutic alliance to be the strongest predictor of positive outcomes for clients (e.g., Orlinsky, Grawe, & Parks, 1994; Strauss et al., 2006; Zuroff & Blatt, 2006). Moreover, within the psychodynamic framework, interventions hinge on the therapist's way of being with and understanding of the client and thus "always exist in the context of the therapeutic relationship" (Silverman, 2005, p. 309). Pastoral counselors and other allied professionals may thus focus much of their attention on the real relationship that emerges through therapy with their clients. Although this may seem more manageable in long-term work, short-term psychodynamic approaches share in this focus on the therapeutic relationship (Lewis, Dennerstein, & Gibbs, 2008, p. 446), extending the breadth with which such approaches may be shared across the helping alliance.

One particularly common focus for professionals using relationship-based interventions involves the concepts of *transference* and *countertransference,* which originate in psychodynamic theory. A salient and dynamic force, transference involves the client relating to the therapist in a manner that reflects the client's relationship with some other significant person in her or his life, past or present (often an authority figure such as the client's parent, employer, or even her or his relational concept of God). The therapist, in turn, responds to the present moment by highlighting how those interactions may indicate unresolved conflicts and/or stifled development. Well-trained, grounded professionals may also be able to use their own countertransference toward the client to facilitate new self-awareness and relational understanding for that individual (Tuckett, 2005).

In outlining key competencies for psychodynamic practice, Sarnat (2010) highlights the impact of relational interventions:

> One might assume that intervention from a psychodynamic point of view means primarily interpretation. From a relational perspective, however, the distinction between interpretation and relationship participation is understood to be an arbitrary one, and insight and change are understood to result from both. . . . How one intervenes—that is, how one participates in the relationship and how one interprets unconscious material—springs directly from the clinician's working conceptualization. Ideally, he or she intervenes only after becoming able to bear the transference/countertransference situation, and avoids reacting directly out of it. . . . In theory, if a psychotherapist is in an analytic frame of mind, an intervention will tend to be well-timed and useful to the client because it will arise naturally from the psychotherapist's unconscious link to the client. (p. 24)

This latter point regarding an unconscious link between therapist and client directs us to consider another source of common ground across allied psychodynamic approaches. Reik (1983) names the phenomenon as listening to the client "with a third ear," which is understood as a connection between the two individuals' unconscious minds in a manner that informs and facilitates the therapeutic intervention. Ogden (1999) expands this notion of an "analytic third" as consisting of a third subject, co-created by analyst and client. Pastoral counselors may further conceive of this unspoken, unnamed "connection" as having some mystical or spiritual component. And although secular professionals may be hesitant to concur, there are many psychodynamic practitioners who would at least subscribe to Cooper-White's (2007) inference that this connection stems from "the shared pool of conscious and especially unconscious wisdom" (p. 233). Whether conceived of as an unconscious link, a co-created third subject, some shared pool of unconscious wisdom, or something more explicitly spiritual, psychodynamic practitioners at large are likely to find common ground in their recognition of and response to this facilitative medium.

Jungian analysis. The Jungian approach offers additional common ground for interventions across the allied professions. Pastoral counselors are often drawn to this perspective given its depth of potentially and explicitly spiritual language and content. For instance, Jung describes the ultimate goal of psychodynamic intervention as a "transcendent function," writing, "In actual practice . . . the suitably trained analyst mediates the transcendent function for the patient, i.e., helps him to bring conscious and unconscious together and so arrive at a new attitude" (as cited in Campbell, 1971, p. 279). Although Jung clarifies this term as nothing particularly spiritual, his use of the term *transcendent* reflects an openness to metaphysical processes that characterize much of his writings and have been adopted by pastoral counselors and other practitioners alike. As Corbett and Stein (2005) propose, "Is psychoanalysis not a quest to discern the central mysteries of human existence and to consider its major riddles, if not answer them?" (p. 67). Jung would likely not disagree, and professionals practicing Jungian interventions would share in this common ground.

In particular, Jung worked with an added dimension of the unconscious, called the *collective unconscious*, which all humanity shares. Stemming from this idea, Jungian interventions often include special attention to *archetypes* and other symbols that represent common human experiences, help inform the client's struggles, and identify possible paths of healing. Jung posited parallel stories and accounts from archetypal legends; pastoral counselors, too, may draw from such grand narratives, including those of both secular and more explicitly religious/spiritual natures. A Jungian intervention might therefore consist of inviting a client to get in touch with her experience of "Sophia" or "wisdom" to facilitate self-affirmation and self-efficacy in accepting and/or promoting personal changes in her life. Or, for example, I once invited an Orthodox Jewish client to consider whether there was a story of struggle to be found in his holy scriptures—a similar story such as Job's, which might parallel his experience of suffering, confusion, and/or identity questing. Such identifications can augment the client's connection with a greater, collective source of insight and awareness, ultimately mobilizing and empowering the client.

Jungian practitioners remain open to moments of *synchronicity*, and their interventions often focus on exploring the *balance* between polarities in an individual's life (Sneck, 2007). This latter notion of balance resonates not only with pastoral counselors but with many allied professionals today who respond to the call for a more holistic approach to well-being. In particular, Jungian interventions seek to promote such a balance between a client's persona and shadow, biological gender and anima/animus, and the dimensions of personality (e.g., through the Myers-Briggs Type Indicator® [Myers, McCaulley, Quenk, & Hammer, 1998], an assessment steeped in Jungian theory and used across the spectrum of the helping professions).

Although not requiring a religious or spiritual affiliation, interventions based in Jungian theory are particularly attractive to pastoral counselors given their attention to the power of enduring religious symbols and invitingly spiritual language. In a final example, Dourly (2004) comments on the spiritual and even theological implications of Jung's perspective on raising awareness:

> Jung equates the recovered memory of one's totality with apocatastasis. . . . Both paradise and the end time are to be approximated and experienced in the present as moments in natural processes of maturation or individuation no longer distinguishable from divinization. When Jung connects such memory with the experience of immortality he understands immortality as the sense of the individual's continuity with the total human experience past and future. ("The Anamnesis of the Nothing and Apocatastasis," para. 2–3)

Accordingly, professionals who employ Jungian interventions to promote individuation and wholeness are participating in a common endeavor that recognizes or at least operates from within the possibility of spiritually transformative, therapeutic experiences.

Adlerian interventions.   The Adlerian approach to psychodynamic interventions also provides common ground for the allied health professions. Many helping professions endorse Adler's positive, collaborative approach to naming and pursuing individual strengths and goals. *Encouragement* is one such intervention that might be employed across disciplines. Literally seeking to "promote courage," encouragement can take various shapes and forms. Sweeney (2009) explains,

> Encouragement inspires or helps others toward a conviction that they can work on finding solutions and that they can cope with any predicament . . . [and consists of] assisting individuals to minimize the impact of noncontrollable factors and to maximize their use of controllable factors in enriching their own life experiences. . . . In short . . . [encouragement entails] helping individuals establish goals, attitudes, and competencies they need to cope with life as they experience it. (pp. 72–75)

Such common-ground interventions may include accompaniment; thought stopping; rehearsal and role-playing; focusing on assets, efforts, and progress, small and large; and patience with inconsistency and forgiveness for errors.

Many of these interventions stem from another commonly held focus in Adlerian theory: awakening *social interest.* Adler (1964b) writes, "The task . . . is to give the patient the experience of contact with a fellow man, and then to enable him to transfer this awakened social interest to others" (p. 341). Fostering client participation in activities that serve others is an intervention commonly used by social workers and in clinical rehab centers and community workshops as well. Although a pastoral counselor could have an additional religious/spiritual motivation or understanding behind pursuing such an intervention (e.g., perhaps some theological orientation that community service and fellowship are inherently good), the practice itself would likely appear identical across professions.

Another manner in which pastoral counselors often align with the Adlerian model and thus share ground with other professionals involves the commonly expressed notion of being a "co-journeyer" with clients. This approach to collaborative work with clients resonates with Adler's emphasis that therapists not view or comport themselves as superior to or above the client. According to Adler (1964b), "One of the most important devices in psychotherapy is to ascribe the work and the success of the therapy to the patient at whose disposal one should place oneself in a friendly way, as a coworker" (p. 338). A variety of professions share in this collaborative approach to promoting client self-efficacy.

Finally, one of the foundational tools of Adlerian theory, the *lifestyle assessment*, equally attracts pastoral counselors and other allied professionals. Practitioners use such broad-based assessments to gather information on the client's patterns of struggles, attitudes, beliefs, and responses. Similar to this shared Adlerian approach, Estadt (1991) elucidates how "as pastoral counselors, we approach clients with wide-angle lenses and attempt to scan the mystery of the human person in all its complexity" (p. 6). Although some practitioners may not identify with the spiritual language of such a claim, those rooted in Adlerian theory will nonetheless recognize the similarity of looking for patterns in client narratives as a means of promoting awareness and facilitating change.

Object relations and God image.   A final subset of psychodynamic interventions bears mentioning given the saliency with which it highlights the common ground of pastoral counseling and other allied professions. A popular development within psychodynamic theory is that of object relations, wherein the therapist recognizes how individuals are influenced by the internalization of significant childhood relationships (Miller & Worthington, 2012; Winnicott, 1965). Allied professionals operating from within the psychodynamic framework are thus encouraged to raise these internalized relationships to the awareness of their clients to promote insight, growth, and change.

These internalizations are also thought to influence a client's God image, that is, her or his affective, relational experience of a divine attachment figure (Moriarty & Davis, 2012; Rizzuto, 1979). Just as paying particular attention to internalized family relationships can be a highly effective intervention, pastoral counselors and other allied professionals can also facilitate healthy change by focusing on a client's God image (Cheston, Piedmont, Eanes, & Lavin, 2003; Sperry, 2005; Tisdale et al., 1997). An individual's God image can have both positive and deleterious impacts on her or his overall psychospiritual well-being. When the latter are more pronounced, mental health professionals can use psychodynamic interventions to address those negative impacts via revelatory explorations and healthy adjustments. More specifically, interventions focusing on clients' unhealthy internalized relationships and God image commonly aim for a *corrective emotional experience* (Alexander & French, 1946) mediated by the therapist through the acceptance, compassion, and validation of the psychotherapeutic relationship.

Despite having their roots in psychodynamic theory, interventions that interact with object relations and God image may also be found within cognitive behavioral and narrative theoretical frameworks (Davis, Moriarty, & Mauch, 2013; Moriarty & Davis, 2012). What remains is a common intervention for allied professionals seeking to promote positive change for clients by engaging their internalized relationships, whether those include family members, peer groups, or God images.

Final Thoughts

Pastoral counselors' attraction to psychodynamic interventions is matched by the potential for other professionals to view these interventions in spiritual terms. According to Rizzuto (2005), "Spirituality, to the extent that it is mediated through the mind, is subject to the same psychodynamic conditions as other phenomena because transcendent realities are also apprehended through psychic processes" (pp. 47–48). Shafranske (2005) adds, "Psychoanalysis provides a dynamic heuristic to grasp many of the psychological, developmental, and cultural contributions to an individual's experience of and relationship with transcendent realities" (p. 112). Not only do the history, depth, and breadth of psychodynamic approaches provide a suitable platform for common-ground interventions, but the dynamics of the theory also provide a suitable overlap and easy entrance for pastoral themes and emphases. Although the content and intention may vary, the practical nature of the interventions remains uniform across the allied professions.

Cognitive Behavioral Approaches

 We can't change the past, so we change how people are thinking, feeling and behaving today.
—Albert Ellis (Epstein, 2001, p. 72)

The allied professions find common ground in psychodynamic interventions given the historical roots and cultural breadth of that paradigm. A second common platform, cognitive behavioral therapy (CBT), has grown dramatically in scope and popularity due largely to current emphases on empirically based and data-driven therapeutic strategies. Thousands of research studies have established the efficacy of CBT interventions. The specific, empirical nature of the theory lends clarity and ease with which its practices can be defined, demonstrated, and measured. Such scientific support further attracts the attention of managed care providers who prefer practitioners to engage in evidence-based interventions.

For these reasons, large numbers of professionals across the allied spectrum have adopted and used CBT practices to respond to various concerns and populations. For instance, due to their empirically validated efficacy, CBT interventions are particularly espoused in treating depression and anxiety across the developmental spectrum (Gloaguen, Cottraux, Cucherat, & Blackburn, 1998; Richardson, Stallard, & Velleman, 2010; Samad, Brealey, & Gilbody, 2011; von der Embse, Barterian, & Segool, 2013). They may be used by school counselors working to address behavioral problems (Gable, Hester, Rock, & Hughes, 2009; Kavanagh et al., 2009), within language therapy (Nye et al., 2013), and in sports psychology (Rumbold, Fletcher, & Daniels, 2012). Social workers may employ the interventions in assisting with work disabilities (Pomaki, Franche, Murray, Khushrushahi, & Lampinen, 2012), occupational trauma (Graham, 2012), and family concerns (Welsh, Viana, Petrill, & Mathias, 2007; Zarit & Femia, 2008). CBT also remains a very popular modality across the allied professions for the treatment of addiction (e.g., Fink et al., 2012; Lee & Rawson, 2008). Physicians and nurse practitioners may employ these strategies not only in response to psychosis (Bird et al., 2010) but also in helping with older patient dementia (Hopper et al., 2013) and even cancer patient rehabilitation (Fors et al., 2011; Kangas, Bovbjerg, & Montgomery, 2008). Chaplains and pastoral counselors equally incorporate CBT modalities and interventions in their work, finding opportunities for religious and spiritual integration in the thought content and behaviors of their clients (Propst, Ostrom, Watkins, Dean, & Mashburn, 1992; Snodgrass, 2009; Tan & Johnson, 2005; Wicks & Buck, 2011).

Modalities and Interventions

As exemplified in this section's opening statement by Albert Ellis, CBT differs markedly from psychodynamic theory and interventions. In particular, CBT theory de-emphasizes the psychodynamic notion of an unconscious rooted in childhood experiences. Instead, pastoral counselors and other professionals using CBT focus on the client's current thought processes and the way in which unhealthy thought patterns or *cognitive distortions* can be identified and modified to change one's present experience of and interaction with the world.

Numerous derivatives of CBT exist, and most are founded on the classic principles established primarily in Ellis's rational emotive behavior therapy (REBT) and Beck's cognitive therapy (CT; Nevid, 2012). Ellis (1962) postulated a model of understanding that a client's emotional experience and behavioral consequences ("C") of a particular, activating event ("A") are in fact mediated by some client thought or belief ("B"). As such, therapists can intervene at the point of the thought/belief to elicit new affective and behavioral experiences from the client. In a similar vein, Beck (1963) articulated the notion of a *cognitive triad* in which individuals perceive themselves, their world, and their future negatively. Professionals thus inquire into those three areas of an individual's thoughts to identify cognitive distortions and their influence on the client's well-being (Reinecke & Freeman, 2003). A third foundational principle of CBT recognizes several common categories of cognitive distortions—such as mind reading, dichotomous thinking, catastrophizing, and ("should" statements, which "tilt objective reality in the direction of self-deprecation" (Corey, 2009, p. 288). CBT professionals work to identify and help their clients to identify such unrealistic or maladaptive cognitions and replace them with healthier, more realistic thoughts.

Common CBT interventions.   Toussaint, Webb, and Keltner (2012) offer the following overview of a CBT-oriented approach:

> The bottom line in [cognitive behavioral] therapy is the basic, inescapable, intertwined connection between thoughts, emotions, and behaviors and the commonly accepted evidence-based view that modification of thoughts has great power in the subsequent modification of emotion and behavior. . . . [Furthermore,] the object of therapeutic intervention is not to change thoughts, per se, but to change thought processes. (p. 346)

From the basic principles of CBT, a number of practical and direct interventions emerge. Any pastoral counselor or allied professional who draws from this psychotherapeutic paradigm is likely to employ some of the following strategies.

One of the foremost interventions is the direct confrontation of the client's fallacious or maladaptive cognitive patterns. As such, the cognitive behavioral professional is likely to employ a direct style of confrontation to highlight those unhealthy thoughts, combined with a supportive teaching modality that allows for pathways of change to emerge collaboratively. In challenging distorted cognitions, for instance, a therapist might *question the evidence* or *decatastrophize*. The therapist might help the client *examine options and alternative possibilities* or *reality check* via *scaling*.

The professional demonstrates these helpful approaches, such as *thought stopping*, to *model* for the client how she or he might practice these strategies on her or his own. In a similar fashion, CBT practitioners often assign homework for clients to pursue between sessions. These assignments are usually fairly specific and can range from *journaling* or keeping a *thought record* to seeking out educational or personally challenging activities. Again, professionals using cognitive behavioral interventions teach their clients about how cognitions work and how one can practice developing and maintaining healthier thought patterns. Practitioners of CBT often employ *psychoeducational* strategies, offer reading materials (*bibliotherapy*), and encourage or host educational workshops.

CBT interventions may also involve more explicitly behavioral approaches such as *systematic desensitization*. Pastoral counselors trained in this paradigm, like other helping professionals, might combine a fear hierarchy with intentional relaxation training or meditation to confront a specific client struggle. Similarly, CBT professionals may engage in other forms of *role-playing, rehearsal,* or *in vivo exposure* and might also advocate for other *trainings* such as those designed to promote social skills or assertiveness (Reinecke & Freeman, 2003).

Pastoral CBT strategies.   In addition to working with nonreligious content, pastoral counselors may also apply CBT strategies to more explicitly religious and/or spiritual content. Tan and Johnson (2005) underscore how Ellis (2000) himself recognized the effectiveness of treating religious clients with REBT and further note how researchers have developed a number of "spiritually oriented CBT approaches" (SO-CBT). For example, Snodgrass (2009) has formulated a spiritually integrative approach to CBT with older populations, Wicks and Buck (2011) have advanced an approach to incorporate CBT and native psychology in pastoral ministry, and Propst et al. (1992) have demonstrated the lasting impacts of "religious CBT" interventions.

The potential for pastoral practitioners to incorporate CBT strategies remains strongly inviting. As Toussaint et al. (2012) note, "Theoretical and empirical connections exist between religiousness, spirituality, and mental health, particularly in the realm of cognitions, emotions, and behavior" (p. 346). For instance, many clients struggle in their belief systems with the concepts of self and deity. These struggles often stem from cognitive distortions wherein individuals believe that positive, optimistic, and rational beliefs about God apply to others but not to themselves. Distorted views of self and/or of God can also have subsequent, negative impacts on each other (Toussaint et al., 2012, p. 347).

CBT interventions that respond to cognitive, religious content are very similar in nature to other nonreligious CBT strategies. For instance, professionals might carefully use scriptural evidence to dispute irrational or self-defeating beliefs that run counter to the client's own faith. They may also use religious imagery to decrease anxiety or offer scriptural reading as bibliotherapy and/or prayer as cognitive homework (Tan & Johnson, 2005, p. 81). Another pastoral intervention, reminiscent of the dysfunctional thought record mentioned earlier, involves the use of a *God image automatic thought record* (Moriarty, 2006). This tool helps clients systematically identify and distinguish their irrational and maladaptive automatic thoughts about God from the positive, encouraging, "real God" proclaimed by their particular scriptures, teachings, and/or religious leaders.

An additional intervention that closely aligns with CBT entails focusing on a client's *religious coping*—the patterns of religious or spiritual beliefs and practices that people use as resources for managing stress (Miller & Worthington, 2012, p. 115). Using an approach developed by Pargament (1997), professionals focus on helping clients with ineffective coping styles to identify maladaptive thoughts and behaviors and develop healthier alternatives (Krumrei & Rosmarin, 2012). Pargament (2007) notes that this process not only serves to cultivate positive religious coping and replace negative religious coping but can also lead to positive change in client God images (p. 195), furthering the overall therapeutic impact of interventions that focus on religious coping.

Final Thoughts

One can see how such pastoral practices are classically CBT in nature. Toussaint et al. (2012) pinpoint that uniting principle found in applying CBT to religious–spiritual content: "Once [the cognitive distortions are] identified, logic and consistent disputation can reverse deleterious effects on mental health" (p. 347). Although focused on religious content, such pastoral interventions reflect the basic principles and approaches of CBT, forming connections with allied professionals who similarly employ CBT-based interventions. Furthermore, the connection need not be unidirectional; there is much potential for all counselors to consider some of the pastoral adaptations of CBT in their own work. Pargament (2007) suggests that, "Any psychology of human behavior remains incomplete without an appreciation for the motivation to know and connect to the sacred" (p. 343). The growing trend of spiritually oriented therapies invites professionals across the allied spectrum to at least consider this extra dimension of human experience and well-being in their own service of holistic health.

Humanistic and Existential Approaches

The first duty of love is to listen.
—Tillich (1957)

The humanistic and existential paradigms of psychotherapeutic intervention serve as another common ground for pastoral counselors and the allied professions. These schools of thought may be especially alluring for pastoral practitioners inasmuch as their ways of being and understanding include an openness to fellowship, compassion, and wrestling with the unknown. In addition, one of the founders of humanistic psychology, Abraham Maslow (1962), proposes, "The human being needs a framework of values, a philosophy of life, a religion or religion surrogate to live by and understand by, in about the same sense he needs sunlight, calcium, or love" (p. 206). Paul Tillich (1957), an existential philosopher whose thought greatly influenced existential psychotherapy, notes, "Man's ultimate concern must be expressed symbolically, because symbolic language alone is able to express the ultimate" (p. 47). Such notions are inviting to pastoral counselors who, in exploring a client's ultimate concerns and purpose-driven motivations, will often recognize and work within that individual's particular framework of meaning and meaning making.

Humanistic–existential approaches are used across mental health disciplines, and the principles and practices of these schools of psychotherapy are common across the allied professions. This is largely because the standard training received by a wide breadth of different helping professions is rooted in the basic helping skills, presence, and attentive listening espoused by humanist theorist Carl Rogers. As such, one can find a similar tendency in how many social workers, nurses, human resource staff members, counselors, and so on, engage clientele. In addition, existential theory's attention to themes of life and death, purpose and meaning, and identity and relationship holds value for various professionals. Counselors, chaplains, spiritual directors, and medical personnel, for instance, are called to recognize such themes in patients dealing with debilitating or terminal conditions (Ekedahl & Wengström, 2008; Piderman et al., 2011). Existential concerns are not limited to end-of-life issues but can arise when people endure life-changing experiences at almost any point along the life span. The themes and practices of humanistic and existential theory thus offer a common invitation to a number of helping professions.

Modalities and Interventions

Humanistic and existential modalities are often discussed hand in hand due to some poignant similarities in their theoretical orientation and therapeutic approaches. As Farber (2010) summarizes, "[The two approaches] share a focus on helping clients make the most of their psychological potentialities" (p. 28). Within this shared focus, the humanistic dimension concentrates more on the provisions required for promoting an individual's natural actualizing potential, whereas the existential dimension stresses an individual's struggle to accept and engage her or his agency and responsibility in light of certain uncontrollable limitations. Allied professionals who operate from a humanistic orientation will tend to adhere to its corresponding emphasis on *congruence*, recognizing human pathology as an incongruence between self-concept and personal experience (Bohart, 2003; Maslow, 1962; Murdock, 2013; Rogers, 1961). Existentialists recognize certain themes of life and death, angst, self-awareness, purpose and meaning, identity and relationships, and freedom and responsibility as inherent to the human condition (Frankl, 1984; Schneider, 2003; Schneider & May, 1995; Yalom, 1980).

Humanistic interventions.   "Humanistic interventions" may be a bit of a misnomer as the paradigm does not approach therapy from the orientation of techniques and strategies (Corey, 2009, p. 176). Still, there is a common way of proceeding that is grounded in this paradigm—namely, an emphasis on the therapeutic relationship itself. Many pastoral counselors and other allied professionals recognize the importance of *process* and *being with* a client toward the work of facilitating change. These are basic skills endorsed in trainings across the helping professions. In relating with the client, the practitioner not only witnesses, supports, and accepts the individual as she or he is but also models congruence and self-acceptance that fosters the client's self-actualizing potential.

Carl Rogers (1961), the originator of this client-centered approach, espouses, "Change is facilitated . . . when one is willing to be what one truly is" (p. 176). By entering into the client's subjective world, professionals encourage the client to do likewise. Guiding the client to access her or his own deeper feelings and true self facilitates the therapeutic congruence needed for client growth. This process is known as *attunement*, increasing trust in one's own experience, and is marked by nurturing a client's self-exploration and self-acceptance to promote an independent and integrated sense of self (Corey, 2009, p. 177).

Bohart (2003) summarily notes that the real function of the humanistic therapist exists in providing an optimal, supportive environment to foster the individual's innate capacity for self-healing and self-fulfillment. Such *support* is not mundane or commonplace but rather quite intentional in the therapeutic interaction. It involves being fully present with and accepting of the other in a natural, authentic relationship. To do so, humanistic pastoral counselors and other practitioners focus on the three "necessary and sufficient" conditions (Rogers, 1957, p. 95) that allow the relationship to be the key healing factor in therapy: *genuineness* (authenticity, congruence, immediacy), *empathy* (active listening, supportive and nondirective reflection), and *unconditional positive regard* (acceptance, compassion). In fostering these traits and skills, the professional moves toward creating an ideal, therapeutic environment for positive change. In addition, through a process of *modeling* to the client her or his own self-attunement, self-exploration, and interpersonal communication, humanistic practitioners allow the client to experience, participate in, and practice those essential, salutary skills.

Fleischman (1990) also notes that there are powerful, spiritual undertones to this humanistic emphasis on being with a client. He labels the phenomenon "witnessed significance" and explains how "patients talk about the need to be seen, known, responded to, confirmed, appreciated, cared for, mirrored, recognized, identified. . . . Being known and knowing are essential human needs" (pp. 7, 14). Rogers (1980) similarly identifies this essential human need and how meeting or overlooking it can affect human well-being. He writes, "When I am not prized and appreciated, I not only *feel* very much diminished, but my behavior is actually affected by my feelings. When I am prized, I blossom and expand, I am an interesting individual" (Rogers, 1980, p. 23). Beier (2007) responds to this phenomenon by suggesting that pastoral counselors have a "particular responsibility" to address individuals' need to have their existence affirmed (p. 701). Beyond this specific encouragement for pastoral counselors, however, humanistic practitioners in general are likely to intervene similarly to facilitate clients' growth by addressing their need to be seen and known.

Although the humanistic approach may seem to lack the "concrete" interventions of other approaches, it is by no means lacking in vitality or effect. Again, researchers have consistently identified the therapeutic relationship as the key factor in determining positive outcomes for clients. Pastoral counselors and other allied professionals who draw from humanistic theory are engaging that same potential. Furthermore, the humanistic practice of "just listening" is no simple task (Kaplan, 2009). Rather, therapeutic listening is a skill that requires great personal presence, congruence, and self-acceptance and only comes with years of training.

Existential interventions.   Akin to the humanistic approach, practitioners of existential therapy would likely not use the term *interventions*, considering themselves more as "philosophical companions" than menders of "broken psyches" (Vontress, 2008, p. 161). Still, this theoretical approach offers an understanding of what healthy functioning looks like and how it can be fostered in the therapeutic relationship. In particular, these professionals respond to those existential concerns listed previously by seeking to collaboratively assist people in the process of living with greater ease and expertise (Van Deurzen, 2007, 2009, 2012). Such a process may even involve a series of "phases" in which individuals first learn to identify and examine their values, assumptions, and beliefs about the world and then exercise their agency and responsibility by putting newly developed orientations into transformative action (Corey, 2009, pp. 151–152). This latter emphasis on value exploration, among other humanist–existential principles, resonates with the tenets of positive psychology, which also has great appeal to many pastoral counselors and other allied professionals (Elkins, 2005; Seligman & Csikszentmihalyi, 2000; Shafranske & Sperry, 2005; Sperry, 2005).

Farber (2010) identifies two core competencies of humanistic–existential approaches: "(1) facilitating experiential awareness and (2) using the psychotherapy relationship to promote change" (p. 29). The existential professional may facilitate experiential awareness through questions about the client's present experience and awareness or by highlighting an incongruence between what a client says and how she or he says it. And through an honest, courageous, and integrated relationship of genuine acceptance, the existential helper "invites clients to view their struggles with compassion, and to accept who they are as a starting point for a process of considering who they want to become" (Farber, 2010, p. 30).

The existentialist perspective on therapeutic relationship further evokes Martin Buber's (1958) concept of the "I–Thou" relationship, which is mutual, intimate, and caring; honest, intentional, and present; and marked by profound respect for the prized humanity of the other. The existential emphasis on facilitating experiential awareness also resonates with what are known as "experiential" therapies. Gendlin (1981) espouses an approach, for instance, that promotes an individual's ability to *focus* on her or his present experience. This therapeutic strategy, in turn, echoes the meditative practices that have become widely used in pastoral counseling, nursing, medicine, and other allied professions across the board (Fortney & Taylor, 2010; Ireland, 2012). The *Gestalt* approach also employs active experiments and exercises to foster a client's experience of the here and now, including such popular techniques as role-playing and the empty chair (Perls, 1973). The immediacy involved in these approaches appeals to various helping professionals who, through attunement, may check in with clients' needs and/or with their experience of the relationship at any given time (Farber, 2010, p. 32).

An additional emphasis within existential therapy that unites pastoral counselors and other professionals operating from this paradigm involves a focus on *presence*. Schneider (2003) identifies presence as the essential element of existential–humanistic approaches, describing its ability to reconnect people to both their experiences and opportunities for positive transformation. He suggests that therapy consists of two aims: "(1) to cultivate presence (i.e., attention, choice, and freedom), and (2) to cultivate responsibility (i.e., ability to respond) to that presence" (p. 169). Farber (2010) explicates,

> Presence creates a space for the psychotherapist to sense deeply the experiential world of the client, thereby facilitating empathic understanding . . . help[ing] the client feel supported and secure . . . illuminat[ing] qualities of the client's subjective world and . . . enhanc[ing] the client's willingness to remain present with increasing degrees of depth in self-experiencing. (p. 30)

This existential emphasis on presence connects with the approach of many pastoral counselors who may be naturally oriented toward imparting a "healing presence" in their practice.

Pastoral integration.   There are other ways in which the humanistic and existential paradigms foster pastoral counseling interventions. Existential therapies, for instance, are deeply rooted in philosophy, and many pastoral counseling approaches imply the need for philosophically integrated methods and considerations in responding to client struggles (e.g., Evans, 2005; Kruger, 2002; Louw, 2011). Louw (2011) espouses the following with regard to existential integration:

> In order to understand human attitude [*phronesis, habitus*] one has to make a pastoral diagnosis of the belief systems that determine human behaviour directly or indirectly, as well as the intentionality as related to a vivid hope and the anticipation of a meaningful future. (p. 28)

Snodgrass and Sorajjakool (2011) further elucidate a specific therapeutic potential for exploring spiritual themes in older adulthood, given the natural prevalence of existential concerns and spiritual perspectives that emerge for this age group. Tan and Wong (2012) enumerate various opportunities for blending Christian biblical perspectives with existential therapy. They also supply a wise caution that in such "integrative" pursuits, practitioners not veer into an overly directive or dogmatic stance but allow for self-originating, authentic, and personal truth to emerge from the client's experience. Such a guideline serves as an example of how pastoral counselors, although in some way identifying personally with a particular religious or theological orientation, are not necessarily inclined to "preach" to their clients. Rather, in keeping with existential and humanistic principles, they respect and allow for a client's own development of meaning and values, much as any other helping professional is encouraged to do.

A pastoral counselor's inclination to consider and attend to the religious and spiritual dimensions of her or his clients' lives further elicits particular ways of intervening that align with the humanistic–existential interventions elucidated earlier. Transcendentalist spirituality, for example, espouses a focus on engaging the world in a specific and personal manner, celebrating an individual's uniqueness, and exploring greater dimensions of meaning and transcendental purpose (Buell, 2006). Ignatian spirituality, a subset of Catholic religious identity, also resonates with existential theories, as individuals are invited to actively and authentically participate in finding God in the here and now, as well as in all things, including both joys and sorrows (Martin, 2010). The vast variety of spiritual and religious orientations tends to offer some manner of addressing individuals' existential anxieties. Accordingly, as pastoral counselors work within those client frameworks, they will often find themselves using interventions similar to those of the humanistic–existential paradigms.

Beyond these general connections, there are also pastoral approaches that seek a more explicit integration of spirituality and humanistic–existential principles. Richards (2005), for instance, in his own blend of "theistic integrative psychotherapy," stresses the use of Rogerian empathy and facilitating client exploration and emotional experience. He also indicates that his integrated approach is influenced by the existential perspective that "therapeutic healing best occurs in the context of a genuine 'I–Thou' relationship" (p. 282). Elkins (2005) delineates another approach to spiritually oriented psychotherapy within which he identifies what he feels are naturally occurring spiritual constructs within the larger humanistic paradigm, such as "the soul," "the sacred," and transcendent values and meaning. And in what he refers to as a "*cura animarum*" or "cure of the soul," his definition of *love*, which he identifies as "the most powerful healer of the suffering soul," echoes explicit, humanistic principles: "Love takes the form of empathy, respect, honesty, caring, and acceptance" (Elkins, 2005, p. 140).

Final Thoughts

The relevance of humanistic and existential psychotherapeutic interventions for pastoral counseling is evident. The emphasis on human potential, present experience, and meaningful values frequently appeals to pastoral counseling's recognition of transcendent frameworks operating in people's lives. These two paradigms are common psychotherapeutic theories that provide a foundation for interventions practiced across the allied professions.

Furthermore, one might recognize a certain movement in humanistic–existential approaches toward a more *holistic* conception of well-being, a perspective frequently adopted by pastoral counselors as well. With the growing appreciation for holistic approaches to health, other professionals may benefit from considering such spiritually integrated modalities in their own practices. In referencing William James's (1902) seminal work, *The Varieties of Religious Experience*, Elkins (2005) espouses a similar invitation from his integrated humanistic approach, writing,

> Any psychotherapy that explores the deeper regions of the human psyche will eventually come to the brink of this spiritual realm, whether the client and therapist recognize the place or not. It is my opinion that human personality and spirituality exist on the same continuum and that a more complete psychology would encompass that entire continuum in terms of theory, research, training, and practice. (p. 131)

The connection, therefore, between pastoral counselors and other practitioners of humanistic–existential principles goes both ways. Just as pastoral counselors partake in commonly used psychotherapeutic practices, other professionals remain similarly invited to consider the potential for spiritual integration inherent in these approaches.

Family Systems Approaches

The basic building block of any emotional system is the triangle.
—Bowen (1978)

A fourth therapeutic approach used by mental health professionals involves an appreciation for the systems within which individuals are located. Although other paradigms may consider such influences on individual health, the family systems approach places this focus at the center of its therapeutic orientation. Stemming back to the early to mid-20th century, general systems theory draws from the biological sciences, understanding a "system" to be a group of different elements that interact with one another (von Bertalanffy, 1968). Systems can further be understood as seeking to maintain homeostasis, exchanging information via positive and negative feedback loops, and maintaining their structure via rigid or diffuse boundaries (Kaslow, Dausch, & Celano, 2003). Families comprise one such system and are themselves embedded in other systems such as community, society, and culture (Goldenberg & Goldenberg, 2008).

Most allied professionals recognize the way in which families and other systems contribute to the psychological health and well-being of their individual constituents. Accordingly, many approach and treat those family systems almost as if they were living entities, with dynamic phenomena, historical narratives, and varying levels of effective functioning. Professionals using family therapy interventions can be found within the fields of psychiatry, social work, psychology, counseling, and pastoral counseling, and they also exist as a particular group of practitioners known as MFTs.

Modalities and Interventions

There are several schools of family therapy, including some that stem from other therapeutic paradigms. Researchers vary on how to categorize the different approaches, but most acknowledge distinct subsets within this otherwise unanimous focus. These include psychodynamic, transgenerational, experiential–humanistic, structural, strategic, systemic, and cognitive behavioral approaches. They differ according to emphases on past versus present and intrapsychic versus interpersonal dimensions, and they also vary in terms of their therapeutic structure, goals, processes, and techniques (Kaslow et al., 2003). Integration of these different approaches is not uncommon, however, and the interventions that follow, although attributed to a particular school, are often recognized across multiple family therapy models.

Common interventions in family therapy.   Early forms of family therapy developed in concert with psychodynamic paradigms. These approaches apply familiar techniques from individual psychodynamic work to the larger family system. Such interventions include exploring defense mechanisms within family members and the family unit as a whole, processing resistance and transference within therapy, and developing interpretations linking past and present family dynamics. Additional psychodynamic strategies more specific to family therapy include exploring the impact of *birth order*

(Adler, 1964a), entering the family system as a *catalyst* to raise awareness of unspoken conflicts (Ackerman, 1966), and creating a *holding environment* for reparenting the family as a "good enough" parent (Framo, 1992).

Psychodynamic family approaches further evolved over time, leading to transgenerational and contextual models of family therapy pioneered by Bowen (1978) and Boszormenyi-Nagy (1987). Goldenberg and Goldenberg (2008) explain how Bowen's family systems theory serves to bridge psychodynamic and systems approaches, viewing the family as "an emotional unit, a network of interlocking relationships, best understood when analyzed within a multigenerational or historical framework" (p. 175). Interventions from this perspective involve developing a *genogram* or pictorial representation of at least three generations of family relationships, promoting *differentiation of self* to separate individual members' intellectual and affective experiences, and *de-triangulating* unfair "two-against-one" triads. Boszormenyi-Nagy's (1987) contextual therapy similarly emphasizes multiple generations of family dynamics, combined with an *ethical balance* between entitlement and indebtedness—that is, what family members earn for themselves and what they owe one another. In addition to facing these ethical issues, contextual interventions also include *multidirectional partiality*—recognizing each family member's perspective—and identifying and addressing *invisible loyalties*—unconscious responsibilities inherited from past generations (Boszormenyi-Nagy & Spark, 1973).

Allied professionals may also draw from the experiential–humanistic models of family therapy, which reflect the tenets of their individual therapy paradigms described previously. Virginia Satir's human validation process model (Satir & Baldwin, 1983), for example, focuses on helping families realize their natural, nourishing potential and inclinations toward growth and development. Promoting access to and legitimizing clients' true feelings facilitates movement from dysfunctional to congruent *communication styles*, thereby building self-worth and self-determination for individuals and families. Carl Whitaker's symbolic-experiential family therapy (S-EFT; Whitaker & Bumberry, 1988) recognizes important symbolic factors underlying the surface of therapy. *Joining in* with the family system, practitioners model self-acceptance and self-expression of those hidden, underlying impulses and fantasies, encouraging the family members to do likewise. Experiential interventions also promote *spontaneity*, *creativity*, and *play* and are aimed at fostering individuation and family cohesion.

The structural approach to family therapy views a family's function or dysfunction as hinging on its underlying organizational structure and flexibility in responding to change (Minuchin, 1974). Also akin to S-EFT, these therapists join in the family dynamic, with special attention to *accommodating* or imitating the family's style and *tracking* their structural particulars, including hierarchies and subsystems, alignments and coalitions, operational rules, and the continuum of enmeshed to disengaged boundaries. Subsequently, the therapist engages in a leadership role to restructure the family by *enacting* family conflicts, *unbalancing* current power dynamics, and constructing healthier *boundaries*.

Taking that leadership role a step further, strategic family therapy locates the therapist as an active director of change, defining problems and devising strategies to achieve short-term goals (Haley, 1984; Madanes, 1981). Adding to structural understandings of triangles and hierarchies, strategic theories view family symptoms as maladaptive sequences of dysfunctional patterns that therapeutic interventions are correspondingly designed to disrupt. These interventions include action-oriented directives and nonharmful *paradoxical interventions* designed to challenge the family's organization by shifting power and control to the practitioner and/or by leading directly to clients abandoning their problematic behaviors.

The systemic model of family therapy shares theoretical foundations with structural and strategic approaches. It distinguishes itself, however, in its movement away from strategic behavioral interventions toward a greater emphasis on questioning family belief systems and examining the different meanings family members ascribe to relationships, thoughts, behaviors, and perceptions (Boscolo, Cecchin, Hoffman, & Penn, 1987; Selvini-Palazzoli, Cirillo, Selvini, & Sorrentino, 1989). Interventions associated with the systemic model include espousing *positive connotations* for negatively viewed symptoms to augment volition, designing *rituals* to disrupt established family patterns, presenting *counterparadoxes* to challenge paradoxical family communications, and using *circular questioning* to reveal multiple perspectives of the family's internal dynamics.

Cognitive behavioral paradigms also extend to working with family systems. Similar to individual CBT, these family approaches infer a linear causality and use formal assessments to ascertain family member beliefs, attributions, and expectations (Goldenberg & Goldenberg, 2008; Kaslow et al., 2003). Subsequent interventions focus on *restructuring* family members' distorted cognitions and cognitive processing of their own and each other's behaviors. The whole family is rarely brought into session, as particular family dyads or triads are usually the greater focus of therapy (e.g., couples, parents). Psychoeducational interventions, homework, and contracts are used to promote communication skills, foster reinforcement, and gradually shape more adaptive behaviors.

Spiritually integrated family therapy.   Although few explicitly spiritually integrated family therapies exist, research continues to grow in support of attending to religious and spiritual dimensions of meaning in family work (Beeber et al., 2007; Mulder, 2012; Wolf & Stevens, 2001). Pastoral counselors and other trained professionals can attend to families' religion and spirituality in ways that foster family cohesion and resilience (Landau, 2007; Vakalahi, 2001) and mitigate the familial suffering associated with serious illness (McLeod & Wright, 2008; Wright & Bell, 2009). Specific interventions include encouraging access to imagination and metaphor, facilitating a family's coauthoring of new beliefs and narratives, and maintaining an openness to include spiritual perspectives in those reinterpretations.

Attending to religious and spiritual dimensions in family therapy also allows practitioners to address religious beliefs or orientations that may be exacerbating family conflict or dysfunction. A family may experience significant discord with regard to different religious views among its members, especially when those views include certain moral prescriptions (Caddy, 2012; Kubicek et al., 2009). Practitioners respond to these powerful, ideological disagreements in various ways that correspond with the interventions described previously. Yanni (2003), for example, even developed a measure of "positive religious detriangulation" for disentangling God from parent–child conflicts and promoting a healthier form of spiritual coping that allows God to be an advocate for familial love and harmony. Beyond such specific interventions, the general invitation remains for practitioners across the allied spectrum to acknowledge and attend to families' religious and spiritual orientations (Walsh, 1999).

Final Thoughts

Approaches to family therapy are presented here as a distinct paradigm inasmuch as they stem from an orientation that recognizes the unique problems and processes involved in family systems. Pastoral counselors and other allied health professionals are equally likely to respond to this particular set of needs and draw from the interventions purported by the various schools of thought described here. In addition, pastoral counseling's attention to religious and spiritual content is highly appropriate for dealing with family dynamics and dysfunction, given the depth and impact of traditionally held religious beliefs and spiritual meaning-making systems. Such attention need not be unique to the work of pastoral counselors but, with the appropriate training, can extend across other mental health professions.

Other Common Approaches

Do not ask who I am and do not ask me to remain the same.
—Foucault (1972)

Postmodern Modalities and Interventions

Beyond the four major schools of psychotherapeutic thought—psychodynamic, cognitive behavioral, humanistic/existential, and family systems—there are other common approaches shared by pastoral counselors and allied professionals. For instance, contemporary practitioners have adopted themes from postmodern philosophical and cultural currents, as well as developed corresponding methodologies and interventions. From a *social constructionist* perspective, professionals work collaboratively within an individual's historical–cultural framework and language to promote new dialogical meanings and possibilities (Anderson & Goolishian, 1992; Burr, 2003; Gergen, 2009). In *narrative therapy*, a constructivist, postmodern modality, intervention strategies include using metaphor, externalizing conversations, and thick descriptions to explicitly "reauthor" or "restory" the client's personal account and experience of life (White, 2007; White & Epston, 1990).

Pastoral counselors may be drawn to such paradigms not only for the way in which they reflect the person-centered respect and compassion of humanistic approaches but also for the way in which religious and spiritual identities often include a "narrative" orientation toward life (e.g., "my story," "God's story," "God's story for me," "a collective story of God's people"). In her writings on Jewish spiritual teachings and "sacred therapy," Frankel (2003) explores how such interventions can further augment well-being by connecting people to a collective, sacred narrative:

> When we go beyond our personal predicaments and . . . open doors to the sacred dimension . . . we come to experience our lives as resonant with a much greater matrix of meaning, in which any transition we undergo . . . may initiate us into the larger mysteries of life. . . . Instead of being overly identified with our problems and pathologies, we can begin to appreciate our perfection and purpose. And instead of feeling isolated and alone in our pain, we can begin to experience ourselves as part of a larger whole in which our individual stories reflect the larger story of which all people are a part. (p. 2)

In depicting this common ground of postmodern, narrative interventions, Frankel's words illumine the inherent potential for spiritual integration via these approaches.

Diversity and Specific Populations

Therapeutic interventions can also vary depending on particular populations and the issues with which they are struggling. Pastoral counselors, like other professionals, may vary in their specialization for treating individuals, groups, or families; children, adolescents, or older adults; and addiction, personality disorders, acute psychoses, and so on. The therapeutic strategies and interventions employed reflect the particulars of the specific client and still remain commonly linked to the literature and evidence used by other professionals. Pastoral counselors may also serve in consulting, educating, and supervisory roles, and their strategies will likewise be similar to other practitioners operating within those functions (see Chapters 19 and 20, this volume). Finally, it remains to be noted that pastoral counselors are not limited to serving any one type of client but share a common ethical code of sensitivity to treating diverse populations, with corresponding trainings and intervention strategies to match (see Chapters 10 and 14–18, this volume).

Holistic Collaboration

The holistic tendencies inherent in many pastoral counselors' orientations facilitate a collaborative approach to treating clients. Pastoral counselors often refer and consult with psychiatrists, social workers, and school counselors to provide a more complete response to client needs. In addition, although the field recognizes and responds to the growing emphasis on empirically based treatments (APA Presidential Task Force on Evidence-Based Practice, 2006; McHugh & Barlow, 2010), many of its practitioners also remain open to various holistic practices. As such, some may incorporate or refer to other professionals who practice interventions such as meditation, alternative medicine (including acupuncture, massage, reiki, chiropractics, etc.), and/or traditional medicine (including psychopharmacology as well as other holistic measures—e.g., checks for hypertension, hyperthyroidism, etc.). Pastoral counseling recognizes that through the collaborative efforts of a professional alliance, including assessments, advocacy, education, and religious and community integration, clients' needs can be served in a more thorough and wholly integrated manner.

CONCLUSIONS

When it comes to defining what pastoral counselors *do*, the truth is that there is much common ground across the mental health spectrum. And like other professionals, the interventions employed by a pastoral counselor will reflect the psychotherapeutic tradition with which she or he is most heavily aligned. Uniquely "pastoral" interventions are explored in the following chapter. This present discussion of common ground, however, has demonstrated the similarity shared between pastoral counseling interventions and those used by other mental health practitioners. The content and timing of a pastoral intervention may reflect a pastoral counselor's unique formation, reflective of particular ways of being and understanding. Nonetheless, the overarching framework of those interventions tends to parallel approaches found across the allied health professions, which remain unified by their common grounding in historical and contemporary psychotherapeutic orientations.

On a final note, if I were to offer a comparative perspective from a more pastoral orientation itself, I would take the reader back to the opening quote of this chapter, by Erich Fromm (1956). In essence, what we often do as pastoral counselors is *love* our clients. This word surely requires clarification, which might be considered unfortunate as there are many things done in the name of "love" that do not promote a fuller human flourishing. Alternately, one might find it natural that *love* require clarification inasmuch as it ascribes to something that many relate to the ineffable mystery of the Divine.

Although this chapter falls short of any comprehensive treatise on the nature of love, what it has aimed to do is to illustrate how love takes many forms, and many can be cultivated and practiced across the spectrum of allied health professions. Love can involve sitting quietly with a suffering human being, holding the person and her or his experiences in honest reverence. Love can involve facilitating another's self-understanding and promoting his or her self-efficacy and self-agency. It can entail encouraging people's strengths and their participation in helping others as well. It might involve a corrective emotional experience or helping someone to replace self-destructive cognitions or behaviors with healthier alternatives. These interventions reflect the "art of love" and emerge from the practitioner's ways of being and understanding. Still, the practices themselves, as instruments of facilitating human flourishing and holistic well-being, provide a common ground for all who choose to use them in the loving service of another.

REFLECTION QUESTIONS

1. According to Rizzuto (2005), "Spirituality, to the extent that it is mediated through the mind, is subject to the same psychodynamic conditions as other phenomena because transcendent realities are also apprehended through psychic processes" (pp. 47–48). In the context that it was cited in this chapter, how does this statement inform your understanding of your own religious tradition? Of your theoretical approach as a pastoral counselor?
2. When considering the spiritual undertones of the humanistic approach and the interventions detailed in this chapter, who in your life has helped you feel both prized and appreciated? In what ways?
3. Pastoral counselors employ an integrated approach to counseling by blending psychological and spiritual or religious wisdom. In your opinion, are particular theoretical orientations, as presented in this chapter, better suited to integration with spiritual and religious wisdom? Explain your answer.

REFERENCES

Ackerman, N. (1966). *Treating the troubled family*. New York, NY: Basic Books.

Adler, A. (1964a). The origin of the neurotic disposition. In H. Ansbacher & R. Ansbacher (Eds.), *The individual psychology of Alfred Adler: A systematic presentation in selections from his writings* (pp. 365–383). New York, NY: Harper & Row.

Adler, A. (1964b). Understanding and treating the patient. In H. Ansbacher & R. Ansbacher (Eds.), *The individual psychology of Alfred Adler: A systematic presentation in selections from his writings* (pp. 326–349). New York, NY: Harper & Row.

Alexander, F., & French, T. M. (1946). *Psychoanalytic psychotherapy: Principles and applications*. New York, NY: Ronald.

American Association of Pastoral Counselors. (2014). *Licensing*. Retrieved from http://www.aapc.org/links-resources/mental-health-resources/licensing/

Anderson, H., & Goolishian, H. (1992). The client is the expert: A not-knowing approach to therapy. In S. McNamee & K. J. Gergen (Eds.), *Therapy as social construction* (pp. 25–39). Newbury Park, CA: Sage.

APA Presidential Task Force on Evidence-Based Practice. (2006). Evidence-based practice in psychology. *American Psychologist, 61*(4), 271–285. doi:10.1037/0003-066X.61.4.271

Ballou, M. (Ed.). (1995). *Psychological interventions: A guide to strategies*. Westport, CT: Greenwood.

Beck, A. (1963). Thinking and depression: I. Idiosyncratic content and cognitive distortions. *Archives of General Psychiatry, 9*, 324–333. doi:10.1001/archpsyc.1963.01720160014002

Beeber, L. S., Cooper, C., Van Noy, B. E., Schwartz, T. A., Blanchard, H. C., Canuso, R., . . . Emory, S. (2007). Flying under the radar: Engagement and retention of depressed low-income mothers in a mental health intervention. *Advances in Nursing Science, 30*, 221–234. doi: 10.1097/01.ANS.0000286621.77139.f0

Beier, M. (2007). On being wanted to exist: A spiritual dimension in pastoral counseling and psychoanalysis. *Pastoral Psychology, 55*(6), 701–710. doi:10.1007/s11089-007-0084-z

Bird, V., Premkumar, P., Kendall, T., Whittington, C., Mitchell, J., & Kuipers, E. (2010). Early intervention services, cognitive-behavioural therapy and family intervention in early psychosis: Systematic review. *British Journal of Psychiatry, 197*(5), 350–356. doi:10.1192/bjp.bp.109.074526

Bohart, A. C. (2003). Person-centered psychotherapy and related experiential approaches. In A. S. Gurman & S. B. Messer (Eds.), *Essential psychotherapies: Theory and practice* (2nd ed., pp. 107–148). New York, NY: Guilford.

Boscolo, L., Cecchin, G., Hoffman, L., & Penn, P. (1987). *Milan systemic family therapy*. New York, NY: Basic Books.

Boszormenyi-Nagy, I. (1987). *Foundations of contextual therapy: Collected papers of Ivan Boszormenyi-Nagy*. New York, NY: Brunner/Mazel.

Boszormenyi-Nagy, I., & Spark, G. (1973). *Invisible loyalties: Reciprocity in intergenerational family therapy*. New York, NY: Harper & Row.

Bowen, M. (1978). *Family therapy in clinical practice*. New York, NY: Jason Aronson.

Buber, M. (1958). *I and thou* (R. G. Smith, Trans.). New York, NY: Scribner's.

Buell, L. (Ed.). (2006). *The American transcendentalists: Essential writings*. New York, NY: Random House.

Burr, V. (2003). *Social constructionism* (2nd ed.). New York, NY: Routledge.

Caddy, G. (2012). Family pathology and the creation of madness: A case study of mind control. *American Journal of Family Therapy, 40*(4), 297–319. doi:10.1080/01926187.2011.614843

Campbell, J. (Ed.). (1971). *The portable Jung*. New York, NY: Penguin.

Cheston, S. E. (2000). A new paradigm for teaching counseling theory and practice. *Counselor Education and Supervision, 39*(4), 254–269. doi:10.1002/j.1556-6978.2000.tb01236.x

Cheston, S. E., Piedmont, R. L., Eanes, B., & Lavin, L. P. (2003). Changes in clients' images of God over the course of outpatient psychotherapy. *Counseling and Values, 47*, 96–108. Retrieved from http://www.aservic.org/counseling-and-values/

Clinebell, H., & McKeever, B. C. (2011). *Basic types of pastoral care and counseling: Resources for the ministry of healing and growth* (3rd ed.). Nashville, TN: Abingdon.

Cooper-White, P. (2007). *Many voices: Pastoral psychotherapy in relational and theological perspective*. Minneapolis, MN: Fortress.

Corbett, L., & Stein, M. (2005). Contemporary Jungian approaches to spiritually oriented psychotherapy. In L. Sperry & E. P. Shafranske (Eds.), *Spiritually oriented psychotherapy* (pp. 51–73). Washington, DC: American Psychological Association.

Corey, G. (2009). *Theory and practice of counseling and psychotherapy* (8th ed.). Belmont, CA: Thomson Brooks/Cole.

Curtis, R. C., & Hirsch, I. (2003). Relational approaches to psychoanalytic psychotherapy. In A. S. Gurman & S. B. Messer (Eds.), *Essential psychotherapies: Theory and practice* (2nd ed., pp. 69–106). New York, NY: Guilford.

Davis, E. B., Moriarty, G. L., & Mauch, J. C. (2013). God images and god concepts: Definitions, development, and dynamics. *Psychology of Religion and Spirituality, 5*(1), 51–60. doi:10.1037/a0029289

Dourly, J. P. (2004, September 2). *Memory and emergence: Jung and the mystical anamnesis of the nothing*. Paper presented at the International Association for Analytical Psychology, Barcelona, Spain. Retrieved from http://www.iaap.org

Ekedahl, M., & Wengström, Y. (2008). Coping processes in a multidisciplinary healthcare team—A comparison of nurses in cancer care and hospital chaplains. *European Journal of Cancer Care, 17*(1), 42–48. doi:http://dx.doi.org/10.1111/j.1365-2354.2007.00801.x

Elkins, D. N. (2005). A humanistic approach to spiritually oriented psychotherapy. In L. Sperry & E. P. Shafranske (Eds.), *Spiritually oriented psychotherapy* (pp. 131–151). Washington, DC: American Psychological Association.

Ellis, A. (1962). *Reason and emotion in psychotherapy*. New York, NY: Lyle Stuart.

Ellis, A. (2000). Can rational emotive behavior therapy (REBT) be effectively used with people who have devout beliefs in God and religion? *Professional Psychology: Research and Practice, 31*, 29–33. doi:10.1037//0735-7028.31.1.29

Epstein, R. (2001). The prince of reason: An interview with Albert Ellis. *Psychology Today, 34*(1), 66–68, 70–72, 74–76. Retrieved from http://www.psychologytoday.com

Estadt, B. K. (1991). Profile of a pastoral counselor. In B. K. Estadt, M. C. Blanchette, & J. R. Compton (Eds.), *Pastoral counseling* (2nd ed., pp. 1–17). Englewood Cliffs, NJ: Prentice Hall.

Estadt, B. K., Blanchette, M. C., & Compton, J. R. (Eds.). (1991). *Pastoral counseling* (2nd ed.). Englewood Cliffs, NJ: Prentice Hall.

Evans, B. A. (2005). Ancient and classic pastoral counsel: Approaches to anxiety, doubt and guilt. *Journal of Psychology and Christianity, 24*(1), 80–88. Retrieved from http://caps.net/membership/publications/jpc

Farber, E. W. (2010). Humanistic-existential psychotherapy competencies and the supervisory process. *Psychotherapy Theory, Research, Practice, Training, 47*(1), 28–34. doi:10.1037//a0018847

FindCounseling.com. (2014). *Types of mental health professionals.* Retrieved from http://www.findcounseling.com/glossary/

Fink, A., Parhami, I., Rosenthal, R. J., Campos, M. D., Siani, A., & Fong, T. W. (2012). How transparent is behavioral intervention research on pathological gambling and other gambling-related disorders? A systematic literature review. *Addiction, 107*(11), 1915–1928. doi:10.1111/j.1360-0443.2012.03911.x

Fleischman, P. (1990). *The healing spirit: Explorations in religion and psychotherapy.* St. Paul, MN: Paragon House.

Fors, E. A., Bertheussen, G. F., Thune, I., Juvet, L. K., Elvsaas, I. Ø., Oldervoll, L., . . . Leivseth, G. (2011). Psychosocial interventions as part of breast cancer rehabilitation programs? Results from a systematic review. *Psycho-Oncology, 20*(9), 909–918. doi:10.1002/pon.1844

Fortney, L., & Taylor, M. (2010). Meditation in medical practice: A review of the evidence and practice. *Primary Care, 37*(1), 81–90. doi:10.1016/j.pop.2009.09.004

Foucault, M. (1972). *The archaeology of knowledge & the discourse on language* (A. M. S. Smith, Trans.). New York, NY: Pantheon.

Framo, J. (1992). *Family-of-origin therapy: An intergenerational approach.* New York, NY: Brunner/Mazel.

Frankel, E. (2003). *Sacred therapy: Jewish spiritual teachings on emotional healing and inner wholeness.* Boston, MA: Shambhala.

Frankl, V. E. (1984). *Man's search for meaning.* New York: Pocket Books.

Freud, S. (1964). An outline of psycho-analysis. In J. Strachey (Ed. and Trans.), *The standard edition of the complete psychological works of Sigmund Freud* (Vol. 23, pp. 144–207). London, UK: Hogarth. (Original work published 1940)

Fromm, E. (1956). *The art of loving.* New York, NY: Harper.

Gable, R. A., Hester, P. H., Rock, M. L., & Hughes, K. G. (2009). Back to basics. *Intervention in School and Clinic, 44*(4), 195–205. doi:10.1177/1053451208328831

Gendlin, E. T. (1981). *Focusing.* New York, NY: Bantam.

Gergen, K. J. (2009). *An invitation to social construction* (2nd ed.). Thousand Oaks, CA: Sage.

Gladding, S. T., & Newsome, D. W. (2010). *Clinical mental health counseling in community and agency settings* (3rd ed.). Upper Saddle River, NJ: Pearson Education.

Gloaguen, V., Cottraux, J., Cucherat, M., & Blackburn, I. M. (1998). A meta-analysis of the effects of cognitive therapy in depressed patients. *Journal of Affective Disorders, 49*(1), 59–72. doi:10.1016/S0165-0327(97)00199-7

Goldenberg, H., & Goldenberg, I. (2008). *Family therapy: An overview* (7th ed.). Belmont, CA: Thomson Brooks/Cole.

Graham, J. (2012). Cognitive behavioural therapy for occupational trauma: A systematic literature review exploring the effects of occupational trauma and the existing CBT support pathways and interventions for staff working within mental healthcare including allied professions. *The Cognitive Behaviour Therapist, 5*(1), 24–45. doi:10.1017/S1754470X12000025

Haley, J. (1984). *Ordeal therapy.* San Francisco, CA: Jossey-Bass.

Hopper, T., Bourgeois, M., Pimentel, J., Dean Qualls, C., Hickey, E., Frymark, T., & Schooling, T. (2013). An evidence-based systematic review on cognitive interventions for individuals with dementia. *American Journal of Speech-Language Pathology, 22*(1), 126–145. doi:10.1044/1058-0360(2012/11-0137)

Ireland, M. (2012). Meditation and psychological health and functioning: A descriptive and critical review. *Scientific Review of Mental Health Practice, 9*(1), 4–19. Retrieved from http://www.srmhp.org/

James, W. (1902). *The varieties of religious experience.* New York, NY: Longmans, Green.

Jung, C. G. (1954). *Collected works: The practice of psychotherapy* (G. Adler & R. Hull, Eds. & Trans.; Vol. 16). New York, NY: Bollingen.

Kangas, M., Bovbjerg, D. H., & Montgomery, G. H. (2008). Cancer-related fatigue: A systematic and meta-analytic review of non-pharmacological therapies for cancer patients. *Psychological Bulletin, 134*(5), 700–741. doi:10.1037/a0012825

Kaplan, D. (2009). *Can we please remove just from just listening?* [Web log post]. Retrieved from http://www.counseling.org/news/blog

Kaslow, N., Dausch, B., & Celano, M. (2003). Family therapies. In A. S. Gurman & S. B. Messer (Eds.), *Essential psychotherapies: Theory and practice* (2nd ed., pp. 400–462). New York, NY: Guilford.

Kavanagh, J., Oliver, S., Lorenc, T., Caird, J., Tucker, H., Harden, A., . . . Oakley, A. (2009). School-based cognitive-behavioural interventions: A systematic review of effects and inequalities. *Health Sociology Review, 18*(1), 61–78. doi:10.5172/hesr.18.1.61

Kruger, A. (2002). Counseling and philosophy: A personal existential view. *American Journal of Pastoral Counseling, 6*(1), 51–62. doi:10.1300/J062v06n01_04

Krumrei, E. J., & Rosmarin, D. H. (2012). Processes of religious and spiritual coping. In J. D. Aten, K. A. O'Grady, & E. L. Worthington Jr. (Eds.), *The psychology of religion and spirituality for clinicians: Using research in your practice* (pp. 245–273). New York, NY: Routledge.

Kubicek, K., McDavitt, B., Carpineto, J., Weiss, G., Iverson, E. F., & Kipke, M. D. (2009). "God made me gay for a reason": Young men who have sex with men's resiliency in resolving internalized homophobia from religious sources. *Journal of Adolescent Research, 24*(5), 601–633. doi:10.1177/0743558409341078

Landau, J. (2007). Enhancing resilience: Families and communities as agents for change. *Family Process, 46*(3), 351–365. doi:10.1111/j.1545-5300.2007.00216.x

Lee, N. K., & Rawson, R. A. (2008). A systematic review of cognitive and behavioural therapies for methamphetamine dependence. *Drug and Alcohol Review, 27*(3), 309–317. doi:10.1080/09595230801919494

Leichsenring, F., & Leibing, E. (2007). Psychodynamic psychotherapy: A systematic review of techniques, indications and empirical evidence. *Psychology & Psychotherapy: Theory, Research & Practice, 80*(2), 217–228. doi:10.1348/147608306X117394

Lewis, A. J., Dennerstein, M., & Gibbs, P. M. (2008). Short-term psychodynamic psychotherapy: Review of recent process and outcome studies. *Australian and New Zealand Journal of Psychiatry, 42*(6), 445–455. doi:10.1080/00048670802050520

Louw, D. J. (2011). Philosophical counselling: Towards a "new approach" in pastoral care and counselling? *HTS Theological Studies, 67*(2), 22–28. doi:10.4102/hts.v67i2.900

Madanes, C. (1981). *Strategic family therapy.* San Francisco, CA: Jossey-Bass.

Martin, J. (2010). *The Jesuit guide to (almost) everything: A spirituality for real life.* New York, NY: HarperOne.

Maslow, A. H. (1962). *Toward a psychology of being.* New York, NY: Van Nostrand Reinhold.

McHugh, R. K., & Barlow, D. H. (2010). The dissemination and implementation of evidence-based psychological treatments: A review of current efforts. *American Psychologist, 65*, 73–84. doi:10.1037/a0018121

McLeod, D. L., & Wright, L. M. (2008). Living the as-yet unanswered: Spiritual care practices in family systems nursing. *Journal of Family Nursing, 14*(1), 118–141. doi:10.1177/1074840707313339

Miller, A. J., & Worthington, E. L., Jr. (2012). Connection between personality and religion and spirituality. In J. D. Aten, K. A. O'Grady, & E. L. Worthington Jr. (Eds.), *The psychology of religion and spirituality for clinicians: Using research in your practice* (pp. 101–129). New York, NY: Routledge.

Minuchin, S. (1974). *Families and family therapy.* Cambridge, MA: Harvard University Press.

Moriarty, G. L. (2006). *Pastoral care of depression: Helping clients heal their relationship with God.* Binghamton, NY: Haworth/Routledge.

Moriarty, G. L., & Davis, E. B. (2012). Client God images: Theory, research, and clinical practice. In J. D. Aten, K. A. O'Grady, & E. L. Worthington Jr. (Eds.), *The psychology of religion and spirituality for clinicians: Using research in your practice* (pp. 131–160). New York, NY: Routledge.

Mulder, C. (2012). Variations in religious and spiritual practices among mothers and grandmothers in three generational households. *Journal of Religion & Spirituality in Social Work, 31*(4), 372. doi:10.1080/15426432.2012.716294

Murdock, N. L. (2013). *Theories of counseling and psychotherapy: A case approach* (3rd ed.). Boston, MA: Pearson.

Myers, I., McCaulley, M., Quenk, N., & Hammer, A. (1998). *MBTI manual: A guide to the development and use of the Myers-Briggs Type Indicator* (3rd ed.). Palo Alto, CA: Consulting Psychologists Press.

Nevid, J. S. (2012). *Essentials of psychology: Concepts and applications* (3rd ed.). Belmont, CA: Wadsworth.

Nye, C., Vanryckeghem, M., Schwartz, J. B., Herder, C., Turner, H., & Howard, C. (2013). Behavioral stuttering interventions for children and adolescents: A systematic review and meta-analysis. *Journal of Speech, Language, and Hearing Research, 56*(3), 921–932. doi:10.1044/1092-4388(2012/12-0036)

Ogden, T. (1999). The analytic third. In S. Mitchell & L. Aron (Eds.), *Relational psychoanalysis: The emergence of a tradition* (pp. 459–492). Hillsdale, NJ: Analytic Press.

Orlinsky, D., Grawe, K., & Parks, B. (1994). Process and outcome in psychotherapy. In A. E. Bergin & S. L. Garfield (Eds.), *Handbook of psychotherapy and behavior change* (4th ed., pp. 270–376). New York, NY: John Wiley.

Pargament, K. I. (1997). *The psychology of religion and coping: Theory, research, practice.* New York, NY: Guilford.

Pargament, K. I. (2007). *Spiritually integrated psychotherapy: Understanding and addressing the sacred.* New York, NY: Guilford.

Perls, F. (1973). *The gestalt approach & eye witness to therapy.* New York, NY: Bantam.

Piderman, K. M., Mueller, P. S., Theneau, T. M., Stevens, S. R., Hanson, A. C., & Reeves, R. K. (2011). A pilot study of spirituality and inpatient rehabilitation outcomes in persons with spinal cord dysfunction and severe neurological illnesses. *Journal of Pastoral Care & Counseling, 65*(3–4), 1–13. Retrieved from http://www.jpcp.org/

Pomaki, G., Franche, R., Murray, E., Khushrushahi, N., & Lampinen, T. M. (2012). Workplace-based work disability prevention interventions for workers with common mental health conditions: A review of the literature. *Journal of Occupational Rehabilitation, 22*(2), 182–195. doi:10.1007/s10926-011-9338-9

Propst, L., Ostrom, R., Watkins, P., Dean, T., & Mashburn, D. (1992). Comparative efficacy of religious and nonreligious cognitive-behavioral therapy for the treatment of clinical depression in religious individuals. *Journal of Consulting and Clinical Psychology, 60*(1), 94–103. doi:10.1037/0022-006X.60.1.94

Ramsay, N. J. (2004). *Pastoral care and counseling: Redefining the paradigms.* Nashville, TN: Abingdon.

Reik, T. (1983). *Listening with the third ear: The inner experience of a psychoanalyst.* London, UK: Macmillan.

Reinecke, M. A., & Freeman, A. (2003). Cognitive therapy. In A. S. Gurman & S. B. Messer (Eds.), *Essential psychotherapies: Theory and practice* (2nd ed., pp. 224–271). New York, NY: Guilford.

Richards, P. S. (2005). Theistic integrative psychotherapy. In L. Sperry & E. P. Shafranske (Eds.), *Spiritually oriented psychotherapy* (pp. 259–285). Washington, DC: American Psychological Association.

Richardson, T., Stallard, P., & Velleman, S. (2010). Computerised cognitive behavioural therapy for the prevention and treatment of depression and anxiety in children and adolescents: A systematic review. *Clinical Child and Family Psychology Review, 13*(3), 275–290. doi:10.1007/s10567-010-0069-9

Rizzuto, A. (1979). *The birth of the living God: A psychoanalytic study*. Chicago, IL: University of Chicago Press.

Rizzuto, A. (2005). Psychoanalytic considerations about spiritually oriented psychotherapy. In L. Sperry & E. P. Shafranske (Eds.), *Spiritually oriented psychotherapy* (pp. 31–50). Washington, DC: American Psychological Association.

Rogers, C. R. (1957). The necessary and sufficient conditions of therapeutic personality change. *Journal of Consulting Psychology, 21*, 95–103. doi:10.1037/h0045357

Rogers, C. R. (1961). *On becoming a person*. Boston, MA: Houghton Mifflin.

Rogers, C. R. (1980). *A way of being*. New York, NY: Houghton Mifflin.

Rumbold, J. L., Fletcher, D., & Daniels, K. (2012). A systematic review of stress management interventions with sport performers. *Sport, Exercise, and Performance Psychology, 1*(3), 173–193. doi:10.1037/a0026628

Samad, Z., Brealey, S., & Gilbody, S. (2011). The effectiveness of behavioural therapy for the treatment of depression in older adults: A meta-analysis. *International Journal of Geriatric Psychiatry, 26*(12), 1211–1220. doi:10.1002/gps.2680

Sarnat, J. (2010). Key competencies of the psychodynamic psychotherapist and how to teach them in supervision. *Psychotherapy Theory, Research, Practice, Training, 47*(1), 20–27. doi: 10.1037/a0018846

Satir, V., & Baldwin, M. (1983). *Satir step by step: A guide to creating change in families*. Palo Alto, CA: Science & Behavior Books.

Schneider, K. J. (2003). Existential-humanistic psychotherapies. In A. S. Gurman & S. B. Messer (Eds.), *Essential psychotherapies: Theory and practice* (2nd ed., pp. 149–181). New York, NY: Guilford.

Schneider, K. J., & May, R. (1995). *The psychology of existence: An integrative, clinical perspective*. New York, NY: McGraw-Hill.

Seligman, M. E. P., & Csikszentmihalyi, M. (2000). Positive psychology: An introduction. *American Psychologist, 55*(1), 5–14. doi:10.1037/0003-066X.55.1.5

Selvini-Palazzoli, M., Cirillo, S., Selvini, M., & Sorrentino, A. (1989). *Family games: General models of psychotic processes in the family*. New York, NY: Norton.

Shafranske, E. P. (2005). A psychoanalytic approach to spiritually oriented psychotherapy. In L. Sperry & E. P. Shafranske (Eds.), *Spiritually oriented psychotherapy* (pp. 105–130). Washington, DC: American Psychological Association.

Shafranske, E. P., & Sperry, L. (2005). Addressing the spiritual dimension in psychotherapy: Introduction and overview. In L. Sperry & E. P. Shafranske (Eds.), *Spiritually oriented psychotherapy* (pp. 11–29). Washington, DC: American Psychological Association.

Silverman, D. K. (2005). What works in psychotherapy and how do we know? What evidence-based practice has to offer. *Psychoanalytic Psychology, 22*(2), 306–312. doi:10.1037/0736-9735 .22.2.306

Sneck, W. J. (2007). Jung: Mentor for pastoral counselors. *Research in the Social Scientific Study of Religion, 18*, 35–52. doi:10.1163/ej.9789004158511.i-301.21

Snodgrass, J. (2009). Toward holistic care: Integrating spirituality and cognitive behavioral therapy for older adults. *Journal of Religion, Spirituality & Aging, 21*(3), 219. doi:10.1080/ 15528030902803913

Snodgrass, J., & Sorajjakool, S. (2011). Spirituality in older adulthood: Existential meaning, productivity, and life events. *Pastoral Psychology, 60*(1), 85–94. doi:10.1007/s11089-010-0282-y

Sperry, L. (2005). Integrative spiritually oriented psychotherapy. In L. Sperry & E. P. Shafranske (Eds.), *Spiritually oriented psychotherapy* (pp. 307–329). Washington, DC: American Psychological Association.

Strauss, J. L., Hayes, A. M., Johnson, S. L., Newman, C. F., Browne, G. K., Barber, J. P., . . . Beck, A. T. (2006). Early alliance, alliance ruptures, and symptom change in a nonrandomized trial of cognitive therapy for avoidant and obsessive-compulsive personality disorders. *Journal of Consulting and Clinical Psychology, 74*, 337–345. doi:10.1037/0022-006X.74 .2.337

Sweeney, T. (2009). *Adlerian counseling and psychotherapy: A practitioner's approach* (5th ed.). New York, NY: Routledge.

Tan, S., & Johnson, W. B. (2005). Spiritually oriented cognitive-behavioral therapy. In L. Sperry & E. P. Shafranske (Eds.), *Spiritually oriented psychotherapy* (pp. 77–103). Washington, DC: American Psychological Association.

Tan, S., & Wong, M. (2012). Existential therapy: Empirical evidence and clinical applications from a Christian perspective. *Journal of Psychology and Christianity, 31*(3), 272–277. Retrieved from http://caps.net/membership/publications/jpc

Tillich, P. (1957). *Dynamics of faith.* New York, NY: Harper & Row.

Tisdale, T. T., Key, T. L., Edwards, K. J., Brokaw, B. F., Kemperman, S. R., Cloud, H., Townsend, J., & Okamato, T. (1997). Impact of treatment on God image and personal adjustment, and correlations of God image to personal adjustment and object relations development. *Journal of Psychology and Theology, 25,* 227–239. Retrieved from http://journals.biola.edu/jpt

Toussaint, L., Webb, J. R., & Keltner, W. (2012). Religion, spirituality, and mental health. In J. D. Aten, K. A. O'Grady, & E. L. Worthington Jr. (Eds.), *The psychology of religion and spirituality for clinicians: Using research in your practice* (pp. 331–356). New York, NY: Routledge.

Tuckett, D. (2005). Does anything go? Toward a framework for the more transparent assessment of psychoanalytic competence. *International Journal of Psychoanalysis, 86*(1), 31–49. doi: 10.1516/R2U5-XJ37-7DFJ-DD18

Vakalahi, H. F. (2001). Adolescent substance use and family-based risk and protective factors: A literature review. *Journal of Drug Education, 31*(1), 29–46. doi:10.2190/QP75-P9AR-NUVJ-FJCB

Van Deurzen, E. (2007). Existential therapy. In W. Dryden (Ed.), *Handbook of individual therapy* (5th ed., pp. 195–226). London, UK: Sage.

Van Deurzen, E. (2009). *Everyday mysteries: A handbook of existential psychotherapy.* London, UK: Routledge.

Van Deurzen, E. (2012). *Existential counseling and psychotherapy in practice* (3rd ed.). London, UK: Sage.

von Bertalanffy, L. (1968). *General systems theory: Foundations, development, applications* (Rev. ed.). New York, NY: George Braziller.

Von der Embse, N., Barterian, J., & Segool, N. (2013). Test anxiety interventions for children and adolescents: A systematic review of treatment studies from 2000–2010. *Psychology In the Schools, 50*(1), 57–71. doi:10.1002/pits.21660

Vontress, C. E. (2008). Existential therapy. In J. Frew & M. D. Spiegler (Eds.), *Contemporary psychotherapies for a diverse world* (pp. 141–176). Boston, MA: Lahaska.

Walsh, F. (Ed.). (1999). *Spiritual resources in family therapy.* New York, NY: Guilford.

Welsh, J. A., Viana, A. G., Petrill, S. A., & Mathias, M. D. (2007). Interventions for internationally adopted children and families: A review of the literature. *Child & Adolescent Social Work Journal, 24*(3), 285–311. doi:10.1007/s10560-007-0085-x

Whitaker, C., & Bumberry, W. (1988). *Dancing with the family: A symbolic-experiential approach.* New York, NY: Brunner/Mazel.

White, M. (2007). *Maps of narrative practice.* New York, NY: Norton.

White, M., & Epston, D. (1990). *Narrative means to therapeutic ends.* New York, NY: Norton.

Wicks, R. J., & Buck, T. C. (2011). Reframing for change: The use of cognitive behavioral therapy and native psychology in pastoral ministry and formation. *Human Development, 32*(3), 8–14. Retrieved from http://www.humandevelopmentmag.org/

Wicks, R. J., Parsons, R. D., & Capps, D. (Eds.). (1993). *Clinical handbook of pastoral counseling* (Vol. 1, expanded ed.). Mahwah, NJ: Paulist Press.

Winnicott, D. W. (1965). *The maturational process and the facilitating environment.* London, UK: Hogarth.

Wolf, C. T., & Stevens, P. (2001). Integrating religion and spirituality in marriage and family counseling. *Counseling & Values, 46*(1), 66–75. doi:10.1002/j.2161-007X.2001.tb00207.x

Wolitzky, D. L. (2003). The theory and practice of traditional psychoanalytic treatment. In A. S. Gurman & S. B. Messer (Eds.), *Essential psychotherapies: Theory and practice* (2nd ed., pp. 24–68). New York, NY: Guilford.

Wright, L., & Bell, J. (2009). *Beliefs and illness: A model for healing.* Calgary, Canada: 4th Floor Press.

Yalom, I. D. (1980). *Existential psychotherapy.* New York, NY: Basic Books.

Yanni, G. M. (2003). *Religious and secular dyadic variables and their relation to parent–child relationships and college students' psychological adjustment* (Doctoral dissertation). Retrieved from ProQuest Dissertations and Theses database. (Order No. 3114955)

Zarit, S., & Femia, E. (2008). Behavioral and psychosocial interventions for family caregivers. *Journal of Social Work Education, 44*(3), 49–57. doi:10.5175/JSWE.2008.773247711

Zuroff, D. C., & Blatt, S. (2006). Therapeutic relationship in the brief treatment of depression: Contributions to clinical improvement and enhanced adaptive capacities. *Journal of Consulting and Clinical Psychology, 74*, 130–140. doi:10.1037/0022-006X.74.1.130

Christina Jones Davis

12

SET APART: THE DISTINCTIVENESS OF PASTORAL COUNSELING INTERVENTIONS

DEFINING OURSELVES: PASTORAL COUNSELING AS A PROFESSION

In many ways, the current developmental stage of pastoral counseling as a profession is analogous to Erik Erickson's adolescent stage of "identity versus role confusion" (Sollad, Wilson, & Monte, 2009, p. 285). According to Erickson, our sense of identity is achieved by sustaining an affinity for our community's history while also "being at one with oneself" (Erikson, 1974, p. 27). Pastoral counseling exists in a substantial community of related disciplines and professions. Although psychology and theology are considered its perennial sources, it exists alongside several other sister professions, including professional counseling, clinical social work, and marriage and family therapy.

Using Erickson's developmental stages as a guide, pastoral counselors must continue to work through this important developmental task of distinction to grow professionally. We are tasked with defining ourselves in a way that acknowledges our community's history and professional heritages as well as distinguishes ourselves from other similar professions in a manner that achieves oneness with ourselves. To best contextualize an exploration of distinctiveness, a brief historical review is useful here (see Chapter 2 for a more thorough treatment of the history of pastoral counseling). Pastoral counseling's unique history reveals the web-like communal identity within which the field was formed and its identity was shaped.

A Brief Historical Sketch

The two theoretical bodies of knowledge that combined to create pastoral counseling were the disciplines of psychology and theology. In the early 20th century, pastors and pastoral care providers were becoming more and more influenced by popular psychology. In response, the pastoral counseling movement was formed by combining psychotherapy and theology as part of a larger movement going on at the time of combining science and religion. Elwood Worcester, influenced by the Clark University Lectures of Freud and C. G. Jung, was the first to advocate blending psychotherapy with religious instruction (Cooper-White, 2004). Subsequently, the interest of clergy and religious leaders in using the theoretical body of knowledge and clinical skills of contemporary helping professions such as psychiatry, psychology, and social work within church ministry continued to grow (Estatdt, Blanchett, & Compton, 1991).

In 1963, the American Association of Pastoral Counselors was formed and the integration of psychological principles and practices with pastoral care developed into a formalized discipline (Everly, 2008). This juncture in history can be considered the birth of pastoral counseling as an organized profession. A review of pastoral counseling's professional heritage sets the stage for the discipline's contemporary identity dilemma.

ISSUES OF DISTINCTION: A CONTEMPORARY DILEMMA WITHIN PSYCHOTHERAPEUTIC COMMUNITIES

Following the professionalization of pastoral counseling, many pastoral counselors ventured out of church settings exclusively and into a wide variety of alternative occupational settings. For this expansion to occur, it was necessary for pastoral counselors to acquire education and training that would enable ethical and legitimate practice within nonreligious contexts. Specifically, pastoral counselors needed to meet the criteria for state-sanctioned counseling licensures. This need to meet state requirements for clinical practice has been a chief contributor to the blurring of lines between pastoral counselors and other related fields.

To meet the criteria for state licensures, pastoral counseling training programs adopted the content and training components necessary to fulfill state licensing board requirements. As a result, features of secular counseling degrees became commonplace within pastoral counseling degree programs. Students of these programs often graduated with dual identities as both pastoral counselors as well as another professional title such as marriage and family therapist or social worker. Just as graduates of these programs became prepared to function in more than one counseling profession, many pastoral counseling training institutions were also designed to skillfully integrate secular psychological concepts and clinical training with the theological and spiritual aspects of pastoral care.

Upon securing state licensure, pastoral counselors continue to experience a merger of professional identities as they establish a presence in a variety of secular settings alongside other mental health professionals in hospitals, group practices, schools, and community mental health organizations. What's more, pastoral counselors are now often found serving on secular state licensing boards and in leadership positions within a variety of secular professional guilds, roles in which they exercise great relevance and effectiveness. The reach of pastoral counseling as a profession has greatly expanded over the course of the past five decades, and pastoral counselors are located in almost any sector of practice in which one would find any other counseling professional. The expansive habitat of pastoral counselors has been useful as it allows for a two-way exposure effect. It underscores pastoral counseling's relevance to communities beyond the scope of the church, and it also provides innumerable contexts and settings for pastoral counselors to exercise their gifts and graces for working with a broad range of clients.

In addition to the increasingly broad reach of pastoral counselors beyond religious settings into a variety of secular ones, a similar expansion has been occurring in secular professional counseling arenas. In the spirit of addressing diversity issues of ethnicity, gender, and sexual orientation, mental health professionals are being called to view spirituality as an important dimension of cultural diversity and, therefore, urged to create a spiritually sensitive context for practice (Canda & Furman, 1999). As a result, there have been efforts to integrate issues of spirituality into coursework in secular counseling programs, and spiritual topics are often advertised in continuing-education courses offered by secular counselors and counseling organizations.

Overlap in the teaching and training that pastoral counselors receive and the recent inclusion of spirituality into secular professional counseling contribute to the reality that pastoral counselors share much in common with other counseling professionals. In lieu of this convergence, the important developmental question remains: Does our common identity as pastoral counselors result in any distinctive approaches to our therapeutic work?

Although pastoral counseling shares much in common with approaches from other fields, I argue that it maintains meaningful aspects of its individuality. Therefore, the purpose of this chapter is to identify how pastoral counselors are different from other counseling professions. One way of defining a profession is by examining its unique theoretical foundation and underpinnings. However, as noted previously, as the variety of mental health practitioners continues to expand, the designations between the professions remain unclear (Raphel, 2001).

Another manner of distinguishing professions from one another is by giving attention to what the clinician does, or the profession's set of therapeutic techniques. Therapeutic techniques are the tools or methods therapists use to facilitate effective therapy or positive client behavior change (Hill, Butman, & Hood, 1999). Therapists' techniques and interventions—what therapists do to help clients during the session—offer useful defining characteristics among classifications of professional counseling. For this reason, an exploration of the distinctiveness of pastoral counseling interventions is an appropriate entrée into understanding what sets pastoral counselors apart.

WHAT IS A PASTORAL COUNSELING INTERVENTION?

The word *intervention* is derived from the Latin word *intervenīre*, meaning "to come between" (Stone, 1994). In the context of psychotherapy, interventions are understood as the proactive role on the part of the therapist to best meet client goals (Wells, 1982). In other words, it is the action of the therapist to address a client's presenting problem.

Discussing the interventions of pastoral counselors may unintentionally suggest a focus only on the *doing* of pastoral counseling. However, there exists and unavoidable relationship between what the pastoral counselor *does* and who the pastoral counselor *is* (Townsend, 2009). There are several reasons this interconnection holds true.

First, a therapist's techniques and interventions include what therapists do or do not do to help clients during their session (Hill et al., 1999). In this way, when a therapist chooses to refrain from doing something in the room, inaction, in itself, is a method of responding to the client. Second, pastoral counselors aspire to a particular "way of being" that is reflected in the degree of empathy expressed, the values demonstrated, and the boundaries that are set in the creation of an environment where change can occur (Cheston, 2000). As such, lines between who the pastoral counselor is and what the pastoral counselor does are inextricably related. Third, formal interventions are a single aspect of the response of the therapist. For many therapists, counseling is not simply enacting a set of techniques. It is primarily facilitating an intimate encounter between therapist and client (Benner, 2003). This manner of intimate encounter shaped by the pastoral counselor is another by-product of who the pastoral counselor is with clients.

The intersubjective space—space shared between the counselor and counselee—also serves as a bridge between a therapist's being and doing. Relational pastoral psychotherapist Pamela Cooper-White argues that intersubjectivity occurs as one inevitably draws from, and is influenced by, the thoughts and feelings that are created between the other and the self (Cooper-White, 2004). Cooper-White argues that even what is reflected on by the therapist outside of the room is brought into the room in the therapist's unconscious and is acting in the therapeutic space. The therapist's reflection holds the power to generate openness and greater possibilities while with the client (Cooper-White, 2004). In this way, the counselor becomes a facilitator and a guide who shapes the therapeutic moment. The intersubjective dynamic of therapy further reinforces the relationship between the being and doing of pastoral counseling.

Given the interconnection between being and doing, it follows that a question about the particularity of pastoral counseling interventions starts with an exploration of the training and formation pastoral counselors receive. The formative nature of pastoral counseling training shapes the pastoral counselor's self and is the rudiment from which the distinctive interventions of pastoral counselors organically emerge.

Pastoral Counseling Training

The distinctive training that pastoral counselors receive is the ground in which distinctive interventions are cultivated. Among the elements of training and formation most salient to shaping pastoral counseling interventions are clinical integration, pastoral formation, and the development of a spiritual orientation.

Clinical Integration

Fundamentally, pastoral counselors are trained in two disciplines as opposed to one, allowing for the integration of knowledge and training from both psychology and theology. The term *clinical integration* refers to the incorporation of religious or spiritual beliefs, values, and methods into the process of pastoral counseling that results in a different way of being a counselor, understanding the client, or doing therapy (Hall, Lewis, & Hall, 1997). The skillful application of this kind of theoretical and clinical integration is a central component of the uniqueness of pastoral counseling training.

Pastoral Formation

Closely related to the clinical integration pursued by pastoral counselors is the profound personal and pastoral formation that pastoral counselors often undergo themselves. This formation is considered an integral aspect of training within this profession. Such a commitment echoes the belief that how we are in relationship with our clients is hugely shaped by who we are as a result of our formation. For example, pastoral counselors are trained to listen in a way that is not only about attention to detail and ascription to a particular theoretical orientation but in a way that is marked by its "soul-fulness" (Stairs, 2000). In this way, pastoral counselors' personal engagement with matters of the soul is intended to affect the nature and quality of listening offered to clients.

Spiritual Orientation

The spiritual orientation that many pastoral counseling training programs promote and reinforce is the assumption that all clients are inherently spiritual (Benner, 2003). According to Brenner (2003), the pastoral counselor recognizes that before he or she enters the life of the individual seeking pastoral counseling, transcendent reality is already present and active in that life. This assumption is critical because a pastoral counselor who assumes spiritual presence and activity will look for the presence of these phenomena in the client's life, and counselors tend to find that for which they are looking. Likewise, if other counseling professions look for psychopathology or for unconscious problems, they will find them as well (Benner, 2003).

In addition to the spiritual assumptions that undergird pastoral counseling training, many pastoral counselors have spent time, or are charged with spending time, embracing the image of the holy—or that which is sacred—within themselves and in the other. Recognition of the sacred in the face of the other speaks to the inherent dignity, worth, and value that the pastoral counselor ascribes to her clients. This recognition can often be felt and discerned by clients, even when not explicitly stated by the pastoral counselor.

Training Matters

Training affects the ability of professional counselors to address issues of spirituality confidently and effectively. In a study among a random sample of American Psychological Association members, Shafranske and Maloney (1990) found that although 60% reported that clients regularly expressed their personal experiences in religious language, approximately one third of the psychologists sampled felt competent in dealing with religious or spiritual issues in therapy. In this way, training is a critical foundation to what sets pastoral counseling apart as it establishes the foundation for preparedness to offer informed and effective pastoral counseling interventions.

PASTORAL COUNSELING: GOALS AND OBJECTIVES

The unique training and formation of pastoral counselors lays the groundwork for the development of interventions. To best understand the connection between training and interventions that follow, it is helpful to discuss key goals and objectives of pastoral counselors in their clinical work. Primary objectives of pastoral counseling include accountability to the theological, spiritual growth; healing versus cure; and joining with a transcendent reality.

Accountability to the Theological

Among the most distinguishing objectives of pastoral counselors is their accountability to the theological. For pastoral counselors, moral and religious attitudes constitute the assumptive background of pastoral psychotherapy. It is within this view of human nature and the world that the use of psychological understandings and interventions takes place (Wicks, Parsons, & Capps, 1993).

In addition, there is a moral imperative for pastoral counselors not to collude with larger powers and principalities that attempt to recruit individuals into hegemonic ideologies that control, oppress, and disempower. Kaner and Pringler (2005) contend that therapists are sought out to help individuals adapt to life when they are unable to do so themselves. In contrast, pastoral counselors at times seek to help a client "maladjust" to their sociopolitical environment to attain the health and wholeness they seek

(Neuger, 2001). Pastoral counselors do so by employing a variety of interventions that promote advocacy and "power-with" to liberate from oppressive structures (Cooper-White, 2012).

Spiritual Growth

Another distinctive goal of pastoral counseling is spiritual growth. Clinebell (1995) asserts that the pastoral counselor should strive to become an expert in spiritual growth—knowing how to stimulate it and how to help remove the things that block it. He continues by saying that pastoral counseling has a quality of uniqueness about it that stems from regarding spiritual growth as an essential objective in counseling. An emphasis on spiritual growth as a goal of pastoral counseling continues today.

Contemporary pastoral counselors understand spirituality in a number of ways. For example, some view spirituality as mysterious, creating an inherent ambiguity to the spiritual aspect of clients' lives (Benner, 2003). For others, everyday life is seen as spiritual (Watkins Ali, 1999). Spirituality that is facilitated by pastoral counselors of this orientation has to come from a person's everyday life to be useful (Mitchem, 2002). Although pastoral counseling practitioners conceive of spirituality in a variety of ways, spiritual growth is often a shared goal nonetheless.

Healing Versus Cure

The matters for which "troubled persons" seek out pastoral counseling are often those of "ultimate concern" and meaning making (Clebsh & Jaekle, 1983). In these matters, healing rather than cure is the most appropriate goal. Healing allows for a more flexible, dynamic, and fluid understanding of the goal of therapy as shaped by the counselee. Employing a social constructionist viewpoint allows one to see the ways in which realities regarding health and unhealth are socially constructed. As Emily Townes (1998) explains, health is not the absence of disease; it is a cultural production. For this reason, most pastoral counselors tend to find it more just, empowering, and culturally appropriate for clients to define what health and unhealth is for themselves rather than always ascribing to a medical model of pathology.

The term *cure* falsely suggests a fixed, universal, and objective remedy to a person's pain that results in the absence of suffering. However, many pastoral counselors understand the human condition to entail brokenness and suffering as part of an ongoing existential situation. This existential reality does not make humanity any less holy or devoid of divine purpose. So although many pastoral counselors may not see absolute cure as attainable, it is not necessary for the goal of healing to occur.

Joining With the Transcendent

The goals of pastoral counseling are multivalent. At their distinctive core, however, is the goal to join with transcendent realities in sacred play in a way that brings about freedom and openness to being liberated by infinite possibilities (Grant, 2001). This occurs through a relational process between the pastoral counselor and one's transcendent reality in the therapeutic space, in addition to the relationship between the pastoral counselor and the counselee. Most psychotherapies name the client–therapist alliance as the primary healing agent in therapy necessary for attaining any therapeutic goal (McWilliams, 2004). Although this concept is similar among psychotherapies, pastoral counseling possesses a distinct understanding of how this relationship also includes a sort of third party of the divine.

DISTINCTIVE PASTORAL COUNSELING INTERVENTIONS EMERGE

The distinctive interventions that spring forth from this professional training process can emerge clearly. Three primary pastoral counseling interventions are derived from this foundation: spiritual assessment, theological reflection, and clinical–theological integration.

Spiritual Assessment

Spiritual assessment is a distinctive method of intervention used by pastoral counselors. It can be performed in formal and informal ways. Formal methods include tests, questionnaires, and other rubrics useful for gathering insight into the spiritual life and well-being of an individual, family, or community. These tools are discussed in detail in Chapter 8 of this volume. However, I will outline a few examples of formal and informal methods of spiritual assessment.

One example of a formal spiritual assessment tool is the Spiritual Assessment Inventory (SAI; Hall & Edwards, 2002). This tool is a relationally based measure designed to assess two dimensions of spiritual development: awareness of transcendent realities and quality of relationship with that reality. According to Hall and Edwards (2002), this scale was developed to address the need for the use of a relationally based, psychometrically sound measure of spiritual development from a broad theistic perspective. The model engages both levels of awareness, from a spiritual standpoint, and measures levels of relational maturity, from a psychological standpoint, as fundamental components of spiritual development (Hall & Edwards, 2002).

In addition to employing formal methods of spiritual assessment such as the SAI, informal methods are also used by pastoral counselors. Informal spiritual assessment includes questions asked of one's self and the client that focus on the client's spiritual needs. This often starts with gathering a spiritual/religious history of the client. To guide this inquiry, one may ask, "What denomination or religious tradition is the client affiliated with?" "Is there an intergenerational affiliation?" "What role(s) has the client held within his or her faith tradition or community?" "How has the client's faith evolved over time?" "What core values and beliefs shape the client's faith convictions?" A spiritual assessment also includes drawing from social, psychological, and other contextual information to create a "thick description" of the client's situation (Geertz, 1973).

In addition to gathering a spiritual history, such an assessment may also include an examination of one's own countertransference. This level of spiritual assessment begins with the therapist recognizing his or her own subjective feelings and experiences of the other that may be drawn from the shared co-created reality between counselor and counselee (Cooper-White, 2004). To accomplish this, the pastoral counselor allows his or her imagination to roam freely and playfully, followed by an examination of the images, thoughts, feelings, and fantasies that arise in ways that may illuminate the pastoral situation at hand (Cooper-White, 2004).

Pastoral counselors and their secular counterparts may both use spiritual assessment tools such as those mentioned here. However, I contend that pastoral counselors often possess a more skillful approach to the use of these tools and the application of the information gathered from the use of these tools due to the nature of their training. I liken this difference to the way a master chef makes a more skillful use of a professional kitchen than a home cook, or the way that a radiologist can make more accurate deductions from an x-ray than can a general practice physician. The distinctive training of pastoral counselors prepares clinicians to accomplish skillful interpretations and applications derived from spiritual assessments.

Theological Reflection

The primary reason theological reflection is considered a pastoral counseling intervention is due to a belief that what is reflected on by the therapist is brought into the room in the therapist's unconscious in the form of countertransference. Pastoral counselors can engage in theological reflection in a variety of ways. Whichever the type of theological reflection method used, its shared purpose is to deepen the pastoral counselor's understanding of the client's situation from a pastoral perspective. What follows is a set of methods that are often used by pastoral counselors to accomplish this kind of intervention.

Methods of theological reflection generally include a form of prayer or meditative reflections that invite spiritual insight about an individual's or a family's situation. Pastoral counselors may start by asking themselves what theological, spiritual, or religious themes come to mind when considering a case and reflect on the associations that may emerge. Possible associations may include a sacred story, a sacred image, an overarching scriptural theme, a sacramental theme, a theological image, a theological theme, or a theological song (Cooper-White, 2004).

After an image or association emerges, pastoral counselors may reflect on how this theme sheds light on the client's experience and use these insights to plan for further interventions. For example, perhaps a mother–son relationship within a family brings to the counselor's mind thoughts of the scriptural story of Sarah and Isaac. Perhaps this association is related to the hopes and dreams the mother projects onto her son similar to the way that Sarah understood Isaac as the fulfillment of a long-held hope for the future. Such an image could provide insight into the use of methods that would encourage the mother to own her projections and for the son to learn how not to enact these projections in unhealthy ways.

Pastoral counselors often do not see theological reflection as a one-time engagement. It is a process that is revisited repeatedly while working with the same client (Cooper-White, 2004). Theological reflection is thus a useful intervention that employs a distinctively pastoral set of skills and sensibilities.

Clinical–Theological Integration

Clinical–theological integration involves the inclusion of spiritual issues in therapy by drawing on spiritual resources. As with other pastoral counseling interventions, clinical–theological integration can occur in implicit and explicit ways. Explicit integration refers to an overt approach that directly addresses spiritual or religious issues in therapy and uses spiritual resources. In contrast, implicit clinical–theological interventions refer to a slightly more covert approach in which the counselor does not initiate the discussion of religious or spiritual issues and does not overtly use spiritual resources in counseling (Tan, 1996).

Pastoral counselors are unique in their ability to use, implicitly and explicitly where appropriate, many kinds of spiritual resources. Some include individual and conjoint prayer; a belief in the power of intercessory prayer; a unifying and explanatory spiritual worldview; the utility of confession; engagement of a faith-based social support system; the use of rituals and sacraments; the use of spiritual language, scripture, and religious symbols; and making recommendations regarding spiritual practices (Benner, 2003). Although secular counseling practitioners may employ these resources as well, they often do not feel comfortable doing so, and I argue that pastoral counselors exercise an added measure of training and skill when it comes to applying these resources helpfully.

Of the many spiritual resources from which pastoral counselors may draw, I will explore in more depth the skillful application of scripture in clinical–theological pastoral counseling interventions. There are several models pastoral counselors can be trained in when it comes to using scripture in pastoral counseling practice. In general, there are four models most commonly used. These include the dynamic use, the moral instructional use, the disclosive use, and the narrative use (Capps, 1990).

Within the dynamic approach, scriptures are employed based on their relevance to the psychological dynamics of the client as a way of addressing the presenting problem—for example, using a scripture that emphasizes the importance of Sabbath rest with a counselee who suffers from anxiety and being perpetually overcommitted, or a scripture about forgiveness with a counselee who is being overcome with resentment. The moral instructional approach is less about psychology and more about selecting scripture that may influence the moral behavior of the counselee. For instance, a scripture encouraging one to treat others as one treats oneself could be employed by a pastoral counselor who wanted to influence a narcissist to have more empathy. The disclosive approach engages the text's ability to reveal meaning and provide insight. This approach often employs the use of parable and metaphor found in scripture from which multiple meanings can be explored and applied to the counselee's experience. For example, the biblical parable about a prodigal son who leaves his family of origin and is readily welcomed back may be explored with a young adult counselee struggling with individuation and belonging. Finally, in the narrative approach, the pastoral counselor works with the counselee to identify the mythology undergirding the problem and reauthors that mythology into a preferred story using similar scriptural stories as frames of reference (Wimberly, 1994). Using this approach, a counselee who believes a myth that he was unlovable and abandoned by his birth parent when put up for adoption as a child may reauthor this narrative by using the story of Moses. Moses' mother seemed to lovingly place him in a basket in the river with the belief that it was more dangerous for her child to stay with her than it would be for someone else to care for him.

Although sacred texts are an important clinical–theological therapeutic resource, they exist alongside other inspirational readings to which many pastoral counselors refer and use in similar ways (Benner, 2003). Spiritual resources are tools with which pastoral counselors are especially aware and learned in using in appropriate and healing ways. In both implicit and explicit ways, these resources support an array of clinically integrated and distinctive interventions of pastoral counselors.

CONCLUSIONS

Pastoral counseling as a profession, now more than 50 years old, continues to wrestle with its identity amid a larger community of counseling and psychotherapeutic disciplines. Although there is great diversity within and among individual pastoral counselors themselves, a distinguishable common identity is discernable. As discussed here, pastoral counselors share distinctive interventions that are born out of particular ways of being and a particular set of goals and objectives. Ours is a distinctiveness that is dynamic rather than static as our profession continues to grow and respond with relevance to changing client needs and social contexts. Explorations such as these will remain important as we continue to discover our uniqueness within an ever-broadening professional landscape.

REFLECTION QUESTIONS

1. Describe in your own words the difference between *cure* and *healing*. Give an example of each. How do you understand the functions of cure and healing in your own pastoral counseling practice?
2. What does the statement "At their distinctive core, however, is the goal to join with the transcendent realities in sacred play in a way that brings about freedom and openness to being liberated by infinite possibilities" mean to you?
3. When might the use of implicit clinical–theological interventions be most appropriate? Describe what this could look like in a session.

REFERENCES

Benner, D. (2003). *Strategic pastoral counseling: A short-term structural model*. Grand Rapids, MI: Baker Academic.

Canda, E. R., & Furman, L. D. (1999). *Spiritual diversity in social work practice: The heart of helping*. New York, NY: Free Press.

Capps, D. (1990). Bible, pastoral use and interpretation. In H. Rodney (Ed.), *Dictionary of pastoral care and counseling* (pp. 82–85). Nashville, TN: Abingdon.

Cheston, S. E. (2000). A new paradigm for teaching counseling theory and practice. *Counselor Education & Supervision, 39*(4), 254–269. doi:10.1002/j.1556-6978.2000.tb01236.x

Clebsch, W. A., & Jaekle, C. R. (1983). *Pastoral care and counseling in historical perspective*. New York, NY: J. Aronson.

Clinebell, H. J. (1995). *Counseling for spiritually empowered wholeness: A hope-centered approach*. New York, NY: Haworth Pastoral Press/Haworth.

Cooper-White, P. (2004). *Shared wisdom: Use of the self in pastoral care and counseling*. Minneapolis, MN: Fortress.

Cooper-White, P. (2012). *The cry of Tamar: Violence against women and the church's response* (2nd ed.). Minneapolis, MN: Fortress.

Erikson, E. H. (1974). *Dimensions of a new identity: Jefferson lectures, 1973*. New York, NY: Norton.

Estatdt, B. K., Blanchett, M. C., & Compton, J. R. (Eds.). (1991). *Pastoral counseling* (2nd ed.). Englewood Cliffs, NJ: Prentice Hall.

Everly, G. S., Jr. (2008). Pastoral crisis intervention: Toward a definition. *International Journal of Emergency Mental Health, 2*(2), 69–71. Retrieved from http://georgiadisaster.info/Mental Health/MH04%20DMHTraining/Pastoral%20Crisis%20Intervention.pdf

Geertz, C. (1973). *Interpretations of cultures: Selected essays*. New York, NY: Basic Books.

Grant, B. W. (2001). *A theology for pastoral psychotherapy: God's play in sacred spaces.* New York, NY: Haworth Pastoral Press.

Hall, M., Lewis, E., & Hall, T.W. (1997). Integration in the therapy room: An overview of the literature. *Journal of Psychology and Theology, 25*(1), 86–101. Retrieved from https://getinfo .de/app/Integration-in-the-Therapy-Room-An-Overview-of/id/BLSE%3ARN026011073

Hall, T. W., & Edwards, K. J. (2002). The Spiritual Assessment Inventory: A theistic model and measure for assessing spiritual development. *Journal for the Scientific Study of Religion, 41*(2), 341–357. doi:10.1111/1468-5906.00121

Hill, P., Butman, R., & Hood, R. (1999). *Measures of religiousness.* Birmingham, AL: Religious Education Press.

Kaner, A., & Pringler, E. (2005). *The craft of psychodynamic psychotherapy.* Lanham, MD: Jason Aronson.

McWilliams, N. (2004). *Psychoanalytic psychotherapy: A practitioner's guide.* New York, NY: Guilford.

Mitchem, S. Y. (2002). *Introducing womanist theology.* Maryknoll, NY: Orbis.

Neuger, C. C. (2001). *Counseling women: A narrative, pastoral approach.* Minneapolis, MN: Fortress.

Raphel, M. M. (2001). *The status of the use of spiritual/religious interventions in three professional mental health groups* (Unpublished doctoral dissertation). Loyola College of Maryland, Baltimore.

Shafranske, E. P., & Maloney, H. N. (1990). Clinical psychologists' religious and spiritual orientations and their practice of psychotherapy. *Journal of Psychotherapy, 27,* 72–78. doi: 10.1037/0033-3204.27.1.72

Sollad, R. N., Wilson, J. P., & Monte, C. F. (2009). *Beneath the mask: An introduction to theories of personality* (8th ed.). Hoboken, NJ: John Wiley.

Stairs, J. (2000). *Listening for the soul: Pastoral care and spiritual direction.* Minneapolis, MN: Fortress.

Stone, H. W. (1994). *Brief pastoral counseling: Short-term approaches and strategies.* Minneapolis, MN: Augsburg Fortress.

Tan, S. Y. (1996). Religion in clinical practice: Implicit and explicit integration. In E. P. Shafranske (Ed.), *Religion and the clinical practice of psychology* (pp. 365–387). Washington, DC: American Psychological Association.

Townes, E. (1998). *Breaking the fine rain of death: African American health issues and a womanist ethic of care.* New York, NY: Continuum.

Townsend, L. L. (2009). *Introduction to pastoral counseling.* Nashville, TN: Abingdon.

Watkins Ali, C. (1999). *Survival and liberation: Pastoral theology in African American contexts.* St. Louis, MO: Chalice.

Wells, G. L. (1982). Attribution and reconstructive memory. *Journal of Experimental Social Psychology, 18,* 447–463. doi:10.1016/0022-1031(82)90065-8

Wicks, R. J., Parsons, R. D., & Capps, D. (1993). *Clinical handbook of pastoral counseling* (Vol. 1). New York, NY: Paulist Press.

Wimberly, E. P. (1994). *Using scripture in pastoral counseling.* Nashville, TN: Abingdon.

PASTORAL COUNSELING AND SPIRITUAL DIRECTION

Mark is a 38-year-old European American Army officer who has recently returned from active duty in the battlefield to his wife and two children, ages 6 and 8. As is the case for many in the military who return from overseas deployment, Mark has found reintegrating himself into his former life to be challenging. Not only does his life have an entirely different rhythm to it, but it also lacks the close camaraderie and intimacy that he shared with his fellow soldiers when deployed in a remote area. Instead, Mark finds himself surrounded by people who simply have no idea of what his experience has been and who have no comfort or wisdom to offer him—and this group includes his wife and children. Since his return, Mark and his wife have had a strained relationship without much intimacy, and he feels like he is just going through the motions. Moreover, he has had several blowups with his elder son, whose special needs have manifested in behavioral problems since Mark's deployment.

These challenges in his personal life have only exacerbated the emotional challenges that have also begun to manifest themselves. Mark is reluctant to give too many details but says that he was involved in a couple of disturbing firefights in which he says he "did what no human being should ever do." He keeps seeing one particular scene in his mind again and again, but he won't specify exactly what happened, except that he holds himself responsible for the outcome. He has tried everything he can to get that vision out of his head and simply can't. It intrudes into his days and nights, and he says he has anxiety attacks whenever he is in an enclosed public space, which he now avoids. He also reports being short-tempered, anxious, and unable to sleep.

Although he knows that he should take advantage of available resources to cope with his emotions, Mark is hesitant to do so. He says that he doesn't want to be absolved by a therapist for the grave moral failing he showed. Mark grew up in a family that was nominally Catholic, but after his First Communion, he rarely went to church. Sometimes, he has thought of going to confession to address his moral qualms, but at other times, he isn't sure that Christianity makes any sense for him as a warrior. A friend introduced him to the *Meditations* of the Stoic Emperor Marcus Aurelius, and he felt a kindred soul there. He did some reading on Stoicism and has even started practicing Stoic visualization exercises to help him cope with his emotions. But because there is no local Stoic church, he isn't sure where to go from here. In addition, he is not so sure that he wants to be part of a faith community because he does not want to "take on a whole bunch of beliefs and responsibilities." He also still feels like being Catholic is his identity, because all his family are still occasional churchgoers.

All of these disturbing questions have led Mark to wonder what he really should be doing with the rest of his life. He wonders what legacy he will leave behind as an absent father who comes home to yell at his children and as an officer whose achievements primarily seemed to be orchestrating death. He would call his experience a midlife crisis if that term didn't connote something that to him seems so petty.

Mark's situation is becoming increasingly common in the world of counseling. It is complex, urgent, overwhelming, and distressingly resistant to separating the mental health issues from moral or spiritual concerns. Yet it also seems too big to be addressed by just one helper. He shows signs of a mental health disorder that would call for treatment by a licensed clinician. There are issues regarding psychosocial, spiritual, and career development. There is the phenomenon of moral injury (Brock & Lettini, 2012), which needs to be worked through with someone knowledgeable about pastoral care. And there are the emerging questions of Mark's spiritual and religious identity and where he is going on his journey, which seem to call for spiritual companionship by someone knowledgeable about Stoicism and Christianity. Someone trained in pastoral counseling may possess the skills necessary to address Mark's myriad concerns, but should a pastoral counselor take all of this on? If so, where is someone trained in pastoral counseling to begin? And who else should be involved?

This chapter examines the relationships between pastoral counseling and spiritual direction with an eye to how these related disciplines can work together to provide holistic care for clients facing the complex problems of modern life. Beginning with a historical overview, it reviews the common ancestor of spiritual direction and psychotherapy in the care for the soul in Western philosophical and religious traditions, tracing their separation in the past century. With this history in mind, it distinguishes between these two modes of helping and creates a typology in which to locate their work. Then, it considers these ideas from an interfaith and contextual perspective and raises questions for the future of pastoral counseling based on cultural differences and emerging social trends.

THE HISTORY OF CARE FOR THE SOUL IN THE WEST

In those cultures rooted in the Christianity of late Greco-Roman antiquity, there is a common ancestor to today's helping professions, the *cura animarum* or care for the soul (McNeill, 1951). This model, which was propagated by monastic and philosophical culture in the West, continued as a prominent model until the 20th century and continues in some ways to the present.

Although Christian sources included the Wisdom literature in Hebrew Scripture and the pastoral writings of the New Testament, many of the practices involved in Western soul care can be traced to ancient Hellenistic philosophy. Contrary to the modern picture of the philosopher as someone with abstract and obscure interests far removed from the real world, the philosophers of the ancient West viewed philosophy as a way of life, with the philosopher as the "physician of the soul" (Hadot, 1995). Competing schools such as Stoicism, Cynicism, Skepticism, Neoplatonism, and Epicureanism all likened their exercises and arguments to a kind of medical treatment that helps the soul flourish and achieve the ability not to be disturbed by the trials of life (Nussbaum, 1994). Many of the spiritual exercises that these schools recommended, such as attention, visualization, investigation, and dialogue, were baptized by Christian monastic theologians and linked to scripture and the ideas of sin and grace (Hadot, 1995). In this way, the practices and their ideals were passed down into the Latin and

Greek churches of the Middle Ages, and the priest took on the role of physician of souls (Purves, 2001). Although monks kept the focus on cultivating a way of life based on a rule, the laity in the Latin church increasingly received spiritual guidance mediated through the confessional, leading in some ways to a two-tiered system of spirituality. Nonetheless, the psychological and spiritual care for people was seen as a single phenomenon.

The Reformations of the 16th century brought an increased focus on the life of the laity but retained an integrated psychospiritual model of care. Martin Bucer, the South German reformer, devised a scripturally based scheme for pastoral care in which the pastor would draw the alienated to Christ, restore those fallen away, have the sinful amend their lives, strengthen the weak, and preserve the healthy for service to God (Purves, 2001). Protestant approaches tended to be skeptical of any monastic and ancient philosophical practices, in large part leaving this tradition behind except in select cases such as John Wesley (1749), the progenitor of Methodism, who translated many spiritual treatises for contemporary audiences. Meanwhile, Roman Catholic leaders such as Francis de Sales introduced the "devout life" of the classical tradition to the laity (de Sales, 1950), and the work of the French and Spanish schools added nuance to ancient accounts of the soul's progress, which have become widely influential in contemporary spiritual direction. All of these models, Catholic and Protestant, had integrated psychospiritual goals, summarized by Clebsch and Jaeckle (1964) in the functions of healing, sustaining, guiding, and reconciling.

With the birth of modern psychology in the late 19th century, the care of souls in the Western Christian tradition underwent a significant transition as it attempted to integrate the insights of this new, modern science of the mind and emotions, a science that specifically saw itself as independent of the value commitments of religion. Nonetheless, many pastoral thinkers found much to appreciate in this modern approach. For instance, Anton Boisen's experience with mental illness convinced him of its theological power and potential for spiritual integration, leading him to advocate reading "human documents" as just as theologically formational as the documents of scripture (Dykstra, 2005). By the middle of the 20th century, Protestant pastoral care had changed emphasis from "salvation to self-realization" (Holifield, 1983), and Catholic pastoral care had moved its focus from "confession to therapy" (Gillespie, 2001). With these changes came the first widespread separation of psychotherapy from spiritual direction in the West. The ancient monastic and philosophical traditions lived on in Roman Catholic, Anglo-Catholic, and Eastern Orthodox "spiritual direction." Mainline Protestantism sought to integrate pastoral ministry with emerging approaches to psychotherapy, marked by Clinebell's (1984) addition of a fifth function of pastoral ministry, nurturing.

This history suggests that the distinction between psychotherapy and spiritual direction is a phenomenon of the modern West that came about through the specific trajectories of Christian theology and psychological science, especially within English-speaking cultures. Although a more integrated sense of soul care remained in some more conservative Evangelical traditions or African American Christianity, in the 20th century, there emerged at least two disciplines caring for the soul, which was understood to be two potentially interrelated entities: the mind and the spirit. Each of these disciplines now had an extensive theoretical literature and, in the case of psychotherapy, an extensive record of empirical research, such that mastering both realms became quite difficult.

DISTINGUISHING CLINICAL COUNSELING FROM SPIRITUAL DIRECTION

In contemporary discussions, counseling and spiritual direction are presumed to be separate fields with their own definitions. The American Counseling Association (2010) has defined counseling as "a professional relationship that empowers diverse individuals, families, and groups to accomplish mental health, wellness, education, and career goals." By contrast, a widely cited definition by Barry and Connolly (1982) states that spiritual direction is:

> help given by one Christian to another which enables that person to pay attention to God's personal communication to him or her, to respond to this personally communicating God, to grow in intimacy with this God, and to live out the consequences of the relationship. The *focus* of this type of spiritual direction is on experience, not ideas, and specifically on religious experience, i.e., any experience of the mysterious Other whom we call God. (p. 8)

It is important to note that these definitions are quite general and leave much open in the way of how people understand, interact with, and intervene with clients. Nonetheless, these general definitions, and more specific ones, have led to a widespread opinion that "there are several similarities between spiritual direction and psychotherapy [or clinical counseling], but they are fundamentally different enterprises" (May, 1982, p. 12). Therefore, although noting similarities, such as concern for the whole person, attention to history, teaching, help with decision making, and a caring motivation (Galindo, 2004), most authors take care to distinguish between the two helping relationships, as may be seen in Table 13.1. Although these authors represent a variety of Christian traditions from Roman Catholicism, mainline Protestantism, and Pentecostalism, their distinctions have some common features. Whereas clinical counseling or psychotherapy tends to be focused on problems, is psychological in focus, and intends to restore clients to mental and emotional functionality, spiritual direction is explicitly mindful of God's grace and presence and seeks to build a connection with God that will bear spiritual fruit for the community. The place of pastoral counseling in this typology is often described as overlapping both categories, but practitioners are encouraged to focus on one or the other.

Therefore, were someone like Mark to come to the office of a pastoral counselor, that person would have a choice to make: whether to focus more on issues of trauma and anxiety and symptom reduction, alongside some work with family dynamics, or to focus more on Mark's emerging spiritual identity and how he might mature in his relationship with the Ultimate. The assumption would be that simply too much training and work are needed to focus on either part of his presenting problems and that trying to address both would simply lead to confusion.

AN INTEGRATED MODEL

Although these distinctions are helpful, they tend to presume that counseling or spiritual direction relationships are not often caught up in issues more properly belonging to the other. It is not so easy to separate which aspects of our lives can only be described by some ultimate reference to theology from those that do not need to refer to anything

TABLE 13.1 Distinguishing Between Counseling/Psychotherapy and Spiritual Direction

AUTHOR	CHARACTERISTICS OF COUNSELING/PSYCHOTHERAPY	CHARACTERISTICS OF SPIRITUAL DIRECTION
May (1982)	• Goal is more functional living in culture, increased autonomy • Focus on mental and emotional dimensions • Medical, expert attitude	• Goal is liberation from attachments, surrender, rejecting worldly values • Openness to grace • Focus on evaluating experiences, discerning spiritual fruits, prayer life, religious experiences, and sense of relationship to God • Attentiveness to God; prayerful attitude
Galindo (2004)		• Healing is redefined as going forth in the community • Requires maturity • Helping relationship goes beyond crisis • Attention to the operation of grace • Faith in God is central • Assumes a context of a community of faith and prayer • Broader temporal focus • Issues of surrender or conversion • Deals with primarily healthy individuals
Barrette (2004)	• Reliance on psychological theories • Focus on here and now, chronos, specific problem	• Scripture and discernment are resources • Focus on eternal point of view, kairos, ongoing
Moon and Benner (2004)	• Normal making • Removes impediments to growth • Empathy is central	• Abnormal making • Helps directee attend and respond to God • Focus never merely on oneself
Tracy (2004)	• Neutral and nondirective • Professionalized	• Compassionate but willing to be directive • Can include laity, friends, or small groups
Leech (2001)	• Focuses on human growth	• Focuses on relationship to divine
Stairs (2000)	• Deals with all persons • Starts with a presenting concern	• Deals with adults • Starts with spiritual needs
McMahon (2004)	• Focus on relief of pain	• Focus on charismatic gifts, testimony, scripture
Stewart-Sicking (2008)	• Using wisdom tradition to solve problems	• Using wisdom tradition to promote flourishing

beyond this material world. In fact, in those traditions believing in a transcendent God who acts in human lives, this distinction is only possible in the abstract, not in real life. For these reasons, some have proposed a single, integrated model that combines the two perspectives.

The most systematic presentation of an integrated model is offered by Sperry (2002), who notes that the concerns that clients bring to helpers tend to fall into five general categories: (a) those centering on relationship with God, prayer, discernment, or spiritual experiences; (b) issues involving meaning, purpose, life decisions, and self-development; (c) moral or ethical issues involving the self, relationships, or community; (d) losses, relational conflicts, work, or family problems and mild to moderate symptoms or impairment; and (e) moderate to severe symptoms or impairment, including personality disorders, addictions, or consequences of early life trauma. Sperry notes that Category 1 issues have been the principal focus of modern spiritual direction, Category 2 issues are often explored in spiritual direction or counseling, Categories 4 and 5 have been the primary focus of clinical counseling, and few helpers in either camp are comfortable exploring Category 3, which was often the core of the classic *cura animarum*.

Sperry (2002) then provides an integrated model for pastoral counseling that addresses all of these dimensions across several meta-domains: transformation (involving all dimensions of being human), moral (involving the development of virtues), spiritual (involving practices of faith), and psychological (involving self-capacities). This integrated approach provides a way for those with training in both counseling and spiritual development (e.g., pastoral counselors) to negotiate the sometimes artificial boundaries between these two endeavors and allow subsequent sessions to flow naturally between these poles. However, the competence and knowledge required to pursue this model would seem to require extensive training and mentoring, which makes May's (1982) admonition to make a clear choice between the two in any given relationship seem like a good default position for most helpers. Nonetheless, Sperry's observations about the continuity between counseling and spiritual direction make it complicated to draw the boundaries for such a choice. For instance, when do issues of values clarification, images of God, meaning making, choice of a vocation, or fostering development cross into an area that is off limits? Any of these areas might be explored in either counseling or spiritual direction, especially by those with training in pastoral counseling. Increasingly, counseling and psychotherapy have moved to include issues of wellness, development, and flourishing as explicit aims, and many therapists are gaining expertise in using spiritual and religious resources in treatment. These shared domains need to be addressed more explicitly in any model of how counseling and spiritual direction are related.

Consider the case of Mark, who has described challenges in at least the first four domains of Sperry's (2002) model. It is likely that many counselors working with him might examine issues of meaning making and clarifying values in addition to helping to reduce the problems he is encountering through the aftermath of his experience of trauma. In fact, because research indicates that spirituality can aid in healing from trauma (Werdel & Wicks, 2013), even secular counselors might seek to include this content for the purpose of helping Mark to cope with his life. Sperry's model acknowledges this impulse and gives practitioners a framework for pulling aspects of this practice together. But it also raises the question of whether such an integrated approach would necessarily result in the best care for someone like Mark. For instance, might he do better to focus primarily on issues of mental health alongside working with a spiritual companion knowledgeable about the traditions he is exploring? And might Maslow's (1943) recognition of a hierarchy of needs suggest that he largely resolve issues of psychological distress before he takes on his spiritual journey in any specific way? Finally, isn't there a difference between using spiritual and religious resources for therapeutic purposes and engaging in critical theological reflection with a client in a manner that moves his or her theological language past naïve understandings of God (Doehring, 2009)? In what ways would an integrated model be able to distinguish this type of pastoral counseling?

HAPPY, HEALTHY, AND HOLY: A THREEFOLD TYPOLOGY

If counseling, pastoral counseling, and spiritual direction are both overlapping and distinct, what concepts give us the best chance to distinguish them? One useful lens is the goals of each approach and the ways these goals dictate the understanding of what is going on, the nature of the relationship, and the ways in which spiritual traditions are included.

Modern psychology's scientific aspirations have meant that much of counseling and psychotherapy have remained focused on utilitarian ends such as reducing emotional pain that can be honed through scientific experiment. However, there have always been streams in depth psychology and humanistic psychology that have not remained content with seeing human health solely in terms of regulated mood. The emergence of positive psychology in the 2000s added to this emphasis by concerning itself with the use of psychological research to promote human happiness and flourishing (Seligman & Csikszentmihalyi, 2000).

In its development, positive psychology has provided helpful distinctions that are useful in describing how counseling, pastoral counseling, and spiritual direction are both similar and different. In their review of the literature, Deci and Ryan (2008) describe two prominent approaches to positive psychology: *Hedonic* psychology has been concerned with identifying factors that influence subjective well-being, comprising the number of negative emotions one experiences, the number of positive emotions one experiences, and one's sense that one's life has been well lived. This approach has much in common with ancient Epicureanism and modern utilitarianism in that it attempts to look at happiness without any appeal to a theory of human nature or the good life. The *eudaimonic* approach has argued that psychology has always had specific accounts of healthy development and ideas of how life should be lived. This approach, which draws on Aristotle's virtue of ethics, argues that happy mood is not everything and has tried to find ways to measure and predict aspects of healthy development such as self-acceptance, purpose in life, and personal growth, among others (Ryff, 1989).

The distinction between hedonic and eudaimonic approaches provides some insight into why it is difficult to distinguish between counseling and spiritual direction. Although counseling tends to address hedonic concerns such as mood disorders much more than spiritual direction, both tend to address eudaimonic concerns. For instance, many counselors (both pastoral and clinical mental health) are interested in promoting cognitive, psychosocial, and faith development, and these concepts also inform spiritual direction; both relationships would be likely to cover ideas such as images of God. However, this does not seem like the sole distinction to be made. Just as Thomas Aquinas adopted Aristotle's eudaimonic approach and reconfigured it to reflect the gift of divine grace, another category is needed to reflect spiritual direction's primary focus.

As seen in Table 13.1, a great deal of spiritual direction's focus is on perceiving and receiving the gift of God's grace, being transformed, and going forth in loving service to others. Therefore, spiritual direction's central focus is primarily on experience and fostering the supernatural virtues of faith, hope, and love, which are the result of God's grace working within human lives. For this reason, the real agent of spiritual direction in the Christian tradition is the Holy Spirit, and much of the work of spiritual direction involves opening oneself up to God's presence. It is in this sense that spiritual direction is not primarily "normal making" but "abnormal making,"

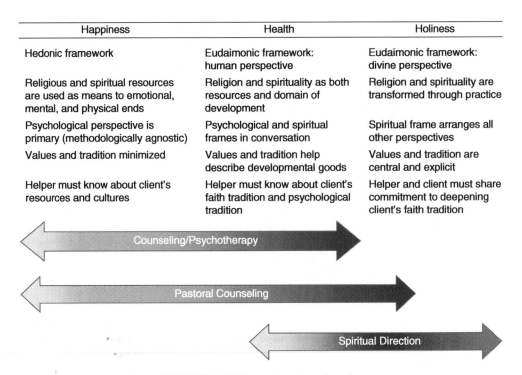

Happiness	Health	Holiness
Hedonic framework	Eudaimonic framework: human perspective	Eudaimonic framework: divine perspective
Religious and spiritual resources are used as means to emotional, mental, and physical ends	Religion and spirituality as both resources and domain of development	Religion and spirituality are transformed through practice
Psychological perspective is primary (methodologically agnostic)	Psychological and spiritual frames in conversation	Spiritual frame arranges all other perspectives
Values and tradition minimized	Values and tradition help describe developmental goods	Values and tradition are central and explicit
Helper must know about client's resources and cultures	Helper must know about client's faith tradition and psychological tradition	Helper and client must share commitment to deepening client's faith tradition

FIGURE 13.1 Three domains of goals.

to use Moon and Benner's (2004) distinction. With this third category, we can make useful distinctions between counseling and spiritual direction and examine how pastoral counseling relates to each (see Figure 13.1).

Counseling and psychotherapy are predominantly focused on helping people in distress return to a state of happiness and emotional balance, but they also draw extensively on psychological theories of healthy development. Therefore, although focused on alleviating suffering, counseling also looks for opportunities through which suffering or other life circumstances can promote development and self-actualization. In these goals, counseling may draw on a client's spirituality but not in great depth and usually as a means for therapeutic ends. It also can be agnostic about whether the client's spirituality is actually true, because the focus is on its practical effects, a feature that makes this approach appealing to many practitioners.

Spiritual direction is primarily focused on goals that might be described in terms of wisdom, contemplation, and holiness. However, these spiritual goals also allow one to understand what true happiness and health really are. Therefore, many spiritual directors see developmental theory in the spirit of Thomas Aquinas (1964 translation), who notes that "grace does not destroy nature but perfects it" (I.1.2), and are open to using the insights of modern psychology alongside their understandings of spiritual maturity. After all, the spirit, body, and mind are not separate entities, so spiritual direction cannot claim to be only about the spirit or indifferent to questions of emotional well-being or human development. In practice, this means that spiritual directors will often use concepts such as personality and faith development to help set goals or conceptualize directees' challenges while also seeking to discern God's will and presence through experience or to understand difficulties in prayer.

Finally, pastoral counseling is comfortable across the entire spectrum of goals, although unlike counseling in general, it is committed to the reality of the spiritual realm, and pure spiritual direction would not normally be included in its purview.

Therefore, a key feature of pastoral counseling is approaching issues of happiness and healthiness in ways that allow these experiences to be open to spiritual growth, even if this growth takes place only implicitly through the pastoral counseling relationship. To achieve this goal, pastoral counselors must develop the habit of theological reflection in which they call on their theological education and formation to work with clients and help them to move beyond naïve theologies toward more critical ones and the ultimate understanding that all theological statements are provisional (Doehring, 2009).

Consider the use of mindfulness techniques by these different approaches. Mark might encounter mindfulness in counseling as a technique for overcoming the anxiety of stuck thoughts. He may be told of its origins in Buddhist thought, but this will not be emphasized so much as the fact that it "works," a fact that scientific study has shown. Little if any thought would be given to the potential of mindfulness practice to lead to a spiritual awakening, because this is not in the purview of therapy. In fact, mindfulness could be reduced to being *merely* therapeutic, a kind of substitute for medication. In pastoral counseling, Mark might also be taught mindfulness, but the pastoral counselor also has been formed to know how this practice can lead to spiritual development and the ways in which it can open doors to new understandings of Ultimate Reality. Therefore, the pastoral counselor might explore how the practice is interfacing with Mark's interest in Stoicism and how his experiences might refine his spiritual views. Finally, a spiritual director would likely work with Mark only when he is at a baseline level of psychological functioning, and in this case, mindfulness would be pursued for its own sake, connected to traditions of contemplation in Christianity, Stoicism, and perhaps Buddhism. This work in spiritual direction could occur concurrently and even in coordination with Mark receiving pastoral counseling or mental health counseling.

The need to mention specific traditions shows a key feature of the spiritual direction relationship. More than counseling or pastoral counseling, it depends heavily on the tradition of the good life one is pursuing and a shared commitment to that life in a community (Stewart-Sicking, 2008). Moreover, many of its practices only make sense when pursued within that communal tradition, and any even basic account of spiritual direction must use the language of the tradition(s) in which it is being practiced. Therefore, although the idea of grace is crucial to the Christian understanding of spiritual direction, a Theravada Buddhist account would find this language problematic in that it interferes with the laws of karma and of dependent origination. By contrast, pastoral counseling often engages tradition by way of negation or critique, seeing through the limitations of all of our spiritual language in the face of human suffering and engaging the mystery of God.

BREAKING DOWN DISTINCTIONS

This threefold distinction of goals to distinguish counseling, pastoral counseling, and spiritual direction depends on the presence of Western psychology. Scholars working in a more global perspective have long noticed the limitations of a Western view of psychotherapy as a distinct entity. For instance, Lartey (2003) notes that although some Western concepts are helpful, pastoral caregivers should be aware that analogues of psychotherapy have existed for centuries in Africa and must be integrated into one's approach. Moreover, he asserts that care for the whole person must take an intercultural stance in a pluralistic world, affirming the contextuality of all views and behavior, the existence of multiple perspectives, and the need for authentic participation. Lartey's intercultural approach would suggest that any distinctions among counseling, pastoral counseling, and spiritual direction not be presented as universal or self-evident.

In fact, this division of labor might be profoundly at odds with the views of the human person or the good life of many cultures. For this reason, it is often better to take a tradition-informed, contextual approach to soul care than to speak of this activity in the abstract, meaning that issues of pluralism must also be paramount.

When soul care is considered in different global contexts, additional features rise to the surface. For instance, traditional accounts of soul care in the Western tradition have not included the concepts of liberation and empowerment (Lartey, 2003). However, these concepts are central for understanding the faith and pastoral needs of marginalized peoples when they are allowed to speak in their own voices (Gutiérrez, 1984). An approach that includes the goal of liberation means that counseling must be willing to work for community change, that pastoral counseling encourages clients to claim their own spiritual voices, and that spiritual direction not be limited to fostering experience if it does not foster action. Although these concerns are largely being pursued in each helping field, they stretch the distinctions between them seen earlier in this chapter.

Another feature of soul care that a global context highlights is the lack of a distinction between psychotherapy and spiritual practice in many contexts. For instance, Buddhism has managed to address the problems of human suffering for millennia without this distinction, exploring the phenomenology of thought, perception, and emotion in great detail (Anuruddha & Bodhi, 2000) for the purposes of enlightenment and ethics.

Finally, current cultural trends in the West provide a special challenge to spiritual direction as articulated previously in this chapter as a helping relationship deeply embedded in a tradition, especially the forms of spiritual direction rooted in Christian monasticism. Although there is a potential new "Great Awakening" (Bass, 2012) of multiplicity, flux, and creativity in the realm of spirituality, many of the classic models of spiritual direction and the cure of souls rely on assumptions—such as geographical stability, regular participation, mentoring, or lifetime affiliation with a single faith tradition—that are not true for most. For this reason, the distinctions and ethical challenges among varieties of soul care become even more of a problem, because spiritual exploration is likely to occur for some in relationships such as counseling when there is no community from which to draw a spiritual companion, and spiritual companionship relations that are ostensibly found within a single tradition (an Episcopalian directing an Episcopalian) will likely cross religious boundaries to include other faith traditions (e.g., Tibetan Buddhist–inflected Anglican Christianity).

CONCLUSIONS

In today's fluid cultural situation surrounding religion and spirituality in the West, there are no simple conclusions to be drawn about how we will distinguish among helping professions. Even within the scope of this chapter, many aspects of these disciplines have been glossed over: distinctions within and among approaches to counseling and spiritual direction; multiple approaches to relating religion and science; problems defining the very terms under discussion, including religion, spirituality, and theology; the growth of non-Christian and nontheist spirituality in the West; the "re-enchantment" of the world in the West; and the lack of the category of the secular in some cultures. This flux is both unnerving and exciting.

Ultimately, what can be said is that the distinctions among counseling, pastoral counseling, and spiritual direction are breaking down, but the work of being a helper is not. Yet, although there is more evidence than ever that such distinctions are culturally bound and may not even work, the specialized knowledge required for even small parts of this spectrum has become such that a team of people is required. Thus, it is likely that current practitioners will need to learn to be both broadly formed and also knowledgeable of their own specialties, training, and limits. Because this is a hallmark of pastoral counseling, there will be a key role for this discipline going forward even if the terms, names, and boundaries continue to evolve.

REFLECTION QUESTIONS

1. The author traces the historical development of soul care in the West. Briefly describe the key contributors to modern notions of soul care.
2. How would you summarize the key distinctions made by the author between counseling and spiritual direction? In what ways are these practices similar? In what ways are they distinct?
3. What are the key elements of Sperry's (2002) integrated model for pastoral counseling? In what ways might this model be advantageous when working with clients? For whom might this model be inappropriate?
4. In what ways do the hedonic and eudaimonic approaches differ? How might they inform the work of the pastoral counselor?
5. The author notes that there are few distinctions between psychotherapy and spiritual practice in many cultural contexts. In what ways is this relevant with the clients you are currently serving?

REFERENCES

American Counseling Association. (2010). *20/20: Consensus definition of counseling*. Retrieved from http://www.counseling.org/knowledge-center/20-20-a-vision-for-the-future-of-coun seling/consensus-definition-of-counseling

Anuruddha & Bodhi, B. (2000). *A comprehensive manual of Abhidhamma: The Abhidhammattha Sangaha of Ācariya Anuruddha*. Seattle, WA: BPS Pariyatti Edition.

Barrette, G. (2004). Spiritual direction in the Roman Catholic tradition. In G. W. Moon & D. G. Benner (Eds.), *Spiritual direction and the care of souls: A guide to Christian approaches and practices* (pp. 55–77). Downers Grove, IL: InterVarsity.

Barry, W. A., & Connolly, W. J. (1982). *The practice of spiritual direction*. New York, NY: Seabury.

Bass, D. B. (2012). *Christianity after religion: The end of church and the birth of a new spiritual awakening*. New York, NY: HarperOne.

Brock, R. N., & Lettini, G. (2012). *Soul repair: Recovering from moral injury after war*. Boston, MA: Beacon.

Clebsch, W. A., & Jaeckle, C. R. (1964). *Pastoral care in historical perspective: An essay with exhibits*. Englewood Cliffs, NJ: Prentice-Hall.

Clinebell, H. J. (1984). *Basic types of pastoral care & counseling: Resources for the ministry of healing and growth*. Nashville, TN: Abingdon.

Deci, E. L., & Ryan, R. M. (2008). Hedonia, eudaimonia, and well-being: An introduction. *Journal of Happiness Studies, 9*, 1–11. doi:10.1007/s10902-006-9018-1

de Sales, F. (1950). *Introduction to the devout life* (J. K. Ryan, Trans.). New York, NY: Harper.

Doehring, C. (2009). Theological accountability: The hallmark of pastoral counseling. *Sacred Spaces: The e-Journal of the American Association of Pastoral Counselors, 1*, 4–34. Retrieved from http://www.aapc.org/news-events/sacred-spaces

Dykstra, R. C. (2005). *Images of pastoral care: Classic readings*. St. Louis, MO: Chalice.

Galindo, I. (2004). Spiritual direction and pastoral counseling. In G. W. Moon & D. G. Benner (Eds.), *Spiritual direction and the care of souls: A guide to Christian approaches and practices* (pp. 205–218). Downers Grove, IL: InterVarsity.

Gillespie, C. K. (2001). *Psychology and American Catholicism: From confession to therapy?* New York, NY: Crossroad.

Gutiérrez, G. (1984). *We drink from our own wells: The spiritual journey of a people*. Maryknoll, NY: Orbis Books/Dove Communications.

Hadot, P. (1995). *Philosophy as a way of life: Spiritual exercises from Socrates to Foucault*. Malden, MA: Blackwell.

Holifield, E. B. (1983). *A history of pastoral care in America: From salvation to self-realization*. Nashville, TN: Abingdon.

Lartey, E. Y. (2003). *In living color: An intercultural approach to pastoral care and counseling*. London, UK: Jessica Kingsley.

Leech, K. (2001). *Soul friend: Spiritual direction in the modern world*. Harrisburg, PA: Morehouse.

Maslow, A. H. (1943). A theory of human motivation. *Psychological Review, 50*, 370–396. doi:10.1037/h0054346

May, G. G. (1982). *Care of mind, care of spirit: Psychiatric dimensions of spiritual direction*. San Francisco, CA: Harper & Row.

McMahon, O. (2004). Spiritual direction in the Pentecostal/Charismatic tradition. In G. W. Moon & D. G. Benner (Eds.), *Spiritual direction and the care of souls: A guide to Christian approaches and practices* (pp. 152–170). Downers Grove, IL: InterVarsity.

McNeill, J. T. (1951). *A history of the cure of souls*. New York, NY: Harper.

Moon, G. W., & Benner, D. G. (2004). *Spiritual direction and the care of souls: A guide to Christian approaches and practices*. Downers Grove, IL: InterVarsity.

Nussbaum, M. C. (1994). *The therapy of desire: Theory and practice in Hellenistic ethics*. Princeton, NJ: Princeton University Press.

Purves, A. (2001). *Pastoral theology in the classical tradition*. Louisville, KY: Westminster John Knox Press.

Ryff, C. D. (1989). Happiness is everything, or is it? Explorations on the meaning of psychological well-being. *Journal of Personality and Social Psychology, 57*, 1069–1081. doi:10.1037/0022-3514.57.6.1069

Seligman, M. E. P., & Csikszentmihalyi, M. (2000). Positive psychology: An introduction. *American Psychologist, 55*, 5–14. doi:10.1037/0003-066X.55.1.5

Sperry, L. (2002). *Transforming self and community: Revisioning pastoral counseling and spiritual direction*. Collegeville, MN: Liturgical Press.

Stairs, J. (2000). *Listening for the soul: Pastoral care and spiritual direction*. Minneapolis, MN: Fortress.

Stewart-Sicking, J. A. (2008). Virtues, values, and the good life: Alasdair MacIntyre's virtue ethics and their implications for counseling, *Counseling & Values, 52*, 156–176. doi:10.1002/j.2161-007X.2008.tb00099.x

Thomas Aquinas. (1964 translation). *Summa theologiae: Latin text and English translation, introductions, notes, appendices, and glossaries*. Cambridge, UK: Blackfriars.

Tracy, W. D. (2004). Spiritual direction in the Wesleyan-Holiness tradition. In G. W. Moon & D. G. Benner (Eds.), *Spiritual direction and the care of souls: A guide to Christian approaches and practices* (pp. 115–136). Downers Grove, IL: InterVarsity.

Werdel, M. B., & Wicks, R. J. (2013). *Primer on posttraumatic growth: An introduction and guide*. Hoboken, NJ: John Wiley.

Wesley, J. (1749). *A Christian library consisting of extracts from and abridgments of the choicest pieces of practical divinity, which have been publish'd in the English tongue. In fifty volumes*. Bristol, UK: Felix Farley.

Kathleen J. Greider

14

RELIGIOUS LOCATION AND COUNSELING: ENGAGING DIVERSITY AND DIFFERENCE IN VIEWS OF RELIGION

This chapter explores religious differences between counselors and their clients. These differences exist whether or not counselors or clients are religious. The notion of "religious location," referenced in the chapter's title, calls our attention to the actuality that, *whether or not we are religious, all persons inhabit a particular location relative to religion*. Whether we call ourselves religious or not, are appreciative of religion or skeptical or ambivalent, we embody attitudes and positions toward religion that affect clinical work. Religious differences exist not simply because we have different religious beliefs or different beliefs about religion. Religious differences arise from the much more complex ground of our diverse religious locations. Religious location is akin to social location, our particular identities in social contexts, and personal location, the particularities of our individuality and our family and life history. Our religious location is but one aspect of—and also always dynamically interacting with—our complex cultural identity as a whole, which includes all aspects of our identity, such as personality, age, sexuality, economic status, gender, ethnicity and race, nationality, and first language.

The chapter begins by setting out the foundational concept of "language care" (Bueckert & Schipani, 2006), a part of which involves clarification of some terminology. A second section explores religious location, including one aspect of religious location that can pose what is arguably the only insurmountable barrier when the counselor and client occupy different religious locations. The chapter then reflects on forms and degrees of religious difference, challenges posed by religious differences in counseling, and the significance in counseling of the counselor's religious location. Therapeutic relationality is of concern throughout the chapter, but a brief concluding section examines a few practices especially valuable for nurturing therapeutic relationality given differences in clients' and counselors' religious locations. The spirit of these themes infers the chapter's thesis: religious particularity and differences between counselors and clients are ever present and, with appropriate attention, have the potential to contribute to more profound clinical relationships.

In addition to those readers for whom counseling and psychotherapy are their primary professional practices, this chapter also will have relevance for chaplains and congregation leaders. They often must provide counseling even if it is not their primary responsibility or specialization and, as the chapter argues, differences in religious location exist everywhere, even within congregations. Although I refer mostly to counselors and clients, I have formed these reflections also with supervisors and supervisees in mind, knowing that diversity in religious location also affects the relationship and process of supervision. Although the chapter may have relevance beyond the United States, the analysis addresses readers presumed to be located in the U.S. context, where English-language expression of certain Christian beliefs, practices, and values forms a dominant and majority culture.

Of course, my own religious location is inextricably related to the chapter's claims; throughout the chapter, I note some of its influences and those of other aspects of my personal and professional locations. Here I offer some grounding for those later reflections. I was born into and have lived all my life immersed in the diversity of beliefs and practices that are called Christian. My education in predominately White, liberal Protestant undergraduate and graduate schools preceded my ordination and entry into the vocation of caregiving and pastoral counseling. My earliest professional experiences were as a chaplain in a major urban medical center and as a pastoral counselor in a working-class city comprising mainly Portuguese immigrants. Later I worked as a mental health counselor in a state inpatient psychiatric facility, a pastoral counselor for the psychiatric unit in the Roman Catholic hospital, and a congregational pastor. I have an ongoing practice in psychotherapy and spiritual direction. However, most of my professional life has been spent as professor of practical theology, spiritual care, and spiritually integrative counseling in a so-called progressive graduate theological school characterized by significant religious, racial/ethnic, and national diversity. As a pastoral and practical theologian, I place care at the center of my concerns and practices, with attention especially to damage done by social and interpersonal violence. These commitments cause me to favor theological and social science theories and practices constructed for the sake of liberation and empowerment by persons-in-communities with histories of having been subjugated and traumatized. The school of psychotherapy that most foundationally informs me is relational–cultural theory, which is psychodynamic by heritage but primarily informed by the experiences of girls and women, feminist and womanist theory, and core values of authenticity, vulnerability, and mutuality.

LANGUAGE CARE

The power of language to disclose and obscure requires attention to semantics and the discussion of terminology used throughout the chapter. Indeed, I am persuaded by Bueckert and Schipani's (2006) discussion of "language care" that careful attention to language is arguably the most essential practice for effective counseling amid any kind of difference and a primary factor that makes it possible to engender meaningful care and counseling in relationships characterized by religious difference. As they note, caring for persons through the language we use, as well as caring for language itself, especially by being attentive to the significance of the exact words used by our clients, goes a long way toward acknowledging and bridging the gaps frequently caused by religious difference. In fact, without painstaking attention to the meaning of the words spoken by client and counselor, we may think we understand each other when we do not. Instead, religiously significant gaps will undermine the therapeutic work.

For now, it is necessary to address two matters of foundational terminology. First, I favor definitions that point toward a close relationship between "religion" and "spirituality." Definitions used by Worthington, Hook, Wade, Miller, and Sharp (2008, citing Hill & Hall, 2002) meet this criteria. Spirituality can be described as "a person's search for the sacred" (p. 17) and religion as "a person's search for the sacred within an organized worldview of specified beliefs and values that are lived out within a community of faith" (pp. 17–18). I will refer primarily to religion and less frequently to spirituality precisely because religious difference tends to be more noticed and divisive than differences in spirituality. Nonetheless, most of our reflection will be relevant to counselors and clients whose religious locations are aligned more with spirituality than religion.

Second, I understand religion to be one aspect of culture and cultural diversity, not separable or fully distinguishable from other aspects of cultural diversity. Therefore, counseling amid religious difference is one dimension of intercultural (or multicultural) counseling. Intercultural competence is required for effective counseling amid religious difference, and competence amid religious difference is required for effective intercultural counseling. It is a gross simplification to discuss it, as for the most part I must do here, as if it were not affected by particularities, interconnectedness with, and power dynamics related to race and ethnicity, class, gender, nationality and first language, and other marginalized and dominating identities.

RELIGIOUS LOCATION(S) AND ONE INSURMOUNTABLE BARRIER

As intercultural and multicultural counseling theories have been arguing for decades, all aspects of human particularity are at play in clinical work. Self-knowledge sufficient for clinical practice is not composed of declaring that we are or are not religious. Even if we are not religious—humanist, agnostic, spiritual, atheist—our attitudes and experiences relative to religion constitute a location, a position, that influences our clinical work. In part because religion is a dominant and often volatile aspect of human relations, our religious location merits the deep self-reflexivity we have learned to bring to our social and personal locations. Such reflection is the purpose of this chapter, especially the diverse, dynamic, and complex effects of religious location—our own and that of our clients—in clinical work.

Even among those of us who consider ourselves pastoral counselors, clinicians inhabit diverse religious locations. Some of us were born into religious families and communities, others of us into families or communities where religion was barely noticed. We may have grown to be antireligion, blasé, or positive toward religion. Surveys consistently report that counselors are less religious than the general public but also report that many of us consider ourselves spiritual, even if not religious (Onedera & Greenwalt, 2008). We may be a lifelong or occasional student of religion, had religious education only when we were children, or never had any education in religion. We may be leaders in religious communities, religious communities may have shunned us, or we lead from marginalized positions within religious communities. Among those of us who make our living doing work that concerns religion, some chose that work because of religion's positive potentials, others because of its dangers, most of us out of concern for religion's capacities both to harm and to help. We may belong to a tradition that is denied the status of a religion, such as indigenous "traditions" or something others call a "cult." Counselors and clients bring all these variations in religious location to counseling relationships.

Still, the situation is even more complex than these initial differentiations imply. Our particularities are not simple demographic markers. They are neither discrete categories nor static. They are alive, synergistically evolving. As with other aspects of identity, through our lifetimes, we inhabit more than one religious location. We become more, less, or differently religious. Our love of or neutrality toward religion is destabilized or destroyed by trauma done to us in the name of religion. We are religious but shaped by multiple religions, not only one, having been born into cultures and families where migration, immigration, and colonialism have created religious multiplicity. In these and many other ways, our relationship to religion is characterized by more than one experience, more than one location, sometimes more than one location in any given moment.

The diversity of our religious locations is demanding and perhaps daunting. Still, little evidence exists that diversity in religious location is inherently an obstacle to clinical work. Quite the opposite. A growing literature argues almost exclusively that with adequate education and clinical consultation, as well as the use of referral for specific religious counsel when needed, counselors and clients from diverse religious locations can work together effectively. Indeed, it is not uncommon to find in the literature documentation through clinical examples that difference in religious location is sometimes treasured by clients because they feel that they could not speak freely with someone from their own tradition (Hanada, 2012; Walsh, 2010). This chapter presumes that under those specified conditions, counselors can work meaningfully with clients whose religious locations differ from the counselor's, with the following crucial caveat.

Counselors and clients do not have to agree about religion to do good clinical work together. Indeed, this chapter argues that significant religious difference *and disagreement* are at play in every clinical relationship, even if religion never surfaces as an explicit subject. However, therapeutic relationality amid religious difference and disagreement require counselors to be open to the *possibility* that there is something of value in religious locations other than our own, even when we disagree vehemently. This is a challenge that is always demanding and becomes excruciating when a client conveys condemnation of our religious location(s) or other identities. It raises an intense question for contemplation: What values and practices will cultivate such openness, when we are impelled to judge, withdraw, strike back?

We each must find our own path to such openness and to practices that will help sustain us on that difficult path. I will offer here, though, a few words about my own religious locations relative to these demands, for the purposes of illustration. Decades of clinical teaching and practice have crafted in me a devotion to what I experience as the mysteriousness and ambiguities of life, which relativize my religious and clinical locations, as well as those of all others. Except for the enduring reality of this unfathomable quality of life, I have come to experience all other aspects of my worldview as partial, at best. Similarly, in my experience, both religion and the science of psychotherapy are partial; neither have proven adequate by themselves to prevent violence or cure woundedness. Thus, personally and professionally decentered, humility is required of me even and especially when I am required by professional codes of ethics to intervene in clients' behaviors or compelled by my ethics or morality to express some disagreement with a client. The practices of religion and spirituality I engage are to a large extent for the purposes of cultivating capacity for this openness and defusing any negativity I experience in relation to the religious locations of others.

But what if we find ourselves in a clinical relationship that exceeds our capacity to offer respectful openness to clients regarding their religious location? What if we find ourselves unable to shake our judgment, fear, voyeurism, or idealization toward a client's religiosity? First, to find ourselves unexpectedly in such a situation suggests that we failed to do a sufficiently thorough initial assessment of either the client's religious location and its interrelatedness with the clinical issues presented or our religious competence with respect to that client's religious particularity. We may need to revise how we do intake and history taking. Second, we need immediately to seek education and supervision to remedy our inadequate training relative to this client's religious location. Codes of ethics usually prohibit us from simply referring clients because we discover differences—religious or otherwise—between ourselves and clients (see, e.g., American Counseling Association, 2014, p. 8). Once we have made a commitment to care for a client, we are required to work diligently to develop competence in the area of religion to meet the client's needs. It is unethical for us precipitously to refer a client because we discover conflicts in deeply held values about, for example, gender roles, sexual practice, race relations, abortion, or military combat.

But, again, what if after our diligent effort to gain education and supervision, we still find ourselves unable to shake our judgment, fear, voyeurism, or idealization toward a client's religiosity? Counselors who cannot foster openness to the possibility of value in clients' religious locations need to refer. Counselors who dismiss, disallow, or otherwise disdain their clients' religious location need to refer. Our codes of ethics may not have adequately grappled with the reality that education and supervision often are insufficient to transform our most passionately held beliefs. Not unlike some of our clinical beliefs, some religious beliefs are nonnegotiable. Just as there are uncompromising disagreements among clinicians about clinical truths (the politics of symptomology and diagnostic criteria, for example), there are uncompromising disagreements among clinicians about what constitutes religious truth or truth about religion. Often referred to as attitudes of exclusivity, I respect that some persons hold those beliefs in good conscience. I am arguing here only that attitudes of exclusivity regarding differences in religious location pose an insurmountable barrier *in counseling* (not necessarily in other professional practices). How can therapeutic relationality be fostered if religious counselors regard a client's religious location as damning or if nonreligious counselors find clients' religious commitments nonsensical? As we will see, like precipitous referral, such personal beliefs also pose a serious ethical dilemma: They fail to meet the minimum criterion regarding religion in our codes of ethics, that of respect. Clients will readily detect when counselors have attitudes of superiority with regard to religion. They are likely to detect it even when we cloak our feelings of superiority in silence. It is intriguing that the old adage about polite conversation—avoid talking about religion and politics—seems strangely descriptive of counseling as well. Perhaps the widespread silence in counseling about religion (and politics) is our effort to mask our religious disagreements? But this is futile. As I argue later, our religious locations and differences are revealed, indirectly if not directly, when we and our clients delve into the profound issues of meaning and value that are at the heart of counseling.

FORMS AND DEGREES OF RELIGIOUS DIFFERENCE

As public attention is drawn to the necessity of dealing constructively with persons who differ from us religiously, emphasis is usually placed on similarities. We should and can treat with respect people whose religion differs from ours because, as this approach goes, religions share many common values. Or, if we encounter persons who are not religious, we can and should treat them with respect because, as humans, we are more alike than different. Focus on similarities is valuable and reassuring.

Focus on similarities is, however, insufficient by itself. The need to augment our awareness of similarity with attentiveness to religious difference is emphasized in this chapter for several reasons. Religious difference is highly prevalent, as I argued earlier. Furthermore, their religious particularity is usually important to clients, whether they are religious or not religious. Most somberly, inattentiveness to difference, along with misperception because of difference, fuels violence (Prothero, 2010). Finally, as has been widely argued in the health sciences, religion can and often does play a role in well-being, but this benefit is not generic. Rather, clients benefit not from religion in a generic way but from particular traditions, practices, and communities. Thus, attentiveness to religious difference is necessary to access religion's contributions to well-being.

The three vignettes that follow are merely suggestive of the three major forms of religious difference commonly encountered in counseling. I encourage you to pause as you read to try to identify situations in which you have experienced other examples of these three kinds of difference.

Interreligious (or Interfaith) Difference

The most widely recognized form is *interreligious* (or *interfaith*) difference: Clients and counselors may identify with different religions. But when we consider religious location and not only belief in religion, we can see that this difference also occurs when one values religion and the other does not.

Near the end of their fourth session, the therapeutic alliance is rocked by the emergence of religious difference. Jared and Dinah Butler have come to counseling with their two teenagers, Elijah and Tamara, because their once peaceable family life has become a battleground where parents and children are regularly fighting over values, behaviors, and their choice of friends. The family has participated for years in a Christian church where African American families like themselves try to instill the values and teach the behaviors that, among other purposes, equip them to resist racism nonviolently and with dignity. Thus, Elijah's recent declaration that he does not believe in God and feels like a hypocrite when he attends church has fueled the family conflict.

Also African American, their counselor, Aliyah, has cautiously assisted them in previous sessions to reflect on the role Christian values play in their conflicts and not only in the closeness that seems under threat. Now, as their fourth session draws to a close, Aliyah asks to reschedule their appointment for next week because of a religious holiday. This surprises Jared and Dinah—"What holiday is next week?" they ask Aliyah. "It is Eid-al-Fitr," she replies, "when Muslims celebrate the end of Ramadan." By the look on their faces, Aliyah can see that Jared and Dinah are stunned. "You are Muslim?" they ask. "Not Christian? Why didn't you tell us?" As Aliyah tries in the few remaining minutes to figure out why her Muslim identity seems to be troubling the parents, the kids enthusiastically say to their parents, "That's great! You have been talking all the time about how great Aliyah is, and now you'll see that there is nothing wrong with our being friends with the Muslims at school!" But Aliyah knows the rocky history between African American Christians and African American Muslims. And since her conversion several years ago, she has been struggling to manage her skepticism toward clients and colleagues who are not religious, as Elijah now describes himself. She knows the gaps now uncovered will not be easily bridged.

Intrareligious (or Intrafaith) Difference

Clients and counselors may differ significantly even when they are located within the same tradition. The relative lack of attention to this form—*intra*religious or *intra*faith difference—is problematic because this form may be more challenging than interreligious difference. When clients and counselors know a tradition from the inside and are committed to it, the differences can be more recognizable, troubling, and divisive.

This vignette represents a composite of my own experience as a Christian counseling Christians. A similar dynamic could occur between counselors and clients who are both not religious or both identify with a religion other than Christianity.

In our first session, Luisa speaks of the divorce that has left her struggling financially as a single mother. Her beliefs about divorce and the behavior that precipitated it—inculcated by Mexican cultural values, her family, and the pastor and ethos of her Pentecostal Christian megachurch—leave her feeling shame, she says, and sometimes suicidal. "Are you a Christian?" she asks me. "It's really important to me that my counselor is a Christian."

I was born into a mainline Christian denomination in a theologically conservative and evangelically oriented community. Now, after years of life experience and of education in "progressive" theologies, I name myself a follower of Jesus. I know my understanding of Christianity is considerably "left of center" among Christians, many of whom would not consider me a Christian. I scramble to find words to respond to this complex question and the even more complex relational and contextual situation it references as we strive to find common ground.

Differences Due to Religious Multiplicity

Historically and globally, engaging in more than one religious tradition is not uncommon. Recently, this way of being religious is becoming more public and widely practiced in the United States. This third form of religious difference stems from what is often called *religious multiplicity*. The next vignette illustrates only one of the many ways this religious location is embodied. (For further discussion, see Greider, 2011.)

A student is preparing his application for his first position as a mental health practitioner, hoping to work as a counselor at the local Jewish Family Services Center. This job matters very much to Joshua, not only because it will be his first job after graduation but also because he has always wanted to work for a Jewish organization. Joshua experiences his religious identity, beliefs, and practices as inextricably related with his view of and commitment to the work of counseling. But he is struggling to write the application and is already preoccupied with the interview, wondering what they will ask him about his Jewish identity. Joshua treasures the Jewish culture that his parents taught to him and his siblings and that remains the foundation of their family life. Both his parents are rabbis in the conservative branch of Judaism, so he also knows well the religious history and practices of his Jewish heritage. Still, Joshua is not an observant Jew, religiously speaking, and is, in fact, atheist. He has joined the ranks of the many Jews who find in Buddhism the worldview, values, and practices that now serve as his spiritual foundation. He has studied Buddhism extensively with respected teachers. Over time, he feels that he has finally found himself, come home to himself, spiritually—he is a Jewish Buddhist and a Buddhist Jew. But how can he explain his multiplicity of religious identities to the interviewers? Will they be assessing whether he is an adequate representative of Judaism? Is he? Will they understand and embrace his complex religious identity? His family is still struggling to understand and accept it.

Degrees of Difference

Inherent in these forms is a spectrum of degrees of difference, ranging from comfortable or even intriguing variation within and between religious locations to extreme differences that give rise to anger or a sense of threat. As with the tendency to emphasize similarity, we may be tempted to focus on relatively manageable differences. Also, as in the three vignettes just presented, the actual or feared degree of difference may, with care and competence, be initially challenging but navigable. This makes all the more noteworthy a case study published by Aten (2011) in which religious difference constituted "opposing worldviews" (p. 81) that threatened to derail Aten from his clinical obligations. In this refreshingly honest examination of his clinical work with "Bill," Aten details the clash between his own religious beliefs and Bill's affiliation with Odinism. Never having encountered an Odinist, Aten asks Bill to tell him more about it.

> Client: My religion is an ancient Northern Scandinavian religion, it is a pagan religion. . . . It is a white Aryan religion. And it is the guiding philosophy behind lots of white supremacy groups. I consider myself a Nazi. . . .
> Therapist: Silence. (p. 82)

Aten wryly sketches how he worked with his thoughts, feelings, and behaviors in the aftermath of Bill's religious self-explanation, eventually finding a religious location from which to cultivate empathy for and be of some help to Bill. From this disorienting experience in interreligious counseling, Aten gleaned guidelines for clinicians working with religious differences, some of which we consider in the final section of the chapter. For now, it is sufficient to note that this case illustrates how serious degrees of difference in religious location, if unattended, might derail a clinical relationship.

CHALLENGES RELATED TO DIFFERENCES IN RELIGIOUS LOCATION

Within the forms and degrees of religious difference are embedded additional complications especially crucial in counseling: exacerbated power dynamics, the remoteness of foundational meanings and values, and inadequacies in education and supervised clinical training.

Exacerbated Power Dynamics Due to Religious Difference

Difference in religious location exacerbates what Bueckert and Schipani (2006) aptly call the "inherent asymmetry" of professional relationships of care and counseling (p. 251). Certainly, the extent to which clients and counselors are conscious of these dynamics varies considerably. To engage these complications effectively, it is first necessary to develop our consciousness that *counselors and clients meet not merely as persons but as groups.* To analyze the complex meta-environment in which persons meet also as groups, Grefe (2011) deftly employs social psychology, social identity theory, intergroup theory, and theory and practice in interreligious dialogue and interfaith spiritual care. Although Grefe is addressing a broader context than ours, her analysis helps us see how, as in all aspects of our living, clients and counselors embody and enact not only our individuality but also the culture and history of the groups to which we belong. Multicultural counseling theory has made clear that intercultural competence requires us to look beyond the influence of the family groups to which we and clients belong. More sophisticated is the capacity to take into account how membership in other collectivities is affecting counseling relationships. Clients, counselors, and the clinical work itself evidence the history and current realities of all the broader cultures to which we and clients belong: less emphasized historically significant cultures of age, ability, and education, as well as the more widely recognized cultures and histories related to gender and sexuality, race and ethnicity, language and national origin, and so forth. Obviously, the culture and history of the groups associated with our religious locations are similarly at play.

Second, embedded in all these dimensions of our group belongingness are *power differentials between groups*. These power differentials are rarely benign. To the contrary, the history of intergroup contact is a record of oppression and suffering. What have come to be referred to handily as the "isms" constitute a painful legacy of pervasive misunderstanding, fear, stereotyping, and prejudice, which has festered into contemporary and impervious patterns of domination by the more powerful of the less powerful, enforced by subjugation and, too often, genocide. Because it concerns nothing less than ultimate meanings and values, religious location is arguably one of the most potentially inflammatory power dynamics in intergroup contact. When meeting in counseling, counselors and/or clients may well see in each other someone who represents this excruciating legacy: Blacks may see descendants of White slave owners, Jews may see Christian inheritors of a long tradition of anti-Semitism, women may see men heedless of misogyny's history, and impoverished Third World people may see oblivious First World consumers.

This analysis may seem to be overly focused on the underside of religious difference. Such a perception, however, may well be evidence of the function of *religious privilege*. The notion of privilege—special advantages, rights, or immunity granted to a specific group of people—has become a crucial aspect of understanding dynamics within systems of domination and oppression. In contrast to emphasis on intentional acts of oppression and the disadvantages of belonging to oppressed groups, the concept of privilege calls our attention to advantages that accrue to being members of dominant groups. As McIntosh (1988) described it in her now oft-cited reflections on White privilege and male privilege, "Privilege is like an invisible weightless knapsack of special provisions, assurances, tools, maps, guides, codebooks, passports, visas, clothes, compass, emergency gear, and blank checks" (pp. 1–2). The privilege we enjoy is obvious to those who do not benefit from it but difficult for us to see because we are so immersed in and reliant on it. Also, we are socialized not to see it, lest conscience cause us to disturb the very social order that privileges our people.

As noted earlier, the privilege associated with our dominance also enables us to distance ourselves, if we choose, from the struggle and suffering endured by those our group dominates. If we choose it, this lack of awareness deforms us not only with regard to our ignorance in the present time but also with regard to history. We can think that the legacy of dominance and subjugation is not as bad as it seems to overpowered groups. We can easily overestimate the degree to which we and our groups foster just and fair relationality.

The concept is now being extended to privilege in the realm of religious difference. It is noteworthy that it was a colleague in counseling, Schlosser (2003), who offered one of the early examinations of religious privilege. Schlosser notes that he came to an awareness of religious privilege as he engaged in the process of identifying the invisible advantages he enjoys as a Caucasian male. Illustrating the complexity of power dynamics that we have been exploring, he notes that his privileges "led to the neglect and denial" of a dimension of his experience in which he experiences oppression—his "identification as a member of a minority religious group" in the United States, that is, a religious group other than Christianity (p. 46). In the United States, Christians are dominant insofar as we far outnumber persons affiliated with other religious groups. Our dominance accrues much more, however, from the fact that Christians far outnumber persons of other religious locations in positions invested with sociopolitical and economic power. Not all Christians enjoy the same level of privilege: The Christian majority discriminates against and marginalizes some of its own—for example, the Metropolitan Community Church, Latter-day Saints (Mormons), Seventh Day Adventists, and Jehovah's Witnesses. Also, as with Whites and males, our dominance does not prevent Christians from claiming and sometimes experiencing disadvantage. At a meta-level, however, Christians in the United States enjoy religious dominance and privilege.

Thus, it is significant when Schlosser (2003) describes speaking of Christian privilege as "breaking a sacred taboo" (p. 44). Similarly significant is the argument by two other colleagues that "religious bigotry" is "the neglected 'ism' in multicultural psychology and therapy" (Negy & Ferguson, 2004, p. 61). In both cases, the exacerbation of power dynamics due to religious difference is being referenced. We can also see this exacerbation in the preceding vignettes. The cultural dominance and privilege associated with being Christian, as well as religious bigotry, are the meta-environment in which Jared and Dinah presume Aliyah is Christian, assume that it was her responsibility to correct their presumption, and for undisclosed reasons seem troubled that Muslims are becoming important persons relative to their family life. The power invested in Aliyah because of her professional role is undermined by her membership in a minority religious group toward which bigotry is often expressed. Yet, it is Elijah whose religious location may be most religiously disadvantaged in this counseling situation, given the global bias and discrimination against atheists (U.S. Commission on International Religious Freedom, 2013). Religious bigotry and privilege exist within communities, as exemplified by the acrimony between so-called conservative and liberal Christians, and the fledgling connection between Luisa and her pastoral counselor is now tested by that culture war. As a Jew and a person of multiple religious identities, Joshua is a member of two minority religious groups. But also, knowing the devastation wreaked upon the Jewish community by genocide and other costs of anti-Semitism, he understands that Jewish interviewers might well resent his religious choices, feeling they contribute to the diminishment of Judaism.

Remoteness of Meanings and Values Rooted in Religious Location

Religious location is often equated with conscious cognitions and observable practices. For example, we are clear that we believe in God or that we think religious belief is superstition. We participate in religious rituals as members of a religious community, or we do not. These easily accessible beliefs and concrete behaviors are, indeed, typically part of our religious location. This can give the mistaken impression that religious location is easily accessible, even obvious.

However, religious location is also associated with deep structures of meaning and value, sometimes referred to as our worldview or philosophy of life. These structures are characterized by remoteness. They are remote relative to consciousness, visibility, and malleability. As we experience regularly, it is not always possible to say what our thoughts and feelings are with regard to profound matters. It is often the case that we behave in ways that conflict with the values we state most insistently. Our worldviews are so resistant to change that often only dramatic experiences like trauma or ecstasy can substantially transform them.

The influence of these profound meanings and values is ubiquitous, and few mental health professionals argue any longer that counseling is value free. What is not so widely acknowledged, however, is that the *meanings and values at the heart of counseling often have their roots in the religious location of both clients and counselors*. Negy and Ferguson (2004) put it bluntly: "Although psychology generally purports to be divorced from religious values, judgments about 'deviant' and 'optimal' behavior often are based on Western cultural values, which themselves are partially derived from a broader Judeo–Christian culture" (p. 67).

When global and cultural variation is respected (not merely tolerated or assessed according to the judgments of our groups or personal choices), we are more able to recognize that religious location affects many, maybe all, of the issues of meaning and value that arise in counseling. The religious valence that inheres in these issues will vary in its characteristics: according to religious location, of course, but also from negative to positive, unconscious to conscious, determinative to disregarded, deeply considered or embraced with little thought, historically obscure or prominent in current media.

However, the religious valence is there. In the vignettes just presented, deep differences in meaning and value that have their roots in religious location will be most obvious in whatever clinical judgments Aliyah makes about parenting and, as Luisa's pastoral counselor, I make about divorce. But consider questions that suggest other religiously influenced clinical issues: Do human beings tend toward goodness or toward offense? In what situations might guilt and shame be warranted? Why is granting forgiveness given more attention than earning forgiveness? What is a family? When my obligations to myself and to others appear to conflict, which should I favor? Why do we try to influence each other's health-related choices—diet, exercise, disease prevention, use of substances? What makes variation in gender, sexual identity, sexual expression, and sexual fidelity so incendiary? Why does nonconformity among humans cause problems? Given the vulnerability of children and the documented extent of neglect and abuse, why do we treat parenthood as an inalienable right? Why do we judge each other's choices related to how we choose to die—attitudes toward dying, resuscitation, euthanasia, suicide, treatment of the body after death?

Perhaps most significant in counseling is how our religious location affects our most deeply held positions on issues of ultimacy and authority. What constitutes a life well lived? What matters most? How do we live with brokenness and losses that are irreparable? What distinguishes honor over dishonor? As the popular slogan asks, why do we kill people who kill people to show that killing people is wrong? Why is military combat valorized and suicide stigmatized? If love and compassion are obviously good, why are they so often absent? When we disagree about what matters most, who decides? When religion and science diverge, or when my religious location diverges from my counselor's, or vice versa, whose authority prevails, and why?

This variation and uncertainty inheres in the remoteness of our meanings and values, calling for our sustained personal and professional reflection and study. Otherwise, as with religious privilege, the close relationship between religion and the meanings and values at issue in counseling will continue to go without our notice. Without mindfulness and responsible behavior regarding how our attitudes toward religion are intertwined with what we deem to be healthy and good, we are at risk of practicing religious bigotry. This is the case whether we are religious, not religious, or against religion (Negy & Ferguson, 2004). Of course, counselors' responsibility in these dynamics is greater than that of clients. "Arguably, the most insidious form of religious bigotry occurring in therapy is when therapists naïvely believe that their guidance is based on clinical judgment when such judgment really reflects therapists' own personal ideology" (Negy & Ferguson, 2004, p. 69).

Professional Competence and Ethics Challenged by Differences in Religious Location

Standards of professional competence and codes of ethics across the mental health professions now usually include at least a mention of religion. Most commonly, it is stated that clinicians are expected to *respect* clients' religious identity and practices.

Some go a step further to state the need for *competence* with regard to clients' religion and/or to caution clinicians from practicing outside the scope of their training with regard to religion. But what constitutes respect and competence with regard to religion? The few codes that do specify competencies make clear that developing such competence requires extensive education and supervised clinical practice, far beyond that which is provided by most degree programs in mental health disciplines. The following extracts are illustrative.

In the statement of its ethical principles and code of conduct, the American Psychological Association (APA; 2010) includes religion in a lengthy enumeration of factors that psychologists are said to be "aware of," "respect," and "consider":

> Psychologists are aware of and respect cultural, individual, and role differences, including those based on age, gender, gender identity, race, ethnicity, culture, national origin, religion, sexual orientation, disability, language, and socioeconomic status, and consider these factors when working with members of such groups. (p. 4)

Also, psychologists are described as aware and respectful of these factors in sections addressing "Human Relations," specifically Section 3.01 on Unfair Discrimination and Section 3.10 on Other Harassment (APA, 2010, pp. 5–6). These expectations set a high bar. Appropriately, then, the APA (2010) includes religion in Section 2.01, which addresses boundaries of competence. Part (b) states that:

> where scientific or professional knowledge in the discipline of psychology establishes that an understanding of factors associated with age, gender, gender identity, race, ethnicity, culture, national origin, religion, sexual orientation, disability, language, or socioeconomic status is essential for effective implementation of their services or research, psychologists have or obtain the training, experience, consultation, or supervision necessary to ensure the competence of their services, or they make appropriate referrals, except as provided in Standard 2.02, Providing Services in Emergencies. (p. 5)

In what clinical situation would these factors *not* be essential for effective practice? Multicultural theory and practice has firmly established that all of the aforementioned dimensions of culture are significant and influential in therapeutic work and research. Thus, all psychologists who do not already have education and training necessary to ensure the competence of their work regarding religious location are obliged to seek it. Alternatively, the APA code of ethics requires that they seek consultation or supervision with, or refer their clients to, colleagues with such competence.

The American Association of Pastoral Counselors (AAPC) exists to provide credentialing of, and continuing education and collaboration for, the development of exactly such competence. That the first words of the AAPC (2012) code of ethics go beyond the simple signifier "religion" is modest evidence of such a mission:

> As members of the American Association of Pastoral Counselors, we are respectful of the various theologies, traditions, and values of our faith communities and committed to the dignity and worth of each individual. (p. 1)

Similarly, Principle III, addressing client relationships, notes that competence in this arena of living goes beyond "religion" and places obligations on the clinicians regarding their own religious location.

We show sensitive regard for the moral, social, and religious values and beliefs of clients and communities. We avoid imposing our beliefs on others, although we may express them when appropriate in the pastoral counseling process. (p. 3)

Interestingly, the American Counseling Association (ACA) links its code of ethics to 14 competencies that go a long way toward making clear the substantial education and supervised practice necessary to develop clinical competency regarding religion. A division of the ACA, the Association for Spiritual, Ethical, and Religious Values in Counseling (ASERVIC), has developed a document entitled *Competencies for Addressing Spiritual and Religious Values in Counseling* (2009). ASERVIC (2009) articulates competencies in six categories:

- Culture and Worldview: knowledge sufficient to compare and contrast spirituality and religion and knowledge of core beliefs of major traditions in spirituality, religion, agnosticism, and atheism; recognition of the interplay between clients' worldview and functioning and their beliefs regarding religion and spirituality
- Counselor Self-Awareness: active development of awareness of one's own position relative to religion; continuous evaluation of its effects on the counselor's clinical work and clients; awareness of, and development of resources to offset, the limitations of one's knowledge regarding religion and spirituality
- Human and Spiritual Development: knowledge of models of development and capacity for appropriate clinical use
- Communication: acceptance and sensitivity regarding clients' communications regarding religion and/or spirituality; use of concepts consonant with clients' communications; capacity to recognize religious and/or spiritual themes in client communications, assess their therapeutic relevance, and address them appropriately
- Assessment: during intake and assessment, seeking information from clients or other sources to understand clients' religious and/or spiritual perspective
- Diagnosis and Treatment: recognition of the role of religion and/or spirituality in clients' well-being, problems, and symptoms; goal setting consistent with clients' spiritual and/or religious perspective; ability to modify therapeutic technique and use spiritual and/or religious practices when appropriate and acceptable to clients' viewpoints; ability to use theory and research therapeutically that supports inclusion of clients' religious and/or spiritual beliefs and practices

Development of the competencies identified by ASERVIC can result only from substantial formal education about religious difference, disciplined and ongoing self-reflexivity regarding religious location, and clinical practice under the guidance of teachers and supervisors who possess these competencies. Again, a high bar is set.

Our codes of ethics and standards for competency put us in a bind. *It is unethical to ignore religion, and it is unethical to attend to religion incompetently.* Our ethics require us to seek to understand and build competence regarding religious difference. But the curricula and credentialing of mental health fields outside of pastoral counseling rarely and inadequately address religious location, so how many clinicians actually have these competencies? Does this gap between high expectations, a dearth of clinicians who actually meet those expectations, and the widespread influence of religious location and difference in counseling mean that many clinicians are working outside their scope of practice? Technically, the only ethical pathway out of this conundrum is consultation with and referral to colleagues with the kind of competencies identified here, such as pastoral counselors. But our vignettes point toward a more complex reality: Aliyah, Joshua, and I (any many other counselors) find that religiously tinged issues and religious difference are so prevalent and so intricately interwoven with other clinical issues and our own religious locations that we could benefit from seeking consultation on a daily basis! The very ubiquity of religious location and difference means that although referral and consultation are sometimes essential, we need also to be learning "in place," working every day toward developing these competencies.

The remainder of the chapter delves into two aspects of such learning: self-reflexivity regarding our own religious location and clinical practices that directly address the gap between our competencies and clients' needs regarding religion. The effectiveness of combining these two emphases can be understood as akin to the synergy of self-differentiation and connection argued by family systems theory to be the fundamentals of effective relationality.

SELF-DIFFERENTIATION: THE SIGNIFICANCE OF THE COUNSELOR'S RELIGIOUS LOCATION

As we have seen, the religious location of the counselor matters in the clinical process. Like all aspects of our identities, whether we understand ourselves to be religious, spiritual but not religious, agnostic, humanist, atheist, utterly disinterested, or in some other position relative to religion, these locations influence the clinical process. There are sometimes good clinical reasons to try to imaginatively "bracket" our religious location, to minimize certain effects of it. These skills notwithstanding, we cannot fully neutralize our religious location(s). More to the point, as counselors, we should be well practiced in self-reflexivity—disciplined, accountable practices to decrease our unconsciousness and increase in depth our understanding of our life narrative, sense of self, participation in relationships, and social–historical location. Extending self-reflexivity to how our religious location is affecting our clinical work should be possible for all of us, even without specialized training regarding religion. Toward that end, we will reflect here on three mutually reinforcing areas of self-reflexivity that are akin to those identified in the category of Counselor Self-Awareness in the ASERVIC (2009) competencies:

- Self-reflexivity regarding our own religious location
- Self-reflexivity regarding the effect of our religious location on clients and clinical situations
- Self-reflexivity regarding our limitations and offsetting them

Self-Reflexivity Regarding Our Own Religious Location

We begin by acknowledging that, as with other dimensions of our identity and self-awareness, our identity, awareness, and self-differentiation regarding religion are fluid. Our personal and group relatedness to religion and spirituality is, hopefully, not stagnant. Thus, the need for this aspect of self-reflexivity is ongoing. It is important to note here that although self-reflexivity does often lead to change, change is not a requirement of self-reflexivity. Out of respect for religious freedom, it is crucial not to expect that we (or others) will be changed in our religious location by self-reflexivity, although that may happen. Rather, the expectation here is the awareness of and, as needed, the capacity to articulate our positions relative to religion. As noted in the vignettes, Aliyah, Joshua, and I all face situations in which our readiness to speak explicitly about our religious location is needed.

Much of our self-reflexivity about religiosity will happen in our most personal contemplation. Religion is one of the tender and controversial matters that may seem to require the relative safety of one's private musings. Yet, clinicians know that solitary reflection by itself is insufficient for clinical responsibility. Given denial, projection, and other forms of unconsciousness and defense, fullness of self-reflection regarding our religious location depends on augmentation through relationships of accountability. The expectation that counselors will seek both psychotherapy and supervision for themselves testifies to our professional acknowledgment that we need the perspective of others to reduce the risk of harm to clients. Similarly, we will also seek *relational* self-reflexivity for accountability as we consider our religious location. We therefore discuss our religious location and its clinical significance with our therapists, supervisors, and consultants. For counselors with a religious orientation, a commonly stated expectation in our codes of ethics is that we maintain relationships of support and accountability with our religious communities (AAPC, 2012). Another excellent, religiously relational resource for our self-reflexivity is the tradition of spiritual direction, a form of spiritual guidance developed in numerous religious and spiritual traditions.

Three domains of self-understanding and the interplay between them are important. Perhaps most obviously, we seek to comprehend the *personal and familial domains* of our religious location. We seek understanding of our personal life philosophy or worldview and consciousness of the particular beliefs that comprise them. Of course, this entails increasing realization of our beliefs about religion, whether we are religious, spiritual, agnostic, atheist, or actively antireligion. But our worldview entails far more, as indicated by the illustrative questions included previously in this chapter, in our reflection on the remoteness of foundational meanings and values. What are your responses to those questions and others like them?

Self-reflexivity in this domain includes attention to the familial aspects of our religious location. What might appear at first glance to be only our personal beliefs are revealed, when we trace the religious aspects of our genealogy, to be weighted with family history and ancestry. Of special value in this aspect of self-reflexivity is the spiritual genogram, because it nuances relative to religion a tool already widely embraced in clinical practice (Frame, 2000). Developing our own genograms with attention to the influence of religion and spirituality in our family history and discussing them in therapy and/or in supervision and consultation groups will substantially advance our cognizance of our religious location. Hodge (2003) describes two other tools—spiritual histories and spiritual life maps—that are designed for use with clients but can easily be adapted for counselors' use to trace the personal and familial domain of our religious location. But any practice that we might suggest to clients as they engage in self-reflexivity relative to their religious location are available to us to use as we work with ourselves, such as retreats, journaling, meditation, prayer, and artistic expression.

We need also to practice self-reflexivity with regard to a second domain of religious location: *the historical, sociopolitical, economic, and global terrain in which we are religiously located.* We investigate the role played by people of our religious location in the long record of interactions between groups inhabiting different religious locations. Especially, when and with whom were people of our religious location agents of violence and injustice or targets? We chart the gains and losses of sociopolitical and economic power and privilege of people in religious locations similar to ours. Just as important, now that migration globalizes almost all of our interactions, is how we are located relative to the history and the contemporary situation of religion around the globe. The clinical tools of spiritual ecomaps and ecograms (Hodge, 2003) can be modified to help us chart these aspects of our own religious location.

A third domain of our religious location crucial for self-reflexive work *is our appraisal of religious plurality*: How do you understand the relationship between the many religious and spiritual traditions, with their sometimes conflicting truth claims? Self-reflexivity in this domain is difficult to practice without the benefit of education in theological and religious studies. However, most major traditions offer books and articles that explore this question and can be used for independent reading. Knitter's (2008) *Introducing Theologies of Religions* differentiates diverse Christian attitudes toward religious plurality and painstakingly charts the strengths and limits of each for navigating a religiously diverse world. It may serve as a prototype for persons of other traditions. Self-reflexive study of books like it will help us avoid the kind of cheap religious tolerance most clients will quickly detect and find alienating.

As noted earlier, if our religious location includes attitudes of religious superiority or exclusivistic beliefs, those likely pose an insurmountable barrier for clinical work related to religious location. But neither is it sufficient to claim religious tolerance blithely. Rather, long consideration is needed to identify how we tend to adjudicate religious differences and conflicts. As mentioned earlier, mystery is at the heart of my theology, and that core value results in large measure from decades of self-reflexivity about religious plurality. But there are countless alternatives, such as some represented by a metaphor widely used in interreligious dialogue: Are we all climbing the same mountain by different paths? Are we climbing different mountains? Are we all on a path but not all climbing mountains?

It is common that pastoral counselors write statements of belief, sometimes called a credo. These are written as part of our process of ordination, AAPC certification, and/or academic work. Such statements depend in large measure on years of self-reflexivity about our religious location. Of course, they reflect the fruits of our self-reflexivity only at the time of writing and not later developments. Examples of such statements can be found in Grefe (2011) and Greider (2013).

Self-Reflexivity Regarding Effects of Our Religious Location on Clients and Clinical Situations

Self-differentiation requires self-reflexivity regarding our relationships. Clinical relationality continuously interweaves our particular religious location with the diverse religious locations of our clients, also with the religious valence of the issues discussed in counseling. Most foundationally, we can detect the relational effects of religious location in our *countertransference*. When Aten (2011) discusses his reaction to his White supremacist Odinist client, one of the first questions he poses to himself is, "Why was I having such a strong reaction?" This is an excellent question for all of us!

The following observations illustrate the use of self-reflexivity about my religious location to establish a reliable baseline that helps me identify when my religiously related countertransference is likely fueling my strong reactions in clinical situations: I know Christianity better than any other religious or spiritual location, intellectually and experientially. Therefore, clinically, when relating to Christians, I perceive similarity and difference at very nuanced levels and frequently have strong cognitive and emotional reactions that I am sure are not hidden. With Christians who appear to share my location within Christianity, these countertransferential reactions are usually positive, unless I discover that I misperceived, and then my countertransference quickly cools or turns negative. Negative projections may seem the more problematic aspect of countertransference, causing us to withdraw or become antagonistic.

However, even if the countertransference remains positive, it can negatively affect my clinical work. I might, for example, run roughshod over the ambivalence a client, supervisee, or other colleague feels toward his or her religious location.

At a deeper level than mere difference and similarity is the psychospiritual and relational valence associated for me with doctrinal disagreement about matters such as atonement, sin and salvation, mission and evangelization. These are important intellectual differences but for me are also laden with experiential memory of painful judgments and exclusion. In the vignette, Luisa's question—"Are you a Christian?"— set off in me a chain reaction of countertransferential remembering that accounted for my having to scramble as I tried to decide how best to respond. By comparison, because I know other religious and spiritual traditions only as an outsider and only at the most superficial levels (if at all), it is relatively easy to show respect for other traditions or to stay composed even when confronted by aspects of other traditions that trouble me. Of course, my religiously related countertransference is made more complex by the transference of others, especially when it is related to their religious location.

The self-reflexivity we carry out concerning our own religious location pays off in another invaluable way as we examine differentials in power and privilege in clinical work. Again offering my own self-reflexivity as an example, in all clinical situations but especially with clients whose religious location has been assailed by Christians, I strive to be mindful of and responsive to questions like these: How is the cultural dominance of Christianity affecting my clients and clinical work? Is the history of Christians being agents or targets of violence pertinent to this particular client's personal or ancestral religious location? What religious privilege do I have in the clinical relationship, whether because of my close relationship to Christianity or perhaps because of my extensive education in theological and religious studies?

Finally, self-reflexivity about our religious location alerts us to how our religious location(s)—especially our personal beliefs—inform our clinical judgment and the positions we take in clinical work. Worthington et al. (2008) offer an illustrative example. They argue that marriage counselors who value "conscientiousness-based virtues" and those who value "warmth-based virtues" (Worthington & Berry, 2005) will "push" clients in different ways, probably unaware of their values-based bias:

> In most marital therapy, the therapist gives little conscious attention to the virtues he or she most strongly advocates. Nevertheless, therapists' personal sense of virtue will often shape some of their therapeutic behaviors. Therapists who are oriented toward the conscientiousness-based virtues will likely push couples toward demonstrating truth, responsibility, honesty, and self-control. Therapists who are oriented toward warmth-based virtues will push their clients to manifest forgiveness, compassion, mercy, and sympathy. (Worthington et al., 2008, p. 20)

We may be able to trace the effects of our religious location "backward": What can you learn about your religious location from the values toward which you tend to "push" clients and supervisees?

Self-Reflexivity Regarding Our Limitations and Offsetting Them

Self-reflexivity about our religious location and its effects on clients and clinical work will inevitably confirm that most of us need remedial education if we are to avoid working outside the scope of our practice. It is fortunate that some form of such education can now be accessed online from anywhere in the world. Those of us who want to specialize in working with religion and spirituality can take advantage of degree programs offered by theological schools, whether in pastoral or spiritually integrative counseling or other areas relevant to clinical practice. Certificate programs and ongoing programs of continuing education offer less intensive alternatives. Face-to-face (in person or video) supervised clinical education is essential. More immediately, when we have clients in religious locations unfamiliar to us, we treat this like any other clinical issue we encounter that is new to us: We immediately research it, whether through reliable Internet or other resources, and/or through consultation.

Also, as with other areas outside our scope of practice, networks of professional collaboration and referral are essential. The clinically certified members of the AAPC comprise a referral and consultation network of clinicians who have expertise relative to religious location; they can be located through the Referral Directory on the AAPC website and through other online directories of clinicians. We also seek consultants from academic settings, for example, faculty at educational institutions that offer accredited degree programs in pastoral counseling. We have a supervisor or peer consultation group with whom we work explicitly on self-reflexivity about religious location, as described earlier in this section of the chapter.

THERAPEUTIC RELATIONALITY: CONNECTION AMID RELIGIOUS DIFFERENCE

Clinical relationship is served by all of the reflections in this chapter. Still, here we will reflect on a few practices that help us address religious location and difference precisely because they do not rely on extensive knowledge about religion. First, meeting constructively amid religious difference encourages more *power sharing*, which may also help offset the negative effects of religious privilege and/or bigotry. For example, it is entirely appropriate to ask clients about their religious location(s), stating explicitly our desire to know about their tradition from their point of view. Aten (2011) calls this a "teach me" approach. Although never to be used in lieu of our own research, this is a "perspective shift" during which counselors make themselves students of their clients' religious knowledge and experience (Aten, 2011, p. 83). The humility involved in sharing power and in risking a perspective shift may also help relativize our religious privilege and reduce the risk of our religious bigotry. In his case study, Aten describes that, after a period of self-reflexivity, although still repelled by Bill's religious location, he was able to approach his client with questions posed with genuine concern and interest. Aten wisely asked, "How did you come to believe what you believe? Are there significant events in your life that have shaped your religious beliefs? How does your faith impact your life?" (Aten, 2011, p. 83). Only then did Bill reveal that he had embraced Odinism after being imprisoned as a teen and experiencing physical assault in prison. Bill aligned himself with Odinism because it was the religious location of the dominant White supremacist culture in the prison, which Bill hoped would protect him. This perspective shift did not change Aten's disagreement with Bill, but it seems to have created in Aten some empathic understanding that allowed the clinical work to go forward. The counselor's willingness to yield power by learning from the client seems to have had connective, therapeutic power.

Sharing power is also a valuable practice with regard to assessment amid religious difference. The diversity of religious location as we have been exploring it dramatically relativizes our capacity for accurate clinical assessment. Our assessment of clients' religious location is ethical only insofar as we have adequate education and supervised clinical training in religion. This limitation is greatly offset, however, by the value of clients engaging in their own assessment of their religious location and its effects. Again calling on clients' greater knowledge of their tradition and their desire to be reflective, we share power by making their assessment at least as important as any we might eventually be able to form. We might ask questions like these: How does your tradition describe well-being and its absence? Are there teachings in your tradition about [the clinical issue]? Are there differing interpretations of that teaching? How do others in your tradition approach [the clinical issue]? How do you assess the influence of your tradition in the ways you are experiencing [the clinical issue]? Sharing the power to assess is not abdication. Rather, our clinical aptitudes allow us to serve as consultants to clients as they seek to grow in understanding of how their religious location both serves and complicates the clinical issues they face.

A second practice that serves us well amid religious difference is that of *language care*, the concept of Bueckert and Schipani (2006) mentioned earlier, arguably the bedrock of care amid difference of any kind. Care for language can deepen therapeutic relationality in at least two directions. We care *for* language. We have an interest in what clients say, in the exact words they choose. When clients say they "believe in God" or "don't believe in God," we express interest in their views of "God" and experience of "believing" and not believing. With Luisa, I bring to her use of the words *divorce* and *shame* the same level of attentiveness I bring to her use of the word *suicidal*, gently inquiring to understand more exactly her meanings and range of experiences, embedded in her choice of those specific words. We also care *through* language by trying to use words in common with clients whenever we can do so with integrity. This can be understood as a form of the multilingualism that deepens therapeutic connection between religiously different clients and counselors. If I strive to learn and speak the language of clients' religious location, although I will often not know what I am saying or may use the language wrongly, my effort will mean a great deal to clients and help our therapeutic relationality to mature.

Finally, therapeutic relationality is served well by allowing differences in our religious locations to *modify the kind of presence we offer* to clients. This practice is more ineffable and thus more difficult to articulate than power sharing and language care. However, arguably its most foundational element is an increased sense of what many religious traditions call *humility*—a modest, unpretentious, unassuming way of engaging. I am not referring to self-debasement, a mere caricature of humility. Mature humility is founded on comprehension of ourselves and our roles in accurate perspective, which serves as a moderating influence that tempers our presence.

When we allow for the possibility that there is value in religious locations other than our own, something of value beyond the truth we perceive, our humanness in relating to clients is not equated with or limited to our being the expert. Counselors and clients meet as companions, all seekers relative to life's most perplexing dilemmas. Respect grows beyond mere tolerance or passive acceptance into a kind of *devotion to the integrity of clients' difference* from us. Our willingness to learn from our clients conveys explicitly that we honor them—their religious location and all aspects of their humanness, as we do our own.

Certainly, because we are providing a professional service, for which clients are likely paying a fee, the focus of the relationship remains on the needs of clients. Moreover, we have a *confident* humility with regard to clients' religious locations: We know our competencies and that they are valuable, but we also see them in perspective. Counselors remain ethically responsible guides on this path of seeking. But in clinical situations where religious difference is especially influential, clients sometimes guide, too. We feel just as responsible but not as big and imposing. Our presence is now comfortably relativized alongside clients' knowledge and responsibilities for their own therapeutic work. Both counselor and client have authority and competence.

Consciousness of the extent of religious diversity, the bounds of our expertise, the profound questions and unsolvable paradoxes of clinical work, the ambiguity and mystery of life—consciousness of all this *humanizes* our presence. More consciousness of our limits and thus of our vulnerability lends to our presence greater mutuality and authenticity. In this kind of therapeutic presence, our interactions with clients are tenderized. Counselor and client may feel and show their tears more readily. Both of us can speak more readily of our emotions, uncertainties, of seeking what we have not yet found. We are likely to talk more about transience, transcendence, mortality. In the midst of these acknowledgments, we and our clients may have a sense of awe, the sacred, even holiness.

Indeed, honoring religious difference and acknowledging mystery and inscrutability tend to cultivate in our presence *a quality of reverence*, most definitely a *reverent curiosity* offered to our clients. Reverent curiosity is an outward expression of our devotion to the integrity of clients' difference from us. Reverent curiosity is expressed in noninvasive but determined movement toward connection with clients, especially in areas of existential divergence. It is a gentle inquisitiveness that is brave and motivated enough to move toward our most profound differences with clients, precisely because mystery allows that something of spiritual value may be encountered other than where we are located, other than where we expect to find it. Reverent curiosity does not resolve our differences. It does, however, decenter those differences. It impels us to move especially toward those with whom we disagree vehemently, with a commitment to try to comprehend how another human could value something abhorrent to us. It is a spirit of reverence for the mystery of the difference, not necessarily the difference itself. It enables connection when we cannot afford to be divided by our differences.

This chapter has argued that particularities and differences in religious location are ever present between counselors and clients and, with appropriate attention, can increase the profundity of clinical relationships. The variety of insights and practices explored here suggest that whatever our positions relative to religion, those differences do not have to divide us but can be acknowledged and inquisitively engaged to open up new ways to connect with ourselves and with clients. Clients such as the Butler family and Luisa, professionals such as Joshua and his supervisors, counselors such as Aliyah, myself, and you—we embody different locations relative to religion precisely because we share but have not mastered the human condition. We meet amid a common existential journey about which we often do not agree. Yet, this brief, challenging human existence leaves all of us seekers to one degree or another. Our different religious locations, whatever they are, can serve us well, if we allow them to inform or perhaps even relativize our therapeutic theories and goals. What seems to be only disagreement about religion can turn out also to be agreement that all of us are searching. Our divergences can impel us to search together, for something *more*, perhaps something like wisdom.

REFLECTION QUESTIONS

1. Engaging in the self-reflexivity described in the chapter, what are some important aspects of your religious location—your background, attitudes, and practices with regard to religion?

2. How might your religious location be affecting your current clinical practice, giving special attention to power dynamics and deeply held meanings and values?
3. In light of the competencies and ethical codes discussed in the chapter, what steps can you take to be a more effective clinician amid religious difference?

REFERENCES

American Association of Pastoral Counselors. (2012). *Code of ethics.* Retrieved June 2, 2014, from http://www.aapc.org/media/142577/aapc_code_of_ethics.pdf

American Counseling Association. (2014). *ACA code of ethics.* Alexandria, VA: Author. Retrieved July 1, 2014, from http://www.counseling.org/resources/aca-code-of-ethics.pdf

American Psychological Association. (2010). *Ethical principles of psychologists and code of conduct.* Retrieved June 1, 2014, from http://www.apa.org/ethics/code/principles.pdf

Association for Spiritual, Ethical, and Religious Values in Counseling. (2009). *Competencies for addressing spiritual and religious issues in counseling.* Retrieved June 2, 2014, from http://www.aservic.org/resources/spiritual-competencies/

Aten, J. D. (2011). Addressing religious differences in therapy: A case study from behind bars. *Journal of Psychology and Christianity, 30,* 81–84.

Bueckert, L. D., & Schipani, D. S. (2006). Interfaith spiritual caregiving: The case for language care. In L. D. Bueckert & D. S. Schipani (Eds.), *Spiritual caregiving in the hospital: Windows to chaplaincy ministry* (pp. 245–263). Kitchener, Canada: Pandora Press, in association with the Institute of Mennonite Studies.

Frame, M. W. (2000). The spiritual genogram in family therapy. *Journal of Marital & Family Therapy, 26,* 211–216. doi:10.1111/j.1752-0606.2000.tb00290.x

Grefe, D. (2011). *Encounters for change: Interreligious cooperation in the care of individuals and communities.* Eugene, OR: Wipf and Stock.

Greider, K. J. (2011). Religiously plural persons: Multiplicity and care of souls. In I. Noth, C. Morgenthaler, & K. J. Greider (Eds.), *Pastoralpsychologie und religionspsychologie im dialog [Pastoral psychology and psychology of religion in dialogue]* (pp. 119–135). Stuttgart, Germany: Kohlhammer.

Greider, K. J. (2013). Do justice, love kindness, walk humbly: A Christian perspective on spiritual care. In D. S. Schipani (Ed.), *Multifaith views in spiritual care* (pp. 85–108). Kitchener, Canada: Pandora.

Hanada, J. C. (2012). "Listening to the Dharma": Integrating Buddhism into a multifaith health care environment. In J. S. Watts & Y. Tomatsu (Eds.), *Buddhist care for the dying and bereaved* (pp. 249–269). Boston, MA: Wisdom.

Hill, P. C., & Hall, T. W. (2002). Relational schemas in processing one's image of God and self. *Journal of Psychology and Christianity, 21,* 365–373.

Hodge, D. R. (2003). *Spiritual assessment: Handbook for helping professionals.* Botsford, CT: North American Association of Christians in Social Work.

Knitter, P. F. (2008). *Introducing theologies of religions.* Maryknoll, NY: Orbis.

McIntosh, P. (1988). *White privilege and male privilege: A personal account of coming to see correspondences through work in women's studies* (Working paper 189). Wellesley, MA: Center for Research on Women.

Negy, C., & Ferguson, C. J. (2004). Religious bigotry: The neglected "ism" in multicultural psychology and therapy. In C. Negy (Ed.), *Cross-cultural psychotherapy: Toward a critical understanding of diverse clients* (pp. 61–73). Reno, NV: Bent Tree Press.

Onedera, J. D., & Greenwalt, B. C. (2008). Introduction to religion and marriage and family counseling. In J. D. Onedera (Ed.), *The role of religion in marriage and family counseling* (pp. 3–13). New York, NY: Routledge.

Prothero, S. (2010). *God is not one: The eight rival religions that run the world—And why their differences matter.* New York, NY: HarperCollins.

Schlosser, L. Z. (2003). Christian privilege: Breaking a sacred taboo. *Journal of Multicultural Counseling and Development, 31,* 44–51. doi:10.1002/j.2161-1912.2003.tb00530.x

U.S. Commission on International Religious Freedom. (2013). *Annual report 2013*. Washington, DC: Author. Retrieved July 2, 2013, from http://www.uscirf.gov/sites/default/files/resources/2013%20USCIRF%20Annual%20Report%20(2).pdf

Walsh, F. (2010). Spiritual diversity: Multifaith perspectives in family therapy. *Family Process, 49*, 330–348. doi:10.1111/j.1545-5300.2010.01326.x

Worthington, E. L., & Berry, J. W. (2005). Character development, virtues, and vices. In W. R. Miller & H. D. Delaney (Eds.), *Human nature, motivation, and change: Judeo-Christian perspectives on psychology* (pp. 145–164). Washington, DC: APA Books.

Worthington, E. L., Hook, J. N., Wade, N. G., Miller, A. J., & Sharp, C. B. (2008). The effects of a therapist's religion on the marriage therapist and marriage counseling. In J. D. Onedera (Ed.), *The role of religion in marriage and family counseling* (pp. 17–34). New York, NY: Routledge.

15

EARNING CLOSENESS WITH OUR MAKER: A TORAH-BASED APPROACH TO COUNSELING

The moral and ritual system of Judaism is meant to govern all areas of daily life, from how Jews pray to how they conduct business, from how Jews dress to how they interact with their families. So, too, the wisdom of Judaism, as contained in the reservoir of divine teachings known as the Torah, is intended to guide the Jew's outlook in all areas in life, including one's vocation. Indeed, for the Jewish mental health counselor, the Torah provides a holistic method of facilitating well-being in clients that has much in common with pastoral counseling at large. This chapter aims to elucidate the workings of "Torah therapy" by drawing on what Cheston (2000) describes as the three points of focus essential to all counselors: the counselor's way of understanding clients, the counselor's way of being with clients, and the counselor's way of intervening in the therapeutic process. The chapter concludes by comparing and contrasting Torah therapy and pastoral counseling as it is traditionally understood.

It should be noted that the following chapter reflects the outlook of Orthodox Jewish counselors; it is not necessarily representative of all denominations of the Jewish faith. Indeed, there are several subcategories of Judaism, each with an individualized approach to Jewish outlook and ritual. For their part, Orthodox Jews believe that God gave the Torah, His timeless set of life instructions, to the Jewish People at Mount Sinai. Accordingly, Orthodox Jews place the highest premium on serving God by adhering to the statutes of His Torah. For Orthodox Jews, though, the goal of Torah is not unthinking submission and robotic performance of God's commandments. Instead, Orthodox Judaism and the Torah therapy from which it stems encourage a passionate quest on the part of human beings to reveal the greatness of God in all of their challenges and life tasks, no matter how difficult or seemingly mundane.

TORAH THERAPY: A WAY OF UNDERSTANDING

To acquire an understanding of Torah therapy, it is important to first discuss the purpose of Creation from a Jewish perspective, as the two subjects overlap. According to Jewish sources, God created the world to serve "as an arena in which human beings could face the challenges of spiritual elevation" (Mishell, 1991, p. 24). This process of spiritual and ethical growth, known in Hebrew as *tshuva* or "return," is sometimes misunderstood to be corrective action in response to sin. As Bechhofer (2013) insists, however, *tshuva* is actually independent of transgression but is rather a "lifelong process of self-improvement directed towards returning the world to its ultimate perfection" (p. 15). Fundamentally, therefore, the work of the counselor, as he assists clients in becoming "more productive and greater actualized" human beings, is essential to the general goal of Creation (Bechhofer, 2013, p. 52).

According to Torah sources, God has several objectives in calling human beings to lives of personal growth. First, by creating human beings in an underdeveloped state and demanding that they elevate themselves, God ensures a system whereby people can accrue merit for their growth. According to Luzzato (1999), God's insistence that one must *earn* one's spiritual keep emanates from His abundant kindness. "God's wisdom . . . decreed that for such (reward) to be perfect, the one enjoying it must be its master. He must have earned it for himself, and not given it accidentally" (p. 39). To further ensure the necessity for growth, God sees to it that each person receives a fundamental challenge (or series of challenges) with which he must struggle during his lifetime. In Hebrew, this challenge is known as one's *tikkun*, or soul correction, and often requires outside assistance to accomplish successfully (Y. Bergman, personal communication, November 4, 2013). According to Lamden (2006), the significance of the soul correction, as well as the therapy that often accompanies it, cannot be understated for "the world around us benefits from our personal *tikkun* . . . Torah encourages us to [elevate] the world by working on ourselves" (p. 132).

Indeed, this notion of *tikkun* is extremely important for it alludes to a key distinction between the Torah-based therapist and his secular counterpart. Whereas the secular counselor works to facilitate change so that a client might enjoy a higher quality of life, the Torah-based clinician pursues a goal that is more expansive in nature. In Jewish thought, only a life of *tshuva* justifies mankind's existence, for the more a person grows and thus adheres to the will of God, the more he or she becomes a part of God's master plan (Twerski, 2012). At the core of Jewish counseling, therefore, is the hope that with enough effort and determination to transcend their challenges, clients will claim their rightful place in God's unfolding story of history and uplift the world in the process.

The second objective of mankind's task to grow has to do with *tshuva's* necessary component of character development. When human beings develop the latent godliness within and conduct their lives with the pristine virtues of their Maker, they create the possibility of relationship with God. As Lieberman (2008) puts it, "The more we resemble our Creator, by emulating His ways, the greater is our connection to God. This is because closeness is not measured in terms of physical space but through levels of awareness that manifest from similarities" (p. 135). From this point of view, God commands us to elevate ourselves so that we might actualize the most fervent wish of our psyche—to be close to our Divine Source. Indeed, "the [most] basic human instinct inherent in all of mankind [is] to reunite with our common Creator" (Lamden, 2006, p. 21). This last point is essential for the Jewish clinician to know, for no matter what the presenting problem is that a client brings to therapy, ultimately, every client feels distant from God. Torah therapy and, for that matter, Judaism in general are considered God-given systems to repair the painful breach that comes with being human (Lamden, 2006).

A third objective of man's task to actualize himself has to do with moving our world toward transcendence. According to M'Liadi (1979), the *neshomo* or godly soul that God places within each human being is literally a piece of God Himself. This is a tremendous responsibility, Roll (Y. Roll, personal communication, November 9, 2013) insists, for if human beings recognize that they are created in the image of God and uplift themselves accordingly, they become capable of channeling God's presence into an otherwise empty and immoral world. From a Jewish perspective, though, it is not enough to merely introduce God's light into this world. Instead, the zenith of Creation occurs when all people freely choose to dedicate their lives to God, disseminating His teachings and serving His children. From this perspective, the purpose of Creation has to do with what a mere mortal can provide to God: nothing less than a partner with whom God might preside over His Kingdom. Indeed, at the ultimate level of spiritual development, the will of human beings and the will of God are one (Mishell, 1991).

There is a large gap, however, separating the gratification-based orientation of childhood and the absolute devotion to one's Maker that stands at the height of Creation. Mishell (1991) stated that there are actually five developmental stages for the soul, beginning with the "elemental" or physical level of the soul, whose primary needs are survival and self-satisfaction. The next level is the "social level" of the soul, where a person works to develop his sense of identity, especially in relationship to others, and of achievement. The third level of the soul is the "religious level," where one unifies one's life into a spiritual and altruistic whole. It is here that one makes a fundamental shift from taking to giving, a significant milestone in one's task to emulate and thus earn closeness to one's Maker.

The two highest levels of spiritual development, the "transcendent" level and "absolute level," respectively, are purely spiritual in nature and involve increasingly higher levels of devotion to serving God's children, disseminating God's Torah, and assisting in the fulfillment of God's Divine Plan (Mishell, 1991). In contradistinction to some schools of therapy, however, Torah makes clear that spiritual development is not the result of some primitive biological drive but rather the outcome of a personal choice, fueled by the deepest yearning of one's soul.

In His wisdom, however, God saw fit to create an oppositional force within human beings to militate against their completing the very mission of growth that God calls them to do. This force, known in Hebrew as the *yetzer hara* (evil inclination) is identified with the human ego and resides in the "elemental" component of the soul described previously in this chapter (Lieberman, 2008). Although the *yetzer hara* is denounced in the Talmud in the most negative of terms, it is also seen as perhaps the greatest example of God's kindness, as only in the presence of the propensity to do evil does one's quest to improve one's life become real and meaningful. Without an alternative to spiritual growth—that is, without a choice between soul-based growth and ego-based stagnation—there would be no possibility for reward or punishment, condemnation or praise. According to Mishell (1991), "If the 'self' were nothing more than a string of predetermined responses we would have neither the opportunity to elevate ourselves nor the responsibility to do so" (p. 55). Free will, or the independence to choose on one's own whether or not one will engage in the process of spiritual elevation, is accordingly one of the keys of Creation.

According to Lieberman (2008), free will is actually that which makes human beings most like their Maker:

> What do we mean when we speak of man being created in the image of God? It means that human beings have the freedom to forge their own reality. In that way we resemble God, Who is completely free and independent. (p. 39)

With respect to Torah therapy, the ability to rise above one's painful circumstances stands at the height of free will. When, on the other hand, one wallows in the upset or unfairness of past events, one forfeits his Divine birthright of free will and, by definition, sinks into emotional disease.

Indeed, the notion that human beings are given the freedom to fashion their own attitudes and behaviors is at the core of Torah therapy. With the recognition that each client is completely free to construct a subjective "life script" or way of interacting in the world, Torah-based clinicians can quickly dispel the notion that external circumstances are to blame for a client's pathology, difficult though a client's past may have been. On the contrary, it is only when we assume that the client is completely responsible for everything he is doing, feeling, and thinking in the present that the hope of therapeutic change exists. Lieberman (2008) summed up the matter of change thusly: "All positive change [for a client] begins with some version of, 'I am responsible and nothing in my life will change for the better unless I change'" (p. 41). Accordingly, one of the most important goals of the Torah-based therapist is to help clients assume increasingly greater amounts of responsibility for their feelings, actions, and lives.

Facilitating change is not easy, however. Lamden (2006) stated that emotional and spiritual disease stem from clients' "negative life scripts," highly individualized series of thoughts, feelings, and attitudes that human beings create as children to make sense of their experiences. As youngsters, Lamden tells us, we "define ourselves according to the reactions we solicit from those surrounding us, accompanied by our personal interpretation of these reactions" (p. 11). When a small child who lacks adult-based thinking sees his mother angry, for example, he may egocentrically conclude that he is the cause of his mother's moodiness (Lamden, 2006). With enough repetition of this scenario, a child may eventually come to believe that he is defective and "no good" in general.

Although the conclusions that one draws about oneself may have no basis in reality, one will behave throughout life as though one's self-image is completely accurate and truthful (Lamden, 2006). A child who comes to see himself as incapable, for example, will not take the risks necessary to achieve great things. Worse, the child (and later, the adult) may sabotage any success that he does experience in an attempt to maintain the apparent "truth" of one's self-image, no matter what the personal cost. Even so, it seems that God set up the world in such a way that almost everyone enters adulthood with the baggage of a stubbornly ingrained "life script" to overcome (Lamden, 2006).

> This is God's will. By allowing man to construct a subjective—and therefore false—self-image, God enables him to reach that point at which he is equally drawn to good (which is his basic Divine nature), or evil (which results from a negative self-image). (Lamden, 2006, p. 65)

Indeed, much of the growth that God calls human beings to do is to escape their self-made prisons constructed in childhood. To understand better the mechanics of negative "life scripts" as well as how to treat them, it is worthwhile to examine the basic structures of the psyche according to the Torah. Luzzato (1999) identified three primary components of the human soul, or, for our purposes, psyche: the *nefesh*, which stores man's baser instincts and drives; the *ruach*, which is the place of emotion; and the *neshomo* or godly soul, which is the seat of higher cognition and transcendence. According to Mishell (1991), the *nefesh*, *ruach*, and *neshomo* align with the "elemental," "social," and "religious" levels of the soul mentioned earlier.

As children lack the higher cognitive abilities of the *neshomo* and eschew the painful emotions that are registered by the *ruach*, they tend to operate from the *nefesh* and its primal needs for survival, comfort, and gratification. Accordingly, when children experience painful feelings associated with the *ruach*, the *nefesh*-based ego steps in to provide psychological protection, repressing uncomfortable feelings with negative self-assessments, cognitive distortions, and other dysfunctional defense mechanisms.

Although the resulting "life script" serves to protect the child from unbearable emotional pain, it also keeps the child (and later, the adult) locked in the *nefesh*, unable to move past the elemental level of spiritual development and stunted in terms of one's duty to become the caring and altruistic adult that God calls one to be (Y. Roll, personal communication, November 9, 2013).

One of the prime tasks of Torah therapy, therefore, is helping clients to process the disowned emotional energy of their childhoods. To make better decisions in the present, one must be willing to rise above the defensive impulses of *nefesh* and ascend into the emotional pain of the *ruach*. Stated differently, at the core of Torah therapy is the goal of helping clients to learn more about themselves, including their deepest feelings and needs from which they may be long estranged (Lamden, 2006). Although painful, such emotional discovery and integration help clients to heal the initial "rupture" between themselves and God, paradoxically, by helping them accept that such a breach occurred in the first place. With the previously repressed pain of the *ruach* successfully released and the need for the psychological defenses of the *nefesh* obviated, clients can focus their attention on fulfilling the desires of their true, *neshomo* selves: ever increasing spiritual growth and connection with God, solidified through the learning of the Torah and observance of *mitzvohs* (commandments; Lamden, 2006).

It must be made clear, however, that therapy from a Jewish perspective is about more than simply releasing the emotional pain of the past. Instead, the Torah-based therapist makes a concerted effort to help clients to reconstruct past hurts in a positive light (Lamden, 2006). With sufficient work, the client comes to see that the painful circumstances of his life "are not arbitrary arrows of some cruel fate. Since God is their source, they must have meaning and purpose" (Lamden, 2006, p. 277). The process of reframing one's past, known in Hebrew as *mituk hadin* (sweetening the judgment), reveals the Jewish belief in God's ultimate goodness, even through the most painful of circumstances. As the Talmud makes clear, Jews are to "bless God for the bad just as they bless Him for the good" (Babylonian Talmud, Tractate Brachos, 54a). Through successful therapy, one will come to accept one's sufferings with equanimity, even appreciation, knowing that past hardships were essential to the unique mission of growth and contribution for which one came to this world in the first place. In a certain sense, therefore, Torah therapy seeks to reconnect clients with the reality of God's innate goodness, as well as their own.

TORAH THERAPY: A WAY OF BEING

As facilitating the acceptance of responsibility by a client is one of the overarching goals of Torah therapy, the stance taken by the Jewish clinician is that of an equal helper and not one of supreme authority. As clients must ultimately take responsibility for their lives, clinicians must be careful to leave room for clients to exercise their own choices and to learn to trust their own feelings. One helpful model of involvement that comes to mind is that of labor coach. Although the labor coach provides presence and empathy through the pain of childbirth, it is the expectant mother who must ultimately give birth. So is the case with counseling: The clinician's goal is to support the client through the discomfort of spiritual and emotional growth, knowing full well that the client's choice to transcend his negative patterns is ultimately his alone.

In terms of how a clinician actually sits with a client, Torah sources strongly corroborate the validity of the counseling approach espoused by Carl Rogers (Bechhofer, 2013). As Bechhofer (2013) explains, Rogerian theory, as it touts the importance of empathy, unconditional positive regard, and congruence, correlates closely with the

Torah definition of friendship. In the Torah sense of the word, a friend views his companions favorably, endeavors to bring them to higher levels of truth by sharing feelings and values, and, perhaps most important, shares in their joys and sorrows, successes and failures. For the Torah-based therapist, empathy is particularly critical to success, as it constitutes "the basis of understanding all human conditions, and the prime qualification for leadership in Judaism at all times in history" (Bechhofer, 2013, p. 41).

According to Lamden (2006), empathy, unconditional positive regard, and the other features of a Torah way of being are about more than simply making the therapeutic encounter more pleasant. Instead, one's way of interacting with a client may, for the first time in the client's life, alert the client to his inestimable worth. Indeed, Lamden (2006) tells us, the "speech, body language, and eyes . . . should help to bring across the idea that the patient is a worthy and unique person, made in the likeness of God, innately pure and beautiful" (p. 242).

Moreover, it is only by offering nonjudgmental understanding of a client's problematic lifestyle that change happens at all. "First, (the client) must be comprehended in depth. Then, when we have gained his trust . . . the change evolves almost naturally" (Lamden, 2006, p. 246). In general, a Torah way of being, by offering absolute attentiveness and acceptance, amounts to "an unprecedented experience of being interesting and of value . . . one of the greatest compliments that a person can receive" (Lamden, 2006, p. 247). In the gentle space of the safety provided by the counselor, the client can, perhaps, feel comfortable enough to "reveal himself truthfully for the first time" (p. 247).

In sum, Lamden (2006) contended that the counselor's desire to see past the client's prickly exterior and make contact with innate goodness within is perhaps the most therapeutic part of Torah therapy, for it is the bond of a "deep human relationship which is our primary goal. Solving people's problems is secondary" (p. 248).

TORAH THERAPY: A WAY OF INTERVENING

As important as the clinician is to facilitating a client's progress, Torah therapy maintains that the therapist is but a messenger, an agent through whom God delivers help to the psychologically ill (Lamden, 2006). Accordingly, it is incumbent "upon all those who suffer, physically or mentally, to seek help from the one and only healer—God" (p. 117). The Torah-based clinician must likewise bear in mind the limits of his power. The necessity and duty for both client and counselor to continually ask for God's assistance, therefore, is imperative throughout all stages of therapy.

In addition to blessing the efforts of clients and clinicians, God involves Himself directly in a client's recovery by providing life tests to clients whereby they are called on to rise above different aspects of their negative "life scripts." Known in Hebrew as a *nisayon*, the life test represents a Divine invitation to human beings to create within themselves new abilities by exercising their free will in better directions. The Torah-based therapist would do well therefore to bring to clients' attention the strong possibility that God will test them in the areas in which they are weakest, particularly when their therapists are out of town.

Jewish sources describe the front line in the battle to overcome one's negative life script as the "point of choice" (Dessler, 1964; Lamden, 2006). Anything "below" one's point of choice, whether good or bad, represents one's present, automatic life script, whereas anything "above" one's point of choice represents as yet, unconquered spiritual territory (Lamden, 2006). The client would be wise, therefore, to greet each set of difficulties with a sense of wonder and gratitude rather than anger or discouragement. When a person chooses to accept the Jewish maxim that "everything is from God," he can look for the opportunity for growth inherent in each life test, thus raising his "point of choice" even higher.

Indeed, one's use of free will is as important to recovery as any other factor. The 13th-century anonymous work known as the *Sefer HaChinuch*, or *The Book of Mitzvah Training*, presents one of the most important Jewish axioms about the human condition: "A person is conditioned according to his actions" (*Sefer HaChinuch*, 1990, p. 16). In other words, one's behavior has an unparalleled impact on the heart and mind. One simply cannot persist in dysfunctional behavior for 6 days a week, come to therapy for 1 hour on the seventh day of the week, and hope to see improvement.

What this means for Torah-based intervention is that the regular assignment of homework to clients is essential to the success of treatment. As Lamden (2006) stated, "The patient's improvement is proportional to the effort he invests in the periods between therapy sessions" (p. 254). On a simple level, therefore, homework assignments are critical to keeping a client engaged in, and responsible for, his recovery. On a deeper level, homework assignments encourage clients to practice the skills learned in therapy throughout the week, thus reinforcing behaviors that are most likely to have a therapeutic effect on one's psyche.

One of the most simple but important homework assignments that a therapist can give a client is practice with deep breathing. The Torah (Exodus 6:9) teaches us that shortness of breath is a telltale sign of emotional distress. Deep breathing, on the other hand, as it "serves to reorganize and reunite our spiritual, mental, and emotional energies," allows a person to rise above the stress of his external circumstances and find peace in the present moment (Lamden, 2006, pp. 252–253). Perhaps this is why the Hebrew word for soul, *neshama*, is so closely related to the Hebrew word for breath, *nashima*, for it is through focusing the breath that one is able to overcome the anxieties of the animalistic *nefesh* and reconnect with one's true, spiritual self. Another benefit of breath work is that by breathing into an area affected by emotional and even physical pain, one can diminish his discomfort and promote continued healing (Lamden, 2006).

According to Roll (Y. Roll, personal communication, November 9, 2013), the primary work of short-term Torah therapy is to dispense with the emotional insecurity of the ego-based "life script" and to embrace the self-esteem and self-confidence of the *neshomo*. As Roll (Y. Roll, personal communication, November 9, 2013) explained, all emotional disease is rooted in ego-generated anxiety. Anxiety, in turn, stems from a lack of awareness of the greatness of one's true soul-self. Accordingly, when one is plugged into the reality of his God-given abilities and virtues, pathology melts away. To enable clients to recognize and honor their soul-selves, Roll employs what he calls "identity therapy," an effective system of Torah-based interventions used to treat anxiety at the *neshama* (cognitive), *ruach* (emotional), and *nefesh* (physical, behavioral) levels of the psyche.

At the cognitive or *neshomo* level of the soul, identity therapy uses an intervention called the "Wheel of Strengths," a handy tool that organizes one's personality strengths into six areas: intellect, social skills, spirituality, character traits, family, and accomplishments. While in session, Roll prompts clients to identify their strengths in the six respective areas while he completes the wheel. For example, if a client says, "I was at the top of my class in high school," Roll might write "high school scholar" under the "accomplishments" section of the wheel. A completed "Wheel of Strengths" provides clients with a handy weapon to be used against the self-esteem–depleting attacks of the *yetzer hara*, whose primary goal is to sap victims of their power to persevere through the challenges of life.

The fourth area listed, "traits," is particularly spiritual. It refers to the "Thirteen Attributes of God's Mercy" as described in the Torah (Exodus 34:6–7). As Roll (Y. Roll, personal communication, November 9, 2013) explained, God deposits one, two, or three of His signature traits into each and every person. When a client identifies the godly trait(s) that he carries, he can immediately experience a greater sense of self-esteem, knowing that God entrusts him with a piece of Himself, as well as responsibility for God's tasking him with the duty of expressing this particular trait properly.

Combating the insidious effect of cognitive distortions, or patterns of faulty thinking, is another intervention at the *neshomo* level of the psyche. Whether the cognitive distortion in question is "discounting the positive," whereby a person ignores all of the good in a given situation and focuses exclusively on what's negative, or "emotional reasoning," whereby a person decides that reality is what he *feels* it is, cognitive distortions preclude positive ways of thinking and coping with life (Y. Roll, personal communication, November 9, 2013). For the purposes of therapy, it is important that therapists educate their clients about the presence of cognitive distortions, as many clients do not realize that cognitive distortions represent unhealthy and unrealistic thinking in the first place.

The Torah maintains that the way one thinks about a given situation is critical to the way one feels and responds to it. From a Jewish point of view, perspective is not a matter of looking at reality positively or negatively. Rather, according to Lieberman (2008), one's choice of perspective is what *creates* the reality. The power to create one's reality cannot be understated for in the power of perspective is the key to coping effectively in any situation. If, for example, a person chooses to see unpleasant events as personal affronts to his dignity, then life becomes a most frustrating struggle. If, however, a person chooses to view the same difficulties as opportunities for spiritual growth, then life becomes a highly meaningful journey of personal development and drawing closer to God.

At the emotional or *ruach* level of the soul, Roll (Y. Roll, personal communication, November 9, 2013) introduced several more interventions, including diaphragmatic breathing and guided imagery. When one's feelings are hurt, diaphragmatic breathing can be employed to restore a person's sense of calm and balance. Similarly, guided imagery, whereby one imagines a favorite accomplishment or destination, can offset negative emotions in the present with positive memories of the past. Finally, Roll (Y. Roll, personal communication, November 9, 2013) recommended that clients maintain an awareness of what is at stake in terms of the responses they choose in the presence of difficult feelings. Simply put, the choice to rise above hurt feelings keeps one rooted in one's *neshomo*, whereas the choice to give in to anger turns a person over to *nefesh* and the body. One must remember one's general mission to reflect God's light into this world. When one responds to difficult situations by filling oneself with egocentric bouts of rage, one cannot fulfill one's spiritual duty.

Finally, identity therapy targets the *nefesh*, the seat of one's actions. Roll (Y. Roll, personal communication, November 9, 2013) recommended that to plug into the power of the godly self, one must keep one's focus on the present. The only power we have, according to Roll, is over *our* thoughts, feelings, and actions, in the now. When we focus on controlling outcomes or on the feelings of others, we grow egocentric and weak. On a deeper level, focusing on things over which one has no control represents a lack of faith as it indicates the individual's belief that he would run the world better than God. Focusing on one's "circle of influence," therefore, keeps one rooted in faith, power, and emotional health.

Although identity therapy is extremely effective, it is not recommended when a client's functioning is severely impaired by psychosis. As a general rule, the deeper a client's pathology, the stronger the need to engage in "inner child" emotional cleansing associated with long-term work (Y. Roll, personal communication, November 9, 2013). Lamden (2006) described the trajectory of longer term therapy as a sort of inverted funnel, whereby a client begins by discussing relatively superficial present relationships, followed by "middle-level" relationships with childhood friends and acquaintances, and concluded with the parental relationships that were most influential over the development of one's negative life script. There, at the core of our pain, we realize that whatever our experience with mother and father, there is an even deeper source of relational failure in our psyche: our relationship with ourselves and, by extension, God (Lamden, 2006).

As Lamden (2006) stated, "Treatment must deal with one's self-image, within which his emotions are rooted, as well as with man's connection with God, which is the basic component of his spiritual makeup" (p. 105). At the core of one's being, a client can choose to embrace the long-repressed feelings of loneliness, separation, and heartbreak at the core of one's separation from God, while simultaneously letting go of the negative self-image that for so many years blocked them. It is this sense of reunification with oneself and with God that signifies a profound step in one's healing, for as Lamden (2006) noted, "Reconnecting man with God and with his own higher self is what health is all about . . . so does the pain gradually disappear" (p. 105).

In summary, we are yanked away from our heavenly union with God and thrust into the heartbreaking state of separateness that characterizes our world. This is painful, to be sure, although our distance affords us an awesome opportunity: Through our own choice to transcend our emotional wounds, we can *earn* permanent closeness with our Maker. Lieberman (2008) sums up the matter of *tshuva*, the Divine command to transcend one's negative life script thusly: "When we break a bone in our body, the set bone, once properly healed, is usually thicker and even stronger than the uninjured bone surrounding the break" (p. 94). So it is with life, each of us is "broken" in certain respects; the work of therapy and of life in general is for us to repair the break and, in so doing, to grow much stronger than we would ever have otherwise.

TORAH THERAPY AND PASTORAL COUNSELING

What distinguishes pastoral counselors from their secular counterparts is the pastoral counselor's interest in the "transcendent strivings" that clients bring to counseling (Estadt, 1991). "When clients deal with issues of forgiveness, conversion, surrender, faith, trust, love, and commitment . . . [that] is uniquely pastoral" (Estadt, 1991, p. 7). According to Estadt (1991), one general goal of pastoral counseling is a "threefold reconciliation," a reconciliation within oneself, with others, and with God (p. 10). This "threefold reconciliation" overlaps with the objective of making peace with oneself and with God that is central to Torah therapy. Accordingly, Torah therapy and pastoral counseling share a common goal: to increase the harmony in one's life.

Torah therapy intersects with pastoral counseling in other ways, too. According to Townsend (2009), the spiritual component of pastoral counseling has to do with " 'big picture' questions or universal human issues of mystery, purpose, and meaning" (p. 94). Torah therapy, in its insistence that part of healing is finding the good in painful events, shares this goal of making meaning. At the same time, Orthodox Jews recognize that there are some events in life whose meaning we simply cannot know during our lifetimes; in this sense, Torah therapy embraces the sense of mystery characteristic of pastoral counseling at large.

What perhaps distinguishes Torah therapy from pastoral counseling is Lamden's (2006) insistence that one need not be a professional counselor to be a Torah therapist. Instead, one must be a faithful servant of God, well versed in traditional Jewish law and philosophy, and someone who has had his or her share of successfully navigating the ups and downs of life. In fact, Lamden insists that Torah therapy need not even be a weekly session of counseling. "Rather, [it] is living life in the service of (God), with emphasis on offering help and counsel to whomever seeks it" (p. 287). By contrast, one who wishes to work as a pastoral counselor must have the state-mandated credentials to do so.

In sum, Torah therapy overlaps with pastoral counseling in large measure but not perfectly, for whereas the government places educational and licensing demands on the pastoral counselor, one may reach the status of Torah therapist less formally and officially.

REFLECTION QUESTIONS

1. According to the author, "Whereas the secular counselor works to facilitate change so that a client might enjoy a higher quality of life, the Torah-based clinician pursues a goal that is more expansive in nature." This goal is "a life of *tshuva*" or ethical and spiritual growth as part of a return to God. Are the goals of the secular counselor and the Torah-based counselor distinctive or related? How so?
2. The author draws parallels between the Torah-based counselor's "way of being" and a Rogerian approach to counseling. Explain the similarities in the two approaches.
3. Torah-based therapy and pastoral counseling, according to the author, both embrace a sense of mystery. How do you understand the author's use of the term *mystery*? How does mystery influence your own counseling practice?

REFERENCES

Bechhofer, Y. G. (2013). *Judaism and counseling: Comparisons and perspectives*. Monsey, NY: CreateSpace Independent Publishing Platform.

Cheston, S. E. (2000). A new paradigm for teaching counseling theory and practice. *Counselor Education and Supervision, 39*(4), 254–269. doi:10.1002/j.1556-6978.2000.tb01236.x

Dessler, E. (1964). *A letter from Eliyahu*. Bnei Brak, Israel: Committee for the Publication of the Writings of E. E. Dessler.

Estadt, B. K. (1991). Profile of a pastoral counselor. In B. K. Estadt, M. C. Blanchette, & J. R. Compton (Eds.), *Pastoral counseling* (2nd ed., pp. 1–17). Englewood Cliffs, NJ: Prentice Hall.

Lamden, E. (2006). *Torah therapy*. Jerusalem, Israel: Feldheim.

Lieberman, D. (2008). *Real power*. Lakewood, NJ: Viter.

Luzzato, M. (1999). *The way of God*. Nanuet, NY: Feldheim.

Mishell, J. (1991). *Beyond your ego*. Lakewood, NJ: C.I.S. Publishers and Distributers.

M'Liadi, S. Z. (1979). *The Tanya*. Brooklyn, NY: Kehot Publication Society.

Sefer HaChinuch [The book of mitzvah training]. (1990). Bnei Brak, Israel: Mishor Holy Books.

Townsend, L. (2009). *Introduction to pastoral counseling*. Nashville, TN: Abingdon.

Twerski, A. J. (2012). *Twerski on machzor—Yom Kippur*. Brooklyn, NY: Shaar.

Shahnaz Savani

16

REFRAMING PASTORAL COUNSELING: TOWARD DEVELOPING A MODEL OF PASTORAL CARE WITHIN MUSLIM COMMUNITIES

Pastoral counseling is the use of therapeutic techniques by trained members of the clergy or laypeople to assist others with personal or emotional problems. Most often individuals, couples, and families who engage in pastoral counseling are committed to a religious tradition and/or spiritual practice, and pastoral counselors are trained to integrate clients' spiritual and religious beliefs within mental health treatment. As a concept, pastoral counseling does not translate entirely or accurately in the Muslim community. It is a clinical practice that is a fairly new development that originated in a Judeo–Christian context. Within Muslim communities, there are currently no known models of such practice. Different denominations within the Muslim community have echelons of leadership among them, but none of them are specifically trained to provide any kind of counseling or therapeutic services. Muslim religious leaders do not offer professional counseling to the members of their faith communities. Rather, Muslim leaders are more likely to offer prayers for the easing of troubles and advice based on individual wisdom and experience. Furthermore, the members of the faith who seek such help from religious leaders are oftentimes purely seeking advice and do not mean to seek treatment or therapy. Religious leaders in most Muslim communities are well-meaning, well-intentioned individuals who want to provide help to members of the faith, but often they have no background or expertise to do so. Therefore, the notion of pastoral care as it exists in the Muslim context bears little semblance to the way that it is understood in its broader professional context. When facing hardship, individuals from religious communities tend to seek support from their own religious leaders more so than from other professionals. Reluctance to seek professional help when faced with difficulties is commonplace in many Muslim communities (Graham, Bradshaw, & Trew, 2008).

In this chapter, I attempt to offer some thoughts on exploring the possibility of developing a model of pastoral counseling in Muslim communities. I write as a Muslim woman who has lived and worked in North America for most of my career and has worked with Muslim populations around the world. I also write as a professional in the field of mental health trained to attempt to alleviate human suffering among those I seek to serve. My unique perspective in working within a particular denomination of the Muslim community has afforded me special insights in this area. My experience in starting a unique program offering social services within a cultural and faith context has been a significant journey, personally and professionally. This unique perspective—as a social worker operating within a faith community and trying to provide mental health and related services to members of the community—continues to be meaningful.

WHO ARE AMERICAN MUSLIMS?

In the classes that I have taught, I have challenged my students with questions about who American Muslims are, what they look like, what they do for a living, and what their outlook on life is. Even at the university level, it is interesting to see the simplistic stereotypes that emerge. Beliefs that Muslims are violent, oppressive toward women, narrow-minded, and not very educated are commonly expressed during these discussions. I ask my students to draw on a piece of paper a "Muslim woman." Invariably, many of my students draw a female figure with a veil or a head covering. Next I inquire whether or not there could be women who are Muslim who don't wear the veil. My personal example is that from the Shia Ismaili tradition of the subcontinent where nobody in my family or wider local community wore the veil for even a single day in her life. What it is that makes a person distinctly Muslim is a much deeper question requiring a much more complex response.

A comprehensive nationwide survey of Muslim Americans finds them to be not very different from other Americans (Pew Research Center, 2007). They are largely well integrated in their wider communities, happy with their lives, and moderate with respect to many of the issues that have divided Muslims and Westerners around the world. Most American Muslims do not stand out as different and appear to be harmonious with the rest of society. They are also decidedly "American" in their outlook, values, and attitudes. Overwhelmingly, they believe that education and hard work pay off in this society. This outlook is reflected in Muslim American income and education levels, which by and large mirror those of the general public (Pew Research Center, 2007). American Muslims more or less watch the same amount of television as others, play the same video games, are engaged with the same types of activities in their communities and neighborhoods as their non-Muslim peers, have a pretty balanced and modern outlook toward life, and are contributing members of their society.

Islam is far from a monolithic religion, and Muslims are anything but a homogeneous group of people. Muslim Americans are a highly diverse population, one largely composed of immigrants. First-generation Muslim Americans come from many countries around the world. About 40% are immigrants from the Middle East or North Africa, whereas about a quarter come from South Asian nations, including Pakistan, Bangladesh, and India (Pew Research Center, 2007). Muslims in the United States belong to diverse religious traditions within Islam. Half identify with Sunni Islam, the largest Muslim tradition worldwide (Pew Research Center, 2007). The second largest segment of the Muslim American population—about one fifth of the total (22%)—reports that they are Muslim, without any more specific affiliation. An additional 16% identify with Shia Islam, which is the second largest Muslim tradition worldwide (Pew Research Center, 2007).

Muslims around the world strongly reject violence in the name of Islam. In the United States, more than 10 years after 9/11, Muslims continue to reject extremist ideas. All segments of the Muslim American population share the ideal of being a God-fearing and peace-loving community and oppose violence in the name of religion. There is no indication of increased alienation or anger among Muslim Americans with respect to concerns about "home-grown" Islamic terrorists according to a comprehensive public opinion survey (Pew Research Center, 2007). Also, there is no evidence of rising support for extremism among Muslim Americans. American Muslims are even more likely than Muslims in other countries to firmly reject violence in the name of Islam. In the United States, most Muslims (81%) say that suicide bombing and similar acts targeting civilians are *never* justified (Pew Research Center, 2007). By and large, Muslim communities in the United States are well educated and well integrated, sharing the ideals of hard work, peace, and service for the betterment of all.

KEY PHILOSOPHICAL BELIEFS AND IMPLICATIONS

Belief in One God and His Messenger

Muslims in the United States and around the world have a set of distinct beliefs and practices. Belief in one God (Allah) and the Prophet Muhammad as the final messenger of God is universal among Muslims. The Muslim *shahada*, profession of faith, is recited as *La ilaha illa Allah Muhammad rasul Allah: there is no god but Allah and Muhammad is the prophet of God.* This recitation embodies the two fundamental elements of the faith: belief in one God and His messenger. Deeply associated with the belief in God is the powerful acknowledgment of His mercy, generosity, and magnanimity. Before the commencement of any important task, pronouncing the phrase *Bismillah ir-Rahman ir-Rahim (in the name of Allah, the most beneficent, the most merciful)* is customary among Muslims.

Predestination and Free Will

Another tenet of the faith that has significant implications for counseling practice is the belief that God's will and knowledge are absolute and that nothing happens in their absence. This is epitomized in the verse from the holy Qur'an, which states that not even a leaf falls without His knowledge (Qur'an 6:59). It is common among Muslims to respond to a question by saying *Inshallah (if God wills)* as if responding to it in the affirmative. A simple question such as "Will you be coming to the counseling session next week?" might yield a response of *inshallah*, which typically means "Yes, if God wills."

Coupled with the strong belief in God's absolute will is the inherent power of human effort and determination. Muslims believe in the idea of free will, the ability and power to create change for the better. Not only does a person have the ability to make things happen for oneself, but one is obligated to do so to better one's condition and the conditions of others. The idea of accountability for one's deeds and omissions is reflected in the belief in the Day of Judgment and the afterlife. Muslims believe that life on earth is a short passage in eternity and that human beings have to account to God for what they do in this life. Hard work, good deeds, and service to God and His creatures are part of this ethic of the faith and much behavior is driven by it. The Qur'an, by its own claim, invites human beings to come to the right path through effort and hard work (Rahman, 2009).

Although there may seem to be some tension between the idea of God's absolute will and the ability of the believer to choose his own path in life, it is widely accepted that human beings are obligated to work toward their goals and that God's blessings, mercy, and kindness follow those who make the effort. This belief is reflected in several verses of the Qur'an. The most direct of these indicates that Allah does not change people's conditions until they change themselves (Qur'an 13:11).

The Concept of Suffering

Within the Muslim ethos, difficulties and challenges are seen as opportunities to realign one's belief in and submission to Allah. Medical illnesses, problems within the family, financial troubles, and even mental health issues are seen as divinely designed to test human beings so that they may ground themselves and seek Allah's blessings (Qur'an 2:155). When afflicted with difficulties, the normal response would be to seek forgiveness and blessings from Allah and hope that the difficulties subside. The fact that suffering is a sign from God and is a calling for humility and submission somewhat hinders seeking help, particularly for emotional and psychological problems. It also frames some problems as though they are related to the supernatural and might require some divine, rather than human, intervention.

It is not uncommon for some believers to seek faith-based solutions to complex problems, especially those pertaining to severe mental illnesses. A poignant example that I have encountered in my practice was that of a woman in her mid-50s with multiple health and mental health problems who for many years went from one religious authority to another seeking solutions for her problems. In working with this woman, I began to understand the magnitude of her suffering over the preceding 30 years, the power of her belief system that inextricably linked her problems to some divine design, and the conviction that the problems could only be confronted by a similar divine intervention. The reason that she even sought services from a social worker was because an enlightened religious figure instructed her to do so.

Although there is a belief that suffering cannot be eliminated from human life, there is also a strong conviction that human effort is instrumental in addressing such suffering. The faith encourages people to make an effort to better their condition and that of others. Hard work and good intentions, coupled with prayer for Allah's grace and mercy, lead to lasting happiness.

It is very helpful for the practitioner to acknowledge this Muslim view on suffering and articulate interventions as part of the human effort to alleviate this suffering. What science has taught us over the course of human history is to be used to improve the quality of life for all people. To not use what we know as evidence-based interventions would be to not make adequate enough effort to improve the human condition and that is not what God would have desired for human beings. This concept, when used insightfully within practice, is a powerful acknowledgment for believers that problems require more than a religious solution and that scientific knowledge and interventions have an important role to play.

Islam as a Way of Life

Islam is not just a religion; it is a way of life. The spiritual and material realms of one's life are inextricably woven together. Asceticism is frowned on, and people are expected to perform all of their worldly duties as a part of their faith obligation. Muslims are required to live in their own historical time and seek contemporary solutions to practical problems of human existence drawn from the knowledge base of society in their own time. In other words, Muslims are encouraged to use the resources available in the present, rather than rely on practices from the past.

In my own practice with Muslim individuals and families, I have often found this idea to be a powerful tool in inviting clients to consider interventions that they would not normally have considered. In working with one young man with severe anxiety, the client found some relief in the recitation of prayer and was hesitant to consider any other interventions. After a few months of working together and pointing out to him that God desires for him to seek scientific and contemporary solutions to alleviate his suffering and that of his family, he started using antianxiety medications that yielded very positive outcomes. His symptoms became very well managed, and there was an overall improvement in his well-being. Even in very serious cases of domestic violence or sexual abuse, the idea of making an effort to seek scientific and knowledge-based solutions to improve one's condition as part of the faith obligation is a powerful one.

The Role of Service

In many Muslim traditions, including my own, the concept of service to fellow Muslims and fellow human beings is highly valued. The themes of generosity and service to the vulnerable, the poor, the sick, and the less fortunate are repeated throughout the Qur'an. The scripture also offers clear direction to share wealth and excess resources with the poor and those in need. Growing up within the Shia Ismaili tradition of Islam, the ethic of service was so infused within the day-to-day activities that it became part of the psyche of many members of the community. Working with an individual from this tradition means acknowledging the role that community service plays in her or his life. A well-documented and well-understood ethic of the faith in all Muslim traditions is giving in charity of one's wealth, resources, and intelligence for the benefit of those who are less fortunate. On the basis of this principle of service to others, the Shia Ismaili community in the United States runs an array of well-organized institutions and programs aimed to improve the quality of life of its members. These programs are offered by a number of talented volunteers from all walks of life who give generously of their time and resources for the well-being of others. A key factor in the success of such programs is the service offered by these volunteers. Being involved in such a tradition of service and offering clinical services within this framework necessitate the use of religious sensitivity and even caution in addressing some of the issues presented by Muslim clients. In keeping with this tradition of service is the potential for the development of a more robust model of pastoral counseling for the Muslim community.

The Institution of Marriage and Position of Women

Muslim communities have received much criticism from the wider society based on the perceived notion that the status of women is inferior to that of men. The permission for Muslim men to have four wives is greatly maligned and misunderstood. It is important to remember that Muslims in many parts of the world live in traditional, patriarchal societies and conduct themselves according to the norms of these societies. Much of what is believed and practiced in relation to women is cultural rather than religious. At this point, a discussion about the position of women in pre-Islamic times is relevant. In the pre-Islamic tribal culture of Arabia, women had no significant status. They were treated like property, and men married an unlimited number of women. Women could not hold property or assets in their own names and could be divorced multiple times without any rights or any means of livelihood. With the advent of Islam and the revelation of the Holy Qur'an, women were given rights that they did not previously have. Female infanticide and forced marriages were prohibited by the Qur'an. Several verses of the Qur'an gave specific rights to women within marriages and if they were divorced. Women were given rights to own property and gained rights to receive inheritance. The Holy Qur'an elevated the status of women from what it had been in pre-Islamic Arabia. When viewed in this historical context, Islam actually made significant reforms in the area of women's rights in its own historical time (Haque & Kamil, 2011).

The Qur'an allowed men to marry up to four wives *only* if they could treat all of them fairly. The oft-quoted verse of the Qur'an that talks about men being able to marry four wives goes on to explain that it is impossible for any husband to be fair to all four wives and, therefore, it is advisable to marry only one wife. In North America, most Muslims are in monogamous marriages per the law of the land. With regard to the relationship between men and women in the context of the family, a few themes are prominent. The first one that merits mention is the inherent equality of the sexes. The Qur'an proclaims that men and women were created from a single soul (Qur'an 4:1). Another prominent theme in the Qur'an is the iteration of men and women as partners to each other who live with one another in peace and mercy (Qur'an 30:21). The Qur'an also talks about men and women serving as friends and protectors of one another (Qur'an 9:71). The other themes of exhibiting kindness and compassion toward women and settling disputes equitably also appear interspersed throughout the scripture. Marriage in Islam is a contract, not a sacrament. Either party can leave the marriage with specific conditions and rights. This makes divorce permissible and legitimate, granting a number of rights to women on separation. The Qur'an states that couples should either remain together equitably or part from each other with kindness (Qur'an 2:229). The overarching ideals of partnership, love, mercy, and compassion between men and women within marriage are distinctive (Abugideiri, 2011).

Family issues frequently arise from the perceived role and function of women in their families and communities. For centuries, the Qur'an has been translated and interpreted largely by men. Although there have been prominent female figures in Muslim history, the status and role of women have largely been viewed through a patriarchal lens, subjecting women to a subordinate status in the practical day-to-day world.

Therapy is usually not a place to change a culture. Within a therapeutic context, it is important to understand the intersection of religion and culture and how it plays out in the family dynamic. An exploration of the belief system of the client with respect to his or her own role and status within the family dynamic is critical. Do the religious teachings of Islam or the lived culture of Muslims confer a lower status to women? In being with a client where he or she is, this exploration is a significant therapeutic journey. Practical examples of the kinds of family issues brought to surface by women are those related to domestic abuse, marital discord, discord among extended family members, and issues between parents and youth related to different expectations.

More often than not, the conventional solutions of feminist practice (involving law enforcement, separating from the family, and pursuing a legal battle) do not sit well with many Muslim women. However, there are instances when such interventions are adopted for safety reasons, but they are not readily considered. In many instances, a more conciliatory approach between the parties having a conflict seems to be a better option. In my experience in working with Muslim women, many women endure significant suffering in the name of religion. They often come to therapy to learn to coexist with the problem rather than seek a solution, because they are convinced that no solution is possible that is consistent with their belief system. Interventions that involve breaking up the family, rebellion, or confrontation between family members are not accepted readily among some Muslim families. Having said this, it is critical to remember and to remind the female client in therapy that God in His infinite mercy could not have possibly intended for women to suffer abuse at the hands of other humans and that kindness and compassion are the hallmarks of a marital relationship according to the Holy Qur'an.

Viewing Muslims through the exclusive lens of their religion can become very problematic when attempting to provide care in the context of mental health and mental well-being. An individual's identity and sense of self come from many dimensions of his or her life—religion being one of them. For some, religion may mean more to their identity than others. These ideas should in no way be considered finite, and each client must be treated as an individual human being first and then a Muslim.

REFLECTION QUESTIONS

1. According to the author, pastoral counseling, as defined in Christian contexts, is virtually unknown within American Islam. How might you describe the nature and function of pastoral counseling to a client or colleague who practices Islam and is unfamiliar with pastoral counseling paradigms?
2. To whom are Muslim families most likely to turn for help when experiencing distress?
3. In what ways are the key philosophical beliefs outlined by the author similar to and different from your own? How might those similarities and differences affect your work with a Muslim client?
4. The author asserts that "therapy is usually not a place to change a culture." What challenges might a Muslim client or colleague face when seeking care or working in an American religious or secular cultural environment?

REFERENCES

Abugideiri, S. E. (2011). Domestic violence. In S. Ahmed & M. M. Amer (Eds.), *Counseling Muslims: Handbook of mental health issues and interventions* (pp. 309–328). New York, NY: Routledge.

Graham, J. R., Bradshaw, C., & Trew, J. L. (2008). Social worker's understanding of the immigrant Muslim client's perspective. *Journal of Muslim Mental Health, 3*, 125–144. doi:10.1080/15564900802487527

Haque, A., & Kamil, N. (2011). Islam, Muslims and mental health. In S. Ahmed & M. M. Amer (Eds.), *Counseling Muslims: Handbook of mental health issues and interventions* (pp. 3–14). New York, NY: Routledge.

Pew Research Center. (2007). *Muslim Americans: Middle class and mostly mainstream.* Retrieved from www.pewresearch.org

Rahman, F. (2009). *Major themes of the Qur'an* (2nd ed.). Chicago, IL: University of Chicago Press.

Stephen Clarke

17

KALAMITRA: A BUDDHIST APPROACH TO PASTORAL COUNSELING

This chapter focuses on Buddhist approaches to the work of pastoral counseling and the role of the counselor. Since what we call pastoral counseling is a field of study that developed over the past 100 years in the West, and Buddhism developed over 2,500 years ago in the East, it is important to contextualize the recent intersection of Buddhist philosophy and practice and the discipline of pastoral counseling. This chapter explores the topics of Buddhism and pastoral counseling as separate entities, looks at how they can be joined, and presents unique elements of working with Buddhist and non-Buddhist clients. Lastly, it introduces the notion of the Buddhist pastoral counselor as the *kalamitra*, or spiritual friend.

BUDDHISM

Buddhism began with the teachings of Siddhartha Gautama (643–557 BCE), the historical Buddha, and has evolved since as it spread through Southeast Asia, West and East Asia, and north into Tibet and Mongolia. It continues to evolve as it spreads outside of Asia and even now as it comes back to Asia from the West. Many people since the time of the Buddha have studied, practiced, clarified, added, debated, and elucidated the teachings of the Buddha for further generations of people. Buddhism, like Christianity, Judaism, and Islam, has many subsects, mostly divided among the regions of Asia and defined by the time periods in which they developed. In India, where Buddhism originated, sects developed within two generations after the Buddha died. Before it spread outside of India, Buddhism had several schools, the two primary schools being *Sthaviras* and *Mahasanghikas* (Skilton, 2004). Southern India remained *Sthaviras* or *Theravadin*, Sanskrit for "teaching of the elders," relying on the study of older texts in Pali, a pre-Sanskrit language that most texts were written in and that continues to be the liturgical language of Theravada Buddhism. From middle/upper India, the *Mahasamghika* branch later evolved into the *Mahayana*, Sanskrit for "great vehicle," school of Buddhism. The Mahayana has greatly influenced all the schools of modern Buddhism, including Theravadin. Northern Indian Mahayana Buddhism mixed with Hindu esoteric practices, becoming the *Vajrayana*, Sanskrit for "diamond vehicle." Buddhism has always mixed with the indigenous religions and spirituality of the places to which it spread, which has provided a unique look and feel within each area. In Southeast Asia, including Thailand, Laos, Cambodia, Burma, and beyond, southern Indian Theravadin Buddhism mixed with local animistic religions. In China, Mahayana Buddhism mixed with Confucianism and Taoism. After spreading through China, Buddhism mixed with Shintoism in Japan. Confucian, Taoist, and Shintoist philosophies, religious practices, and celebrations give Chinese and Japanese Buddhism the unique Zen philosophies. In Tibet, Mongolia, Nepal, and Bhutan, northern Indian Vajrayana Buddhism mixed with Pon, an animistic religion similar to Native American spirituality, giving Tibetan Buddhism its unique philosophy (Snellgrove & Richardson, 1995). Buddhism in the West today is undoubtedly mixing with Christianity, Judaism, Islam, atheism, and a scientific worldview. The many subsects or derivations of Buddhism hold the main body of teachings in common but emphasize specific teachings or focus on a teacher who reinterpreted the Buddhist teachings. However, almost all Buddhists, including the Theravadin, Zen, Pure Land Buddhists of Japan and Vajrayana Buddhists, fall under the category of the Mahayana teachings of Buddhism, which emphasize an understanding of compassion and encourage ethics and helping others.

Today, there are many non-Buddhists who practice Buddhist meditation to supplement their spirituality. Chogyam Trungpa (1971), one of the first Tibetan teachers to come to the West, said that the three main religions of the West (Christianity, Judaism, and Islam) were losing their meditative and mystical traditions and therefore were becoming parched deserts of spirituality. He predicted that Buddhism would be like rain, nourishing and replenishing their spiritual traditions. As one Jesuit priest once told me, "My religion is Catholicism, but my spirituality is Buddhism." Buddhism's lack of theistic figures or dogmatic beliefs allows for many people to study and practice without having to become Buddhist or give up the religion or spirituality they already have.

Even though Buddhism has been a significant force in Asia for over 2,500 years, it is only since the early 1960s that Buddhism has begun to attract adherents and find general acceptance in North America and Europe. Buddhism has grown significantly in the West since the Diaspora of Tibet after the Chinese communist invasion in 1959 and the rise of the counterculture in North America and Europe in the 1960s. It was popularized by the writings of Jack Kerouac (1986), Alan Watts (1985), Allen Ginsberg (1997), Herman Hesse (1998), and many others. It also spread when Westerners traveled to the East to study with Buddhist teachers. Some Westerners came back as teachers themselves, such as Jack Kornfield (2008) and Sharon Salzberg (1995). Many of the Eastern teachers started coming to the West at the request of their Western students. Many Buddhist terms have gained a place in the popular vernacular such as *karma*, *nirvana*, *samsara*, and *mindfulness*.

A Buddhist Approach: Cessation of Suffering

According to Chodron (2013), the Buddha said he taught two things: that suffering exists and the path to end suffering. Buddhist philosophy states that it is more important to end suffering than adhere to any dogma or philosophy. Tsering (2006) stated, "Buddhism does not consider the root cause of our problems to be an external agent of this life, but rather an internal agent developed over many lifetimes—the habitual tendencies of our own mind" (p. 3). According to Brach (2003), suffering is the state in which one is stuck in a "trance of unworthiness and alienation" that keeps us thinking that we and the present moment are not good enough and that we are separate and unconnected (p. 6). When we are stuck in this struggle moment after moment, day after day, year after year, and, as traditional Buddhist philosophy states, lifetime after lifetime, we are stuck in *samsara*, Sanskrit for the cycle of suffering. In fact, the word

Buddha, meaning "one who is awake," points to how one can "wake up" from the illusions that bind us in suffering, *dukha* in Sanskrit. Suffering is due to the "trance," to use Brach's word, meaning we feel we have to crave and grasp after pleasure and comfort and avoid pain and discomfort. As the famous adage states, "Pain is inevitable, suffering is optional"; suffering is distinguished from pain and pleasure. It is the pursuit to control our outward and inward feelings, surroundings, and mental states that keeps us in a constant state of anxiety (*dukha*, dissatisfaction, suffering), never really relaxing or accepting things as they are. A key concept in Buddhism is impermanence, the understanding that everything is in a constant state of flux. Much of what creates our suffering is not being in tune with this truth and not allowing pain and pleasure to come, be, and go without avoiding or grasping. As Mipham (2003) stated, we are always looking for the "Goldilocks zone," the zone where everything is "just right" (p. 20). This zone is where we minimize our suffering and maximize our pleasure. But it is this struggle itself that creates most of our suffering.

Western psychology has focused on the components of personality and the development of the "healthy sense of self" (Epstein, 2007). Tsering (2006) stated, "Rather than harmonizing the disharmonious elements of the psyche so it becomes whole, and hence reifying the concept of the self, the goal of Buddhist teachings is to transcend the very concept of the self" (p. 2). The patterns and habits of avoidance and grasping make up what Buddha called the "ego." Ego is what we think of as a self, me, mine, and I. Ego, from a Buddhist perspective, has no permanent, lasting, or independent existence. As Ponlop (2010) stated,

> We expend so much effort just to convince ourselves that we've found something we can call "me." We try to freeze the moment-to-moment flow of experience that is our life and make something solid out of it. But somehow, it just doesn't work. Our efforts only produce more anxiety because we're going against the way things truly are. (para. 10)

The ultimate goal of Buddhist practice is egolessness or no self. According to Welwood (2000),

> Identifying with a self-concept is an attempt to give ourselves some shape, some hold on things, some security. Experience may change, but at least, so we hope, the experiencer endures. But in fending off its continual impending dissolution into openness, the experiencer gets in the way of its own experience, becoming an obstruction that prevents direct contact with our true nature, with others, and with the larger sweep of life. (p. 46)

Later, Welwood (2000) stated that on the way to egolessness, we need to respect the self as simply a stage on the path. As Engler (1983) wrote, "You have to be somebody before you can be nobody" (p. 36). The Buddhist pastoral counselor understands the self as a necessary condition of selflessness. When there is self-cherishing, there can also be self-hatred (Trungpa, 1971). Brach (2003) recounted the following about a group of Western Buddhist teachers and psychologists who met with the Dalai Lama to dialogue about emotions and health:

> During one of their sessions, an American vipassana teacher asked him to talk about the suffering of self-hatred. A look of confusion came over the Dalai Lama's face. "What is self-hatred?" he asked. As the therapists and teachers in the room tried to explain, he looked increasingly bewildered. "Was this mental state a

nervous disorder?" he asked them. When those gathered confirmed that self-hatred was not unusual but rather a common experience for their students and clients, the Dalai Lama was astonished. How could they feel that way about themselves, he wondered, when "everybody has Buddha nature." (p. 11)

This pursuit to solidify a sense of self brings us further and further away from the true nature of things *as they are*, which is *shunyata*, or emptiness. In this translation, emptiness means empty of concept and permanence. Another way to translate *shunyata* is fullness, meaning that when things are empty of concept and permanence, they are full of the things themselves: the direct experience. One could say that the essence of Buddhism is abandoning anything that hides truth. One of the truths of Buddhism is that true reality is Buddha, awake. In realizing emptiness and seeing our nature and the nature of everything as already enlightened or as Buddha, we can relax more and more with our primordial goodness, *domine zangpo*, in Tibetan. Our enlightened nature is naturally awake, peaceful, loving, kind, sane, and wise. As emphasized in Vajrayana Buddhism, "We practice being our enlightened nature" (Kilts, 2008, p. 279). Renouncing what separates us from our true nature and resting more and more in that true nature is the thrust of Buddhist psychology. By doing this, we stop the struggle to stave off suffering and relax more with things *as they are*.

Central to the philosophy of relaxing with things *as they are* is the nontheistic nature of Buddhism. Chodron (2000) defines *nontheism* as follows:

> The difference between theism and nontheism is not whether one does or does not believe in God. . . . Theism is a deep-seated conviction that there's some hand to hold [that there is some ground or belief one can hold onto]. . . . Non-theism is relaxing with the ambiguity and uncertainty of the present moment without reaching for anything to protect ourselves [or hold onto] . . . it is total appreciation of impermanence and change. (p. 39)

Nontheism is taking salvation into our own hands and realizing an ultimate personal responsibility. In the *Nikayas* and *Samannaphala Sutra* (Bhikkhu, 2004), the Buddha rejected speculating on the existence of a creator deity, refused to endorse many views on creation, stated that questions on the origin of the world are not ultimately useful for ending suffering, and listed materialism, amoralism, nihilism, and eternalism as wrong views that lead to suffering. As Ato Rinpoche once said about the philosophy of emptiness, "If one is serious about emptiness, one has to even see Buddha and Buddhism as empty. There really is nothing to hold onto" (personal communication, September 5, 2001).

PASTORAL COUNSELING AND THE BUDDHIST PASTORAL COUNSELOR

The Buddhist pastoral counselor focuses on working with both Buddhist and non-Buddhist clients from a Buddhist psychological perspective. The Buddhist pastoral counselor studies the connection between health and Buddhist psychology and practice. Buddhism and its practice embody the personal and professional orientation of the Buddhist pastoral counselor.

Buddhism incorporates the "inner sciences" of meditation and psychology and the "outer sciences" of astronomy, astrology, cosmology, medicine, and more. Buddhist philosophy recognizes the "inner sciences" as primary to the "outer sciences" (Tsering,

2006). Many Buddhist teachers have high regard for Western psychology and science, in general, as a way of understanding and intervening in the suffering of people, and they also see it more as a tool, similar to the "outer sciences" already held in Buddhism. Christianity and many other Western traditions previously integrated the inner and outer sciences; however, when Western science began challenging the dogma of the religion, rather than change, the inner and outer sciences became adversarial. Buddhism is more about freeing people from suffering than about any dogma. As the Dalai Lama has said, if science can prove any Buddhist philosophy wrong, Buddhism will abandon that philosophy (Goleman, 2003).

Buddhism, meditation, yoga, mindfulness, and compassion practices are beginning to have a significant impact on the world of Western psychology and will therefore continue to influence pastoral counseling. Pastoral counseling has been primarily dominated by Christian practitioners and faith, but as Buddhism influences Western psychology and as Buddhism grows, there will be more pastoral counselors who are Buddhist or associate themselves with Buddhist practices to guide their own tradition or faith and their work with clients and supervisees.

Buddhism has an "inner science" or psychology and "therapeutic" interventions that have been developed over the past 2,500 years. Buddhist psychology offers pastoral counselors generally, and Buddhist pastoral counselors specifically, a lens for understanding their clients and their situations. Buddhist pastoral counselors possess training and experience in meditative disciplines and/or religious practices from the Buddhist tradition of which they are a part. That being said, they may also draw on other theories or non-Buddhist religious practices they have experienced or that the clients have as their own framework. As there are currently no Buddhist pastoral counseling programs, many Buddhist pastoral counselors receive training from Christian-based pastoral counseling programs using Western psychological theory and practice. Many have worked in settings requiring them to use Western psychological theory and interventions. Many current psychological theories have been influenced by Buddhism and mindfulness practices such as Acceptance and Commitment Therapy (Hayes, Strosahl, & Wilson, 1999), Dialectical Behavioral Therapy (Koerner & Linehan, 2011), Mindfulness-Based Stress Reduction (Stahl & Goldstein, 2010), Mindfulness-Based Cognitive Therapy (Sega, Williams, & Teasdale, 2012), and more. Many Buddhist pastoral counselors may use these theories as they are generally accepted as evidence-based practices (Greco & Hayes, 2008). Buddhist psychology has been and will continue to be interwoven with the major Western psychological theories. Some of the people instrumental in interweaving Buddhist and Western psychological theories are Epstein (2007) with psychodynamic theory, Wallin (2007) with attachment theory, and Welwood (2000) with existentialism and focusing, among others. As Buddhists train in pastoral counseling programs, pastoral counselors become interested in Buddhism, and as Buddhist philosophy and practice, such as mindfulness meditation, become an interest of Western psychology generally, pastoral counseling and Buddhism will shift and change.

Working With Buddhists

Naturally, we tend to seek out those like us, and in looking for a counselor, many Buddhists seek out a Buddhist counselor. Among Buddhists, there are those who are Eastern Buddhists and those who are Western Buddhists. Eastern Buddhists are those raised in an Eastern culture either in the East or as first-generation immigrants to the West. Some Eastern Hindus believe that Buddhism is another form of Hinduism, so some Eastern Hindus will also be a part of this group. Eastern Buddhists tend to rely more on their family, religion, or culture to cope with issues that many Westerners bring to counseling. Asian children often deal with areas of family enmeshment and difficulties with self-differentiation yet often have stronger ego strength and less object relation complexes due to closer knit family structures (Welwood, 2000). Eastern Buddhists, when they do come to counseling, whether for personal or relationship issues, tend to treat the counselor like the expert or doctor and want advice or a prescriptive intervention. Western Buddhists tend to be raised in the West and therefore possess an openness to psychology or to seeking professional counseling. Welwood (2000) states that more Western children grow up in fragmented families plagued by narcissism and loss of meaning than is typically found in the East. When Western Buddhists seek a Buddhist pastoral counselor, they are typically looking for Buddhist psychological understanding and interventions that come from the Buddhist contemplative and meditative traditions. Unlike Eastern Buddhists, Western Buddhists are less likely to look for prescriptions and expert advice and are more likely to want to process and tell their stories. In this writer's experience, both Eastern and Western Buddhists generally want to use their faith or practice to address the issues that they face, and most come to counseling to address issues such as depression, anxiety, and relationship issues.

Looking at the possible pitfalls associated with working with those who identify with and practice spirituality, and specifically Buddhism, Trungpa (2002) stated, "The problem is that ego can convert anything to its own use, even spirituality" (p. 14). In this same vein, Welwood (2000) coined the term *spiritual bypassing* to mean "using spiritual ideas or practices to sidestep personal, emotional, 'unfinished business,' to shore up a shaky sense of self, or to belittle basic needs, feelings, and developmental tasks, all in the name of enlightenment" (p. 207). One area that may arise as a trap or unique expression of spiritual bypassing by Buddhist clients is using meditation or the Buddhist philosophy to detach from *what is* and to avoid one's inner or outer experience. An example of this is shown in the clinical case of Sam, who came to therapy to work on depression and anxiety. Sam had been experiencing a recurrence of depression for the past several months after graduating college on the West Coast. He had moved back home to the East Coast, had no friends at home anymore, and was unable to find a job. Sam had learned meditation in college and wanted to bring his study and practice of meditation to the work of therapy. When asked what he liked about meditation, he stated that it allowed him to "blank out" and not think about his problems. He liked this effect and already tended toward dissociation, a skill he learned to cope with his parents' vicious arguments while growing up. Now that he was home again and his parents' arguments had not improved, he wanted to dissociate from it all again. He was finding it hard to blank out or dissociate back at home around his parents' fighting. Without a job and friends, he was stuck around his parents' fighting again. His meditation was not working, and so he had begun drinking alcohol to numb the discomfort he felt. He was trying to use alcohol and meditation to bypass the work of staying with the feelings and chaos he felt. It takes one well versed in the pitfalls of spiritual practice, and our tendency to convert anything to ego defense, to recognize clients' use of spiritual ideas and practices to escape or "bypass." The two most common pitfalls of the Buddhist pastoral counselor include the assumption of similar worldviews or understandings of their clients and joining with their client in spiritual bypassing. One other possible pitfall is that the relationship of counselor–client may become hijacked by the more traditional teacher–student relationship found in Buddhism. To counteract these, Buddhist pastoral counselors need to maintain awareness and reflection of their interactions and unconscious motivations just as in any other form of counseling.

Working With Non-Buddhists

Non-Buddhist clients come to a Buddhist pastoral counselor for several reasons: openness to a Buddhist view, a desire to include a mindfulness practice, the assumption that a Buddhist pastoral counselor will be open to their spiritual tradition/view, the conception of a Buddhist counselor as exotic, a lack of success with other types of counselors, or for reasons similar to why any counselor is selected such as location, price, or referral. Working with non-Buddhists may ultimately be similar to working with Buddhists, yet one main difference is the counselor's awareness of whether the client is open to a Buddhist framework in assessing and intervening. An initial assessment to determine this includes the client's level of understanding and acculturation with the language, experience, and practice of Buddhism or other spiritual traditions. Cultural sensitivity is required on the part of the Buddhist pastoral counselor to use effectively Buddhist philosophy, psychological tenets, and practices in a manner commensurate with the client's understanding or desire and helps the client feel respected and understood. Like any counselor, the Buddhist pastoral counselor needs to be sensitive to the needs and wishes of the client. Informed consent, both as a formal signed agreement at the start of counseling and as ongoing informal verbal informed consent, is essential in working with any client and especially those with different backgrounds and viewpoints. Including what is to be expected, a basic theoretical framework, possible damaging effects, and all the other generally agreed-upon areas of informed consent is as important for a Buddhist pastoral counselor as any other counselor. Because most Buddhist pastoral counselors may be theoretically eclectic or have worked in settings with non-Buddhist clients for training and/or licensure, they typically have the experience and clinical language that would allow a non-Buddhist client to feel comfortable.

Possible pitfalls for the Buddhist pastoral counselor working with non-Buddhist clients are the same for any form of counseling, including colluding with the client, boundary violations, misunderstanding the needs or wishes of the client, and so on. One major pitfall already discussed is not being sensitive to the culture, beliefs, and language of the client by pushing a Buddhist "agenda" or worldview. For example, when I first started as a Buddhist pastoral counselor, I gave everyone a copy of a book by a Buddhist author that I thought summarized my point of view of the counseling process and goals of counseling, regardless of the client's orientation and beliefs. A woman who came for her first session to work on anxiety and depression identified herself as New Age and stated she was part of an area New Age church. She thought I would be open to her point of view and had the understanding that Buddhism and New Age philosophies were "related." I gave her the book and described my orientation. When she returned the next week, she gave the book back to me and said that she didn't think she was going to continue with me after reading about the Buddhist concept of "hopelessness" in the first few chapters of the book. We explored her reaction and possible ways to see this concept differently and possibly that it may already be held within her tradition. She was not open to this discussion and felt I was trying to convince her. On reflection, I realized I was trying to convince her. After realizing this, I have altered to whom and how I give the book and try to refrain from discussions in which I may be imposing my point of view. Buddhist pastoral counselors, as much as every other counselor, regardless of theoretical or religious/spiritual orientation, need to maintain awareness and reflection of their interactions and unconscious motivations.

TRAINING AND SUPERVISION

Until relatively recently, only one Buddhist psychology training program existed in the West at Naropa University in Boulder, Colorado. This is quickly changing, with a growing number of university programs in the United States, Europe, and Australia that focus on both training and research in Buddhist psychology and/or mindfulness orientations and interventions. Buddhist pastoral counselors may not have received training or supervision from a Buddhist supervisor due to this historical shortage. Many mental health professionals first studied with a Buddhist teacher and later integrated their personal and professional interests or vice versa. Buddhist pastoral counselors often receive supervision from those of other faith traditions and therefore develop their own methods for working with clients and their own supervisees. Buddhist pastoral counselors have traditionally taken up the task of integrating Buddhist philosophy and practice within Western psychological frameworks for both clinical and supervisory practice. As there is no Buddhist pastoral counseling supervision theory per se, Buddhist supervisors often borrow liberally from other models of supervision. Some of these models might include a Western psychological theoretical model, a developmental model, a cross-cultural model, or any other model or combination of models.

Training and supervision require Buddhist pastoral counselors to engage in personal experience with the study and practice of Buddhist psychology and meditation. Buddhist psychology is based on personal meditative experience. It would likely be the case that a Buddhist pastoral counseling supervisor may encourage a supervisee interested in this approach to develop a personal meditative practice, attend retreats, study modern or ancient texts, and/or become involved with a Buddhist community. This may require the supervisee to study with a Buddhist teacher and to develop several years of personal experience before applying the principles and practice in counseling.

RESEARCH

Many teachers and leaders of Buddhism say that Buddhism is not a religion but a "science of mind" or a "philosophy, science and psychology" (Yeshe, 2003, p. 5). Both Western science and Buddhism use empiricism as the method of inquiry. Although Western science uses the scientific method and Buddhism uses mindfulness/insight meditation, as the Dalai Lama noted, "Buddhism and science are not conflicting perspectives on the world, but rather differing approaches to the same end: seeking the truth" (as cited in Goleman, 2003, p. xiii). The Dalai Lama has asked Buddhist meditators to volunteer themselves for the study of their brains, behavior, emotions, and cognitions to see what effect can be documented by Western science. The hope that Buddhist meditative practice can be shown to help reduce human suffering has been a priority of Buddhism since the time of the Buddha, Siddhartha Gautama. Today, we use science to verify evidence of the efficacy of Buddhist practice. Neuroscience research on meditation and mindfulness, most notably the research of Dr. Richard Davidson at the University of Wisconsin, indicates that Buddhist meditators have higher activation of the left prefrontal cortex, associated with improved mood and feelings of contentment (R. Siegel, 2010). When people with no connection to Buddhist meditation, higher right prefrontal cortex activity, and symptoms of depression, anxiety, and hypervigilance were taught meditation over 8 weeks, they showed decreased right prefrontal cortex activity and increased left prefrontal cortex activity (R. Siegel, 2010).

In addition to advances in neuroscience, many new quantitative measures and scales have been developed related to mindfulness, loving-kindness, detachment, and other factors prominent in meditation. These scales include the Mindful Attention and Awareness Scale (MacKillop & Anderson, 2007), the Toronto Mindfulness Scale (Lau et al., 2006), the Kentucky Inventory of Mindfulness Skills (Baer, Smith, & Allen, 2004), the Freiburg Mindfulness Inventory (Walach, Buchheld, Buttenmuller, Kleinknecht, & Schmidt, 2006), Self–Other Four Immeasurables Scale (Kraus & Sears, 2009), and the Self-Compassion Scale (Neff, 2003), among others. Buddhist pastoral counselors use these scales as anyone using psychological measures might, to identify strengths and weaknesses. This allows the counselor to tailor interventions more specifically to address the identified areas. Additional qualitative research is needed. As Mace (2008) stated, "The continuing failure to utilize qualitative research methods in the articulation of mindfulness within psychology remains, in my view, mindless" (p. 38). The available literature and research in all areas of Buddhist principles and meditation will continue to increase as more people become interested in this approach. So far, much of the research has "borrowed" a concept or practice from Buddhism but not looked at Buddhism and its psychology as a whole. According to Greco and Hayes (2008), research has been pulling Buddhism apart to create theories and methods that can be put to the scientific test. "Some think this can be avoided merely by defining Buddhism as scientific, but that only works if science itself is redefined" (Greco & Hayes, 2008, p. 4). Using a metaphor from Buddhism, it is like three blind men standing near three different areas of an elephant trying to describe the elephant. One is touching the trunk and describing the elephant as long and cylindrical, another is touching the ear and describing the elephant as thin and flat, and last is describing the body as enormous and round. Each has a piece and yet doesn't see how it all works together to be an elephant. It is yet to be determined whether testing the parts is effective or whether you need the whole. Generally, Buddhists are fine with testing particular interventions as whatever is of help to those suffering should be used. Where this becomes problematic is testing a practice, like mindfulness, and expecting quick results. It is generally understood that it takes time to shift and change a mind because of the habitual tendencies. In fact, traditional Buddhist philosophy states it takes "lifetimes."

KALAMITRA

Being Whatever Is Needed: The Kalamitra

Metaphors for counselors and caregivers include the shepherd, the physician, the wounded healer, and more. Buddhism posits several images as well: the sage/yogi, the provocateur/crazy wisdom holder, the teacher/guru, the king/queen, and the physician/shaman, among others. Different traditions offer unique understandings of the "helper/healer" relationship. In Mahayana Buddhism, the teacher is often termed *kalamitra*, Sanskrit for spiritual friend. The kalamitra functions in all of the aforementioned roles as the kalamitra does whatever is needed. *Kala* literally means "time" in English and refers to being beyond time or to the spiritual experience of timelessness.

Kala can also mean the time of awakening or golden age. *Mitra* means friend or friendly. Together, they are translated as spiritual friend and refer to the *bodhisattva*, Sanskrit for "awakened being." Summing up the seventh-century Buddhist scholar Shantideva (1997) in the *Bodhisattvacharyavatara*: May I be the doctor, nurse, and medicine for those ailing; may I be the food and drink for those starving; may I be the boat, raft, or bridge for those who need to cross the body of water; may I be the slave for those who need a servant. Shantideva points to the kalamitra or bodhisattva ideal: to be what is needed, no matter the circumstance. Because of the bodhisattva's compassion, he or she is willing to be whatever the person needs to arrive at awakening and to end suffering. The kalamitra, or spiritual friend, is one who has walked the path and knows how the path unfolds as well as the traps along the way. Understanding the habitual tendencies of ego clinging and how the mind creates suffering within oneself, the kalamitra sees this tendency in the other to do the same. The kalamitra as counselor is one who has worked with his or her own mind and therefore knows the workings of the mind and how the mind creates suffering. When one has studied and worked with one's own mind and the states of mind that arise, one gains insight into how the mind works and how to intervene when one is being afflicted by unhelpful and damaging states of mind. Buddhists contend that everyone can have every state of mind that anyone else can. This gives rise to the need to study and work with one's own mind first and then apply that knowledge and experience to another. Part of this work is to be willing to remain present with anything that arises in the mind and remain curious. Another aspect of this work is the willingness to develop an attitude and stance of friendliness with *what is*, whatever that may be.

Working With One's Own Mind

If it is essential to work with one's own mind first, then what is mind? Languages such as Pali, Sanskrit, Tibetan, Chinese, and Japanese have evolved to talk more precisely about aspects and qualities of the mind as described in Buddhist texts and by the practitioners of meditation. In Tibetan, for example, there are at least 20 different words or conjugations of words that refer to the mind or an aspect of the mind. One primary distinction is between the words *sem* and *rigpa*. *Sem* is Tibetan for ordinary or conceptual mind, whereas *rigpa* means primordial awareness or wisdom mind. According to Sogyal (1992), "Sem is the discursive, dualistic, thinking mind, which can only function in relation to a projected and falsely perceived external reference point" (p. 46). Sogyal defines *rigpa* as "a primordial, pure, pristine awareness that is at once intelligent, cognizant, radiant, and always awake. It could be said to be the knowledge of knowledge itself" (p. 47). This distinction in Western Zen Buddhism is often termed *small mind* and *big mind*, respectively. Small mind here refers to the self-referential and self-conscious mind, which in traditional Buddhism describes the mental factors and especially *kleshas*, or afflicted emotions. Big mind refers to the non–self-conscious mind that simply perceives and knows. *Rigpa*, or big mind, is like the sky, and the small mind is like the clouds passing in the sky. We often identify with this small mind or clouds and think that they are ultimate reality. This identification with small mind leads directly to suffering as we solidify and lose any malleability of the mind. We do not often identify with the sky in which the clouds occur or space in which thought happens. One purpose of mindfulness or insight meditation is to identify with *rigpa* and not hold *sem* as ultimate reality. From one perspective, meditation is like mental exercise. It is by the repeated process of placing one's mind on an object of meditation (breath, sense perceptions, mantra, visualization, *koan*) and bringing the mind back when it has left the object that one develops a strength, clarity, and peace of mind to be present (Mipham, 2003). It is also by practicing the mind's analytical curiosity, detachment, and open-heartedness that one develops the skills of insight, precision, loving-kindness, and compassion to more directly rest with *what is*. It is by learning to rest more in big mind that one can experience this state more often and suffer less. We have the seeds of Buddha within us already, so the question is whether we water these seeds or water the seeds of confusion by identifying with small mind.

Buddhist psychology gives many resources and practices for studying and working with the mind and its states (Chodron, 2001; Goleman, 2003; Hahn, 2010; Kornfield, 2002; Salzberg, 1995; Tsering, 2006; Yeshe, 2003). Most of these, however, are understood primarily through direct experience by learning from teachers their philosophy (view) and practice (method). An example of a practice that addresses the fear of death could be meditations on the fear of death. We could meditate on our own and everyone else's death, visualizing our own and other's bodies decomposing. Similar to exposure therapy, the more one is able to stay with the meditation, the less fear one has as the attachment to the body begins to disappear. One outcome of this kind of meditation is to lessen the fear of death, but another is the process of "staying with" or being mindful of one's anxiety or other emotions and thoughts that arise and are elicited by this image. This *staying with* or being mindful of the process within oneself is of vast importance. Mindfulness is both the willingness to be present with whatever arises and the lack of conceptual overlay and judgment about what arises. Another example of a meditative or contemplative method of working with the mind is analytical explorations of thoughts, emotions, and experience. If we choose to explore the emotion of fear again, we can elicit something that produces fear by thought or experience and, once it is elicited, analytically start investigating. We may start by developing a detached observer stance toward the mind and the fear that arises in our experience. In this process, we can first simply have the felt sense of what fear feels like in the body and mind. Then we can look at the reactions the fear elicits using our curiosity to get to know and break down the fear and its stimulus. After this, we could develop an unconditional friendliness toward the fear and our reaction. Next, we can look at where fear comes from and where it goes after the stimulus is absent. Finally, we can look at what remnants are left after it is no longer there. Although Buddhist pastoral counselors may lead their clients through similar exercises, the primary intervention would be counselors' willingness to stay with their own states of mind, especially those that frighten them, and to have worked with this type of analysis in their own practice. If counselors are willing to go where the clients are or have gone and can develop the skills necessary to work with any state of mind, it will help develop an authentic and courageous presence on the part of the counselor. An authentic and courageous presence is essential in creating attachment and attunement with the client. It is developed by meditative training and working with one's own mind. In this way, the kalamitra acts as a guide who knows the territory very well. The kalamitra has become *shinjang*, Tibetan for "thoroughly processed." As the counselor has traveled the path and done the work of developing a mind that is strong, clear, and calm, the kalamitra becomes able to lead another.

Developing Compassion and Loving-Kindness

Although Buddhist practitioners develop a detached observer stance in order not to follow or identify with afflicted emotions, the ultimate goal is not to be separate from what we experience or from our connections to sentient beings and the world itself.

Mindfulness is a nonjudgmental, compassionate, and friendly stance toward the present moment. The present moment contains not only the "nice or pleasant" experiences but also the experiences that are painful. Being mindful allows our heart/mind to be touched intimately as there are fewer boundaries separating us from what is directly happening. Similar to all counseling, the Buddhist pastoral counselor will still rely on the relationship with the client as the main process and intervention of counseling. D. Siegel (2010) contends that the presence of the therapist and the attunement of the therapist with the client are the most crucial factors affecting the client's healing process. It is through effort in developing mindfulness that one can increase presence, which can directly lead to attunement (D. Seigel, 2010). According to D. Siegel (2010), "Our most powerful therapeutic tool is trust—and this can only happen with authentic presence as we move forward with kindness and compassion to face whatever arises in the journey to heal" (p. 87).

Buddhism places *bodhicitta* or "awakened heart," loving-kindness, and compassion into two categories: aspiring and entering. *Aspiring* is developing the wish and intention of helping others (including ourselves in all references to "another" as we can be another to ourselves), and *entering* is committing the action that helps others. As compassion and loving-kindness are capacities of the mind, it is possible to develop and cultivate them in the aspiration phase of meditation. Mindfulness practice itself will accomplish this, and there are specific practices in the Buddhist tradition to nurture these within us. Some of those practices are the contemplations on the *four immeasurables* or divine abodes, *tonglen* meditation, deity visualizations, and prayer. Entering bodhicitta or enacting the aspiration is the willingness to be with the suffering of others. The etymology of the word *compassion* means "being-with-suffering." It is through being-with-suffering, in all of its forms, that bodhicitta takes hold. When one can be present with the suffering of another and allow one's training or natural wisdom to arise to meet the suffering, that entering becomes manifest. We do not simply rely on the wish to be of benefit; we also need training. A helpful metaphor for this is when someone needs cardiopulmonary resuscitation (CPR). If we have not had training in CPR, we will only have the intention to help. We also need the means of helping, in this case CPR training, as well as the intention. This same principle applies to psychology. We may have the intention to help, but we also need the means (methods) to help. Because Buddhism is not dogmatic and, in fact, is mostly a pragmatic philosophy, whatever will be of help is what the kalamitra or Buddhist pastoral counselor should do. In that way, the kalamitra marries the aspiration with entering in being of service.

Working With Another's Mind

For most contemplative traditions, it is essential for one to have personal experience with meditation or contemplation before leading another. Kabat-Zinn (2003) states this about mindfulness-based stress reduction (MBSR) training:

> In our experience, unless the instructor's relationship to mindfulness is grounded in extensive personal practice, the teaching and guidance one might bring to the clinical context will have little in the way of appropriate energy, authenticity, or ultimate relevance, and that deficit will soon be felt by program participants. For how can one ask someone else to look deeply into his or her own mind and body and the nature of who he or she is in a systematic and disciplined way if one is unwilling (or too busy or not interested enough) to engage in this great and challenging adventure oneself, at least to the degree that one is asking it of

one's patients or clients? How will one know how to respond appropriately and specifically to their questions if one cannot draw on one's own lived experience, not just on book knowledge and concepts, when the practice itself is all about seeing clearly and transcending (not getting caught up in and blinded by) the limitations of the conceptual mind while, of course, not rejecting the conceptual mind or the power and utility of thought within the larger context of awareness? (p. 150)

If one has worked with one's own mind and has a good grasp of how to intervene (i.e., stay with, hold compassionately, analytically investigate) with one's own mind and its states, then one begins to know how the mind works and can begin to apply the same method/understanding to the situation of another. Although there is a great deal of commonality between most mind states such as anger, jealousy, and fear, the origins can be quite different. This is where one's own lived experience may not completely cover the depth and extent of suffering that is experienced by others. As this is often the case, one can only go with another as far as one has gone with oneself. Interestingly, another factor can come into play at this moment. If one can stay open and not become overwhelmed, there is an inner wisdom (Buddha nature) that can help. Sometimes it is through a willingness to stay in unknowing with the intention to help that something arises. It could be sensing an inward voice that gives a word or phrase, it could be expressing the "not knowing," or it could be something that is genuine but one would never say in one's "right mind." Whatever this is, it is listening to one's inner wisdom and wakefulness. It is also by relying on one's training in healing by way of theory, experience, or other means that can be applied to help. All of these factors come together in the present moment of intervening with another being. First, it is staying or being with what arises in another. Second, it is being willing to see the similar experience, being willing to remember one's own mind state and the effect it had. Then it is seeing how to hold that for oneself and possibly to analytically investigate it. Third, it is relying on everything one has at hand to intervene. That intervention could be anything from meditative/contemplative practices to cognitive behavioral therapy to affirmations. This is how the kalamitra works; being whatever is needed and not tied to any one way of helping or necessarily to what the result should be.

CONCLUSIONS

Although Buddhist pastoral counseling is fairly new to the pastoral counseling field, Buddhism and mindfulness have had a significant influence on psychology for the past 20 years and most notably the past 10 years. Buddhism and mindfulness will continue to influence psychology, and therefore Buddhist pastoral counseling as a discipline will continue to grow. As there are many Buddhists, there are many ways of understanding Buddhism and styles of presentation. This chapter presents only one. Hopefully, many other Buddhist pastoral counselors will add their voice to this dialogue.

In that same vein, there is a need for more research. The Buddhist orientation is very open to research and wants to further human knowledge to free people of suffering. As research begins to use and investigate meditation, especially with those who have trained their minds, the investigations have revealed some interesting and potentially helpful discoveries to add to human knowledge. May all beings be free of suffering.

REFLECTION QUESTIONS

1. According to the author, "We are always looking for the 'Goldilocks zone,' the zone where everything is 'just right' (Mipham 2003, p. 20). This zone is where we minimize our suffering and maximize our pleasure. But it is this struggle itself that creates most of our suffering." In what ways do you agree or disagree with this assertion? What implications does this have for work with clients experiencing suffering as the result of systemic oppression and discrimination?

2. In this chapter, you read about Sam's experience of "spiritual bypassing" to cope with his feelings of depression and anxiety. How do you understand "spiritual bypassing"? Can you think of a time you, a friend, a loved one, or a client engaged in spiritual bypassing? How did this affect the individual's spirituality and psychological health?

3. The body of literature researching Buddhist psychology and mindfulness techniques continues to expand. According to the author, "Where this becomes problematic is testing a practice, like mindfulness, and expecting quick results. It is generally understood that it takes time to shift and change a mind because of the habitual tendencies. In fact, traditional Buddhist philosophy states it takes 'lifetimes.'" What are the pros and cons of researching spiritual interventions, in Buddhism or other traditions, to determine their effectiveness in fostering mental well-being?

4. *Kalamitra* or spiritual friend is posited as a fitting metaphor for the pastoral counselor. The kalamitra first works with his or her own mind to guide and assist others on the journey. If you were to adopt this metaphor for your role and practice as a counselor, what implications would this have for your own training and/or practice?

REFERENCES

Baer, R. A., Smith, G. T., & Allen, K. B. (2004). Assessment of mindfulness by self-report: The Kentucky inventory of mindfulness skills. *Assessment, 11*(3), 191–206. doi:10.1177/1073191104268029

Bhikkhu, T. (2004). *Handful of leaves: Vol. I. An anthology from the Digha and Majjhima Nikayas.* Valley Center, CA: The Sati Center for Buddhist Studies & Metta Forest Monastery.

Brach, T. (2003). *Radical acceptance: Embracing your life with the heart of a Buddha.* New York, NY: Bantam.

Chodron, P. (2000). *When things fall apart: Heart advice for difficult times.* Boston, MA: Shambhala.

Chodron, P. (2001). *Tonglen, the path of transformation.* Halifax, NS: Vajradhatu.

Chodron, P. (2013). *How to meditate.* New York, NY: Sounds True.

Engler, J. H. (1983). Vicissitudes of the self according to psychoanalysis and Buddhism: A spectrum model of object relations development. *Psychoanalysis and Contemporary Thought, 6*(1), 29–72.

Epstein, M. (2007). *Psychotherapy without the self: A Buddhist perspective.* New Haven, CT: Yale University Press.

Ginsberg, A., Ko, U., & Kim, Y. (1997). *Beyond self: 108 Korean Zen poems.* New York, NY: Parallax.

Goleman, D. (2003). *Destructive emotions: How can we overcome them? A scientific dialogue with the Dalai Lama.* New York, NY: Bantam.

Greco, L. A., & Hayes, S. C. (2008). *Acceptance & mindfulness treatments for children and adolescents: A practitioner's guide.* Oakland, CA: New Harbinger and Context Press.

Hahn, T. N. (2010). *Reconciliation: Healing the inner child.* Berkeley, CA: Parallax Press.

Hayes, S. C., Strosahl, K. D., & Wilson, K. G. (1999). *Acceptance and commitment therapy: An experiential approach to behavior change.* New York, NY: Guilford.

Hesse, H. (1998). *Siddhartha.* New York, NY: Dover.

Kabat-Zinn, J. (2003). Mindfulness-based interventions in context: Past, present, and future. *Clinical Psychology Science and Practice, 10*(2), 144–156. doi:10.1093/clipsy.bpg016

Kerouac, J. (1986). *The Dharma bums.* Cotchogue, NY: Buccaneer Books.

Kilts, T. (2008). A vajrayana Buddhist perspective on ministry training. *Journal of Pastoral Care and Counseling, 62*(3), 273–282.

Koerner, K., & Linehan, M. M. (2011). *Doing dialectical behavior therapy: A practical guide.* New York, NY: Guilford.

Kornfield, J. (2002). *The art of forgiveness, lovingkindness, and peace.* New York, NY: Bantam.

Kornfield, J. (2008). *The wise heart: A guide to the universal teachings of Buddhist psychology.* New York, NY: Bantam.

Kraus, S., & Sears, S. (2009). Measuring the immeasurable: Development and initial validation of the self-other four immeasurable (SOFI) scale based on Buddhist teachings on loving kindness, compassion, joy, and equanimity. *Social Indicators Research, 92*(1), 169–181. doi:10.1007/s11205-008-9300-1

Lau, M. A., Bishop, S. R., Segal, Z. V., Buis, T., Anderson, N. D., Carlson, L., . . . Carmody, J. (2006). The Toronto mindfulness scale: Development and validation. *Journal of Clinical Psychology. 62*(12), 1445–1467. doi:10.1002/jclp.20326

Mace, C. (2008). *Mindfulness and mental health: Therapy, theory and science.* London, UK: Routledge.

MacKillop, J., & Anderson, E. J. (2007). Further psychometric validation for the Mindful Attention Awareness Scale (MAAS). *Journal of Psychopathology and Behavior Assessment, 29,* 289–293. doi:10.1007/s10862-007-9045-1

Mipham, S. (2003). *Turning the mind into an ally.* New York, NY: Riverhead.

Neff, K. D. (2003). The development and validation of a scale to measure self-compassion. *Self and Identity, 2*(3), 223–250. doi:10.1080/15298860309027

Ponlop, D. (2010). Ego: Myth of the self. *Elephant Journal.* Retrieved from http://www.elephant journal.com/2010/06/ego-myth-of-the-self-dzogchen-ponlop-rinpoche/

Salzberg, S. (1995). *Loving-kindness, The revolutionary art of happiness.* Boston, MA: Shambhala.

Sega, Z. V., Williams, J. M., & Teasdale, J. D. (2012). *Mindfulness-based cognitive therapy for depression.* New York, NY: Guilford.

Shantideva. (1997). *The way of the bodhisattva.* Boston, MA: Shambhala.

Siegel, D. J. (2010). *The mindful therapist: A clinician's guide to mindsight and neural integration.* New York, NY: W. W. Norton.

Siegel, R. D. (2010). *The mindfulness solution: Everyday practices for everyday problems.* New York, NY: Guilford.

Skilton, A. (2004). *A concise history of Buddhism.* Cambridge, UK: Windhorse.

Snellgrove, D., & Richardson, H. (1995). *A cultural history of Tibet.* Boston, MA: Shambhala.

Sogyal, R. (1992). *The Tibetan book of living and dying.* New York, NY: HarperCollins.

Stahl, B., & Goldstein, E. (2010) *Mindfulness-based stress reduction workbook.* New York, NY: New Harbinger.

Trungpa, C. (1971). *Garuda: Tibetan Buddhism in America.* Boulder, CO: Karma Dzong.

Trungpa, C. (2002). *Cutting through spiritual materialism.* Boston, MA: Shambhala.

Tsering, T. (2006). *Buddhist psychology, the foundation of Buddhist thought* (Vol. 3). Boston, MA: Wisdom Publications.

Walach, H., Buchheld, N., Buttenmuller, V., Kleinknecht, N., & Schmidt, S. (2006). Measuring Mindfulness—The Freiburg Mindfulness Inventory (FMI). *Personality and Individual Differences, 40,* 1543–1555. doi:10.1016/j.paid.2005.11.025

Wallin, D. J. (2007). *Attachment in psychotherapy.* New York, NY: Guilford.

Watts, A. (1985). *The way of Zen.* New York, NY: Vintage.

Welwood, J. (2000). *Toward a psychology of awakening: Buddhism, psychotherapy, and the path of personal and spiritual transformation.* Boston, MA: Shambhala.

Yeshe, L. (2003). *Becoming your own therapist.* Boston, MA: Lama Yeshe Wisdom Archive.

18

HINDU APPROACHES
TO PASTORAL COUNSELING[1]

Hindus who seek counseling want solutions to problems. It is unlikely that a Hindu may seek out a pastoral counselor for spiritual problems or for the problems of daily living. However, understanding Hinduism may be helpful to pastoral counselors who work with clients who identify as Hindu or for clients who read about Hinduism. Hindus who experience existential dilemmas may seek out a *guru* or a spiritual leader who may help them evolve spiritually. For example, Richard Alpert, more popularly known as Ram Dass, found a guru in Neem Karoli Baba (Dass, 1971). In contrast, another famous Hindu, Mahatma Gandhi, worked independently and found the inspiration to evolve spiritually by reading the *Bhagavad Gita* (Easwaran, 2011).

DIVERSITY AMONG HINDUS

South Asians from the Indian subcontinent are the third largest immigrant group in the United States, and a significant number of these individuals identify as Hindus. Other terms used to describe this population are East Indians, East Asians, and Asian Indians (Baptiste, 2005). Within India, Hindus represent a diverse group based on caste, class, languages spoken, geographical and regional subcultures, cuisine, and skin color (Baptiste, 2005; Hodge, 2004; Pillari, 2005). In India, there are 18 official languages and more than 1,652 dialects (Pillari, 2005). Despite the common beliefs that Hindus hold, the religious practices and daily rituals may vary among these subgroups. Although a majority of Hindus may be of Indian nationality, others may be citizens of Trinidad, Guyana, South Africa, Uganda, Nepal, Ceylon, or Indonesia, and their daily lives may be influenced by their nationality. Although it is beyond the scope of this chapter to capture the full diversity that Hindus represent, an attempt will be made to reduce Hinduism's complexity so that the Hindu worldview can be better understood. Two factors that affect the degree to which Hindus practice their religion may be determined by (a) immigration and/or the length of time lived in the home country and/or in the United States and (b) the desire and commitment to acculturate to the mainstream American culture (Das & Kemp, 1997; Shariff, 2009).

In 2012, there was a 50% increase in U.S. green cards issued to citizens of India from the previous year (2011). A green card allows the bearer all the privileges that American citizens enjoy, except for the right to vote, and is usually considered to be a precursor to citizenship. Approximately 35,500 Indians with a work visa obtained a green card in 2012 in contrast to 6,000 individuals from the previous year ("Green Cards," 2013). There are close to 1 million Hindus residing in the United States, and Hinduism is the largest Asian religion in the country. In the United States, there are at least 412 Hindu centers and one accredited university, located in Iowa, called the Maharishi University of Management (Hodge, 2004; Pillari, 2005). This Hindu subgroup is a growing population in the United States, and those in pastoral counseling and other helping professions will benefit from understanding the Hindu worldview.

CULTURE VERSUS RELIGION

Hinduism started in India and is one of the oldest religions in the world (Hanna & Green, 2004). Hinduism is more than 3,000 years old and dominates the Indian landscape today. However, the culture has been in existence since 7000 BCE, before national boundaries were carved by politics (Shariff, 2009). Shariff (2009) described the culture as a "common way of life . . . of shared values and traditions" (p. 36) that includes diverse nationalities, ethnicities, religions, and languages. Many Hindus consider the Hindu culture to be the Indian culture (Hodge, 2004). Teasing apart the culture from the religion is a necessary first step in providing culturally sensitive counseling to clients. A cultural influence would apply to *most* people, irrespective of religion, class, and caste. In contrast, religious influences or beliefs may be relevant to only one subgroup of a culture or country. A few of the cultural practices prevalent in India are described in the text that follows.

Consanguineous Marriage

A common and acceptable practice in India is consanguineous marriages within a family. Cousins may marry each other. In some subgroups, a niece may marry her uncle. This is prevalent among the many subgroups that coexist together in India; Zoroastrians, Muslims, and Hindus practice consanguineous marriages. However, each subgroup may have unique rules that allow some consanguineous relationships and forbid others. For example, in the Mangalore Brahmin community, a marriage between cousins who have the same family name is forbidden, whereas this practice is sanctioned in the South Indian Muslim community. What does this mean? A Mangalore girl may marry her maternal first cousin but may not marry a distant paternal cousin (related to her through her father) because they have the same last name. In contrast, many subgroups in North India forbid consanguineous marriages.

Dating and Courtship

On the Indian subcontinent, dating is not permitted, particularly for women. A woman who dates may very well be "ruined for marriage" even if she is not sexually active (Albright, 1948/2012, p. 4). A cultural value in the Indian subcontinent is sexual modesty. Women are selected for marriage based on their behavior (Das & Kemp, 1997). A chaste reputation is required to be considered a suitable candidate for an arranged marriage. In addition, being engaged to be married for an extended time period is discouraged. Once the decision to be married is made, the wedding ceremony usually takes place within a week to 6 months. Traditionally, marriages are arranged between the parents of the bride and groom. Even if a couple decides independently (without the prior consent of their parents) to be married, the couple is urged to marry soon. This is a cautionary measure to ensure that an agreement to marry is not broken. The ending of an engagement or a marriage can be misunderstood as a scandal that may limit future choices.

"You Don't Just Marry the Man but Also His Family"

The message often conveyed to young women is that they are not just marrying the man but his entire family. Traditionally, a young bride lives with her husband's family. Sometimes that may involve living with four generations under the same roof. The male members are blood relatives, and the women are the mothers, wives, unmarried daughters, or widowed relatives. When Indians refer to "family," this can include several households, sometimes in different locations, that help each other financially (Das & Kemp, 1997). However, with modernization in India, it is becoming more acceptable for a young couple to break away from the larger family and live independently.

Culturally, the practical benefits of marriage typically outweigh the romantic aspects of marriage. Romantic marriage proposals are not yet a cultural norm, and ensuring the consent of the parents takes precedence. For example, on national television, talk-show host Oprah Winfrey asked Aishwarya Rai, the former Miss World 1994, how her fiancé had proposed to the "most beautiful girl in the world." Ms. Rai did not have a quick and romantic response to this query. Culturally, a proposal usually comes from the groom's family and not the groom himself, and betrothal is not expected to be a romantic event.

HINDUISM

Hinduism is described as a way of life that is not defined by a central administration or a single founder (Hodge, 2004; Pillari, 2005; Thillainathan, 2009). Hodge (2004) stated that Hinduism has "an extraordinary degree" of diversity; basic terminology among Hindus can have "divergent and discrete" significance among the many spiritual traditions (p. 28). Hinduism is a philosophical approach to life and its problems, in which the "concepts of community, interdependence, divinity" and interconnections are implicit (Hodge, 2004, p. 28). Some of these beliefs are described in the following text.

"My Suffering Today Is a Result of My Past Deeds"

Karma means action. Karma is a fundamental concept used to explain how a life unfolds and provides an explanation for privilege, destiny, and suffering. Hindus strongly believe in reincarnation (Hanna & Green, 2004). Karma means facing the consequences of past actions, even if these actions occurred in past lifetimes. If people do good, then good will return to them, either in this life or the next. *Samsara* refers to being caught in the cycle of birth and rebirth. According to Hindu belief, people go through an endless cycle of birth and rebirth, paying for or benefiting from one's past deeds. Ultimately, universal justice prevails through the concepts of karma and samsara (Hodge, 2004; Swami Nikhilananda, 1949). The ultimate goal of human life is to be liberated from karma or past actions and the cycle of birth and death. This liberation in Hinduism is called *moksha* or *mukti*, and among Buddhists it is called *nirvana* (Paranjpe, 2013). Karma can galvanize Hindus in the implementation of free will with the hope of improving their future but can also restrict their sense of agency in dealing with difficult life situations. For example, Kanti, a 34-year-old married woman in South India, had a son who died at age 16 years due to a sex-linked genetic disorder called Duchenne muscular dystrophy. Kanti decided to have another child and became pregnant soon after. It was suggested to her that she determine the gender of the child and avail herself of other options such as abortion if the unborn child was determined to be a boy. Kanti refused the use of ultrasound to determine the child's gender and decided that she would bear the consequences of her karma if that was what was destined for her. Unfortunately, her second child was also a boy who also began to show the signs of muscular dystrophy as a toddler. An abortion is socially and religiously accepted in Hindu society, but Kanti's belief that she could not alter her fate led to the refusal of technology and to the lack of exploration of all options that were available to her.

"Do Your Duty"

One of the guiding principles by which Hindus live is the concept of *dharma* or righteous duty (Hodge, 2004; Thillainathan, 2009). Dharma means to do the duties that are expected from one's position in life and society. Young people are often admonished by their parents to do their duty, even if it is unpleasant to fulfill that duty. For example, the dharma of a young man in college is to study, be studious, and be respectful to his teachers. If he has additional roles to play, be it that of a husband or employee, he is expected to put the time and effort into fulfilling those roles by working hard and providing for his family financially. Doing one's dharma properly stops the accumulation of new negative karma and can reduce suffering in the future. However, perceptions of one's duties can be confusing, particularly when the duty interacts with acculturation to the mainstream U.S. culture.

Collectivist cultures emphasize the sacrifice of one's personal desires for the well-being of the family. Hindu children are raised by their parents to be dependent on their families, and parents continue to influence their children and grandchildren (Das & Kemp, 1997; Shariff, 2009). For the young career-oriented Hindu woman, the freedom and autonomy allowed in American society may make traditional gender expectations at home stifling. Perceptions of what constitutes one's duties, as men and women break out of traditional gender roles, make the concept of dharma harder to implement, particularly in relation to the extended family. For example, Leila, a 35-year-old married doctor, came to see a therapist because of a lack of work–life balance. Leila felt angry about the expectations that her mother-in-law had of her. Leila was expected to run the house with very little support from her husband and her in-laws, despite a full work schedule. In addition, her mother-in-law asked her to continue the family tradition of celebrating the Hindu festivals with ritualistic prayer or *pooja* and to continue daily worship at the shrine in their house. Leila's mother-in-law was also involved with her children, discouraging the children from eating American food at home. Leila felt guilty about her anger toward her mother-in-law and was confused about what decisions were hers to make and what decisions her mother-in-law had the "right" to make about the family.

Worship of Many Gods

Hindus practice idol worship and pray to many different Gods. Hindu mythology has many different tales about the relationship between these Gods and wars that were fought against evil. Some of these Gods are symbols of personal or familial aspirations. For example, *Lord Ganesha,* the elephant-headed God, represents success. People pray to Ganesha before embarking on a major life event or business enterprise. The *Goddess Laxmi* is prayed to for wealth and prosperity. Despite the numerous Gods, Goddesses, and demigods that are recognized by Hindus, the major powers lie with the *Trinity* comprising of *Brahma,* the Creator; *Vishnu,* the Preserver; and *Shiva,* the Destroyer. Vishnu is believed to have been reincarnated on earth numerous times. Among the most famous of these avatars are *Rama, Krishna,* and the *Buddha.* To hint at the diverse beliefs of Hindus, the sacred book *Srimad Bhagavata Mahapurana* states that Krishna, not Vishnu, is the source of all incarnations. Beyond the Trinity lies *Brahman* or *Brahm,* who has no attributes and whose description defies human words and concepts (Swami Nikhilananda, 1949). The *Upanishads,* one of the sacred texts of Hinduism, refers to Brahm as "eternal and omnipresent, all-pervading and extremely subtle; which is imperishable and is the source of all beings" (Swami Nikhilananda, 1949, p. 28). Brahm is symbolized by the sound *Aum* or *Om.* The individual soul, which is an extension of the Brahm, is located at the heart organ of each person (Swami Nikhilananda, 1949; Swami Prabhupada, 1986). Brahma, Vishnu, and Shiva are three functions of the one God, Brahm.

Hinduism promotes the cyclical view of the world. For instance, people go through lifetimes and life stages in cycles through rebirth. Time is seen to exist in endless cycles of day and night. During the *Day of Brahm,* life is manifested through form as perceived by the sense organs. Once the Day of Brahm runs its course, the *Night of Brahm* follows, when all forms of life go back to their seed state awaiting the rebirth of the cosmos through another cycle of the Day of Brahm. Each phase of this cycle is 100 Brahm years, and one day of Brahm is "total to 311 trillion and 40 billion earth years" (Swami Prabhupada, 1986, p. 436). The average Hindu who does not read the sacred books may not be aware of the deeper concepts in Hinduism and may only be aware of the mythological stories about the relationships and the interactions of the Gods.

According to Hinduism, an individual's life falls into four periods. The *Brahmachari* or student phase starts anywhere from 5 to 8 years of age until the individual is 25 years old and requires the student to live with his teacher or guru. The *Grihastha* or householder phase involves marrying, raising a family, and performing civic duties based on each person's role. The *Vanaprastha* stage starts with retirement. In ancient India, this involved living in the forest to meditate and pray. The last phase is *Sanyassa,* when in old age the individual practices detachment from the world and lives like a hermit (Taylor, 1948).

Worship among Hindus may vary. Traditional Hindus in India worship at temples where Brahmin priests chant in the ancient language of Sanskrit. Sermons and hymns are not a part of the religious service. In contrast, in the United States, Hindus may congregate at any Hindu center and listen to sermons spoken in English or Hindi. Songs and dance may be an integral part of the service. Arya Samaj, Chinmaya Mission, and the International Society of Krishna Consciousness are some of the institutions that make the religion accessible and meaningful to North American Hindus. Most Hindus keep a shrine or altar in their homes where ritualistic prayers are offered in front of the deity.

Many Ways to Reach God

Hindus believe that there are many paths to God. The best way is determined by what fits well with an individual's temperament. Therefore, Hindus are not interested in converting people of other faiths to Hinduism. The *Bhagavad Gita*, one of the sacred texts in Hinduism, lists many ways by which people can reach moksha, or the liberation from the cycle of birth and rebirth. The *Gita* is a conversation about the metaphysical laws of the world between Sri Krishna, who is considered to be an *avatar* or reincarnation of Vishnu, and his cousin Arjuna. Krishna informed Arjuna that the paths to liberation are *Bhakti yoga*, *Karma yoga*, and *Dhyana yoga*. Bhakti yoga or devotional service is practiced when the devotee feels pure love for Krishna or any other personal deity. Dhyana yoga is a mechanical meditative practice that controls the individual's senses and helps the individual focus on God. This meditation results in the spiritual knowledge that one's soul or *atman* is Brahm in its true form (Hanna & Green, 2004). One is freed from the illusionary power of *maya* (illusion) that blinds the individual to his own divinity (Hodge, 2004). Karma yoga is practiced when all of one's actions are conducted without being attached to the consequences of those actions. One acts according to the law of dharma or righteous duty and is thus freed from the clutches of one's karma (Hodge, 2004). For example, a student working hard in school without thinking about the rewards that come with success or the negative consequences that inevitably follow failure would be practicing karma yoga.

Caste System

Hindu society is organized into a rigid and hierarchical structure based on division of labor. The caste system is unique in that one is born into a strata of society and cannot change this placement despite innate talents, hard work, or the desire to break free. The four caste groups are *Brahmins*, *Kshatryias*, *Vaisyas*, and *Sudras* (Hodge, 2004; Pillari, 2005). The Brahmins enjoyed the highest status in Hindu society. Traditionally, Brahmins were educated and by profession were the priests, healers, and teachers. The Brahmin culture traditionally reflects values of nonmaterialism, cleanliness, austerity, simple living, and preoccupation with one's spiritual growth. Kshatryias, the warriors, held the second highest caste and were the administrators who governed the land. The Kshatryias served their kings by being a part of the defense forces. Vaisya were the merchants and farmers who ran the economy. Traditionally, the Kshatryias and the Vaisyas lived a life of material comfort and valued wealth and hard work. The lowest caste was the Sudra, who did the menial work that was considered spiritually unclean. Over time, the caste system became oppressive and the upper castes curtailed the freedom of the lower castes (Pillari, 2005). For example, in ancient India, the Sudras were not allowed entry into temples. The caste system is still prevalent in India. It continues to shape the identities of individuals and groups. Parents prefer to marry their adult children into the same caste. In India, caste intersects with socioeconomic status and determines individual privileges. The impact caste can have on an individual or family may be subtle and/or obvious and may be expressed in innumerable ways. Politically, the government of India has set up opportunities for lower castes to have opportunities for higher education and jobs in the public sector.

Preference for Male Children

Having a son is important to Hindu families because only men are allowed to participate in some rituals, such as the cremation of parents on their demise. It is also the
male descendants who "discharge the spiritual debt owed" to the ancestors (Hodge,
2004, p. 29). Traditionally, sons are responsible for their aging parents and are expected
to financially support their parents. In contrast, a daughter is "given away" in marriage
and becomes a member of her husband's family. Male privilege is widely prevalent
in Hindu society. Differential parenting practices for sons and daughters result in
greater restrictions placed on girls within almost every aspect of their lives, from careers
to freedom of movement (Das & Kemp, 1997). Among Hindus, women mate only
once in their lives. Today, although women may marry again, the practice of widow
remarriage for women is not widely practiced. In India, in some Hindu communities,
dowry, or the practice of "buying" a groom for their daughter to marry, makes the birth
of a girl child a financial burden for parents. This preference for boy children can be
seen in the experience of Tara, a 35-year-old South Asian client who sought genetic
counseling services at a community agency in Detroit, Michigan, because of a family
history of genetic disorders. Tara had three daughters with her husband, who was
also Hindu. Tara informed the genetic counselor about her concerns about the pregnancy because of her advanced maternal age and family history of genetic disorders.
During the session, the counselor informed Tara that the test results were normal and
that the fetus was a girl child. A week later, the counselor received a call from a dis-
traught Tara. Tara told the counselor that she was at an abortion clinic with the intention
of terminating her pregnancy because she was carrying a girl child and asked whether
the counselor made a mistake about the gender of the child.

PROBLEM SOLVING AMONG HINDUS

Hindus believe that events in their lives are inevitable and predestined. When a
child is born, the child's horoscope is read and a rough trajectory of the future is determined for each individual. Information needed for a horoscope includes the time,
date, and place of birth. A horoscope determines how the position of the planets
affects events in the individual's life. Thus, when a person is encountering problems,
the first response of a traditional Hindu is to have his or her horoscope read to find
out if and when a "bad" time will end.

There are many ways of foretelling the future in India. Some of the more modern
methods include numerology and dousing. For example, Lata, a 60-year-old widow
living in Austin, Texas, struggled to pay her bills on a meager salary. In the past 6
months, she encountered many problems consecutively that ranged from a threat
of being laid off at work to her house requiring numerous repairs plus maintenance
costs. Lata contacted her brother in India to have her horoscope read by a priest. Lata
learned that she was going through *Shani*, or the strong influence of the planet Saturn, which resulted in her current problems. Lata was told to wait out the influence
of Saturn and to pray to mitigate the harmful effects of this planet. The karmic consequences of past lives can also be determined from horoscopes. Tanvi, a 26-year-old
woman living with her parents in Chennai, India, had her horoscope read because
she felt "stuck." She was not married, had no job, and wanted to study abroad but
was not admitted into any university and was still treated like a child at her parents'
home. She had the past-lifetime segment of her horoscope read and learned that her

feelings of stagnation were a consequence of not having cared for her parents in a previous lifetime.

ACCULTURATION

American-born Hindus navigate two cultures: the culture of their families and the mainstream American culture. Parenting among traditional Hindus is hierarchical and authoritarian. Children are expected to obey their parents (Das & Kemp, 1997). The culture values education and economic success (Baptiste, 2005). Many Hindu parents pressure their children to pick high-status occupations such as medicine and engineering. American Hindus who wish to acculturate to the mainstream culture and maintain their unique identity must navigate a bicultural world that may involve asserting their values and beliefs in the face of opposition from their families (Das & Kemp, 1997; Shariff, 2009).

Culturally, lighter skin is viewed favorably. American-born Hindus who are educated to be sensitive to stereotypes and racial discrimination often resent judgments made by the older immigrant members of their families about race and skin color. In India, for women in particular, lighter skinned women are more likely to make a "favorable" marriage to husbands who are chosen for their incomes and occupations. American-born Hindu women who wish to assimilate by dating sometimes do not have the support of their families because the family would want them to maintain their chastity (Das & Kemp, 1997).

Immigrants in the United States continue to arrange marriages for their adult children, with potential life partners residing in the United States or even internationally. Sometimes, American-born Hindus may reject the notion of an arranged marriage and may choose to marry based on the American idea of romance and love (Baptiste, 2005). However, in reality, this process is negotiated by parents and their adult children, with some children wanting the privileges to choose freely and to have a long courtship. Often, parents in the United States introduce their children to other eligible Hindus, and young couples are then allowed to build a relationship with each other, often over long distances, before making an independent decision to marry. In the United States, the most important criterion for marriage is common religious affiliation, and exogamous factors, such as languages spoken, caste, and ethnicity, become secondary in choosing a life partner. In the United States, the traditional requirement of compatible horoscopes of the bride and groom also becomes secondary to the desire to choose a life partner within the religion.

INTERVENTIONS WITH HINDU CLIENTS

Although both cultural and religious concerns affect Hindu clients, teasing apart distinct cultural and religious interactions may be challenging. Often, Hindu clients may present a cultural concern but may want a solution that is aligned with their religious beliefs and values. For example, modern Hindus may struggle to overcome caste distinctions because of their belief that every person shares the same universal spark of divinity. Conversely, some Hindu clients may have difficulty translating Hindu ideas into their daily lives. For example, a male client who may want to follow his dharma or righteous duty may be unwilling to take sides in a conflict between his mother and his wife. Most helpful interventions with Hindu clients integrate both cultural and religious solutions.

In India, most Hindus are discouraged from sharing their personal woes and intimate problems with "outsiders" (Das & Kemp, 1997; Pillari, 2005; Shariff, 2009). People who are indiscreet about their personal lives, particularly if they complain about another family member whom they are expected to honor and respect, are criticized and judged harshly. "Outsiders" are trusted only if a personal relationship has already been built or can be built with the service provider. Typically, the family doctor, who monitors the health of the individual, may also have the privilege of hearing about the client's problems. Hindu clients who have problems are more likely to use prayer and worship and may struggle to be open about their culture and their feelings with a counselor (Thillainathan, 2009).

Seeking counseling services could be the very last and desperate attempt to find a solution to a problem (Sharma, 2011). Although priests may be called on to read horoscopes, an individual is unlikely to reveal her or his personal problems to a traditional priest. A traditional Hindu Brahmin priest is expected to know Sanskrit chants and prayers. A Hindu priest will not have any training in counseling or psychology and may operate from a traditional worldview. Hindus belong to a collectivistic culture, and counseling that promotes Western values such as self-promotion, individual identities, and interpersonal defiance may result in premature termination (Baptiste, 2005; Das & Kemp, 1997; Hodge, 2004; Pillari, 2005).

It is important that the counselor convey understanding and acceptance of the client's Hindu values without making assumptions about what these values might be. Thillainathan (2009) believed that client-centered therapy with a focus on building trust in oneself and on "becoming the self one truly is" (p. 51) would mirror the Hindu belief about recognizing the divinity of each individual. Empathy and direct questioning may be appropriate for helping clients explore problems (Hodge, 2004). Interventions to facilitate change must be offered very slowly, and the counselor should check in frequently with the client to determine that an accurate reading of the client has been done and to evaluate client reactions to interventions. Counselors should be neutral and resist taking sides among the members of the family (Baptiste, 2005). Dialogue among family members struggling with acculturation and intergenerational conflicts can be facilitated by "cultural brokering," or externalizing or shifting the blame from an individual family member to the culture (Speigal, 1982). Particularly when working with adolescents, relabeling family problems as a transition to the mainstream culture can allow youths to feel more empowered within the Hindu family system. Because the Hindu family is patriarchal and hierarchical, counselors who address the husband and the oldest members of the family will honor the cultural value of deference to the elders (Hodge, 2004). In addition, intervention that promotes confrontation of parents by their children or the confrontation of a husband by the wife may be culturally discordant (Baptiste, 2005). As clients, Hindus are typically less interested in insight-oriented counseling, and interventions that are behaviorally focused are viewed as more credible. Therefore, a short-term, solution-focused, cognitive behavioral intervention model of counseling may work best with this population (Shariff, 2009).

Hinduism has provided four goals that individuals should aspire to in their lifetimes: dharma (righteous action), moksha (liberation from the cycle of birth and death), karma (the process of improving one's future), and *artha* (the accumulation of wealth through righteous ways) (Pillari, 2005). The *Bhagavad Gita* lists three *gunas* or modes of the material world: *Sattva* or the mode of goodness, *Rajas* or the mode of passion, and *Tamas* or the mode of ignorance (Swami Prabhupada, 1986). Sri Krishna in the *Bhagavad Gita* stated that living from Sattva is preferable. A Sattvic person prefers a simple lifestyle that reflects self-discipline and the renunciation of pleasures. A Sattvic person values compassion, truthfulness, humility, and contentment. Mahatma

Gandhi would be an example of a Sattvic person. A Rajasic person seeks worldly success and recognition but may be discontent even when he or she is successful. In their interpersonal interactions, they may ridicule other people and consider themselves better than other people. Tamasic people are hateful, angry, and slothful. They live in ignorance. Hindus who are Rajasic or Tamasic in their thoughts and actions and whose aim in life is material gain may not be in a spiritual struggle to develop Sattvic qualities. However, every aspect of life can be analyzed by the three gunas. For example, charitable donations given with the intention of being socially recognized as a philanthropist would be Rajasic in quality. Donations made because of guilt will be Tamasic in nature. Determining the *right* amount to be given to the *right* person at the *right* time for the *right* reasons will be Sattvic. Helping Hindu clients understand the motives for their actions and to assist them to determine how they can integrate their life goals into their everyday lives through the process of counseling may make the client feel "heard" by the therapist.

Although the aim of this chapter is to provide the pastoral counselor with a "working hypothesis" (Hodge, 2004, p. 28) about Hinduism and the culture of South Asian Hindus, it is no substitute for the recognition of the uniqueness of each individual who seeks counseling. Ultimately, clients should be allowed the freedom and the right to correct the counselor's knowledge about the culture and the religion based on their lived experiences and their interpretation of Hinduism.

Although it is unlikely that a Hindu client will seek out a pastoral counselor to specifically address religious or spiritual issues, pastoral counselors are likely to encounter clients who identify as Hindu in a variety of settings such as hospitals and community agencies. If pastoral counselors are alert to both the cultural and religious aspects of their Hindu clients' lives and can identify the Hindu clients' levels of acculturation (culture) and/or the developmental stage of their spiritual evolution, then pastoral counselors are more likely to make a positive impact in the lives of their Hindu clients.

REFLECTION QUESTIONS

1. According to the author, in what ways do culture and religion intersect and interact for Hindus? What might be considered distinctively religious, rather than cultural?

2. In what ways are the concepts of karma and dharma congruent with your own worldview? What challenges might you face when working with a client who sees these principles differently than you do?

3. Imagine that a Hindu client came to see you. He tells you that he has just entered the Vanaprastha stage of his life and wants to reflect more on the Brahmachari and Grihastha stages of his life as he contemplates Sanyassa. What developmental models from your training might you draw on to better understand the client's development?

4. Describe three ways in which common Hindu problem-solving and help-seeking strategies differ from your own.

NOTE

1. The author thanks Jayani Parikh for sharing her knowledge about Hinduism.

REFERENCES

Albright, M. (2012). *Prague winter: A personal story of remembrance and war,* 1937–1948. New York, NY: HarperCollins. (Original work published 1948)

Baptiste, D. A. (2005). Family therapy with East Indian immigrant parents rearing children in the United States: Parental concerns, therapeutic issues, and recommendations. *Contemporary Family Therapy, 27*(3), 345–366. doi:10.1007/s10591-005-6214-9

Das, A. K., & Kemp, S. F. (1997). Between two worlds: Counseling South Asian Americans. *Journal of Multicultural Counseling and Development, 25*(1), 23–33. doi:10.1002/j.2161-1912 .1997.tb00313.x

Dass, R. (1971). *Be here now.* New York, NY: Crown.

Easwaran, E. (2011). *Gandhi the man: How one man changed himself to change the world* (4th ed.). Tomales, CA: Nilgiri.

Green cards issued to Indians soar six fold in a year. (2013, August 14). *India Herald,* p. 6.

Hanna, F. J., & Green, A. (2004). Asian shades of spirituality: Implications for multicultural school counseling. *Professional School Counseling, 7*(5), 326–332. Retrieved from http://eric .ed.gov/?q=Asian+shades+of+spirituality%3a+Implications+for+multicultural+school +counseling.&id=EJ704649

Hodge, D. R. (2004). Working with Hindu clients in a spiritually sensitive manner. *Social Work, 49*(1), 27–31. Retrieved from http://allianceforclas.org/wp-content/uploads/2013/05/ WorkingwithHinduClients.pdf

Paranjpe, A. C. (2013). The concept of Dharma: Classical meaning, common misconceptions and implication for psychology. *Psychology Developing Societies, 25*(1), 1–20. doi:10.1177/ 0971333613477302

Pillari, V. (2005). Indian Hindu families. In M. McGoldrich, J. Giordano, & N. Garcia-Preto (Eds.), *Ethnicity & family therapy* (pp. 395–406). New York, NY: The Guilford Press. Retrieved from https://whsresearch.wikispaces.com/file/view/Ch.+29+Indian+Hindu+Families.pdf

Shariff, A. (2009). Ethnic identity and parenting stress in South Asian families: Implications for culturally sensitive counselling. *Canadian Journal of Counselling, 43*(1), 35–46. Retrieved from http://files.eric.ed.gov/fulltext/EJ832723.pdf

Sharma, B. (2011). *The differences between first-generation American-born Asian Hindus and immigrated Asian Indian Hindus on measure of acculturation, self-concept, and attitudes towards counseling: A mixed methods study* (Doctoral dissertation). Retrieved from http://gradworks.umi.com/ 34/48/3448056.html

Speigal, J. (1982). An ecological model of ethnic families. In M. McGoldrick, J. K. Pearce, & J. Giordana (Eds.), *Ethnicity and family therapy* (pp. 31–51). New York: Guilford.

Swami Nikhilananda. (1949). *The Upanishads: A new translation* (Vol. 1, 5th ed.). New York, NY: Ramakrishna-Vivekananda Center.

Swami Prabhupada. (1986). *Bhagavad-Gita as it is.* Los Angeles, CA: The Bhaktivedanta Book Trust.

Taylor, W. S. (1948). Basic personality in orthodox Hindu culture patterns. *Journal of Abnormal and Social Psychology, 43,* 3–12. doi:10.1037/h0056297

Thillainathan, N. (2009). Rogers to reincarnation: Counselling people of Hindu faith. *Psychotherapy in Australia, 15*(4), 51–52. Retrieved from http://www.psychotherapy.com.au/fileadmin/ site_files/pdfs/InterfaceAugust2009.pdf

Michael T. Garrett, Cyrus Williams, Russ Curtis,
Iain Tucker Brown, Tarrell Awe Agahe Portman,
and Mark Parrish

19

NATIVE AMERICAN SPIRITUALITIES AND PASTORAL COUNSELING

Some of my fondest memories of when I was still a little one go back to times spent with my grandfather, Oscar Rogers, who was Eastern Cherokee. We would spend time sitting on the rocks by the Oconaluftee River in Cherokee, North Carolina. "What do you see when you look into the water?" he would inquire, as he sat on a rock enjoying the afternoon sun. I would look closely to see the water rushing quickly downstream. My eyes would catch the glimpse of a fish, water beetles, flies touching the water, soaked wood floating along at the will of the water, rocks, and green plants.

"I see the water," I said. "What else do you see?" he asked. "Well, I see the fish," I answered, because there were little minnows swimming around in the water. "What else do you see?" he asked. "I see the rocks," I said. "What else do you see?" he asked again. My eyes began to water themselves as I stared intently, wanting so much to please my grandfather by seeing everything he saw.

"Ah, I see my reflection," I responded proudly. "That's good," he replied confidently. "What you see is your whole life ahead of you. Know that the Great One has a plan for you to be the keeper of everything you see with your eyes, 'cause every living thing is your brother and sister." "Even the rocks?" I questioned. "Yes, even the rocks," he answered, "because they have elements of Mother Earth and Father Sky, just as we do."

"Remember to give thanks every day for all things that make up the Universe," said my grandfather. "Always remember to walk the path of Good Medicine and see the good reflected in everything that occurs in life. Life is a lesson, and you must learn the lesson well to see your true reflection in the water."
—M. T. Garrett (1996a, p. 12)

The family story just presented evokes very simple but powerful lessons offered by the image of a grandfather spending precious time with his young grandson on the riverbank on a reservation in western North Carolina. However, the story also illustrates a number of concepts central to the experience of Native people in general, with an extraordinary emphasis on the harmony and balance required to survive and thrive from a cultural standpoint by remaining grounded in oneself, while deeply connected to family, community, traditions, natural surroundings, and the Creator. Although my (Garrett) great-grandfather was a Cherokee traditionalist, he also served as a lay minister in the local church and frequently engaged in pastoral care, a meeting of worlds that is not uncommon in many reservation communities. Therefore, in his spiritual work he represented the crossroads between both indigenous and Christian-based systems of faith, with an eye toward best fulfilling his sacred responsibility by helping others in need. To understand better how pastoral counseling relates to the spiritualities and spiritual needs that exist in the lives of Native peoples in the United States, it is important to understand their stories and experiences and from where they have come. This chapter provides an overview of traditional Native American spiritualities and life ways as systems of faith, then discusses the role and influence of Christianity, and, finally, offers implications for pastoral counseling with Native people from a culturally based perspective.

TRADITIONAL NATIVE AMERICAN SPIRITUALITIES

The Creation

Some Native American creation stories say they came into their land by climbing up from the world or worlds below. Others believe they traveled to this Middle World on a journey to find the exact place where they were supposed to live. Sometimes the beings of the sky, sun, moon, or stars guided the First People to the Center of the World, as in the Zuni concept of their homeland. In other cases, the plants or animals of the Middle World led the First People to the place where they were to live and flourish. Each of the tribes in North America has its own story about where they came from and why they chose to settle where they were at the time the Europeans arrived.

Most Native American nations have no word in their language for the European concepts of "religion," "Indian," or "Native American." Instead, they have a concept of themselves as "The People," as distinct from the First Animals, who were people in the Before Time, a sacred time when animals were the first beings to live on the earth. The animals planned what the First People would look like, how these new creatures called humans would live, and maybe even where they would live. From a Native perspective, every living thing in the world is related to human beings.

Not a Typical Religion

When most people think of religion, they picture a church, synagogue, or mosque. Tribal groups in North America in times past built temples made of earth or stone, but for the most part, it is the natural world where tribes prayed and made sacrifices to their concept of the Supreme Being. For Native peoples today, their place of worship might be a mountaintop, a spring, or a small sweat lodge in a canyon deep in the woods. This diverse group of people spawned a wide array of ideas about what constitutes a religion and how religious ideas are expressed. People have often referred to the Native American concept of the sacred or the holy as the Great Spirit, and it is true that most Native Americans believe in a single creator. But in some cases, Native American people believe that the creator or creators are both male and female. Some tribes believe that a feminine spirit was responsible for the creation of the world and humans. Others believe in a gender-neutral creator—that is, a creator who is neither male nor female but has the power to create the world and all that is in it.

Spirit and the Natural World

The cultures and religions of Native Americans are greatly influenced by their surroundings, and their beliefs and spiritual practices reflect the variety of those natural settings. Today, tribes maintain many traditions first started by their ancestors. The Native peoples who lived in the Southwest, called the Pueblos by the Spanish because of the villages they established, were at first primarily farmers. Water and rainfall were precious, and so much of the religion of these Hopi and Zuni people, among other groups, was focused on prayers for rain. Those people who lived in the near-arctic regions remained nomadic hunters. The harshness of their environment, with its terrible winter storms and less abundant food supply, made them often appear to be equally harsh, at least to outsiders. Because both humans and animals had to kill to survive, the Inuit people of the far north assumed that the powerful animals they hunted, such as the polar bear, had powerful spirits, too. The people who settled in the Pacific Northwest, on the other hand, had abundant resources, unlike the peoples to their north and south, and consequently, the religion of the Northwest coastal tribes included ceremonies designed to curb greediness, a human tendency they believed would be displeasing to the spirits they looked to for help and guidance.

The Influence and Role of Animals

Animals are also important in the lives and beliefs of traditional Native Americans. Native people generally do not consider themselves superior to animals but believe the animals' role in the world as a resource for people—meat, skins, or bone for tools—is something the animals, at some point, voluntarily chose to perform when approached with reverence and respect. In fact, in many Native American spiritual traditions, animals play an important part in the creation of people and usually have human traits such as speech or virtues such as bravery or generosity as conveyed through tribal legends as part of the oral tradition.

Native Humor as Spiritual Tradition

The use of humor in Native tradition has contributed to the survival of many Native nations as a coping skill, to harmony and balance among Native people as an everyday communication skill that preserves connections, and to the life-learning of younger generations as an oral tradition. As a spiritual tradition, Native humor has served a number of important purposes, including the maintenance of Native culture, controlling social situations, teaching people how to live, creating unity, increasing social and political awareness, testing others' identity or cultural competency as Native, and simply as a way of interacting and enjoying being together (Deloria, 1988, 1994). Furthermore, Native humor takes many different forms, including stories, anecdotes, teasing or razzing, songs, dance, art forms, cultural symbols, and so forth (Herring & Meggert, 1994).

One of the most common forms that Native humor has taken traditionally is that of stories intended to both entertain and educate. Many tribal oral traditions emphasize important life lessons through the subtle humor expressed in these stories and legends. Often, it is the arrogant, manipulative, vain, clown-like figure of Rabbit, Possum, Coyote, Dog, Turtle, or Raven, among others (the character depends on the tribe but is always the one who thinks he or she knows it all), that ends up learning a hard lesson in humility in the end (thereby restoring balance to all things), much to the amusement of others and maybe as a reminder to others (J. T. Garrett & Garrett, 1996; M. T. Garrett, 1998; Herring, 1994). Humility and a sense of generosity are cultural values that seem to pervade Native nations across the United States (M. T. Garrett, 1996a). Stories and anecdotes are but one means of reinforcing and reminding in-group members of the cultural values and unspoken rules by which they live. Many Native people live for laughter, which plays a very important role in the continued survival of the tribal community. After all, laughter relieves stress and creates an atmosphere of sharing and connectedness. As George Good Striker (Blackfoot) puts it, "Humor is the WD-40 of healing" (as cited in M. T. Garrett, 1998, p. 137).

Cultural Symbolism of the Eagle Feather

Eagle feathers, considered infinitely sacred among many Native peoples, are used for a variety of purposes, including ceremonial healing and purification as well as the embodiment of a sacred connection with the Creator. Native traditionalists refer to "Eagle Medicine," which represents a state of being achieved through diligence, understanding, awareness, and completion of "tests of initiation" such as the Vision Quest or other demanding life experiences (Deloria, 2006; M. T. Garrett & Garrett, 2012). Highly respected elder status is associated with Eagle Medicine and the power of connectedness and truth. It is through experience and patience that this medicine is earned over a lifetime. And, it is through understanding and choice that it is honored. There is an old anecdote that probably best illustrates the lessons of the eagle feather by reminding us about the power of perspective: Once while acting as a guide for a hunting expedition, an Indian had lost the way home. One of the men with him said, "You're lost, chief." The Indian guide replied, "I'm not lost, my tipi is lost."

The eagle feather represents duality in existence and serves as a lasting symbol of resilience through connectedness to the greater whole. It tells the story of life by symbolizing harmony and balance through which life has been able to persist. It tells of the many dualities or opposites that exist in the Circle of Life, such as light and dark, male and female, substance and shadow, summer and winter, life and death, peace and war (M. T. Garrett & Myers, 1996; M. T. Garrett & Portman, 2011). The eagle feather has both light and dark colors, dualities and opposites. Although one can make a choice to argue which of the colors is most beautiful or most valuable, the truth is that both colors come from the same feather, both are true, both are connected, and it takes both to fly (J. T. Garrett & Garrett, 1996; M. T. Garrett & Portman, 2011). As one elder put it,

> The Eagle feather teaches about the Rule of Opposites, about everything being divided into two ways. The more one is caught up in the physical, or the West, then the more one has to go in the opposite direction, the East, or the spiritual, to get balance. And it works the other way too—you can't just focus on the spiritual to the exclusion of the physical. You need harmony in all Four Directions. (J. T. Garrett, 1991, p. 173)

Therefore, the colors of the eagle feather could be perceived as opposite, but they are part of the same truth. The importance of the feather lies not in which color is most beautiful but in finding out and accepting what the purpose of the feather as a whole may be. In other words, there is no such thing as keeping the mountains and getting rid of the valleys; they are one and the same, and they exist because of one another. This stands as a constant reminder of the need to strive for balance in all things as a basis for Native American spiritual practices and beliefs.

Spiritual Belief Systems

The spiritual beliefs of any individual Native person depend on a number of factors, including her or his level of acculturation (traditional, marginal, bicultural, assimilated, pan-traditional), geographic region, family structure, religious influences, and tribally specific traditions (M. T. Garrett & Pichette, 2000; LaFromboise, Coleman, & Gerton, 1993). However, it is possible to generalize, to some extent, about a number of basic beliefs characterizing Native American traditionalism and spirituality across tribal nations (M. T. Garrett, Torres Rivera, Dixon, & Myers, 2009). The following, adapted from Locust (1988, pp. 317–318), describes a number of basic Native American spiritual and traditional beliefs. This list of beliefs crosses tribal boundaries. It is, by no means, a comprehensive list. It does, however, provide insight into some of the assumptions that may be held by a "traditional" Native client.

1. There is a single higher power known as Creator, Great Creator, Great Spirit, or Great One, among other names (this being is sometimes referred to in gender form but does not necessarily exist as one particular gender or another). There are also lesser beings known as "spirit beings" or "spirit helpers."
2. Plants, animals, and inanimate beings such as rocks, like humans, are also part of the spirit world. The spirit world exists side by side with, and intermingles with, the physical world. Moreover, the spirit existed in the spirit world before it came into a physical body and will exist after the body dies.
3. Human beings are described as having a body, mind, soul, and spirit. All of these facets (body, mind, soul, and spirit) of the human experience are interconnected; therefore, illness affects the mind and spirit as well as the body.
4. Wellness is indicated through the experience of balance and harmony at the physical (body), mental (mind), soul (emotional), and spiritual levels of human existence. Likewise, unwellness or disease is a result of imbalance.
5. Natural unwellness is caused by the violation of a sacred social or natural law of Creation (e.g., participating in a sacred ceremony while under the influence of alcohol, drugs, or having had sex within 4 days of the ceremony).
6. Unnatural unwellness is caused by conjuring (witchcraft) from those with destructive intentions.
7. Each of us is responsible for our own wellness by keeping ourselves attuned to self, relations, environment, and universe.

The most common way to conceptualize Native spirituality is in a basic holistic (cardinal) directions frame, although specific symbolism or meanings can vary from tribe to tribe; overall, seven directions provide the foundation of belief systems that inform life's journey:

1. *The East* is the direction of spirit and spiritual connectedness. This direction is the way of new beginnings, representative of a new day of life. In this direction, information becomes knowledge only when it is in service of the creation of balance and harmony in all directions of living.

2. *The South* is representative of the Earth plane, or the body, consisting of the same elementals as all other beings on the planet (the standing nations [plants], the four-leggeds [animals], the winged ones, the ones that crawl on the earth, and the finned ones [those that swim in the ocean]). In this direction, all beings are equally valuable and important in the larger scheme of things.
3. *The West* is the direction of the soul, or more operationally conceptualized as the emotions. This direction provides an awareness of the energy that informs the day-to-day decisions that we make; balance and harmony are intrinsically interrelated with emotional awareness and regulation.
4. *The North* is representative of the mind and the thought processes that inform how to journey most effectively through this lifetime. This direction represents the wisdom of life's experiences and the importance of passing on knowledge to inform future generations.
5. *The Sky (Above)* is the knowledge provided through our awareness of the cosmos, the ethereal, referring to the upper reaches of the atmosphere. This direction is representative of the things that we do not fully understand but that we know to be true, such as the importance of living in a good way to produce balance and harmony along our journey.
6. *Below* represents our connection to the earth and the earth elements: earth, wind, fire, and water.
7. *All Around (or Center)* is representative of our awareness of self within the larger picture. It is our sense of personal space and grounding resulting from our experiences of past, present, and future. In other words, it represents our self-actualized and self-determined self and active connection to all things.

All things exist in the seven directions within the universal circle of life (M. T. Garrett & Garrett, 2002). This basic directions model provides a frame for understanding Native spiritual beliefs. However, it is important to understand that tribes have different stories and archetypes assigned to each direction.

Native American Spiritualities and Religion

Traditional Native American ceremonies are still practiced by many tribes, and the older spiritual belief systems are still held by many of the "traditional" people, often "elders" and therefore, keepers of that special wisdom passed down from generation to generation. These spiritualities might be more "pure" in terms of tradition or may accompany adherence to another faith as well, which might represent a person's primary religious identity, therefore representing a blending of traditions or faiths in reality. Although much Native American spiritualism exists on a tribal–cultural continuum and as such cannot be easily separated from tribal identity itself, certain other more clearly defined movements have arisen among "traditional" Native American practitioners, these being identifiable as "religions" in the stricter sense of the word. Traditional practices of some tribes include the use of sacred herbs or substances such as tobacco, sweetgrass, corn pollen, or sage as a means of cleansing and offering prayer. Also involved might be forms of fasting, singing, and specific prayer or prayer chants in the ancient languages of their people, and sometimes drumming or rattle shaking is also common. Another significant religious faith among Native peoples, to be discussed further in the following section, is the Native American Church. It is a synergistic church incorporating elements of Native spiritual practice from a number of different tribes as well as symbolic elements from Christianity. Finally, there are Native people who practice Christianity or other major religious faiths rather than the traditionalism of their Native traditional heritage or origin but may or may not consider that aspect of their lives as detracting from their sense of themselves as Native American.

THE ROLE AND INFLUENCE OF CHRISTIANITY

In terms of faith and belief, Christianity has had the greatest influence on Native Americans. Christian missionaries were among the first Europeans to arrive in the Americas, and many explorers saw converting the "savage Indians" as a key part of their job. The history of Christian influence on Native Americans is a mixed one, blending care and consideration with outright hostility and various forms of harm. Only in recent years have Christian denominations embraced the original spiritual beliefs of Native Americans and begun to include some of those beliefs in the rituals of Christian services. Chumash dancers can be seen performing at Catholic services in California. Native American–designed vestments are worn by priests and ministers in the Southwest. Music influenced by Native American style is used in a variety of Christian services. Theologians and ministers seek ways to combine the message of Jesus with Native American themes, such as in creation stories and in the Christian call for service or humility.

Some individual Christian churches have been more accepting of traditional activities related to ceremonial practices, especially songs in tribal languages and drums and rattles for song-chants used with funerals and special youth ceremonies. The American Indian Church, located in Garden Grove, California, is one example of a new Christian denomination based on traditional spirituality. It was founded in 1978 to combine Christian teachings with respect for tradition among Native people. Earlier in the 20th century, a church of the Christian sect called the Shakers was established among the Yakimas of Washington state. Missionaries first started the group, but it was soon run by Native Americans themselves, combining traditional spiritual practices with Shaker rites and beliefs.

Some tribes continue to worry about the "outsider" influence of Christian churches. There remain memories of earlier policies that demonized or cast aside traditional Native American beliefs and imposed Christian ones. However, today there is a greater sensitivity to tribal sacred sites, for instance, or to the use of pipe ceremonies and dances. There is also clearly more open-mindedness among the various Christian churches for traditional, spiritual ways. This is especially true in urban areas where there are large numbers of Native Americans, such as Denver, Los Angeles, and New York.

Today, although they continue to keep and hold a variety of Native American spiritual beliefs and customs, many Native Americans are part of a wide variety of Christian denominations. Their relationship to one another is part of the ongoing story and evolution of Native American spiritualities and systems of faith.

Native American Church

The Native American Church (NAC) originated in Oklahoma and is a religious denomination that practices the Peyote religion, the most widespread indigenous religion among Native Americans in the United States. Quanah Parker is credited as the first big leader of the Native American Church, which was introduced to North American

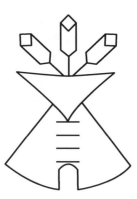

FIGURE 19.1 Native American Church insignia.

tribes in the 1880s and was formally incorporated in Oklahoma in 1918. Parker adopted the Peyote religion after being gored by a bull in South Texas and surviving the attack with the help of peyote. Parker taught that the Sacred Peyote Medicine was the Sacrament given to all Peoples by the Creator and was to be used with water when taking communion in some Native American Church medicine ceremonies, which also incorporate elements of Christianity. The peyote ritual is believed to allow communion with God and the deceased and to give power, guidance, and healing. The healing may be emotional, physical, or both (Figure 19.1).

Although specific Peyotist beliefs vary from tribe to tribe, all Peyotists believe in a supreme God. The "Peyote Road," as it is known, calls for Native American brotherly love (often taking the form of Native American nationalism), family care, self-support through work, avoidance of alcohol, and avoidance of recreational drug use. The use of peyote, a type of cactus bud that produces psychedelic or hallucinogenic effects when eaten, is an ancient practice considered sacred among cultures in North and South America. In the late 19th century, several Southwestern Native American tribes began to use peyote in more organized religious contexts. In peyote religions, followers eat small portions of peyote, called buttons; sing songs; and perform a variety of ceremonies. In many cases, they blend Christian beliefs and ideas with the traditional use of peyote, which they say gives them a higher and deeper understanding of and connection to the spiritual world.

As the practice spread more formally, opposition arose on local and federal levels, and a variety of legislation was passed banning the practice. Some tribes, such as the Navajo in 1940, also later tried to outlaw the use of peyote. The objections came about because of peyote's drug-like nature. Just as people objected to alcohol or marijuana use, they felt that peyote was a narcotic. Some users were jailed, and raids were carried out on ceremonies while they were under way. Followers kept using the substance, however, and in 1918 in Oklahoma, they formed the Native American Church as a way to help protect their practices. Similar groups were founded in other states, and in 1944, a national Native American Church group was founded. In defending itself against the legal challenges it faced, the church argued that its use of peyote is a sacrament of their church, similar to the Christian Eucharist (the ceremony in which Christians remember Christ's Last Supper; they eat bread and wine that has been consecrated according to their denomination's beliefs.)

The 1994 amendment to 1978 American Indian Religious Freedom Act, among other things, legalized the use of peyote in religious ceremonies. Today, peyote religions are practiced in some form by perhaps 25% of Native Americans who use peyote in churches that are both Christian and more traditionally Native American. Peyotism is now practiced in more than 50 Native American tribes, mostly in the West, and has around 250,000 practicing members.

PASTORAL COUNSELING WITH NATIVE AMERICANS

Pastoral counseling in the global community is a significant challenge for those who endeavor to help the many communities of faith that may be represented in their congregation (Barry & Connolly, 1982; Benner, 2002; Cobb, 1991; Wicks, Parsons, & Capps, 1985). The primary focus for pastoral counselors is healing or care of the soul by helping clients who are experiencing any combination of mental, emotional, and/ or spiritual crisis and pain become more aware of God's presence in their lives through therapeutic work and techniques such as dialogue, prayer, and personal reflection (Moon & Benner, 2004). According to Silva-Netto (1992), however, a challenge exists for pastoral counselors in terms of the cultural relativity of working with and:

> defining the "optimal person" [as] one who is able to function appropriately and effectively, maximize abilities and talents, and actualize potentials within given contextual limitations . . . [without basing it on] some definition of what it means to be human as that is commonly held by the dominant culture [or systems of faith]. (pp. 131–132)

Essentially, cultural competence is critical in pastoral counseling with ethnic and spiritually marginalized groups such as Native Americans due to historical struggles, mistreatment, and a resulting potential for mistrust (Mazur-Bullis, 1984; Means, 1997; Reyes-Netto, 1985; Silva-Netto, 1992).

Although Native Americans represent many different tribes with cultural and ethnic uniquenesses, for the most part, existing literature suggests that Native Americans are family oriented, may be suspicious of counseling as a form of authority tied to dominant culture, may tend to try to solve personal problems within the family or community context, or may seek help first or exclusively from Native American spiritual leaders and tribal elders (Brucker & Perry, 1998). Additionally, some tribal groups attach great stigma to mental health problems, and thus, clients may be guarded because they do not know whether the information shared will be disclosed to their communities and cause further problems (Granbois, 2005).

In regard to help-seeking behaviors and spirituality, Native Americans who do seek help outside of their community may have an expectation of some form of advice or advising as opposed to psychotherapy. Native Americans who pride themselves on living out their spirituality in the traditional cultural sense may practice their spirituality by listening and talking to the Creator throughout the day; this too may be an impediment to receiving counseling from individuals who do not understand their practice of spirituality (M. T. Garrett & Garrett, 2002). These cultural issues, coupled with the training or lack thereof, present potential problems for the practice of pastoral counseling with these clients.

Indigenous ways of knowing (IWOK) are defined by Grayshield and Mihecoby (2010) as "a multidimensional body of lived experiences that informs and sustains people who make their homes in a local area and always takes into account the current socio-political colonial power dimensions of the Western world" (p. 6). As a general framework, IWOK can help pastoral counselors to understand the unique cultural worldview of Native Americans, as well as necessary approaches to assessing and assisting with spiritual needs, health, and well-being (D. Dell & Hopkins, 2011). According to Deloria (as cited in Grayshield & Mihecoby, 2010), indigenous forms of knowledge are "the result of keen observations in the experience of daily life and in the interpretive messages received from spirits in ceremonies, visions and dreams" that coincide with a reality for tribal people based on "the experience of the moment coupled with the interpretive scheme that had been woven together over the generations" (p. 5). From the perspective of IWOK, the true purpose of the helping process would be to promote engagement in activities that increase one's awareness of nature and many of the inherent universal truths of which one becomes aware through that experience as a basic and fundamental construct of overall health, well-being, and resilience.

As a central concept in spiritual well-being, resilience is defined as "a balance between individual strategies of coping with adversity and the availability of community support" (as cited in D. Dell & Hopkins, 2011, p. 109), reflecting an emphasis that also is central to an indigenous worldview and ways of knowing. C. Dell, Hopkins, and Dell (2004) explain how the "traditional Native world view highlights one's spirit as the core of one's self—the motivator and animator of one's life . . . the spirit is what gives one the ability to bounce back . . . the spirit is not a material form, so it is indestructible" (as cited in D. Dell & Hopkins, 2011, p. 109).

Spirit is central to one's resiliency as a life force connected to all other life forces across time and space from a Native perspective, and thus, one also has to be attuned to aspects of transcending historical oppression and current-day adversity that span generations in spiritual, mental, and physical effects as well as pathways for healing. Therefore, it is important that pastoral counselors take into account the Native perspective on a sense of community and one's intentionality toward respecting and maintaining that sense of community as paramount to understanding the indigenous experience. D. Dell and Hopkins (2011) expand on this notion that:

> from an Indigenous cultural worldview, knowing oneself comes from a connection to the universal family of creation, one's biological and extended family, and community. It is through this connection that one is nurtured in awareness of self in relation to others. Choosing self and acting with intention from a cultural perspective is about choosing a life path that is reflective of cultural identity, intrinsically motivated by one's spirit and one's spiritual connection to family and community. Cultural knowledge facilitates an understanding about the "truth," purpose, and meaning of one's life, which sets the foundation for "giving self." (p. 110)

Cultural knowledge and practices form the basis for indigenous resilience rooted in family and community strength. Although Native Americans face many obstacles, members of this population also possess strengths that have helped them survive racism, forced relocation, and genocide (Brave Heart & DeBruyn, 1998). Goodluck (2002) conducted a meta-analysis that focused on identifying the strengths of Native Americans. Results of the analysis yielded 42 specific strengths of Native Americans that were combined into three categories: extended family, spirituality, and social connections. These strengths are important to acknowledge within a body of literature about Native people that tends to focus on struggles and obstacles rather than cultural strength and resilience. Furthermore, these help to guide effective, culturally responsive practice in pastoral counseling with this population that is focused on honoring and using as a resource when possible the strength of Native American life ways as a method for spiritual healing.

Native people have always believed in and encouraged the gifts and potential of their people. In a way, they embraced the concept of resiliency long before it was named "resilience" (HeavyRunner & Morris, 1997; Kirmayer, Dandeneau, Marshall, Phillips, & Williamson, 2011). Resilience theory with a strength-based perspective may be a good match for pastoral counselors to adopt or at least consider when endeavoring to understand and work with this population (Arrington & Wilson, 2000). This perspective honors the power of the self to heal and right itself with the help of the environment, the need for healthy alliances, and hope that life can get better (Saleebey, 1992). Although acknowledging the prevalence of generational poverty and other risk factors, there is a need to identify the strengths and resources of this client population. As HeavyRunner and Morris (1997) assert,

> Cultural resilience is a relatively new term, but it is a concept that predates the so-called "discovery" of our people. The elders teach us that our children are gifts from the Creator and it is the family, community, school and tribe's responsibility to nurture, protect and guide them. This traditional process is what contemporary researchers, educators and social service providers are now calling resilience. Thus resilience is not new in our people; it is a concept that has been taught for centuries. The word is new but the meaning is old. (p. 28)

A common core of values has been discussed in the literature characterizing Native traditionalism across tribal nations as a source of strengths and protective resources. These commonalities include the importance of community contribution, sharing, acceptance, cooperation, harmony and balance, noninterference, extended family, attention to nature, immediacy of time, awareness of the relationship, and a deep respect for elders (M. T. Garrett & Portman, 2011). These traditional values show the importance of honoring, through harmony and balance, what Native people believe to be a very sacred connection with the energy of life and the whole of biodiversity. This provides the basis for a traditional Native worldview and spirituality across tribal nations that have served as the foundation for strength and resilience in the face of adversity over many generations as an indigenous way of knowing and being.

With this in mind, to work most effectively with Native clients concerning issues around mental health and spirituality, it is important to understand the nature of the cultural experience from which they come but also how important it is to see the uniqueness of each and every client. The cultural dimensions emphasized here allow the pastoral counselor to conceptualize current issues in a cultural context and select methods of approaching that client and issue(s) so that cultural values, beliefs, practices, and experiences are used as strengths and valuable resources for the client.

Attending to Common Presenting Issues and Recommendations

A summary of common presenting problems for Native Americans is provided in Table 19.1 based on a synthesis of those revealed in the literature. Although these lists are not necessarily all-inclusive, they do represent common themes or issues that seem to emerge for Native clients at the respective age levels. Recognizing common presenting issues across age groups and areas of attention for cultural responsiveness in therapeutic intervention, Herring (1999, pp. 56–57, 76) summarized a set of specific recommendations (see Table 19.2) pertinent to working with Native Americans.

TABLE 19.1 Common Presenting Problems for Native Americans by Age Group

CHILDREN	ADOLESCENTS	ADULTS
• Failure to develop a strong ethnic identity and self-identity	• Difficulty developing a positive self- and ethnic identity	• Difficulties stemming from overcoming myths and stereotypes that the Native culture is evil, savage, and inferior
• Adverse effects of misperceptions about Native peoples in general	• Reactions to stereotypical misperceptions of Native peoples	• Negative effects of injustice, discrimination, hardship, and degradation
• Adverse effects of discrimination and hatred toward Native peoples, both generally and specifically	• Communication conflicts such as English as a second language or a preference for nonverbal communication	• Negative effects of poverty
• Distrust of European American schools and helping professionals based on historical and contemporary negative interactions	• Conflicts between family loyalty and peer pressures	• Diverse cultural characteristics
• Limited standard English skills or limited use of English	• Effects of misunderstandings and misperceptions of school personnel	• High suicide rate and low life expectancy
• Nonverbal communication style conflicting with European American verbal expectations	• Low academic achievement	• Language difficulties and nonverbal communication misunderstandings
• Difficulty reconciling Native cultural values and mainstream values	• Substance use and abuse	• Midlife crises
• Lower academic achievements after the fourth grade	• Adverse effects of discrimination and bias	• Substance use and abuse
• Conflicts resulting from changing from an extended family-centered world to a peer-centered one	• Generational conflicts resulting from varying degrees of acculturation	• Low self-concept and feelings of inferiority/rejection
• Differences in physical appearance, psychosocial differences, and possible intellectual differences (including learning style differentiations)		• Low educational attainment

Source: Adapted from Herring (1999, pp. 59, 76).

Each of these recommendations is intended to assist pastoral counselors in becoming more effective with Native clients from a variety of backgrounds and with a variety of presenting issues (Brucker & Perry, 1998). However, beyond the logistics of working in one-on-one or group contexts, it is also important to consider systemic, environmental, and other contextual factors that influence the health and well-being of Native clients.

TABLE 19.2 Therapeutic Recommendations for Working With Native Americans

---

1. Address openly the issue of dissimilar ethnic relationships rather than pretending that no differences exist.

2. Evaluate the client's degree of acculturation.

3. Schedule appointments to allow for flexibility in ending the session as needed.

4. Be open to allowing the extended family or other valued persons (such as indigenous or faith-based healers) from the community to participate in the session as needed or requested by the client.

5. Allow time for trust to develop before focusing on the problem.

6. Use strategies that elicit practical solutions to problems, and focus on the positives/strengths as a rule with a coinciding potential for change.

7. Establish eye contact sufficient to subtly match the client and create comfort nonverbally.

8. Respect the use of silence.

9. Demonstrate honor and respect for the client's culture and show interest without being intrusive or presumptuous, and with openness, be willing to admit your ignorance.

10. Provide assistance to Native clients in exploring ethnic identity issues as needed.

11. Maintain the highest level of confidentiality.

12. Listen with your heart and your mind.

Source: Adapted from Herring (1999, pp. 56–57, 76).

Understanding Identity, Family, and Acculturation

A first step in the counseling relationship, and a sign of respect, lies in the pastoral counselor's effort to identify the client's tribe and whether the client is directly affiliated with that tribe (federal, state, and/or community recognition). It is not the job of pastoral counselors to pass judgment on who is Native American and who is not. Thus, a pastoral counselor should not ask a Native client "How much Native American are you?" or relate personal stories of Native American heritage in his or her family as a way of connecting with that client. That is often a quick way to lose a Native person's receptivity and trust. If a client says that he or she is Native, then a pastoral counselor must assume that it is so. This acceptance of client self-report is a way to understanding that client without having to get into the painful (and sometimes irrelevant) politics of categorization. More important, it gives the pastoral counselor insight into that person's perception of her experience and place in the world.

When working with a Native American client, it is important to get a sense of that person's level of acculturation. This can be assessed through the client's (a) values (traditional, marginal, bicultural, assimilated, pan-traditional), (b) geographic origin/residence (reservation, rural, urban), and (c) tribal affiliation (tribal structure, customs, beliefs) and history as well as any family issues and history (see M. T. Garrett & Pichette, 2000). Both verbal and nonverbal cues offer pastoral counselors a sense of a Native American client's level of acculturation (M. T. Garrett & Pichette, 2000). If questions remain, it is important to pose them in a respectful, unobtrusive way. Following are some examples of general leads intended to respectfully elicit important culturally relevant information:

- Where do you come from?
- Tell me about your family, clan, and/or community.
- What tribe/nation are you? Tell me a little bit about that.
- Tell me about you as a person, culturally and spiritually.
- Tell me about your life as you see it, past, present, or future.

To further determine acculturation and subsequent worldview, the pastoral counselor should gather information on the spiritual beliefs, family history and structure, and community of origin versus community of choice. Pastoral counselors must avoid making assumptions about the cultural identity of Native American clients without gathering further information about both the individual's internal and external experiences. As mentioned earlier, one cannot assume because a person "looks Native American" that he or she is traditional in his or her cultural and spiritual ways or that, because a person "does not look Native American," he or she is not traditional. Instead, it is important to explore the meaning of the core values and beliefs that characterize what it means to be Native for any given client.

Facilitating Healing From Historical Trauma

Given the historical and current context of social and political issues facing Native people, a major underlying and ongoing issue in therapeutic work with most Native clients, regardless of the setting, is the establishment of trust, as is true with many oppressed peoples (Grayshield & Mihecoby, 2010). The question that the pastoral counselor must ask of herself or himself is, "What can I do to create and maintain trust with a Native client?" It may be time well spent to bring up the topic of oppression with the client, asking him or her to relate growth-fostering experiences that have had an impact on his or her life, both in joyful and hurtful ways. Pastoral counselors can ask where the client is from and, likewise, where his or her family is from. It also might be helpful to ask further about some of the experiences across generations that have affected the client and helped to shape how he or she sees the world. Specifically, pastoral counselors should inquire as to what ways family and intergenerational history may be playing into what has brought the client in for help.

Brave Heart (2000) and other scholars (Brave Heart & DeBruyn, 1998; Crazy Thunder & Brave Heart, 2005; Grayshield & Mihecoby, 2010) have identified three aspects of the historical experience as critically important in creating trauma: colonization, the boarding school experience, and forced assimilation. According to McLeigh (2010), colonization is an apt description for the experience of Native peoples subjugated through European conquest, including the impact of infectious diseases, the introduction of alcohol (which had not been part of indigenous cultures), and other major traumatic events such as massacres and forced migration that had and continues to have long-lasting repercussions. The historical trauma response (HTR) is the constellation of features in reaction to historical trauma that may include substance abuse (a vehicle for numbing the pain associated with trauma) and other types of self-destructive behavior, including suicidal thoughts and gestures, depression, anxiety, low self-esteem, anger, and difficulty recognizing and expressing emotions (Brave Heart, 2003). Historical unresolved grief often accompanies the trauma; this grief may be considered impaired, delayed, fixated, and/or disenfranchised (Brave Heart & DeBruyn, 1998). Brokenleg (2012) offers an example of the trauma and grief common to many adults:

I spoke with a woman in Winnipeg who was a smartly dressed, articulate, intelligent school teacher. When she was five years old, a plane landed in the community. The officials aboard took all of the five-year-olds away and they never went home again. She does not know what happened to her parents or if she has brothers or sisters. (p. 11)

For this Native person, the trauma of the boarding school experience in childhood is still very real. Her narrative represents a vivid illustration of cultural genocide and a reminder of the soul wound that many Native clients carry (Duran, 2006; Duran, Firehammer, & Gonzalez, 2008). Across Native populations in the United States and throughout the world, boarding schools were consistently used as an instrument of forced assimilation through removal from, and denigration of, traditional culture. McLeigh (2010) contends that the transgenerational effects of the residential schools include disruption of families and communities; confusion of parenting with punitive institutional practices; impaired emotional response (a reflection of the lack of warmth and intimacy in childhood); repetition of physical and sexual abuse; loss of knowledge, language, and tradition; and the systematic devaluing of Native identity. These consequences of residential schools not only affect the adults who directly experienced these dislocations but often have significant impacts on adults' abilities to parent youths in the ways that they and their communities may desire.

According to Brave Heart (2003, 2005), both prevention and treatment need to focus on ameliorating the HTR and fostering a reattachment to traditional Native values. These values may serve as protective factors to limit or prevent both substance abuse as well as further transmission of trauma across generations (Brave Heart, 2003, 2005). These practices often promote improved parenting skills and parent–child relationships. Improved relationships across generations may further serve as protection against both substance abuse and the transfer of the HTR to subsequent generations of children and adolescents (Gone, 2009). Furthermore, Native ceremonies often require discipline and commitment, delaying gratification, and healthy role modeling of skills needed to defend against substance use and other problematic behaviors.

The goal for pastoral counseling to help address historical trauma could be three-fold. The first goal would be to provide an opportunity for trauma and grief resolution, including a decrease in hopelessness as well as an increase in joy. The second goal would be to foster an increase in positive tribal identity when possible. The third goal would be to facilitate an increase in protective factors and a decrease in risk factors for substance abuse and other harmful behaviors while fostering parental relationships with children and family relationships across generations. By educating themselves about the history of tribes from which Native clients come and culturally based treatment modalities, pastoral counselors can better understand the impact of institutional racism and acculturation, as well as the meaning of the Native American experience for any given client, and begin the process of healing in a way that incorporates culture as a central focus.

Integrating Spirituality

It is important that pastoral counselors recognize the vast diversity of spiritual traditions and customs that can be tribally specific as well as those that may be influenced or replaced by forms of Christianity or other belief systems. Pastoral counselors might want to invite the client to identify his or her need for spiritual support or ceremony and how that might be best achieved within the context of pastoral counseling. As stated, Native spirituality manifests itself in many different forms, such as traditional tribal ways, Christian traditions, Native American Church, or other faith traditions altogether. With a client who seems to have more traditional values and beliefs, it may be particularly helpful to suggest that family or a Medicine person participate in the process to support the client as he or she moves through important personal transitions and subsequent personal cleansing. It should be noted that a general understanding of Native American spirituality does not prepare pastoral counselors to participate in or conduct Native ceremonies as part of the counseling process (M. T. Garrett et al., 2011; Matheson, 1996). That is the responsibility of those who are trained as Native Medicine persons. These individuals can serve as an important resource to pastoral counselors working with Native clients in a spiritual context.

Building on Cultural Symbolism to Seek Spiritual Balance

An understanding of indigenous perspectives on seemingly contrasting opposites (right and wrong, happy and sad, day and night, open and closed, good and bad, etc.) is essential for working with Native American clients who may be experiencing dissonance in their lives but who perceive this in a much different way than might be expected within the majority culture context. Asking the right questions and being open to what is not readily perceived bridges the gap between what pastoral counselors see and what exists underneath perceived facades. Given the understanding that, from the Native worldview, everything has meaning and purpose, one goal of counseling is to help Native clients discover their purpose, examine their assumptions, seek an awareness of universal and personal truths, and make choices that allow them to exist in a state of harmony and balance within the Circle of Life. Talking with the client about his or her powerful cultural symbols, such as the eagle feather or any other significant cultural symbol as discussed earlier in the section on "Cultural Symbolism of the Eagle Feather," and what they represent to that particular client may help facilitate an opening to a dialogue that lends insight into current issues, internal and external resources, and needed approaches, including the use of spiritual metaphor. For instance, a pastoral counselor might say to a client, "How does the eagle feather or symbolism of the eagle feather help offer guidance or clarity on your situation or issue?" Again, from an indigenous worldview, cultural symbols can help provide powerful insight into potential therapeutic goals for achieving harmony and balance among the four directions—mind, body, spirit, and natural environment.

Using Therapeutic Humor

Humor can provide another powerful avenue for understanding and/or healing through spiritual connection and perspective taking. Although humor is one of the important Native coping mechanisms, it should only be used if the client invites it, thereby trusting the pastoral counselor enough to connect on that level (M. T. Garrett, Garrett, Wilbur, Roberts-Wilbur, & Torres-Rivera, 2005). What, in one situation, can be humor between two people, in another can be interpreted as ridicule or being disingenuous. Pastoral counselors therefore have to be sensitive to using humor in a way that does not reinforce various means of oppression that the client may have endured for all of his or her life. However, on the opposite side of this issue lies the opportunity to connect with the client on his or her own ground and share humor through mutual trust that seems appropriate while following the client's verbal and nonverbal cues. In sum, although pastoral counselors working with Native clients should exercise caution when using humor, they definitely should not overlook it as a powerful therapeutic technique. Native American humor serves the purpose of reaffirming and enhancing the sense of connectedness as part of family, clan, and tribe. To the extent that it can serve that purpose in the counseling relationship, it is all the better.

Incorporating Social Justice and Client/Community Advocacy

Many Native communities today are faced with the daunting task of linguistic and cultural revitalization of their respective tribal traditions and customs, as well as addressing the numerous challenges and ongoing risk factors faced by Native youth resulting from current and historical oppression (Grande, 2004; Turner & Pope, 2009). Pastoral counselors working from a social justice and advocacy perspective must have a clear understanding that oppression occurs on many levels (ethnical backgrounds, gender, worldviews, national origins, social economic statuses); therefore, it is vital that pastoral counselors advocate for Native individuals at the individual, community, and national levels. Choudhuri, Santiago-Rivera, and Garrett (2012) discuss the need for helping professionals to focus on three main levels of practice from an advocacy and social justice counseling perspective: client and student advocacy, school and community advocacy, and public arena advocacy.

In client and student advocacy, the pastoral counselor implements direct counseling strategies based on understanding the social, political, economic, and cultural contexts in which clients live and facilitating self-advocacy on the part of the client. For instance, a pastoral counselor might join an organization offering counseling services to returning Native American veterans and their families. Furthermore, the pastoral counselor may directly address external barriers that impede the client's development that the client himself or herself is unable to address due to lack of resources, access, or power. In school and community advocacy, the pastoral counselor might get involved in assisting community organizations that are working for change, such as developing a cultural sensitivity training program for volunteers at a food bank or helping with a mentoring program to connect community elders with youth in need. Furthermore, pastoral counselors might get involved by going to a larger stage to maintain a direction for change that will affect macro levels of access and resources. An example of this may be to join in ongoing lobbying efforts to maintain funding and services for Native American–based ex-offender employment and rehabilitation programs. Finally, in public arena advocacy, pastoral counselors might get involved in disseminating information widely to raise social consciousness that assists in deepening understanding. So, pastoral counselors might write an article for the local newspaper on systemic influences on spiritual and mental health concerns for Native American clients, sensitizing public awareness of ongoing discrimination. Furthermore, pastoral counselors might get involved with working on large social issues that will then indirectly affect the experience of Native American clients.

On a cautionary note, it is also necessary that nontribally affiliated service providers maintain an awareness of a long history of mistrust that has developed between agency-affiliated persons and tribal people (Matheson, 1996). In other words, an underlying mistrust for non-Native people in their service to Native people and their communities has been fostered in the types and levels of services and resources that have been provided or promised to Native people and their communities throughout American history. Numerous government and church agencies have historically misused and affectively abused the relationships that were established with the intention of "helping" Native people live in a system that is drastically different from the one they were taught to value. Thus, social justice and advocacy efforts should be engaged vehemently with the specific intention of promoting the programs and processes that have been previously established by the specific tribal nations themselves.

Many tribes and tribal communities themselves have formed advocacy groups to address the numerous challenges they face such as cultural and linguistic revitalization, health and nutrition, economic and environmental stewardship, education and vocation advancement, and a whole host of other social and political interests. This may mean attending community meetings, educating the general population, organizing activities to highlight the needs of Native Americans, and actively participating in the policy-making process. Native American clients who are not affiliated with their respective tribe(s) may themselves be at varying places in their tribal/indigenous identities and may be subject to the whims of displaced pan-Indian processes and products that essentially lead to further confusion for Native people in their search for meaningful identity. However, nontribally affiliated pastoral counselors and service providers can effectively develop the skills needed to encourage and galvanize individuals and communities to participate in the social justice activities that they identify as important to them and to the healthy functioning of their communities for generations to come.

CONCLUSIONS

A culturally responsive approach to understanding the spiritual needs and challenges of Native peoples acknowledges intrapersonal and interpersonal connections through a metaphor of concentric circles that move outward from the self, much like the rippling effect of water (see Figure 19.2), and also resonates back to the self, according to indigenous teachings. Circles of life energy surround us, exist within us, and make up the many relationships of our existence. In all, we each have a circle of self, comprising the many facets of our own development (e.g., mind, body, spirit, and natural surroundings); a circle of immediate family, extended family, tribal family, community, and nation; a circle consisting of all our relations in the natural environment; and a circle of our universal surroundings.

Within the cultural context of an understanding of concentric circles, statistics show that Native Americans face many difficult challenges that include being at greater risk for substance abuse, suicide, accidental death, violence, and mental health problems, as well as contextual factors that include communities characterized by high rates of unemployment, poverty, physical and mental health disparities, violence, and lower levels of educational achievement. At the same time, there are many positive efforts within Native communities throughout the country directed at fostering resilience among Native Americans and promoting positive growth and development based on indigenous ways of knowing. With this in mind, the overall purpose of this chapter was to offer a comprehensive overview and understanding of culturally sensitive and competent pastoral counseling practice with Native people by discussing traditional Native American spiritualities, the role and influence of Christianity, and implications for effective pastoral counseling with Native peoples.

FIGURE 19.2 Circles within circles represent interrelationship from a Native perspective.

Through culturally responsive pastoral counseling, as we turn to an approach that is more congruent with traditional Native worldviews, we listen to the life stories of Native elders, adults, and youngsters alike and begin to understand the spiritual needs and challenges from the perspective of indigenous ways of knowing. We see the powerful influences of history and systems of faith converging. We become more attuned to the importance of the stories—the meanings, language, experiences, images, and themes—of our Native clients. In that process, we begin to learn, as it has traditionally been taught by so many Native elders, that true learning is a lifelong process, just as a story unfolds and offers the gift of its life to us. The following quote from a Native elder illustrates the power of tradition and community to many Native people as he was asked to respond to the question, "Who are you as a Native person?":

Well, I think the stories probably gave me a sense of connection with the Indian side more than anything else. What I remember most of all is everything that my grandfather ever said because to me, he must have been the tallest man in the world. I was such a little boy, and I'd look up at him, and he was tall, tall and slender. Boy, I thought he was such a fine man. The first thing he'd say every time I'd see him was "Ceo Tsayoga," in other words, hello there little bird, how you doing. The first thing he would always do is he'd put me up on his shoulders, I remember that, and take me down to the creek bank. He'd say, "Come on, let's go to the creek bank . . . gonna do some fishin'." I never fished. I never got a chance to fish. I don't know that he ever fished. It's like if he had a chance to take me fishing, that was a chance to tell me stories, teach me values. And one that I do remember very much was when we'd look in the water because I really enjoyed as a little kid just looking at the little minnows, seeing the fish in the water. And he'd let me look for hours, and I don't know whether he was fishing or not, I think he was. We never brought home any fish. I think he would always put the fish back, even if he caught one. (M. T. Garrett, 1996b)

Somewhere even now, a young child may be sitting by the riverside with a grandparent, looking at the water and at himself or herself, one and the same. The elder and the child sit together, honoring Mother Earth and all that she has to offer us, honoring life and its constant motion. The elder and the child sit together, one and the same. Stories might be shared, and many generations will hear their words flow alongside the trickling of the river's water. Someday, the little boy or girl may earn that first eagle feather or other symbol of cultural and spiritual significance. And in doing so, he or she may earn the responsibility and the joy of looking to the surface of the river's water and seeing the true reflection of his or her own grandchild looking back. In this way, the Circle continues to move and shift with the all the gifts of life and mysteries of what it means to live well in a spiritual way from a Native perspective.

REFLECTION QUESTIONS

1. What do the authors mean when they assert that Native American spiritualities are not "typical" spiritualities? In what ways are the spiritualities that they describe different from and similar to other spiritualities with which you are already familiar?
2. What important roles does the natural world play in Native American spiritualities? How might you include this important dimension in your work, both with Native American clients and those from other backgrounds?
3. The authors describe seven common elements of Native American spiritual belief systems. Which of these paradigms are most similar to your own ways of seeing the world and conceptualizing health and distress? Which of these is most dissimilar from your ways of seeing the world?
4. According to the authors, what have been some of the significant impacts of Christianity on Native American spiritualities and practices? What are points of connection between these traditions? What are points of divergence?
5. How might indigenous ways of knowing (IWOK) be integrated into a pastoral counseling approach? In what ways should a counselor be thoughtful before integrating IWOK into her or his work?

REFERENCES

Arrington, E. G., & Wilson, M. N. (2000). A re-examination of risk and resilience during adolescence: Incorporating culture and diversity. *Journal of Child and Family Studies, 9*, 221–230. doi:10.1023/a:1009423106045

Barry, W. A., & Connolly, W. J. (1982). *The practice of spiritual direction.* New York, NY: Seabury.

Benner, D. G. (2002). Nurturing spiritual growth. *Journal of Psychology and Theology, 30*(4), 355–361.

Brave Heart, M. Y. H. (2000). Wakiksuyapi: Carrying the historical trauma of the Lakota. *Tulane Studies in Social Welfare, 21–22*, 245–266.

Brave Heart, M. Y. H. (2003). The historical trauma response among Natives and its relationship with substance abuse: A Lakota illustration. *Journal of Psychoactive Drugs, 35*, 7–13. doi: 10.1080/02791072.2003.10399988

Brave Heart, M. Y. H. (2005). *Substance abuse, co-occurring mental health disorders, and the historical trauma response among American Indians/Alaska Natives* (Research monograph). Washington, DC: Bureau of Indian Affairs, Department of Substance Abuse Prevention.

Brave Heart, M. Y. H., & DeBruyn, L. M. (1998). The American Indian holocausts: Healing historical unresolved grief. *American Indian and Alaska Native Mental Health Research, 8*(2), 55–78. doi:10.5820/aian.0802.1998.60

Brokenleg, M. (2012). Transforming cultural trauma into resilience. *Reclaiming Children and Youth, 21*, 9–13.

Brucker, P. S., & Perry, B. J. (1998). American Indians: Presenting concerns and consideration for family therapists. *American Journal of Family Therapy, 26*(4), 307–319. doi:1080/01926 189808251109

Choudhuri, D. D., Santiago-Rivera, A. L., & Garrett, M. T. (2012). *Counseling and diversity: Central concepts and themes for competent practice.* Boston, MA: Cengage/Lahaska.

Cobb, J. B. (1991). Pastoral counseling and theology. In H. W. Stone & W. M. Clements (Eds.), *Handbook for basic types of pastoral care and counseling* (pp. 18–40). Nashville, TN: Abingdon.

Crazy Thunder, D., & Brave Heart, M. Y. H. (2005). *Cumulative trauma among tribal law enforcement officers: Search, rescue, & recovery at Ground Zero and on the reservation.* Washington, DC: Bureau of Indian Affairs, DASAP.

Dell, C., Hopkins, C., & Dell, D. (2004). Resiliency and holistic inhalant abuse treatment. *Journal of Aboriginal Health, 1*(2), 4–12.

Dell, D., & Hopkins, C. (2011). Residential volatile substance misuse treatment for indigenous youth in Canada. *Substance Use & Misuse, 46*, 107–113. doi:10.3109/10826084.2011.580225

Deloria, V., Jr. (1988). *Custer died for your sins: An Indian manifesto.* Norman, OK: University of Oklahoma Press.

Deloria, V., Jr. (1994). *God is red.* Golden, CO: Fulcrum.

Deloria, V., Jr. (2006). *The world we used to live in: Remembering the powers of the medicine men.* Golden, CO: Fulcrum.

Duran, E. (2006). *Healing the soul wound: Counseling with American Indians and other Native peoples.* New York, NY: Teachers College Press.

Duran, E., Firehammer, J., & Gonzalez, J. (2008). Liberation psychology as the path toward healing cultural soul wounds. *Journal of Counseling & Development, 86*, 288–295. doi:10.1002/j.1556-6678.2008.tb00511.x

Garrett, J. T. (1991). Where the medicine wheel meets medical science. In S. McFadden (Ed.), *Profiles in wisdom: Native elders speak about the earth* (pp. 167–179). Santa Fe, NM: Bear & Company.

Garrett, J. T., & Garrett, M. T. (1996). *Medicine of the Cherokee: The way of right relationship.* Santa Fe, NM: Bear & Company.

Garrett, M. T. (1996a). Reflection by the riverside: The traditional education of Native American children. *Journal of Humanistic Education and Development, 35*, 12–28.

Garrett, M. T. (1996b). "Two people": An American Indian narrative of bicultural identity. *Journal of American Indian Education, 36*. Retrieved from http://jaie.asu.edu/v36/V36S1pt1.htm

Garrett, M. T. (1998). *Walking on the wind: Cherokee teachings for harmony and balance.* Santa Fe, NM: Bear & Company.

Garrett, M. T., & Garrett, J. T. (2002). "Ayeli": Centering technique based on Cherokee spiritual traditions. *Counseling and Values, 46*, 149–158. doi:10.1002/j.2161-007x.2002.tb00285.x

Garrett, M. T., & Garrett, J. T. (2012). *Native American faith in America* (2nd ed.). New York, NY: Facts on File.

Garrett, M. T., Garrett, J. T., Wilbur, M., Roberts-Wilbur, J., & Torres-Rivera, E. (2005). Laughing it up: Native American humor as spiritual tradition. *Journal of Multicultural Counseling and Development, 33*, 194–204. doi:10.1002/j.2161-1912.2005.tb00016.x

Garrett, M. T., & Myers, J. E. (1996). The rule of opposites: A paradigm for counseling Native Americans. *Journal of Multicultural Counseling and Development, 24*, 89–104. doi:10.1002/j.2161-1912.1996.tb00292.x

Garrett, M. T., & Pichette, E. F. (2000). Red as an apple: Native American acculturation and counseling with or without reservation. *Journal of Counseling and Development, 78,* 3–13. doi: 10.1002/j.1556-6676.2000.tb02554.x

Garrett, M. T., & Portman, T. A. A. (2011). *Counseling and diversity: Counseling Native Americans.* Boston, MA: Cengage/Lahaska.

Garrett, M. T., Torres-Rivera, E., Brubaker, M., Portman, T. A. A., Brotherton, D., West-Olatunji, C., Conwill, W., & Grayshield, L. (2011). Crying for a vision: The Native American sweat lodge ceremony as therapeutic intervention. *Journal of Counseling and Development, 89,* 318–325. doi:10.1002/j.1556-6678.2011.tb000096.x

Garrett, M. T., Torres-Rivera, Dixon, A. L., & Myers, J. E. (2009). Acculturation and wellness of Native American adolescents in the United States of North America. *Perspectivas Socials/Social Perspectives, 11,* 39–64.

Gone, J. P. (2009). A community-based treatment for Native American historical trauma: Prospects for evidence-based practice. *Journal of Consulting and Clinical Psychology, 77,* 751–762. doi:10.1037/2326.4500.1.S.78

Goodluck, C. (2002). *Native American children and youth well-being indicators: A strengths perspective.* Portland, OR: National Indian Child Welfare Association. Retrieved from http://www.nicwa.org/research/03.Well-Being02.Rpt.pdf

Granbois, D. (2005). Stigma of mental illness among American Indian and Alaska Native nations: Historical and contemporary perspectives. *Issues in Mental Health Nursing, 26,* 1001–1024.

Grande, S. (2004). *Red pedagogy: Native American social and political thought.* Lanham, MD: Rowman & Littlefield.

Grayshield, L., & Mihecoby, A. (2010). Indigenous ways of knowing as a philosophical base for the promotion of peace and justice in counseling education and psychology. *Journal for Social Action in Counseling and Psychology, 2,* 1–16.

HeavyRunner, I., & Morris, J. S. (1997). Traditional Native culture and resilience. *Research and Practice, 5,* 28–33.

Herring, R. D. (1994). The clown or contrary figure as a counseling intervention strategy with Native American Indian clients. *Journal of Multicultural Counseling and Development, 22,* 153–164. doi:10.1002/j.2161-1912.1994.tb00461.x

Herring, R. D. (1999). *Counseling with Native American Indians and Alaska Natives: Strategies for pastoral counselors.* Thousand Oaks, CA: Sage.

Herring, R. D., & Meggert, S. S. (1994). The use of humor as a counselor strategy with Native American children. *Elementary School Guidance & Counseling, 29,* 67–76.

Kirmayer, L. J., Dandeneau, S., Marshall, S., Phillips, M. K., & Williamson, K. J. (2011). Rethinking resilience from indigenous perspectives. *The Canadian Journal of Psychiatry, 56,* 84–91.

LaFromboise, T. D., Coleman, H. L. K., & Gerton, J. (1993). Psychological impact of biculturalism: Evidence and theory. *Psychological Bulletin, 114,* 395–412.

Locust, C. (1988). Wounding the spirit: Discrimination and traditional American Indian belief systems. *Harvard Educational Review, 58,* 315–330.

Matheson, L. (1996). Valuing spirituality among Native American populations. *Counseling and Values, 41,* 51–58. doi:10.1002/j.2161-007x.1996.tb00862.x

Mazur-Bullis, R. (1984). Pastoral care in a Native American context. *Journal of Pastoral Care, 38,* 306–309.

McLeigh, J. D. (2010). What are the policy issues related to the mental health of Native Americans? *American Journal of Orthopsychiatry, 80,* 177–182. doi:10.1111/j.1939-0025.2010.01021.x

Means, J. J. (1997). Pastoral counseling: An alternative path in mental health. *Journal of Pastoral Care, 51*(3), 317–328.

Moon, G. W., & Benner, D. G. (2004). Spiritual direction and Christian soul care. In G. Moon & D. Benner (Eds.), *Spiritual direction and the care of souls* (pp. 11–28). Downers Grove, IL: InterVarsity Press.

Reyes-Netto, B. (1985). Hidden agenda in cross-cultural pastoral counseling. *Journal of Pastoral Care, 39,* 342–348.

Saleebey, D. (1992). The strengths perspective in social work practice: Extensions and cautions. *Social Work, 41,* 296–304. doi:10.1093/sw/41.3.296

Silva-Netto, B. (1992). Pastoral counseling in a multicultural context. *Journal of Pastoral Care, 46*, 131–139.

Turner, S. L., & Pope, M. (2009). North America's Native peoples: A social justice and trauma counseling approach. *Journal of Multicultural Counseling & Development, 37*, 194–205. doi: 10.1002/j.2161-1912.2009.tb00102.x

Wicks, R. J., Parsons, R. D., & Capps, D. E. (Eds.). (1985). *Clinical handbook of pastoral counseling*. New York, NY: Paulist Press.

Jason Hays

20

PASTORAL COUNSELING AND QUEER IDENTITIES

I received a call from a person named Alex who had been given my name by a local pastor. Alex wanted to explore the possibility of "finding someone to talk with about troubles I'm having" and was interested in working with a pastoral counselor "because spirituality and faith are really important to me." At the same time, Alex wanted to make sure I was "open-minded and accepting." I briefly disclosed to Alex my LGBTQI (lesbian, gay, bisexual, transgender, queer, intersex)-affirming theological commitments as a pastoral counselor and clergyperson within the United Church of Christ and my clinical experience working with LGBTQI-identified persons who have consulted me for pastoral counseling. During our initial conversation, I learned that Alex grew up in a Roman Catholic home in the southwestern part of the United States, graduated from high school, and attended community college while working as a server at a local restaurant. Last year, at the age of 28, Alex graduated from university, which was located several hours from home, and is now working as a teller at a bank in a large urban city. On moving to the city, Alex began attending a Christian congregation that describes itself as independent and postdenominational. We explored together the areas of Alex's life that were troubling, which included Alex's experiences of "rejection" and "judgment" by family, difficulty with "being authentic and true to who I am" at work, and feeling "sad and angry because I don't seem to fit in anywhere." These troubling experiences were, in Alex's assessment, related to being "queer." For Alex, queer meant being "attracted to people regardless of their gender" and "expressing my gender as sometimes more male and sometimes more female." Alex decided that it might be helpful to work together on some of these concerns through counseling, and we negotiated another conversation.[1]

This chapter explores how pastoral counselors might work with queer-identified persons. The first section reviews theories of sexual orientation and some literature establishing gay/lesbian-affirming approaches to pastoral counseling. The next section considers emerging theories regarding "queer" identities and how such identities are related to prevailing constructs of gender and sexuality in psychotherapeutic discourses. After reflecting on how queer persons' life experiences challenge pastoral counselors to reconsider embedded theoretical commitments and theological anthropologies, the chapter concludes by identifying several themes common to the queer experience and key competencies for pastoral counselors working with persons who identify as queer.

SEXUAL ORIENTATION AND IDENTITY

There is significant literature addressing the historical discourses of sexuality and the construction of sexual "orientation" as a category of identity (Foucault, 1990; Hansen, 1989; Wilchins, 2004).[2] Analysis of these discourses on sexuality generally, and same-gender attraction specifically, is beyond the scope of this chapter. But it is worth noting that there are two distinct historical trajectories that affect pastoral counselors working with queer-identified persons. The first historical psychological and psychotherapeutic discourse regarding the experience of same-gender attraction and/or sexual intimacy generally viewed homosexuality as indicative of pathology. In the 20th century, the fields of psychology, psychotherapy, and counseling began to experience a major shift in this regard, and more recent psychotherapeutic approaches with gay men and lesbians are generally more affirming (Bieschke, Perez, & DeBord, 2007; Bigner & Wetchler, 2012; Ritter & Terndrup, 2002). Homosexuality was officially classified as a mental disorder in the first *Diagnostic and Statistical Manual of Mental Disorders* (*DSM*; American Psychiatric Association [APA], 1952). And although it was removed in 1973, a new diagnosis of *ego-dystonic homosexuality* emerged in the *DMS-III* (APA, 1980) to label the experience of psychological stress resulting from same-gender attraction. (Interestingly, this diagnosis did not take into account how such psychological stress is often a result of living in a heterosexist world.) By 1987, the *DSM-III-R* (APA, 1987) removed homosexuality from the section on "Sexual Disorders." Malony (2001) makes the point that this shift raised significant questions about the extent to which pastoral counselors should be influenced by other mental health professionals and guilds that quickly abdicated the pathological view of homosexuality, especially pastoral counselors who maintain that homosexuality is a sin.

The second historical discourse regarding the experience of same-gender attraction and/or sexual intimacy is theological, which generally viewed same-gender attraction and/or intimacy as sinful and contrary to the intended nature of creation (Boswell, 1980). John J. McNeill (1976) broke new ground with *The Church and the Homosexual*, which challenged the prevailing assumption that the Bible condemns loving homosexual relationships and constructed a moral theology that argued same-gender love and intimacy was not contrary to God's creative plan for humanity. During the 1980s, while professional guilds in psychology, psychotherapy, and counseling were revising their positions on therapeutic responses to gay and lesbian persons, several important resources in pastoral counseling emerged that sought to challenge the historical theological discourses on homosexuality. These pastoral counseling (and care) approaches began developing affirming clinical models of working with gays and lesbians, shaped largely by liberationist, feminist, and gay/lesbian liberation theologies.[3] These included Topper's (1986) work on spirituality of gay men and lesbians in counseling and Struzzo's (1989) work, entitled "Pastoral Counseling and Homosexuality." Shortly thereafter, the second volume of *Clinical Handbook of Pastoral Counseling* was released with a chapter on counseling with lesbians (Unterberger, 1993) and another on working with gay men (Byrne, 1993). This was followed by Marshall's (1997) pastoral counseling text *Counseling Lesbian Partners*; Graham's (1997) *Discovering Images of God: Narratives of Care Among Lesbians and Gays*; Switzer and Thornburg's (1999) *Pastoral Care of Gays, Lesbians, and Their Families*; and Tigert's (1999) *Coming Out Through Fire*. By the early 2000s, the pastoral counseling field was increasingly considering affirming models of working with gay men and lesbians with texts such as Malony's (2001) edited volume *Pastoral Care and Counseling in Sexual Diversity*, which includes several contributed chapters from many gay- and lesbian-affirming perspectives (although not all).

A growing number of authors in African American communities began to write about the experiences of LGBTQI persons in their congregations, primarily from a pastoral care or theological approach. These include Wilson's (1998) essay "I Don't Mean to Offend, but I Won't Pretend," Douglas's (1999) *Sexuality and the Black Church: A Womanist Perspective*, Comstock's (2001) *A Whosoever Church*, and Griffin's (2006) *Their Own Receive Them Not*.

More recently, Tanis (2003) and Tigert and Tirabassi (2004) engage questions of transgender spirituality, pastoral care, and counseling, and Kundtz and Schlager's (2007) *Ministry Among God's Queer Folk* offers a queer-affirming approach to pastoral care. It's worth noting, too, that many introductory and overview texts in pastoral counseling have also begun to include sections or chapters on gay- and lesbian-affirming approaches (Clinebell & McKeever, 2011; Culbertson, 2000; Townsend, 2009).

These contributions to the field have much to offer pastoral counselors working with gay men and lesbians from an affirming approach, and counselors are encouraged to become knowledgeable about these resources before working with gay and lesbian persons in counseling. One of the limitations of this literature, however, is that most gay- and lesbian-affirming approaches do not consider with any great detail the experience of persons who identify as queer, sexually fluid, and/or bisexual. Many make brief mention of queer fluid identities and bisexual-identified persons. One notable exception to this claim is Blevins's (2005, 2009) work, which seeks to engage queer theory not as an apologetic approach to pastoral counseling but as a theoretical starting point. Notwithstanding the work of Tanis (2003) and Tigert and Tirabassi (2004), there are even fewer resources in the field of pastoral counseling for working with persons who are transgender, genderqueer, and/or intersex. Because of this, and because there are significant resources already available on pastoral counseling with gay and lesbian persons (as opposed to queer, bisexual, genderqueer), this chapter focuses more on counseling with those who identify as queer, sexually fluid, bisexual, and/or genderqueer.

WHAT IS *QUEER*?

Although many counselors may be wary to use the word *queer* because of its historical use as a pejorative term, more recently, a growing number of persons are reclaiming the term as a positive, nuanced identity of resistance within the discourses of identity politics. There is no universal definition of *queer*, nor is there a monolithic queer identity. *Queer* is often used as a general umbrella term referring to the increasingly expanding acronym of LGBTQI. In this way, *queer* is broadly defined as *anything other than heteronormative*. In a more specific way, queer is used as a gender and/or sexual identity suggestive of such metaphors as crossing, blurring, turning upside-down, and/or contrary to the dominant binary constructions of gender and sexuality (Robinson, 2002). In other words, it is an identity that disrupts binary categories.

It seems to be the case that younger persons are more likely to use *queer*, whereas older persons may identify more specifically as gay, lesbian, bisexual, or pansexual. Some critique the umbrella use of *queer*, arguing that queer identity is *specifically* different from *gay* or *lesbian*, primarily because *queer* is indicative of fluidity between, or transgression of, the dominant binary construct of sexuality and gender. Understood this way, queer is a more transgressive political identity. Because there are rich and accessible resources for working with gay- and lesbian-identified persons within the field of psychotherapy and pastoral counseling, this chapter uses the latter definition of *queer*: queer as fluid and transgressive of binary categories of gender and sexuality.

Queer as a Verb

Queer is also used as a verb, meaning "to queer" an idea or an institution or a relationship. In this way, queer is a worldview or positionality that intentionally disrupts hegemonic systems of normative binary gender and sexuality. To queer is "to frustrate, to delegitimize, to camp up—heteronormative knowledges and institutions, and the subjectivities and socialities that are (in)formed by them and that (in)form them" (Sullivan, 2003, p. vi). As a disruptive methodology, queer theory has also gained growing interest in the fields of theology, hermeneutics, and ethics (Althaus-Reid, 2000, 2003; Goss, 2002; Loughlin, 2007; Stone, 2004; Stuart, 1997, 2003).

Queer as a Sexual Identity

Alex's sexual identity is *in between* and *fluid*. Alex describes being "attracted to people regardless of their gender." In our conversation, I remain curious whether this means that the gender identity of Alex's partners is unimportant or irrelevant to Alex's attraction and emotional connection to such partners or whether it means that the gender identity of Alex's partners is important and relevant but Alex experiences attraction and emotional connection to many different gender identities. For some queer-identified persons who are attracted to persons of different genders (note I didn't say "both" genders), gender is unimportant; there are other characteristics of their partners that are more attractive. Other queer-identified persons claim that the gender identity and expression of their partners is particularly important, although the person is open to a spectrum of gender identities or gender expressions to which the person is equally attracted (Hays, 2013).

In addition to *queer*, other similar terms of identities similarly seek to articulate this in between, either-or, and/or fluid expressions of sexuality. They include *bisexual, sexually fluid, pansexual, polyamorous,* or *hyphenated* (e.g., gay-identified bisexual, bi-identified lesbian). For some persons, *queer* encompasses these more particular identities, but for others it does not. Either way, an important consideration here is that queer sexual identities may not remain the same over time. In other words, queer-identified persons are likely to experience their sexual attraction and interpersonal intimacy as changing or fluid over time. As addressed in more detail in the text that follows, the problem is that prevailing personality and psychotherapeutic theories assume that acceptance and stability (not change and fluidity) are indicators of a healthy sexual identity.

Most prevailing gay- and lesbian-affirming psychotherapies (including many pastoral counseling approaches) often identify as a psychotherapeutic goal the acceptance of a clearly defined and stable gender or sexual orientation identity. In other words, the assumption is that to be a healthy, fully self-actualized, and differentiated person, one needs to identify, accept, and fully integrate a *stable* sexual identity, and for affirming psychotherapeutic theories, that means adopting a gay/lesbian or straight identity (Cass, 1979, 1984; Coleman, 1982; Grace, 1992; Troiden, 1979, 1989). This assumes an either-or construction of sexuality: One is *either* gay/lesbian *or* straight. Queer persons for whom sexual attraction and identity are not fixed (e.g., the attraction is to multiple genders or changes over time) are thus considered to have not fully accepted themselves or to have not completely integrated their sexual identity (orientation). In essence, persons are pathologized because their sexuality is fluid, not fixed.

As pastoral counselors, there is more at stake in this question than prevailing personality and sexual orientation theories. The lived experiences of queer-identified persons challenge pastoral counselors to reconsider our embedded assumptions of theological anthropology: What are our operative criteria of what it means to be a healthy person? Who are we as gendered persons created in the image of God? What is the meaning of human sexuality as an embodied experience? How are ambiguity, fluidity, and transgression important theological concepts that shape, and are shaped by, our operative definitions of personhood? And who gets to decide the boundaries of practice and identity within these theo-anthropological discourses?

Working with queer-identified persons in counseling necessarily challenges both Western psychological discourses and theological discourses regarding gender and sexuality.[4] We are challenged to take into account the idea that sexuality is fluid—not static or fixed—and that such fluidity may, indeed, be more normal than we have been led to believe. There is far more variability and fluidity in many people's sexual experiences (i.e., attraction, fantasy, intimacy, identity) than most theoretical notions tend to provide (Firestein, 2007): "The tendency is to deny the legitimacy of one's erotic responsiveness to either males, or females; thereby, one assumes that all people are either basically heterosexual or homosexual" (Paul, 2000, p. 11). In this way, fluid sexuality presents an existential crisis for persons—especially persons who come from religious communities—because such fluidity transcends and transgresses binary categories found in normative theological discourses on embodiment and human sexuality.

THEORIES OF SEXUAL IDENTITY

There is no monolithic queer sexuality experience: Some are emotionally attracted to and/or partnered with person(s) of the same gender; some are attracted to and engage in sexual intimacy with any gender; some remain in monogamous relationships but also remain attracted to others whose gender is different from their partner's; and some view sex and gender as irrelevant. There is considerable literature considering historical constructs of same-gender sexual and emotional attraction that is beyond the scope of this chapter (Foucault, 1990; Wilchins, 2004). In the 20th century, several theorists attempted to construct models to explain human sexuality generally and same-gender attraction specifically. Early theorists of sexuality, such as Kinsey and his colleagues at the Institute for Sex Research (Kinsey, Pomeroy, & Martin, 1948; Kinsey & Institute for Sex Research, 1953/1998), focused on sexual behavior and how same-gender behavior varied among research participants. Kinsey developed his 0- to 6-point scale of human sexuality (based on self-reported experiences of sexual behavior) by which one end of the spectrum was exclusively homosexual, the other end was exclusively heterosexual, and bisexuals were somewhere in between. In other words, persons who had no sexual contact or arousal with persons of the same sex were considered exclusively heterosexual, whereas persons who had sexual contact or arousal with persons of the same sex were considered exclusively homosexual. There is significant criticism of Kinsey's work, largely because it was based primarily on sexual behavior and did not take into account the distinctions between emotional affection, physical attraction, sexual arousal, and social identity. That said, it is important to acknowledge that Kinsey's work proposed an entirely new paradigm to understanding sexuality: relying on a *spectrum* of sexual experiences rather than a binary of heterosexual and homosexual. This fundamental principle that sexuality is a spectrum, not a binary category, remains an important theoretical concept in understanding queer sexual identities.

Kinsey's work was based only on behavior, which left several important questions unanswered: What if one is attracted to someone but does not express one's attraction in sexual behavior? What if one identifies with one sexual identity but never engages in sexual intimacy with anyone? In response to these questions, Klein (1993) developed the Sexual Orientation Grid, which included additional criteria: sexual attraction, behavior, fantasies, emotional preference, social preference, lifestyle, and self-identification. The Klein grid was used to categorize persons using a numerical scale from 1 (straight) to 4 (bisexual) to 7 (gay or lesbian) for each of these criteria. Although more nuanced than Kinsey's scale, the Klein grid didn't take into account how sexuality may change over time: What if a person is involved in a monogamous relationship with a same-gender partner but had a previous heterosexual relationship? Or what if a person is in a committed polyamorous relationship with more than one person (Burleson, 2005)?

In our work together, I learned that Alex first began experiencing sexual attraction to multiple genders while in high school. This was "scary" because Alex's parents were "traditional Catholics, even though we didn't go to Mass very much." "I was hooking up with different people. It was really exciting because I was having all these new experiences and exploring these new parts of myself." These sexual experiences with different genders led Alex to originally identify as "lesbian," since Alex was raised as a girl/woman and found those sexual experiences with other women as most congruent in terms of sexual identity. But by the time Alex began attending community college, Alex realized that "lesbian didn't fit as the right word" because "I found myself attracted to both men and women—I didn't want to have to choose one or the other."

The challenge for developing any model of sexual identity is that it requires theorists to make several key assumptions regarding sexuality—namely, is sexuality comprised by emotions or attraction or behavior or self-identity? More germane to our discussion of queer identity, two additional questions must be considered: (a) How does the model take into account the role that gender plays in sexual identity, and (b) to what extent does the model account for change over time?

The first question raises an important point that sexual orientation is, after all, primarily about gender and not sexuality. Categories of sexual identity are predicated on the relationship between one's gender and the gender of one's partner. In other words, sexual attraction and intimacy between a man and man is "gay" because they are of the same gender. Likewise, sexual attraction and intimacy between a woman and a man is constructed as "straight" because they are of different genders. But what happens when the woman in that "straight" relationship is transgender and transitions from woman to man? The couple is now a man with a man. Is the couple now a "gay" couple? Did the sexual orientation of both partners change? The relationship has not changed. The persons in the relationship have not changed. But the gender of one partner did. This is particularly important, for example, for a female-to-male transgender person who is attracted to women and who may have been viewed by the dominant homonormative gaze as a lesbian woman but whose internal sense of identity has always been "straight man" (Jenness & Geis, 2011). Moreover, what if a relationship includes one or both partners who identify as man sometimes and woman sometimes (gender fluid), or neither man nor woman (genderqueer or intersex)? The point here is that our understanding of sexuality, especially in counseling contexts, is predicated on particular assumptions we make about gender and the relationship between two or more persons' genders.

Pastoral counselors working with queer-identified persons—especially in couples and family therapy—are thus challenged to critically reflect on and intentionally deconstruct the ways in which dominant discourses of gender and sexuality have become embedded in our operative psychotherapeutic approaches. When we think about sexual orientation with persons who come to us for counseling, what assumptions are we making about gender and sex? How are we defining terms such as *gay, lesbian, bisexual, queer, intersex, transgender, fluid, polyamorous,* and *ambiguous*? And perhaps most important, what theological or spiritual commitments do we hold that are shaping our understanding of these identities?

The second question related to models of sexual identity asks in what ways the model accounts for change over time. This question challenges theories of sexual orientation to take into account the lived experiences of persons for whom sexuality is not fixed. Most prevailing theories on coming out are predicated on a stage theory of human development (Cass, 1979, 1984; Coleman, 1982; Grace, 1992; Lewis, 1984; Troiden, 1979, 1989). These sexual identity models assume identity stability as healthy, and they implicitly characterize continued identity change or fluidity as an indicator of psychosexual immaturity. Two notable exceptions come from the field of bisexuality studies: Weinberg, Williams, and Pryor's (1994) model of bisexuality provides for "open gender schema" and Zinik's (1985) "dual-gender" sexual orientation and identity.

Queer persons are increasingly challenging psychotherapeutic discourse and counselors to suspend and deconstruct the fixed and binary assumptions embedded in prevailing personality theories (Moon, 2008, 2010). For example, if you are a gay- and lesbian-affirming pastoral counselor, how do you make assessments of persons who are experiencing "confusion" or "questioning" their sexuality? Many gay- and lesbian-affirming counselors are likely to encourage the person to explore the meanings of those feelings and experiences and are likely to disclose their commitment to being an affirming counselor as an act of ethical transparency. The counselor then seeks to facilitate exploring the emerging self-understanding of same-gender attraction, identifying fears and consequences of disclosing this new awareness to family and friends and workplace, and identifying supportive resources and relationships to equip the person to claim a new identity as gay/lesbian. The conclusion of this process—the psychotherapeutic goal of counseling—is acceptance of the person's new preferred sexual identity.

Such an approach may be relevant in working with many gay and lesbian persons, but a problem arises when the person does not choose a new gay/lesbian identity but also does not wish to continue identifying as "straight." Here the counselor may conclude that the person's failure to claim a new stable identity is indicative of not fully accepting one's "true" sexual orientation, internalizing homophobia, or an unwillingness to deconstruct heteronormative religious discourses necessary for the person to accept a gay/lesbian identity. In response, the counselor may continue to encourage the person to accept the new gay/lesbian identity (assuming the failure to claim a gay/lesbian identity is pathological) and does so as an act of affirmation and encouragement. But in actuality, doing so may result in an imposition of a homonormative binary construct of sexuality.

IMPLICATIONS FOR PRACTICE

During my conversations with Alex, I had to remain self-aware of my own internal thoughts and responses. I noticed that I was wondering whether Alex was internalizing the homophobic and heterosexist discourses of power that make it very difficult for someone to fully claim and embrace a nonstraight identity. I found myself wondering about how the beliefs from Alex's Roman Catholic upbringing may be internalized and how the church's teachings that being gay or lesbian was an "objective disorder" might be unknowingly discouraging Alex from fully experiencing same-gender relationships (Ratzinger, 1986). As a bisexual-identified pastoral counselor who works from a queer-affirming approach, I found myself experiencing an impulse to encourage Alex not to give up a lesbian identity. I certainly did not believe that what Alex was experiencing was "just a phase" or "experimenting," and I wanted to be transparent that I was a pastoral counselor with strong commitments to LGBTQI affirmation and liberation. In an effort to be encouraging, I could have used the power of my position as a counselor to ask questions that directed Alex toward (what I thought) was full acceptance and affirmation of a lesbian identity—the goal of most sexual orientation models in psychotherapy. But I did not. Had I done so, it would have reified and imposed a homonormative binary construct of sexual orientation on Alex. Of course, it was also important for me to remain vigilantly aware of how my own fluid sexuality and male gender identity are both a helpful resource for inviting counseling conversations with persons experiencing their own nonheterosexual experiences and a problematic resource inasmuch as it may lead me to conflate my own experience with Alex's or to make assumptions about Alex's experiences out of my own. Ultimately, Alex preferred to use *queer* as a descriptor for sexual identity, because "bisexual sounds too medical."

Page (2007) interviewed bisexual persons about their experiences with psychotherapists who thought they were being affirming but who ended up causing harm. One respondent said, "I thought I might want to talk to the therapist about bisexual issues when I first went for therapy. She made a comment that one could be 'either straight or gay' . . . meant to convey her openness about orientation but [this was] uncomfortable for me to hear" (Page, 2007, p. 60). Pastoral counselors should consider several important theoretical commitments in working with queer-identified persons:

- Recognize that sexual fluidity is a valid, psychologically healthy sexual identity (orientation) and that one's subjective experience and identity may change over time.
- Be cautious of conflating sexuality with counseling goals/objectives. Sometimes sexuality is the presenting problem for persons seeking counseling, but often it is not. It is important to decenter ourselves as counselors in ways that allow the person seeking counseling to establish his or her own goals.
- Be conversant and competent in providing intercultural care, as many queer-identified persons are socially located differently than many pastoral counselors.
- Recognize the limitations of our knowledges and competencies. Consult, refer, and seek supervision as an ethical practice of queer-affirming counseling.

Ethical Implications of Fluid Sexual Identities

Sexual fluidity challenges prevailing theories of monosexism by critiquing the assumption that sexual orientation is naturally fixated on one easily identifiable sex and is static over time (Robinson, 2002). This poses a critical challenge to essentialist constructions of sexual orientation because it implies choice, rather than an inherent nature of one's "true" sexual self. This also poses a dilemma for the contemporary gay and lesbian liberation movement, which has sought human and civil rights as a legally protected class based on essentialist constructions of sexual orientation. Similarly, essentialist constructions of sexual orientation have also dominated the theological arguments of LGBTQI inclusion and affirming movements within Christian congregations, arguing that sexual orientation is immutable, unchangeable, not a choice, and persons are "born this way."

This presents three key ethical questions for pastoral counselors to consider in their queer-affirming clinical practice. First, the LGBTQI-affirming position argues that persons don't choose to be gay, lesbian, bisexual, transgender, intersex, or queer. But persons do make significant choices in response to their sexuality or gender. For example, a transgender person may *choose* to transition from one gender to another; a gay man may *choose* to never come out or engage in sexual intimacy with another man; a bisexual person may *choose* to remain exclusive with one partner, even though she is attracted to all genders. In response to these examples, Kundtz and Schlager (2007) conclude that "*being* bisexual, transgender, lesbian, or gay is almost never a choice . . . this is the same for all: human beings very rarely choose their sexual orientation or gender identity—possibly never" (p. 6). But this claim becomes more problematic when one shifts from fixed, essentialist sexual orientation theories toward fluid, socially constructed sexual identity theories. In other words, if queer (and bisexual) persons are equally attracted to persons of any gender, then heterosexist theological perspectives can argue they should *choose* the so-called natural or moral option of an opposite-gender partner (Siker, 2007). Most queer-affirming pastoral counselors would find this conclusion problematic. As a result, pastoral counselors who work with queer-identified persons are faced with the decision of how to ethically communicate our stance on the ethics of choice. What criteria do we bring to our work as pastoral counselors that establish limits and boundaries for ethical choices? If a person seeking counseling identifies as queer and is sexually intimate with multiple partners of different genders, does the pastoral counselor disclose her or his ethical commitments regarding exclusivity or polyamory? Is this behavior a choice or a condition of a sexually fluid embodiment? If we regard commitment and covenant as prerequisite criteria for sexual intimacy, how do we respond to persons who hold very different criteria for sexual intimacy? It is important that pastoral counselors critically reflect on our embedded and operative moral theology of sexual ethics in preparation for working with persons who, by their very embodiment, will challenge dominant constructs of sexual relationship.

Second, if sexual orientation is fluid and unfixed, then supporters of "conversion therapy" or "reparative therapy" can argue for the conversion of homosexuals. If sexuality can change over time, as is often the case for queer- (and bisexual) identified persons (Burleson, 2005; Firestein, 2007), then it may also be argued that sexuality can *be changed*. Most counselors (queer affirming or not) would find this claim ethically indefensible. Even so, sexual fluidity begs the question: When one argues that sexuality changes over time, how and why does it change? If it is the case that the complex and nuanced embodied experience of sexuality ebbs and flows naturally and inherently over time, can it be controlled or changed or modified externally by therapy or a person's own will? This, of course, remains a point of contention with some neo-orthodox and conserving (i.e., conservative) Christian counselors who maintain that nonheterosexual orientations are a result of a fallen humanity and can be redeemed through therapy (Nicolosi, 2001). That said, nearly every major professional organization in the fields of psychology, psychiatry, psychotherapy, counseling, medical, and social work has rightly taken positions against "reparative therapy" (Human Rights Campaign, 2014b). The point here for pastoral counselors is to recognize that when we shift our operative theory of sexual orientation away from fixed, essentialist concepts toward fluidity and socially constructed spectra, subsequent ethical and theological implications need to be addressed. Pastoral counselors should consider these implications and prepare their responses.

Third, there is a growing effort to conduct research on genetic and other psychobiological explanations for same-gender sexual attraction. Many support this research to find a "gay gene" or other inherent biological marker, which would prove that homosexuality is a natural biological variation of the human species. Doing so is an understandable effort to resist the historical oppression of gays and lesbians perpetuated, in no small part, by moralist discourses and institutions in the Christian and other traditions that have said homosexuality is sinful and contrary to the nature of creation. A few queer critics, however, are questioning this approach because it risks a return to the pathologizing of same-gender attraction and intimacy—this time as a genetic disorder (De Cecco, 1987). In other words, if the "gay gene" is found, queer folks are then pathologized as having a genetic disorder for which gene therapy can be developed.

The question for pastoral counselors is simply the following: What is our operative theory and theology of human sexuality? Is sexuality a genetic condition? Is it a biosocial experience that combines brain chemistry, hormones, and socialization? Is it a gift from God? It is critically important for queer-affirming pastoral counselors to clearly identify the theological, scientific, psychological, anthropological, and sociological conclusions we make about human sexuality because each of these assumptions shapes our clinical practice.

Queer as a Gender Identity

Recall that in addition to sexuality, Alex's gender identity and expression also does not fit within the binary categories of male and female. Alex identifies and expresses gender differently in different contexts and within different relationships. Although much of the time, Alex identifies as *more* female, there are times in which Alex expresses gender as *more* male, or as *neither* male *nor* female. For example, sometimes when going to work at the bank, Alex wears a tie and jacket. Dressing this way, along with having short hair, allows Alex to express gender in more masculine ways. Even though Alex knows doing so may "create trouble" at work with the bank's management and exposes Alex to higher risk of hate crime violence (Sprinkle, 2011), Alex found it "exciting" and "freeing" when "customers came into the bank and were unable to figure out whether I was a man or a woman." In this regard, Alex's preferred identity is genderqueer: *in between* male and female.

Here, the argument is that gender is a socially constructed, performative identity, which brings a person's inner sense of gender into dialectic relationship with inscribed gender discourses that demand sex-based binary gender identities (Butler, 1993, 2004, 2005). Thus, gender is less correlated with chromosomal sex and/or physical characteristics of one's genitalia but more with one's inner sense of gender identity and how one expresses that identity within culturally embedded practices of gender socialization. For most persons, one's gender identity is congruent with one's sex. But for some, like Alex, they are less correlated. And for intersex persons, one's fluid gender identity may indeed be a result of one's chromosomal sex and/or genitalia. When Alex and other genderqueer persons who seek pastoral counseling embody a queer fluid gender expression, they are creating a paradox of liberation and oppression vis-à-vis disciplinary regimes of normalcy (Foucault, 1965, 1975, 1977). On the one side, expressing one's gender in queer or ambiguous ways can be a liberating experience by which one finds congruity between one's inner sense of gender and how one is perceived or "read" by others. On the other side, doing so within a strictly binary gendered society can create conflict, disruption, and violence for the person.

This opens up important opportunities for pastoral counselors to explore questions of personal agency, subjugated power, and capacity building with the person seeking counseling. For example, I was curious how it was possible, given the feelings of rejection and isolation caused by the family's reactions to Alex coming out as queer (fluid sexual identity), that Alex was able to embody a genderqueer identity at work. This action to go to work as "more male" seemed to be bold, in my view, in light of Alex's experience of rejection and isolation from family. This piqued my curiosity, and I learned that Alex had been "experimenting with passing as a guy" when going out with friends. This facilitated Alex's agency and capacity to express gender in this ambiguous way with supportive friendships, which helped to build confidence that doing so was possible in the workplace. These resources were important for Alex to access when several coworkers made derisive remarks and in anticipating questions from the branch manager.

Gender Fluidity and Pathology

Although the *DSM-IV* (American Psychiatric Association, 2000) used the nomenclature of *gender identity disorder* to describe the clinical criteria for gender fluidity and/or transition, the *DSM-5* (American Psychiatric Association, 2013) has sought to use a more general term of *gender dysphoria* in an attempt to reduce the stigma associated with the term *disorder*. The diagnostic criteria include not only the desire to identify as a gender other than one's assigned gender at birth ("natal gender") but also distress or impairment associated with this gender incongruence (American Psychiatric Association, 2013). The *DSM-5* recognizes that there is growing variability in gender expression along a spectrum, and emphasizes that clinical diagnosis should be limited only to transgender persons who experience significant distress or impairment as a result of their gender identity (American Psychiatric Association, 2013). Indeed, some genderqueer and gender-fluid persons do not experience diagnosable distress in response to their gender identity. The problem is that most transgender persons are required to be diagnosed as having gender dysphoria in order to begin key steps in seeking professional assistance in transition from one gender to another. According to the World Professional Association for Transgender Health's "Standards of Care," (Coleman et al., 2012) which is the prevailing set of guidelines for mental health and medical professionals working with transgender persons, diagnosis of gender dysphoria from a mental health professional is recommended for hormone therapy and is required for breast/chest (one referral) and/or genital surgery (two referrals). In other words, to access surgical services so one's body is congruent with one's gender identity, a person is required to seek a mental health diagnosis. It is interesting to note, however, that nontrans persons are not required to have a psychiatric diagnosis to have access to prescribed hormones and/or cosmetic plastic surgery.

Just as with fluid sexual identities and the term *genderqueer*, there are no uniform or universal definitions of *transgender* and *genderqueer*. Transgender seeks to capture a wide variety of identities, orientations, and behaviors. Some transgender persons use the term as a wide umbrella for all gender variation, including cross-dressing, male-to-female (MTF) or female-to-male (FTM), genderqueer, and transsexuals. Others prefer to use the term more specifically: *transgender* for persons who have transitioned (or seek to transition) from one gender identity to another and *genderqueer* for the wider definition for gender-variant identities (Jenness & Geis, 2011, p. 224). In the context of transgender persons who transition (MTF, FTM), the binary gender regime continues to be reified inasmuch as a transgender person transitions from one singular gender to the other singular gender. By contrast, a genderqueer person locates one's gender identity outside or in between the binary male/female gender construct (Girshick, 2008; Stryker, 2008; Tanis, 2003).

Prevailing counseling objectives with gender dysphoria remain binary: to successfully transition from one (singular) gender identity to another (singular) gender or to assist the person in accepting the gender into which the personal was socialized as a child. For most transgender persons, this is helpful and consistent with the goal of transitioning to, and living as, the preferred gender identity. But for genderqueer persons, the goal of transition is more problematic. It is important that the pastoral counselor not assume that transition is preferred; the person's preferred objective may very well be forging a third gender or a gender-fluid identity.

IMPLICATIONS FOR PRACTICE

Counseling objectives are shaped by embedded assumptions, theoretical and theological commitments, and the person's life experience. This is particularly true when pastoral counselors consider working with trans and genderqueer persons. Pastoral counselors are encouraged to seek continuing education and specialized training before working with persons who are transgender, especially those who are actively seeking gender transition (Tanis, 2003). For our purposes here, it might be helpful to highlight a few of the competencies developed by the American Counseling Association (ACA) for working with transgender persons, especially the competencies that seem to correlate with the unique work of pastoral counselors integrating theology, religious discourse, and spirituality into counseling practice (Burnes et al., 2010).

- "Identify the gender normative assumptions present in current lifespan development theories and address for these biases in assessment and counseling practices" (p. 142). In addition to deconstructing development theories, pastoral counselors should similarly identify and evaluate embedded *theological anthropologies* of gender shaping their work with transgender persons.
- "Be aware of the sociopolitical influences that affect the lives of transgender individuals, and that stereotyping, discrimination, and marginalization may shape one's developmental processes, self-esteem, and self-concept" (p. 142). Pastoral counselors should similarly consider the ways in which heterosexist theological discourses and institutional practices within the Christian tradition have contributed to this marginalization. This is an important opportunity to deconstruct dominant theological discourses that negatively affect transgender persons and to work with the person to co-construct a transpositive theology helpful for the person's own sense of identity and relationship to God.
- "Recognize that gender identity formation, self-acceptance of transgender identity, and disclosure of transgender status are complex processes that are not necessarily permanently resolved and may be experienced repeatedly across one's lifespan" (p. 143). Pastoral counselors should identify and vet community resources

in order to refer the transgender person to supportive networks and resources, especially trans-affirming communities of faith or congregations. Doing so creates opportunities for supportive relationships that will help support the person through recurring struggles with identity formation, self-acceptance, and disclosure throughout the life span.

- "Acknowledge that the oppression of transgender people is a component of sexism, heterosexism and transphobia and reflects a worldview and value-system that undermines the healthy functioning and autonomy of transgender people" (p. 143). Pastoral counselors committed to justice, liberation, and transformation in our work might also consider ways in which the counseling work we facilitate not only resources the transgender person but also contributes to the dismantling of sexism, heterosexism, and transphobia within broader theological discourses and ecclesial structures.

- "Recognize that spiritual development and religious practices may be important for transgender individuals, yet it may also present a particular challenge given the limited transpositive religious institutions that may be present in a given community, and that any transgender individuals may face personal struggles related to their faith and their identity" (p. 144). Pastoral counselors play a vital role in this regard, especially as many of us inhabit a liminal location between faith communities and the mental health field. This social location presents an opportunity to connect and reconcile the transgender person with transpositive congregations and transpositive theologies.

INTERLOCKING SYSTEMS OF OPPRESSION

At the beginning of this chapter, I reviewed several theories of sexual orientation and identity that are common in gay- and lesbian-affirming counseling and emphasized the importance of pastoral counselors deconstructing our own embedded theological and theoretical assumptions regarding sexuality and gender. Then, after nuancing the definitions of *queer*, *transgender*, and *genderqueer*, I identified several competencies (in conversation with the ACA) for working with transgender persons that opened up specific opportunities for pastoral counselors. Before moving to pastoral counseling issues related to genderqueer and sexually fluid persons, it's important to consider the ways in which gender and sexuality are interconnected with other categories of social location and identity.

Queer sexuality and genderqueer identities are constructed within contexts of heteronormative (i.e., straight is normal and nonstraight persons are "other") and homonormative (i.e., persons are born either gay/lesbian or straight) disciplinary discourses. These discourses also occur within other interlocking systems of power and oppression, especially gender and race. For example, queer-identified women (who are engaged in sexual activity with men) are accused of bringing sexually transmitted diseases into the lesbian community or are accused of being traitors to feminism (Burleson, 2005, p. 24). The argument is that any sexual act with a man is inherently patriarchal and thus contrary to feminist principles. Moreover, there is a notable critique by some feminist lesbians of FTM transmen arguing that a woman becoming a man is the ultimate act of internalized misogyny. Here we see echoes of Adrienne Rich's (1980) "compulsive heterosexism," which continues to influence the ways in which queer women have been received by the wider feminist movement. The implication is that questions of gender identity and sexual relationships between men and women are interconnected with broader questions of gender, patriarchy, and sexism.

Pastoral counselors working with genderqueer and transgender persons are thus challenged to be self-aware of not only our own embedded assumptions of patriarchy but also the importance of inviting persons who consult us for counseling into reflection about and deconstruction of patriarchy in their own lives.

The same intersection of oppression occurs in terms of race. Raymond Scott (2007) asserts that African American queer identities represent opportunities to undermine two binaries common to the dominant U.S. culture and to "Africentric patriarchal constructions": the binary male–female gender/sex systems and the binary homosexual/heterosexual concepts of sexual orientation (p. 216). He argues that psychotherapists have historically practiced a predisposition to pathologize as an internal personality disorder what is, more accurately, a survival response to injustice, racism, and social invalidation. Scott makes this point as it relates to bisexual-identified persons:

> Multiracial bisexuals of African descent "actively" construct their identities and experience often in opposition to the moral, political, and ideological concerns of their families of origin and communities. . . . Reading bisexuality in this manner redirects the psychotherapeutic focus toward intersecting narrative of cultural histories, invalidation, and class dynamics that shape bisexuality and homoerotic desire. At times the story line reflects a critical reflexive movement away from the individual's psyche toward a socially and historically informed focus on the particulars in that client's experiences of oppression, ostracism, or liberation. (p. 207)

The clinical implication of this intersection of race, gender, and sexuality is that we, as pastoral counselors, are challenged to shift our psychotherapeutic attention (or what Foucault (1975) called the "clinical gaze") away from the pathology of the individual's psyche toward systems of power and oppression. Here the so-called psychiatric disorders imposed on queer-identified persons may be more likely the result of living in a heterosexist world than an inherent disorder of the psyche.

In the current postmodern era, psychotherapists and researchers are increasingly problematizing the notion of unitary fixed identities beyond questions of sexuality and gender. This has led to a rich discussion of the subjectivity of hybrid identities. In this way, hybridity in racial and ethnic identities has much to offer the changing field of gender and sexual identity formation. As was discussed previously in this chapter, although some fluid persons are using a broad queer identity to encompass a wide range of changing experiences, others are claiming a more particular experience of hybrid or hyphenated identity (e.g., gay-identified bisexual, bi-identified lesbian). It may be helpful at this point to consider the contribution that *mestizo* theology might have on the discussion of pastoral counseling with queer-identified persons. Daisy Machado's (2003) work on racial hybridity and borderlands argues that *mestizaje* is a reality that is not limited to racial hybridity but is about belonging and not belonging, about centers and margins, about one being seen by others and community.

> We are daily border-crossers who must learn early on to interpret life from both sides—life in the dominant culture and life in the Latino community. This is how we learn to survive and how we are able to be truly ourselves. It is in this very paradox—of belonging yet not really belonging—where the history of Latinos begins to be understood, not just nationally, but within our own denominational histories as Protestants and Roman Catholics. (p. xx)

Here we see an interesting echo between queer-identified persons who describe navigating the in-between places of gender and sexuality, of belonging and not belonging, and Machado's description of the borderland experience. It is important to not conflate these two experiences but merely to note how intersections of race and gender and sexuality present unique challenges for fluid and hybrid-identified persons—especially belonging and not belonging. Similarly, J. Fuji Collins (2007), writing from a queer Asian Pacific perspective, says, "The borderlands are a place where one is marginalized because of ethnic background and then additionally marginalized by heterosexuals and homosexuals alike" (p. 231).

In my work with Alex, I learned that hybridity was an important resource of resiliency and capacity. Alex's family lineage is Mexican American. As I explored the intersectionality of sexuality and gender with other discourses such as race, ethnicity, and class, I became curious about other places beyond sexuality and gender where Alex experienced not fitting in or a double bind. Some of the narratives Alex shared with me were of painful feelings of being different, not belonging, or being an outsider. Alex said, "When I was younger I felt like I wasn't fully Mexican and not fully American. I was, like, stuck in between two worlds. My family was Mexican, but my school was mostly White. So I didn't really know where I belonged." But eventually Alex began to embrace the Mexican American hybrid identity, saying, "Now that I'm older I think it's good. I can celebrate the great things about being Mexican; all the traditions and music and food and Spanish. I can also say that I'm an American and not feel like I'm rejecting my family." My work with Alex led me to invite deconstruction of the hegemonic discourses of race that inscribe race-based systems of privilege, and I was also able to invite Alex into considering how those experiences and narratives of not fitting in, neither/nor, or being in the borderlands were not only painful experiences but also opportunities to identify strength, resilience, and agency necessary for Alex to navigate similarly painful experiences as these related to gender and sexuality.

Intersectionality of gender, sexuality, racial/ethnic, and class identity is receiving important consideration in the field of pastoral theology (Cooper & Marshall, 2010; Ramsay, 2014), as are intercultural models of pastoral counseling that take into account sexual orientation (Marshall, 2009). In 2010, the American Association of Pastoral Counselors (AAPC) adopted *Antiracist Multicultural Competencies* for pastoral counselors working across racial and ethnic counseling relationships. As growing awareness of intersectionality continues to shape our clinical theories and practice as pastoral counselors, perhaps the AAPC might soon follow the lead of the ACA, AAMFT (American Association for Marriage and Family Therapy), and American Psychiatric Association in moving forward with competencies for working with LGBTQI persons.

Pastoral Counseling Strategies With Fluid Persons

This chapter began with the lives of persons who do not experience their sexuality and/or gender as fixed, reviewed prevailing theories of sexual orientation and identity that are common in gay- and lesbian-affirming psychotherapy, and considered the importance of pastoral counselors deconstructing our own embedded theological and theoretical assumptions regarding sexuality and gender. Several competencies for working with transgender persons were correlated with possible pastoral counseling considerations, which were followed by a discussion of the intersectionality of sexuality, gender, and race. We now move to conclude by discussing several concerns that pastoral counselors should consider when working with genderqueer and sexually fluid persons.

As already mentioned, there is no singular, monolithic experience of queer-identified persons. Queer folk experience challenges and life problems similar to those of other persons: fear, loss, grief, life transitions, joy, being overwhelmed, difficulty with relationships, violence, and trauma (to name a few). And for many queer-identified persons seeking counseling, the presenting problem is not always related to gender and/or sexuality. Pastoral counselors should be cautious about immediately assuming that all problems a queer person is experiencing in life are related to being queer. That is not to say that issues of gender and/or sexuality do not intersect with all areas of life; it is impossible to compartmentalize life in ways that result in a mutual exclusivity between gender and sexuality and the rest of one's life. Living and navigating disciplinary binary gender regimes often result in many queer persons experiencing problems with fear, loss, grief, life transitions, joy, feeling overwhelmed, relationships, violence, and trauma (at much higher rates than their nonqueer peers). The point is not that one's queerness causes them problems; the point is that living in a heterosexist and transphobic world does.

There are five important considerations pastoral counselors should keep in mind when working with fluid persons: (a) identity change is normal, (b) double-bind marginalization is common, (c) deconstructing gender and sexuality correlates with deconstructing God, (d) a new ethic of transgression is needed, and (e) marriage and covenant making need modifying.

Identity Change Is Normal

The most important theoretical shift necessary to work effectively and ethically with queer-identified persons is the suspension of the fixed-identity model of sexual orientation. When a person changes sexual identity, it does not mean the person is confused. It is not uncommon for a person to begin identifying as gay for a few years, then shift to queer, then bisexual, then in some contexts gay-identified bisexual but in other contexts polyamorous, then back to queer. In these cases, the person is seeking to put into language an embodied experience that is nearly impossible to put into words. It may be that the person's own experience of sexuality remains constant over time but doesn't easily fit within the binary categories of gay/lesbian or straight/heterosexual. Or it may mean that the person's actual experience of sexuality changes. This does not mean the person is confused or in transition or "on the fence." These are often euphemisms for imposing a binary model of sexual orientation on the person. Rather, the person may very well be experiencing *actual change* in such experiences as sexual attraction, sexual behavior, fantasies, emotional preference, relational intimacy, social identity, and community identification. These changes occur for some during different seasons of a person's life, for others with different persons at different times, and still for others in different contexts and communities (Firestein, 1996, 2007).

It's important to remember that most cultural contexts in which queer persons are living are deeply grounded in binary constructs of maleness and femaleness. The division of gender, and the often violent (and deadly) response to persons who embody a transgressive or fluid gender, means that there is great pressure to conform (Sprinkle, 2011). As such, it takes a great deal of capacity and inner resources, as well as external support, for one to resist internalized social norms to live authentically and congruently with one's preferred gender or sexual identity. This pressure often results in experiences of stress, anxiety, depression, and suicidal thoughts. These life problems and/or diagnoses can't be addressed in the counseling process without also address-ing the real effects of a queer person living in a heterosexist and homophobic world. Because queer persons experience the hegemonic binary in nearly every context and setting in life, it is critically important that pastoral counselors suspend fixed models of gender and sexuality within the counseling experience.

Once gender and sexual identity change is recognized as normative and not pathological, the objective of counseling then becomes exploring the identity change process as way of understanding identity itself. Thus, if we understand what invites or motivates persons to change the ways in which they experience and language their sexual selves—or the ways in which they resist being labeled by others—we can better map the landscape such persons are navigating and can assist the person in identifying the resources and capacities needed to live a preferred way of being in the world.

Double-Bind Marginalization

Allport (1954) concluded that persons who experience ridicule, disparagement, and discrimination often manifest four common characteristics: social withdraw and pas-sivity, anxiety and suspicion, denial of members in their minority group, and self-hatred. Many researchers of gay and lesbian communities have noted similarities to Allport's work with the experiences of gay men and lesbians living in a heterosexist world (Herek, 1991). As it relates to queer-identified persons, however, these four effects of marginalization are experienced a bit differently than gay and lesbian persons. Pas-toral counselors should keep in mind how, despite recent gains in social acceptance of gay men and lesbians in the United States, the prevailing dominant discourse of sexuality remains hetero- and homonormative. In other words, being gay or lesbian is increasingly accepted as a minority class, but there remains limited acceptance if one is queer, bisexual, pansexual, or fluid (Burleson, 2005; Firestein, 2007).

Alex originally shared with me that experiences of "rejection" and "judgment" by family, as well as difficulty with "being authentic and true to who I am," were most troubling in life. This is common to the coming-out experience, especially for persons who come from families and congregations who hold more conserving beliefs and practices with regard to sexuality (Tigert, 1999). Often this means that gay and lesbian persons find support and acceptance with others in gay and lesbian communities, and these affirming relationships remain critically important for navigating the pain and loss of familial rejection (although the experience of family rejection is begin-ning to change). This is not always the case for queer persons, especially sexually fluid queer persons, however. One of the consequences of fluid sexuality is the criti-cism by some gay and lesbian communities that queer- and bisexual-identified per-sons are "riding the fence," "going through a phase," or "afraid to come totally out of the closet."

Alex says, "At first I used to feel welcome in the lesbian community, but now that I've been dating a man I feel that a lot of the gay and lesbian people I know think I'm using 'straight privilege' or that I just am afraid to fully come out as lesbian." This experience creates a double bind of marginalization. As a queer-identified person who is experiencing sexual fluidity, Alex is experiencing marginalization from family and straight friends who are unaccepting and rejecting. At the same time, Alex is also experiencing marginalization from gay and lesbian communities that are equally unac-cepting and rejecting of Alex's fluidity.

God Imaging and the Construction of Identity

Queer persons who identify as genderqueer, transgender, or gender fluid and who are seeking pastoral counseling are often integrating their gender identity within their own operative theological anthropologies. Beliefs about who God is and what God's gender is, beliefs about imago Dei and creation, and beliefs about the body and the morality of engaging in sexual intimacy play an important role for the person seeking to find a sense of wholeness and justice in life. There seems to be a correlation between deconstructing images of God and deconstructing one's own gender and/or sexual identity. As queer persons consider their gender or sexuality in between the dominant binary constructs, similar reflections occur about how God is similarly imaged between dominant binary constructs (Hays, 2013). In other words, as Alex explores the idea that there are other gendered metaphors for God beyond male, or that God may embody both (or all) genders, or that God is beyond gender, Alex is able to find more self-acceptance of Alex's own queer gender. This is deconstructive theological anthropology. And it raises important considerations for pastoral counselors to invite persons within the Abrahamic traditions who consult us for counseling to consider the correlation between their operative God images and their own self-identities. Practitioners working within the context of other religious traditions are similarly invited to consider how the person's embedded theological commitments and cosmologies correlate with the person's own self-identity. Is this correlation problematic or oppressive, or is it liberative and restorative? Feminist pastoral counselors have long described this strategy in counseling with women, but with queer persons, there is an additional opportunity for liberation in the theological claim that God's gender is not static or fixed but is fluid and ambiguous.

This raises several important areas for exploration: What might be the implications of being in relationship with and/or being in covenant with a God who is liminal and fluid over time? How might that shape the person's own values and ethics of sexual covenant making? What might be the consequences of embodying relational justice with a God who is ambiguous? How might queering God open up erotic opportunities for mystical union with the Divine?

These questions require pastoral counselors to suspend our own operative theories of binary gender and sexual orientation in order to open up space in the therapeutic/pastoral relationship for persons to explore their own fluid gender and/or sexual identities. This presents a powerful opportunity for liberation, healing, and justice making, particularly in light of binary disciplinary regimes within faith communities and society that deny the existence of gender and/or sexual fluidity in the first place. Here I'm suggesting that suspending our operative theories and theologies of binary gender and sexual orientation is not only helpful to persons seeking care, but doing so is also an act of public theology within wider discussions of gender and sexuality in faith communities.

Transgressive Ethics

The lived experiences of genderqueer and gender-fluid persons within the context of binary theological discourses—discourses that often reject gender and sexual fluidity—represent an opportunity for transgressive acts of resistance. Keeping in mind that queer is an identity that suggests crossing, blurring, turning upside-down, and/or contrary to dominant categories, queer is also used as a verb to cross, blur, turn upside-down, or disrupt. Many queer persons are increasingly using biblical texts and faith narratives with a queer hermeneutic to claim them as agential and/or constitutive resources in the construction of their fluid, queer, or ambiguous identities. Such texts and narratives include Jesus embodying a fluid or ambiguous identity himself and engaging in ethical practices that transgressed binary norms, as well as other biblical characters who similarly transgress binary norms. This represents an important opportunity for pastoral counselors working from liberative and emancipatory perspectives to queer (i.e., disrupt) homophobic theological discourses and to construct queer-affirming sacred texts and faith narratives.

Genderqueer persons increasingly choose to express their preferred gender in multiple community settings, including congregations. For example, a genderqueer person might attend religious services one week expressing one gender and another week expressing a different gender. This is a transgressive act but also a liberating one. And it has real consequences. Depending on the congregation, some find acceptance, and the changing of one's gender expression does not raise much notice. But in other congregations, the person might experience disapproving looks, inappropriate questions, or outright rejection. Trans and genderqueer persons experience significantly higher rates of hate crime and violence compared to both gay/lesbian and straight populations—especially trans and genderqueer persons of color (National Coalition of Anti-Violence Programs, 2014; Sprinkle, 2011). Pastoral counselors can assist trans and genderqueer persons in fully embodying their preferred gender identity while, at the same time, helping persons to navigate the risks and real effects of doing so.

Marriage and Covenant Making

Genderqueer and sexually fluid persons are challenging many assumptions about marriage and covenantal relationships. Several denominations have developed marriage and holy union liturgies for same-gender couples.[5] Many states are making legal provision for same-gender marriage, and the political movement for federal recognition of same-gender marriage appears imminent. This is good news for same-gender-loving persons who wish to have their relationships legally recognized as marriage. Some couples specifically do not wish to participate in the institution of marriage and, instead, have developed other covenant-making practices within their communities. But this raises an important consideration regarding queer persons who choose not to marry/make a covenant with one other person.

Pastoral counselors working with couples and families are even more affected by these issues, particularly as queer-identified persons also queer their relationships, marriages, and covenants. Thus, counseling queer couples and families not only requires an intentional deconstruction of our theoretical models of marriage and family (this is especially the case for those trained in family systems therapy) but also requires a critical self-assessment of our operative theological assumptions about marriage, vows, covenants, mutuality, families, and children.

Polyamory and multiple intimate partners is a considerable component of queer sexuality. For some queer-identified persons, this means multiple partners at the same time; for others, it means varying degrees of intimacy with different people; and for others, it means sexual intimacy with different gendered partners at different times in their lives (Hays, 2013). Polyamory challenges the hegemony of the exclusive two-person committed relationship, which is prevalent in the ethics of many contemporary religious traditions, including LGBTQI-affirming Christian ethics. Indeed, this may be an important discussion in the field of queer theology and ethics in the years to come. This, in turn, challenges pastoral counselors to become critically self-aware of our assumptions and biases regarding the intersections of sex, marriage and covenanted relationships, and monogamy. Although there may be queer sexual practices that might be ethically defendable, there may also need to be limits on practices that are unjust, that harm others, or that are not life giving. So how do we, as pastoral counselors, construct our own ethical boundaries around sexual intimacy? And how do we ensure that our ethical commitments regarding sexual intimacy and relationships do not lead us to impose inappropriate norms and therapeutic objectives on the person? Finally, are we making our own ethical positions regarding questions of justice transparent?

CONCLUSIONS

This chapter began with the lived experience of Alex, a queer-identified person seeking pastoral counseling. Through Alex's life, we explored concepts of queer identity and critiqued theories of sexual orientation and identity that are common in gay- and lesbian-affirming psychotherapy. Throughout this discussion, I have emphasized how important it is for pastoral counselors to deconstruct and critically assess a wide variety of assumptions—especially clinical theories regarding sexual orientation and theological commitments regarding embodiment, sex, gender, and relationships. I argue that in order for pastoral counselors to engage in ethically and theologically grounded counseling with queer-identified persons, we must queer our own practice. In other words, we must disrupt, frustrate, and turn upside-down the embedded heterosexist assumptions within our practices that lead us to conclude that gender is fixed, that sexuality is fixed, or that identities are fixed. I am confident that doing so will be difficult and uncomfortable and will demand that we enter into intentional relationships of professional accountability to do so. It is, however, possible. This is, after all, what queer persons who consult with us for counseling do every day of their lives.

REFLECTION QUESTIONS

1. Some readers may not be familiar with the use of the word *queer* as addressed in this chapter. How does the author understand *queer*? What is included in this concept?
2. The author outlines several historical developments in writing and talking about LGBTQI individuals within pastoral counseling. What are some of the major milestones in this development?
3. What does it mean "to queer" something? How is *queer* different as a verb than an adjective or noun?
4. Hays asserts that "working with queer-identified persons in counseling necessarily challenges both Western psychological discourses and theological discourses regarding gender and sexuality." What does he mean by this? What are some of the most significant ways in which psychological and theological discourses are challenged in this work?
5. The author notes that we can sometimes do harm even when attempting to be affirming and inclusive. What are your points of vulnerability in this type of work? In other words, where might you be likely to mean well but do harm?

NOTES

1. This case is a composite of persons in my pastoral counseling practice, rather than a specific case. Because I take my commitment to maintain confidences seriously, and because of the power differential in seeking consent, I prefer to use composite cases to illustrate the concepts and strategies presented here.
2. This work will use sexual *identity* rather than orientation because it is more suggestive of the ways sexuality is socially constructed within dominant discourses of binary categories of identity. It is noteworthy that the Association for Lesbian, Gay, Bisexual, and Transgender Issues in Counseling (Harper et al., 2013) uses "affectional orientation," although doing so seems to disembody the nature of human sexuality. Discussion regarding the tension between socially constructed, essentialist, and biological/genetic models of sexual orientation is considered in this chapter.
3. I recognize that for some pastoral counselors, this remains a debatable point and that there is not agreement among religious traditions and denominations on homosexuality and same-gender intimacy. Discussions about whether or not pastoral counselors should work from an affirming perspective are easily accessed through the literature mentioned here. For a discussion of varying models of affirming pastoral counseling with LGBTQI persons, see Marshall (1997, 2001, 2009) and Graham (1997). This chapter already assumes an LGBTQI-affirming stance and seeks to move the conversation beyond apologetics toward more nuanced questions of theological anthropology, embedded clinical theories of human identity and development, and queer-affirming practice.
4. Although most of the theological resources engaged in this chapter come from the Western Christian tradition, questions of gender fluidity and transgender identity have long histories in other religious traditions, including Islam (Davies, 2010; Kugle, 2010), Hinduism (Pattanaik, 2002), and Native American (Jacobs, Thomas, & Lang, 1997). For a diverse collection of essays on queer identities in world religions, see Boisvert and Johnson (2012) and Machacek and Wilcox (2003).
5. The predominantly LGBTQ denomination, Universal Fellowship of Metropolitan Community Churches (UFMCC), has been authorizing same-gender marriages and holy unions since 1969. More recently, in 2005, the United Church of Christ's General Synod officially called on its local congregations to affirm full marriage equality. In 2009, the Evangelical Lutheran Church in America officially allowed same-gender unions to be blessed liturgically on a congregation-by-congregation basis. In 2012, the General Convention of the Episcopal Church adopted a liturgy for the blessing of lifelong covenant for same-gender unions but specifically did not call the rite a marriage. In 2014, the General Assembly of the Presbyterian Church (United States) recognized same-gender marriage. For more details on official positions from a wide variety of faith traditions and religious organizations, see Human Right Campaign's "Faith Positions" (2014a).

REFERENCES

Allport, G. (1954). *The nature of prejudice.* Reading, MA: Addison-Wesley.

Althaus-Reid, M. (2000). *Indecent theology: Theological perversions in sex, gender and politics.* London & New York: Routledge.

Althaus-Reid, M. (2003). *The queer god.* London, UK: Routledge.

American Psychiatric Association. (1952). *Diagnostic and statistical manual of mental disorders.* Washington, DC: American Psychiatric Press.

American Psychiatric Association. (1980). *Diagnostic and statistical manual of mental disorders* (3rd ed.). Washington, DC: American Psychiatric Press.

American Psychiatric Association. (1987). *Diagnostic and statistical manual of mental disorders* (3rd ed., rev.). Washington, DC: American Psychiatric Press.

American Psychiatric Association. (2000). *Diagnostic and statistical manual of mental disorders* (4th ed., text rev.). Washington, DC: American Psychiatric Press.

American Psychiatric Association. (2013). *Diagnostic and statistical manual of mental disorders* (5th ed.). Arlington, VA: American Psychiatric Press.

Bieschke, K. J., Perez, R. M., & DeBord, K. A. (Eds.). (2007). *Handbook of counseling and psychotherapy with lesbian, gay, bisexual, and transgender clients*. Washington, DC: American Psychological Association.

Bigner, J. J., & Wetchler, J. L. (2012). *Handbook of LGBT-affirmative couple and family therapy*. New York, NY: Brunner-Routledge.

Blevins, J. (2005). *Queer as This May Sound: Toward New Language and New Practices in Psychology, Theology, and Pastoral Care*. Unpublished doctoral dissertation, Candler School of Theology, Atlanta, GA.

Blevins, J. (2009). Hospitality is a queer thing. *Journal of Pastoral Theology, 19*(2), 104–117.

Boisvert, D. L., & Johnson, J. E. (2012). *Queer religion*. Santa Barbara, CA: Praeger.

Boswell, J. (1980). *Christianity, social tolerance, and homosexuality: Gay people in Western Europe from the beginning of the Christian era to the fourteenth century*. Chicago, IL: University of Chicago Press.

Burleson, W. E. (2005). *Bi America: Myths, truths, and struggles of an invisible community*. New York, NY: Harrington Park Press.

Burnes, T. R., Singh, A. A., Harper, A. J., Harper, B., Maxon-Kann, W., Pickering, D. L., . . . Hosea, J. (2010). American Counseling Association: Competencies for counseling with transgender clients. *Journal of LGBT Issues in Counseling, 4*(3–4), 135–159. doi:10.1080/15538605.2010 .524839

Butler, J. (1993). *Bodies that matter: On the discursive limits of "sex"*. New York, NY: Routledge.

Butler, J. (2004). *Undoing gender*. New York, NY: Routledge.

Butler, J. (2005). *Giving an account of oneself*. New York, NY: Fordham University Press.

Byrne, R. (1993). Pastoral counseling of the gay male. In R. J. Wicks & R. D. Parsons (Eds.), *Clinical handbook of pastoral counseling* (Vol. 2, pp. 267–295). New York, NY: Paulist Press.

Cass, V. C. (1979). Homosexual identity formation: A theoretical model. *Journal of Homosexuality, 4*(3), 219–235. doi:10.1300/J082v04n03_01

Cass, V. C. (1984). Homosexual identity formation: Testing a theoretical model. *Journal of Sex Research, 20*(2), 143.

Clinebell, H., & McKeever, B. C. (2011). *Basic types of pastoral care & counseling: Resources for the ministry of Healing and Growth*. Nashville, TN: Abingdon.

Coleman, E. (1982). Developmental stages of the coming out process. *Journal of Homosexuality, 7*(2–3), 31–43. doi:10.1300/J082v07n02_06

Coleman, E., Bockting, W., Botzer, M., Cohen-Kettenis, P., DeCuypere, G., Feldman, J., . . . Zucker, K. (2012). Standards of care for the health of transsexual, transgender, and gender-nonconforming people, version 7. *International Journal of Transgenderism, 13*(4), 165–232. doi:10.1080/15532739.2011.700873

Collins, J. F. (2007). Counseling at the intersection of identities: Asian/Pacific American bisexuals. In B. Firestein (Ed.), *Becoming visible: Counseling bisexuals across the lifespan* (pp. 229–245). New York, NY: Columbia University Press.

Comstock, G. D. (2001). *A whosoever church: Welcoming lesbians and gay men into African American congregations*. Louisville, KY: Westminster John Knox Press.

Cooper, K. J., & Marshall, J. L. (2010). Where race, gender, and orientation meet. In J. Stevenson-Moessner & T. Snorton (Eds.), *Women out of order: Risking change and creating care in a multicultural world* (pp. 115–127). Minneapolis, MN: Fortress.

Culbertson, P. L. (2000). *Caring for God's people: Counseling and Christian wholeness*. Minneapolis, MN: Fortress.

Davies, S. G. (2010). *Gender diversity in Indonesia: Sexuality, Islam and queer selves*. London, UK: Routledge.

De Cecco, J. P. (1987). Homosexuality's brief recovery: From sickness to health and back again. *Journal of Sex Research, 23*, 106–114. doi:10.1080/00224498709551346

Douglas, K. B. (1999). *Sexuality and the Black church: A womanist perspective*. Maryknoll, NY: Orbis.

Firestein, B. A. (Ed.). (1996). *Bisexuality: The psychology and politics of an invisible minority*. Thousand Oaks, CA: Sage.

Firestein, B. A. (Ed.). (2007). *Becoming visible: Counseling bisexuals across the lifespan*. New York, NY: Columbia University Press.

Foucault, M. (1965). *Madness and civilization: A history of insanity in the age of reason* (R. Howard, Trans.). New York, NY: Pantheon.

Foucault, M. (1975). *The birth of the clinic: An archaeology of medical perception* (A. Sheridan, Trans.). New York, NY: Vintage.

Foucault, M. (1977). *Discipline and punish: The birth of the prison* (A. Sheridan, Trans.). New York, NY: Pantheon.

Foucault, M. (1990). *The history of sexuality* (Vintage Books ed.). New York, NY: Vintage.

Girshick, L. B. (2008). *Transgender voices: Beyond women and men*. Hanover, NH: University Press of New England.

Goss, R. (2002). *Queering Christ: Beyond Jesus acted up*. Cleveland, OH: Pilgrim Press.

Grace, J. (1992). Affirming gay and lesbian adulthood. In N. J. Woodman (Ed.), *Lesbian and gay lifestyles: A guide for counseling and education* (pp. 33–47). New York, NY: Irvington.

Graham, L. K. (1997). *Discovering images of god: Narratives of care among lesbians and gays*. Louisville, KY: Westminster John Knox Press.

Griffin, H. L. (2006). *Their own receive them not: African American lesbians and gays in black churches*. Cleveland, OH: Pilgrim Press.

Hansen, B. (1989). American physicians' earliest writings about homosexuals, 1880–1900. *Milbank Quarterly, 67*(Suppl. 1), 92–108. doi:10.2307/3350187

Harper, A., Finnerty, P., Martinez, M., Brace, A., Crethar, H. C., . . . Hammer, T. R. (2013). Association for Lesbian, Gay, Bisexual, and Transgender Issues in Counseling competencies for counseling lesbian, gay, bisexual, queer, questioning, intersex, and ally individuals. *Journal of LGBT Issues in Counseling, 7*(1), 2–43. doi:10.1080/15538605.2013.755444

Hays, J. D. (2013). *Ambiguous embodiment: Constructing poststructuralist pastoral theologies of gender and sexual fluidity* (Unpublished doctoral dissertation). Brite Divinity School, Texas Christian University, Fort Worth, TX.

Herek, G. M. (1991). Stigma, prejudice, and violence against lesbians and gay men. In J. C. Gonsiorek & J. D. Weinrich (Eds.), *Homosexuality: Research implications for public policy* (pp. 960–980). Newbury Park, CA: Sage.

Human Rights Campaign. (2014a). *Faith positions*. Retrieved from http://www.hrc.org/resources/entry/faith-positions

Human Rights Campaign. (2014b). *The lies and dangers of efforts to change sexual orientation or gender identity*. Retrieved from http://www.hrc.org/resources/entry/the-lies-and-dangers-of-reparative-therapy

Jacobs, S., Thomas, W., & Lang, S. (1997). *Two-spirit people: Native American gender identity, sexuality, and spirituality*. Urbana, IL: University of Illinois Press.

Jenness, V., & Geis, G. (2011). Transgender lives and lifestyles. In C. D. Bryantp (Ed.), *Routledge handbook of deviant behavior* (pp. 223–230). London, UK: Routledge.

Kinsey, A. C., & Institute for Sex Research. (1998). *Sexual behavior in the human female*. Bloomington, IN: Indiana University Press. (Original work published 1953)

Kinsey, A. C., Pomeroy, W. B., & Martin, C. E. (1948). *Sexual behavior in the human male*. Philadelphia, PA: W. B. Saunders.

Klein, F. (1993). *The bisexual option* (2nd ed.). New York, NY: Haworth.

Kugle, S. A. (2010). *Homosexuality in Islam: Critical reflection on gay, lesbian, and transgender Muslims*. Oxford, UK: Oneworld Publications.

Kundtz, D., & Schlager, B. S. (2007). *Ministry among God's queer folk: LGBT pastoral care*. Cleveland, OH: Pilgrim Press.

Lewis, L. A. (1984). The coming-out process for lesbians: Integrating a stable identity. *Social Work, 29*(5), 464–469. doi:10.1093/sw/29.5.464

Loughlin, G. (Ed.). (2007). *Queer theology: Rethinking the western body*. Malden, MA: Blackwell.

Machacek, D. W., & Wilcox, M. M. (2003). *Sexuality and the world's religions*. Santa Barbara, CA: ABC-Clio.

Machado, D. L. (2003). Rethinking the melting pot. *Harvard Divinity School Bulletin*. Retrieved March 30, 2011, from http://www.hds.harvard.edu/dpa/news/bulletin/articles/machado.html

Malony, H. N. (Ed.). (2001). *Pastoral care and counseling in sexual diversity*. New York, NY: Haworth Pastoral Press.

Marshall, J. L. (1997). *Counseling lesbian partners*. Louisville, KY: Westminster John Knox Press.

Marshall, J. L. (2001). Pastoral care and the formation of sexual identity. *American Journal of Pastoral Counseling, 3*(3–4), 101–112. doi:10.1300/J062v03n03_08

Marshall, J. L. (2009). Pro-active intercultural pastoral care and counseling with lesbian women and gay men. *Pastoral Psychology, 59*(4), 423–432. doi:10.1007/s11089-009-0203-0

McNeill, J. J. (1976). *The church and the homosexual*. Kansas City, MO: Sheed Andrews and McMeel.

Moon, L. (Ed.). (2008). *Feeling queer or queer feelings? Radical approaches to counselling sex, sexualities and genders*. London, UK: Routledge.

Moon, L. (Ed.). (2010). *Counselling ideologies: Queer challenges to heteronormativity*. Farnham, UK: Ashgate.

National Coalition of Anti-Violence Programs. (2014). *Lesbian, gay, bisexual, transgender, queer and HIV-affected hate violence in 2013*. New York, NY: Author.

Nicolosi, J. (2001). A developmental model for effective treatment of male homosexuality: Implications for pastoral counseling. In H. N. Malony (Ed.), *Pastoral care and counseling in sexual diversity* (pp. 87–100). New York, NY: Haworth.

Page, E. (2007). Bisexual women's and men's experiences of psychotherapy. In B. Firestein (Ed.), *Becoming visible: Counseling bisexuals across the lifespan* (pp. 52–71). New York, NY: Columbia University Press.

Pattanaik, D. (2002). *The man who was a woman and other queer tales from Hindu lore*. New York, NY: Harrington Park Press.

Paul, J. P. (2000). Bisexuality: Reassessing our paradigms of sexuality. In P. Rust (Ed.), *Bisexuality in the United States: A reader and guide to the literature* (pp. 221–249). New York, NY: Columbia University Press.

Ramsay, N. J. (2014). Intersectionality: A model for addressing the complexity of oppression and privilege. *Pastoral Psychology, 63*(4), 453–469. doi:10.1007/s11089-013-0570-4

Ratzinger, J. (1986). *Letter to the bishops of the Catholic Church on the pastoral care of homosexual persons*. Congregation for the Doctrine of the Faith, Rome, Italy.

Rich, A. (1980). Compulsory heterosexuality and lesbian existence. *Signs, 5*(4), 631–660.

Ritter, K., & Terndrup, A. I. (2002). *Handbook of affirmative psychotherapy with lesbians and gay men*. New York, NY: Guilford.

Robinson, M. (2002). *Bisexuality and the seduction by the uncertain*. Retrieved March 3, 2013, from http://www.margaretrobinson.com/scholarly/bisexuality.html

Scott, R. L. (2007). Addressing social invalidation to promote well-being for multiracial bisexuals of African descent. In B. Firestein (Ed.), *Becoming visible: Counseling bisexuals across the lifespan* (pp. 207–228). New York, NY: Columbia University Press.

Siker, J. S. (Ed.). (2007). *Homosexuality and religion: An encyclopedia*. Westport, CT: Greenwood.

Sprinkle, S. (2011). *Unfinished lives: Reviving the memories of LGBTQ hate crimes victims*. Eugene, OR: Resource Publications.

Stone, K. (2004). *Practising safer texts: Food, sex and bible in queer perspective*. London, UK: T & T Clark International.

Struzzo, J. A. (1989). Pastoral counseling and homosexuality. *Journal of Homosexuality, 18*(3–4), 195–222. doi:10.1300/J082v18n03_10

Stryker, S. (2008). *Transgender history*. Berkeley, CA: Seal Press.

Stuart, E. (1997). *Religion is a queer thing: A guide to the Christian faith for lesbian, gay, bisexual, and transgendered people*. London, UK: Cassell.

Stuart, E. (2003). *Gay and lesbian theologies: Repetitions with critical difference*. Aldershot, UK: Ashgate.

Sullivan, N. (2003). *A critical introduction to queer theory*. New York: New York University Press.

Switzer, D. K., & Thornburg, J. (1999). *Pastoral care of gays, lesbians, and their families*. Minneapolis, MN: Fortress.

Tanis, J. E. (2003). *Trans-gendered: Theology, ministry, and communities of faith.* Cleveland, OH: Pilgrim Press.

Tigert, L. M. (1999). *Coming out through fire: Surviving the trauma of homophobia.* Cleveland, OH: United Church Press.

Tigert, L. M., & Tirabassi, M. C. (2004). *Transgendering faith: Identity, sexuality, and spirituality.* Cleveland, OH: Pilgrim Press.

Topper, C. J. (1986). Spirituality as a component in counseling lesbians-gays. *Journal of Pastoral Counseling, 21*(1), 55–59.

Townsend, L. L. (2009). *Introduction to pastoral counseling.* Nashville, TN: Abingdon.

Troiden, R. (1979). Becoming homosexual: a model of gay identity acquisition. *Psychiatry, 42*(4), 362–373.

Troiden, R. (1989). The formation of homosexual identities. *Journal of Homosexuality, 17*(1–2), 43–73.

Unterberger, G. L. (1993). Counseling lesbians: A feminist perspective. In R. J. Wicks & R. D. Parsons (Eds.), *Clinical handbook of pastoral counseling* (Vol. 2, 228–266). New York, NY: Paulist Press.

Weinberg, M. S., Williams, C. J., & Pryor, D. W. (1994). *Dual attraction: Understanding bisexuality.* New York, NY: Oxford University Press.

Wilchins, R. A. (2004). *Queer theory, gender theory: An instant primer.* Los Angeles, CA: Alyson Books.

Wilson, D. M. (1998). I don't mean to offend, but I won't pretend. In K. B. Lyon & A. Smith, Jr. (Eds.), *Tending the flock: Congregations and family ministry* (pp. 145–172). Louisville, KY: Westminster John Knox Press.

Zinik, G. (1985). Identity conflict or adaptive flexibility? Bisexuality reconsidered. In F. Klein & T. J. Wolf (Eds.), *Bisexualities: Theory and research* (pp. 7–19). Binghamton, NY: Haworth.

Elizabeth Denham Thompson

21

REFERRAL, CONSULTATION, AND COLLABORATION

It is increasingly evident that the need for appropriate, effective, and timely referral, consultation, and collaboration is more critical and necessary than ever. This fact can be overwhelming. How can a pastoral counselor continuously be up-to-date on the latest theories and practices? How can a pastoral counselor know that a particular practice might be more helpful for a client or would be helpful to suggest in tandem with what the pastoral counselor is offering? Access to information via the Internet provides immediacy but not necessarily clarity of information or professional competency. When is collaboration, consultation, or referral beneficial? How will the pastoral counselor decide when to use one versus the other or to do all three? How can clients, therapists, religious leaders, physicians, and other allied helpers work together so that there are not too many "chiefs" providing guidance? These questions, and a host of others, can make the process of connecting with others bewildering and problematic. However, enlarging the circle of care and expertise can also be a tremendous gift that brings others into a community of care for people who are hurting.

Any attempt at a definitive discussion on best practices in consulting, collaborating, and referring is a bit like a lava lamp. At any given moment in time, the shape shifts and morphs based on what is happening in the system, what is heating up or what is cooling down, and what resources are or are not available. The key elements are there and can be seen, but the shape keeps evolving and changing. We all operate within a variety of spheres or systems that are like concentric as well as overlapping circles—family, congregation, work, volunteer groups, hobbies, school, friends, group activities, legal entities, neighborhood, city, state, country, religious groups, ethnicity, language, education, and socioeconomic placement, among others. Each of these influences the individual and is influenced by the individual. Family systems theories, social systems theories, and their many iterations help us to know that although any single individual can and does exist with his or her own identity, it is also imperative to acknowledge the multiple systems within which we operate and the influences they have on our lives.

Although overwhelming and problematic at times, the idea of referral, consultation, and collaboration can be understood as connecting critical resources that include the larger systems within which we function, interact, and live. We need to recognize that connecting with other partners in caring for people can strengthen our work and others'. Pastoral counselors need not feel as if they are "lone rangers" even if they may be the first and potentially ongoing provider of care. Pastoral counselors and therapists, as well as religious leaders, can reach out, and by actually going through the process of referral, consultation, and collaboration, they will begin to build the knowledge of how to do it and will be even more effective the next time around. This chapter is designed as a way to help the reader think through what each of these might look like, think more broadly about potential partners, provide some parameters and best practices for discerning next steps, and provide clarity on how pastoral counseling fits into these activities.

This chapter approaches the topics of referral, consultation, and collaboration from the perspective of the pastoral counselor, although religious leaders and allied professionals in other related fields should be able to benefit from the conversation. The terms *pastoral counselor*, *counselor*, and *therapist* are used interchangeably, although there are distinctions among them addressed elsewhere in this book. In a like manner, the term *religious leader* is used through this chapter as an all-inclusive identifier for the variety of ministers; clergy; rabbis; imams; ordained, appointed, and/or elected spiritual and theological leaders in congregations. The terms *clergy, ministers,* and *religious leaders* are used interchangeably, although obviously there are distinctions among them. Today, most pastoral counselors credentialed by the American Association of Pastoral Counselors (AAPC) also carry credentials as marriage and family therapists, psychologists, or licensed counselors. Other therapists may see themselves as a licensed therapist first and a pastoral counselor second. There are religious leaders who serve in a variety of settings, including those who may both serve as pastors of a congregation and maintain a pastoral counseling practice, sometimes in the same facility. All of these mental health professionals are included under the terms *counselor, pastoral counselor,* and *therapist.*

DEFINING *REFERRAL, CONSULTATION,* AND *COLLABORATION*

Although referral, consultation, and collaboration overlap and take different forms, it is important to clarify the definitions and implications of these three practices.

Referral

When a referral is offered by a professional, it is usually because someone has asked for assistance and the professional is not in a position to offer the assistance. The professional then refers, sends, or suggests another person or place where what is wanted or needed by the person asking may be obtained (i.e., treatment, help, advice, support services). The person asking for the referral may be an acquaintance, friend, client, potential client, or even another professional. The person may or may not follow through with the referral, but the professional giving the referral believes that it would be helpful if he or she did. The assumption is that, for any number of reasons, the professional with whom a person first connects is unable to provide the help that is needed. Therefore, a referral to another professional is desirable to access timely and appropriate care. At times, a referral does not end the existing relationship but may be in addition to or in tandem with the current relationship. When we get into the section on referrals, these will be explored in more depth.

Consultation

In a pastoral counseling context, consultation is understood as the process of obtaining input from another professional regarding the clinical work that is being done with a client. Consultation is understood as existing between peers, even if one has more expertise than the other or is licensed to practice in a particular area that the other is not. Depending on the circumstances and length of consultation, this may be a free consultation, or the services may involve a fee. Clinical consultation is placed in juxtaposition to clinical supervision. Supervision connotes a hierarchy with professional and legal implications for all parties involved in the supervisory contract (supervisor, supervisee, and client). Consultation implies a triadic relationship "with the involvement of a consultant and one or more consultees and clients" (Erchul & Martens, 2010, p. 4). In this case, the consultee is the therapist seeking clinical consultation. However, the professional and legal responsibilities continue to reside within the therapist–consultee and client's relationship. There are different ways to receive clinical consultation and different reasons for seeking consultation, which are explored later. We also explore the idea of pastoral counselors providing consultation with clergy, religious leaders, congregations, organizations, and judicatories, in addition to individual clients.

Collaboration

> Collaborative care involves providers from different specialties, disciplines, or sectors working together to offer complementary services and mutual support, to ensure that individuals receive the most appropriate service from the most appropriate provider in the most suitable location, as quickly as necessary, and with minimal obstacles. Collaboration can involve better communication, closer personal contacts, sharing of clinical care, joint education programs and (or) joint program and system planning. (Craven & Bland, 2006, p. 9S)

This definition, drawn from a report commissioned in 2004 to improve the mental health and well-being of Canadians, is a complete yet concise definition. Collaboration is probably the broadest of the practices addressed in this chapter because it can include just about anyone and can be of any duration for an unlimited number of reasons.

What is common among referral, consultation, and collaboration is that the professional is seeking additional assistance from another professional and/or external resource(s) to support and extend care for an individual, family, or organization. The distinction among them is how that additional assistance is obtained, who is asking or offering it, how many others are involved in providing it, the legal and ethical implications involved, and with whom the client does or does not have an ongoing formal relationship.

The chapter addresses why and when a pastoral counselor would choose to work with a client without any additional outside professional resources and why and when a pastoral counselor would choose to obtain consultation, request collaboration, or provide a referral or some variant combination of these. Sometimes it is more helpful to explore these choices with a particular situation in mind. Therefore, what follows is a brief case study to keep in mind throughout the reading of the chapter. It is intended to spur questions, discussion, implications, applications, and practical discernment processes.

CASE STUDY[1]

Joelle is a 38-year-old, single, female client who has come to see Samantha Jones, a pastoral counselor. Joelle has one child, a son Bobby, who is 9 years old and in elementary school. The father is a boyfriend, with whom she lived for several years (never married), but they have now separated and he has very little to do with Joelle or their son. Joelle is coming for therapy at this point because she has struggled with depression much of her adult life, with at least one suicide attempt in her history. A couple of weeks ago, she voiced out loud, again, that sometimes it would be easier if she were dead, and her mother became concerned. Her mother still lives in town, in the house where Joelle grew up. She and Joelle's father are divorced and she has not remarried. Joelle and her mother have a conflicted relationship, but "she's my mother and Bobby's grandmother," so Joelle sees her mother every few days, often in connection with her mother helping to care for Bobby. Joelle's father has remarried and moved to another part of the state. He sends money as needed but has moved on with his life. Joelle has two other siblings, an older brother and a younger sister. Her brother seems happily married and lives in another part of the country with his wife and two children, occasionally coming home for visits at the holidays. Her sister lives in town and seems to be the primary connector for the family, reaching out to the disparate family members and trying to keep them from wandering off too far. Joelle loves her sister but also reacts to what she thinks are "intrusive questions" about her life.

Joelle's mother is involved in a local congregation, and after she heard Joelle's suicidal comment, she called her minister for help. The minister gave her the names of a couple of counselors, including Samantha. Joelle's mother pushed Joelle to call and schedule an appointment and encouraged her to call Samantha in particular because her mother liked the idea of having some kind of spiritual support available. Joelle, who has been in therapy before for depression and was hospitalized in the state's major city following a suicide attempt when she lived there, agreed to call and schedule an appointment with Samantha. Joelle is not really sure that anything will be different this time around, although she likes the idea of working with someone who might bring a spiritual perspective.

As Joelle and Samantha work together in therapy, more information comes to light. Joelle reports that she was sexually abused by her father and tried to protect her younger sister from her father. She and her sister have never really talked about this abuse, because her sister becomes very uncomfortable when Joelle's abuse is mentioned, quickly changing the topic. So Joelle doesn't know whether she was successful in diverting her father's attention away from her sister or whether he also abused her as well. Her mother lives with bipolar disorder, and Joelle never felt particularly safe with her mother due to significant mood swings. She is clear that her mother did not protect her from her father. Joelle, alongside her history of depression, has also been diagnosed with attention deficit hyperactivity disorder (ADHD). She's completed enough therapy with other therapists to be able to name, identify, and understand some of the dynamics that are problematic for her from her family of origin. Despite this knowledge, she continues to have difficulty making and sustaining primary relationships outside the family. Her son has provided a sense of stability and focus for her, but she also senses that she focuses too much on him, even obsessing about his safety and what he needs and whether she's a good enough mother. With her ADHD and mistrust of authority, she has difficulties with supervisors as well as staying on task, so she struggles to keep a job. Funds are always an issue, so she feels caught between wanting to cut off completely from her father and needing to ask her father for money to pay for essentials.

As she works with Joelle, Samantha is faced with the primary questions that every pastoral counselor faces—or any professional for that matter—when getting to know more of a client's story. "Can I work with this client? If so, is there anything else I need in order to provide appropriate and effective care? What other resources might be more helpful or at least additionally helpful to this client? Who else is already involved and can we/should we collaborate to care for this client?" How Samantha answers these questions and others, as well as how she keeps answering them as she assesses her work with Joelle, will determine whether she considers herself competent to handle Joelle's therapy herself or whether she should seek consultation, request collaboration, and/or refer Joelle elsewhere.

Keep this case study in mind as you read through the three overarching topics. Make a list of the information you would still want answered that is not provided. We will return to it toward the close of the chapter.

CONSULTATION

As noted earlier, consultation carries different legal implications than does supervision, although both involve asking for input from another professional. Supervision assumes a hierarchy whereby the counselor is understood to still be in a learning stage, and the supervisor takes on a legal responsibility for how the student counselor is working with a client. In consultation, the assumption is that both the counselor and the consultant are professionals of equal standing. The counselor who is now the consultee may choose to accept the suggestions and insights of the consultant or not, and the counselor/consultee continues to carry the legal and ethical weight of caring for the client. The underlying assumption is that the therapist remains the key link for a client and will act as a type of conductor, bringing in different resources as needed to provide the best care that promotes healing for the client. Not quite a gatekeeper, the therapist is at least the key figure in accessing, inviting in, interpreting, and integrating the information that comes from the various resources on behalf of the therapist's work with a client.

Assuming that the pastoral counselor has obtained a legal status in the state to provide services without clinical supervision, why would a pastoral counselor seek consultation? Key reasons include the desire to continue one's ongoing individual learning, to ensure quality and expertise in working with a particular client or type of client, to certify that one is abiding by one's professional code of ethics, and to clarify legal issues pertaining to one's clinical work. Pastoral counselors may also seek consultation when feeling "stuck" in working with a client; when a therapist is seeking alternative treatment options and modalities; when there are cultural, racial, national, religious, or spiritual differences between the client and therapist; or when the therapist would like to use expertise that is cross-disciplinary between the therapist and the client.

Ongoing Consultation

There are four basic forms that clinical consultation can take for an individual pastoral counselor. The first is ongoing consultation for the counselor in either a peer group model or an individual consultation model. In this form of consultation, the pastoral counselor proactively seeks out or forms a relationship with other therapy professionals, possibly across disciplines, to meet on a regular basis to discuss their cases and seek input and consultation on how to proceed. This can be an enriching experience for all professionals involved, expanding each person's knowledge, skills, and personal insights and reducing a counselor's isolation and potential for unethical behavior. An ongoing peer consultation group or individual consultation arrangement can proactively build a support network for the counselor and provide immediate resources when encountering a particularly difficult or interesting clinical situation or client. A peer group can be self-facilitated or the group can contract with an outside facilitator to lead them, keeping them on track and maintaining the group norms as established by the group. Generally, three types of peer consultation groups exist: case centered (in which the case is central and there may be a variety of therapeutic viewpoints presented to assist in understanding the case), process centered (in which all cases presented are used to deepen the knowledge of a particular modality of therapy), or a combination of these two (Truneckova, Viney, Maitland, & Seaborn, 2010).

Consultation Limited to a Particular Client

The second basic form of consultation is ongoing consultation that is limited to a particular client. In this model, the counselor seeks out a specific colleague to work more effectively with a particular client but may ask for an ongoing connection as long as he or she is working with that client on that issue. The consultation may even include the client meeting with the other professional for assessment (such as a neurological evaluation for brain injury or some form of psychological testing). After obtaining written permission from the client, the consultation may also include others who operate within the sphere of service for that particular client. These may include religious leaders, medical practitioners, therapists working with other members of the family or with the client, parole officers or legal system representatives, victim advocates, psychiatrists, 12-step sponsors, social workers, pediatric or geriatric specialists, congregational caregivers, hospital or other inpatient facility staff, or alternative medical practitioners such as acupuncturists, herbalists, massage therapists, or occupational therapists.

Onetime or Limited Consultation

The third basic form of consultation is onetime or limited consultation. This overlaps a bit with ongoing consultation that is limited to a particular client but is understood from the beginning to be a limited relationship. Again, the client may meet with the other professional for an assessment. The consulting professional most often provides the pastoral counselor with an assessment report or findings to help guide ongoing treatment. The same sphere of service providers may be listed in this section as well, but with the idea that, with the client's permission, the counselor will talk with the service provider on a limited basis to obtain additional information and insight that would be helpful for the counselor in providing ongoing treatment. The counselor may also reach out to another professional who has expertise on a particular type of incident or issue, expertise in a treatment modality, or understanding or accessibility in a particular geographic region and so may be asking for general information without needing to share any information about the particular client.

Educational Consultation

Finally, educational consultation, which is more about expanding one's knowledge rather than focusing on resourcing a particular client, can be another way to access consultation, especially when a pastoral counselor is connected with an organization.

A counselor could be part of a pastoral counseling center or may be able to create a network with others that is more didactic in nature. The center or network may bring in resources on a regular basis for training and education from within or outside the community. These could include bringing in religious leaders from diverse religious backgrounds to learn how their particular religious polities work and how they can be a resource to clients; bringing in specialists trained in other modalities such as EMDR (eye movement and desensitization reprocessing), acupuncture, herbal or Chinese medicine; bringing in community educators with knowledge about differing sexual orientations and community resources; inviting a psychiatrist to discuss recent developments in psychological medication and treatments; or seeking specialists to educate on particular cultural, racial, ethnic, national, or spiritual issues. These can be self-contained events for the counseling center or group members, or these could be open meetings for anyone interested in learning more about the particular topic. Some counseling centers will contract with a specialist for a year to lead clinical case conferences and to bring their particular expertise to bear on case studies presented monthly by the staff. This arrangement provides specific consultation for a therapist with a particular client, but over the course of the year, as all the staff participate and hear the discussion, it also provides a larger context of how to use this consultant's approach for all staff working with a broad range of clients. Over the course of several years, as different specialist consultants are brought in, the staff deepens and broadens their knowledge.

Consultant Fees

One thing to keep in mind is the financial cost of asking for and/or providing consultation, professional to professional. If the client is seeing another professional directly, even when being recommended to do so by the lead therapist, then the client or the client's insurance (if available) is usually paying the cost to see the other professional, including the time to write a report or share results with the lead therapist. However, if the therapist is the one asking for consultation to enhance and support his or her work with a client, the information is most likely being shared directly between the professionals. In this scenario, the therapist, as the consultee, bears the cost of paying the fee of the consultant. Some therapists/specialists consider their time presenting educational events as marketing their expertise and building their referral base or as a public service to the community. Therefore, some may not charge or would expect only a small honorarium. Others see the service as a billable use of their time and will expect full compensation. Depending on the history of their relationship, the length of the consultation process, whether it involves a scheduled monthly phone call or a chat at a conference, whether they are colleagues in a counseling center or have never met before, whether the consultant is salaried and this is "part of the job" or is paid by the hour, as well as what the norms are for that particular consultant or industry, are all factors that will determine whether there is a fee to be exchanged or not and how much the fee is.

A Special Note Regarding Confidentiality

When working with those from other professions, be aware that there are different standards for confidentiality that vary from state to state and profession to profession (Butler & Zamora, 2013). The legal standards that define confidentiality for a pastoral counselor or licensed marriage and family therapist are different from those for a minister, lay care provider in a local congregation, an acupuncturist, or a psychiatrist. Also critical to keep in mind are the current legal restrictions and accessibility requirements identified in the Health Insurance Portability and Accountability Act (HIPAA) enacted in the United States in 1996 (U.S. Department of Health & Human Services, n.d.). The Office for Civil Rights enforces the HIPAA Privacy Rule, Security Rule, and Breach Notification Rule. So, when consulting or collaborating with anyone, it is helpful to be clear and transparent at the outset about how confidentiality will be handled. This may also need to be talked through with the client so that he or she is also aware of the varying legal standards around confidentiality and may make choices about what to share and with whom.

Pastoral Counselors as Consultants to Others

Pastoral counselors may also be called on or wish to offer their services as a consultant to others in the community, particularly with local clergy and other religious leaders. Research indicates that local clergy are often the first line of service for individuals and families in crisis and provide a significant percentage of mental health support within the community (Friedman, 2005; Weaver, Koenig, & Ochberg, 1996). Often they can become the only line of service, such as when there are limited financial resources, limited geographic accessibility to other resources, distrust of medical and therapeutic professionals, appreciation for the knowledge of the larger family connections, or because of a religious leader's own desire to be helpful and caring. Some denominations set clear standards and limit clergy in how many counseling sessions they may offer before they must refer, even if the person has extensive training in counseling. Other denominations do not have any restrictions. Even if there is a referral or transferal for professional support, the minister usually maintains an ongoing relationship with the individual or family and interacts with them on a regular basis. Sometimes mental health issues can spill over into issues within the congregation vis-à-vis leadership, organization, staff, or problematic behavior at congregational events and with other congregants. In cases such as these, a pastoral counselor can be a significant resource to a minister not only one-on-one but also in the larger congregational setting.

In addition, a pastoral counselor may support religious leaders in initiating discussions on the nature of mental health issues within the congregation in an objective, yet compassionate and theologically relevant manner. This could take the form of encouraging religious leaders to offer workshops within the congregation, developing resources on how to incorporate stories about mental health needs into sermons and writings, or identifying mental health issues in various biblical characters that normalizes the experience. Alternately, a pastoral counselor could support a religious leader to develop ministries that can effectively respond to congregants with varying mental health needs within the congregation and community. Pastoral counselors can teach workshops in the congregation or at regional clergy gatherings that strengthen the resources of religious leaders (Address, 2003). These and others are all ways that a pastoral counselor can be a resource consultant with ministers, their congregations, and with judicatories.

Developing working relationships with local religious leaders can provide them access to a pastoral counselor's specialized skills of integrating theology, spirituality, and psychology. This could be on an as-needed basis, or the counselor may choose to create an ongoing consultation group comprising religious leaders who bring their own cases from congregants (or staff) with whom they are working. This could provide religious leaders with an ongoing resource, much as the ongoing professional peer consultation group is supportive of the pastoral counselor. Such a group increases the religious leader's knowledge and skills, strengthens his or her ability to name and address mental health issues compassionately, and at the same time reduces the possibility of ethics violations and burnout. Such a group could even become an income provider for the pastoral counselor who charges for facilitating and offering clinical consultation to group members.

The call for pastoral counselors to provide consultation on behalf of judicatories is also growing. The term *judicatory* is used generically to refer to the governance structures used by all denominations and faith groups for their organization, communication, resourcing, and administrative oversight. Although each group uses specific nomenclature for their particular structure and leaders, they usually are structured with local, regional, national, and often global entities that allow connection internally and between the various faith groups. Judicatories from various denominations and faith groups are generally working with smaller resources and less staffing than in previous years. As the emerging church continues to break apart and re-form the way denominations and religious institutions operate, judicatories are looking for outside resources that honor their particular tradition, polity, and theological stance and that can provide services that meet the needs of their religious leaders and congregations. Types of services include clergy psychological assessments for ordination, training leaders around boundary issues and healthy systems, therapeutic intervention and assessment when religious leaders and/or their families are struggling or have crossed boundaries, and consulting with religious leaders, congregations, and judicatories as a whole when dealing with congregational problems, staffing difficulties, strategic planning, or transitional issues.

More pastoral counselors are being approached by congregations and are now seeking training in providing consultation with congregations, judicatories, and even nonprofits and other nongovernment organizations. Sometimes the consultation takes the form of coaching the leadership (i.e., the religious leaders, executive directors, lay leaders, and chief operating officers running the organizations). This type of consultation and coaching is focused around organizational structure, staff and leadership issues, conflict resolution, and visioning/strategic planning. Pastoral counselors who have training in family systems theory can build on that training with an eye toward larger organizational systems. They provide a unique perspective when consulting with religious and lay leaders to understand dynamics that may be going on within their congregation and their community. Pastoral counselors are a specialized resource as they are also trained in integrating the theological and spiritual dimensions with family and organizational systems theory and can bring that to bear in working with a congregation or nonprofit organization.

REFERRAL

As mentioned earlier in the chapter, there are many overlapping concerns, questions, and answers that would inform a therapist when choosing to refer rather than the therapist asking for a consultation. But the key focus is that the therapist, for a variety of reasons, may not be able to be the therapist, or at least the sole therapist, for a particular client. These reasons could include a clear sense that the therapist or pastoral counselor would be practicing outside his or her competency, the therapist's schedule may be full, or the client's schedule does not line up with when the therapist has openings. There may be a conflict of interest that the therapist may or may not be able to explain to the client without breaching confidentiality elsewhere. The therapist may decide to refer a client for a particular type of work that needs to be done by someone else and will then resume seeing the client again once that work is completed. The underlying assumption is that the therapist may be stepping aside from being the key figure on behalf of a particular client. The therapist is now actively suggesting that the client is able to seek treatment from someone else and may in fact be "handing off" the client entirely. However, the therapist may remain a key link for a client or may step into the background while someone else becomes the lead. In this instance, Howard Clinebell's (1984) admonition for clergy who are making referrals is appropriate for a therapist or pastoral counselor as well: "Referral is a means of using a team effort to help a troubled person. It is a *broadening* and *sharing*, not a total *transfer* of responsibility. It employs the division-of-labor principle that is the basis of interprofessional cooperation" (p. 311, emphasis added). As a therapist and client discern what is needed, desired, available, and affordable, the decision will need to be made whether the client remains an ongoing client of the therapist, while at the same time accessing the other resources, or whether the active client–therapist relationship is ended.

If a therapist has determined that a referral is needed and appropriate, the next question is how to make the referral. A general referral (such as "You need to see someone who specializes in posttraumatic stress disorder [PTSD]"), without giving some specific names or resources for PTSD, is less than helpful. Therefore, developing and updating local referral resources is critical. Reaching out to other practitioners and finding out their areas of expertise is one way to start making a list. Check out websites on the Internet and social media sites, paying particular attention to organizational websites for credentialed/licensed providers. The AAPC is an example, but so too is the American Association for Marriage and Family Therapy (AAMFT) or similar credentialing organizations. Ask other professionals who also are in the practice of providing referrals. Ask area clergy, family doctors, hospital social workers, other therapists, school counselors, victim advocacy programs, funeral directors, and others to whom they refer and why. As a therapist with your own training, background, and personal preferences, you may decide that some of the resources you hear about are not appropriate for referrals. Be sure to develop as broad and diverse a resource list as possible because other resources may offer a viewpoint or expertise that is needed. Attempt to find resources that will work with a broad range of incomes so that you are able to refer, no matter the price point, insurance coverage, or special need. You may also hear about resources that others do not like because of ethical breaches or viewpoints that are harmful. Make a note of those as well.

If you are in a large city, the process of developing a resource list may feel overwhelming because there may be so many resources that it is hard to narrow down who is competent. It may also be harder to get to know other professionals or to create connections. It may seem like there are too many specialists with very narrow areas who have carved out niches in their counseling practices. In an opposite manner, if you are in a tightknit community or rural area, there may be a sense that there are too few resources from which to choose, and the potential for conflict of interest increases exponentially (Helbok, 2003). If so, look for complementary resources in neighboring towns or cities. The possibility of trading referrals across a larger region expands the potential sources of clients as well as the list of potential resources.

Seek out regional gatherings and conferences sponsored by credentialing organizations. These are great ways to receive contact hours or Continuing Education Units (CEUs; often required for state licensure) and to meet others from that geographic region. If possible, locate centers that provide multiple services, multiple therapists, multiple locations, and multiple areas of expertise. Pastoral counseling centers are often not for profit and offer an adjusted fee scale and/or scholarship funds. Many of them employ practitioners who take many types of insurance. This is a wonderful resource because, with one referral, a therapist has the ability to help a variety of clients. If possible, provide two or three resources to ensure that the client has a choice and can decide whom to see. Depending on one's professional organization's code of ethics, this may have ethical as well as legal implications for the person making the referral.

Another factor to consider in building a resource list is identifying what seem to be the primary needs within your community. Is there a military base nearby? If so, then knowledge of that branch of the military, PTSD, Veterans Administration services, and military family services are resources that you would be more likely to need. Is there a particular religion or ethnic population that is significant? Again, knowing something about the population and/or finding professionals and organizations who are knowledgeable about them will be helpful.

Up to this point, I have focused on external resources and names or organizations that can be placed on a resource list. Equally important are the internal resources, specifically knowing one's own limitations and gaps in knowledge so that a referral is made in a timely manner. Unfortunately, it is easy (easier than we'd like to admit) to get hooked into working with a client with whom we get dragged into areas that we are not prepared for and may do harm. Proactive and routine involvement with peer consultation or some other quality assurance practice is one way to strengthen one's internal resources. When bringing cases to talk about with others, we find out more about what we do know as well as what we do not know. We all need to create safe professional connections where we can build on our strengths, explore our limitations, and grow in new skills and insight so that we establish clear boundaries and are more self-aware when working with clients.

It is important to note that there are times when it is not appropriate to make a referral, even if under "normal" circumstances we might do so. Listed in the following text are some of the situations that may determine whether to refer someone or seek consultation while working with someone. This is not an exhaustive list, but it is hoped that it will stimulate discussion about what may be involved in discerning appropriate referrals.

Conflict of Interest in Rural Areas

The codes of ethics for credentialing organizations are generally designed with an assumption that conflict of interest can be and should be avoided and that there are adequate resources available to make that happen. However, in rural areas and smaller communities, that is often not the case. An ethical stance that says that a therapist cannot have any personal connections or do business with a client outside of the office may be disregarded when the only grocery store in town is owned and managed by one's client, or the new client knows more about you personally than professionally because his son is in the same class as your child at the only elementary school in town. In these situations, the question is not whether there are blurred boundaries but whether there is a clear conflict of interest. Serving as the therapist for one's child's teacher would be a conflict of interest, but not necessarily so for the parent of the child's classmate.

Limited Resources

Access to resources is an issue in multiple ways for rural, remote, and smaller communities. Although a therapist may not be an expert in particular issues or treatment modalities, if there is no child therapist in town, then one may be compelled to accept a child client. It is imperative to continue to indicate what is or is not one's area(s) of competency, but if there are limited resources in the community, then a therapist may become more of a generalist than might happen in a large city. This also holds true for therapists who may be practicing in a global setting where therapy is not prevalent, is not considered acceptable within that culture, or is not easily available. Even in large cities within the United States, there may be limited access to diverse therapeutic resources in underprivileged, isolated, close-knit, or ethnically defined parts of the community.

Military Personnel

When a therapist is also a member of the military and is offering therapy or counseling as a part of military duties, even as a chaplain, multiple relationships are operant. Dual loyalties and multiple relationships can occur when a unit is deployed and the therapist is now stationed within an overseas compound, when the therapist's client outranks the therapist, or when the client becomes a comrade when the unit is engaged in a combat scenario. The needs, demands, and situations within the military may supersede the needs and demands of the client and even one's professional code of ethics, which would recommend or even require a referral (Zur & Gonzalez, 2002).

Language and/or Cultural Expertise

Although having expertise in specific languages or cultures may provide a referral stream, it may also provide a potential difficulty in referring a client elsewhere. It may also mean that there is a close-knit community from which clients are drawn, providing the therapist with more information about a client, or the client may have more information about the therapist than would normally be the case. The therapist may be working with people on varying sides of a situation that might otherwise be considered a blurring of boundaries.

Financial Considerations and Insurance Coverage

Being on a particular insurance panel or offering an adjusted fee scale may mean accepting and continuing work with a client who is boxed in by financial considerations, someone one might otherwise refer to others.

Trust Issues Between the Client and Therapist

There are times when a therapeutic alliance has formed or may have formed in other ways prior to therapy, and that alliance produces therapeutic benefits that are beyond the specific tools or modality a therapist may be using. If the referral can be made in conjunction with ongoing interaction between the current therapist and client, then a referral may work. But if referral means terminating the current relationship, then that breach of trust may create more problems than it helps.

Transportation and Accessibility

Clients come with all sorts of life situations, and access to transportation or physical disabilities can limit where a client may seek help. For example, if a client does not have a car, then accessing therapeutic services depends on who has an office accessible from a bus or light rail route. Similarly, if a client is dependent on others for transportation or for physical assistance or needs an interpreter, then it becomes more difficult to make an appropriate referral.

Virtual Access to Consultation

Clients, issues, and scenarios that might have required referral at one point in time are now being maintained by therapists, partly due to the explosion in virtual technology that allows for consultation, supervision, and therapeutic encounters over longer distances. Previously, it could be cost-prohibitive to access consultation or supervision, because it was assumed (even required) to be done face-to-face with the therapist bearing the brunt of the costs to get to the consultant or supervisor. Although this is an area that is still developing with codes of ethics and laws changing to keep up with the evolving technology, there are still ways to maintain appropriate boundaries. Virtual consultation is becoming much more prevalent in the medical community as well as within the therapeutic community. As technology improves with more secure modes of communicating, and as more helpers and professional organizations become comfortable with the benefits and the challenges of technology, the ability to use technology in receiving consultation and supervision will be a significant resource for therapists.

COLLABORATION

As indicated earlier, collaboration is the broadest of the three practices under consideration. It can include just about anyone, at just about any level, for just about any length of time. I have left this as the last of the three overarching practices because there is such a diversity of collaborative practices. Although collaboration can occur related to a specific client, collaboration often happens on an organizational level around topics or events irrespective of any particular client. Let's begin with the collaboration that can occur around a particular client and build our way out to the broader scope.

Collaboration Focused on a Particular Client

Collaboration is similar to consultation in that many of the same situations that would lead a therapist to seek consultation would also lead a therapist to invite collaboration. Many of the same challenges regarding confidentiality and financial costs apply as well. An underlying assumption with collaborative treatment is that the therapist does not step back but remains a significant player in the treatment of the client, in conjunction with others who also play significant ongoing roles in treating/supporting the client. This is both the good news and the bad news.

First the bad news: It takes a lot more time and energy to provide collaborative treatment, sometimes without being paid for the extra time that is invested in making it happen. The more entities that are involved, the amount of time grows exponentially.

Coordinating schedules to find a time when several or all of the collaborating partners can debrief on a regular basis can be difficult, and that includes where and how to meet and who must travel or set up a virtual connection. There can also be disagreement among the entities on what is the best course of treatment or at least potentially conflicting information that is given to the client that the client is then left to sort out. Different professionals have different ways of working, which can be problematic. It can also be higher in cost for the client, paying for multiple services as well as what's needed in coordinating them. Collaboration takes more time for the client as well. Instead of an hour or two a week, the client is now potentially attending several regular appointments and meetings, which may create its own problems with finances, work, energy, family commitments, or transportation. Collaboration implies that everyone involved is invested in working collaboratively, but there may need to be a point person who helps keep all parties active and committed or else there is a potential for things to slowly unravel as time goes along. Sometimes several services are available within one organization or center, which makes the collaboration easier, but most often services are offered by distinct and separate entities.

The good news is that collaborative care, in its fullest form, is often most needed when a client is addressing multiple issues and multiple needs that can overwhelm an individual therapist. Sometimes referred to as "wraparound care," multiple professionals paying attention to and being on call for a client can significantly ease the emotional and legal weight that an individual therapist alone might be carrying. Knowing that a client is attending regular Al-Anon meetings, is being seen regularly by a psychiatrist for medication monitoring, is participating in parenting classes, is going to a massage therapist biweekly, is being visited by a minister and a congregational lay visitor monthly, is participating in a job training program or anger management course, is under the care of an agency who handles her budget and expenses, and has a social worker who is monitoring her living situation can be a resource for the therapist as well as the client. If the collaborative care involves other professionals, family members, spiritual community, voluntary support groups, and/or educational components, then the client has a number of people in varying capacities on whom she can call, who are paying attention and can intervene if something becomes problematic. And if any entities are unavailable, there are still others who are available to the client if needed.

Gratefully, most collaborative care is far less extensive and may only include two or three entities that really need to be actively collaborating in providing treatment, such as the client's psychiatrist, social worker, and the anger management instructor. A client may attend worship and be in contact with the minister, but that does not mean there is regular, ongoing connection between the therapist and the minister. The same might be true with a massage therapist or attendance at an Al-Anon meeting. So the therapist and the client need to be clear as to who is involved in the collaborative care and plan accordingly, with clear understanding of how confidentiality will be handled.

Collaboration Between Organizational Entities

This type of collaboration is a completely different type of collaboration that is not about a particular client but is about organizations. Organizational collaboration is about breaking down silos within and in between professional communities, providing services and resources that would be much more difficult to do individually, pooling resources to provide services that are more effective and efficient, qualifying for grants and other funds focused on collaborative projects, and increasing learning opportunities within the larger community.

Educational events may be conjointly sponsored for the community such as Mental Health Day for congregations, a suicide prevention workshop, or an alcohol dependency workshop for religious leaders, thus increasing their knowledge and skills to intervene with congregation members. Several organizations may come together to offer an annual conference for lay and ministerial caregivers with breakout sessions led by professionals in the community. The alphabet soup of professional credentialing and membership organizations (i.e., the AAPC, AAMFT, Association of Clinical Pastoral Education [ACPE], Association of Professional Chaplains [APC], National Association of Catholic Chaplains [NACC], National Association of Jewish Chaplains [NAJC], and American Psychological Association [APA] to name a few) may work together to conjointly sponsor annual regional conferences, bringing in a named speaker with time for breakout workshops that encourage cross-disciplinary dialogue and services. Additionally, educational materials, workshops, and training events may be developed and offered for particular congregations, judicatories, or between similarly minded denominations. An example of this is *Web of Care*, a congregational care ministry and training workshop that was developed for theologically progressive churches, using input from clergy from two different denominations (Thompson & Whitehead, 2009).

An emerging trend in the collaboration between physicians and therapists occurs when physicians create an office (or two or three) within their medical clinic for a therapist to see patients/clients. Other collaborations include the placement of pastoral counselors in homeless shelters, private and parochial schools, or community centers. Who does the billing, pays the rent, and carries the legal liabilities needs to be worked out, but it provides a unique collaborative model. This mirrors the historical practice of placing a pastoral counselor in an office space within a church, temple, or mosque to provide therapy within a religious setting. These are collaborative models of two or more organizations working together to provide resources in a more convenient and appropriate space that allows for better access and more solid referral, consultation, and collaboration among the professionals serving clients.

RETURNING TO THE CASE STUDY WITH JOELLE AND SAMANTHA

Based on this understanding of consultation, referral, and collaboration, let us return to the case study to see how these practices might be relevant within Samantha's counseling with Joelle. Pay attention to what is happening within the system's lava lamp, what is heating up and what is cooling down, and what is or could be affecting the various elements as they shift, merge, and separate again.

First, Samantha must assess whether she has the appropriate qualifications to work with someone like Joelle and whether there are other resources available that would be more appropriate. For example, Samantha may feel confident working with depression, especially in adult women, but may be unsure about working with someone with sexual abuse in her history. So although she may be working within her therapeutic competency in one arena, she would be outside her competency in another arena. That is not a reason to refer a client per se but would be an excellent reason to ask for consultation from others who know more about abuse and its effects on women.

Samantha may decide that she not only lacks the expertise to work with someone with a history of childhood sexual abuse but also does not have the professional interest in trying to learn more about it. It could be that Joelle is exhibiting symptoms of PTSD, not just depression, so Samantha may refer Joelle to a specialist who works with trauma or sexual abuse or is trained in EMDR. This may be a referral to someone in a larger city, or hopefully, if Samantha has done her homework and has developed a list of potential resources to make these referrals, then Samantha may know of another therapist in a town nearby who is trained and has an interest in working with trauma.

Joelle lives and Samantha works in a smaller community, which possibly has limited resources. So even if Samantha might make a referral if they were living in a larger city, she may be the best and most appropriate resource given the smaller community. In this case, seeking consultation would ground her provision of care for Joelle. Samantha may want to seek legal consultation on whether she is bound by law as well as her professional code of ethics to report the father for abuse of a minor, given that the last incidence of abuse was over 20 years earlier. States vary in their laws about reporting requirements, so Samantha needs to clarify in what state(s) the abuse occurred and when the statute of limitations expires in that state. Additionally, the laws continue to be reviewed and are changed periodically. In some states, there is now a need to report if there is knowledge that the abuser is in a current position to abuse a minor (such as access to grandchildren). Receiving and paying for legal consultation will help Samantha know how to proceed and will also be a topic that she will need to discuss with Joelle so they both know what the ramifications are regarding any content Joelle may share.

Samantha may also check to see whether there are any county- or community-based support groups for victims of abuse, victim advocacy programs, or financial counseling organizations in the area. Even though there is no history of alcohol abuse in Joelle's story at this point, a support group such as Al-Anon might be a resource as it provides education and a group environment to deal with one's own behavior that developed in response to a dysfunctional family system. Different Al-Anon groups vary in being open to broader participants. Depending on what Samantha finds, she might encourage Joelle to get involved in one or more of these groups to begin to build a support system outside of her family. Another possibility is for Samantha, with Joelle's permission, to consult with the minister who made the initial referral. There may be a lay caregiver's ministry at the congregation that could reach out to Joelle. Or Samantha may seek to understand more of the theology important in that congregation to have a better idea of what may be helpful or harmful for Joelle or Joelle's mother.

Because Joelle has had difficulty in maintaining long-term relationships, Samantha may determine that it is important to remain the constant figure in Joelle's therapeutic life, assuming that Joelle will keep coming to sessions. So although a referral might be important to address the trauma, the trust that Joelle has developed with Samantha may override the referral pattern of moving from therapist to therapist to therapist that would only reinforce Joelle's experience of short-term relationships.

If Samantha agrees to continue seeing Joelle, she may be concerned about her son, Bobby, as well as Joelle's mother and how the family system operates. Samantha might consider referring Joelle and Bobby to a play therapist so that they can work on their mother–son relationship. Samantha and the play therapist, with Joelle's permission, could then consult with each other on how best to strengthen each other's work with the family. Samantha may talk with Joelle about whether it would be helpful to bring Joelle's mother into some of their sessions and what they hope to accomplish by doing so.

Samantha may confirm that Joelle is under the care of a family physician or psychiatrist who is prescribing and monitoring antidepressants or some other treatment that might help with her obsessive thoughts. She may collaborate with the doctor to monitor how the medication(s) are working, whether Joelle is complying with the treatment plan, or even if some additional medication for ADHD might be helpful so that Joelle can maintain focus at work and thus be more likely to maintain a stable job and income.

Samantha may have already developed an ongoing consultation resource with other therapists in her community or may travel once a month to participate in a peer consultation group with therapists across various disciplines. Samantha could bring her concerns about working with Joelle to the peer consultation group, asking for resources to help her stay grounded in her work with Joelle. Alternately, she might participate in an online educational program on working with trauma and abuse clients to educate herself better on potential areas of concern, asking for a onetime consultation with the presenter afterward to better understand what may be happening with Joelle. If Samantha finds that she is often feeling like a lone ranger in providing pastoral counseling in a small community, she may seek out a larger pastoral counseling center in the city and find out whether it would be possible for her to operate as a satellite office from it. This may provide her with collegiality, clinical resources, and even business and accounting support. There would be a cost to joining a center, but the connection may more than offset any sense of financial loss she might have.

Samantha might also begin conversations with other professionals in the community—social workers, school counselors, teachers, religious leaders, medical personnel—to offer a workshop on recognizing, understanding, and treating depression and/or the lasting effects of childhood abuse. The workshop could be offered at a community center or may be hosted by an area congregation, with an additional section that addresses the spiritual dimensions inherent in depression using various sacred texts as a resource.

All of these, and more, are examples of potential ways that Samantha may pay attention to the elements within the lava lamp and could use consultation, referral, and collaboration to strengthen her work as a pastoral counselor with Joelle as well as with other clients, to strengthen connections within the community, and to make her work with Joelle more effective and life giving for both of them.

Questions for Further Discussion

There is nothing in the case study to indicate the ethnicity, race, language, religion, sexual orientation, geographic location, or cultural background of Joelle, her family members, or of Samantha. Nor is there much indication of the family's socioeconomic situation, other than Joelle's current financial struggles. There is a reference to a "minister," which is often used as a general term for any clergy, rabbi, priest, or imam, even though the term is prevalent in Protestant denominations. What difference would it make in the conversation if one of the more specific religious titles were to be used? Joelle has a child from a heterosexual relationship, but there is no indication whether she is comfortable or presently identifies as a heterosexual. Her history of depression and suicidal ideation could be a result of wrestling with her sexual identity. If so, would that make a difference in her treatment—spiritually, emotionally, socially, or psychologically? Also, there is no age given for Samantha or any information provided about her specific training, spiritual background, credentials, or license other than that she identifies as a pastoral counselor.

It would be interesting to go back over the case study and offer variations with these aspects in mind. How would these details change the discernment process for seeking consultation, collaboration, or providing a referral? What assumptions were made in the absence of specific content? What additional questions are raised when various social locations and cultural backgrounds are identified? Such factors further influence how the shapes shift and morph within the lava lamp as these various elements come into play.

REFLECTION QUESTIONS

1. This chapter focuses on the activities of referral, consultation, and collaboration. What do these practices have in common? In what ways are they distinctive?
2. When are the most appropriate times to use each of the practices? When are they contraindicated?
3. Who are the most likely partners in your professional sphere to approach for these types of referral, consultation, and collaboration? How might you practically develop a wider network of colleagues for these purposes?
4. In your community, what might be the most salient challenges to confidentiality when engaging in these practices? In other words, does it make a difference if you are in a rural or urban setting? A culturally homogeneous setting?

NOTE

1. Joelle, Samantha, and Bobby are fictitious names. All other names, identifying information, and circumstances have also been changed, blended, and created to develop this particular case study. Although this case study no longer represents an actual client, the circumstances, themes, and issues are common in many clients and families so is "true" in the larger sense.

REFERENCES

Address, R. F. (Ed.). (2003). *Caring for the soul R'fuat HaNefes: A mental health resource and study guide developed by and for the Union of American Hebrew Congregations*. New York, NY: UAHC Press.

Butler, M. H., & Zamora, J. P. (2013). Ethical and legal concerns for MFTs in the context of clergy-collaborative care: Is what I share really confidential? *American Journal of Family Therapy, 41*, 85–109. doi:10.1080/01926187.2012.677713

Clinebell, H. (1984). *Basic types of pastoral care & counseling*. Nashville, TN: Abingdon.

Craven, M. A., & Bland, R. (2006). Executive summary. *Canadian Journal of Psychiatry, 51*(1), 9S. Retrieved from https://ww1.cpa-apc.org

Erchul, W. P., & Martens, B. K. (2010). School consultation: Conceptual and empirical bases of practice. In M. Roberts (Ed.), *Issues in clinical child psychology* (3rd ed., p. 4). New York, NY: Springer Science+Business Media.

Friedman, D. A. (Ed.). (2005). *Jewish pastoral care: A practical handbook from traditional & contemporary sources* (2nd ed.). Woodstock, VT: Jewish Lights Publishing.

Helbok, C. M. (2003). The practice of psychology in rural communities: Potential ethical dilemmas. *Ethics and Behavior, 13*(4), 367–384. doi:10.1207/s15327019eb1304_5

Thompson, E. D., & Whitehead, J. (2009). *Web of care: Basic lay care training & congregational care ministry*. Denver, CO: Author.

Truneckova, D., Viney, L. L., Maitland, H., & Seaborn, B. (2010). Personal construct peer consultation: Caring for the psychotherapists. *The Clinical Supervisor, 29,* 128–148. doi:10.1080/07325223.2010.519248

U.S. Department of Health & Human Services. (n.d.). *Health information privacy.* Retrieved from http://www.hhs.gov/ocr/privacy/

Weaver, A. J., Koenig, H. G., & Ochberg, F. M. (1996). Posttraumatic stress, mental health professionals, and the clergy: A need for collaboration, training, and research. *Journal of Traumatic Stress, 9*(4), 847–856. doi:10.1002/jts.2490090412

Zur, O., & Gonzalez, S. (2002). Multiple relationships in military psychology. In A. A. Lazarus & O. Zur (Eds.), *Dual relationships and psychotherapy* (pp. 315–328). New York, NY: Springer Publishing Company.

Danielle LaSure-Bryant

22

SHEPHERDING THE FLOCK: SUPERVISING PASTORAL COUNSELORS IN TRAINING

The process of becoming a professional counselor is one of personal and professional formation. Professionally speaking, becoming a counselor, whether a pastoral counselor, a clinical mental health counselor, or a substance abuse counselor, requires the acquisition of advanced knowledge and demonstrated proficiency using a specialized skill set. Organizations such as the American Counseling Association (ACA), the American Association of Pastoral Counselors (AAPC), and the National Board for Certified Counselors (NBCC) provide policies, procedures, and best practices for counselor skill development. Personal formation as a pastoral counselor is often more internalized than professional identity formation. Pastoral counselors in training engage in personal formation by reflecting on the session as a way to improve client care, reconciling professional shortcomings related to intuition and practice, and refining expectations with regard to personal limitations. Without the appropriate guidance and structure, the continual formative process of becoming a professional counselor can be difficult both for a neophyte and for a more experienced professional.

Clinical supervision is the mechanism that helps to manage the continuous process of both personal and professional formation. Ogden and Sias (2011) contend that the process of supervision may minimize anxiety and increase the level of skill development among supervisees. According to Bernard and Goodyear (2014), every professional counselor will eventually be called on to supervise junior professionals. Through the process of supervision, pastoral counselors in training learn to sharpen skills, engage in case conceptualization, and provide their clients with competent care (Bornsheuer-Boswell, Polonyi, & Watts, 2013). For these and other reasons, supervision is a salient part of counselor education and crucial to the personal and professional formation of emerging and advanced pastoral counselors alike.

This chapter describes the practice of supervision used across the spectrum of clinical mental health counseling to train pastoral counselors. To this end, the supervision of pastoral counselors-in-training in both academic and clinical mental health settings is addressed. In addition, this chapter advocates for the need for pastoral counseling supervisory training and certification at the state licensure level. Finally, the chapter highlights practices that may be used to address spiritual and religious issues within the supervisory process.

DEFINING *SUPERVISION*

Generally, *supervision* is categorized as a clinical practice that occurs between individuals in a professional setting. For example, Bernard and Goodyear (2014) define *supervision* as one experienced member of a profession overseeing the skill development, knowledge attainment, and attitude adjustment of an inexperienced member of that particular profession. By labeling supervision as an "intervention," Bernard and Goodyear (2004) identify a procedural practice of directly influencing client care, monitoring the accuracy of documentation, and remaining the last line of defense against sanctioning individuals inappropriate for the profession.

In the organization's *2009 Standards*, the Council for Accreditation of Counseling and Related Educational Programs (CACREP; 2009) defines *supervision* as a systemic method more germane to counselor training:

> tutorial and mentoring form of instruction in which a supervisor monitors the student's activities in practicum and internship, and facilitates the associated learning and skill development experiences. The supervisor monitors and evaluates the clinical work of the student while monitoring the quality of services offered to clients. (p. 63)

Although this definition is more aligned with the curriculum for training emerging pastoral counselors, advanced counselors may also benefit from the oversight supervision provides to client care. For example, the American Counseling Association's (2014) *Code of Ethics* acknowledges that the primary responsibility of a supervisor is to "monitor client welfare and supervisee performance and professional development" (p. 12). The monitoring of client welfare can be especially precarious given that some client populations are more difficult to manage than others. For advanced pastoral counselors, peer consultation related to client care (typically used as supervision) can be helpful in providing additional support, information, and resources. West and Clark (2004) also underscored the importance of supervision for all practicing counselors, stating that it provides quality control, acts as a conduit for developing professional competence, and is one of the primary methods by which mental health counseling is monitored and evaluated. When cultivating clinical competence in supervisees, supervisors must consider multicultural competence, which includes addressing the client's spirituality, an issue addressed later in the chapter.

Ideally, a supervisor who shares, at the very least, the core training and vocational identity of pastoral counseling supervises the supervisee. Idealism aside, the reality shows that more multidisciplinary work in the field of mental health has led to an increase in interprofessional supervision (Binnie, 2011). Corsini, Wedding, and Dumont (2008) pointed out that professionals, including rehabilitation counselors, substance abuse counselors, and medical personnel, such as psychiatric nurses, have historically provided clinical mental health services and supervision of counselors in training. As trends go, it appears that the initial acceptance has become less acceptable in the field, however. The AAPC appears to lead in this initiative certifying pastoral counseling supervisors. The organization has a certification process for becoming a pastoral counselor supervisor. Regretfully, every pastoral counselor supervisee will not have a supervisor certified by the AAPC. While seeking state licensure, pastoral counselors in training will seek employment in secular agencies that lack a pastoral counseling supervisor. The formation process for the pastoral counselor in training is no less important because of one's position. Indeed, as pastoral counselors continue to become more prevalent and more embedded in the field of clinical mental health counseling, the need for qualified supervisors to supervise pastoral counseling supervisees continues to increase. This increasing need can be seen in the number of states requiring certification for professional counselors providing supervision for license-eligible clinicians, including those trained as pastoral counselors. Supervisor training and certification is one way to ensure that pastoral counselors in training and, for that matter, all counselors in training receive supervision that attunes the client's spirituality/religion into biopsychosocial assessment and treatment.

THE NEED FOR SUPERVISOR TRAINING

In recognition and understanding of the impact of clinical supervision for emerging and practicing pastoral counselors, accrediting organizations such as the Council for Accreditation of Counseling and Related Educational Programs (CACREP) and the Association of Counselor Education and Supervision (ACES) have specific curriculum requirements for the practice of supervision. Not surprisingly, more accreditation bodies are mandating training in supervision for future supervisors (Baker, Exum, & Tyler, 2002). Such training bodies have specific requirements related to how much time should be spent in supervision, the types of modalities used for supervising, the specifying of supervisor credentials, and the nature of the supervisory process.

State boards are increasingly requiring formal procedures for documenting specialized training in clinical supervision as well (Faiver, Eisengart, & Colonna, 2004; Hipple & Beamish, 2007). Some areas of specialization for clinical supervision include addictions and marriage and family. The author contends pastoral counseling should be considered an area of specialization as well. The current movement toward requiring professional counselors to gain specialized training in clinical supervision as a condition of certification is beneficial to supervisees, clients, and the field of clinical mental health counseling broadly and pastoral counseling specifically. Pastoral counseling supervisees benefit from supervisor certification by knowing that their supervisors are trained in how to supervise in spiritual integration and are recognized by a state accrediting board to do so. Clients benefit from supervision because it offers an extra layer of clinical care and oversight. State certification for pastoral counselors in clinical supervision offers a level of protection for reporting unethical supervisory behavior. Last, pastoral counselors licensed as state professionals will likely promote the theories, practices, and processes of clinical mental health and pastoral counseling, thereby promoting and advocating for both professions.

Academic Supervision

Supervisors are trained, not made. The deliberateness of preparing counselors to become supervisors debunks the myth that "experience sufficed, leading to the conclusion that experience as a counselor and as a supervisee is sufficient for becoming a supervisor" (Baker et al., 2002, p. 15). The clinical preparation for pastoral counselors in training begins in the academic setting.

Supervision with supervisees in an academic setting can take on several forms. For example, supervisors may oversee supervisees individually, in dyads, or as a group. In an academic setting, the supervisor may teach a variety of counseling courses to prepare supervisees for clinical practice. According to Faiver et al. (2004), the format of most university programs includes a course or seminar for supervisees to attend on a weekly or biweekly basis. Many graduate training programs employ a progressive or graduated curriculum structure that promotes foundational knowledge before clinical practice. For example, it is common for training programs in pastoral counseling and allied clinical mental health practices to require prerequisite coursework that must be completed before a student may begin a practicum or internship experience. Academic courses related to life-span development, professional ethics, theoretical foundation, basic interviewing and attending skill development, and diagnostic assessment, to name a few, may be required in an effort to build the foundational knowledge of the emerging counselor before formally entering a clinical setting.

Supervisors in an academic setting can help themselves and their supervisees by becoming familiar with course syllabi, objectives, and assignments completed by the supervisees prior to the initial supervision session. Becoming familiar with the curriculum provides the supervisor with greater insight into the academic preparation gained by the student. Knowing that a supervisee completed a course in psychopathology, for example, lets the supervisor know that the supervisee can be expected to have basic knowledge of diagnostic assessment. Also, for counseling training programs that do not have a spiritual integrated curriculum, the supervisor must take responsibility for the introduction of said material. At times, however, a student may have received a passing grade in the course but has not yet mastered the course material. Therefore, assessing the knowledge level of the supervisee may become more apparent as the supervisory relationship develops. To this end, the supervisor can individualize the learning aims of the supervisee based on the academic preparation of the supervisee or lack thereof.

In addition to academic knowledge, supervisors must include cultural competence as a learning aim for the supervisee. The *Code of Ethics* of the ACA (2014) mandates that "counseling supervisors are aware of and address the role of multiculturalism/diversity in the supervisory relationship" (p. 13). Many counselor training programs contain a course in multiculturalism/diversity as part of the curriculum. As a result, a supervisor in an academic setting should encourage and expect supervisees to have some sensitivity to issues of multiculturalism/diversity with their clients. Supervisors can remind supervisees that client spirituality and religion are intrinsic elements of multiculturalism/diversity. Client spirituality and religion are often overlooked as a clinical characteristic, especially in nonpastoral counseling programs. By assessing client spirituality, the supervisee can identify "how the client's conscience, beliefs, values, spiritual experiences, meaning, responsibility, and practices contribute to the ways the client experiences the problem and to ways the client might cope with the problem" (Gill, Harper, & Dailey, 2011, p. 33). Supervisors not trained as pastoral counselors can encourage supervisees to discuss spirituality and religion with their clients (providing the client is open to the discussion) and expect supervisees to include information related to client spirituality and religion in clinical case documents. The client's religious affiliation and spiritual background can be identified along with social and medical history, for example, thereby painting a holistic picture of the individual. Supervisors can also encourage supervisees to reflect on pastoral themes, religious concerns, or value conflicts that may arise with a client by requiring a one- to two-page personal essay following the session.

Supervising in academic settings may present unique challenges for clinical supervisors. In an academic setting, clinical supervisors may also be faculty members and clinical program administrators. Faiver et al. (2004) reminded us that a supervisor is also an educator who is there to enrich academic training. Thus, supervisors in an academic setting are expected to engage with supervisees as educators who both teach theoretical principles and cultivate clinical skills. In pastoral counseling training programs, faculty members are also expected to help supervisees engage in the process of formation through dialogue, reflection, and discernment practices. Although there are pedagogical similarities between teaching and supervision, the two disciplines are not the same. For example, unlike the student–teacher relationship, the supervisor and supervisee enter into a supervisory relationship that is required, is evaluative, and extends over time. Also, unlike a teacher, the supervisor has the additional tasks of monitoring the quality of client care, enhancing professional effectiveness, and acting as the proverbial "gatekeeper" for the profession.

Another challenge for supervisors in academic settings includes the necessity to assume various supervisory roles. For instance, in its *Best Practices in Clinical Supervision* publication, the ACES (2011) cautions supervisors to minimize and manage multiple roles and relationships with supervisees. Within an academic setting, it is common for a newly appointed supervisor to have previously been a course instructor or an academic adviser or research mentor to the supervisee. Clinical supervisors in academic settings are presented with a unique perspective when given the opportunity to interact with the supervisee in situations outside of the supervisory milieu. The academic supervisor may be privy to additional (personal) information about the supervisee that was shared in class either by spoken or written word. Consider the following example:

Bea was in her second semester of a clinical internship with Dr. Renee, a professor she had previously for another course. In an academic course with Dr. Renee, during a discussion about trauma, Bea shared in class how years ago she delivered a child who was stillborn. The class members were able to absorb her comments, offer words of support, and move on with the lesson. In a subsequent clinical course with Dr. Renee, Bea appeared to be experiencing countertransference toward the sexually active adolescent females she counseled in her internship. During a video presentation showing Bea counseling an adolescent girl, she was questioned by one of her classmates about her (seemingly) judgmental approach toward the client. Bea stated, "She doesn't respect that life is a miracle . . . I guess it makes it hard for me to respect her." Dr. Renee was mindful but not forthcoming about the knowledge of her personal history. The class addressed the statement as a conflict in values, and their feedback reflected the context. Dr. Renee, on the other hand, immediately identified the issue as likely that of countertransference. As a result, Dr. Renee met with Bea separately to explore the issue further and provide additional feedback.

Academic supervisors must also address ethical and legal issues while supervising. As a proactive measure, supervisors can obtain informed consent from supervisees before entering into a supervisory relationship. In addition, supervisors and supervisees can sign contractual agreements that delineate policies, scope of practice, and other clinical concerns. Adherence to ethical laws regarding confidentiality, the Health Insurance Portability and Accountability Act of 1996 and the Family Educational Rights and Privacy Act of 1974, is also expected while supervising in an academic setting. In other words, the frank discussion of a supervisee's clinical performance is best saved as fodder for formal consultation rather than a hallway sidebar. With that said, what supervisor hasn't been so rushed for time that a hallway sidebar must suffice? The point is to simply try to minimize cavalier interactions masked as supervision or consultation. As a supervisor, it is beneficial to seek consultation routinely from other professionals, especially those who may also supervise one's supervisees. Another proactive measure for supervisors is to attend training opportunities that focus on ethical/legal issues in supervision. All of the identified activities can help supervisors minimize professional liability, increase client safety, and create an ethical learning environment for the supervisee.

To summarize, clinical supervisors in academic settings face unique challenges. Clinical supervisors may assist in both the academic preparation and the clinical preparation of the supervisee. Consequently, supervisors assume a variety of roles within an academic setting. Supervisors must be mindful of dual or multiple roles and relationships to appropriately assess and evaluate clinical learning aims. Learning aims focusing on multicultural competence must include the spiritual and religious dimensions of the client. Clinical supervisors can learn ways to incorporate spiritual/religious dimensions of the client included in the therapeutic process. Finally, an academic supervisor can minimize malpractice liability by becoming aware of ethical and legal considerations of the supervisee in the supervisory process.

Agency Supervision

Much like the academic supervisor, the agency supervisor plays a fundamental role in the professional development of the supervisee as well. It is at the practicum or internship site where the student becomes a supervisee. During the clinical internship, pastoral counselors in training are expected to become competent practitioners (Tang et al., 2004). The clinical internship experience is also a training ground for novice supervisors. According to Lewis, Lewis, Daniels, and D'Andrea (2011), most counselors will be called on to supervise a variety of human services workers, including volunteers, paraprofessionals, and new and experienced clinicians. With this expectation in mind, pastoral counselors in training working in secular organizations may have a supervisor unfamiliar with pastoral counseling. In many agency settings, a supervisee may be assigned to a particular supervisor based on factors such as the fullness of caseload, theoretical orientation, level of expertise, or specific educational or licensure requirements. It is unlikely that supervisees will have a choice as to who will be selected to provide supervision. In a clinical mental health setting, supervisors are expected to supervise those who are either interns or provisionally licensed counselors. Although it was suggested that a supervisor and supervisee may benefit from having a shared theoretical orientation and ideology, researchers also offer a divergent view by suggesting that a supervisee may be challenged to grow professionally with a supervisor who does not share a similar style (Faiver et al., 2004). In a clinical mental setting where resources, including staff, are often limited, there may or may not be the option to match supervisors and prospective supervisees who have similar theoretical orientations or similar knowledge of spirituality-integrated psychotherapy. The situation is much like the academic supervisor who may not choose which students sign up for a supervision class. In both the agency and the academy, this fact demonstrates the importance of supervisors receiving training to conduct supervision across the spectrum of professional training and pursuing supervisory certification when relevant.

The formative role that agency supervisors play in the development of the supervisee supersedes the monitoring of caseloads and signing of paperwork (Faiver et al., 2004). Because supervisors assume legal responsibility for the actions of their supervisees (Hipple & Beamish, 2007), supervisors may need to have more than a peripheral involvement with the clinical activities of their supervisees. That said, what follows are the duties supervisors in clinical mental health settings may be expected to perform:

- Assign or refer clients to supervisee
- Review and approve notes in the client file (paper record) or chart (electronic record)
- Review supervisee skills via live supervision and/or recorded review
- Provide ongoing feedback (both written and verbal)
- Attend to multicultural issues, including race, gender, religion, sexual orientation, and other dimensions of diversity
- Continuously gauge client welfare while under the care of the supervisee
- Maintain contact with the educational institution (student) or state licensure board (provisionally licensed)
- Complete necessary paperwork to verify supervised clinical experience
- Provide ongoing training in theory, skill development, and therapeutic process
- Arrange daily, weekly, and monthly supervision meetings
- Co-facilitate groups or engage in co-therapy with the supervisee

Although this list is not exhaustive, it indicates that an agency supervisor must serve in a variety of roles, including that of an educator, consultant, and therapist (Bernard & Goodyear, 2014; Pearson, 2004). Recognizing the potential for impropriety, the ACES (2011) cautions, "Supervisors should minimize potential conflicts" (p. 3).

Supervisors not trained to assess, interpret, and integrate client spirituality into counseling may feel unprepared to address the subject with a supervisee. In fact, Ogden and Sias (2011) identified three reasons why agency supervisors in secular settings avoid raising the issue of spirituality in clinical practice and supervision: (a) supervisors have not received formal training, (b) the multidisciplinary approaches make it difficult to agree on client conceptualization and needs, and (c) supervisors do not understand spiritual differences and practices. Despite the tendency to avoid the spiritual realm, supervisors in community mental health settings should address client spirituality and religion as it relates to clinical diagnosis, case conceptualization, and treatment goals. Lewis et al. (2011) contend that "clients religious/ spiritual identity may play an important role in the way they construct meaning-of-life experiences, interpret personal difficulties they encounter in life, and cope with stressful situations" (p. 55). Supervisors who seek to practice spiritually integrative supervision validate to supervisees that religion and spirituality are an integral aspect of client functioning.

For the supervisor not trained as a pastoral counselor, there are several ways to competently practice spiritual integration with supervisees. To begin, if one has little training in this area, one may want to seek out more experienced colleagues for guidance and consultation. The AAPC website (www.aapc.org) is a good place to start looking for professionals in one's geographical area. Another resource used to connect with potential colleagues can be found within a professional organization such as the ACA, where counselors interested in practicing, researching, and teaching about the integration of counseling and spirituality join the Association for Spiritual, Ethical, and Religious Values in Counseling (ASERVIC; www.aservic.org). Also, conferences, workshops, and seminars related to counseling and spirituality can be helpful in providing knowledge and resources for further information and training.

Supervisors can also assist pastoral counselors in training in becoming competent to integrate client spirituality and counseling in several ways. Beginning at the point of intake, clients may be asked about their religious affiliation, whether their faith plays a role in their ability to cope with situations, and whether they want their faith integrated into counseling sessions. These questions may appear on agency intake forms and then used to help the supervisee segue into the topic in subsequent sessions. Gill et al. (2011) acknowledged that counselors who are unaware of the importance of spirituality and religion could miss important therapeutic concerns or intervention strategies for greater functioning. By asking about the client's spirituality and religion from the outset, supervisors reinforce that supervisees are mindful to address this potentially salient influence. In addition to asking pertinent questions on client intake forms, supervisors may introduce the supervisee to the value of using spiritual assessments. The use of spiritual assessments may provide greater insight into client religious and spiritual beliefs, values, and practices. For instance, the Assessment of Spirituality and Religious Sentiments (ASPIRES), for example, provides data identifying the client's religious coping practices (Piedmont, Kennedy, Sherman, Sherman, & Williams, 2008). These practices, which include prayer, reading religious material, and attending religious services, may help to motivate a client to better handle periods of stress and thus may be considered part of treatment planning. As such, the supervisor and the supervisee can discuss the best way to use the information for the benefit of client care. For a more detailed approach to spiritual assessments, please see Chapter 8 in this volume.

Models of Supervision

A supervisor entering into a supervisory relationship with a supervisee must decide when, how, and by what means the supervision will occur. At the beginning of the supervisory relationship, the supervisor may find it necessary to construct a learning plan that is individualized and systematic in its approach (Leddick, 1994). There are a myriad of models by which effective supervision is delivered. This chapter does not address any one model in detail; it provides a categorical overview of the models currently identified within the field. The reader is directed to the works of Leddick (1994) and Bernard and Goodyear (2014) for a more detailed rendition of the common models of supervision.

Bernard and Goodyear (2014) noted that three main categories describe the myriad of clinical supervision models proposed by researchers: therapy based, developmental, and process. Therapy-based models of supervision are based on specific theories of psychotherapy such as systemic, solution-focused, or cognitive behavioral theory. In therapy-based models of supervision, theory is integrated within the supervisee's clinical practice and within clinical supervision. Developmental models operate on the premise that the supervisee's skill level evolves over time and the supervision adapts to the changing needs of the supervisee. Neophyte supervisees may require a more direct presence and involvement than those who are near the end of the clinical internship experience. Last, process models are concerned with the interpersonal dynamics of supervision. In other words, process models examine the interactions that occur between the supervisee and the supervisor during supervision.

Much like a pastoral counselor who adopts a theoretical orientation as a means to anchor clinical practice, a supervisor must do the same. In other words, "models of supervision provide a conceptual framework(s) for supervisors" that provide structure to the supervisory process (Bernard & Goodyear, 2014, p. 21). Therefore, it is in the best interest of the supervisor to find a way of supervising that resonates personally and professionally while still developing supervisee skills and maintaining quality control.

Methods of Supervision

Supervisors may employ a variety of methods by which to oversee supervisees. Two of the most commonly used methods are reviewing recorded sessions (either audio or video) and live observation. These are the supervision methods endorsed by the accrediting bodies of the CACREP and AAPC. As outlined in the 2009 *Standards* from CACREP, the supervisee is expected to "develop program-appropriate audio/ video recordings for use in supervision or to receive live supervision of his or her interactions with clients" (p. 17). Also, during the process of reviewing recorded counseling sessions, the supervisor has an opportunity to identify the student intern's strengths and areas of improvement or "growing edges."

Both clinical mental health agencies and counselor preparation programs use recorded counseling sessions as training tools. Recordings, digital or otherwise, can be crucial to understanding interpersonal interactions between the supervisee and the client by providing an opportunity to focus on microprocesses. During the session, subtle indicators of anxiety (in the client or the intern) that may be present in the folding of arms or a shifting stance can be interpreted for additional information.

Consider the following example:

The supervisee shares a video of her counseling a client, a 32-year-old woman currently separated from her husband. After 8 months of separation and 6 months of counseling, the client is considering reconciling with her husband "even though I hate the way he speaks to me and the kids and nothing I do is good enough." The supervisee sits back in her chair, crosses her arms, and sighs. "It sounds like you've made up your mind to go back anyway," the supervisee tells the client. At this point, the supervisor stops the videotape to process the interactions. Having the ability to see the nonverbal actions of the supervisee allows the supervisor to identify the behavior as counterproductive to the counseling relationship. When the supervisee is asked to explain her verbal and nonverbal reaction toward the client, she blurts out, "I couldn't believe she wanted to go back to him. I spent so many sessions constructing a plan for her to be independent. I thought I was making progress."

The supervisor used the session content on the video to gain greater insight into the motivation (and countertransference) of the supervisee. The tape provided a valuable means of capturing clinical skills and demonstrating the unpredictability of the therapeutic process. Discussion regarding the content of the tape included issues of countertransference, gender, and power. Although an audio recording of the session would have revealed the content of the session, the visual content helped the supervisee to see that which needed to be seen. Supervisors must also have clear expectations for the visual and audio quality of the recorded sessions. To this end, the supervisee should review the recording in advance before presenting it for supervisory review. The supervisor can work with the supervisee to identify potential areas for review, including impasses or demonstration of a new technique. Audio-recorded sessions can also serve as a means of providing a transcript or verbatim of the session. Specific recall of the discussion is then available for interpretation and greater understanding of the content of the therapy session. As a general rule, if video is unavailable, audio recording may be considered a substitute.

When using either audio or video recordings, care should be taken to make sure that the environment is conducive to recording a counseling session. Besides the consideration of minimizing background noise levels and having adequate space, client consent and confidentiality are primary considerations. In other words, recording should not occur if the client does not give consent or if client confidentiality cannot be protected or maintained during the session.

Consider the following example:

A supervisee accepted an internship at a private high school. Because of space limitations, the supervisee was instructed to conduct a counseling session in the school's auditorium. Eager for the opportunity to counsel a student, the supervisee did not consider the ramification of recording in an open environment. After the third interruption by school personnel, the supervisee began to feel uneasy about the arrangement. He realized that he could not maintain confidentiality and turned off the recorder. He spoke with his on-site supervisor, who agreed with his assessment of the situation and commended him on being proactive and behaving ethically. The supervisee and the student were escorted to a smaller, more secure environment for a confidential session.

Finally, when considering what aspects of the session to present, it can be beneficial to show the beginning, middle, and end of the recorded session. This chronological viewing offers the opportunity to witness difficult moments and successful interventions. Moreover, it provides data for discussing the overall structure, tone, and direction of the session.

Another training method used by clinical supervisors is live supervision. This method is often used in academic settings as a way to provide immediate feedback to the supervisee either as the session occurs or shortly thereafter and provide evidence of skill demonstration for academic assessment. As pointed out by Bernard and Goodyear (2014), the method involves direct observation while employing a method of communicating clinical feedback with the supervisee during the live session. Live supervision can occur with the supervisor observing the session through a one-way mirror or with the supervisor in the room during the counseling session. Live supervision can also occur by viewing the session remotely using digital recording software. The ways in which supervisors communicate with supervisees while under observation have changed with the advances in digital technology. In the past, supervisees were subjected to various interruptions such as in-room telephones to signal feedback from their supervisor. Presently, supervisors can provide immediate feedback either with or without physical interruption or time delay through the use of wireless technology, and interruptions for feedback can be negotiated beforehand.

Special logistical considerations may be necessary to facilitate live supervision. Clinical supervisors seeking to use live supervision as a training method should consider the level of professional training of the supervisee and how to structure the feedback process. In other words, the method has the potential to intimidate some inexperienced supervisees and arrest rather than enhance the supervisory relationship. The practice may also have the potential to restrict the development of the supervisee's own unique style of counseling. Also, live supervision can be time-consuming for the supervisor and resource consuming for the agency as two individuals become involved with serving one client. All things considered, live supervision often offers a sense of comfort and safety for both the supervisee and the client. Despite the protective elements of live supervision, the practice may not work well in some agency settings. The space needed to accommodate adjacent rooms that share a one-way mirrored wall, for example, may not be the best use of resources for a nonprofit social service agency squeezed for office space. Live supervision, as a method of clinical supervision, may find more utility in graduate training programs.

CONCLUSIONS

This chapter addressed the practice of clinical supervision in both academic and agency settings with pastoral counselors in training. Pastoral counseling training and certification at the state licensure level for supervisors is advocated to further promote the profession. In addition, the chapter outlined how supervisors, untrained as pastoral counselors, can incorporate dimensions of spirituality and religion into clinical practice and supervision.

REFLECTION QUESTIONS

1. The author notes that pastoral counselors in training are likely to be supervised by professionals from other, related disciplines. What are the advantages and drawbacks of this multidisciplinary approach to supervision?

2. What qualities are essential in an effective supervisor? Can those qualities be taught through supervisor training? What are the most effective means for supervisors to enhance their supervision skills?

3. What are some of the distinctive challenges for supervisors serving in academic settings? How do these challenges differ from those of supervisors in clinical settings?

4. The author outlines several models of supervision. At this point in your professional development, what type(s) of supervision would be most helpful to you? What type(s) are you best equipped to offer?

5. We often supervise in the ways that we have been supervised by others. What methods of approaching supervision have you drawn from your own experience being supervised? How might those affect your future supervision of others?

REFERENCES

American Counseling Association. (2014). *ACA code of ethics*. Retrieved from http://www.counseling.org/resources/aca-code-of-ethics.pdf

Association for Counselor Education and Supervision. (2011). *Best practices in clinical supervision*. Retrieved from http://www.acesonline.net/resources/

Baker, S. B., Exum, H. A., & Tyler, R. E. (2002). The developmental process of clinical supervisors in training: An investigation of the supervisor complexity model. *Counselor Education & Supervision, 42*(1), 15. doi:10.1002/j.1556-6978.2002.tb01300

Bernard, J. M., & Goodyear, R. K. (2004). *Fundamentals of clinical supervision* (3rd ed.). Needham Heights, MA: Allyn & Bacon.

Bernard, J. M., & Goodyear, R. K. (2014). *Fundamentals of clinical supervision* (5th ed.). Upper Saddle River, NJ: Pearson Education.

Binnie, J. (2011). Structured reflection on the clinical supervision of supervisees with and without a core mental health professional background. *Issues in Mental Health Nursing, 32*(9), 584–588. doi:10.3109/01612840.2011.576325

Bornsheuer-Boswell, J., Polonyi, M. M., & Watts, R. E. (2013). Integrating Adlerian and integrated developmental model approaches to supervision of counseling trainees. *Journal of Individual Psychology, 69*(4), 328–343. Retrieved from http://utpress.utexas.edu/index.php/journals/journal-of-individual-psychology

Corsini, R. J., Wedding, D., & Dumont, F. (2008). *Current psychotherapies* (8th ed.). Belmont, CA: Thomson Brooks/Cole.

Council for Accreditation of Counseling and Related Educational Programs. (2009). *2009 Standards*. Retrieved from http://www.cacrep.org/2009standards.html

Faiver, C., Eisengart, S., & Colonna, R. (2004). *The counselor intern's handbook* (3rd ed.). Belmont, CA: Thomson, Brooks/Cole.

Family Educational Rights and Privacy Act of 1974, 20 U.S.C. § 1232g; 34 C.F.R. pt. 99 (1974).

Gill, C. S., Harper, M. C., & Dailey, S. F. (2011). Assessing the spiritual and religious domain. In C. S. Cashwell & J. S. Young (Eds.), *Integrating spirituality and religion into counseling: A guide to competent practice* (pp. 31–62). Alexandria, VA: American Counseling Association.

Health Insurance Portability and Accountability Act of 1996, Pub. L. No. 104–191, 110 Stat. 1936 (1996).

Hipple, J., & Beamish, P. M. (2007). Supervision of counselor trainees with clients in crisis. *Journal of Professional Counseling: Practice, Theory, & Research, 35*(2), 1–16. Retrieved from http://www.highbeam.com/publications/journal-of-professional-counseling-practice-theory–research-p142246

Leddick, G. R. (1994). *Models of clinical supervision.* Greensboro, NC: ERIC Clearinghouse on Counseling and Student Services. Retrieved from http://www.eric.ed.gov/contentdelivery/servlet/ERICServlet?accno=ED372340

Lewis, J. A., Lewis, M. D., Daniels, J. A., & D'Andrea, M. J. (2011). *Community counseling: A multicultural-social justice perspective* (4th ed.). Belmont, CA: Brooks/Cole.

National Board of Certified Counselors. (2013). *NBCC code of ethics.* Retrieved from http://nbcc.org/Assets/Ethics/NBCCCodeofEthics.pdf

Ogden, K. R. W., & Sias, S. M. (2011). An integrative spiritual development model of supervision for substance abuse counselors-in-training. *Journal of Addictions & Offender Counseling, 32*(1), 84–96. doi:10.1002/j.2161-1874.2011.tb00209.x

Pearson, Q. M. (2004). Getting the most out of clinical supervision: Strategies for mental health. *Journal of Mental Health Counseling, 26*(4), 361–373. doi:10.1037/13487-000

Piedmont, R. L., Kennedy, M. C., Sherman, M. F., Sherman, N. C., & Williams, J. E. G. (2008). A psychometric evaluation of the Assessment of Spirituality and Religious Sentiments (ASPIRES) Scale: Short form. *Research in the Social Scientific Study of Religion, 1,* 163–182. doi:10.1163/ej.9789004166462.i-299.55

Tang, M., Addison, K. D., LaSure-Bryant, D. R., Norman, R., O'Connell, W., & Stewart-Sicking, J. A. (2004). Factors that influence self-efficacy of counseling students: An exploratory study. *Counselor Education & Supervision, 44*(1), 70–80. doi:10.1002/j.1556-6978.2004.tb01861.x

West, W., & Clark, V. (2004). Learning from a qualitative study into counseling supervision: Listening to supervisor and supervisee. *Counseling & Psychotherapy Research, 4*(2), 20–26. doi:10.1080/14733140412331383903

Joanne L. Miller

23

UNDERSTANDING PASTORAL COUNSELING RESEARCH

We have no instruments capable of detecting the presence or absence of God. Neither can we test the ultimate truth of religious claims. However, we can consider the question of the uniqueness of religion on a different set of grounds, the empirical.
—Pargament, Magyar-Russell, and Murray-Swank (2005, pp. 666–667)

There is impetus in our field to prove our worth and to prove the "pastoral" part of pastoral counseling. The "search for the sacred" (Pargament, 2007), the "unique domain" (Richards & Bergin, 1997) of spirituality and religion in clinical mental health, is one aspect of what constitutes pastoral counseling, and as pastoral counselors, we believe these constructs have an essential place along with other valuable constructs in psychology. However, as pastoral counselors, we also understand "truth" to be far more than we can learn through scientific exploration alone.

There is no universally agreed-on definition of pastoral counseling. However, most definitions contain some combination of aspects of religion, theology, psychology, and counseling. All of these fields contribute to the understanding of the human condition. Pastoral counseling research, then, is a combination of research in these same fields. The language of statistics and faithful application of research methods allow pastoral counselors to speak to and with related disciplines. This chapter presents common research methods, both qualitative and quantitative, including how the researcher influences what is being measured, challenges and opportunities in measuring religion and spirituality, and cultural implications of the measurement of religion and spirituality. Although research in many different areas is of interest to pastoral counselors, for the purposes of this chapter, all of the examples are specific to research involving the ways that religion and spirituality intersect the fields of counseling and psychology. There are many complexities within research demonstrating the benefits of religion and spirituality and empirically supporting spiritual interventions as valuable tools in counseling and psychotherapy. However, even with these complexities, this research shows that a link to the transcendent can, but does not always, promote greater well-being in people.

WHAT DO THE TERMS *RELIGION* AND *SPIRITUALITY* MEAN?

From an assessment viewpoint, the concepts of religion and spirituality have been conjoined and confused for quite a while, and there are no common definitions in the field. Hill et al. (2000) state that "both spirituality and religion are complex phenomena, multidimensional in nature, and any single definition is likely to reflect a limited perspective or interest" (p. 52). Hill et al. go on to explain how the schism between the two terms evolved, as disillusionment with organized religion grew in the Western world during the 1960s and 1970s, with more pleasant associations growing around the concept of spirituality in an increasingly secular society, leading to descriptions of "bad" religion and "good" spirituality in Western contexts.

Kapuscinski and Masters (2010) describe research showing that individuals maintain consistent evaluation criteria for religion and spirituality within themselves, but these criteria are not consistent between individuals; therefore, a person is consistent in how he or she uses the terms, but there is often inconsistency in use of the terms among people. Kapuscinski and Masters summarize the current, Western understanding:

> It appears that there is significant, but not complete, overlap in the common understanding of religiousness and spirituality, with belief in a higher power constituting a core aspect of both, but with religiousness alone necessitating involvement with institutionalized practices, groups, and beliefs. (p. 193)

However, whatever these two constructs are, they are probably distinct. Through structural equation modeling with spiritual and religious constructs, Piedmont, Ciarrochi, Dy-Liacco, and Williams (2009) found that Western spirituality and religiosity are at the same time highly correlated but distinct enough statistically to continue using both concepts.

As Emmons and Paloutzian (2003) point out, religious and spiritual variables are being included in epidemiological studies. Without conceptual clarity, differing meanings of the terms from study to study cloud the results and make comparisons unlikely. Researchers have their own perceptions of what the terms *religion* and/or *spirituality* mean, the participants may have other interpretations of religion and/or spirituality, and those who read the research study may have yet other interpretations. When reading reports of research on the impact of religion and spirituality on psychological constructs, pastoral counselors must consider what the researcher intended to capture, as this may be different from the pastoral counselor's personal definitions of religion or spirituality.

RESEARCH METHODS

All research seeks to increase our knowledge and understanding. Pastoral counseling falls in the broad category of the social sciences. There are two general categories of social science research: quantitative research and qualitative research. Quantitative research, the use of surveys and scales to measure the relationship between variables or to see whether a given treatment is more effective than another, is what most people associate with the term *research*. Ponterotto (2005) describes differing research paradigms in psychology research, noting different ways of knowing and understanding truth.

Quantitative research lies at one end of the spectrum, grounded in an epistemology that posits that objective realities can either be known or known imperfectly. Within this paradigm, the researcher can, theoretically, exercise objectivity through the use of and adherence to standardized statistical methods. In quantitative methodologies, the world is considered objectively knowable and, through the use of large sample sizes, idiosyncrasies are minimized and the data point to a knowable truth. Quantitative research seeks to explain and predict. In quantitative research, a study's design is based on what one expects to find. Hypotheses are generated, and the research tests the hypotheses.

Qualitative methods exist on the other end of the epistemological spectrum Ponterotto (2005) describes. Instead of accepting a single imperfectly knowable reality as with quantitative research, qualitative research assumes that multiple realities exist and are equally valid based on the lived experiences of the participants (Morrow, 2007; Ponterotto, 2005). Qualitative research seeks a depth of understanding, rather than the breadth and universality that quantitative research seeks. In that sense, qualitative research also examines the outliers so that understanding the unique experiences of that "case" matter and may affect the overall understanding of the research study. Qualitative research lends itself to development of theories, rather than the testing of hypotheses. The two types of research can be used together; qualitative methods are used to develop theories and hypotheses, and quantitative methods are used to test the hypotheses once they are developed.

Duffy and Chenail (2008) state that "quantitative research translates human experiences into numbers, and qualitative research translates human experiences into words" (p. 26). Both types of research are important in the field of pastoral counseling. Qualitative research can minimize some of the issues that arise while researching religion and spirituality, as we discuss later. Quantitative research is more common and is being used to demonstrate the value of spirituality or spiritual interventions in addition to other psychological constructs, such as social support and personality.

Quantitative Research

A baseline level of knowledge about statistics is important to understand this chapter. A *variable* is, in very simple terms, a characteristic or value that can assume different values in people. Age, ethnicity, level of depression, or prayer frequency are all examples of variables. Variables are said to be *correlated* with each other when there is some association between them that is greater than one would expect to find by chance. For example, the variables of "church attendance" and "prayer frequency" are, most likely, correlated such that participants with higher levels of church attendance also have higher levels of prayer frequency. However, simply because items are correlated does not mean that one causes the other. Church attendance does not cause prayer frequency, nor does prayer frequency cause church attendance. Correlation is not causation. Correlation signifies that the variables are somehow related. What is underneath that relation is still to be determined. That unknown relationship is often important in the analysis.

Variables are broken up into two general categories: dependent variables and independent variables. A *dependent variable* is the item or items that we wish to explain or predict. Dependent variable(s) are the focus of the research hypothesis or hypotheses. For example, we may wish to know how or whether prayer frequency affects depression. Depression would be the dependent variable, whereas prayer frequency (and possibly others) would be *independent variables*, also known as predictor variables. The analysis would assess whether differing levels of these independent variables could predict levels of depression. We will look at several different types of quantitative analysis, using research in spirituality and religion as examples.

Multiple Regression

Multiple regression is used when there are multiple independent variables with a single dependent variable. This series of independent, predictor variables can be used to come up with a linear combination that maximizes the predictive power of each to create a comprehensive explanatory model. Multiple regression recognizes that multiple constructs can explain and interpret the dependent variable. For example, Webb, Dula, and Brewer (2012) assessed the impact of various types of forgiveness (forgiveness of self, forgiveness of others, feeling forgiven by God) on aggression. In this example, the types of forgiveness are independent variables, whereas aggression is the dependent variable. These three types of forgiveness have elements in common such that each is, most likely, correlated to the other two and contain a shared variance that could make analysis of the individual types difficult. However, multiple regression accounts for this kind of shared variance. Therefore, by using multiple regression as the tool to analyze this phenomenon, the researchers assess the unique contribution of each type of forgiveness, determining which had the greatest impact on aggression. They found that forgiveness of others had the greatest impact on aggression. This finding can be used to tailor programs that seek to curb violence and aggression by promoting interventions that increase forgiving other people, knowing that increases in forgiving others should help lessen aggression overall.

Although researchers have not produced a universally accepted definition of either religion or spirituality, there appears to be agreement that the two constructs are overlapping, such that aspects of religiousness appear in spirituality and vice versa. Because there is an overlap of constructs, there is also shared variance between measures, which multiple regression accounts for. There have been multiple scales developed to assess the impact of religiosity and spirituality. Multiple regression, given that it allows for shared variance, is an effective way to capture the contributions of both religious and spiritual variables in the same studies. Religious scales that moderately correlate with each other can be used in the same study to "tap into different aspects of religiousness" (Gorsuch, 1988, p. 210), and multiple regression allows us to evaluate the unique contribution of each.

Incremental Validity

The concepts of religiosity and spirituality often overlap with other psychological concepts, such as emotions, virtues, and personality variables (Emmons & Paloutzian, 2003); attitudes and behaviors (Gorsuch, 1988); or social support (Joiner, Perez, & Walker, 2002). The incremental validity paradigm is a special case of hierarchical multiple regression. With an incremental validity approach, a researcher can account for these psychological concepts first and then assess the impact of religion or spirituality. This allows for the unique contribution of the spirituality variables to be highlighted. This is important not only to demonstrate the worth of religiosity and spirituality but also to assess where religious and spiritual variables may hurt well-being, such as in the case of some types of religious coping mechanisms. In other words, the theory drives the analysis, such that new research expands on existing, well-documented, and accepted research to show that the new construct or new way of looking at the issue lends something more to the discussion.

For example, Golden, Piedmont, Ciarrocchi, and Rodgerson (2004) performed a study on clergy burnout. Research on burnout in other work situations indicates that two factors are prominent: work environment and personality factors. To assess the role of spirituality factors in clergy burnout, the researchers first accounted for the impact of work environment and personality. The statistical analysis showed one of the spiritual elements, prayer fulfillment, had a small but significant contribution to burnout, which the authors discuss:

> The less one feels oneself in intimate relationship with the Divine, the greater the likelihood of burnout. The implication of this is that when it comes to dealing with the work-related distress of burnout, the ability to lose oneself in prayer or meditation is different than the ability to lose oneself in other areas of life such as in a hobby or in service. (Golden et al., 2004, p. 123)

If the analysis had only looked at the spiritual components, the researchers may have been open to criticism that the spiritual components encompass some of the known psychological factors related to burnout.

This is a common criticism of research into the impact of religion and spirituality. For example, social support is often a component of participation in a religious community. Social support has psychological benefits, whether the social support is from a religious community or from a book club. If a researcher uses religious and spiritual constructs in an analysis, especially behavioral factors such as participation in religious services, other researchers may question whether the demonstrated benefits of the religious and spiritual constructs are due to social support instead of religion or spirituality (George, Ellison, & Larson, 2002; Hoyt, Imel, & Chan, 2008; Joiner et al., 2002). By measuring incremental validity, an analysis can be performed by first accounting for the impact of psychological factors known to affect the phenomenon under observation, then assessing whether or to what extent the religious and spiritual variables have an impact over and above what has already been accounted for by the known psychological constructs.

The incremental validity approach has been championed as a way to demonstrate the contribution of religious and spiritual constructs. Kapuscinski and Masters (2010), in their critical review of scale development for religiosity and spirituality constructs, recommend that more research be conducted using an incremental validity approach with well-established personality constructs, such as the five-factor personality model (FFM; McCrae & Costa, 1997). There are a plethora of scales purporting to measure religious and spiritual variables, and what these scales actually measure is uncertain. However, by using strongly grounded psychological constructs as a basis and then using an incremental validity approach for the religious and spiritual values, a researcher who finds a significant variance then demonstrates that there is *something* there and something worthy of studying and of understanding. What that *something* is has yet to be fully understood, if it is even possible to fully understand that which is transcendent.

For example, in the development of the Spiritual Transcendence Scale (STS), Piedmont (1999) used an incremental validity approach to assess the contribution of a new measure of spirituality above existing psychosocial constructs. After correlating the STS subscales with psychosocial outcomes, such as prosocial behavior, interpersonal orientation, and sexual attitudes, Piedmont then performed hierarchical multiple regression to assess whether the STS subscales added unique variance over and above the impact of personality on those same psychosocial outcomes. For each of the psychosocial outcomes, at least one of the three STS subscales, Connectedness, Universality, or Prayer Fulfillment, demonstrated incremental validity over and above the impact of personality. The rigor of the scale development and the use of STS in an incremental validity approach have been cited as examples of good practices in our field (Kapuscinki & Masters, 2010; Slater, Hall, & Edwards, 2001).

Multivariate Analyses

"Because religion takes so many forms, because there are a host of potential moderators of the relationships between religion and well-being, and because well-being is itself a complex phenomenon, simple answers to evaluative questions about religion are simply impossible" (Pargament, 2002, p. 169). Research in the scientific study of religiosity and spirituality needs to reflect the complexity of the constructs themselves, the overlapping understandings between the broad constructs of spirituality and religion, and the overlapping understandings among spirituality, religion, and psychosocial constructs. Many components of these constructs are unobservable. Someone can be defined as "religious" if he or she attends services and prays, both observable and quantifiable behaviors. However, depending on the person's definition of religion, there may be other aspects such as connection to a higher power that are not observable. Few, if any, definitions of spirituality contain any aspect of observable behaviors. Therefore, to research religion and spirituality, we need insight into these unobservable, latent dimensions. These very complexities are what multivariate analyses are designed to address.

Multivariate analyses can simultaneously assess the interaction of multiple independent and dependent variables and explore the complex relationships among these variables. Hypotheses about religious or spiritual constructs can be grouped together in an analysis and, through factor analysis, a type of multivariate analysis, the items that are related to each other are identified. For example, Davis et al. (2014) studied relational spirituality and forgiveness, specifically assessing whether certain negative spiritual appraisals impede forgiveness: "viewing the offender as evil, anger toward God, and viewing the transgression as a desecration" (p. 103). By using factor analysis, Davis et al. evaluated items in a scale designed to assess one of these negative spiritual appraisals, the Viewing the Offender as Evil-23 scale. The research illuminated two factors contributing to this negative spiritual appraisal, Dehumanization and Dissimilarity. The researchers then used both multivariate analysis and multiple regression to evaluate hypotheses about these negative spiritual appraisals impeding forgiveness. Davis et al. found that:

> all three negative appraisals of relational spirituality were positively related to unforgiveness. Moreover, the two newer constructs (i.e., viewing the offender as evil and anger toward God) uniquely predicted unforgiveness. . . . These findings converge with prior theoretical and empirical work suggesting that some R/S [religion and spirituality] phenomena may hinder the forgiveness process, perhaps by fueling motivated reasoning to avoid forgiveness. (p. 110)

This kind of detailed analysis provided insight into the complex phenomena of both forgiveness and spirituality.

Technology has allowed us to create a more solid scientific foundation for our spiritual and religious constructs by using multivariate techniques. As statistical software has become more advanced, multivariate statistical analyses are more accessible to researchers. These technological advances allow us to refine and advance earlier research into religion and spirituality. For example, the Religious Orientation Scale of

Allport and Ross (1967) purported to measure intrinsic and extrinsic religiousness, following the theory that intrinsic religiousness was more internalized and lived by the individual, whereas extrinsic religiousness was more outwardly focused. This study correlated the Religious Orientation Scale to other scales in use at the time and to outcome measures about prejudice, because the conceptual basis of the study assumed that specific ways of being religious were correlated with prejudice. Allport and Ross found that extrinsic religiousness was correlated with prejudice, but intrinsic religiousness was not. That rudimentary conclusion was revolutionary at the time. However, we have learned much more about both statistics and religiousness since that time. Later research looked at the same issue from a multivariate perspective, taking the conceptual scales, which had been revised over time, and performing factor analysis. By using factor analysis, Gorsuch and McPherson (1989) identified two subcategories of extrinsic religiousness: a personal orientation (extrinsic, personal) and a social orientation (extrinsic, social). Thus, multivariate analysis allows for refinement of existing measures. Even without implying causality, these studies show the significant movement from Allport and Ross's (1967) research indicating that ways of being religious correlate with prejudice. This allows us to see beyond the religious motivation that Allport was trying to capture and into a world of complexity about how the religious person understands his or her faith, relates to others within and outside of the faith, and handles threats to faith beliefs.

Qualitative Methodologies

Qualitative methodologies rely on words and observations rather than numbers. Qualitative research seeks to create an in-depth understanding of an experience or a phenomenon. For example, to describe quantitative methods, earlier we used an example of research on the impact of religion and spirituality on depression. In qualitative research, we might interview people who have experienced a loss, such as a miscarriage, asking them to describe their experience and the role of religion or spirituality as part of that experience. In doing so, we allow the participants to define their own experiences instead of asking participants to fit their experiences into the scales that we have chosen. By doing so, we may find an understanding of grief and of depression that would not be captured in quantitative research.

Morrow (2007) discusses the core assumptions within qualitative research: (a) that it is emic and idiographic, being based on insider knowledge and perspectives of the participants and generating knowledge that is specific to these individuals or groups; (b) that it is inductive, as the research begins with a research question rather than a hypothesis; (c) that the researcher is a part of the process and the social location of the researcher in relation to what the researcher is studying matters; and (d) that it is subjective both because it believes that objective reality is not completely knowable and because the researcher becomes a participant in the research itself. Although there are many different types of qualitative research, two forms are highlighted here: phenomenology and grounded theory.

Phenomenology
Phenomenology looks at an experience or event to discern its constructs, both those that are unique and those that may be common to other experiences. The general questions are, "What is it like to experience a particular phenomenon? What is the lived experience?" In the example mentioned earlier in this chapter, people who experienced a miscarriage would be interviewed and invited to tell their stories. Because we are

looking for layers and depth in a particular experience and looking for both common-alities and differences among stories, specific types of participants may be sought. For example, although many people have experienced miscarriages, the researchers may only solicit those in their 40s who remain childless or those who experienced miscarriages and later adopted. The participants share similarities in that all experi-enced the particular phenomenon under consideration. Holloway and Todres (2003) state that phenomenology should give "relevant and transferable insights into what an experience may be like through clarification of its essential structures and textures" (p. 350). Participants discuss actual lived experiences in a concrete fashion. Research-ers then transcribe the interviews. From the transcription, the words are analyzed for patterns, the themes that are present among multiple participants.

As an example of recent research using phenomenology, Swinton, Bain, Ingram, and Heyes (2011) studied the role of spirituality in 14 women who received a breast cancer diagnosis within the past year. In analyzing the interviews, the researchers used this description of spirituality: "Spirituality is the quest for meaning, value and relationship with Self, others and, for some, with God" (p. 644). The three themes that emerged were "Moving inwards: loneliness and reassessment of the Self; Moving Outwards: relational consciousness; Moving Outwards and upwards: ultimate mean-ing" (p. 646). This provides insight to health professionals as to how to better serve women: "It is not enough simply to note that a person has a religious belief. . . . To misunderstand or misrepresent a woman's beliefs may be to misinterpret the very essence of what she perceives to be happening to her" (p. 650). The researchers note that hidden dimensions to a patient's experience are important to understand in order to provide more empathetic care.

Grounded Theory
Grounded theory looks for understanding of a process or event or the shared mean-ing between people. The keyword is *theory*, such that a plausible way of appreciating the complexity of human interaction or understanding is a desired outcome of the research. The focus is on ideas and concepts, and the theory is emergent, such that the researchers acknowledge that the theory is incomplete and will need to be tested in other situations and populations (Holloway & Todres, 2003). This approach is best used for examining process questions or investigating experiences that have differ-ent phases (Creswell, Hanson, Clark, & Morales, 2007). Grounded theory involves interviewing people who are living through or have lived through the phenomenon under investigation.

Charmaz (2006) recognizes that the quality of a grounded theory study depends on the quality of the data. Data should be "rich," not in a sense that there are a lot of data due to the number of participants, but in the sense that data gathered are at a deep enough level to thoroughly examine the participants' experience. When related back to the original research question, additional cases are added through theoretical sampling, "seeking and collecting pertinent data to elaborate and refine categories in your emerging theory" (Charmaz, 2006, p. 96) to reach data saturation, meaning enough cases have been added such that no new themes emerge.

An example of recent research is a study by Tillman, Dinsmore, Hof, and Chasek (2013) about counselor confidence in addressing client religion and spiritual issues in counseling. The researchers went through an extensive process to ensure that the data gathered represented the participants' experiences. Participants "were purposely chosen because they stated they had experienced the phenomenon of becoming con-fident in addressing spiritual and religious issues in counseling" (p. 241). First, each of the 12 participants was interviewed individually, using a semistructured interview with 15 open-ended questions. Then each participant was asked to create a pictorial representation of his or her spiritual development and to describe this drawing. Finally, a focus group discussion was held during which some of the participants collaborated on the themes that were emerging from the data analysis. The researchers developed five themes from these data to explain a process of developing confidence in addressing client religious and spiritual orientations in therapy:

> (a) having a positive foundational sense of things spiritual, (b) having engaged in a personal spiritual journey, (c) having the opportunity to socially construct one's ideas about spirituality or religion, (d) having an inner drive to become confident, and (e) developing the ability to traverse pitfalls when addressing spiritual or religious orientation with clients. (p. 245)

This research allows counselors and counselor educators insight into how to gain confidence or promote confidence in students. Exploring one's own spiritual identity and creating opportunities to share and discuss with others are two such recommendations made by the researchers.

How Can We Ensure That the Research Yields Accurate Results?

Regardless of methodology, researchers and reviewers need to be able to evaluate the research for quality, so that the results of the research are minimally related to error, in quantitative language, or bias, in qualitative language. Validity, from a statistical standpoint, refers to the accuracy of the research and the idea that the research measures what it is designed to measure. The results are then believed to be authentic and defensible. Because the underlying philosophy behind quantitative research is that reality is knowable, this knowledge should also be verifiable. For qualitative research, the concept of validity is still important, because the research should measure what it is designed to measure, but the applications are different and can be based on the type of qualitative research that is being conducted. The concept of validity changes between quantitative and qualitative, from *ensuring* validity in quantitative research to *minimizing threats* to validity in qualitative research. Because the researcher becomes part of the analysis in qualitative research, transparency of the analysis is important. Being explicit about researcher perspective and potential biases and maintaining an audit trail are two ways to create transparency. The qualitative research is then both subjective and reflexive. The balance between reflexivity and subjectivity is achieved through several methods in qualitative research, including data triangulation, member checking, reflexive journaling, bracketing, and thick descriptions (Holloway & Todres, 2003; Morrow, 2005).

Kapuscincki and Masters (2010) recommend using more qualitative methods in spirituality research, noting that in 25 years, only 22 qualitative studies appeared within the seven journals they assessed. Because qualitative methods are not common in the field, the rationale for choosing a qualitative approach instead of the more commonly used quantitative methods should be part of the discussion. Is this research question better answered by qualitative or quantitative methods, and, if qualitative, by using which particular methodology? Charmaz (2006) states that "*how* you collect data affects *which* phenomena you will see, *how*, *where*, and *when* you will view them, and *what* sense you will make of them [emphasis in the original]" (p. 15).

WHAT DO CURRENT DEFINITIONS OF *RELIGION* AND *SPIRITUALITY* MEASURE?

In their review of religious and spiritual scales, Kapuscinski and Masters (2010) state that the "experience of spirituality is not easy to verbalize, and even more difficult to operationalize for empirical investigation" (p. 201). Slater et al. (2001) note that there is strong social pressure in some religious groups to appear spiritually healthy and spiritually mature, which they call illusory spiritual health. This becomes an issue in quantitative research related to social desirability, meaning respondents answer the way they are "supposed to" answer, rather than indicating what they really think or feel. By using quantitative measures to assess spirituality and religiosity, we are inheriting some of the issues with those techniques.

For many years, a single-item measure was used in research studies to capture religion or spirituality, such as a question about the religious denomination of the participant or the degree of spiritual importance. This single-item approach represents what many still think about the role of religion or spirituality, as typified by Baumeister (2002), who stated that "what matters in terms of psychological and health outcomes is whether a person is religious—period. It does not make much difference which religion a person believes" (p. 166). Our knowledge and understanding of religion and spirituality have continued to grow in the years since Baumeister's (2002) statement. As pastoral counselors, we understand that religion and spirituality are far more complex than a single-item measure. Research shows that specific beliefs matter, more so than religion per se. For example, Rosmarin et al. (2011), in assessing belief systems and worry, looked at trust/mistrust in God and intolerance of uncertainty. Rosmarin et al. found that "certain spiritual beliefs are tied to intolerance of uncertainty and worry for some individuals" (p. 697). Trust/mistrust in God can occur in any theistic religion. Park (2007), when addressing religiousness and spirituality as a meaning system, stated that "theological differences in traditions and denominations may powerfully affect a multitude of individuals' beliefs, goals and values, which may influence their health" (p. 326). She referenced the work of Tix and Frazier, who found differences in the efficacy of religious coping between Protestants and Catholics in a medical crisis (as cited in Park, 2007). Exline (2002) asked, "Is it time to zero in on specific doctrines or beliefs?" (p. 246). The role of religion is so complex that, in assessing attributes such as worry or prejudice, the beliefs or doctrines do make a difference in how an individual experiences his or her world and, ultimately, well-being.

Religion and spirituality are yet to be universally defined, and it may ultimately turn out that some constructs now labeled "psychological" or "personality" end up in the distant future to be labeled or understood as spiritual. As Emmons and Paloutzian (2003) state, we "do not yet know whether personality influences the development of religiousness . . . whether religiousness influences personality . . . or whether personality and religiousness share common genetic or environmental causes" (pp. 392–393). However, religion and spirituality can be contentious issues, and the historically secular world of psychology may choose to treat what some might consider spiritual concepts as secular concepts. For example, Emmons and Paloutzian describe several virtues that exist within the major religions of the world: gratitude, forgiveness, and humility. All can exist both outside and inside of the religious context. Some might consider all three spiritual concepts not necessarily religious concepts; others would consider them secular concepts. The perspective of the researcher is important in evaluating the corresponding research. For example, Schuurmans-Stekhoven (2011) looked at what he termed "spiritual faith based beliefs," which appear to encompass both religiosity and spirituality, and virtues, which he defined as "those human qualities that involve an empathetic recognition of our mutuality and inter-dependence" (p. 315). Schuurmans-Stekhoven questioned past research purporting to show that religiosity and spirituality promote well-being because "other explanations are removed by design" (p. 318). He noted that multivariate analyses need to be performed to test other theoretically valid explanations and that these multivariate analyses could help integrate results from other studies, including those about moral reasoning. His argument about prior research also notes that past path analyses have found well-being fully mediated by what he calls secular constructs, such as social support, positive reinterpretation, hope, and optimism, and not what he would consider religious or spiritual factors. Schuurmans-Stekhoven concluded that his multivariate analyses reveal that virtues and not "spiritually based beliefs" predict well-being. He defines virtues as secular, whereas others may define virtues as spiritual, which then changes the argument that spirituality does not predict well-being. The conclusion depends on what is being defined as spiritual.

CULTURAL CONCERNS IN MEASUREMENT

Research in religion and spirituality must consider the culture(s) of those who devise the research and the culture(s) of those who participate. Augsburger (1986) describes a trifold concept of human beings: (a) commonalities exist between all people, with shared human responses and shared experiences that are universal in nature; (b) each person exists within a community or communities that help form the individual throughout his or her life; and (c) each person is unique, with unique experiences that no one else can fully inhabit. When assessing spirituality and religiosity, all of these commonalities and differences are important.

Most assessments of spirituality and religiosity were created by Western research-ers and based in terms of Western religious traditions, most often Protestant Christianity (George et al., 2002; Miller & Thoresen, 2003). Many religious and spiritual assessment scales have been developed using convenience samples of U.S. college students rather than the population to which the scale theoretically applies. The scale may also be based on deductive measures, based on existing theory or existing scales, rather than inductive measures coming from qualitative measures (Kapuscinski & Masters, 2010). These methodological issues need to be noted when assessing research involving religion and spirituality.

For example, the RCOPE, a measure of religious coping, was developed using college students, mostly Caucasian, female, and Christian. To determine whether the scale was useful beyond that demographic, the researchers then confirmed the data by querying elderly hospital patients (Pargament, Koenig, & Perez, 2000). Religious coping will be used to illustrate scale development issues and cross-cultural concerns in the measurement of spirituality constructs. The RCOPE scale was validated with a mostly Christian population in the United States. Rosmarin, Pargament, Krumrei, and Flannelly (2009) noted in development of the JCOPE, a scale measuring religious coping among Jews, that the RCOPE is not as relevant for Jewish populations because "in contrast to other religious traditions that stress the importance of thoughts, feelings, and intentions, the Jewish religion places more importance on religious practices and community involvement" (p. 671). This is a very important difference in the expression of religious coping, such that individuals in the same country, with many similarities in culture, have different experiences with respect to aspects of religiosity.

Tarakeshwar, Pargament, and Mahoney (2003) developed a religious coping scale for use among Hindus and validated it with a population of Hindus in the United States. Tarakeshwar et al. noticed that some of the religious coping mechanisms used were similar to the Christian population previously studied, but the meanings that the participants assigned may be different between the different faiths. Researchers also noted that some of the more traditional Hindu religious coping strategies, such as karmic attribution and yoga/meditation, were less used than may have been expected, with the hypothesis that the dominant culture in the United States does not reinforce those beliefs and practices in ways they might in a country that is predominantly Hindu. Phillips et al. (2009) conducted a qualitative assessment of spiritual coping in Buddhists in the United States, finding that meditation serves as a form of coping, which the researchers noted was not listed as a religious coping form for any of the previous research in coping, with the exception of Hindus. Therefore, a scale that purported to measure religious coping was found to be more specifically focused on religious coping for Christians and needed to be tailored to account for diversity in religious coping between different religions and different cultures.

There are also cross-cultural concerns between different countries or regions of the world with respect to measurement of religiosity and spirituality. Although there are commonalities between religions and in the cultural expression of religion, there are also many differences. Emmons and Paloutzian (2003) discuss the concept of virtues embedded within the major world religions. Using the concept of forgiveness, they describe how this virtue may be universally valued "but still embedded in specific cultural institutions and rituals" (p. 387). They further describe how Western cultures and Eastern cultures may be different with respect to this one value: "Individualistic models of forgiveness would tend to construe forgiveness as a personal decision or choice, whereas individuals in collectivist cultures would tend to operate according to strongly proscribed social norms" (p. 387). Therefore, something that may be an aspect of religion has both universal qualities and culturally embedded qualities, and if we measure the expression of forgiveness in a universal manner, both the individualistic and collectivist aspects should be considered, unless the scale is designed specifically for one or the other.

Cultural bias can exist in research design or scale development. The concept of "good" religion may be culturally biased. In the research conducted by Rican and Janosova (2010), the Prague Spirituality Questionnaire (PSQ) developed by Rican and Janosova, the Spiritual Transcendence Scale (Piedmont, 1999), and the Paranormal Beliefs subscale of the Experiential Spirituality Inventory (MacDonald, 2000) were used to assess whether spirituality comprises a sixth factor of personality, as proposed by Piedmont (1999). The researchers generally support that finding but add as an aside that the PSQ correlates with the Paranormal Beliefs subscale, which is "somewhat disappointing. . . . These beliefs were supposed to be closer to superstition than to spirituality proper. As such, they should *not* correlate with the PSQ or other measures of spirituality or other aspects of genuine, cultured religion" (Rican & Janosova, 2010, p. 11). Paranormal beliefs are parts of some cultural expressions of Christianity within cultures such as Haiti (Germain, 2011), yet this cultural expression may be deemed unworthy or unacceptable in measures of spirituality by researchers. Whether the beliefs are culture specific or completely unrelated to spirituality is irrelevant here; the point is that the researcher made an a priori decision that this is not and should not be considered a part of spirituality, most likely because it is not part of most Western spiritualities.

Finally, we can be limited by language in our cross-cultural assessment of spirituality and religiosity. Spirituality itself is difficult to put into words, let alone put into words and then translate into other languages. Many religious and spiritual assessments have been created in the Western world and cross-validated in other English-speaking countries (Brewcynski & MacDonald, 2006). The cross-cultural issues lie not only in translating the scale to the language in which it will be given but in conceptual issues within the questions themselves. For example, Brewcynski and MacDonald (2006) describe how the concept of "Bible study" has no readily translatable concept in Poland, so the semantics became less important than the context in the translation of the Religious Orientation Scale (Allport & Ross, 1967). Likewise, Rican and Janosova (2010) took an approach of not only translating the Spiritual Transcendence Scale (Piedmont, 1999) but reinterpreting the individual items to more closely match the prevailing atheism of the target population, the Czech Republic, creating the PSQ. Even within the same language, the same word might have different meanings for participants. In a qualitative study by Phillips et al. (2009), some of the Buddhist participants objected to the classification of Buddhism as a religion. Words matter. As Miller and Thoresen (2003) state, "We suspect that any scientific operational definition of spirituality is likely to differ from what a believer means when speaking of the spiritual" (p. 27).

SUMMARY AND CONCLUSIONS

Pastoral counseling research is complex because it crosses multiple disciplines and encompasses concepts that are difficult to define and conceptualize: religion and spirituality. It is important to note that the researcher always affects the results of the research, even when using more empirical methods. With every choice of scale and definition, a researcher imprints his or her own understanding of the issue on the research.

As pastoral counselors, we must consider the context of the research as we read and assess the results. Every client we see has a unique connection to the transcendent and his or her own conceptualizations of what it means to be religious and/or spiritual. When assessing religiosity and spirituality in clinical settings, quantitative measures can be used to evaluate a client's spirituality but should be assessed carefully because most have been created in a Western, Protestant Christian context and could potentially offend a client, for example, if the questions give reference to God when the client is not theistic (Pargament, 2007). Sometimes asking a question might help spur a client's reflection, so scales about spiritual transformation or spiritual coping may help clients just by taking them, regardless of the "scores," or if the pastoral counselor uses the item questions in session rather than requesting the client take the full measure.

Pargament (2007) discusses explicit and implicit spiritual assessment and notes that "spirituality is deeply personal" (p. 201), and the client may not feel comfortable discussing spirituality early in the therapeutic relationship. Explicit questions, such as those designed to elicit a client's spiritual journey, should be used only after the clinician knows the client is comfortable with the religious and spiritual constructs and should use the language with which the client is familiar. This is also important when the cross-cultural consideration is atheism. D'Andrea and Sprenger (2007) suggest that counselors working with atheist or nonspiritual clients ask about celebrations and focus on morals or values. A spiritual counselor may see those as part of spirituality, but the important thing is to value the connotation that the client puts to the concept. It is the client's perspective, not the clinician's perspective, that is important.

As pastoral counselors, we acknowledge the importance of religious and spiritual constructs. Our understanding of religion and spirituality is, most likely, different from other pastoral counselors, from researchers in the fields of religion and spirituality, and from the clients we see. Although a basic understanding of research is important in your pastoral counseling journey, understanding that there is a lens through which each of us interprets religion and spirituality is even more important.

REFLECTION QUESTIONS

1. How do understandings of epistemology and objectivity differ in qualitative and quantitative research? According to the author, both research methods are relevant and important to the work of pastoral counseling and the study of spirituality and religion. Do you agree? Why or why not?
2. Quantitative methods employ both dependent and independent variables. Define these two types of variables and describe how they are used in a multiple regression analysis.
3. Two common qualitative research methods include phenomenology and grounded theory. How are these two approaches similar and distinct?
4. Validity, a study's accuracy and authenticity, differs in qualitative and quantitative studies. How?
5. According to the author, "Religion and spirituality are yet to be universally defined." What are the pros and cons of fluid definitions of religion and spirituality? What impact does this have on empirical research?

REFERENCES

Allport, G. W., & Ross, J. (1967). Personal religious orientation and prejudice. *Journal of Personality and Social Psychology, 5*(4), 432–443. doi:10.1037/h0021212

Augsburger, D. W. (1986). *Pastoral counseling across cultures.* Philadelphia, PA: Westminster.

Baumeister, R. F. (2002). Religion and psychology: Introduction to the special issue. *Psychological Inquiry, 13*(3), 165–167. doi:10.1207/S15327965PLI1303_01

Brewczynski, J., & MacDonald, D. A. (2006). Confirmatory factor analysis of the Allport and Ross Religious Orientation Scale with a Polish sample. *International Journal for the Psychology of Religion, 16*(1), 63–76. doi:10.1207/s15327582ijpr1601_6

Charmaz, K. (2006). *Constructing grounded theory: A practical guide through qualitative analysis.* London, UK: Sage.

Creswell, J. W., Hanson, W. E., Clark, V., & Morales, A. (2007). Qualitative research designs: Selection and implementation. *The Counseling Psychologist, 35*(2), 236–264. doi:10.1177/0011000006287390

D'Andrea, L. M., & Sprenger, J. (2007). Atheism and nonspirituality as diversity issues in counseling. *Counseling and Values, 51*(2), 149–158. doi:10.1002/j.2161-007X.2007.tb00072.x

Davis, D. E., Van Tongeren, D. R., Hook, J. N., Davis, E. B., Worthington, E. R., & Foxman, S. (2014). Relational spirituality and forgiveness: Appraisals that may hinder forgiveness. *Psychology of Religion and Spirituality, 6*(2), 102–112. doi:10.1037/a0033638

Duffy, M., & Chenail, R. J. (2008). Values in qualitative and quantitative research. *Counseling and Values, 53*(1), 22–38. doi:10.1002/j.2161-007X.2009.tb00111.x

Emmons, R. A., & Paloutzian, R. F. (2003). The psychology of religion. *Annual Review of Psychology, 54*, 377–402. doi:10.1146/annurev.psych.54.101601.145024

Exline, J. (2002). The picture is getting clearer, but is the scope too limited? Three overlooked questions in the psychology of religion. *Psychological Inquiry, 13*(3), 245–247. doi:10.1207/S15327965PLI1303_07

George, L. K., Ellison, C. G., & Larson, D. B. (2002). Explaining the relationships between religious involvement and health. *Psychological Inquiry, 13*(3), 190–200. doi:10.1207/S15327965PLI1303_04

Germain, F. (2011). The earthquake, the missionaries, and the future of vodou. *Journal of Black Studies, 42*(2), 247–263. doi:10.1177/0021934710394443

Golden, J., Piedmont, R. L., Ciarrocchi, J. W., & Rodgerson, T. (2004). Spirituality and burnout: An incremental validity study. *Journal of Psychology and Theology, 32*(2), 115–125. doi: 0091-6471/410-730

Gorsuch, R. L. (1988). Psychology of religion. *Annual Review of Psychology, 39*, 201–221. doi:10.1146/annurev.ps.39.020188.001221

Gorsuch, R. L., & McPherson, S. E. (1989). Intrinsic/extrinsic measurement: I/E-Revised and single-item scales. *Journal for the Scientific Study of Religion, 28*(3), 348–354. doi:10.2307/1386745

Hill, P. C., Pargament, K. I., Hood, R. R., McCullough, M. E., Swyers, J. P., Larson, D. B., & Zinnbauer, B. J. (2000). Conceptualizing religion and spirituality: Points of commonality, points of departure. *Journal for the Theory of Social Behaviour, 30*(1), 51–77. doi:10.1111/1468-5914.00119

Holloway, I., & Todres, L. (2003). The status of method: Flexibility, consistency and coherence. *Qualitative Research, 3*(3), 345–357. doi:10.1177/1468794103033004

Hoyt, W. T., Imel, Z. E., & Chan, F. (2008). Multiple regression and correlation techniques: Recent controversies and best practices. *Rehabilitation Psychology, 53*(3), 321–339. doi:10.1037/a0013021

Joiner, T. R., Perez, M., & Walker, R. L. (2002). Playing devil's advocate: Why not conclude that the relation of religiosity to mental health reduces to mundane mediators? *Psychological Inquiry, 13*(3), 214–216. Retrieved from http://www.jstor.org.ezp.lndlibrary.org/stable/1449334

Kapuscinski, A. N., & Masters, K. S. (2010). The current status of measures of spirituality: A critical review of scale development. *Psychology of Religion and Spirituality, 2*(4), 191–205. doi:10.1037/a0020498

MacDonald, D. A. (2000). Spirituality: Description, measurement, and relation to the Five Factor model of personality. *Journal of Personality, 68*(1), 153–197. doi:10.1111/1467-6494.00094

McCrae, R. R., & Costa, P. R. (1997). Personality trait structure as a human universal. *American Psychologist, 52*(5), 509–516. doi:10.1037/0003-066X.52.5.509

Miller, W. R., & Thoresen, C. E. (2003). Spirituality, religion, and health: An emerging research field. *American Psychologist, 58*(1), 24–35. doi:10.1037/0003-066X.58.1.24

Morrow, S. L. (2005). Quality and trustworthiness in qualitative research in counseling psychology. *Journal of Counseling Psychology, 52*(2), 250–260. doi:10.1037/0022-0167.52.2.250

Morrow, S. L. (2007). Qualitative research in counseling psychology: Conceptual foundations. *The Counseling Psychologist, 35*(2), 209–235. doi:10.1177/0011000006286990

Pargament, K. I. (2002). The bitter and the sweet: An evaluation of the costs and benefits of religiousness. *Psychological Inquiry, 13*(3), 168–181. doi:10.1207/S15327965PLI1303_02

Pargament, K. I. (2007). *Spiritually integrated psychotherapy: Understanding and addressing the sacred.* New York, NY: Guilford.

Pargament, K. I., Koenig, H. G., & Perez, L. M. (2000). The many methods of religious coping: Development and initial validation of the RCOPE. *Journal of Clinical Psychology, 56*(4), 519–543. doi:10.1002/(SICI)1097-4679(200004)56:4<519::AID-JCLP6>3.0.CO;2-1

Pargament, K. I., Magyar-Russell, G. M., & Murray-Swank, N. A. (2005). The sacred and the search for significance: Religion as a unique process. *Journal of Social Issues, 61*(4), 665–687. doi:10.1111/j.1540-4560.2005.00426.x

Park, C. L. (2007). Religiousness/spirituality and health: A meaning systems perspective. *Journal of Behavioral Medicine, 30*(4), 319–328. doi:10.1007/s10865-007-9111-x

Phillips, R., Cheng, C., Pargament, K. I., Oemig, C., Colvin, S. D., Abarr, A. N., & Reed, A. S. (2009). Spiritual coping in American Buddhists: An exploratory study. *International Journal for the Psychology of Religion, 19*(4), 231–243. doi:10.1080/10508610903143263

Piedmont, R. L. (1999). Does spirituality represent the sixth factor of personality? Spiritual transcendence and the Five-Factor model. *Journal of Personality, 67*(6), 985–1013. doi:10.1111/1467-6494.00080

Piedmont, R. L., Ciarrochi, J. W., Dy-Liacco, G. S., & Williams, J. G. (2009). The empirical and conceptual value of the spiritual transcendence and religious involvement scales for personality research. *Psychology of Religion and Spirituality, 1*(3), 162–179. doi:10.1037/a0015883

Ponterotto, J. G. (2005). Qualitative research in counseling psychology: A primer on research paradigms and philosophy of science. *Journal of Counseling Psychology, 52*(2), 126–136. doi: 10.1037/0022-0167.52.2.126

Rican, P., & Janosova, P. (2010). Spirituality as a basic aspect of personality: A cross-cultural verification of Piedmont's model. *International Journal for the Psychology of Religion, 20*(1), 2–13. doi:10.1080/10508610903418053

Richards, P., & Bergin, A. E. (1997). The need for a spiritual strategy. In P. Richards & A. E. Bergin (Eds.), *A spiritual strategy for counseling and psychotherapy* (pp. 5–18). Washington, DC: American Psychological Association.

Rosmarin, D. H., Pargament, K. I., Krumrei, E. J., & Flannelly, K. J. (2009). Religious coping among Jews: Development and initial validation of the JCOPE. *Journal of Clinical Psychology, 65*(7), 670–683. doi:10.1002/jclp.20574

Rosmarin, D. H., Pirutinsky, S., Auerbach, R. P., Björgvinsson, T., Bigda-Peyton, J., Andersson, G., . . . Krumrei, E. J. (2011). Incorporating spiritual beliefs into a cognitive model of worry. *Journal of Clinical Psychology, 67*(7), 691–700. doi:10.1002/jclp.20798

Schuurmans-Stekhoven, J. (2011). Is it God or just the data that moves in mysterious ways? How well-being research may be mistaking faith for virtue. *Social Indicators Research, 100*(2), 313–330. doi:10.1007/s11205-010-9630-7

Slater, W., Hall, T. W., & Edwards, K. J. (2001). Measuring religion and spirituality: Where are we and where are we going? *Journal of Psychology and Theology, 29*(1), 4–21.

Swinton, J. J., Bain, V. V., Ingram, S. S., & Heys, S. D. (2011). Moving inwards, moving outwards, moving upwards: The role of spirituality during the early stages of breast cancer. *European Journal of Cancer Care, 20*(5), 640–652. doi:10.1111/j.1365-2354.2011.01260.x

Tarakeshwar, N., Pargament, K. I., & Mahoney, A. (2003). Initial development of a measure of religious coping among Hindus. *Journal of Community Psychology, 31*(6), 607–628. doi: 10.1002/jcop.10071

Tillman, D. R., Dinsmore, J. A., Hof, D. D., & Chasek, C. L. (2013). Becoming confident in addressing client spiritual or religious orientation in counseling: A grounded theory understanding. *Journal of Spirituality in Mental Health, 15*(4), 239–255. doi:10.1080/19349637.2013.799411

Webb, J., Dula, C., & Brewer, K. (2012). Forgiveness and aggression among college students. *Journal of Spirituality in Mental Health, 14*, 38–48. doi:10.1080/19349637.2012.642669

Serena A. Flores and Elizabeth A. Maynard

PASTORAL COUNSELING
AT A DISTANCE

Among the most significant developments in counseling over the past half-century is the use of technology to facilitate client care. The development of distance counseling in the past 2 decades is substantial, as is the demand for knowledge regarding the advantages and disadvantages of these forms of care (Rochlen, Zack, & Speyer, 2004). Pastoral counselors are now challenged to consider ways in which technology may facilitate the development of healing relationships, navigate the technical and ethical aspects of such forms of counseling, and maintain a genuine sense of connection with clients. This chapter serves as a brief introduction to key issues in distance counseling, with particular emphasis on the implications of these practices for pastoral counselors.

WHAT IS DISTANCE COUNSELING?

Several terms have been adopted by mental health professionals to describe the provision of services to clients at a distance. The American Counseling Association (ACA, 2014) defines *distance counseling* as the provision of counseling services by means other than face-to-face meetings, usually with the aid of technology. Other terms used to describe these practices include *cybercounseling, e-counseling, e-therapy, telepsychology, telehealth,* and *psychotechnology.* Each of these terms indicates the use of technology as an element of counseling practice. For the reader's benefit, the term *distance counseling* is used throughout this chapter to describe these practices. Distance counseling technologies include both asynchronous and synchronous formats. Asynchronous formats facilitate communication between the counselor and client but do not involve real-time communication. The most common example of this is the use of electronic mail (e-mail). Synchronous formats involve real-time communication, including telephone, video, or chat-based interactions. Please see the Appendix at the end of this chapter for a summary of these and related practices.

Distance counseling methods are usually distinct from practices common in social media venues such as Facebook and Myspace. Although social media activities have achieved widespread social and cultural acceptance, mental health codes of ethics (American Association of Christian Counselors [AACC], 2014; American Association of Pastoral Counselors [AAPC], 2012; ACA, 2014; American Psychological Association [APA], 2013; National Board for Certified Counselors [NBCC], 2012) discourage counselor engagement with clients through social media sites or virtual communities to avoid multiple relationships, violations of confidentiality, and other potentially harmful practices.

A BRIEF HISTORY

Scholars trace the nascence of distance counseling to the early 1960s and the development of basic computer programs such as *ELIZA* that responded to clients' statements with Rogerian-type responses (Weizenbaum, 1966). Within several decades, distance counseling evolved with the use of the first computer-mediated client resource programs such as *Ask Uncle Ezra* at Cornell University. Recognizing the potential impact of these emerging technologies on counseling, Herr and Best (1984) first identified the need for the counseling profession to establish ethical guidelines for technology use.

Over the past 5 decades, telephone and Internet technologies have become ubiquitous in North America. These technologies have become both more available to the general population and more integrated into everyday life. This integration of technology into everyday life requires both *knowledge* of emerging technologies and *competence* to use these new tools. The infusion of technology in counselor training has also become increasingly common, reflecting these larger social changes. This shift mirrors both client interest in distance counseling and the increasing comfort of counselors with technology.

At a basic level, many practitioners now offer information about their services and credentials through web pages (Centore & Milacci, 2008). Some professionals also offer asynchronous distance communication counseling services through their web pages (e.g., *Ask the Therapist*) by which clients are able to convey a question to the clinician and receive a response using e-mail. An increasing number of counseling professionals now offer distance counseling as one part of their traditional, face-to-face, counseling practices, and a smaller number of counselors practice primarily in a distance format. Rather than supplanting traditional counseling methods, distance counseling has become a supplementary modality for many practitioners interested in serving clients in new ways.

Although mental health treatment and spiritual care have traditionally been delivered using in-person techniques, an increasing number of Americans consult Internet-based resources when seeking solutions to mental health concerns (Wells, 2008). In fact, Wells (2008) found that many individuals and families seek Internet-based mental health resources *before* they seek more traditional mental health resources. This may be a result of the emerging digital culture in which adults (and an increasing number of youths) have access to Internet resources, easy access to the Internet from many locations and during many times of day, and anonymity when seeking aid. Internet resources are widely *accessible* in the sense that many people have access to them; they are also more *portable* than ever before, with many American adults carrying smartphones each day. Users of Internet search engines such as Google and Yahoo receive a plethora of results when keywords such as *online counseling* are explored (McAdams & Wyatt, 2010). Thus, help seekers with phone and Internet access are increasingly likely to use technology to identify a counselor and to receive aid at a distance.

These broader societal developments have also affected the practice of pastoral counseling. Like other forms of counseling, pastoral counseling has traditionally been practiced as a face-to-face activity. Although this remains the most common form of pastoral counseling, many pastoral counselors have begun to embrace distance technologies in their work with clients, so much so that the AAPC has published a statement on best practices for AAPC members (Reith, n.d.). The AAPC, like other professional organizations, recognizes the merits, drawbacks, and complexities of distance counseling.

THE PRACTICE OF DISTANCE COUNSELING

Pastoral counselors are witnessing a new era in communication technologies. Blogs, chat rooms, post-and-thread forums, and video-based Internet counseling are all resources new to counseling in the past 2 decades. Like other forms of counseling, distance counseling is a multidimensional enterprise. In addition to the provision of talk therapy, technology may be used by counselors to support testing and assessment (Barros-Bailey & Saunders, 2010), peer consultation, supervision, and professional training.

When engaging in distance counseling, professionals attend to many of the same therapeutic and practice management issues that arise in face-to-face client services. Counselors seek informed consent, maintain confidentiality, negotiate scheduling, and evaluate the outcomes of distance counseling on a regular basis, attending to both the quality of the therapeutic relationship and the dyad's success using the technologies that they have selected.

At heart, the role of the pastoral counselor remains the same, whether the services are offered in person or at a distance. Counselors are responsible for determining, in collaboration with the client, when distance counseling methods are a useful form of assessment and intervention and when services are more appropriately offered in person by themselves or by referral to others. As part of this process, the counselor considers the client's levels of emotional and intellectual functioning, her or his presenting concerns, and the individual's levels of skill and comfort with Internet-based activities. The client and counselor work together to decide on the use of technology to support the work of counseling, including the types of technology that will be used and for what purposes. For example, a client may desire distance counseling sessions to accommodate family responsibilities but feels "technophobic," whereas another client may be more skilled in Internet-based communication than the counselor. In the first situation, the counselor and client may choose from among several software programs to enhance the client's comfort, and the counselor may include a brief orientation to the technology as part of the counseling work. In the latter situation, the counselor and client may negotiate the use of technologies with which the counselor feels comfortable, and she or he may need to pursue additional training in those technologies before working with the client. It is important to emphasize that distance counseling is not intended to replace entirely conventional modes of pastoral counseling; rather, it may serve as an essential adjunct to traditional methods.

BEST PRACTICES IN DISTANCE COUNSELING

Recognizing the increasing reach of distance counseling, governing bodies such as the NBCC, ACA, APA, and AAPC have established guidelines and statements of best practices in efforts to guide distance counseling practices. Members of these organizations are usually expected to adhere to these guidelines (NBCC, 2012). These guidelines serve as a resource, both to those new to distance counseling and those who are adapting their distance counseling practices in light of emerging legal standards.

Although the standards and suggestions for best practice differ slightly among organizations, several key themes remain consistent across standards: the importance of the practitioner's knowledge and competence in distance practices, the licensure and credentials of practitioners, jurisdiction of practice, the maintenance of existing ethical standards for client care, informed consent, confidentiality, secure transmission and storage of information, professional boundaries, access to services, and cultural and disability considerations.

Pastoral counselors who engage in distance counseling must develop both foundational knowledge of distance practices and the technical skills to offer services remotely. This knowledge and skill may be developed through both formal training in graduate or certification programs such as those offered by the Center for Credentialing and Education (CCE), continuing education courses and workshops, hands-on training in the clinician's practice setting, and supervision by and consultation with more experienced practitioners.

PREPARATION FOR DISTANCE COUNSELING WORK

Up to now, few graduate training programs have equipped counselors for distance work. Flores (2012) found that only a handful of mental health training programs incorporated material to prepare trainees for distance practice. In addition to securing and maintaining state licensure as a mental health professional and/or endorsement from a religious community, the pastoral counselor is encouraged to seek certification as a distance credentialed counselor (DCC; offered by the CCE). Although DCC certification is not required for distance practice in most states, the NBCC endorses the credential as a requirement to practice distance counseling. DCCs adhere to state licensure laws, ethical codes published by their primary professional organizations (AAPC, ACA, APA), and best practices in distance counseling outlined by the CCE (see http:// cce-global.org/DCC for more information). Although not specific to pastoral counseling practice, this type of training may familiarize the practitioner with common technologies, ethical and legal issues, and therapeutic factors involved in distance counseling work. Counselors may also benefit from membership in professional organizations such as the American Distance Counseling Association (ADCA) for consultation and support of distance counseling practice.

In addition to these types of certification and membership, an understanding of *netiquette* (Internet-based etiquette) is essential to successful distance counseling practice, particularly in asynchronous formats. Distance counseling netiquette involves culturally prescribed customs, a general code of conduct in an electronic environment, and the use of traditional counseling skills (Fink, 1999). Common netiquette guidelines include respect for privacy, the use of appropriate language, timeliness in responses to others, and limiting the use of intensifiers to convey meaning (such as capital letters to convey screaming; Shea, 2004). Although the AAPC (Reith, n.d.), ACA (2014), NBCC (2012), and APA (2013) do not address specific netiquette guidelines, each organization outlines ethical practices for electronic communication.

BENEFITS OF DISTANCE COUNSELING

There are a number of notable benefits to the practice of distance counseling. Distance counseling technologies are revolutionary in their potential to serve clients who would otherwise not have access to mental health services. With advances in Internet technologies such as video streaming, many individuals are now able to overcome personal barriers such as problems with transportation, domestic obligations, agoraphobia, or the lack of needed services in their areas to access services that were otherwise not available to them in the past (Derrig-Palumbo & Zeine, 2005).

Clinicians and clients are able to connect for counseling both *to* and *from* remote locations (APA, 2013). Thus, counseling services are now more available to those who live in remote or underserved regions, including rural and developing regions of the United States and other countries. This may also include access to services for those serving in missionary, development, and war contexts. Furthermore, distance counseling also makes it possible for otherwise marginalized clients to seek and receive counseling support, such as the queer adolescent coming out in a region with few "out" models or an ethnically or linguistically underserved client making a connection with a culturally similar helper in another part of the world. Some clients are fearful of face-to-face counseling due to stigma or cultural reservations about seeking mental health care; they may be drawn to distance counseling by the sense of perceived anonymity that this format affords (Hollingsworth, 2014; Rees & Stone, 2005). Despite the many potential benefits to clients, there are also a number of potential limitations to the use of distance counseling.

LIMITATIONS AND CONCERNS

Although distance counseling offers unique opportunities for individuals to engage in mental health services, not all clients may benefit from this form of care. Many clients remain isolated and ineligible for these services due to a lack of access to computers, low levels of technological proficiency, a limited number of pastoral counselors willing to offer care at a distance, and similar obstacles.

Pastoral counselors must assess for the appropriateness of distance counseling and technology use by the client before engaging in this form of care. Furthermore, the counselor must ask not only whether distance counseling is a good fit for this client at this time but also what types of pastoral counseling activities are appropriately offered at a distance. For example, assessment of clients is often complicated in distance counseling, as the counselor may not be able to see or hear the client in ways that she might in an in-person session. Thus, the subtleties of body language and speech tone that so often inform a counselor's impression of a client may be lost. In this way, critics of distance counseling assert that the absence or distortion of nonverbal client observations increases the possibility of misdiagnosis (Alleman, 2002; McAdams & Wyatt, 2010).

Critics of distance counseling also question the ability of counselors to build genuine rapport with clients. At present, it is unclear whether the therapeutic alliance between counselor and client can be firmly established and maintained, particularly when using asynchronous methods (Chester & Glass, 2006). Distance counseling clients have also reported concerns about feeling understood by and connected to the counselor (Centore & Milacci, 2008).

Although distance counseling often allows clients to engage in care in an environment of their choosing, this flexibility may also create challenges. The client and counselor may need to negotiate the location that the client chooses for services. Although the client may be comfortable logging on to "meet" with the counselor in a crowded, noisy, or high-traffic location, this will present challenges to a counselor who wants to support the client's confidentiality or make room for silent reflection during a session.

Furthermore, for some clients, this method of communication may paradoxically reinforce feelings of isolation from others or a sense that the counseling relationship is more virtual than real.

Counselors working at a distance from clients must also take care to verify the identity of the clients they serve. It may be more difficult to confirm that the client is, in fact, the person that he or she claims to be. From a client's perspective, it may also be difficult to confirm that the counselor maintains the licenses and certifications that he or she advertises. The NBCC and ACA suggest verifying the client's identity by using nondescript identifiers such as code words or phrases, particularly when communication with clients is asynchronous (ACA, 2014; NBCC, 2012).

Finally, a common challenge of Internet-based counseling work is the use of the technology itself. Counselors and clients may be thwarted by problems with Internet connectivity, dropped calls/sessions, and poor video or audio quality.

SPECIAL CONSIDERATIONS

Pastoral counselors seek to protect and support our clients' welfare and meet the needs of the client within her or his unique set of life circumstances. For example, the client's physical abilities and childcare situation may make it important that he "meet" with the counselor by Internet rather than making a tiring or lengthy trip to the counselor's office. While responding to the client's unique needs, the counselor must also minimize the potential risks to clients that arise in distance counseling (Ford, 2006). Thus, the counselor must attend first to informed consent and confidentiality.

Informed Consent

Several features of informed consent are particularly important in the distance counseling domain. In addition to the elements of informed consent that pastoral counselors use in their face-to-face work with clients (nature of the care and interventions to be offered, potential risks and benefits of counseling), distance counselors should also describe their distance counseling credentials (such as the DCC certification), clarify the physical location of their practices, and provide reliable contact information. Furthermore, the counselor should describe the risks and benefits of engaging in distance counseling, including the possibility of technology failure (e.g., dropped calls or inability to connect for scheduled sessions due to technology problems). The counselor and client should also take special care to discuss the counselor's anticipated response time to e-mail and voicemail as well as emergency procedures when the counselor is not available. The counselor must also inform the client that distance services might not be covered by insurance. Finally, the counselor should discuss his or her social media policy with the client, outlining appropriate and inappropriate types of distance relationships (e.g., no "friending" on Facebook).

Confidentiality

Maintaining the confidentiality of client's information through electronic means presents novel challenges not present in face-to-face work. Counselors must inform clients about the potential risks related to the unauthorized electronic access of personal records, including transmission of session data (ACA, 2014). That is, electronic records and communications may be "hacked" by outsiders, and many forms of Internet-based video communication are not considered secure. Encryption-protected telecommunication systems are commonly used in the asynchronous and synchronous formats of distance counseling; counselors must take care to use these secure types of technologies unless the client has expressed a preference for and given informed consent to use non-secure technologies. Distance counselors in the United States must also attend to the federal standards established in Health Insurance Portability and Accountability Act (1996) and Health Information Technology for Economic and Clinical Health (HITECH; 2009) legislation, both of which address the secure storage and transmission of client information. The reader is encouraged to review Rummell and Joyce (2010) and Shaw and Shaw (2006) for more specific information on securely transmitting, storing, and disposing of client data.

State Laws and Regulations

Legal standards surrounding distance counseling vary both nationally and globally. One of the most common issues addressed by professional organizations is the offering of services to clients who reside outside of the jurisdiction in which the practitioner is licensed. Although it is common practice for counselors to offer limited telephone support to clients traveling outside the counselor's area for work or leisure, it is often unclear whether or to what extent counselors may offer ongoing services to clients outside their own jurisdictions. Some U.S. states have begun to address this issue, but it remains unclear how to interpret the boundaries of jurisdiction in most states and countries. For example, should a pastoral counselor offer services to a client who lives in another state, province, or country if a qualified pastoral counselor is unavailable in the client's area? May a Mandarin Chinese–speaking pastoral counselor in California provide distance counseling services to a client in Texas who is unable to find a counselor in her area who speaks Mandarin or whom she does not know socially? Until licensure portability is more clearly resolved, pastoral counselors are encouraged to limit their practices to their state(s) of licensure and to monitor the regulations in their own jurisdiction (and that of the client) when offering distance care.

Distance Supervision and Consultation

Distance supervision and peer consultation may permit counselors to seek both regular and specialized supervision from professionals in other locations. This arrangement may have many benefits, such as permitting the counselor to practice in settings where an on-site supervisor is not readily available. Furthermore, distance consultation may assist the counselor in developing knowledge and skills needed to serve an individual or group of clients with whom she or he has little experience. For example, the number of professionals with significant experience serving transgender or pagan-identified adults is limited. A counselor new to these aspects of client identity may find it impossible to find a local professional with whom to consult; rather, she may develop a consultation relationship with a professional in another state or country. It is important that each counselor carefully review the legal codes in jurisdictions that outline the requirements for face-to-face supervision during periods of prelicensure supervised practice, as well as regulations that dictate the number of hours that a supervisor and supervisee must be physically present in the same agency. States and licensure boards often differ significantly in their acceptance of distance supervision to meet licensure standards.

IMPLICATIONS FOR PASTORAL COUNSELING

Like other forms of spiritual and mental health care, pastoral counseling is most often offered to clients as a face-to-face activity. Research in the use of distance technologies in pastoral counseling is limited, but promising. For example, Mills (2011) noted that asynchronous (e-mail) pastoral counseling supported the development of the minister–person relationship and increased the client's positive emotion and emotional well-being.

To borrow from Cheston's (2000) "Ways" paradigm, distance counseling is likely to affect the pastoral counselor's ways of *being, understanding*, and *intervening* with clients. Most obviously, the counselor's way of being will differ significantly depending on whether she uses a synchronous or an asynchronous format for care. If she and the client select real-time video-streaming technology to conduct their sessions, many features of the session will be similar to what might be experienced in a face-to-face meeting. However, the use of e-mail or real-time chat to facilitate pastoral counseling will necessitate a very different (text-based) way of being with the client. Even so, distance counseling may affect the client's and counselor's perceptions of warmth and connection, as well as comfort with the use of specific strategies such as prayer. Particularly for those who understand pastoral counseling as involving the presence and participation of a holy *other* (God), the distance format may require significant adjustment. How is this holy other invited into the distance care relationship by the counselor and client? Is God present in e-mail? When two or more are gathered electronically, is God present there as well?

As previously mentioned, distance pastoral counseling may limit some forms of assessment and understanding of the client and his or her experience and concerns. At the same time, the pastoral counselor may gather information about the client through distance technologies that she or he may have been reticent to share in person but may feel more comfortable sharing with the psychological distance of e-mail or a computer screen. The counselor may come to understand better the client's ways of using technology as a companion, a substitute for other human or transcendent relationships, or a means to forge new spiritual connections.

Distance counseling not only affords the counselor with means to offer care to clients who might not otherwise have access to pastoral counseling but also opens up new methods of intervention within and beyond the session. For example, most counselors refrain from asking clients to pull up potentially helpful websites, inspirational or instruction videos, or spiritual songs during face-to-face sessions, either because the technology is not available in the counselor's office or because it might disrupt the flow of the session. However, the use of these resources may be more compatible with distance counseling, affording the client and counselor a multimodal (and multimedia) experience.

As an emerging practice, distance counseling presents both opportunities and challenges for pastoral counselors. Counselors must weigh the potential benefits of distance pastoral counseling along with the potential risks involved with using electronic media to facilitate client care. Pastoral counselors who develop the knowledge and skills to provide distance care competently and ethically are poised to forge a fruitful union between the pastoral and the technological, extending the reach of pastoral presence and care.

REFLECTION QUESTIONS

1. According to the authors, "Distance counseling is a multidimensional enterprise" that influences talk therapy as well as testing and assessment (Barros-Bailey & Saunders, 2010), "peer consultation, supervision, and professional training." Should the incorporation of technologies be limited to only certain stages in the counseling process or particular practices within the counselor–client or counselor–supervisor relationship? Why or why not?
2. What factors influence the appropriateness of distance counseling with a particular client? Who is involved in making this determination?
3. How do you understand the impact of distance counseling on the counselor's ways of *being, understanding,* and *intervening* with clients?

REFERENCES

Alleman, J. R. (2002). Online counseling: The Internet and mental health treatment. *Psychotherapy: Theory, Research, Practice, Training, 39,* 199–209. doi:10.1037//0033-3204.39.2.199

American Association of Christian Counselors. (2014). *AACC code of ethics.* Retrieved from http://aacc.net/files/AACC%20Code%20of%20Ethics%20-%20Master%20Document.pdf

American Association of Pastoral Counselors. (2012). *Code of ethics.* Retrieved from http://www.aapc.org/about-us/code-of-ethics/

American Counseling Association. (2014). *ACA code of ethics.* Retrieved from http://www.counseling.org/Resources/aca-code-of-ethics.pdf

American Psychological Association. (2013). *Guidelines for the practice of telepsychology.* Retrieved from http://www.apa.org/practice/guidelines/telepsychology.aspx

Barros-Bailey, M., & Saunders, J. L. (2010). Ethics and the use of technology in rehabilitation counseling. *Journal of Applied Rehabilitation Counseling, 41*(2), 60–64. doi:10.1177/0034355210368867

Centore, A. J., & Milacci, F. (2008). A study of mental health counselors' use of and perspectives on distance counseling. *Journal of Mental Health Counseling, 30*(3), 267–282. Retrieved from http://essential.metapress.com/content/q871r684n863u75r/

Chester, A., & Glass, C. A. (2006). Online counseling: A descriptive analysis of therapy services on the Internet. *British Journal of Guidance & Counseling, 34,* 145–160. doi:10.1080/03069880600583170

Cheston, S. E. (2000). A new paradigm for teaching counseling theory and practice. *Counselor Education & Supervision, 39*(4), 254–269. doi:10.1002/j.1556-6978.2000.tb01236.x

Derrig-Palumbo, K., & Zeine, F. (2005). *Online therapy: A therapist's guide to expanding your practice.* New York, NY: W. W. Norton.

Fink, J. (1999). *How to use computers and cyberspace in the clinical practice of psychotherapy.* Northvale, NJ: Jason Aronson.

Flores, S. (2012). *Online counseling and online counselor preparation: A mixed methods investigation* (Unpublished doctoral dissertation). Texas A&M—Corpus Christi, Corpus Christi, TX.

Ford, G. (2006). *Ethical reasoning for mental health professionals.* Thousand Oaks, CA: Sage.

Gautreau, C. (2011). Motivational factors affecting the integration of a learning management system by faculty. *The Journal of Educators Online, 8*(1), 1–25.

Herr, E. L., & Best, P. L. (1984). Computer technology and counseling: The role of the profession. *Journal of Counseling and Development, 63*(3), 192–196. doi:10.1002/j.1556-6676.1984.tb02798.x

Hollingsworth, M. A. (2014). *Distance counseling: Client fit, ethical considerations, and contraindications.* Retrieved from http://www.aacc.net/2014/01/17/distance-counseling-client-fit-ethical-considerations-and-contraindications/

Lee, C. C. (2000). Cybercounseling and empowerment: Bridging the digital divide. In J. W. Bloom & G. R. Walz (Eds.), *Cybercounseling and cyberlearning: Strategies and resources for the millennium* (pp. 85–93). Alexandria, VA: American Counseling Association.

McAdams, C. R., & Wyatt, K. L. (2010). The regulation of technology-assisted distance counseling and supervision in the United States: An analysis of current extent, trends, and
implications. *Counselor Education and Supervision, 49,* 179–192. doi:10.1002/j.1556-6978
.2010.tb00097.x

Mills, S. (2011). Caring through technology: Using e-mail for Christian pastoral counseling. *Interacting With Computers, 23*(2), 106–116. doi:http://dx.doi.org/10.1016/j.intcom.2010.10.005

National Board for Certified Counselors. (2007). *The practice of Internet counseling.* Retrieved from
http://www.nbcc.org

National Board for Certified Counselors. (2012). *Code of ethics.* Retrieved from http://www.nbcc
.org/Assets/Ethics/NBCCPolicyRegardingPracticeofDistanceCounselingBoard.pdf

Rees, C. S., & Stone, S. (2005). Therapeutic alliance in face-to-face versus videoconferenced
psychotherapy. *Professional Psychology: Research and Practice, 36,* 649–653. doi:10.1037/0735-
7028.36.6.649

Reith, S. M. (n.d.). *Best practices for AAPC members in relation to electronic communication endorsed
by the Judicial Ethics Panel of AAPC.* Retrieved from http://www.appc.org

Rochlen, A., Zack, J., & Speyer, C. (2004). Online therapy: Review of relevant definitions, debates
and current empirical support. *Journal of Employment Counseling, 38,* 150–160. doi:10.1002/
jclp.10263

Rummell, C. M., & Joyce, N. R. (2010). "So wat do u want to wrk on 2day?": The ethical implications of online counseling. *Ethics & Behavior, 20*(6), 482–496. doi:10.1080/10508422
.2010.521450

Shaw, H. E., & Shaw, S. F. (2006). Critical ethical issues in online counseling: Assessing current
practices with an ethical intent checklist. *Journal of Counseling & Development, 84,* 41–53.
doi:10.1002/j.1556-6678.2006.tb00378.x

Shea, V. (2004). *Netiquette.* Retrieved from http://www.albion.com/netiquette/book/index.html

Weizenbaum, J. (1966). ELIZA: A computer program for the study of natural language communication between man and manchine. *Communications of the ACM, 9*(1), 36–45. doi:10.1145/
365153.365168

Wells, A. T. (2008). *A portrait of early Internet adopters: Why people first went online—And why they
stayed.* Retrieved from Pew Internet & American Life Project: http://able2know.org/topic/
112301-1

APPENDIX: DEFINITION OF TERMS

1. *Blog:* A web log is a publicly accessible web page, updated regularly and often,
   that serves as a personal journal of the site owner (Lee, 2000).
2. *Chat-based Internet counseling:* Involves synchronous distance interaction between
   counselor and client using what is read via text to communicate (NBCC, 2007, p. 3).
3. *Chat room:* A virtual environment in which numerous Internet users may join and
   converse with one another in synchronous communication through typed text
   (Lee, 2000).
4. *Client/patient:* The recipient of psychological services, whether these services are
   delivered in the context of health care, corporate, supervision, and/or consulting
   services (APA, 2013, pp. 3–4).
5. *Confidentiality:* The principle that data or information is not made available or
   disclosed to unauthorized persons or processes (APA, 2013, pp. 3–4).
6. *E-mail–based Internet counseling:* Involves asynchronous distance interaction between counselor and client using what is read via text to communicate (NBCC,
   2007, p. 3).
7. *Emoticon:* A cluster of punctuation or a small graphical sign or picture that may
   be used in online communication to compensate for the lack of nonverbal cues to
   indicate a facial expression or gesture (Lee, 2000).

8. *Face-to-face counseling:* According to the NBCC, face-to-face counseling is defined as "synchronous interaction between and among counselors and clients using what is seen and heard in person to communicate" (NBCC, 2007, p. 3).

9. *Forum:* A message board or discussion board; a website designated to allow asynchronous group communication (Lee, 2000).

10. *Information system:* An interconnected set of information resources within a system that includes hardware, software, information, data, applications, communications, and people (APA, 2013, pp. 3–4).

11. *In person:* Used in combination with the provision of services, *in person* refers to interactions in which the psychologist and the client/patient are in the same physical space and does not include interactions that may occur through the use of technologies (APA, 2013, pp. 3–4).

12. *Jurisdictions/jurisdictional:* Used when referring to the governing bodies of states, territories, and provincial governments (APA, 2013, pp. 3–4).

13. *Learning management system:* An online learning course design tool facilitated by instructors for students (Gautreau, 2011).

14. *Online counseling:* According to the NBCC (2007), Internet counseling is defined as an "asynchronous and synchronous distance interaction among counselors and clients using e-mail, chat, and videoconferencing features of the Internet to communicate" (p. 3).

15. *Online counseling competence:* A degree of mental competence toward mentally and/or physically using and employing the technological applications and/or equipment necessary to conduct an online counseling session.

16. *Post:* To publish a message on the Internet, including sending a message to an e-mail list or publishing a message in a forum (Lee, 2000).

17. *Security measures:* A term that encompass all of the administrative, physical, and technical safeguards in an information system (APA, 2013, pp. 3–4).

18. *Synchronous:* Coinciding in time of communication that is carried out with all parties present at the same time (e.g., chat) (NBCC, 2007, p. 3).

19. *Technological issues:* An individual experiencing difficulties toward the technological applications and/or equipment necessary to conduct an online counseling session (NBCC, 2007, p. 3).

20. *Technology-assisted distance counseling:* For individuals, couples, and groups involving the use of the computer to enable counselors and clients to communicate at a distance when circumstances make this approach necessary or convenient (NBCC, 2007, p. 3).

21. *Thread:* A multiple-part virtual conversation on a given topic in an e-mail list or a forum composed of a leading message and responses (Lee, 2000).

22. *Video-based Internet counseling:* Involves synchronous distance interaction between counselor and client using what is seen and heard via video to communicate (NBCC, 2007, p. 3).

Bonnie J. Miller-McLemore

25

CHILDHOOD STUDIES
AND PASTORAL COUNSELING[1]

Over the past 2 decades, childhood studies has emerged as a recognized area of academic research bridging several disciplines, similar to programs in gender or race studies. Its appearance is especially prominent in social sciences such as sociology and anthropology. But interest has also arisen within humanities such as art history, literature, and philosophy. In the past decade, childhood studies has even earned a place in the study of religion, becoming a new program unit in the American Academy of Religion (AAR) in 2002, for example, and receiving attention from scholars across a number of disciplines in religious studies.

Scholars in religion, however, have been late in coming to the table (see Miller-McLemore, 2006a). Some regard children as less than respectable subject matter. This is illustrated in the evaluation of such studies by the AAR. When the new program unit of Childhood Studies and Religion sought AAR renewal in 2005–2006, one of the concerns raised by the program committee was the unit's proximity to what the committee described as normative, Christian, and practical interests. Although traits such as normative, Christian, and practical may sound like valid concerns for those engaged in pastoral counseling, they raise red flags for many scholars in religion. Behind such labels lie deeper anxieties about narrow, subjective, confessional, and ministerial biases creeping into academic scholarship in religion. The presumption on the part of program unit committee members seems to be that studying children means lowering one's academic standards and promoting parochial agendas. Even though this judgment seemed to be a gross misperception to those responsible for the unit's programming who took special care to include a range of religious perspectives and scholarly disciplines in their planning, it captures the general anxiety and prejudice that surround the topic of children in religious studies. Children have been misperceived as a low-status subject of little theoretical interest except to those in professional or practical areas such as religious education or pastoral care. Meanwhile, however, even scholars in religious education and pastoral specialists such as chaplains have shown less interest in children than others presume they possess (Lester, 1985, pp. 13–16; Miller-McLemore, 2006c).

This benign neglect has consequences for pastoral counselors who may unknowingly adopt a similar attitude, especially if educated in institutions where such a view prevails. Pastoral counselors may also be unaware of new publications in this area. If the 2001 publication of *The Child in Christian Thought*, spearheaded by Marcia Bunge, marks the advent of childhood studies in religion, then over a decade of scholarship has accrued since Bunge's edited collection. Significant research has occurred, in other words, since classical mid- to late 20th-century works such as Erik Erikson's *Childhood and Society* (1950), Ana-Marie Rizzuto's *The Birth of the Living God* (1979), and James Fowler's *Stages of Faith* (1981) became the primary resources on children, development, and religion.

Pastoral counselors are justified in asking, "What is so distinctive about childhood studies and why does it matter?" After all, the books I just named foreshadow today's burgeoning enterprise of childhood studies, and pastoral counselors have already incorporated their ideas. Although most overviews of childhood studies fail to credit Erikson, Rizzuto, or Fowler, their obvious investment in children played a fundamental role in the creation of a formal enterprise called *childhood studies*. Sigmund Freud, an important figure in pastoral counseling's history, deserves credit for turning public eyes to children, even though his primary interest was not children per se but the relevance of their sexual and emotional experiences for adult pathology (e.g., Freud, 1905/1962). Via Freud and his legacy, pastoral counselors already understand the importance of childhood for adult development, the impact of trust in infancy on adult faith, the influence of parents on God imagery, the connections between early transitional objects and adult ritual, and the progression of faith from concrete to abstract imagery. Has childhood studies really added all that much to the understandings pastoral counselors already have?

This chapter argues that distinct advances have occurred over the past 2 decades that are worthy of greater engagement by the pastoral counseling community. I chart some of the developments and characteristic features in the social sciences and theological studies. I envision my account as largely a research report, designed for those who might benefit from the knowledge but lack the time to analyze this terrain. A good deal of my argument therefore lies in recounting insights within the growing literature itself, which I believe have important implications for pastoral counseling and care, a topic to which I return in the concluding sections. However, I suggest that this body of research is distinguished by two major reconstructions about which pastoral counselors should be informed more generally: Childhood studies in general has consistently promoted children as active agents in families and other social institutions. And childhood studies in religion has shown that children's religious faith is shaped as much by routine practices as by verbal confession of belief claims by parents and religious authorities.

Although I do not spend much time describing my own research, these two transformations are reflected in my books, with *Let the Children Come* (Miller-McLemore, 2003) focused on the dramatic cultural reconstruction of children under way and the question of what Christianity has to contribute and *In the Midst of Chaos* (Miller-McLemore, 2006b) devoted to tracing how religion forms children and children form parents in the midst of the most routine practices of everyday life. I came to the study of children through experiences of birthing and raising three boys, and in another essay (Miller-McLemore, 2011), I identify an earlier book, *Also a Mother* (Miller-McLemore, 1994), as the first in this trilogy. In fact, acute recognition 2 decades ago that few feminist theologians, Christian or otherwise, had addressed the dilemmas of work and family led me to suspend my own pastoral counseling practice and turn to the project on mothers. I felt a real need to give voice to such issues, especially as they have taken shape within the Christian tradition (a perspective that I continue in this chapter), and then the demands of teaching and research kept me from returning to clinical work. I continue to miss engaging in counseling as an intimate and tangible form of healing. But I was troubled then and still find disturbing how women and children are idealized *and* devalued all at once. This chapter is one more effort to correct distortions and expand understanding, and I am grateful for the opportunity to return to the realm of pastoral counseling another way.

CHILDHOOD STUDIES IN THE SOCIAL SCIENCES

One of the most important distinctions between modern psychology and today's childhood studies is the portrait of children themselves. Although some people borrow a phrase from an important book by Swedish social theorist Ellen Key (1909) to designate the past century as the "century of the child," those in childhood studies raise questions about the approach to children characteristic of much 20th-century research in the social sciences, especially psychology. As Key hoped, many Western societies devoted new resources to children's welfare and development. This coincided with increased research on children in education and the social sciences. Child psychology grew especially after World War II. Child experts eventually included not only psychologists and psychiatrists but also pediatricians and educators. Pastoral counselors themselves benefited from these advances and sometimes included children among their clientele.

However, according to Martin Woodhead (2004), a professor in a new childhood studies program in the United Kingdom, there are problems with how these studies "objectify 'the child' as subject of processes of development, socialization or acculturation" (p. x). In his Foreword to *An Introduction to Childhood Studies*, he suggests that childhood studies emerged out of "frustration" with "narrow versions of 'the child' offered by traditional academic discourses" (p. x). Psychology is often held up as the most culpable. In a flagship essay contrasting the old paradigm with the emerging one, Alan Prout and Allison James (1997) use Piaget's (1965) Kantian typology built around modern notions of rationality and universality as an illustration of this problem. His theory of cognitive development assumes "progression from simplicity to complexity of thought, from irrational to rational behavior" as natural and widespread (Prout & James, 1997, p. 10). It also focuses on what children are becoming, their apprenticeship into adulthood, rather than on what they already are. According to Prout and James, this view was uncritically absorbed into other disciplines such as sociology, perpetuating an unfortunate binary, described by sociologist Robert Mackay (1973), between the "immature, irrational, incompetent, asocial [and] accultural" child and the "mature, rational, competent, social and autonomous" adult (as cited by Prout & James, 1997, p. 13), almost as if children and adults were instances of "two different . . . species" (p. 13).

Over and over, in different words but consistent fashion, scholars in childhood studies insist that there is no such cohesive reality as "the child." In fact, there is a problem, according to James (2004), when "a singular term comes to represent an entire category of people" (p. 33). In place of the static universal type studied in abstraction from context in the dominant paradigm, childhood is described as a social construction. French historian (and not coincidentally a friend of Michel Foucault) Philippe Ariès's *Centuries of Childhood* (1962) is pivotal here. Although historians have since debated the veracity of his argument for the modern "invention" of childhood, contending that people of earlier periods did indeed have such a conception as well as endearing connections to children (see de Mause, 1976; Pollock, 1983), his larger insight that historical periods differ in their constructions has endured. Even though childhood is demarcated by biological immaturity across cultures, it is now seen as a "product of culture," an institution created by society that varies considerably "across time and place" (Kehily, 2004, p. 7). In her introduction to the new field, Mary Jane Kehily (2004) describes the "recognition that there may be different ways of being a child and different kinds of childhood" as especially "important" (p. 7). I would go a step further and describe this as a crucial turning point in understandings of children.

The view of childhood as socially constructed is closely linked to a second feature—that children should be seen as actors in their own right, constructing and determining their social lives and the lives and societies around them, rather than "passive subjects" (Prout & James, 1997, p. 8). In line with other movements to empower marginalized groups, a primary intent is to "give a voice" to children as "people . . . and not just . . . receptacles of adult teaching" (Hardman, 1973, p. 87, cited by Prout & James, 1997, p. 8). The problem in the previous century "of the child" therefore is not "an absence of interest." There are abundant studies. The problem is children's "silence" as active contributors (Prout & James, 1997, p. 7).

The novelty today, as James (2004) states, "lies in the ways the academy currently engages with children" (p. 26). Scholars increasingly turn to an ethnographical methodology that grounds theory in children's own words, actions, and thoughts. They are repeatedly dubbed "agents." Childhood is not a stage to be outgrown or a space where adult socialization and religious rituals get enacted or adult pathology develops. Nor is adulthood all about forming children. Children also form adults and the institutions in which they live. As editors Pufall and Unsworth (2004a) remark, research in childhood studies "demonstrates unmistakably that children not only have minds of their own but also have values, aspirations, and societies of their own" (p. xi).

These three features—the social construction of childhood, their agency as active participants in creating knowledge, and the usefulness of ethnography in hearing their voices—are among those listed by Prout and James (1997, p. 8) as part of the emerging paradigm. There is a notable preference in this new kind of analysis for sociology, seen as already sensitive to culture, over psychology, characterized as particularly essentialist in its views of children and their stages of development. But traditional sociology also comes under scrutiny for having ignored and misperceived children, and psychology is seen by some scholars as a discipline capable of being reshaped under the guidance of the new paradigm (see Walkerdine, 2004; Woodhead, 1997). It is also interesting that the primary characteristics of childhood studies cohere with traits common to the rise of postmodernity—questions about objectivity and universality, sensitivity to marginalized groups, promotion of agency and voice, awareness of the relationship between power and knowledge, and appreciation for everyday experiences and ethnography.

I lift up one more attribute that Prout and James (1997) include—the "reconstructive" dimension of childhood studies or what I would call its inevitably normative dimension—and two items they overlook but that are often presumed—the need for advocacy and interdisciplinarity. Although Woodhead (1997) characterizes the impetus behind childhood studies as primarily intellectual—in my words a *concern about proper conceptualization of children*—I think the impetus also arises out of practical and political concerns about *the need to act* on children's behalf. This awareness puts social scientists into an awkward bind, however, given the nonnormative intent of modern science. So, for example, Prout and James observe that although social scientists "seek only to understand the world as it is," their seemingly neutral "findings" are "nevertheless absorbed back into . . . and become constitutive" of the very societies which they study (p. 21). That is, the social sciences not only study childhood but also contribute to childhood's cultural construction. As they recognize, the "detached scholar" is displaced. But they are unsure about "what will replace" this modality

(p. 29). Their own answer is strikingly tentative: Scholars should proceed "cautiously" (p. 21), adopting a "degree of analytical detachment . . . whilst at the same time not denying responsibility" (p. 30). Because children rarely organize on their own behalf, how can adults do so without foisting adult presumptions on children? Hence the need for caution. They are less sure about assuming responsibility. So, most tellingly, they begin their landmark volume, which marks the advent of childhood studies in the social sciences in the 1990s, with comments on war, famine, poverty, and abuse. But in the end, they are more interested in the theoretical question of how escalating awareness of these problems has challenged conventional views of childhood than in addressing the problems themselves.

Recent scholars are more forthright about the need for political advocacy. In editing her *Introduction to Childhood Studies*, Kehily (2004), for example, makes "policy perspectives" the third section of a three-part overview of the emerging field (the other two are "historical approaches" and "sociocultural approaches"). Likewise, the editors and contributors to *Rethinking Childhood* identify addressing children's welfare as a primary motivation. Pufall and Unsworth (2004a) describe the "seed" behind the book's inception as the "rapidly growing triad of abuse, neglect, and poverty afflicting children in our society" and a Coalition for Children created by students and faculty on the campus of Smith College (p. ix). Authors of individual chapters suggest public policies and practices "that are in the best interest of children" (Pufall & Unsworth, 2004b, p. 4).

Rethinking Childhood illustrates one further noteworthy attribute of the field—the heightened value and necessity of interdisciplinary interchange. Studying children in a narrow fashion, "under the methodological glass of each particular academic discipline" (Pufall & Unsworth, 2004a, p. x), makes it almost impossible to respond adequately to the problems children face. Children suffer if only studied in disciplinary isolation and detachment from social implications. The *interdisciplinarity* toward which Pufall and Unsworth (2004b, pp. 7–8) strive differs from a more limited *multidisciplinary* approach in its effort to avoid academic jargon, resist intellectual territoriality, and work toward active listening across disciplines.

CHILDHOOD STUDIES IN RELIGION

At the turn of the 21st century, several journals in religion recognized the growing importance of childhood studies and published issues devoted to the subject.[2] In one of the more distinguished journals, Marcia Bunge (2006) and John Wall (2006) offer overviews. Their essays are useful here in grasping what is happening in religion.

Both articles are a goldmine of bibliographical resources with extensive footnotes listing representative publications. As they both recognize, other scholars have lamented the "undeveloped" state of childhood studies in religion. For Catholic historian Robert Orsi (2002), the oversight is dire because of its direct implications for clergy sexual abuse. A scholarly and priestly community unable to imagine the reality of children's lives leads to travesty. Projection of adult fantasies on children, whether about their innocence, depravity, or innate holiness, "renders them porous to adult need and desire" (Orsi, 2002, p. 29). Ethicist Todd Whitmore (1997) is equally alarmed by the colonization of childhood by a capitalist market bent on exploiting desire. Children face unique suffering in a world where money dictates worth and people are reduced to consumers, products, or burdens. Do religious traditions have any "countervailing understanding[s]" to offer, he asks, comparable to the extensive Catholic teachings, say, on just war (p. 175)?

Given the state of the world's children—the influence of poverty, poor health care, sex and drug trafficking, disintegrating families and communities, advertising and media enticements—Wall (2006) also wonders why theological ethicists have "played such a limited role in social debates," dealing instead with children, if at all, as a subcategory of other issues like abortion or marriage (p. 524). Bunge (2006) rues the condescension among religion scholars who see the subject as "beneath" them or "suitable only for practitioners or educators" (p. 552). Wall is interested in how childhood studies transform the enterprise of ethics itself, a theme he develops into a book-length argument (Wall, 2010a), whereas Bunge is a historical theologian intent on capturing the best that religious traditions have to offer. Modeling his effort after similar movements among feminists and environmentalists, Wall (2006) dubs his approach "childist," a term that has not yet caught on but is still suggestive of the "fundamental rethinking" (p. 524) needed. In this regard, his work is more creative and constructive than Bunge's descriptive and summative efforts. He uses religious and philosophical insights to critique secular assumptions about children's agency, for example. Inversely, he uses the sciences to show how theological ethics has misunderstood dynamics of poverty. At the same time, Bunge has a richer sense of the resources in Christianity and has been especially instrumental in bringing scholars together from diverse contexts to contribute to edited collections (see Bunge, 2001, 2008, 2012) and in creating structures that undergird the emerging field of childhood studies in religion, such as the AAR program unit.

Wall is especially gifted in creating typologies and offering his own improvement on previous paradigms. He divides the evolution of childhood studies into four approaches (Wall, 2006, pp. 525–528) with "developmental-psychological" (e.g., Freud, Erikson, Piaget) and "family-psychological" (e.g., family systems and marriage education therapists) on one side of the "greatest fault line" in the literature, with their more biological and universalist leanings, whereas two other approaches, "politico-sociological" (e.g., James and Prout) and "family-sociological" (e.g., David Popenoe), which focus on children "as they participate in and are constructed by their diverse cultures and societies," stand on the other side. In turning a two-phase development into four parts and including scholars such as Judith Wallerstein (1989) and Popenoe (1988), who actually self-identify more with the marriage movement than with childhood studies, Wall stretches the umbrella farther than I would. Despite what seems to me like a slight misreading of such scholars, Wall does recognize a diverse body of social scientists who share an anxiety about the state of today's children.

Wall (2006) also provides a useful typology for religion and ethics. He names three approaches: "communitarians" such as Stanley Hauerwas and Jean Bethke Elshtain, who believe children need stronger communities that resist modern pressures; "liberationists" such as Pamela Couture and Adrian Thatcher, who find science more useful in returning voice and power to children; and "progressive familists" such as Don Browning and Lisa Cahill, who promote children's inclusion but also recommend strengthening families and parenting (Wall, 2006, pp. 529–533).[3] He uses directional metaphors to elucidate distinctions among these groups based on where they locate authority: top-down (tradition and communities shape children), bottom-up (sciences and children deserve voice), and circular (mutual interaction between tradition and science, parents and children). He returns to this typology in his book where he adds to the top-down and bottom-up groups a "horizontal" or "developmental" approach of those who believe that children only progressively realize their potential over time (Fowler would be a good example here). This approach turns out to be "just as morally ambiguous" as the others (Wall, 2010a, p. 25). That is, in his view, each approach has strengths and limitations, and his intent in both his essay and book is to fashion a more adequate postmodern model that puts "children themselves at the center" (Wall, 2006, p. 533). When he does so, he discovers that the hermeneutical circle is decentered or asymmetrical. That is, the irreducible "otherness" of children turns the circle into an ellipse that orbits around "not one point but two: the interpreter and the interpreter's irreducible other" (p. 537). Children are the same as adults *and* an irreducible mystery, and this is their gift to adult understanding. They "must be allowed to disrupt and constantly open up even the interpretive assumptions adults bring to them" (p. 537). In the end, they reveal the asymmetry of the love demand—that moral responsibility requires "superabundance toward others in the service of realizing a common humanity" (p. 547). In this, children are "morality's greatest test" (p. 547). He illustrates by showing the limitations of the modern ideal, so uncritically promoted by many scholars in childhood studies, of children as agents. Yes, children have influence, but they are also acted on by many forces. Their unique vulnerabilities impel distinct adult response and care.

Whereas Wall stands out for his typologies and constructive agenda, Bunge excels in providing comprehensive synopsis of neglected themes. She organizes the introduction to her first edited collection (2001) and other articles around an itemization of subjects she believes scholars in religion need to address. Here's an example of the range of relevant religious issues from her overview article in the *Journal of Religion*:

> the nature and status of children; distinctions between boys and girls; the duties and responsibilities of children; the role of children in religious practices and rituals; parental obligations to children; the role of religious communities and the state in protecting children and providing them with the resources they need to thrive; the moral and spiritual formation of children; the role of children in the spiritual maturation of adults; children's rights; and adoption. (Bunge, 2006, pp. 551–552)

Like Wall, she urges people to adopt what she calls the " 'lens' of the child" to see theology anew (Bunge, 2006, pp. 555, 574). However, she reveals an ideational bias that presumes new ideas will automatically translate into practice, changing how families and societies advance children's well-being, something that has not exactly been the case in the past. Nonetheless, her leadership in projects covering major bodies of knowledge (e.g., classic theologians, scriptural texts, the three Abrahamic faith traditions) gives her precisely the bird's-eye view necessary to distill what she describes as "at least six important and almost paradoxical perspectives on children" (p. 562) that offset both the reductive views of Christianity as harboring only punitive attitudes and the simplistic or harmful views in culture at large. In the tradition, children are seen in at least the following diverse ways:

- Gifts of God and sources of joy
- Sinful creatures and moral agents
- Developing beings that need instruction and guidance
- Fully human and made in God's image
- Models of faith and sources of revelation
- Orphans, neighbors, and strangers in need of justice and compassion

She says these divergent images must be viewed "together instead of in isolation" (p. 563), thereby underscoring the tradition's complexity on children.

Bunge (2006) also lifts up something called "child theology," a confusing term she does not completely clarify. She describes its origin and some of its practices but offers little critical analysis of its history or orientation beyond what one can learn from its website (see Child Theology Movement, n.d.-b). The term appears to have been used initially by Keith White, a pastor and tutor at Spurgeon's College in the United Kingdom, and then further developed after sparking interest at an international consultation of Christians working with at-risk children in 2000. Now known as the Child Theology Movement, groups of scholars, educators, youth ministers, relief agency leaders, and so forth have continued to gather biannually in Penang, Malaysia, with the intent of "putting the child in the midst of any and every theological issue" to refashion "the whole of Christian theology," words Bunge uses that also appear in various forms on the movement's website (Bunge, 2006, p. 570; see also Child Theology Movement, n.d.-a). The intent is to rethink doctrine and practice from a child's perspective, thus influencing those who seldom approach belief and ministry from this vantage point.

How "child theology" differs from "theologies of children," which seem to include all scholars beyond this movement who also attempt to reconceptualize the methods and substance of theology, is unclear. This is a distinction Bunge (2006, p. 572) uses but does not elucidate clearly enough. Judging from the website, child theology receives structural support from those in the United Kingdom but sustains deep international connections and commitments, especially in the Southern Hemisphere. The language on the website reflects an evangelical orientation, as does a rather flat reading of Jesus putting "a child in the centre of the disciples when they were having a theological argument" as the movement's rationale (Child Theology Movement, n.d.-b, para. 6). As best I can discern, the nonprofit organization serves largely as an umbrella for strategy-based ministries, fostering networking and alliances, with recent efforts to enhance its intellectual foundations beyond newsletters and reports.

Bunge (2006, pp. 572–573) also attempts a one-paragraph summation of recent constructive Christian theologies of children. She mentions books by David Jensen (2005), Kristin Herzog (2005), Marshall and Parvis (2004), and one of my own books (Miller-McLemore, 2003). But it quickly becomes apparent that her one-sentence depictions of publications cannot do justice to either the individual arguments or the magnitude of production that has occurred. Nor can I begin to identify, much less expound on this body of work. At risk of repeating what I have just criticized Bunge for doing, I think it worth expanding her list just to give a sense of the immense literature that has appeared within a 10-year span. Besides those she names, Joyce Ann Mercer (2005), Pamela Couture (2000, 2007), Mary Doyle Roche (2009), Martin Marty (2007), and John Wall (2010a) are among those who have also written constructive theological books. The specific emphasis of each contribution is apparent in their book titles and subtitles. A careful analysis of these works would have real merit. I know of only one such effort by the author of *Godly Play* Jerome Berryman (1995) found in two of his other publications—a *Religious Studies Review* essay (2007) and a chapter of a survey book (2009, pp. 170–195). But I would assess these attempts as less than satisfying. His coverage and summation is limited and his evaluation muddled. In the words of reviewer John Wall (2010b), Berryman's reading is "cursory," "light on historical analysis," skewed toward Protestantism and male scholars "despite [their] coming later to the field," and essentialist in its depiction of the child (p. 3).

Even if we had a good review essay on constructive theological books, this would not begin to cover recent scholarship. There are publications on practical ministries of education and care (e.g., Davis, 2001; Dykstra, Cole, & Capps, 2007; Parker, 2003; Wigger, 2003), sociological studies (e.g., Bales, 2005; Lytch, 2004; Smith,

2005), biblical and historical research (e.g., Bakke, 2005; Murphy, 2013), interreligious exploration (e.g., Browning & Bunge, 2009; Browning & Miller-McLemore, 2009; Bunge, 2012), tools for research on children and religion (e.g., Bales, 2011), and multiple explorations of children's spirituality, including synthetic collections (e.g., Yust, Johnson, Sasso, & Roehlkepartain, 2006). Scholarly attention to children also appears in literature on families more broadly (e.g., Rubio, 2010) and on subissues within childhood studies such as adoption (e.g., Stevenson-Moessner, 2003) and divorce (e.g., Flesberg, 2008). Suffice it to say that rarely has one thematic topic attracted such intense study during such an abbreviated period of time. Even though I do not expect constructive theologies to continue appearing at the current pace, I doubt productivity more generally has reached its climax, particularly as new issues arise and as scholars from other religious traditions besides Christianity make additional contributions (as a start, see authors and bibliography in Browning & Miller-McLemore, 2009; Yust et al., 2006).

One last concern that I would expect among pastoral counselors: Strangely absent in the otherwise fairly comprehensive overviews of Bunge (2006) and Wall (2006) is commentary on literature on child abuse and religion. Wall does not mention this at all, and Bunge does so parenthetically. She is actually more worried about an inverse problem—that the analysis of abuse has swamped the discussion and that this has misled people into thinking negatively about Christianity, assuming that claims about original sin and child discipline are all Christianity has said on children (see Bunge, 2001, pp. 4–5; Bunge, 2006, pp. 560–561).

Unfortunately, disregard for children as a subject of study *and* religious tolerance for their abuse go hand in hand, as Orsi (2002) argues. To omit mention or downplay the significance of the problem and religion's influence seems like a serious oversight and more so in light of pastoral counseling practice, where consequences of abuse for mental health are so obvious. An extensive pastoral literature exists around child abuse and religion, including in particular pastoral theologian Donald Capps's (1995) book *The Child's Song*. Perhaps Wall and Bunge considered this a subject area all its own or, inversely, too narrow and focused to warrant inclusion in the emerging arena of childhood studies. But the two bodies of scholarship have a more complicated connection than appears in the overviews. As Orsi argues, the clergy abuse crisis is not only about bodily urges, celibacy, or immorality; it is about a crisis of theology—the "kind of stories that have been told about children in Christian cultures over time" (p. 27; e.g., as innocent or depraved, innately spiritual or in need of adult authority) and their negative consequences. The solution is to "find ways of making children more authentically . . . present" and "giving them greater voice" (p. 29).

RELIGION AND CHILDREN

So far, I have examined scholarly developments but spoken only indirectly about children's religious experience and the way religion itself is characterized. To gain a sense of some new insights in the study of religion, I want to look briefly at three books outside theology proper in the social scientific study of religion (psychology, sociology, and anthropology, respectively). When I teach a class on children and religion, I use these books to help students understand children from a variety of fresh perspectives or at least to consider how one might go about gaining such an understanding. Of the three authors, only Susan Rigley Bales (2005) explicitly situates her work in relationship to recent developments in childhood studies. Trained in religious studies and sociology of religion, she uses ethnography to enter into a close study of children's everyday experience and perceptions. Robert Coles's (1990) research precedes the more formal advent of the field. But as a result, he shows how 20th-century psychology played a key role in its development and how his own insights are limited by a largely cognitive view of religion. Robert Wuthnow (1999) is an established scholar in an area beyond childhood studies—sociology of American religion—but his examination of "growing up religious" makes an interesting contribution nonetheless. These scholars take us inside children's lives from three different angles—individual and group interview (Coles), adult memory and storytelling (Wuthnow), and ethnographical study of three congregations over a defined time period (Bales). Hence, they each give unique answers to one of the challenging questions in childhood studies: How does one gain knowledge of a population that often lacks the power to speak for itself, especially when it comes to religious needs and ideas?

Coles is a child psychiatrist-turned-field-researcher, influenced by Erikson, Anna Freud, and post-Freudian object relation theorists who see religion as potentially a positive force. We gain two immediate lessons from his work: how to listen to children and the richness of their religious ideation. He is brutally forthright about his own blinders in truly seeing children. This seems surprising from someone well trained as an analyst with a fine reputation for publications based on hours and hours of interviews. Indeed, his book on *The Spiritual Life of Children* (Coles, 1990) is the last in a trilogy on their political (Coles, 1986b) and moral lives (Coles, 1986a), which follows a Pulitzer Prize–winning five-book series *Children of Crisis* (Coles, 1967–1977)—a 30-year period of writing on children all told.

Yet Coles (1990) confesses that only provocative interchanges with Anna Freud sent him back to his field notes to discover what he had missed. When it comes to children and religion, he is powerfully shaped, as are most psychiatrists and psychologists, by residual Freudian biases against religion. Even if many therapists no longer see religion as wish fulfillment or a defense against aggressive and sexual desire, fewer are inclined to take children's religious views seriously.

As Coles (1990) tells it, it is the 6- to 12-year-old children who set him straight, beyond anything he or Anna or even an apparently astute supervisor (Abraham Fineman) could anticipate. Connie, an 8-year-old girl whom he had treated for 2 years, calls him on what he describes as his "wanton imperialist" assumptions caricaturing her religious "delusions." She finally blurts out, "You're not interested in my religion, only my 'problems'" (Coles, 1990, pp. 12–13). Stopped in his tracks, he realizes he has repeatedly disregarded her attempts to let him know more about her Catholic piety. When Coles follows Fineman's advice—"Why not let *her* educate *us* about her Church? [original emphasis]"—Coles discovers her "religious life was far more many-sided than I had been prepared to admit" (pp. 14–15). Her symptoms show evidence not of conflict but of "high aspirations and yearnings sustained by a faithful vision" (p. 18) with religion as an essential dimension.

Coles (1990) models precisely the kind of demeanor one should adopt in approaching children, a refined version of what Freud calls "closely hovering attention" and a foretaste of the mantra now common within childhood studies that the child is the authority. "Let the children help you with their ideas on the subject," Anna herself suggests when Coles is unsure whether to go ahead with his project (as cited by Coles, 1990, p. xvi). So he pushes years of analytic practice of listening to a new level. He gives example after example of what he describes as a "phenomenological acceptance of the immediate" (p. 21). Sometimes this is fostered by not rushing to fill the space. In a Boston Sunday school class, he seems uncannily able to suspend his own plan when the 7-year-olds take over the discussion of what church means for them (pp. 27–35). His vivid account of interview and classroom conversations is sprinkled with comments such as, "We both reflected in silence for ten or fifteen seconds" or "I fell into a silence that lasted long enough for us to know that we had exhausted the subject" (pp. 81–82). In a fourth-grade art history class, he learns "to ask nothing, to say nothing" when a hush falls over the children on viewing a 19th-century portrait of a doctor with a sick girl (p. 110). He knows from experience the children will offer up more than anything he might anticipate.

In Coles's (1990) view, linear developmental categories of "cumulative cognitive awareness" (p. 38) based on what children display when presented with a hypothetical situation are insufficient to measure their resourcefulness if listened to in their own good time. Different from some psychological approaches and most theological analysis, direct observation precedes theoretical classification. Learning happens through prolonged encounters, weekly visits, the development of trust, and an acute sensitivity to context (he learns the hard way that Hopi children will say more in their homes than in a school environment). Coles also makes use of open-ended methods, such as asking children to draw pictures and talk about them. He discovers that they are "as anxious to make sense of [life] as those of us who are farther along in the time allotted us" (p. xvi).

Perhaps reflecting his contextual limitations, Coles (1990) never questions his own male image of God (always capitalized as "He") and what seems like an unquestioned chauvinist reliance on his wife and kids as assistants. But a more serious limitation—where he might have benefited from childhood studies—is apparent when we turn to Wuthnow (1999) and Bales (2005). Even though Coles has moved beyond Freudian interpretations of religion, he still harbors a modernist view. Religion is about cerebral belief in God, examined by asking kids how they picture God's face, hear God's voice, or deal with conceptual frameworks such as salvation. Therefore, Coles assumes he can study religion outside its context. Besides comments about classrooms, hospitals, or Native American reservations, readers have minimal sense of where the children live, where they worship, or what familial and social forces shape their lives. Rather than understanding spirituality and religion as inextricably intermixed and embedded in particular contexts, spirituality is set off sharply from religion, as if one can actually isolate "children as soulful" from their practice of "this or that religion" (p. xviii).

By contrast, Wuthnow (1999) shows how deeply seeded religion is in everyday life. As an empirical sociologist, he designs national surveys and examines biographies and other research on growing up religious as a preliminary step to the qualitative research that lies at the heart of his work. His study of growing up religious centers on semistructured interviews conducted by a team of scholars over a 3-year period with 200 adults chosen through quotas and a snowball technique to foster diversity in age, gender, ethnicity, geographic location, education, and religion. The aim is to ask "ordinary people to talk at length" to determine how they "conceive of their religious upbringing . . . what seems memorable and significant to them" (Wuthnow, 1999, p. xxxi).

Wuthnow (1999) does not study children themselves, in other words. But he is greatly interested in childhood experiences of religion understood in retrospect. He even contends that learning about children's faith requires just the kind of evaluative perspective that adulthood lends—a view that is quite different from current efforts in childhood studies to listen to children instead of adults. In his words, "Accounts of childhood can only be given by people who are no longer children" because they are able to make judgments about "what is actually of value" in such memories (pp. xxxiv–xxxv). Moreover, childhood religiosity is not simply left behind but ripens with age and lives on into the present. Religious upbringing is "part of the continuing experience of adults," not "an event occurring only in childhood." In fact, people who make an effort to reflect on pivotal faith experiences "felt they were able to live a more fully integrated life as a result" (p. xxxvii).

Growing up Religious is chocked full of narratives of "embedded practices" that connect people to those around them—holiday customs, home and congregational rituals, bedtime and table prayers, family bibles and spiritual artifacts, particular foods, and daily routines. These narratives reflect what I see as Wuthnow's most impressive finding, one that stands in contrast to Coles's research: Growing up religious has as much to do with habits and routines as it does with existential reflection on the meaning of existence or God's reality. In fact, few interviewees "remembered being especially curious about metaphysical questions as children" (Wuthnow, 1999, p. xxxvii), although Coles's (1990) research partially disproves this. Like Coles, Wuthnow finds "little evidence" among his interviewees for progress through cognitive stages toward a more sophisticated adult faith (p. xxxvii). Spirituality is fluid, dynamic, and journey-like. But in contrast to Coles, Wuthnow sees religion as "much more deeply rooted in our personal histories, in our families, and congregations, than in anything else" (p. xi). He distinguishes his research from studies over the past half-century that focus on children as "mental machines." Children assimilate religion "more by osmosis than by instruction" (p. xxxvi–xxxvii).

In this vein, Wuthnow (1999) makes several fascinating observations: "Having the Bible read to them as children is not nearly as good a predictor of feeling that one's family took religion seriously as having seen parents reading the Bible themselves" (p. 12). Or, again, "the act of praying was more important than the content" (p. xxxvii). People remember "short simple, rote prayers learned by heart and repeated almost automatically" rather than specific petitions, teachings on the nature of prayer or anything more elaborate (p. 8). They are also "deeply influenced by the pictures and other representations of the sacred that were in their immediate environment," including Bibles, jewelry, and statues (p. 18). In a national study, bible reading and table grace are cited as greater factors in religion's importance than Sunday school (p. 80). And if they did attend Sunday school, being there "was more memorable than anything they may have been taught" (p. xxxvii).

All this is not to negate the value of catechetical instruction but to underscore religion as a "way of life." Over and over, it is clear that material culture and social connections matter: candles, stained-glass windows, clothes and routines in preparation for worship, "ritual" family meals, congregational meals, and congregational picnics. Indeed, children absorb quite a bit more than most people ever consider simply by "staring at the altar, the paintings, and the stained glass windows week after week" (Wuthnow, 1999, p. 70).

Even more radically than Wuthnow, Bales (2005) also challenges what adults think children learn through adult-led classes.[4] She would disagree with Wuthnow that talking to adults about their childhood memories provides the best perspective. She sets her book apart not just from developmental views, which see children as part of a group or category rather than as distinct individuals, but also from efforts to understand children retrospectively. Memory is notoriously inaccurate as a source for reconstructing history and experience. Distinct from both Wuthnow and Coles, Bales accords significant space to what she has learned from childhood studies, although she identifies Coles as a "notable exception" (p. 13) from the tendency to dismiss children's religious experience (and whose example she follows in using drawings to engage children). Her work is an instance of the broader effort in childhood studies to return agency and voice to children. She adopts ethnographic methods that take her into three Roman Catholic parishes, a predominantly African American congregation and Anglo and Latino congregations that share worship space. She spends time observing children and adults in all three settings as they participate in faith formation classes, retreats, and rehearsals in preparation for First Communion, during the Mass itself, and in the aftermath. Her study includes interviews and participant observation.

Although one would think that people would have wondered what children think of their First Communion, scholars have not pursued the question. There is plenty of literature on the Eucharist's role in the rite of initiation. But "why . . . [are] the voices of the primary participants . . . , the children, not included in the scholarship?" (Bales, 2005, p. 2). Bales discovers "that children have their own revealing interpretations . . . that differ from those of adults" (p. 1). This may not seem all that remarkable since adults often assume children do not listen to them. But by and large, the adults she interviews rarely see children as interpreters themselves, evaluating and even transforming the information they receive. In contrast to the adult aims, children do not absorb official beliefs or see the sacrament as a ritual that draws them into the wider universal Catholic Church. They are more focused on joining their particular family and community, "coming to know Jesus," and enacting the ritual correctly (p. 4).

Of greater interest is a second thesis about how heavily children rely on material, physical, and sensual knowledge to construct their interpretations, a finding that partially agrees with Wuthnow's research. As Bales (2005) states, "Much of the information that they use . . . comes through their sense—taste, sound, and movement—rather than through classroom lectures and workbook exercises alone" (p. 1). Children develop what she calls a "theology of taste" (p. 92), understandings based on heightened preoccupation with how the bread will taste. Ryan, a communicant in the African American congregation, captures the theology "most succinctly when he explains that First Communion is 'about tasting and learning about Jesus'" (p. 99). One child even explains her understanding of transubstantiation through taste, saying that the real bread tastes better than the practice bread (p. 101). They also seem to develop what I would call a "theology of movement." That is, they see their belonging to the church as based as much on action as belief and on their ability to emulate the actions of the community. So they are hypervigilant about movement; they want to teach "their bodies to move as the adults moved during the liturgy" (p. 103). In general, Bales helps us see the value of a central theme in childhood studies: Age deserves to be as important a category of analysis as other commonly recognized categories such as gender and race.

Read together and in conversation with each other, Coles, Wuthnow, and Bales offer fresh insight into children's religious experience. They question previous assumptions about children's inability to grapple with existential and highly theoretical questions and the idea that children move in lock-step fashion through faith stages from concrete to symbolic ideation. Through the eyes of all three scholars, children come alive, revealing just how much children construct their versions of life's meaning and value. Children formulate their own unique theories about God, religion, faith, ritual, and so forth. Bales and Wuthnow also disrupt previous presumptions that being religious largely means cognitive belief in God. Children reveal the powerful and lifelong influence of everyday bodily experience and practices, especially material practices and artifacts that have social meaning or occur in the midst of important social relationships. Belief in God's existence almost seems like a relatively minor detail when religion is viewed through children's experience and eyes. In short, these authors reveal that, whether studied through the retrospective reflection, direct observation, or in-depth interviews, children deserve greater consideration as full participants in religious life.

CALLING FOR A NEW PASTORAL CARE OF CHILDREN

As it turns out, the pastoral counseling community has sources for caring for children within pastoral care literature. Two books by pastoral theologians predate the heyday of childhood studies but anticipate its arguments—Andrew Lester's (1985) *Pastoral Care of Children in Crisis* and Herbert Anderson and Susan Johnson's (1994) *Regarding Children*. Only the latter earns honorary mention in Bunge (2001, p. 6; 2006, p. 556) and Wall's (2006, p. 530) footnotes. But both books made unique contributions. Notably, they begin by lamenting the lack of interest in children. Lester titles his first chapter, "The Pastoral Neglect of Children." During marital crises, medical emergencies, and funerals, ministers often fail to consider children even though they are among those most affected. Lester's students recall life-changing struggles when they were children that went unnoticed by their pastors and congregations. The problem is not insensitivity or dislike but simply lack of awareness, magnified by limits of expertise and time. Western society has idealized children, allowing assumptions about their innocence to obscure their struggles. Children do not communicate their needs in verbal ways typical of adults. Yet, at the same time, they are far more aware of what is happening around them than adults realize, even if children misconstrue the meaning and exaggerate their responsibility (e.g., blaming themselves for a parental fight). People devalue children's constructive contributions in home and church, see them as "women's work," and restrict obligation for them to parents alone. Seminaries do not focus on children and, even more than Lester realizes, awareness of clergy abuse makes pastoral attention to them more complicated. But whatever the causes of neglect, the consequences are twofold: Few pastors give "*systematic attention*" to children, and those who do feel inadequately informed (Lester, 1985, p. 27).

Anderson and Johnson (1994) are even harsher in their assessment than Lester. On the first page, they say children are in trouble because "adults disdain childhood" (p. 1). Although this seems overstated, they give instances in which disdain is evident— the unimpeded prevalence of gang warfare and domestic abuse, the unquestioned presumption that parents "own" children, the Christian emphasis on breaking a child's will, the perception of childhood as merely a stepping stone to adulthood, and the corresponding view of children as incomplete. Rather than simply an issue within the pastoral office, they locate the problem at the cultural level—the perpetuation of a "*culture of indifference*" (p. 2, emphasis in original). One of their main aims is attitudinal—to "transform the ways we think about children and childhood" (p. 1), hence the book's title, *Regarding Children*. Adequate response involves ideological change within congregations and society, not just within clerical practice. The church itself must become a "sanctuary for childhood" (p. 111) that makes greater effort to welcome children, support parents, forge partnerships, respond to crises, and challenge social indifference. Adults must regard children as people, fully human, even if their emerging potential is not fully realized and, speaking theologically, as capable of "bearing transcendence" (p. 20) through qualities particularly prominent in childhood of dependence, openness, immediacy, and vulnerability.

To my knowledge, although several pastoral theologians like myself have written about children more generally, it has been almost 20 years since a scholar in the discipline has written a book like Lester's on care and counseling. Apart from a book by pediatric chaplain and pastoral counselor Daniel Grossoehme (1999), which is focused on care of ill children, there is a dearth of pastoral care and counseling literature on children. More significant for this chapter, there has been little attempt among pastoral counselors and theologians alike to take into consideration new findings in childhood studies or new challenges, such as social media, when writing on the pastoral needs of children. I hope this chapter will serve as a clarion call on this score.

At least two major reconstructions in childhood studies and religion should inform any such effort. There is a demand to see children as commanding greater agency and meriting inclusion as full participants within families and congregations, respected for the distinct contributions and needs they bring. For pastoral counselors, this raises the question of how to hear children and include them more completely. Unlike other marginalized groups who at least theoretically have the "adult" capacity and right to speak for themselves, counselors need to ensure that children's voices are adequately represented, especially when their very definition as children suggests their vulnerability, dependency, and emerging maturity.

There is also a demand to see religion in fuller ways. Throughout the 20th century, religion was defined flatly in terms of belief. This view is still alive and well among secularists and fundamentalists. One decides in college, for example, that one is no longer a Christian or a Jew (etc.) because one no longer believes in God. Research on religion reveals that such educated dismissal is not as easy as it seems. As known through truism and underscored by research, children are shaped more by what their parents and extended communities *do* as habitual religious or spiritual practices than by anything they *profess* about religion. One can disassociate from belief, but overthrowing religious formation is harder. Moreover, as families and communities are disrupted, scattered, urbanized, and diversified in today's neoliberal capitalistic society, shared religious practices become less cohesive, pervasive, and persuasive.

IMPLICATIONS FOR PASTORAL COUNSELING

What does this mean for pastoral counselors? Plenty of concrete suggestions for counseling lie between the lines of this chapter's exploration of childhood studies. I lift up a few implications in four areas—the first two focused on religion and theology, the second two on listening to children.

First, in this literature, we discover fresh ways to understand and incorporate religion and theology into clinical practice. Listening for religion and pursuing religion's benefits in securing children's welfare means far more than asking about cerebral *belief* in a *divine figure*. It includes wondering about the very materiality of our daily lives and how material religion shapes and forms children in mundane daily life. So, as vividly portrayed in Wuthnow's (1999) account of growing up religious, clinicians need to consider social structures, community practices, and cultural ideologies as well as routine habits, holiday celebrations, household art and artifacts, and other modalities that clutter our lives but often go unrecognized for their impact on religious understanding and healing. Children absorb a great deal from their surroundings, far more than most adults previously assumed. They glean as much from watching adults worship, pray, read the Bible, and engage in social service, for example, as they do from catechetical instruction on any of these acts. Moreover, when we consider religion as a "way of life" rather than merely cognitive doctrinal confession, we recognize that children also have a spiritually transformative impact on parents and other adults who care for them. We assume adults should form children, but we neglect how much children affect adults. So, clinicians interested in understanding the role of religion in the lives of their clients need to focus on both adults and children and their spiritually formative influence on one another.

Attending to religion as more than intellectual assent to belief also means exploring how the best of such "embedded practices" can be strengthened in a changing world to ensure children's welfare within the daily habits of family and social institutions. Despite their problems and limitations, religious communities and traditions have given children meaning, allayed loneliness, offered material support, countered adolescent peer pressure, provided intergenerational relationships, and so forth. The continued presence of religion (and its absence) in children's lives requires clinical sensitivity and attention, especially as religious communities and traditions face the disruptive pressures of today's society. I dare say pastoral counselors have a responsibility to do what they can, even if only in the most limited way, to sustain the vitality of these wider networks of care and to challenge them when they become destructive—for the sake of their clients.

Second, pastoral counselors not only observe religion as practiced by their clients. They also bring their own constructive religious and theological frameworks for understanding children to the clinical context. They need to become more conscious about these frameworks as they overtly and covertly shape clinical practice. Childhood studies suggests that societies construct images of childhood that have evolved over time and place. In Western society in particular, cultural constructions of children have shifted from premodern images of sinful and adult-like children to 18th-century portraits of the naturally innocent child to today's "Knowing child" who blurs the sharp distinction between adult and child (see Higonnet, 1998; Miller-McLemore, 2003). Each of these images has positive *and* adverse consequences for children. In the turnover of cultural imagery, the wider culture has also happily filled in today's picture of who kids are and what they need with problematic notions. So, for example, prevalent images that romanticize children as innocent and hence less capable or that exploit them economically as commodity, consumer, and burden have serious negative consequences and deserve critique by those in clinical practice (see Mercer, 2005; Miller-McLemore, 2003; Roche, 2009; Whitmore, 1997).

Such imagery requires constant evaluation and correction, especially from professionals such as pastoral counselors who are theologically trained and who see the damaging effects of such imagery in the daily lives of their clients. Although many pastoral counselors within mainline and progressive Christian traditions have hesitated to impose an overtly confessional framework on their counseling practice, more evangelical clinicians, such as Kelly Flanagan and Sarah Hall (2014), have led the way in showing how such theological insights in childhood studies might be incorporated more fully to enrich treatment of families and respect for children (rather than distort or bias clinicians toward Christian confession). Religious traditions—Christianity and beyond—abound with alternative images of children that provide greater respect for their full humanity and their moral and spiritual complexity (Browning & Bunge, 2009; Browning & Miller-McLemore, 2009). Theologians and ethicists, such as Bunge (2001), Couture (2000), Mercer (2005), Jensen (2005), Wall (2010a), and myself (Miller-McLemore, 2003), have called for a revitalized Christian perspective on children as gift, task, agent, vulnerable, and so forth. As Orsi (2002) argues in his writing on the Catholic Church and child abuse, we are obligated to think long and hard about the "kind of stories" that we tell "about children in Christian cultures over time"—as innocent or depraved, innately spiritual or in need of adult authority—and their effect on children and adults (p. 29). Pastoral counselors are in a better position to engage in such storytelling and critique than counselors with less background in the study of religion.

Third, in addition to new ways to approach religion as practiced and as theologically and culturally constructed, childhood studies also suggests fresh ways pastoral counselors might listen to children at both a general and a more concrete level. At the most general level, childhood studies demands, in Orsi's (2002) words, that we "find ways of making children more authentically . . . present" and give "them greater voice" (p. 29). Just as other marginalized groups have insisted in recent years, clinical perspectives must begin to include children as subjects, not merely objects of study. They should be seen as full participants and actors with voice, agency, and authentic responsibilities in contributing to the material and spiritual welfare of families and congregations. As Bales (2005) shows so clearly, children have their own "slant," their own "unique interpretations" that are always more than a mere parroting of adults (p. 58). The push to return agency to children requires a comparable change in adults. We must "regard" children *and* ourselves in new ways, to use Anderson and Johnson's (1994) term. As psychologists such as Alice Miller (1986) already made clear a couple decades ago in their work on the dynamics of child abuse, children should never be used as a means to other ends by parents who dote on their achievements to feel better about themselves, for example, or by congregations that want to increase their numbers, companies that want to sell their products, or even clinicians who hope to resolve family problems.

Fourth, and possibly of most interest to clinicians, childhood studies also offers practical advice for counseling. For the most part, Coles (1990) exemplifies therapeutic practice at its best. He opens himself up for supervisory critique, and his supervisors themselves willingly admit how their own psychoanalytic biases have obscured the richness of children's religious ideation. Scientific proclivities have led them to miss the startling ways children process existential questions about life, death, and their own suffering. Abraham Fineman and Anna Freud demonstrate extremely sound supervisory insight when they suggest that Coles let the children "educate *us*" about their religious experience and beliefs (Coles, 1990, p. 14). As Coles makes clear, this means the clinician must make space for children's participation through such basic moves as allowing for silence rather than filling the lull out of discomfort. He uses nonverbal means of communication such as drawing. He notes the even greater impact of context on children and their ability to enter into conversation. Coles had to go to where Hopi children would talk, and that meant getting away from White schools and entering into their homes.

However, earlier clinicians and researchers, such as Coles (1990) and Lester (1985), were not alert to and did not consider the necessary precautions and ethical boundaries when it comes to meeting with children. We are more aware today than ever before about the prevalence of child abuse, its damaging consequences, and the need to establish proper boundaries when caring for children. However, this should not prohibit the effort and need to attend closely to children; in fact, increased respect for children's vulnerability *and* their distinct knowledge have the potential to deepen our connections. Bales (2005) admires Coles and uses some of his methods, such as inviting children to draw, but she offers an interesting correction and advance on how best to listen, shaped by childhood studies. She shares with readers her constant worries about the "many epistemological, practical, and legal" (p. 54) challenges to entering fully into the children's world—the power differential, the need for informed consent, her racial and religious differences, her ambiguous status in her participatory observation as neither teacher nor child, and so forth. She asks herself continually whether she is "doing everything I could to help them understand what my study was about and why I was conducting it" (p. 54). She grants the children as much agency as she can, envisioning them as "partners and teachers" (p. 64) in the project and conveying this understanding to them, inviting them, for example, to create their own pseudonym, an exercise they love. She asks children themselves to give consent or permission (see Appendix B in Bales, 2005, pp. 186–187), even though this surprises the parents, who mostly buy into cultural assumptions about "innocent" children as "passive entities" whom they protect and "who need not have a say in the activities in which they participate" (p. 63). She knows her perspective constrains her ability to understand the children. She admits that she only shows how they *"represent"* their worlds (p. 55), not necessarily how they actually experience their worlds. Her commitment to thinking seriously about all these questions is apparent in her later work on methods in studying children (Bales, 2011). This is the kind and level of thoughtfulness required of clinical work with children.

Finally, recent scholarship in childhood studies suggests that clinicians also need to reconsider widely accepted linear stage theories of cognitive, moral, and faith development that truncate and underestimate the depth and complexity of children's religious thought and engagement. These theories are based on forced situations in which children are presented with a problem to solve. Their reactions in such settings differ markedly from the insights and declarations that emerge in prolonged and open encounters of longer term relationships. Coles (1990) even implies that "developmental" theory has it backward:

> The longer I do this research, the more I realize how much there is to recover from our Sunday school and Hebrew school past, from our nine-year old or ten-year-old life, when the mysteries of the Bible or the Koran lived hard by the mysteries of childhood itself. (p. 37)

Philosopher Gareth Matthews (1994) has also done research with children that confirms this. He suggests that many educational settings actually discourage children's philosophical acuity—their distinctive eye for incongruity and perplexity—and, I would add, their religious imagination (see Miller-McLemore, 2009).

I have identified in these four areas only some of what I hope are the many possible implications that others may see in the new research in childhood studies for the care of children and families in pastoral counseling. In childhood studies, children and religion both receive fresh interpretations, making children more visible and religion more complex. Childhood studies in religion encourage greater intentionality about children's voice, visibility, and inclusion, on one hand, and more nuanced grasp of how religion shapes their lives, on the other hand. As Anderson and Johnson (1994) stated boldly, fostering respect for children is *"one of the fundamental and urgent agendas of our time"* (p. 18, emphasis in original). As childhood studies in religion suggests more generally, fostering respect for religion in all its complexity is an equally important dimension of understanding children.

REFLECTION QUESTIONS

1. How have psychology, religion, and contemporary society mischaracterized and misunderstood children and what are the consequences?
2. What are your own concerns with how people regard children? Do advances in childhood studies respond to these concerns?
3. What "countervailing understandings" of children do religious traditions offer, to use Todd Whitmore's (1997) phrase?

4. How does this chapter reshape your clinical approach to children and religion? In what ways will you listen to children or regard religion differently?
5. How do you anticipate helping adults, families, religious communities, and the wider society regard and treat children in more inclusive and respectful ways?

NOTES

1. This chapter is a reprint, with minor editorial changes and additions, of an essay that appeared in *Sacred Spaces*, Volume 6, 2014, and is used by permission.
2. See, for example, *Dialogue*, 37(3) (Summer 1998); *Theology Today*, 56(4) (January 2000); *Interpretation: A Journal of Bible and Tradition*, 55(2) (April 2001); *New Theology Review: An American Catholic Journal of Ministry*, 14(3) (August 2001); *Conservative Judaism*, 53(4) (Summer 2001); *The Living Pulpit*, 12(4) (2003); *African Ecclesial Review*, 46(2) (2004); and *Journal of Religion*, 86(4) (October 2006). A new online journal in religion on children, *Journal of Childhood and Religion*, was founded in 2010 (see www.childhoodandreligion.com/JCR/Welcome.html, accessed July 15, 2014).
3. I am ambivalent about Wall's putting my work in this latter group, but I leave that debate for another time.
4. I have written elsewhere about my appreciation for Bales's research in understanding how bodies and sensual experience form religious understandings not just for children but also for adults (Miller-McLemore, 2012, 2016). So I keep my comments here more circumscribed.

REFERENCES

Anderson, H., & Johnson, S. W. (1994). *Regarding children: A new respect for childhood and families*. Louisville, KY: Westminster John Knox.

Ariès, P. (1962). *Centuries of childhood: A social history of family life*. New York, NY: Vintage.

Bakke, O. M. (2005). *When children become people: The birth of childhood in early Christianity*. Minneapolis, MN: Fortress.

Bales, S. R. (2005). *When I was a child: Children's interpretations of first communion*. Chapel Hill, NC: University of North Carolina Press.

Bales, S. R. (2011). *The study of children in religions: A methods handbook*. New York, NY: New York University Press.

Berryman, J. W. (1995). *Godly play: An imaginative approach to religious education*. Minneapolis, MN: Augsburg Fortress.

Berryman, J. W. (2007). Children and Christian theology: A new/old genre. *Religious Studies Review*, 33(2), 103–111. doi:10.1111/j.1748-0922.2007.00162.x

Berryman, J. W. (2009). *Children and the theologians: Clearing the way for grace*. New York, NY: Morehouse.

Browning, D. S., & Bunge, M. (Eds.). (2009). *Children and childhood in world religions: Primary sources*. New Brunswick, NJ: Rutgers University Press.

Browning, D. S., & Miller-McLemore, B. J. (Eds.). (2009). *Children and childhood in American religions*. New Brunswick, NJ: Rutgers University Press.

Bunge, M. J. (Ed.). (2001). *The child in Christian thought*. Grand Rapids, MI: Eerdmans.

Bunge, M. J. (2006). The child, religion, and the academy: Developing robust theological and religious understandings of children and childhood. *Journal of Religion*, 86, 549–579. doi: 10.1086/505894

Bunge, M. J. (Ed.). (2008). *The child in the Bible*. Grand Rapids, MI: Eerdmans.

Bunge, M. J. (Ed.). (2012). *Children, adults, and shared responsibilities: Jewish, Christian, and Muslim perspectives*. Cambridge, UK: Cambridge University Press.

Capps, D. (1995). *The child's song: The religious abuse of children*. Louisville, KY: Westminster John Knox.

Child Theology Movement. (n.d.-a). *About us*. Retrieved from http://www.childtheology.org/about-us/

Child Theology Movement. (n.d.-b). *Home*. Retrieved from http://www.childtheology.org/home-2/

Coles, R. (1967–1977). *Children of crisis: A study of courage and fear*. Boston, MA: Little, Brown.

Coles, R. (1986a). *The moral life of children*. Boston, MA: Atlantic Monthly Press.

Coles, R. (1986b). *The political life of children*. Boston, MA: Atlantic Monthly Press.

Coles, R. (1990). *The spiritual life of children*. Boston, MA: Houghton Mifflin.

Couture, P. D. (2000). *Seeing children, seeing God: A practical theology of children and poverty*. Nashville, TN: Abingdon.

Couture, P. D. (2007). *Child poverty: Love, justice, and social responsibility*. St. Louis, MO: Chalice.

Davis, P. H. (2001). *Beyond nice: The spiritual wisdom of adolescent girls*. Minneapolis, MN: Augsburg Fortress.

de Mause, L. (1976). *The history of childhood*. London, UK: Souvenir.

Dykstra, R. C., Cole, A. H., & Capps, D. (2007). *Losers, loners, and rebels: The spiritual struggles of boys*. Louisville, KY: Westminster John Knox.

Erikson, E. H. (1950). *Childhood and society*. New York, NY: W. W. Norton.

Flanagan, K. S., & Hall, S. E. (2014). *Christianity and developmental psychopathology: Foundations and approaches*. Wheaton, IL: InterVarsity.

Flesberg, E. (2008). *The switching hour: Kids of divorce say good-bye again*. Nashville, TN: Abingdon.

Fowler, J. W. (1981). *Stages of faith: The psychology of human development and the quest for meaning*. San Francisco, CA: Harper & Row.

Freud, S. (1962). *Three essays on the theory of sexuality*. New York, NY: Basic Books. (Original work published 1905)

Grossoehme, D. H. (1999). *The pastoral care of children*. New York, NY: Routledge.

Hardman C. (1973). Can there be an anthropology of children? *Journal of the Anthropological Society of Oxford*, *4*(2), 85–99.

Herzog, K. (2005). *Children and our global future*. Cleveland, OH: Pilgrim Press.

Higonnet, A. (1998). *Pictures of innocence: The history and crisis of ideal childhood*. New York, NY: Thames and Hudson.

James, A. (2004). Understanding childhood from an interdisciplinary perspective: Problems and potentials. In P. B. Pufall & R. P. Unsworth (Eds.), *Rethinking childhood* (pp. 25–37). New Brunswick, NJ: Rutgers University Press.

Jensen, D. H. (2005). *Graced vulnerability: A theology of childhood*. Cleveland, OH: Pilgrim Press.

Kehily, M. J. (Ed.). (2004). *An introduction to childhood studies*. Berkshire, UK: Open University Press.

Key, E. (1909). *Century of the child*. New York, NY: Putnam.

Lester, A. D. (1985). *Pastoral care of children in crisis*. Philadelphia, PA: Westminster.

Lytch, C. E. (2004). *Choosing church: What makes a difference for teens*. Louisville, KY: Westminster John Knox.

Mackay, R. (1973). Conceptions of children and models of socialization. In H. P. Dreitzel (Ed.), *Childhood and socialization* (pp. 27–43). London, UK: Collier-Macmillam.

Marshall, K., & Parvis, P. (2004). *Honouring children: The human rights of the child in Christian perspective*. Edinburgh, Scotland: Saint Andrew.

Marty, M. (2007). *The mystery of the child*. Grand Rapids, MI: Eerdmans.

Matthews, G. B. (1994). *The philosophy of childhood*. Cambridge, MA: Harvard University Press.

Mercer, J. A. (2005). *Welcoming children: A practical theology of childhood*. St. Louis, MO: Chalice.

Miller, A. (1986). *The drama of the gifted child* (R. Ward, Trans.). New York, NY: Basic Books.

Miller-McLemore, B. J. (1994). *Also a mother: Work and family as theological dilemma*. Nashville, TN: Abingdon.

Miller-McLemore, B. J. (2003). *Let the children come: Reimagining childhood from a Christian perspective*. San Francisco, CA: Jossey-Bass.

Miller-McLemore, B. J. (2006a). Children and religion in the public square: 'Too dangerous and too safe, too difficult and too silly.' *Journal of Religion, 86*, 385–401. doi:10.1086/503694

Miller-McLemore, B. J. (2006b). *In the midst of chaos: Care of children as spiritual practice*. San Francisco, CA: Jossey-Bass.

Miller-McLemore, B. J. (2006c). Whither the children? Childhood in religious education. *Journal of Religion, 86*, 635–657. doi:10.1086/505897

Miller-McLemore, B. J. (2009). Redefining children's spirituality. In W. Graeb & L. Charbonnier (Eds.), *Secularization theories, religious identity, and practical theology* (pp. 223–231). Berlin, Germany: LIT Verlag.

Miller-McLemore, B. J. (2011). Feminism, children, and mothering: Three books and three children later. *Journal of Childhood and Religion, 2*(1). Retrieved from http://childhoodandreligion .com/wp-content/uploads/2015/03/Miller-McLemore-Jan-2011.pdf

Miller-McLemore, B. J. (2012). Embodied knowing, embodied theology: What happened to the body? *Pastoral Psychology, 61*, 149–163. doi:10.1007/s11089-013-0510-3

Miller-McLemore, B. J. (2016). Spooning: How bodies shape knowledge. In D. C. Bass, K. A. Cahalan, B. J. Miller-McLemore, J. Nieman, & C. Scharen, *Christian practical wisdom: What it is, why it matters*. Grand Rapids, MI: Eerdmans.

Murphy, A. J. (2013). *Kids and kingdom: The precarious presence of children in the Synoptic Gospels*. Eugene, OR: Pickwick.

Orsi, R. A. (2002). A crisis about the theology of children. *Harvard Divinity School Bulletin, 30*(4), 27–30.

Parker, E. L. (2003). *Trouble don't last always: Emancipatory hope among African American adolescents*. Cleveland, OH: Pilgrim Press.

Piaget, J. (1965). *The moral judgment of the child* (M. Gabain, Trans.). New York, NY: Free Press. (Original work published 1924)

Pollock, L. (1983). *Forgotten children: Parent-child relations from 1500–1900*. Cambridge, UK: Cambridge University Press.

Popenoe, D. (1988). *Disturbing the nest: Family change and decline in modern societies*. New York, NY: A. de Gruyter.

Prout, A., & James, A. (1997). A new paradigm for the sociology of childhood? Provenance, promise and problems. In A. James & A. Prout (Eds.), *Constructing and reconstructing childhood: Contemporary issues in the sociological study of childhood* (pp. 7–32). London, UK: Falmer.

Pufall, P. B., & Unsworth, R. P. (Eds.). (2004a). Preface. In *Rethinking childhood* (pp. ix–xi). New Brunswick, NJ: Rutgers University Press.

Pufall, P. B. & Unsworth, R. P. (Eds.). (2004b). Introduction: The imperative and the process for rethinking childhood. In *Rethinking childhood* (pp. 4–21). New Brunswick, NJ: Rutgers University Press.

Rizzuto, A. (1979). *The birth of the living God: A psychoanalytic study*. Chicago, IL: University of Chicago Press.

Roche, M. M. D. (2009). *Children, consumerism, and the common good*. New York, NY: Lexington Books.

Rubio, J. H. (2010). *Family ethics: Practices for Christians*. Washington, DC: Georgetown University Press.

Smith, C. (with Denton, M. L.). (2005). *Soul searching: The religious and spiritual lives of American teenagers*. Oxford, UK: Oxford University Press.

Stevenson-Moessner, J. (2003). *The spirit of adoption: At home in God's family*. Louisville, KY: Westminster John Knox.

Walkerdine, V. (2004). Developmental psychology and the study of childhood. In M. J. Kehily (Ed.), *An introduction to childhood studies* (pp. 96–107). Berkshire, UK: Open University Press.

Wall, J. (2006). Childhood studies, hermeneutics, and theological ethics. *Journal of Religion, 86*, 523– 548. doi:10.1086/505893

Wall, J. (2010a). *Ethics in light of childhood*. Washington, DC: Georgetown University Press.

Wall, J. (2010b). Review of Jerome Berryman's *Children and the theologians*. *Journal of Childhood and Religion, 1*. Accessed July 15, 2013, from http://www.childhoodandreligion.com/JCR/Book_Reviews_files/Berryman%20review.pdf

Wallerstein, J. S. (1989). *Second chances: Men, women, and children a decade after divorce*. New York, NY: Ticknor & Fields.

Whitmore, T. D. (with Winright, T.). (1997). Children: An undeveloped theme in Catholic teaching. In M. A. Ryan & T. D. Whitmore (Eds.), *The challenge of global stewardship: Roman Catholic response* (pp. 161–85). Notre Dame, IN: University of Notre Dame.

Wigger, B. J. (2003). *The power of God at home: Nurturing our children in love and grace*. San Francisco, CA: Jossey-Bass.

Woodhead, M. (1997). Psychology and the cultural construction of children's needs. In A. James & A. Prout (Eds.), *Constructing and reconstructing childhood: Contemporary issues in the sociological study of childhood* (pp. 63–84). London, UK: Falmer.

Woodhead, M. (2004). Foreword. In M. J. Kehily (Ed.), *An introduction to childhood studies* (pp. x–xi). Berkshire, UK: Open University Press.

Wuthnow, R. (1999). *Growing up religious: Christians and Jews and their journeys of faith*. Boston, MA: Beacon.

Yust, K. M., Johnson, A. N., Sasso, S. E., & Roehlkepartain, E. C. (Eds.). (2006). *Nurturing child and adolescent spirituality: Perspectives from the world's religious traditions*. New York, NY: Rowland & Littlefield.

Joretta L. Marshall

26

FUTURES OF A PAST: FROM WITHIN A MORE TRADITIONAL PASTORAL COUNSELING MODEL

As a child, I remember the tedium of hearing my elders begin a sentence by saying, "Back when I was a child. . . ." This was usually followed by something like, "What is the world coming to?" Now, as I head toward the latter stages of my professional life, I carry an inward dread of sounding like one of those who can't forget the past and who is overly concerned about perceived changes in the future. Yet, my elders in pastoral theology, care, and counseling taught me the wisdom of holding the middle ground wherein one neither forgets the past too quickly nor clings to it too tightly. Honoring the past and building on it meaningfully in the present creates space for the ebb and flow of multiple generations who craft new visions out of long-held commitments and values.

In many ways, my journey in pastoral counseling represents what is often referred to as a more traditional model of formation. Having felt a "call" into ordained ministry early in my life, I enrolled in a Master of Divinity program shortly after college. The school of theology that I chose provided a curriculum that was at once traditional in its scope of courses and offerings, yet progressive and constructive. My work as a pastoral assistant, college chaplain, associate pastor, and staff person in a youth crisis center shaped my pastoral identity in church and community. It did not take me long to realize that there was a great deal that I did not know. I was convinced that if I wanted to be a good pastor, I needed more education than was afforded to me by two classes in pastoral care, one unit of clinical pastoral education (CPE), and cumulative unreflected-upon experience. Hence, I moved into a PhD program with the intent of returning to the parish. Although the journey is a bit more complex and complicated than I suggest here (as is true for everyone I know), my formation was rooted in the integration of theological education, church leadership, and community experience.

As part of my doctoral program, I was expected to gain minimal clinical competency in counseling. With no intent of becoming a pastoral counselor, I engaged in training in a newly founded pastoral counseling center that was part of the outreach of a local church in the community and tangentially related to the divinity school. There I was met with a clinical supervisor who not only was a gifted clinician but also deeply grounded in the theological dynamics of pastoral counseling. Joining the American Association of Pastoral Counselors (AAPC) and becoming a vital member of that organization was an expectation in the training. In this formation model, there was an emphasis on clinical competency alongside deep attention to pastoral formation as shaped by one's theological and ecclesial commitments. Formed by a doctoral program that was clearly grounded in pastoral theology while working alongside pastoral clinicians who brought sophistication to their theological and clinical integration, I began to see the identity of a pastoral counselor emerging among the multiple identities I carried. Ultimately, my interests culminated in a dissertation on the formation of internalized pastoral theological identity and concerns for the pastoral soul (Marshall, 1994).

Most of my professional journey has involved teaching at master's and doctoral levels in theological education. Until the past several years, a consistent part of my work included counseling with individuals and couples while also enhancing skills in supervision. As state regulations changed over the years, and as I moved between institutions in different states, I discovered that maintaining clinical work as a pastoral counselor who does not carry any other professional license made the work increasingly difficult. This story illustrates the changing tides of culture and counseling that many of us experienced: We discovered that to do our work as clinicians, we must also attend to legal requirements that are very different from those of the mid-1960s when the AAPC was first established. I maintain my connections to the AAPC as it has struggled to re-create itself for a new future because I believe there is something redemptive about belonging to an organization that takes seriously the integration of theological construction and clinical work.

I share these parts of my story to lay the foundation for the reflections that follow. As we have come to know, the perspectives expressed in chapters such as these are deeply informed by the social locations of the writers. My story is more common to those of us from an earlier era. Other scholars and writers have noted the shifts and changes that have occurred in the specialization of pastoral care and counseling over the past 2 or 3 decades (Holifield, 2010; Mills, 2010; Townsend, 2009). In addition, the historical developments of such organizations as the Association of Clinical Pastoral Education and the AAPC tell the story of the interaction among theological education, clinical paradigms, and the changing culture around us (King, 2007; Marshall, 2012). My goal here is not to retell the story; rather I am interested in what we can learn from our past that might inform the present as we imagine ourselves and our discipline into the future.

In an attempt to imagine the future out of a more traditional formation model in pastoral counseling, I will draw on my experience and knowledge of the AAPC and briefly look at three things. First, I want to begin with a question that rests in the background: Recognizing that there are many narratives that make up the stories of pastoral counselors, I would like to ponder aloud about what is meant by a "traditional" pastoral counseling model. Second, among the central features of the AAPC in the late 1980s was the importance of formation. This concept and its concomitant practices hold the capacity to assist us in identifying some of the values and commitments for pastoral counselors from one strand of the tradition. Hence, attending to some of the salient formative practices as developed in the AAPC can provide insight into the values that shaped and formed pastoral counselors. I do this not because it is the only story but because it speaks to what many of us see as both the strength and potential failure in the pastoral counseling movement, historically and in the present. Finally, growing out of this traditional sense of pastoral counseling, I would like to suggest some commitments that I hope we sustain, re-create, or co-construct into the future.

IS THERE A TRADITIONAL PASTORAL COUNSELING MODEL?

Many of us related to the AAPC assume, at our own peril, that there is one traditional model out of which all other pastoral counseling movements arise. What began as a movement at the intersection of ministry and community eventuated into an organization related to mental health and spirituality (e.g., the tagline for the AAPC is now "professionally integrating psychotherapy and spirituality"; www.aapc.org). Although the AAPC is the most prominent organization representing pastoral counseling, it is not the only one working toward the integration of mental health and spirituality in our culture. Indeed, psychologists, social workers, and others identify spirituality as a significant theme in contemporary psychotherapy. Although we are historically related to organizations such as the Association for Clinical Pastoral Education (King, 2007) and the younger College of Pastoral Supervision and Psychotherapy (CPSP) (www.pastoralreport.com/), the AAPC's self-understanding is as the overseer and protector of the pastoral counseling movement. My goal here is not to defend this precarious position; rather, I hope to draw on some historical realities evident in the AAPC as a way to address larger concerns. First, it is important to note that a focus in this chapter on the AAPC limits this exploration in three significant ways.

First, for a host of theological and contextual reasons, the historical formation of the AAPC, with a few exceptions, was built around the assumptive world of White, Protestant, moderate to progressive, theologically educated, and ordained men. This is not meant to be an indictment of our history, nor does it suggest that nothing good arose from the movement; rather, it is the sad reality in a culture where issues of race, class, gender, sexual orientation, and mainline denominational power limited the scope of vision for the early founders of this organization. Although the AAPC represents some minimal movements toward inclusion of multifaith and multicultural perspectives, the organization has largely remained Protestant with an ecumenical focus (Steckel, 1993). Roman Catholic and Jewish practitioners, within and outside of the boundaries of the AAPC, were among the early pastoral counselors in the United States. Institutions of higher education in the Roman Catholic tradition continue to develop vital training programs for pastoral counselors. In addition, the growing recognition of the deep need for interfaith pastoral counselors pushes us all to move beyond the realm of the past (Asquith, 2010; Grieder, Clements, & Lee, 2006). There is a growing international movement in pastoral counseling reflected in organizations such as the International Council on Pastoral Care and Counseling (ICPCC) and other indigenous movements (Doehring, 2010; Holifield, 2010; Lartey, 2004). The AAPC is one strand among a host of partners invested in matters of theology, faith, spirituality, and mental health.

A more significant limitation when one focuses on the AAPC as "the tradition" is reflected in the lack of attention until recently to deeper matters of racial/ethnic diversity in pastoral counseling (Townsend, 2009). The ministry of pastoral leaders in faith communities that were more racially diverse always included the embodiment of pastoral counseling. For example, the strong African American legacy of pastoral leaders who informed the care of souls tradition is often lost from view because of the racism inherent in the dominant culture, which the AAPC has often reflected (Townsend, 2009; Wimberly, 2006). My point here is that when we assume that the AAPC is the only tradition of pastoral counseling, our lack of diversity in terms of religious plurality and racial/ethnic diversity reminds us of the limitations of our perspective. As a member and leader of the AAPC, I both regret and accept responsibility for this ongoing cultural and systemic oppression.

Second, many scholars and practitioners note the inherent limitation that comes with identifying a movement as "pastoral." Reflective of the dominance of Protestant images in the formal history of the care of souls, the word *pastoral* carries at least two meanings (Dykstra, 2005). At one and the same time, it "may refer either to the person of the religious leader or to the motivation/attitude characterizing the caregiver" (Mills, 2010, p. 51). When it represents the religious leader, the word almost always refers to someone who is ordained or endorsed by a mainline tradition. When *pastoral* connotes a particular perspective, it almost always refers to a sense of theological wisdom that is shaped through education and supervision. Because deep theological diversity (as opposed to tolerance or respect for theological difference) has not always been prominent in the AAPC, we have retained the use of the word *pastoral*, and unfortunately, it has created tensions because we are not clear any more on its meaning. Other kinds of theological diversity can be found in the Christian counseling movement that has attracted thousands who do not define themselves as "pastoral" but who have deeply embedded theological claims that direct their work. Similarly, faith-based individuals from diverse theological traditions have joined the pastoral care and counseling movement through other licensing organizations. Once again, we see that the AAPC represents only one strand of a larger and more complex pastoral counseling tradition.

Third, the focus on the AAPC illustrates the complex intersection of culture and, in particular, the way in which therapy has come to be understood and valued by the culture. As counseling became more institutionalized, the role of regulatory agencies at state and federal levels also increased. Hence, any historical look at pastoral counseling, particularly from the perspective of an organization such as the AAPC, must account for the ways in which the culture around us has made a difference in the embodiment of our practices and policies. Many members or potential members have not pursued AAPC membership in the past two decades largely because of the need to maintain certification and licensure to survive financially in their practices. For example, there are a large number of ordained pastors licensed through the American Association for Marriage and Family Therapy (AAMFT) and many pastoral counseling training programs affiliate either with this organization or others that offer licensure. As AAPC members sought greater economic value and legitimation within the mental health profession, the AAPC's capacity to retain an emphasis on theological integration often took second place to clinical education (Rogers-Vaughn, 2013). The drop in membership and vitality in the AAPC over the past 2 decades can be traced, in part, to this cultural shift. Hence, this chapter's focus on the AAPC does not adequately take into account the multiple organizations that now support the work of pastoral counselors.

With these caveats and limitations in mind, the question remains: What does it mean to explore a "traditional" model of pastoral counseling? For the purposes of this contribution, I suggest that the AAPC is representative of one strand of a larger pastoral counseling tradition. My argument is not that it is the only "valid" pastoral counseling tradition; rather, I am suggesting here that the AAPC has been a significant leader and conversation partner in defining pastoral counseling. Hence, as one component of more complex narratives, even in the midst of its limitations, it still holds value for consideration as one imagines how pastoral counseling might move into the future.

Although this chapter is narrow in scope and represents the limitations of social location, context, and culture, I believe it can also be instructive as we examine some of the ways in which the organization of the AAPC focused its energies on formative practices that helped solidify something called "pastoral counseling" in mainline denominational life. The trajectories that flow from this particular history relate to embedded values that have been at the center of the AAPC and that are worthy of consideration as we move into the future.

FORMATION IN THE AAPC

Formation has been a central concept in AAPC's model of pastoral counseling. An examination of the formative practices that evolved over time helps identify some of the embedded values in this tradition. Any look at the future must include deliberate decisions related to the values and commitments reflected in these formational processes, not because they are essential in some mandated form but because they are instructive about what has been important over time to a group of people who identify themselves as pastoral counselors. My goal in focusing on formation relates to the fact that naming these formative practices in the AAPC allows us to think more critically about what strands from the past we might carry into the future, alongside which ones might be wise to let go of as we discern new horizons.

Formation refers to the processes we engage to help shape people toward specific intentions around particular content (Marshall, 2009). Formation processes, even those with a particular telos such as the integration of theology and psychology, do not occur in linear paths or isolated arenas. We are constantly in the process of being shaped and formed around multiple identities. Because we never arrive at a stopping point in formation, we are engaged collectively in practices that help shape our thinking, reflecting, being, and doing over time. Formative practices are one way of identifying those series of actions that are developed over time and in community for the purpose of supporting formation. Embedded within these practices in the AAPC are particular values and commitments that reflect the larger ethos and community of pastoral counselors.

In the mid- to late 1990s, some 30 years after the formal incorporation of the AAPC, a task force was developed to reflect on the organization and its vision for the future. Already some of the cultural and theological challenges for traditional pastoral counseling were emerging in ways that encouraged the leadership of the organization to take notice and to be intentional about building toward a future. As the task force began its work, we asked questions typical of organizational planning, such as the following: What would be lost if pastoral counseling and, more specifically, the organization of the AAPC did not exist? What were the distinctive qualities that made pastoral counseling an important resource for the churches, communities, and broader cultures around us? It did not take long for the leaders in that group to identify that the formation processes for pastoral counselors, as embodied in the AAPC, illuminated some distinctive characteristics we wanted to support as we moved forward. For many, these practices represented part of the heart and soul of the organization and of what it meant to claim that one was a pastoral counselor.

Lest one jump too quickly toward a romanticized version of this formation process in the AAPC, it is critical to point out the deep interpersonal wounds that were experienced between members around such practices as supervision and the meeting of membership committees. There were many for whom the process of moving from a novice clinician to a more experienced supervisor was not only a difficult experience but also deeply painful as people were challenged around normative expectations in personal growth, psychotherapeutic modalities, and notions of integration. Those wounds continue to spill out into our corporate life in ways that are intense and quite illustrative of both the healing and destructive power of formation processes that are embedded within the traditional model of the AAPC. Yet, these stories also point to the deeper underlying and embedded value of relationship. The power and importance of relationality will show up in multiple ways in the following pages.

As the AAPC task force worked in the late 1990s, we identified six elements that articulated the historical qualities inherent in the formative processes of a pastoral counselor. Identifying the values that are embedded in these elements can be instructive lest we dismiss formative practices too quickly for the sake of convenience in the marketplace or in order to shorten the time that is required before someone becomes a fully endorsed member of the association. Although the language in the following paragraphs reflects historical realities, some forms of these formative practices continue in the AAPC today.

The first element important to formation was a commitment to lifelong learning. It was clear from the outset that pastoral counselors needed to be cognizant of the growing edges of multiple disciplines related to theology, psychology, and therapy. The integration of these ways of thinking was critical to the formation of pastoral counselors. The corresponding formative practices were particularly evident in the ongoing educational opportunities made available through training centers, regional meetings, and larger organizational conferences. Although fellowship was central at these meetings, equally important was some formal aspect of education through lectures, plenaries, and workshops. In similar fashion, supervision was a formative practice where learning was mutual and expected on the part of both the supervisor and the supervisee. The embedded values of education and lifelong learning reflected deeper commitments to serve others with care. These formative practices occurred in the context of relationships with one another.

Over time, lifelong learning activities emphasized the pressing need for pastoral counselors to increase their clinical competency and effectiveness. Concomitantly, there seemed to be fewer opportunities to deepen sophisticated theological claims, in part because there was an assumption that one's formation of pastoral identity took shape through formal theological education and ecclesial processes that often eventuated in ordination. It was expected, for example, that one could articulate a theological anthropology in papers presented for membership committees because one had theological training. As more persons entered the AAPC without formal theological education or deep connections to ecclesial formation, there was a period of confusion about the importance of these previously normative expectations. Although the deep value in education and lifelong learning in multiple fields of inquiry related to theology and psychology remains, it appears to many of us in the tradition that there is a growing split between theology and the clinical realm. The value of formal and more sophisticated theological inquiry seems to have eroded in the past two decades while clinical competencies remained central.

A second element of formation identified by the task force was the need for ongoing growth in personal self-awareness (emotional, spiritual, theological, relational, and ethical). Part of the historical legacy of pastoral counseling as a movement was its connectedness to theories of personality and clinical work that demanded deeper self-awareness. As a result, formative practices carry expectations for supervision (individual and group), participation in one's own therapy, and transparency about one's self in the written materials prepared for meeting committees for membership as well as in the conversation with the committee itself. There is no doubt that there was an identifiable strength in this emphasis as clinicians—both young and mature— were taught the importance of a self-awareness that decreased the likelihood of perpetrating intentional or unintentional harm on clients. At the same time, there was an assumption that one gained self-awareness largely, and sometimes exclusively, through formal therapy. In some regions of the AAPC, the unofficial expectation was that formal therapy was best done by someone from the psychoanalytic tradition. As the AAPC became more diverse in multiple ways, there was a growing resistance to either a singular therapeutic approach for gaining self-knowledge or the understanding that therapy was the only avenue to greater self-awareness. Yet, the value of self-awareness, particularly to prevent harm with clients, remains central in the AAPC.

A third identified element in formation was a commitment to grow in faith and spirituality, alongside an appreciation for the faith and spirituality of others. Three dimensions related to this concept of faith and spirituality are important to note here. First, as noted previously, the AAPC was built around assumptions that members were shaped and formed by theological education and in the context of ecclesial connections. Although most members of the association maintained a denominational connection, those relationships were often ambiguous and tentative. A central theological issue became that of encouraging members of the AAPC to retain their connections to the church and, in turn, for denominations to claim the work of pastoral counselors as valid ministry (Patton, 1983). At the same time, many pastoral clinicians grew concerned about the destructive power of churches as they processed their own experiences or listened to stories of clients who had been deeply wounded by congregations or denominations. Many AAPC members carry a healthy suspicion of ecclesial and denominational life.

The values of theological education and ecclesial formation were directly tied to denominational endorsement, an issue that became problematic in the mid- to late 1980s for at least three reasons. First, a growing number of persons marginalized from their faith communities or unable to secure ecclesial endorsement wanted to pursue membership in the AAPC. This included Roman Catholic laywomen who were invested in pastoral counseling yet unable to get the hierarchies of their traditions to offer official endorsement. Second, as the number of closeted and self-identified lesbians and gays moved through the supervisory structures of the AAPC and into formal membership, it was clear that many of us would lose our endorsement if our sexual orientation became an issue. The history of denominational endorsement is more complex than can be commented on here fully, but a group of justice-minded advocates moved the association to provide an alternative to denominational processes. Third, the AAPC began to attract and encourage persons to join the organization that brought with them deep commitments to conversations around mental health and spirituality but who were not formally ordained or part of an ecclesial formation process. Many of these people were licensed in a correlative mental health organization, were experienced and valuable clinicians and colleagues, and had no need of ecclesiastical endorsement. All of these variations began to raise questions about the language of "pastoral" and the value of formal theological education. For our purposes here, it is important to note that although earlier in its legacy, the AAPC relied on denominational practices to help shape and form the theological and ecclesial understandings of pastoral identity, those taken-for-granted worlds continue to be tested.

A second dimension related to this aspect of formation rests in the growing popularity of the term *spirituality*, not only among pastoral counselors but also in the broader culture. At the time the task force met, other mental health professionals, such as psychologists, social workers, and psychiatrists, were exploring the meaning of "spirituality" with their clients and in their practices. As AAPC members engaged these multidisciplinary peers, we benefitted from the larger cultural conversation.

However, with the adoption of the language of spirituality, less attention has been paid to the way in which theological training and education supports and deepens understandings and experiences of spirituality and faith. As a result, the language of spirituality often supersedes any critical theological engagement in the AAPC.

A third dimension inherent in this formational element about faith and spirituality reflects the deep respect and value that pastoral counselors carry for the faith journeys of our clients, as well as nurturing our own journeys. From the very beginning, it was clear that pastoral counselors worked diligently not to appear in any way to proselytize others or to be pejorative in their work with people who embodied different spiritual journeys than their own. This valuing of pluralism resulted in pastoral counselors leading ecumenical and interfaith conversations at least with their clients and in the context of the counseling office. This element of formation values multiple forms of faith and spirituality in self and others and continues to be nurtured among AAPC's membership.

The fourth element of formation identified by the AAPC task force in the late 1990s was the importance of honing professional skills and competencies. Building on what has been noted earlier in this chapter, one of the hallmarks of the AAPC and the pastoral counselors formed in this tradition is the recognition that a theological degree and ordination, coupled with well-intentioned good will, was not enough to meet the critical needs of clients. In fact, in many ways, this was the perfect prescription for doing harm. Formative practices centered, once again, on the importance of supervision, continuing education, and a constant vigilance to create good clinical practices. Much of the pastoral counseling literature over the past several decades has deepened skills and competencies needed for working with particular populations or in specific contexts. The value of education and supervision emerges in this formational element as it conveys a commitment to the well-being and health of clients.

A fifth element of formation identified by the task force articulates the need to learn from mentors and supervisors, colleagues and peers, clients and students, and other disciplines. Again, formative practices around supervision were central to the shaping of pastoral counselors. In particular, there was an expectation that other AAPC-related supervisors, alongside colleagues and peers from other disciplines, were essential in the formation process. Likewise, this formational element notes the importance of being open to learn from and with clients and students. In other words, the value of mutual learning while respecting the boundaries that emerged in the context of pastoral counseling required solid supervision. A central commitment to learn from others remains critical in the formational practices within the AAPC.

Finally, and perhaps as a summative vision of formation as a pastoral counselor, the task force included socialization into the AAPC's history, story, tradition, and charism. For many of us from my era, belonging to the AAPC not only was a choice about organizational affiliation but also became a community of colleagues and peers whose history, ethos, and unique perspectives were important not simply for those of us who belonged to the organization but for the churches, communities, and cultures in which we lived. In the AAPC, we found a collegium of others who were invested in the integration of theological and clinical perspectives; committed to the care of individuals, couples, families, and communities; and informed by values and commitments reflective of these formational practices.

Embedded in the process of formation for pastoral counselors were several values that have remained important, although with shifting nuances over time. Perhaps among the most prominent of these values was the belief that our clients deserved theologically and clinically competent pastoral counselors who understood the spiritual elements in life's crises. The formative practices articulated previously in this chapter were developed to provide clients with what we thought was the best pastoral care and counseling we could offer. Other values and commitments emerged alongside, such as formal and informal education in multiple disciplines, including theology and psychotherapy; honest and sometimes intense relationships with one another that mutually transformed and changed us; theological–clinical integration that guided our perspectives; and a deeper awareness of self. The question remains: How might these embedded values assist us in moving forward as pastoral counselors?

Futures of Our Past

Building on the values named in the formational processes just described, at least four commitments will help us imagine the multiple avenues pastoral counseling can develop into the future. There is not one future that we ought to imagine, nor should we automatically suggest that there is one organization that ought to hold together all of the various strands in pastoral counseling. Instead, we are wise to embrace the multiple embodiments that our commitments and values will lead us to into the future. To sustain pastoral counselors individually and within organizational structures, we must be aware that the era of imagining that there is a singular approach to pastoral counseling has long since disappeared. What I want to suggest, however, is that systemic values in the AAPC might become part of the future, whether within that organization or in broader and more complex systems.

First, the AAPC began with a deep commitment to the integration of theological and clinical competencies. The formative practices of building relationships with one another through supervision and collegiality, the expectation of formal education in theology and clinical expertise, and the commitment to ongoing learning were significant aspects of theo-clinical integration. At one time in our culture, it was assumed that pastoral formation occurred in the context of largely Judeo–Christian ecclesial communities. In the postdenominational milieu of our culture, these realities are deeply challenged, and fewer pastoral counselors carry advanced theological development. If there is one value that I hope we collectively wrestle with into the future it is to give serious consideration to the role of critical theological reflection and construction in the lived realities of pastoral counselors. Our clients need a sophisticated and thoughtful theology that can meet the pressing realities of our world. Perhaps because of my own social location, but hopefully more because of what I see happening in our world, it is clear to me that our clients, faith communities, and the cultures around us need critical and thoughtful pastoral counselors who can not only bring the best of our clinical competencies into the room but who can also think with people about the theological and ethical questions that arise in the complexity of life.

Pastoral counseling offers one of the few places in our culture where critical theological engagement is more than an added bonus but is part of the inherent understanding of the field and discipline. Although I draw on language that is clearly Judeo–Christian in heritage because of my own commitments, I am not suggesting that this is the only legitimate religious perspective in pastoral counseling. Instead, what I am suggesting here is that in order for genuine interfaith and interreligious conversations to take place, those of us who explore theology from various Christian perspectives must deepen our thinking self-consciously and self-critically. We need not withdraw from our commitments or language even as we remain open to learning with and from others. We need this deeper engagement with theological discourses for two reasons. First, offering casual understandings of God or unreflective platitudes about spirituality or matters of ethical decision making leaves clients open to destructive interpretations of their lives. A collegium of pastoral counselors who take their theology as seriously as they do clinical competency can offer to clients, churches, and communities a vision of the world that is honest, yet hopeful. Recognizing that sacred texts are not only written historical narratives but the stories of people's lives requires something more than simplistic reflections on what is holy. I am not suggesting here that there ought to be a dominant theology that overrides all others, but I am encouraging us to consider that one of the most unique perspectives we can offer to the world is a more reflective awareness of how theology shapes lives and communities.

People ought to be able to assume that pastoral counselors have a deeper theological ability to assist them in reflecting on their lives in ways that touch on spirituality but are not confined by it. Pastoral theologians and counselors Graham and Whitehead (2006) noted the significance of theological formation when they suggested that:

> to be formed as a pastoral counselor is to be theologically fluent about the multiplicity of sacred stories available to our work and to our clients, and to envision contextually creative ways in which these stories might become resources for healing and transformation. (p. 23)

The sacred work we are called to do with clients requires that we pay deliberate attention to theology. Not to do so leaves the culture, our clients, and faith communities vulnerable to theologies that can ultimately harm people's souls. This perspective, of course, is built around a profound belief that in our deeper theological conversations with one another, we come to know ourselves, others, and the Holy One in new and transformative ways.

A second way in which theology serves us into the future is through our leadership in the ongoing constructions of pastoral theology and counseling. Pastoral theology does not belong solely to a group of scholars who teach in seminaries or offer written reflections. Instead, pastoral counselors need to claim their place within a larger guild that offers constructive theological reflections. Even as we have much to gain from engaging critical theological concepts that have been offered to us through generations of thinkers, the constructive work of pastoral theology arises from the integration of our current work with clients and our critical reflection on what we experience. The clinical work of pastoral counselors assists in developing larger ethical and theological dimensions to clinical competencies, offers new ways of envisioning the sacred, and provides substantive challenges for older visions of God and the world that are confining or that diminish human life. We need pastoral counselors who can respond clearly and not simply empathetically to the theological questions that people bring about, such as norms for relationships and human sexuality, moral debates about reproductive health, and oppressive policies and systems that destroy families and individuals. Such constructive theological reflection is at the core of pastoral counseling (Graham & Whitehead, 2006; Townsend, 2006), and if we dismiss it too quickly, we cannot serve our clients and communities well.

A second commitment that will move us forward in pastoral counseling is reflected in the degree to which we do not simply accept diversity but value it and let it inform and transform our work as pastoral clinicians. Reflective pastoral counselors clearly value the difference that comes to them in their clients. We know how to create safe space for people to share the complexity of their lives without being met by judgment or dismissive moral attitudes. Yet, we have not been as good about creating spaces to learn with diversity in our training centers, our educational venues, or our organizational life. If we are to offer anything to the world beyond us, we must not only talk about the value that we carry for our clients who bring us diverse social locations and issues but also concretely value the bodies and perspectives of those who surround us and engage us with diverse perspectives, life experiences, and wisdom.

Allowing diversity to exist next to us is quite different from engaging that diversity and nurturing it among us. We must draw on our best clinical and intellectual capacities to understand the intersection of such things as race, class, gender, orientation, and more. However, understanding is only a first step toward valuing difference and being committed to enhancing it and giving it space to flourish in our individual and corporate lives. To value diversity, we must continue to deconstruct the structures of pastoral counseling that are oppressive both in practice and in our individual and corporate lives. "Oppression-sensitive" pastoral practice can become a norm rather than something that emerges from time to time (Kujawa-Holbrook & Montagno, 2009). Pastoral counselors who challenge racism in the counseling office as well as in our organizational life can lead us in efforts to change the systems of our world. Such work resists the marginalization of populations who are often considered the "other," such as African Americans, Latinas/Latinos, lesbians and gays, and bisexual and transgender persons. In addition, this kind of valuing of diversity recognizes that Jewish, Muslim, and other multifaithed perspectives are critical to engage in our clinical practices as well as in our world. As we dismantle colonialism and other realities of oppression in pastoral counseling, we will be invited to new ways of engaging one another (Sharp, 2013). Pastoral counselors who deeply value otherness will learn how to sit in the middle of thorny issues of diversity in ways that do not escape their complexity or diminish their contextuality. This includes deeper attention to global issues that not only impinge on the lives of our clients in our offices but also carry an impact on the realities and possibilities for human flourishing in multiple contexts.

I have no doubt that pastoral counseling will continue to reflect greater diversity in its scholarship and practices. We will have more ways of thinking about what good theology or clinical work looks like, and we will be jolted by theologies and theories that counter our assumed worlds. We will learn from disciplines, theoretical perspectives, and pluralistic approaches that will challenge the way that we think about human beings, or what makes for change, or what is needed to create health and wholeness. The disruption of pastoral counseling in these ways is not a bad thing; indeed, if we are to survive as vital and critical agents in the world around us, we must risk the challenges that come with the deepest valuing of diversity in perspective, theology, clinical work, embodied realities, and scholarship.

Third, tending to the wholeness and health of communities must become a central component in the future of pastoral counseling. A central value of the AAPC has always been reflecting on what is in the best interest of clients we serve. Building on this, we must expand our awareness that our clients are not only individuals, couples, and families who meet us in our clinical offices but also the communities around us. Imagining with faith communities and local municipalities about what is needed in order for people to thrive in a whole and healthy community requires our deeper theological and clinical leadership abilities. McClure (2010) notes that because of our expertise and the way in which pastoral counseling values relationships with self, others, and communities, pastoral counselors are in a unique situation to participate in the building of healthy communities.

In the future, pastoral counselors need to pay attention to how power and systems function to diminish the health and wholeness of all, including within the institutions that we serve. Drawing on the language of flourishing, McClure (2010) notes "that psychological flourishing cannot be the only form we seek" (p. 244). Indeed, we must expand our horizons to participate in the creation of institutions that work toward the human flourishing of all at multiple levels of our communities and organizations. "Holding *institutions* and the wider social order accountable to human need makes sense" (p. 220), and this labor becomes part of what we offer as pastoral counselors whose vision is shaped by not only clinical expertise but also theological vision. Finding meaningful ways to get out of the offices that confine us and into the realm of the institutions and communities in which we live can bring a new dimension of genuine health to the world.

Finally, raising our public voice as pastoral clinicians is becoming not only important but also critical in the world. We have much wisdom to bring to issues that are at the forefront of politics in religious communities and society. Drawing on the wisdom of the voices that we carry inside of us—of those who have once been our clients and our teachers—will compel us not only to think about change but also to actively and creatively bring our public voice to the conversations of the culture. We do this not because it will save the AAPC, our denomination, or any other organization but because we have been offered these sacred stories in trust and in hope that they will make a difference in the lives of others.

The role of organizations such as the AAPC in these moments is to capture their organizational wisdom and power in a way that allows them to actively be a voice in the broader cultural realm. We need institutions that are willing to risk complacency in order to speak to issues of mental health and spirituality in new ways. At the same time, such organizations can offer a larger vision, and they have a platform from which to speak about critical social issues that need to be addressed in the larger public square. Pastoral counselors can be leaders in denominations, faith communities, local municipalities, and in the larger conversations about issues related to health, welfare, public good, and the creation of a transformed world only if we see that part of our theological gift goes beyond the realm of clinical offices.

Although these commitments and their potential trajectories seem mundane and predictable to some, to others they will suggest disruptive ways of imagining the future of pastoral counseling. Our pastoral clinical training programs, theological educational institutions, mentors, and supervisors must take seriously the challenges that are before pastoral counseling. I am less invested in returning to the past or the formation practices we have developed over the decades in the AAPC. Instead, I hope that we find new ways to retain values that have been important to the field and discipline over time while also freeing energy to create systems and structures that nurture healing and wholeness in the world. In this way, we will move forward in our efforts to meaningfully contribute to the lives of clients, communities, and the culture beyond us.

REFLECTION QUESTIONS

1. In what ways is or was your own journey similar to and distinct from what the author refers to as the "more traditional model of formation"? How do your social locations (race, gender, sexual orientation, religious identity, age, etc.) influence the formation model you experienced?
2. In what ways does the traditional model of pastoral counseling reflected by the AAPC mirror your own understanding and practice of pastoral counseling? In what ways does it not?
3. According to the author, in the mid- to late 1990s, a task force was developed within the AAPC that reflected on the formation of pastoral counselors. According to the task force, one key element of formation as a pastoral counselor is a "commitment

to grow in faith and spirituality." How was this formational element fostered in your own training? How can pastoral counseling training programs foster this element of the formation process given the increasing religious and spiritual diversity of pastoral counselors in training?

4. The practice of pastoral counseling has changed markedly since the formation of the AAPC in the 1960s. The author advocates four tenets of pastoral counseling that should be carried with us and aid us in moving into the future. They are (a) an emphasis on critical theological reflection; (b) a valuing of and engagement with diversity; (c) care of communities along with individuals, which entails examining systems of power and oppression; and (d) "raising our public voice as pastoral clinicians." What, if anything, is missing from this list of values to help move the discipline into the future? In your assessment, are any of these values more critical than others?

REFERENCES

Asquith, G. H. (Ed.). (2010). *The concise dictionary of pastoral care and counseling*. Nashville, TN: Abingdon.

Doehring, C. (2010). Pastoral care and counseling in a postmodern context. In G. H. Asquith (Ed.), *The concise dictionary of pastoral care and counseling* (pp. 70–74). Nashville, TN: Abingdon.

Dykstra, R. C. (2005). *Images of pastoral care: Classic readings*. St. Louis, MO: Chalice.

Graham, L. K., & Whitehead, J. C. (2006). The role of pastoral theology in theological education for the formation of pastoral counselors. In D. R. Bidwell & J. L. Marshall (Eds.), *The formation of pastoral counselors: Challenges and opportunities* (pp. 9–27). New York, NY: Haworth.

Grieder, K. J., Clements, W. M., & Lee, K. S. (2006). Formation for care of souls: The Claremont way. In D. R. Bidwell & J. L. Marshall (Eds.), *The formation of pastoral counselors: Challenges and opportunities* (pp. 177–195). New York, NY: Haworth.

Holifield, E. B. (2010). Pastoral care movement. In G. H. Asquith (Ed.), *The concise dictionary of pastoral care and counseling* (pp. 74–84). Nashville, TN: Abingdon.

King, S. D. (2007). *Trust the process: A history of clinical pastoral education as theological education*. Lanham, MD: University Press of America.

Kujawa-Holbrook, S. A., & Montagno, K. B. (Eds.). (2009). *Injustice and the care of souls: Taking oppression seriously in pastoral care*. Minneapolis, MN: Fortress.

Lartey, E. Y. (2004). Globalization, internationalization, and indigenization of pastoral care and counseling. In N. J. Ramsay (Ed.), *Pastoral care and counseling: Redefining the paradigms* (pp. 109–131). Nashville, TN: Abingdon.

Marshall, J. L. (1994). Toward the development of a pastoral soul: Reflections on identity and theological education. *Pastoral Psychology, 43*(1), 11–28. doi:10.1007/BF02258959

Marshall, J. L. (2009). Formative practices: Intent, structure, and content. *Reflective Practice: Formation and Supervision in Ministry, 29*, 56–73. Retrieved from http://journals.sfu.ca/rpfs/index.php/rpfs/article/view/220

Marshall, J. L. (2012). A perspective on pastoral theology, pastoral care, and counseling in the United States. In I. Noth & R. Kunz (Eds.), *Nachdenkliche seelsorge—Seelsorgliches Nachdenken* (pp. 326–341). Gottingen, Germany: Vandenhoeck & Ruprecht.

McClure, B. J. (2010). *Moving beyond individualism in pastoral care and counseling: Reflections on theory, theology and practice*. Eugene, OR: Cascade.

Mills, L. O. (2010). Pastoral care (history, traditions, and definitions). In G. H. Asquith (Ed.), *The concise dictionary of pastoral care and counseling* (pp. 51–70). Nashville, TN: Abingdon.

Patton, J. (1983). *Pastoral counseling: A ministry of the church*. Nashville, TN: Abingdon.

Rogers-Vaughn, B. (2013). Pastoral counseling in the neoliberal age: Hello best practices, goodbye theology. *Sacred Spaces: The e-Journal of the American Association of Pastoral Counselors, 5*. Retrieved from http://www.aapc.org/media/127298/2_rogers_vaughn.pdf

Sharp, M. A. (2013). *Misunderstanding stories: Toward a postcolonial pastoral theology*. Eugene, OR: Pickwick.

Steckel, C. J. (1993). Directions in pastoral counseling. In R. J. Wicks, R. D. Parsons, & D. Capps (Eds.), *Clinical handbook of pastoral counseling* (Expanded ed., Vol. 1, pp. 26–36). Mahwah, NJ: Paulist Press.

Townsend, L. (2006). Theological reflection and the formation of pastoral counselors. In D. R. Bidwell & J. L. Marshall (Eds.), *The formation of pastoral counselors: Challenges and opportunities* (pp. 29–46). New York, NY: Haworth.

Townsend, L. (2009). *Introduction to pastoral counseling*. Nashville, TN: Abingdon.

Wimberly, E. P. (2006). *African American pastoral care and counseling: The politics of oppression and empowerment*. Cleveland, OH: Pilgrim Press.

James W. Pruett and F. Morgan Enright

27

INTEGRATIVE PSYCHOTHERAPY TRAINING PROGRAM: A DEPARTMENT OF SPIRITUAL CARE AND EDUCATION

This chapter examines the development and organization of pastoral care within the context of managed care. It illustrates an approach that has been effective at engaging a medical system while providing quality care to patients. It then outlines the structure and staff that are needed to establish quality training and support for counselors within the system. It concludes with a potential plan on how to further establish a training program in the context of educational systems and licensing boards.

CONTEXT

The Affordable Care Act (ACA; Davis, 2014) is one of the most significant factors in the changing health care marketplace and is intended to correct earlier imbalances in health care delivery (Napili, 2013). Its aim is to realign the context of care, service delivery, provider accountability, quality of care, and cost-effectiveness by promoting clear communication and collaboration among providers. Like all health care providers, pastoral psychotherapists are not able to work as effectively if they are isolated within their silos (Knadig, 2011). Instead, services must be integrated seamlessly within a hospital or in a network with a health care delivery system (Shin, Sharac, & Rosenbaum, 2013). This structure fosters mutual accountability and a team commitment to offer excellent services based on the best stewardship of varied skill sets, time, energy, and money. However, pastoral psychotherapy must establish its own distinctiveness in a health care delivery system. Practitioners within this approach wear many hats, including both counselor and psychotherapist. The role of counselor attends to the patient through guidance and facilitation of the patient's conscious choice. Psychotherapists work with the patient to help understand the impetus for change and the intrapsychic, unconscious dynamics that can be part of that drive. They also assess the patient from both an individual and systemic perspective: engaging both to help facilitate change. The provider learns the process of assessing which hat to wear to best serve the patient within each session.

Pastoral psychotherapists have historically been well educated and trained in diverse counseling and psychotherapy clinical theories and methodologies (Roberts, 2003). To be effective in the changing health care marketplace, pastoral psychotherapists also must be established as the health care team's psychotherapy specialists in the care of the soul and the client's integration of faith/spiritual resources. This requires an ability to integrate clinical theory and techniques into rapid assessment, diagnosis, and brief psychotherapy. Finally, it is crucial that pastoral psychotherapists use both research and outcome studies to demonstrate the efficacy of care they provide.

Pastoral psychotherapists offer more than treatment. They help to engage patients and health care systems "soul to soul." Through their skillful use of self across these complex systems, pastoral psychotherapists establish the credibility necessary to advocate for longer term care when it is clinically indicated. Pastoral psychotherapists are attuned to the health care system's response to patient populations. They observe how their clients are offered care in the context of respective patient populations. Health care systems repeatedly ask, "How does your care help lessen (a) the unnecessary and often unreimbursed services provided by the emergency room, (b) the time spent with physicians, and (c) the use of medical procedures and supplies?" Specialists who help health care systems address these concerns are deemed vital to the health care delivery system and remain in the budget.

The term *pastoral* in pastoral psychotherapy typically connotes a specificity of education, training, supervision, and experience. However, use of this adjective in the marketplace is not without problem. In 2013, the Theological and Social Concerns Task Force (TSCTF) of the Membership Division of the American Association of Pastoral Counselors (AAPC) determined that the terms *pastoral, faith, theological,* and *spiritual* individually and collectively have a negative connotation for various segments of society. The TSCTF has begun to search for an inclusive term that captures this specialized expertise for all patients, but to date, no term has been found. Likewise the terms *counseling* and *psychotherapy* evoke interesting responses from society. Most patients still have ambivalence about receiving clinical services and often seek ways to minimize any association with terms that can connote that they are "damaged" or "ill." Yet, services received from pastoral psychotherapists may be viewed more positively than services provided by clinicians of other disciplines.

Psychotherapists specializing in the care of the soul in a health care system typically are positioned in a specific department, section, or division. Often, they serve through the Department of Pastoral Care and Education. In recent years, these departments have made name changes to respond better to the interfaith diversity of their patient population. The Carolinas HealthCare System (CHS), for example, uses its Integrative Psychotherapy Service Center and Training Program to train professionals from varied disciplines to be specialists in the care of the soul. These specialists then may be mainstreamed through the Department of Spiritual Care and Education or embedded within specific CHS departments.

John Santopietro, MD, chief clinical officer, behavioral health, CHS, emphasizes how crucial it is for hospital systems to train and supervise the next generation of spiritually sensitive psychotherapists for integrative care when he declared,

> I think training psychotherapists to be spiritually sensitive is important in all areas, integrative care included. Ignoring patients' spirituality is tantamount to ignoring a large part of what keeps them going in life—usually it boils down to three things—work, relationships, and spirituality. (Personal communication, September 15, 2013)

Dr. Santopietro, a national expert in both patient populations and how health care systems must respond to the changing clinical marketplace, contends that future psychotherapists must integrate a bio-psycho-social-cultural-spiritual perspective and skill set. Two questions emerge from his comments: (a) Who will train these specialists? and (b) What is a useful methodology for this training?

The CHS, through its Integrative Psychotherapy Service Center and Training Program, has accepted this challenge and offers one viable model for consideration as other systems seek to do the same. CHS has established a trusted model that provides more than 40,000 psychotherapy hours annually. Numerous outcome studies are ongoing to verify the significance of these services. CHS uses its Integrative Psychotherapy Training Program (IPTP) to train supervisors from several clinical disciplines to practice with this integration. With the aging of many clinical supervisors nationally, this program also trains clinical supervisors from these disciplines to provide both supervision of psychotherapy and supervision of supervision. The IPTP thus is presented as one example of the key themes and principles that are necessary to deliver such a program.

HISTORY AND CONTEXT

The CHS, located mostly in North and South Carolina with 42 hospitals and more than 900 medical practices, is still rapidly growing. It is second in size only to the Veterans Administration hospital system. Its IPTP was developed by James W. Pruett, PhD, DMin, and David E. Carl, MDiv, in 2008 and was originally entitled the Integrative Pastoral Psychotherapy Training Program. This program is accredited by the AAPC as an approved training program (Levels 1, 2, and 3) and an accredited services center.

CURRENT MODEL

Currently, there are 50 IPTP interns and residents serving within metropolitan Charlotte in these nine types of clinical settings:

1. psychiatric units
2. medical clinics
3. family medicine practices, some connected with the University of North Carolina at Charlotte Medical School's Department of Family Medicine, which also trains physicians
4. trauma units
5. intensive care step-down units
6. kidney dialysis units
7. cancer and oncology institute/practices
8. long-term assisted care facilities
9. rehabilitation hospitals/units

IPTP has established two main training tracks. The first is an IPTP intern track, which is a 1-year minimum placement for graduate students. The IPTP collaborates with more than a dozen graduate programs, seminaries, and divinity schools to create IPTP intern positions. The IPTP intern placements meet both the internship and practicum requirements for students to complete the graduate degrees required to sit for their respective national exams and obtain provisional state licensure.

The second training track is the IPTP residency. Some IPTP interns apply to be IPTP residents. IPTP residents must have completed their required graduate degree, passed the national exam of their discipline, and procured a provisional state license prior to entering the residency. IPTP residents typically continue in the IPTP until they complete their full state license/certification.

The IPTP is formatted to meet the standards for multiple state licenses/certifications and credentials in various allied cognate groups, including fee-based pastoral counseling, professional counseling, marriage and family therapy, social work, and health psychology. Supervisory contracts include the credentials to which the supervisee aspires and how the IPTP helps the person qualify for them. Permanent training records are kept for all students to help them and the IPTP readily document their IPTP supervisory contracts and courses, clinical hours served, and supervisory hours received. Clinical logs and evaluations are included to monitor the supervisee's formation. Each supervisee must maintain $1 million/$3 million liability insurance coverage. A copy of the face sheet for this policy is kept in the permanent training file.

IPTP graduates who seek membership with the AAPC do not need endorsement by their faith/spirituality community; however, those who want to become an AAPC-certified pastoral counselor, fellow, or diplomate must obtain an endorsement from their respective endorser whose faith group is affiliated with the Religious Endorsers Body (REB). IPTP graduates who have received their master's or doctoral degree may apply for certified pastoral counselor if they have completed a formal self-reflective experience, the most common of which is a unit of Clinical Pastoral Education or the AAPC Pastoral Care Specialist training and have provided at least 375 hours of clinical practice while receiving at least 125 hours of individual and group supervision. These supervisees then may elect to pursue further training with the IPTP toward AAPC fellow and later diplomate status based on interest and formation.

IPTP interns and residents keep confidential clinical notes for each patient session. The CHS legal department deems these records to be "educational notes." These notes and the case termination summary are retained by the IPTP in locked files for 7 years. These notes are not a part of the patient's medical record but instead are used to help interns to develop in their counseling formation. Using monthly supervisee reports, CHS researchers continuously track the clinical contacts that all IPTP interns and residents have with every patient they serve. This research is used to examine quality of care and cost savings to the CHS. These statistical reports may influence future program expansion and CHS budgeting.

IPTP interns and residents see clients who pay no fee, and in turn they receive free supervision. CHS researchers conduct this research to build the case for IPTP residents eventually receiving training stipends with hospital benefits. Some IPTP residents who became fully licensed have been hired by the CHS, and efforts are under way to develop other paid training and supervision opportunities. Quality patient experience and documented cost savings for the health care system are foundational for offering these stipends and the hiring of program graduates.

IPTP FACULTY

As a result of the rapid growth of the IPTP, the education and training of supervisors have been critical. The IPTP faculty is composed of both educators and supervisors who are fully credentialed and IPTP supervisors in training from various disciplines who are seeking one or more supervisory credentials. The IPTP provides the supervisors with supervisees and free supervision of supervision. Through individual/triadic and group supervision of supervision, these new supervisors, in parallel with their supervisees, use video clips, case presentation write-ups, and feedback to formulate their theory of supervision, which integrates use of self, psychotherapy practice, research, and supervision of supervision. Faculty members cite the "in vivo" experiences in group supervision of supervision as crucial to their learning. Supervisors in training are amazed at the complexities of how supervision and training in such a vast health care system interface. They consider the diverse, complex interlocking circles within the IPTP clinical arena. The vast differences of supervision in other settings have also been contrasted with supervision in a highly complex health care system.

CHS research has determined that there has been significant cost savings with clients who have seen IPTP interns and residents. This determination has warranted the CHS securing funds through Community Care Partners of Greater Mecklenburg to pay supervisors who have completed a year of supervisory training to enable them to continue with the IPTP faculty. Morgan Enright is one of these supervisors in training who has remained with the IPTP while he obtained various supervisory credentials and became a licensed supervisor in both North and South Carolina. The IPTP aspires to have these supervisors continue with the program long term as paid supervisors and potentially part-time or full-time employees with hospital benefits. Some fully credentialed IPTP supervisors are now drawn from CHS employees whose job descriptions have been reconstructed to allow them a certain number of hours weekly to supervise IPTP interns and residents.

Based on psychiatrist George L. Engel's (1977) "biopsychosocial" model, the IPTP adds the spiritual lens to form the "bio-psycho-social-cultural-spiritual" model. This model assumes that there is no clinical moment void of spiritual meaning and context. Some consider the spiritual dynamic as the container of the bio-psycho-social-cultural components. The hyphens in the resultant model underscore how all four components of experience and the clinical moment must be seen both singularly and as a part of the whole.

The IPTP offers a useful model for how pastoral counseling and psychotherapy is self-differentiating while extending its influence into the complexities of a very large health care delivery system. This model seeks to respond to the changing health care marketplace and to offer both quality patient experience and compliance with the ACA.

The IPTP model seeks to embody (a) best clinical practices; (b) integrative education and training, including from a distance; (c) administrative positioning of IPTP services; (d) coordination with multiple graduate degree programs, leading to varying professional credentials; (e) collaborative means for student recruitment; (f) quality assurance; (g) curriculum development; and (h) hard questions to ask at each level of program development.

PROGRAM STRUCTURE AND PROCESS

Application, Admission, and Placement

After completing the application process and going through an interview process, a placement is selected that best serves both the supervisee and CHS site. If accepted by the site, the supervisee is assigned an on-site administrative supervisor who attends to the practical needs of working in the site and acts as a liaison between the site and the IPTP. A clinical supervisor is also assigned who coordinates clinical supervision and facilitates the supervisee's formulation of an IPTP learning contract. The clinical supervisor also works with the site administrator to foster communication and ensure that both site standards and student learning requirements are being met. To gain clinical context, supervisees attend an orientation related to their respective clinical site and a general orientation class hosted by the CHS.

Practice

Both IPTP interns and residents serve a minimum of 20 hours per week: 16 psychotherapy hours and 4 hours in supervision, research, and writing. All IPTP interns receive 3 hours of weekly group supervision to oversee their entire case load. Some student interns may also receive individual/triadic supervision depending on what is required by their graduate program. IPTP residents receive both weekly group supervision and individual/triadic supervision. Residents can also choose to work more than the required 20 hours as long as they do not exceed the ratio of supervision to clinical hours set by their respective regulatory boards. All clinical supervision is free to the supervisee, a parallel in that clients also do not pay a fee to the CHS.

The supervisee writes an educational note for each psychotherapy session and has it reviewed and cosigned by the clinical supervisor. Case termination notes also are reviewed and cosigned by the clinical supervisor to close a case. The file is placed in the locked IPTP closed cases files, which are maintained by the administrative assistant for the IPTP. All case presentations for group or individual/triadic supervision are written using only patient and counselor initials. IPTP case presentations are written on a formatted IPTP Psychotherapy Case Presentation template (see Appendix C), which includes the IPTP Educational Note(s) (see Appendix E) detailing the clinical process. These appendixes can be found online at www.springerpub .com/maynard-snodgrass.

The completed case presentation template and the pertinent educational notes are sent securely through CHS e-mail to the supervisor and peers by 8:00 p.m. the night before the presentation to assist participants in preparation for the group. The supervisee brings a video clip to supervision that illustrates the learning questions posed. The learning questions and video clip help the supervisees address formation and practice issues. Each supervision group is composed of no more than six persons and has its own secretary who coordinates a balanced schedule for case presentations.

Each IPTP intern, resident, and supervisor in training has a permanent record kept in the IPTP records system, which is managed by the IPTP administrative assistant. Every communication between the supervisor and the supervisee is copied into the individual's file along with all evaluations and reports provided to the respective graduate program and regulatory boards. Thorough records are kept of all clinical and supervisory hours, IPTP courses taken, trainings completed, state licenses/certifications received, cognate group certifications obtained, and evidence of active liability insurance coverage in the amount of at least $1 million/$3 million. This permanent record is an ongoing resource for the IPTP and the supervisee to document what has been completed through the IPTP and helps both persons be intentional about training and supervision. Should the IPTP graduate seek further professional credentialing and state licensure/certification, that person's IPTP training file is available to substantiate what the supervisee has completed. Closed cases with all educational notes and the case termination notes are maintained for 7 years by the IPTP administrative assistant.

Supervision and Training Philosophy

Both IPTP interns and residents enter the IPTP having already taken many courses in aspects of clinical practice, including personality, psychotherapy, systems, ethics, and law. Most supervisees come seeking to integrate their ideas about clinical work with both their use of self perspective and faith perspective. This includes the desire to improve clinical competence and the ability to formulate and articulate their theory of psychotherapy and learn how it is put into practice. Even though the IPTP offers general courses to complement prior learning, the intent is not to promote a particular modality of psychotherapy. Many theories have been effective in serving CHS clients. However, the key to clinical competence and effectiveness with patients has been the clinician's integration of their use of self with their personal theory of practice and theology. The IPTP philosophy of both supervision and training is to promote the best use of self within the bio-psycho-social-cultural-spiritual frame for the psychotherapist, client, and supervisor. The IPTP contends and has observed that faith/spiritually sensitive psychotherapy occurs when supervisees address identity formation within their personal and professional formation. The Supervision of Supervision Case Presentation template (see Appendix F, found online at www.spring-erpub.com/maynard-snodgrass) is designed to foster the supervisor's formation and excellence of practice as well as management of critical incidents with patients.

Personal and Professional Identity

The IPTP concurs with Henri Nouwen (1991), who asserted that identity is born out of tension between self-affirmation and self-denial, self-denial and self-emptying, and self-realization and self-sacrifice.

The formation of identity is furthered through the practice functions identified first by Seward Hiltner (1958) in *Preface to Pastoral Theology* and expounded on by William A. Clebsch and Charles R. Jackle (1964) in *Pastoral Care in Historical Perspective*, Howard Clinebell (1966) in *Basic Types of Pastoral Counseling*, and Andrew D. Lester (1995) in *Hope in Pastoral Care and Counseling*. These practice functions include the following:

- Healing (Hiltner)
- Guiding (Hiltner)
- Sustaining (Hiltner)
- Reconciling (added by Clebsch and Jackle)
- Nurturing (added by Clinebell)
- Liberation (added by Lester)

Faith/spiritually sensitive psychotherapists form through doing their own self-work and being clinically present with patients in their similar and perhaps parallel journeys. The same is true for the parallel process that occurs between supervisor and supervisees. By intentionally balancing the aforementioned life tensions with one's practice functions, both the supervisee and the supervisor may deepen both personal and professional identity while becoming more attuned to the soul and its work.

With Wayne Oates (1974), the IPTP contends that regardless of the psychotherapist's professional identification, social role, or knowledge of expertise, the psychotherapist's work is "pastoral" (faith/spiritually sensitive) when the focus of the psychotherapeutic alliance is on the influence of God/Higher Power to the process of their lives. Work is also pastoral when there is an awareness of God as reality or a conversation about faith in God occurs. The context of the work is pastoral when a psychotherapist's basic knowledge of expertise includes the basic literature of his or her religious or faith background and an understanding of the client's religious culture. Pastoral context also occurs when it is perceived that the psychotherapist represents a church or faith community or speaks from a prophetic context. Last, psychotherapists can be perceived as pastoral if they function as an ethicist or they are seen as being able to give or withhold blessing (Oates, 1974). The pastoral person in these contexts truly is a faith/spiritually sensitive psychotherapist.

The IPTP is sensitive to the isomorphic combination of these dynamics within the supervisee and supervisor as well as their resultant influence on optimal clinical outcome. The IPTP makes every effort to assist supervisees, the site, and clients in differentiating the scope and practice of faith/spiritually sensitive psychotherapy from pastoral care. IPTP interns and residents use a handout in their sites to clarify their role in the respective health care setting (see Appendix A, found online at www.springerpub.com/maynard-snodgrass).

These distinctions are vital in health care because psychotherapists and chaplains often operate in the same context and refer to each other. Formal psychotherapy is established with a contract between the psychotherapist and the client while the pastoral care relationship is less formal.

Supervision of Supervision

The IPTP philosophy of supervision and training extends to supervision of supervision. Following faculty meetings, the IPTP faculty engages in ongoing supervision of supervision. The group secretary coordinates a balanced presentation schedule in which each person has the opportunity to be a part of "in vivo" learning through participation in all of these roles:

  a supervisor who presents a video of supervision of therapy
  a supervisor who supervises the supervisor who is presenting
  a member of the process group that gives feedback regarding the overall process
    observed

The presenter of the video of supervision of therapy sends the IPTP Clinical Supervision template with allied learning questions to the group by 8:00 p.m. the night before the group meets to promote every participant's preparation for the next day's group.

The "in vivo" learning experience can help the faculty form as providers of both supervision of therapy and supervision of supervision. This modality is offered in addition to individual/triadic supervision of supervision. Currently, the two supervision-of-supervision training modalities are led by James W. Pruett, who holds various national and state supervisory credentials. He has presented a number of national and international workshops concerning supervision and psychotherapist formation and has published chapters and articles in pastoral psychotherapy, professional counseling, and marriage and family therapy journals. Other IPTP supervisors are training to lead such supervisory modalities across the CHS facilities. The primary foci of training for supervisors through each modality are (a) development of a personal theory of supervision, (b) integration of this theory with the use of self in supervision, (c) continued differentiation of supervision from the personal practice of psychotherapy, (d) quality assurance of supervision provided to the IPTP interns and residents, and (e) quality assurance of the care that patients receive from the IPTP.

IPTP Coursework

Although the IPTP collaborates with several master's degree and doctoral programs, AAPC Level 3 training program approval standards mandate that the IPTP offers coursework to extend supervisee learning. The IPTP currently offers five courses that can assist the fully licensed IPTP graduate in pursuing the AAPC fellow certification/licensure track.

The following IPTP courses are designed to be applicable for persons without a theological education who need to take them to meet the AAPC Fellow Body of Knowledge requirements:

- Introduction to Integrative Pastoral Psychotherapy
- Pastoral Diagnosis in Integrative Pastoral Psychotherapy
- Theological, Faith, and Spiritual Method in Integrative Pastoral Psychotherapy
- Brief Solution-Focused Pastoral Psychotherapy
- Spiritual Formation and Practice in Pastoral Psychotherapy

The first three courses listed are three-credit courses offered by the Pfeiffer University Master of Arts in Practical Theology Program, and others may elect to take these courses as special students. The introduction course is team taught by persons from these disciplines: pastoral psychotherapy, psychiatry, sleep medicine, family medicine, healing touch, acupuncture, aromatherapy, neurological psychology, and professional ethics. All courses are taught at the Carolinas College of Health Sciences, which provides its own continuing-education units (CEUs). Because the IPTP is an AAPC-approved training program, it offers National Board for Certified Counselors (NBCC) CEUs as a CEU provider. Both provisionally licensed and fully licensed persons can use these courses for state licensure/certification renewal.

Some clinical sites offer didactic trainings to help enrich the IPTP supervisees' understanding of illness and treatment modalities. Elizabeth Family Medicine (EFM), for example, is a training facility for the Department of Family Medicine of the University of North Carolina Medical School at Charlotte. Resident physicians and IPTP interns and residents train together at EFM. IPTP interns and residents typically bring clinical cases and video clips pertinent to the subjects presented during the Mini Med School at EFM to amplify their learning. IPTP persons serving at other sites are invited to attend the Mini Med School. The following schedule is an example of the EFM Mini Med School offerings:

- March 15   Matthew Alexander, PhD   Dreams
- April 10   Lindsay Kuhn, PA   Asthma
- May 17   Allison Knott Bickett   Traumatic Brain Injury
- May 31   Vanessa McPherson, MD   Headaches
- June 7   Rhett Brown, MD   HIV/AIDS
- June 14   Krishna Desai, MD   Fibromyalgia
- July 12   Jamayla Culpepper, MD   Diabetes & Other Metabolic Syndromes
- July 26   Larry Raymond, MD   Lung Cancer
- October 2   Matthew Alexander, PhD   Boundaries
- October 9   Mary, Hall, MD   Women's Issues and Pelvic Pain
- October 23   Dale Waxman, MD   Chronic Obstructive Pulmonary Disease

Uniqueness of the IPTP Clinical Placements

As illustrated by the Mini Med School, IPTP interns and residents have a wonderful opportunity to engage the complexity that CHS sites often afford them. EFM and Cabarrus Family Medicine also integrate Eastern and Western medicine, which provides interesting learning opportunities that may not occur in the usual outpatient training settings. These opportunities include the following:

- learning how to be a vital part of a medical treatment team with an influential voice
- being seen as an extension of the physician and thereby coordinating all legal and ethical implications of practice
- working closely with and making regular recommendations to physicians and specialists
- recognition of the complex and often intertwined isomorphic dynamics of the clinical arena
- functioning as the eyes and ears of the physician regarding medication and care compliance
- discerning what the physicians need to know and not know to serve their common clients and determining what actually goes into the medical records
- developing the fine art of precept contacts for the physicians
- thinking and responding in the "bio-psycho-social-spiritual" model to become the site specialist for the care of the soul and spiritual resources
- using the physician, on-call physician, primary supervisor, on-call supervisor, and Department of Psychiatry to respond to clinical emergencies
- understanding how to use one's own locus of authority well in a vast clinical arena while integrating written theory of psychotherapy into personal practice
- becoming competent with the support of distant learning supervisors to use Skype, Go to Meeting, and other technology to participate in individual/triadic or group supervision when one is out of the geographical area

Clinical supervision and supervision of supervision are used to promote integration of this and other learning. The CHS makes available to the IPTP the technology necessary for supervisees throughout its system to attend classes and supervision from their respective facilities. This technology is becoming more vital as the IPTP develops other service and training sites in such places as Greensboro, North Carolina, and Charleston, Anderson, and Union, South Carolina, as well as other burgeoning sites. These training sites will be developed in concert with the CHS Department of Psychiatry and integrated with a strategic plan to improve quality service delivery and patient experience throughout both states.

Supervisee and Program Evaluations

The IPTP uses the supervisees' written self-evaluations and program evaluations, the supervisors' written evaluations, feedback from the clinical sites, and feedback received in supervisees' exit interviews with the Department of Spiritual Care and Education to improve the IPTP. The IPTP affords an opportunity for all persons involved and for the program itself to learn and form. Ongoing IPTP individual/triadic clinical supervision plus administrative supervision with the clinical services director are intended to address both individual and program formation before evaluations are formulated.

THE FUTURE OF THE INTEGRATIVE PSYCHOTHERAPY TRAINING PROGRAM

The future of the IPTP within the CHS seems bright. There are many key factors. CHS has developed an Annual Healing Summit to bring representatives from all of its sites to consider how the system operates as one with the theme of what can we do better together than separately to deepen patient experience. The IPTP has been presented to those in attendance to foster the receptivity of other CHS sites affiliating with the IPTP. The IPTP is using outcome studies to document the need for increased funding for the IPTP. Such funding might mean that IPTP graduates might be hired, IPTP residents might get training stipends and hospital benefits, and IPTP faculty might be extended with increased income and benefits.

Routinely, new graduate programs are collaborating with the IPTP, and it is reasonable to expect this trend to continue as new CHS sites come aboard throughout the Carolinas. The CHS has technology in place for distance education and training, which can be used by the IPTP to extend its effectiveness. Academic programs that are already a part of the CHS and the IPTP have the opportunity to venture jointly in the development of their own master's- and doctoral-level programs in integrative psychotherapy. Countless internal CHS resources can undergird this endeavor. Faith-sensitive psychotherapy; medical family therapy; and leadership, administration, and supervision of bio-psycho-social-cultural-spiritual service center and training programs are examples of what might be developed.

For the IPTP to take these bold steps in the future, the program must interface well with the CHS mission and strategic plan and, specifically, the divisions of psychiatry and family medicine. Each need to work seamlessly to address the challenging behavioral health needs of both North and South Carolina. Any health care system that wants to serve its geographical context must consider these factors. The CHS is committed to offer consultation services to other health care systems seeking to offer a similar bio-psycho-social-cultural-spiritual program.

The IPTP is prepared to extend the opportunity for each of its hospitals and physician practices to have a faith-sensitive psychotherapist either on site or available through CHS technology. IPTP education, training, and supervision can literally extend to every geographical area served by the CHS with onsite or distance services available with psychiatric backup. IPTP interns and residents can form in the CHS, understand the system, and can be known by it. This opens the door for residents to be hired when fully licensed to serve in new areas. In time, when fully credentialed, these residents would act as team leaders with other interns and residents working under their purview. Some will form as clinical supervisors with the opportunity to have satellite training centers linked to local graduate programs and the technology hub of the CHS for course and distance supervision and supervision of supervision. Throughout the growth of the program, the bio-psycho-social-cultural-spiritual underpinnings will be deepened. There will be balanced care for the individual, couple, and family.

REPLICATION OF A FAITH-SENSITIVE PSYCHOTHERAPY TRAINING PROGRAM IN A LARGE HEALTH CARE SYSTEM

Lessons that have been learned from the design and development of the IPTP of the CHS point to several themes to be considered in the establishment of a similar program in other health care systems.

Top-to-Bottom Buy-In

To develop a bio-psycho-social-cultural-spiritual psychotherapy service center and training program, all levels of administration, the senior medical staff, all treatment team members, and the corporate and departmental budgets must be operating with one set of values, priorities, and stewardship/expenditure of all necessary resources. All energies must operate in concert. All service agreements, memorandums of agreement, and training contract templates must be approved by the legal department of the health care system.

Construction and Development of a Service Center and Training Program

All service and training needs to be contextualized. Integrative psychotherapists are members of specific treatment teams that are accountable to site administration. All care and reporting measures are to be made through the respective physician in charge. Integrative psychotherapists function as the eyes and ears of the physicians between medical visits. In turn, succinct documentation in the patient's electronic medical record apprises the referring physician of the patient's ongoing response to care without compromising confidentiality about specifics in sessions. The administrative needs of each psychotherapist must be coordinated with the clinical service director to foster administrative cohesiveness between sites.

Integrative psychotherapists' education and training must be coordinated with both academic institutions within the health care system and graduate programs. The educational programs will be the referral source for students for training and service placement. Regular meetings with these referring institutions help to promote program cohesiveness and deepen the referral base. Utilization of supervisors from referring institutions as part of the program's faculty also helps promote cohesiveness and diversifies the potential for various supervisory modalities.

Training programs are most marketable and best respond to student need when they educate and supervise for numerous related group certifications and state licensures/certifications. Psychotherapist training is enriched by a cross-pollination of supervisees from various graduate programs with different emphases and approaches. Pathways that lead to provisional licensure, completion of state licensure, and training for various supervisory credentials can help undergird program expansion. Effort should be made to structure each course and supervisory hour so it will count toward multiple credentials.

Case presentations and educational note template standardization that have been designed and approved by the faculty can help unify program learning. A health care system's legal department may be able to protect such clinical progress notes from being subpoenaed when they are entitled "educational notes." Supervisors facilitate best practices and professional formation through signing each educational note for their supervisees. The IPTP supervision of psychotherapy case presentation, educational notes, and supervision-of-supervision templates are located in Appendices A to G (found online at www.springerpub.com/maynard-snodgrass) and may be illustrative for other training programs.

The training program should keep a permanent educational file for each supervisee, including program acceptance; all communication with the supervisees, graduate programs, and regulatory boards; evaluations; clinical logs; supervisory hours; evidence of professional liability insurance; certificates; and certifications/licensures received. These permanent education files provide ongoing documentation for the training program's accreditation as well as for students seeking other credentials or seeking to practice in a new state.

A student handbook should be developed that clearly outlines responsibilities and resources of the supervisee, the program, and the health care system. This handbook may be updated as needed and disseminated through use of a disc or a download from the training program website. The handbook should include a statement to be signed, which indicates that the supervisee has read and understands the handbook. This page is to be a part of the student's permanent file.

Dissemination of program materials can be enhanced by the development of a training program website that is complete with certification and licensure requirements, forms, templates, and other materials to promote continuity in training.

Program Expansion

Program expansion is built on the foundation of how the program is established. Before starting to offer the program, all policies, procedures, and administrative support should be in place. As the program unfolds, new lessons will be learned to fine-tune the initial business plan and program delivery. Health care systems manage budgets tightly. Thus, the program must be prepared to justify, both clinically and financially, how the program fits into best practices with the stewardship of the health care system's finances. Integrative psychotherapists may be asked to participate in outcome studies as a part of documentation. Service bartering between departments may occur and mutual fairness must be sustained to secure the long-range viability of the program. Specific costs to offer services, education, and training must be clearly factored. Offering free services in one service area can lead to expectations for the same policy along other service lines. All sites must agree to minimal standards and resources for placing integrative psychotherapists so that when they do arrive, all is in place. Their buy-in to the program reflects their valuing of the services that supervisees provide. The clinical services director must negotiate such agreements and monitor complicity. Clinical supervisors need to help maintain these agreements to oversee service delivery, best practices, and patient experience.

Use of Technology

Excellent training experiences and the incorporation of best practices are the best forms of marketing. Program leadership needs to be prepared to address students and have descriptive pamphlets and applications in hand to share. In the age of technology, interested applicants first connect with the program through its website. These sites must be user-friendly with PDFs of pamphlets and applications for each training level. The application process must be clearly delineated along with descriptions of available placement sites. Website links to these sites can assist students in understanding more completely what a placement site might be like. Contact information should be highlighted so that interested applicants can ask specific questions and receive clarification. As the website facilitates clear communication, it often serves as the public face for the program and must be updated regularly.

Networking With Regulatory Boards and Cognate Groups

The regulatory boards in the health care system's constituency area must not only know the veracity of the training program but also personally know the program director. The health care network has established its own public perception and its good will. The service center and the training program have the opportunity to carry this good will forward and establish their own. Program standards must be seen as exemplary. Program personnel need to understand regulatory board rules and procedures to maintain standards and help students orient to them. It helps for the program leadership to realize how ominous and onerous it can be for supervisees to complete state licensures and certifications. Supervisees regularly look to their supervisors and the program to help them navigate these professional waters. The program must never speak for how a regulatory board will act. Instead, it can encourage the student to engage the board directly.

Training Program Approval and Accreditation

Some analogous groups approve training programs, whereas others accredit them. Some states require service centers and training programs to be accredited or chartered. The legal department for the health care system can support the program's compliance with state and federal regulations.

When developing an integrative psychotherapy service center and training program, the program must discern the service needs of the health care system. In turn, it determines how a training program might help address these needs, particularly with patients who tend to be underserved or can drain the resources of the health care system. Training programs can then identify what state licensures and certifications potential students are seeking and design its program accordingly. If the training program plans to seek accreditation, the standards and documentation process of the organization must be hardwired into both program structure and business/training plan formulation. The program should invite conversation among all stake holders to help establish strong buy-in and support. The mantra, "What can we all do better together than separately?" helps to establish commonality, voice, and follow-through. The health care system's training program's base can then be understood as a "Consortium Conversation" that helps to deliver the psychotherapy training program as a team. The consortium can then choose whether to become formalized to initiate, develop, and sustain the program. Often accreditation standards require that the training program have either a board of directors or board of advisers. Representatives of this board should be included in the Consortium Conversation.

As the program moves toward achieving accreditation, it is wise to conduct ongoing statistical analyses as well as revisions of policies and procedures. It is also important to keep thorough training files, clinical records, and a record of how decisions are made. These actions should be taken in accordance with the respective reaccreditation standards and documented so that the program's self-study is being written synchronously to sustain the accreditation.

CONCLUSIONS

The fields are "white unto harvest" for health care systems to embark on the training of psychotherapists who practice with a bio-psycho-social-cultural-spiritual model that is inclusive, able to improve patient experience and satisfaction, reduce health care costs, and link together regional resources. The ACA has affected health care in such a way that these programs are not only useful but also essential to the system. Knowing the issues faced and how to respond to them through bio-psycho-social-cultural-spiritual means are keys to deciding the viability of the training program within the health care system. The AAPC-accredited Integrative Psychotherapy Service Center and approved Training Program of the CHS is one model that effectively illustrates how to affect and foster viability.

REFLECTION QUESTIONS

1. The Affordable Care Act (ACA) has had and will continue to have an impact on the provision of pastoral counseling, particularly in managed care settings. How might the ACA affect your practice of pastoral counseling in the next 2 years?
2. How are pastoral counseling and pastoral psychotherapy alike? How do they differ?
3. The authors describe the integration of pastoral perspectives within the Carolinas HealthCare System. What elements of that system are similar to contexts in which you currently work or have worked in the past?
4. Imagine that you are tasked to adopt three significant elements of the model presented by the authors in your clinical setting. What three elements of the model would you most want to adopt? Why? What elements of the model should not be adopted in your setting?
5. What important function(s) does supervision of supervision serve in this system?
6. For a program like this to work well, what features (personnel, resources, buy-in) must be in place?

REFERENCES

Clebsch, W. A., & Jackle, C. R. (1964). *Pastoral care in historical perspective*. New York, NY: Jason Aronson.

Clinebell, H. (1966). *Basic types of pastoral counseling*. Nashville, TN: Abingdon.

Davis, E. (2014, December 9). *The Affordable Care Act—What is it?* Retrieved from http://healthinsurance.about.com/od/adefinitions/g/The-Affordable-Care-Act.htm

Engel, G. (1977, April 8). The need for a new medical model: a challenge for biomedicine. *Science, 196*(4286), 129–136. doi:10.1126/science.847460

Hiltner, S. (1958). *Preface to pastoral theology*. New York, NY: Abingdon.

Knadig, T. (2011). *The spirituality and ethics underlying the Affordable Care Act*. Retrieved from www.uphs.upenn.edu/pastoral/events/Knadig_PRESENTATION_Oct2011.pdf

Lester, A. D. (1995). *Hope in pastoral care and counseling*. Louisville, KY: John Knox Press.

Napili, A. (2013). *Patient Protection and Affordable Care Act (ACA): Resources for frequently asked questions*. Washington, DC: Congressional Research Service.

Nouwen, H. (1991). *Creative ministry*. New York, NY: Doubleday.

Oates, W. E. (1974). *Pastoral counseling*. Philadelphia, PA: Westminster.

Roberts, R. C. (2003). Psychotherapy and Christian ministry. *Sothern Baptist Journal of Theology, 7*(4), 40–47.

Shin, P., Sharac, J., & Rosenbaum, S. (2013). *Assessing the potential impact of the Affordable Care Act on uninsured community health center patients: A nationwide and state-by-state analysis (Geiger Gibson/RCHN Community Health Foundation Research Collaborative policy research brief no. 33)*. Washington, DC: George Washington University, School of Public Health and Health Services, Department of Health Policy.

PERSPECTIVES FROM BEYOND THE FIELD: PSYCHOLOGY AND SPIRITUALLY INTEGRATED PSYCHOTHERAPY

The field of psychology has progressed considerably in its understanding of the importance of religion and spirituality in people's lives since the days of Freud and Skinner, who saw the practice of religion as evidence of pathology, a view also supported by more contemporary leaders in the field such as Ellis (Pargament, 2007; Pargament, Mahoney, Shafranske, Exline, & Jones, 2013). Fifteen years ago, however, Plante (1999) suggested that the relationship between professional psychology and religious institutions continued to be strained or at best indifferent. He also referred to Seymour Sarason's 1992 presidential address to the American Psychological Association (APA), in which Sarason expressed confidence that most APA members would consider themselves agnostic or atheist and view a person who tended to be religious with concern. More recent work (Gonsiorek, 2009) suggests that a negative bias toward religiosity continues within the profession. At the same time, there appears to be an expressed desire on the part of students and program directors to include spiritual and religious content in professional psychology training programs (Brawer, Handal, Fabricatore, Roberts, & Wajda-Johnston, 2002; Hage, 2006). However, inclusion of spiritual and religious content seems to be unsystematic and variable for the most part (Brawer et al., 2002; Hage, 2006; McMinn et al., 2014). The remarkable increase in the past decade in the amount of research on the role of religion and spirituality in human functioning and the development of spiritually integrated treatments suggests that graduate training programs in psychology will have to give more systematic attention to this area.

An indicator of the growth of research in the field of psychology and spirituality can be seen by examining the increase in the number of citations found over the past several decades in the PsycINFO database, which is the premier resource of the APA that provides abstracts of peer-reviewed literature in the behavioral sciences and mental health (EBSCO Industries, 2014). For example, a November 2013 search using the subject term *spirituality* identified only 303 citations for the 10 years beginning with 1980, including only 21 citations from the first 5 years of the decade. From an overall total of 12,185 citations, 2,417 (19.8% of the total) occurred for the years 2011 through 2013. When the search phrase *therapy or psychotherapy* was added, 1,586 hits resulted in all, with only 54 occurring in the 1980s and 9 between 1900 and 1979. As Pargament (2013) noted in the introduction to the recently published massive two-volume

APA Handbook of Psychology, Religion, and Spirituality, research and related applied literature on the topic has accelerated to the point that it can now be considered mainstream.

For a number of years, clients for whom religion or spirituality was central to their lives tended to seek counseling from pastoral counselors, clergy, vowed religious, or spiritual directors usually affiliated with specific religious traditions (American Association of Pastoral Counselors [AAPC], 2005–2012; Clinebell, 1983). To an increasing extent, however, a more diverse group of spiritually and religiously committed clients seeks the services of spiritually integrated psychotherapists who are not necessarily trained in the pastoral counseling tradition (Sperry, 2013). These clients often place a high level of importance on having a therapist who honors their faith tradition or spiritual orientation and whose values and beliefs are consonant with theirs (Worthington, Hook, Davis, Gartner, & Jennings, 2013). According to Sperry (2013), although pastoral counseling, spiritual direction, and spiritually integrated psychotherapy can all lead to spiritual growth, such is the primary focus of pastoral counseling and spiritual direction. Spiritually integrated psychotherapy, on the other hand, emphasizes psychological change while drawing on spiritual or religious resources that may contribute to spiritual growth as well.

My own professional development provides a good example of how some psychologists have grown to incorporate religion and spirituality in their research and practice. When I began my clinical practice and was gaining competence as a professor of developmental psychology at a Catholic university in the late 1980s, I was surprised by the lack of attention to the faith development and religious and spiritual needs of children, adolescents, and adults in the graduate psychology curriculum and in the clinical orientation of many of my professional colleagues. Fortunately, I did find some colleagues for whom faith and religious or spiritual involvement were essential aspects of their personal and professional lives, from whom I was able to learn, and with whom I was able to collaborate to integrate spirituality into my own teaching and clinical practice. Although I, like most of my spiritually oriented colleagues, received no formal training in the integration of religion and spirituality in understanding human behavior and development, my students and clients helped me see how essential it was to understand and embrace this integration.

As I introduced more religious and spiritual content into my psychology courses and developed ties with more religious communities, my clinical and consulting work became more focused on individuals of faith and their faith communities, and many of my referrals came from pastors. Naturally, I needed to prepare myself better for meeting the complex psychological, emotional, and spiritual needs of my clients, as well as my students. As I engaged in considerable reading and study, attended workshops and retreats, and grew as a therapist and researcher, I conducted more workshops for church groups and developed a graduate seminar on the integration of psychology and spirituality with a focus on spiritually integrated psychotherapy in the mid-1990s.

Despite my lack of theological training, I was able to bring to my graduate seminar and workshops more than a dozen years of Catholic education and numerous resources from the education I continued to receive through participation in spiritual direction, retreats, meditation, book discussion groups, faith-based local and international community service, clinical supervision, and continuing-education workshops. As my own learning advanced, I endeavored to bring perspectives from multiple religious and spiritual traditions to this seminar, as well as to my research, workshops, and clinical practice. I developed research tools (e.g., Fenzel, 2002) with which to examine the role of religious and spiritual practice on the stressors of university student life, with particular application to the phenomenon of binge drinking and the use and abuse of other substances and their consequences (Fenzel, 2005). From my education in Ignatian spirituality (Fleming, 2008), I found valuable applications for my personal and clinical practice. This spiritual orientation, based on the work of Ignatius Loyola, the 16th-century founder of the Society of Jesus (Jesuits), emphasizes the active presence of God in our everyday lives and God's availability and desire to work with people to care for the world. It is a reflective approach to discernment and taking action in daily life. One such practice, the *Examen*, which includes a regular review of one's day with respect to a particular focus behavior, has provided a useful framework for homework I have given to some clients.

Today, as chair of an academic department of pastoral counseling, I am particularly interested in effective ways that professionals in pastoral and clinical counseling, psychology, and other mental health professions can meet the needs of an increasingly diverse religious and spiritual clientele. In this department, faculty trained as pastoral counselors or as clinical and research psychologists work together to advance the profession and prepare licensed counselors in a program accredited by both the Council for Accreditation of Counseling and Related Educational Programs (CACREP) and the American Association of Pastoral Counselors (AAPC). The growing interest in integrating spirituality into the behavioral sciences and mental health provides an opportunity for pastoral counselors to assume leadership roles in this endeavor.

A MANDATE FOR PSYCHOLOGY

In 1983, when Howard Clinebell presented a vision for the future of the pastoral counseling profession, he noted that pastoral counselors were the only mental health professionals who were equipped to integrate religion and spirituality in the therapy room. At that time, as I documented earlier in this chapter, the field of psychology was barely paying attention to the role of spirituality in the human experience, and few resources were available to psychologists interested in this area (Pargament, 2013).

Today, with a growing body of research on the relation of religion and spirituality to numerous aspects of human functioning, psychologists and other mental health practitioners and researchers cannot help but recognize the importance of this integration. In addition to the field of psychology, data on the relevance of religion and spirituality is being generated by disciplines in the humanities and the physical and other social sciences to which spiritually oriented psychologists and other mental health therapists need to pay attention (Pargament, 2013).

Still there is much evidence that mental health therapists generally continue to be out of step with their clients when it comes to spiritual and religious beliefs and practices (Bhatia, Madabushi, Kolli, Bhati, & Madaan, 2013; Bilgrave & Deluty, 2002; Pargament, 2007). In addition, our Western society seems to be one in which its citizens are poorly educated on religious and spiritual matters, including diverse traditions, and where informed dialogue is often replaced with extremist pontification (Pargament, Mahoney, Exline, Jones, & Shafranske, 2013). In short, the needs are greater than ever for mental health professionals to seek knowledge of the roles that religion and spirituality play in human development, problem solving, illness, and wellness and to apply that knowledge effectively in prevention and intervention efforts. Given the complexity of the issues, careful study and sensitive research are needed. For example, research studies are just beginning to recognize the cultural contexts in which religion and spirituality are related either positively or negatively to well-being (Diener, Tay, & Myers, 2011; Lun & Bond, 2013).

FROM RESEARCH TO PRACTICE

The possibilities for applying knowledge gained from research on the integration of psychology, religion, and spirituality are numerous and extend from the therapy room to congregations, schools, businesses, hospitals, and community agencies. Spirituality has had a long history in the understanding and treatment of substance use disorders (SUDs) serving as a core component of Alcoholics Anonymous (AA) and Narcotics Anonymous (NA) and also contributing to the understanding of SUDs among religious groups, some of which have viewed alcohol use as sinful and addiction as an idol replacement for God (Johnson, 2013). Some religious leaders have viewed substance addiction as a spiritual quest gone awry, and other traditions and cultures have viewed the use of some substances, such as peyote, as vehicles for approaching the sacred. With new treatment approaches that incorporate religious and spiritual integration being tested and found to be effective, and with the popularity of 12-step programs that incorporate a spiritual focus, therapists need to be open to new ways of understanding SUDs and the role of religion and spirituality in their development and stay abreast of new developments in treatments to provide the best service to their clients (Johnson, 2013). Given the complex role that religion and spirituality have in addiction and its treatment, this would appear to be one area in which secular and faith-based counselors and therapists could benefit from engaging with one another in research, dialogue, and study.

With respect to the community context, psychologists have paid little attention to churches and other religious and spiritual congregations, yet the potential for contributing to the mental health and other needs of congregations and their leaders and members is substantial (Maton, Domingo, & Westin, 2013). For example, programs recently developed by psychologists and other mental health providers have supported the work of ministry leaders in helping to identify and address mental health needs of members following disasters and intervene with adolescents at risk for suicide (Maton et al., 2013). Psychologists have also begun to take a role in helping congregations deal with internal conflicts and assess congregational needs to promote healthy organizational development and also in providing effective community-based services, such as faith-based youth mentoring programs (Maton et al., 2013). Working with congregations in faith-based initiatives is another area in which the collaboration of psychologists, pastoral counselors, and ministers could bear considerable fruit.

PSYCHOLOGISTS' PERCEPTIONS OF PASTORAL COUNSELING

The increased interest among clinicians trained in psychology programs to integrate spirituality in therapy practice suggests the value of collaborating with other clinical counseling professionals who have the training and experience to work effectively with clients seeking this type of integration. Pastoral counselors may be situated to take a leadership role in this collaboration. To assess psychologists' perceptions of the quality of preparation received by pastoral counselors, I conducted two informal investigations: one with students in my master's-level course in the integration of spirituality and psychology in a psychology department and one on a social networking site for professionals in the psychology field (Fenzel, 2014).

Psychology students indicated on a 5-point Likert-type scale the extent of their agreement or disagreement with a series of items (there was a midpoint option of *neither disagree or agree*) that was distributed on the first day of the semester. Five of

21 respondents (24%) endorsed the statement that "most pastoral counselors are pastors or ministers in a church congregation," whereas 52% disagreed; 43% agreed that "pastoral counselors tend to be directive . . . in helping clients see the spiritual issues related to their concerns," whereas 24% disagreed. With respect to clinical competence, most students of psychology (86%) agreed that "pastoral counselors are as capable of conducting effective psychotherapy as psychologists," and only 14% agreed that "pastoral counselors tend not to be as proficient with multiple therapeutic approaches as counseling psychologists are." Finally, 24% of respondents agreed that "pastoral counselors would not be as effective working with clients with severe mental illness as would licensed psychologists (master's or doctoral level)." These findings suggest that these psychology students, who reported a mean of 238 hours of clinical training and had some interest in the integration of spirituality and psychology by virtue of having registered for the course, saw pastoral counselors as capable clinicians who tended to be directive about addressing spiritual issues in therapy.

I received 72 responses from 45 different psychotherapists (psychologists, social workers, and counselors, including pastoral counselors) to a discussion board post (Fenzel, 2014) on a professional social networking site in which I asked, "Are pastoral counselors as prepared as psychologists to practice?" Twenty-eight of the respondents' posts addressed the question at least to some extent. One pastor who later trained as a psychologist indicated that she "was ill-prepared to deal with the plethora and severity of psychological issues with which many church people presented" when she served as a pastor and pastoral counselor and that she "was far more prepared to deal with maladaptive behaviors and deep emotional issues as a psychologist." She, along with other respondents, emphasized the importance of pastoral counselors having master's-level training in counseling, marriage and family therapy, or other counseling or clinical field if they are to work effectively with clients presenting with severe mental health issues.

The prevailing view of respondents to the online post (Fenzel, 2014) was that a graduate degree in professional counseling that included adequate clinical supervision was essential to work as a psychotherapist. Responses indicated a perception that some pastoral counseling programs provided this level of preparation and some did not. Several other respondents indicated that having a theology background would serve as an asset for licensed therapists who work with spiritually or religiously oriented clients. Also, 13 respondents suggested that pastoral counselors generally lacked the skills of licensed psychotherapists to diagnose and treat many or most clients who seek treatment. At the same time, several respondents also indicated that pastoral counselors and psychologists, in addition to other mental health professionals, would have something to offer each other that would enhance the quality of the therapy or counseling each provided. In sum, findings from these informal studies of students and professionals in psychology and related fields suggest that perceptions of pastoral counselors as competent clinicians are mixed, with the majority viewing pastoral counselors as capable as any other licensed therapists.

MINDFULNESS-BASED APPROACHES

One area that blends the psychological and the spiritual and offers an opportunity for collaboration between psychology and pastoral counseling is that of mindfulness-based therapies. The influence of Buddhist psychology and Buddhist mindfulness practices in the West over the past half-century or so has led to an expanded view of spirituality and the search for the sacred. As Pargament (2007) argued, the sacred or spiritual is an inherent aspect of the human person, and journeys to discover one's significance and source of meaning are spiritual pursuits that may well be embedded in the unconscious. Buddhist practices of mindfulness, gratitude, compassion, loving-kindness, and integrity remind us of what Chogram Trungpa (2005) described as our basic goodness and sacredness or what Kornfield (2008) has acknowledged as our inherent nobility. These perspectives of the human person eschew the notion of an inherent human woundedness or deficiency that is endorsed by some religious traditions and that contributes to Western psychology's focus on treating pathology. Kornfield (2008) reported how the Dalai Lama was shocked to learn of the extent of feelings of shame, self-criticism, and self-hatred that existed among Westerners seeking mental health treatment. Fortunately, interventions based on positive psychology principles that focus on human strengths and virtues, such as gratitude, hope, and forgiveness, which are more consistent with the Buddhist perspective of the human person, have been effective (Rye, Wade, Fleri, & Kidwell, 2013).

Buddhism is a psychology and philosophy of living that is seamlessly integrated within an ancient religious tradition.[1] Its central practice of meditation, which has been a part of numerous religious traditions for centuries and takes many forms, has become mainstream in contemporary Western culture, and meditation-based practices are becoming more common in the field of psychology (Kristeller & Rapgay, 2013; Wachholtz & Austin, 2013; Wallace & Shapiro, 2006). The Buddhist concept of mindfulness serves as a key component of several recently developed therapies, including mindfulness-based cognitive therapy (MBCT; Sega, Williams, & Teasdale, 2012) and acceptance and commitment therapy (ACT; Hayes, Strosahl, & Wilson, 1999). In addition, Mindfulness-Based Stress Reduction (MBSR), introduced by Kabat-Zinn (1990/2009) some 25 years ago, is a meditation-based practice with wide appeal and strong empirical support (Kristeller & Rapgay, 2013). Mindfulness approaches have shown considerable success with clients suffering from the stress of physical illness and chronic pain, mood disorders, and eating disorders, as well as with various groups such as athletes, health care providers, urban teachers, and prison inmates to improve focus and help regulate dysfunctional behaviors (Bergemann, Siegel, Belzer, Siegel, & Feuille, 2013; Kabat-Zinn, 1990/2009; Kristeller & Rapgay, 2013; MacDonald & Shirley, 2009). It is no coincidence that Buddhist psychology is able to contribute so much to the development of a spiritually integrated cognitive psychology.

Kornfield (2008) has shown how mindfulness is no stranger to traditional Western psychology, as was demonstrated in Freud's emphasis on analysts paying attention to the revelations of clients and Rogers's notion of unconditional positive regard. Recognition and acceptance of what is really happening in our high-stress lives helps to break through denial and delusion and marks the beginning of change that loosens us from the shackles of worries, judgments, and beliefs we have held and that have brought needless suffering.

Cognitive therapies seem to be particularly compatible with spiritually integrated therapies and the principles of Buddhist psychology. For example, spiritual self-schema (3-S) therapy, which was developed through a joining of cognitive self-schema theory and Buddhist principles, including the notion that craving is the cause of much suffering, has been effective in reducing addictive and HIV risk behaviors among individuals from various religious backgrounds (Avants, Beitel, & Margolin, 2005; Avants & Margolin, 2004). In this therapy program, the client is guided toward replacing a harm-inducing addict self-schema with a spiritual self-schema that incorporates a client's spiritual or religious beliefs and an orientation toward preventing all harm to self or others and embracing compassion and optimism. Research has shown that 3-S clients reduce drug-seeking behaviors while they also report an increase in everyday spiritual practice and spiritual–religious coping (Avants et al., 2005).

SERVICE TO A DIVERSE AND SUFFERING SOCIETY

Many of the themes describing the state of society that Clinebell (1983) articulated over 30 years ago continue to ring true today. For example, his references to a contemporary society of "mind-boggling change" (p. 180) that is experiencing "an epidemic of existential emptiness, ethical confusion, spiritual poverty and pathology" (p. 181) describe current social conditions as well. The emptiness, confusion, and pathology of today are evidenced not only in the outbursts of violence against innocent children in schools but also in the failure to address the violence and its causes with sensible and life-saving (and life-affirming) legislation. Today, we also see an abysmal failure of the oil and gas industries to protect the earth and of politicians to address the widening income and wealth gaps in the United States. These are just some of the symptoms of a society that has lost its soul (Fenzel, 2012; Moore, 1992).

With such a deep spiritual malady infecting our world today, the need for spiritually oriented mental health professionals who attend to the psychological as well as the spiritual needs of individuals and communities is greater than ever. In addressing the challenges of an earlier time, Clinebell (1983) called for a more holistic approach to pastoral care and counseling to help heal brokenness while also promoting wellness and positive human development. In considering what this holistic approach might look like, the fields of study that address mental health needs and counseling may need to reflect on the extent to which it perpetuates the individualism of Western society with its focus on curing what ails the individual with little or no regard for the ways in which individuals remain disconnected from one another while they focus on their personal "issues" (Kornfield, 2008).

The integration of the religious and spiritual provides psychology and pastoral counseling with a pathway to expand their models of care beyond the individual or couple in the therapy room and work together to address solutions to social justice concerns. Such has been the focus to the social justice practices and teachings of religious and spiritual traditions and is also the work of groups such as Psychologists for Social Responsibility (n.d.). Another potential partner in this endeavor, which could provide a vehicle for dialogue and cooperation among mental health professions, would be the Council for a Parliament of the World's Religions (CPWR, 2009), which held its most recent parliament in 2009 in Melbourne, Australia. (A parliament will be held in October 2015 in Salt Lake City, Utah.) The parliament, which promotes and fosters interreligious dialogue to address some of the most pressing global social issues, recognizes the importance of honoring and strengthening each religious tradition and bringing them together in harmony to work together for justice and peace to provide healing for all global citizens (CPWR, 2009). Reflecting on the 1993 parliament, Teasdale (1999) recounted how the presence of the divine in the manner of a "second Pentecost" (p. 9) opened up attendees to a vision of mutual trust, community, cooperation, and shared responsibility for building a new kind of civilization. Teasdale posited that interspirituality, "the sharing of ultimate experiences across traditions" (p. 26), serves as the foundation for the world's religious and spiritual traditions and institutions to form a harmonious community to foster a deeper understanding and sense of responsibility to all of humankind.

The challenges for the world's religions and spiritual traditions are the challenges for psychology and its allied professions, including pastoral counseling. Just as the 2009 parliament focused on issues of healing the earth, peace and justice, overcoming poverty, and other social issues, so must psychology and the other counseling professions. Clinebell (1983) himself called for the field of pastoral counseling to address the societal ills that lie behind personal difficulties and contribute to the care of the earth and all of its living things through social action. He cited liberation theology as a valuable conceptual resource for the profession by which to undertake a "more holistic, socially responsible pastoral counseling" (p. 189). Many psychologists would no doubt be interested in joining with pastoral counselors and learning more about theological perspectives that inform issues of human rights, war, peace, poverty, sustainability, and education. Buddhism, too, could provide a shared spiritual framework for addressing social issues with its emphasis on the care and reverence for all of life and a commitment to healing the suffering of the world and taking political action where needed with a mind that is focused and at peace (Kornfield, 2008).

RESPONDING TO TODAY'S RELIGIOUS AND SPIRITUAL DIVERSITY

Pastoral counseling may be able to contribute to psychology's understanding of the changing landscape of religious and spiritual diversity in which so many adults, including 25% of America's young adults and nearly 18% of adults overall, lack a specific religious identity (Burklo, 2009; Gallup Politics, 2013). In addition, with the percentage of Americans who expressed confidence in "church or organized religion" at its lowest point (44%; Gallup Politics, 2012), psychology, pastoral counseling, and other mental health professions must consider how to broaden its reach and freshen its appeal to address the many spiritual and personal challenges of what Gonsiorek (2009) identified as a "fractionated yet vibrant" American religious landscape (p. 386).

This changing spiritual and religious landscape presents challenges for all mental health professions and further emphasizes the need for training programs to equip graduates with the skills needed to meet the mental health needs of an increasingly diverse clientele. In order for these training programs to be effective, careful attention must be paid to who is providing the training and how it is being conducted. Including religious and spiritual content in a single course or as a part of a course in diversity issues is clearly inadequate. In addition, the training of supervisors in clinical settings will be needed if interns are to be successful at integrating the spiritual with the psychological. Pastoral counselors and religious and spiritual leaders who serve the increasingly diverse religious and spiritual public can work together with psychology programs, as well as other mental health counseling programs, to design and help deliver a curriculum that meets the educational needs of students and the ethical and accreditation standards of the profession.

Pargament (2007) cautioned that training must be designed to avoid problems of spiritual myopia, bias, overenthusiasm, and cockiness in attempting to work with spiritually oriented clients. He recommended that both formal and informal training be incorporated that includes courses in comparative religion and spiritually integrated psychotherapy that helps aspiring clinicians understand and address spiritual and religious themes with respect to presenting problems and solutions. Effective training programs should also include a focus on facilitating students' self-understanding of their spiritual or religious backgrounds and biases (McMinn et al., 2014) as well as increasing their sensitivity to and understanding of the cultural and spiritual worldviews of their clients (Vogel, McMinn, Peterson, & Gathercoal, 2013). In addition, a knowledge of spiritual assessment approaches and measures should be included in the curriculum (Brawer et al., 2002). In all of these areas, pastoral counselors have the knowledge and experience and could contribute their expertise to clinical training programs.

Important to keep in mind also is that instructors and supervisors in these programs will require education and mentoring to develop and advance the knowledge, skills, and dispositions they will need to prepare future clinicians (Brawer et al., 2002). In addition, high-quality continuing professional education must be provided for clinicians and supervisors to maintain and further develop their competencies in spiritual integration.

A host of professionals will be needed to work together to provide the kind of ongoing training that is needed, and pastoral and other spiritually competent counselors and therapists can play an important role in this work. Although the requirements of different accrediting agencies may make this practice difficult in some ways, there is much to be gained when pastoral counseling and psychology faculty are able to contribute to the education of students in both programs. At Loyola University Maryland, students in school counseling and psychology programs take courses in the pastoral counseling department that provide the integration of spiritual and psychological content, and pastoral counseling students take courses in other departments as well. In addition, graduates of Loyola's doctoral program in pastoral counseling have provided continuing-education workshops and supervision for psychologists, clinical social workers, and counselors, and a few have taken faculty positions in psychology and counseling programs.

CONCLUSIONS

The recent publication of the two-volume *APA Handbook of Psychology, Religion, and Spirituality* (Pargament, Exline, & Jones, 2013; Pargament, Mahoney, & Shafranske, 2013) contains 75 chapters that examine the nature of religion and spirituality in the United States and how religion, spirituality, and psychology are being integrated in theory and practice. The release of this work alone is evidence of a growing interest in the integration of psychology and spirituality in research and counseling. As this integrated field of theory, research, and practice develops, good-quality training will be needed to guard against spiritual myopia and harmful practice. Herein lies an important opportunity for the pastoral counseling profession and religious communities and organizations to assume a leadership role to ensure that psychologists who seek to integrate religion and spirituality in their practices do so to the benefit of their clients. The influence of Buddhist psychology on mindfulness-based therapies appears to provide an important growth opportunity for both psychology and pastoral counseling, as well as an area for cooperation and mutual support.

Finally, the social justice challenges of the planet and its people are spiritual issues that are great and urgent and must fall more within the scope of practice for pastoral counseling, psychology, and related professions. In addition, these professions will need to engage with religious communities and organizations to bring an integrated approach to addressing these challenges. Pastoral counseling could provide leadership here as well.

REFLECTION QUESTIONS

1. According to the author, "Although pastoral counseling, spiritual direction, and spiritually integrated psychotherapy can all lead to spiritual growth, such is the primary focus of pastoral counseling and spiritual direction (Sperry, 2013). Spiritually integrated psychotherapy, on the other hand, emphasizes psychological change while drawing on spiritual or religious resources that may contribute to spiritual growth as well." Spiritual growth and psychological change are both goals of pastoral counseling. In your opinion, should primacy be placed on one or the other? Why?

2. The author recommends further collaboration among secular and faith-based counselors regarding the research, study, and treatment of addictions as well as mindfulness-based interventions and related research. In what other areas could collaboration among this diversity of mental health professionals be especially relevant? What unique perspectives and skill sets would these related but distinctive groups of professionals bring to topics identified?

3. The author conducted two informal studies with psychology students and psychologists regarding their perceptions of pastoral counselors' training and skill sets. What surprised you regarding the studies' findings? How do you understand your role in educating others on who pastoral counselors are and what we do?

4. What is the role of pastoral counselors in educating other mental health professionals on the integration of spirituality and religion within counseling? How are pastoral counselors advancing general understandings of integration? How is this knowledge being shared with the broader mental health disciplines?

NOTE

1. The reader is referred to Chapter 17 in this volume by Stephen Clarke for more information about Buddhism and its application to pastoral counseling.

REFERENCES

American Association of Pastoral Counselors. (2005–2012). *Brief history on pastoral counseling.* Retrieved from http://www.aapc.org/about-us/

Avants, S. K., Beitel, M., & Margolin, A. (2005). Making the shift from "addict self" to "spiritual self": Results from a Stage I study of spiritual self-schema (3-S) therapy for the treatment of addiction and HIV risk behavior. *Mental Health, Religion, & Culture, 8,* 167–177. doi: 10.1080/13694670500138924

Avants, S. K., & Margolin, A. (2004). Development of spiritual self-schema (3-S) therapy for the treatment of addictive and HIV risk behavior: A convergence of cognitive and Buddhist psychology. *Journal of Psychotherapy Integration, 14,* 253–289. doi:10.1037/1053-0479 .14.3.253

Bergemann, E. R., Siegel, M. W., Belzer, M. G., Siegel, D. J., & Feuille, M. (2013). Mindful awareness, spirituality, and psychotherapy. In K. I. Pargament, A. Mahoney, & E. P. Shafranske (Eds.), *APA handbook of psychology, religion and spirituality: Vol. 2. Applied psychology of religion and spirituality* (pp. 207–222). Washington, DC: American Psychological Association.

Bhatia, S. C., Madabushi, J., Kolli, V., Bhatia, S. K., & Madaan, V. (2013). The Bhagavad Gita and contemporary psychotherapies. *Indian Journal of Psychiatry, 55,* 315–321. doi:10.4103/0019-5545.105557

Bilgrave, D. P., & Deluty, R. H. (2002). Religious beliefs and political ideologies as predictors of psychotherapeutic orientations of clinical and counseling psychologists. *Psychotherapy: Theory/Research/Practice/Training, 39,* 245–260.

Brawer, P. A., Handal, P. J., Fabricatore, A. N., Roberts, R., & Wajda-Johnston, V. A. (2002). Training and education in religion/spirituality within APA-accredited clinical psychology programs. *Professional Psychology: Research and Practice, 33*(2), 203–206. doi:10.1037/0735-7028.33.2.203

Burklo, J. (2009). *Interspirituality.* Retrieved from http://www.patheos.com/Resources/Additional-Resources/Interspirituality

Clinebell, H. J., Jr. (1983). Toward envisioning the future of pastoral counseling and AAPC. *Journal of Pastoral Care, 37,* 180–194.

Council for a Parliament of the World's Religions. (2009). *Parliament of the world's religions: Melbourne, Australia,* December 3–9, 2009. Retrieved from http://www.parliamentofreligions.org/index.cfm

Diener, E., Tay, L., & Myers, D. G. (2011). The religion paradox: If religion makes people happy, why are so many dropping out? *Journal of Personality and Social Psychology, 101,* 1278–1290. doi:10.1037/a0024402

EBSCO Industries. (2014). *PsycINFO.* Retrieved from http://www.ebscohost.com/academic/psycinfo

Fenzel, L. M. (2002). *The development of the Spiritual Integration Scale: Examining the spiritual lives of late adolescents.* Poster presented at the Biennial Meeting of the Society for Research on Adolescence. Available at www.apa.org

Fenzel, L. M. (2005). Multivariate analyses of predictors of heavy episodic drinking and drinking-related problems among college students. *Journal of College Student Development, 46,* 126–140.

Fenzel, L. M. (2012, December 18). The malady of America's soul. *The Baltimore Sun,* p. A15.

Fenzel, M. (2014, May 20). *I teach in the field of pastoral counseling; I am interested in your view of the PC field. Are pastoral counselors as prepared as psychologists to practice? How do you integrate spirituality in therapy?* [Online forum posting]. Retrieved from https://www.linkedin.com/groupItem?view=&gid=94332&type=member&item=5874432028866281472&qid=deaf67d7-4c55-4058-8cea-9e34a6874d26&trk=groups_items_see_more-0-b-ttl

Fleming, D. L. (2008). *What is Ignatian spirituality?* Chicago, IL: Loyola Press.

Gallup Politics. (2012, July 12). *U.S. confidence in organized religion at low point.* Retrieved from http://www.gallup.com/poll/155690/Confidence-Organized-Religion-Low-Point.aspx

Gallup Politics. (2013, January 10). *In U.S., rise in religious "nones" slows in 2012.* Retrieved from http://www.gallup.com/poll/159785/rise-religious-nones-slows-2012.aspx

Gonsiorek, J. C. (2009). Ethical challenges incorporating spirituality and religion into psychotherapy. *Professional Psychology: Research and Practice, 40,* 385–395. doi:10.1037/a0016488

Hage, S. M. (2006). A closer look at the role of spirituality in psychological training programs. *Professional Psychology: Research and Practice, 37,* 303–310. doi:10.1037/0735-7028.37.3.303

Hayes, S. C., Strosahl, K. D., & Wilson, K. G. (1999). *Acceptance and commitment therapy: An experiential approach to behavior change.* New York, NY: Guilford.

Johnson, T. J. (2013). Addiction and the search for the sacred: Religion, spirituality, and the origins and treatment of substance abuse disorders. In K. I. Pargament, A. Mahoney, & E. P. Shafranske (Eds.), *APA handbook of psychology, religion and spirituality: Vol. 2. Applied psychology of religion and spirituality* (pp. 297–317). Washington, DC: American Psychological Association.

Kabat-Zinn, J. (2009). *Full catastrophe living: Using the wisdom of your body and mind to face stress, pain, and illness* (15th Anniversary ed.). New York, NY: Bantam Dell. (Original work published 1990)

Kornfield, J. (2008). *The wise heart: A guide to the universal teachings of Buddhist psychology.* New York, NY: Random House.

Kristeller, J., & Rapgay, L. (2013). Buddhism: A blend of religion, spirituality, and psychology. In K. I. Pargament, J. J. Exline, & J. W. Jones (Eds.), *APA handbook of psychology, religion and spirituality: Vol. 1. Context, theory, and research* (pp. 635–652). Washington, DC: American Psychological Association.

Lun, V. M., & Bond, M. H. (2013). Examining the relation of religion and spirituality to subjective well-being across national cultures. *Psychology of Religion & Spirituality, 5,* 304–315. doi: 10.1037/a0033641

MacDonald, E., & Shirley, D. (2009). *The mindful teacher.* New York: NY: Teachers College Press.

Maton, K. I., Domingo, M. R., & Westin, A. M. (2013). Addressing religion and psychology in communities: The congregation as intervention site, community resource, and community influence. In K. I. Pargament, A. Mahoney, & E. P. Shafranske (Eds.), *APA handbook of psychology, religion and spirituality: Vol. 2. Applied psychology of religion and spirituality* (pp. 613–632). Washington, DC: American Psychological Association.

McMinn, M. R., Bufford, R. K., Vogel, M. J., Gerdin, T., Goetsch, B., Block, M. M., . . . Wiarda, N. R. (2014). Religious and spiritual diversity training in professional psychology: A case study. *Training and Education in Professional Psychology, 8*(1), 51–57. doi:10.1037/tep0000012

Moore, T. (1992). *Care of the soul: A guide for cultivating depth and sacredness in everyday life.* New York, NY: HarperCollins.

Pargament, K. I. (2007). *Spiritually integrated psychotherapy: Understanding and addressing the sacred.* New York, NY: Guilford.

Pargament, K. I. (2013). Introduction. In K. I. Pargament, J. J. Exline, & J. W. Jones (Eds.), *APA handbook of psychology, religion and spirituality: Vol. 1. Context, theory, and research* (pp. xxiii–xxvii). Washington, DC: American Psychological Association.

Pargament, K. I., Exline, J. J., & Jones, J. W. (Eds.). (2013). *APA handbook of psychology, religion and spirituality: Vol. 1. Context, theory, and research.* Washington, DC: American Psychological Association.

Pargament, K. I., Mahoney, A., Exline, J. J., Jones, J. W., & Shafranske, E. P. (2013). Envisioning an integrative paradigm for the psychology of religion and spirituality. In K. I. Pargament, J. J. Exline, & J. W. Jones (Eds.), *APA handbook of psychology, religion and spirituality: Vol. 1. Context, theory, and research* (pp. 3–19). Washington, DC: American Psychological Association.

Pargament, K. I., Mahoney, A., & Shafranske, E. P. (Eds.). (2013). *APA handbook of psychology, religion and spirituality: Vol. 2. Applied psychology of religion and spirituality.* Washington, DC: American Psychological Association.

Pargament, K. I., Mahoney, A., Shafranske, E. P., Exline, J. J., & Jones, J. W. (2013). From research to practice: Toward an applied psychology of religion and spirituality. In K. I. Pargament, A. Mahoney, & E. P. Shafranske (Eds.), *APA handbook of psychology, religion and spirituality: Vol. 2. Applied psychology of religion and spirituality* (pp. 3–22). Washington, DC: American Psychological Association.

Plante, T. G. (1999). A collaborative relationship between professional psychology and the Roman Catholic Church: A case example and suggested principles for success. *Professional Psychology: Research and Practice, 30,* 541–546.

Psychologists for Social Responsibility. (n.d.). *Who we are.* Retrieved from http://www.psysr.org

Rye, M. S., Wade, N. G., Fleri, A. M., & Kidwell, J. E. (2013). The role of religion and spirituality in positive psychology interventions. In K. I. Pargament, A. Mahoney, & E. P. Shafranske (Eds.), *APA handbook of psychology, religion and spirituality: Vol. 2. Applied psychology of religion and spirituality* (pp. 481–508). Washington, DC: American Psychological Association.

Sega, Z. V., Williams, J. M., & Teasdale, J. D. (2012). *Mindfulness-based cognitive therapy for depression.* New York, NY: Guilford.

Sperry, L. (2013). Distinctive approaches to religion and spirituality: Pastoral counseling, spiritual direction, and spiritually integrated psychotherapy. In K. I. Pargament, A. Mahoney, & E. P. Shafranske (Eds.), *APA handbook of psychology, religion and spirituality: Vol. 2. Applied psychology of religion and spirituality* (pp. 223–238). Washington, DC: American Psychological Association.

Teasdale, W. (1999). *The mystic heart: Discovering a universal spirituality in the world's religions.* Novato, CA: New World Library.

Trungpa, C. (2005). *The sanity we are born with: A Buddhist approach to psychology.* Boston, MA: Shambhala.

Vogel, M. J., McMinn, M. R., Peterson, M. A., & Gathercoal, K. A. (2013). Examining religion and spirituality as diversity training: A multidimensional look at training in the American Psychological Association. *Professional Psychology: Research and Practice, 44*, 158–167. doi: 10.1037/a0032472

Wachholtz, A. B., & Austin, E. T. (2013). Contemporary spiritual meditation: Practices and outcomes. In K. I. Pargament, J. J. Exline, & J. W. Jones (Eds.), *APA handbook of psychology, religion and spirituality: Vol. 1. Context, theory, and research* (pp. 311–327). Washington, DC: American Psychological Association.

Wallace, B. A., & Shapiro, S. L. (2006). Mental balance and well-being: Building bridges between Buddhism and Western psychology. *American Psychologist, 61*, 690–701. doi:10.1037/0003.066X.61.7.690

Worthington, E. L., Jr., Hook, J. N., Davis, D. E., Gartner, A. L., & Jennings, D. J., II. (2013). Conducting empirical research on religiously accommodative interventions. In K. I. Pargament, A. Mahoney, & E. P. Shafranske (Eds.), *APA handbook of psychology, religion and spirituality: Vol. 2. Applied psychology of religion and spirituality* (pp. 651–669). Washington, DC: American Psychological Association.

EPILOGUE

Pastoral counseling is positioned at a crossroads. Significant shifts in the profession over the past half-century have both reinforced the enduring value of pastoral counseling and challenged traditional practices and paradigms. The goal of this book has been to offer the reader an overview of the history and current perspectives in the field, as well as insights into what may lie ahead for pastoral counselors in the coming years.

The authors in this volume have explored the roles and identities of pastoral counselors as both religious leaders and mental health professionals; pastoral views of the human experience and the nature and function of suffering; pastoral models of dysfunction and approaches to diagnosis; and tacit, implicit, and explicit approaches to spiritual assessment. They have explored means by which pastoral counselors attend and respond to explicit and implicit spiritual content in work with clients and many of the important cultural sensitivities imperative to this work. The similarities between pastoral counseling practices and those of allied mental health disciplines have been investigated, along with the distinctiveness of pastoral counseling interventions and spiritual direction practices.

Among the most novel contributions of this volume are those addressing pastoral counseling from Buddhist, Hindu, Islamic, Jewish, and Native American spiritual and cultural perspectives. These authors invite the reader further into the work of intercultural, interspiritual, and interreligious exploration in pastoral counseling. These approaches are complemented by discussion of pastoral counseling to meet the needs of children and those in the queer community.

Pastoral counselors offer meaningful contributions as consultants, collaborators, and sources of referrals to other helping professionals. Pastoral counselors also transmit and transform the traditions of the field in their roles as educators, supervisors, and researchers. Authors from each of these perspectives have enriched this volume. Finally, the future of the field was considered in terms of emerging care delivery models such as distance counseling, and new visions for the field from both within and outside the tradition were posited.

The authors in this volume have offered a diverse range of perspectives on the discipline of pastoral counseling, attending to both theory and practice. It is the hope of the authors and editors that, taken together, this tapestry of perspectives invites the seasoned and novice reader to consider the themes and practices most relevant to the discipline and its development. Furthermore, it is hoped that the reader will be inspired to review and reimagine her identity and roles as a pastoral counselor or allied helping professional. This exploration not only supports the pastoral counselor in her work but also benefits the clients and students we serve.

Elizabeth A. Maynard and Jill L. Snodgrass

INDEX

Pastoral Counseling (Hiltner), 27
pastoral counselors
 community supported by, 1
 confidentiality standards of, 359–360
 consultations provided by, 360–361
 homosexuality and same-gender work
  of, 347
 queer-identified persons working with,
  334, 345–346
 role and identity of, 479
pastoral degree programs, 27
pastoral diagnosis
 ambivalence about, 203–205
 apophatic approach to, 106–107
 assumptions in, 105–106
 Draper coining term, 103
 experience engagement in, 109–111
 from Hiltner, 103, 104
 history of, 102–103
 variables in, 104
pastoral formation, 214
pastoral identity, 118–119
pastoral integration, 196–197
pastoral psychotherapists, 449–451
pastoral strategies, 192, 193
pastoral theology, 444
Pastoral Work and Pastoral Counseling
  (Dicks), 35
A Pastor's Sketches (Spencer), 21
Paul (the apostle), 18
penitential guidelines, 102
Pensees (Pascal), 58
Pentecostalism, 226
personal growth, 258
personalism, 35
personality, religions and, 394–395
personal lives, 299
perspective shift, 252
peyote religion, 309–310
Peyote Road, 310
phenomenology, 391–392
physicians, 23
pleasure (kama), 62
pleasure principle, 34
plurality, in pastoral counseling, 1–2, 14
positionality, 116–117
positive psychology, 229
positive religious detriangulation, 200
postmodern/liberative method, 90–94
postmodern modalities, 201
posttraumatic stress disorder (PTSD), 362,
  363, 368
power differentials, 243
power sharing, 252–253
Prague Spirituality Questionnaire (PSQ), 396

prayer, 106–108, 148–151
predestination, 269–270
Preface to Pastoral Theology (Hiltner), 27, 455
presence, 43, 110, 111, 196
preserver (Vishnu), 295
problem solving, 73, 297–298
progressive familists, 418
prophetic presence, 43
Protestantism, 102–103, 226
Protestant seminaries, 32
providence, 104
proximal development, 60
proximity-seeking behavior, 75
PSQ. *See* Prague Spirituality Questionnaire
psychiatric disorder, 340
psychiatric patients, 63–64
psychodynamic approach, 28, 31, 184–190, 199
psychological revival, 23–24, 88–89
psychology
 areas of respect in, 246
 Buddhism influencing, 279, 287
 Buddhist, 282, 285–286, 469–471
 courses, 466
 developmental, 57
 functionalist, 22, 34
 God in images in, 143–144
 hope as construct in, 153
 mandates in, 467
 methods and intention of helping in, 286
 pastoral counseling perceptions of, 468–469
 pastor's knowledge of, 21
 positive, 229
 psychotherapy and, 22–23
 religion's relationship with, 19, 22–23
 spirituality and research growth in,
  465–466
 spirituality integrated with, 468
 spirituality/religion/theology used with,
  90–91, 95–96
 structuralist, 34
 theology combining with, 211–212
psychophysical exercise (Raja Yoga), 54
psychospiritual themes, 115–116, 122,
  126–128
psychotherapy, 26, 28, 88, 182–183
 brain and research of, 109–110
 emotional balance from, 230–232
 faith-sensitive, 459–460
 gay or lesbian, 330–331
 individual's dance in, 74
 integrative care in, 450
 interventions in, 213–214
 pastoral, 449–451
 pastoral counseling's commitment to, 31–33
 psychology and, 22–23